The ... of
QUATRE BRAS
1815

The Battle of
QUATRE BRAS
1815

MIKE ROBINSON

SPELLMOUNT

First published 2009
This paperback edition published 2010 by Spellmount,
the military history imprint of
The History Press
The Mill, Brimscombe Port
Stroud, Gloucestershire, GL5 2QG
www.thehistorypress.co.uk

© Mike Robinson, 2009, 2010

The right of Mike Robinson to be identified as the Author
of this work has been asserted in accordance with the
Copyrights, Designs and Patents Act 1988.

All rights reserved. No part of this book may be reprinted
or reproduced or utilised in any form or by any electronic,
mechanical or other means, now known or hereafter invented,
including photocopying and recording, or in any information
storage or retrieval system, without the permission in writing
from the Publishers.

British Library Cataloguing in Publication Data.
A catalogue record for this book is available from the British Library.

ISBN 978 0 7524 5760 4

Printed in India by Replika Press Pvt. Ltd.
Manufacturing managed by Jellyfish Print Solutions Ltd

CONTENTS

Foreword	7
Acknowledgements	12
Prologue	14
Chapter 1 'The Prussians have been attacked'	27
Chapter 2 'The French are on the Nivelles road'	46
Chapter 3 'Be ready to march in the morning'	66
Chapter 4 'I am too feeble to remain here for long'	85
Chapter 5 'The suddenness of the danger multiplying its horrors'	103
Chapter 6 'We suspected treachery on the part of the foreigners'	123
Chapter 7 'I know who expects to be killed today'	142
Chapter 8 'The first booming of distant guns'	162
Chapter 9 'We had the wood to retreat into'	180
Chapter 10 'Many found their deaths beneath the hooves'	197
Chapter 11 'A field of rye as tall as our Grenadiers'	214
Chapter 12 'Sir Andrew pointed out which was the French'	232
Chapter 13 'The clash of the fixing bayonet'	251
Chapter 14 'Some had the audacity to draw their swords'	270
Chapter 15 'The ground was literally covered with dead'	290
Chapter 16 'Push on old three tens – pay 'em off for the 44th'	309
Chapter 17 'The separation between soul and body'	328
Chapter 18 'Now men, let us see what you are made of'	344
Epilogue	364
The Army of the Low Countries	381
Bibliography	391
Index	411

FOREWORD

This book is overdue by almost two hundred years.

Major Richard Llewellyn, who fought at the battle of Les Quatre Bras, wrote in 1837: 'Had it not been so closely followed by the very decisive and important, but all-absorbing victory of Waterloo, perhaps the gallant exploits and unexampled bravery that marked that day would have, under other circumstances, excited even more admiration than was actually associated with it.'

My interest in the Waterloo campaign was awakened by a Christmas gift from my parents of Carmigniani's beautiful conception of Lachouque's 'Waterloo', but like many others, I was beguiled by the climactic nature and iconic status that the final battle of the campaign has received. Some eight years ago, a change in circumstance made it possible for me to consider making my own contribution on the subject and it was only after many months of reflection and a moment of inspiration from Philip Haythornthwaite that I heard Llewellyn's voice across time and the germ of an idea started forming in my mind.

History is littered with books on virtually every aspect of the campaign: one can read about grand strategy; weapons; personal experiences and even the weather. But what I discovered was that, despite this immense body of literature, only one book had ever been written that focused solely on the battle of Les Quatre Bras, by a little-known Dutch author named J. P. Jonxis in 1875. Though Alain Arcq has subsequently published his own treatment of the battle in French, there remains no English language work on the subject.

Why has the battle attracted so little attention from historians? At a strategic level, Les Quatre Bras resulted in Napoleon failing in his objective of separating the Allied armies and defeating them in detail; on 16 June 1815 he lost and never recovered the initiative. Despite earlier miscalculations, Wellington gained sufficient time to rectify his mistakes and concentrate his army, but only at the cost of some 5,000 casualties. Though the Prussians were defeated at Ligny on the same day, a French defeat at Waterloo was made infinitely more probable and the two battles can rightly be considered a turning point in the campaign. But whilst this book provides insights into the thinking of those in command, it does not seek to evaluate the performance of the generals, nor offer opinions on strategic or tactical matters.

Les Quatre Bras was a confusing battle in many respects and this has led to many discussions between historians, differences of opinion and not a little controversy. Little is known of the sequence of events; long periods of time and large areas of the fighting remain shrouded in mystery; the commanders committed errors of omission and commission; and the soldiers as ever, were inconsistent, with supposedly élite units behaving poorly and the most unlikely formations performing prodigious feats of valour. These characteristics have not been helped by a degree of historical partiality which would have the English language reader believe that the victory was won by Wellington's redcoats alone, that the German contingents played a negligible role and that the Netherlands troops, to paraphrase Ensign Edward Macready of the 30th Regiment of Foot, 'Behaved vilely'. I have found the reality to be somewhat different.

Finally, I was struck by the drama of the events and the impact that the experience had on those who took part. From the time at which the French invaded in the early hours of 15 June 1815, until the last musket shot was fired at Les Quatre Bras on the evening of the following day, events in southern Belgium escalated to a dramatic conclusion, with anxious Allied generals obliged to disregard orders based on incomplete or faulty intelligence and use their initiative to establish a weak line of resistance. On the day of the battle itself, the French assaults provoked a desperate, improvised defence, which bought time for the arrival of successive reinforcements, each time denying the French the victory that looked inevitable.

What I have set out to do in writing this book is simply to tell the story of this battle: the circumstances that led to it, the fighting itself and the aftermath. History is, after all, an individual's interpretation of the facts available to them and this book comprises my imperfect effort to present an impartial view of events. At an early stage in my thinking, I wanted to present as balanced a view as possible and I felt it was important to draw on as much primary source material as it was possible to obtain. The reader will note that, whilst I have provided references to this material in the end-notes, I have also included secondary sources where this information is more readily accessible. All the conclusions I have drawn from these accounts – whether correct or otherwise – are incorporated in the narrative and I leave it to each of you to come to your own conclusions as to their value.

My starting point was the British Library and the Siborne Collection, but it soon became obvious that the number of British accounts was wholly disproportionate to that of other nations. Despite my best efforts, little of value could be found in French sources, but by a combination of luck and generosity, I was able to access material from Belgian, Brunswick, Hanoverian, Nassau and Netherlands' accounts; much of which has never been published in English. I chose, therefore, to concentrate on events seen from the Allied side of the hill, using French accounts to corroborate where necessary. It is for this reason that there is no examination of the inactivity of the French on the morning of 16 June, no analysis of the peregrinations of General d'Erlon and no space devoted to the increasingly desperate flow of orders from Imperial Headquarters to Marshal Ney.

Foreword

Instead, this is the story of a battle that turned a campaign; a story of triumph and disaster; of glory and dishonour; and most importantly, a story of the intense human experience of those that took part. It is drama of the highest quality.

But it is a drama that would never have been possible to tell without the generosity of those prepared to share unique insights with me. I would like to thank Earl Cathcart for providing access to the journal of the second Earl and to Michael McGarvie for his transcription. Mick Crumplin, possibly the leading expert on military surgery of the period, was kind enough to share his detailed knowledge of this grisly aspect with me. Jean-Pierre Forniaux allowed me to examine the interior of La Bergerie and shared his knowledge of the battle and of the landscape his family has farmed for generations. Julia Muir provided me with Ensign Richard Master's memoirs and kindly permitted me to quote from them. Diana Short furnished me with information about her great-great-great uncle, Ensign Charles Short, possibly the youngest officer at Les Quatre Bras.

A detailed understanding of the battlefield has greatly aided me in interpreting the sequence, timing and location of events. For this, I am deeply indebted to the officers and men of 14 (Geographic) Squadron, Royal Engineers. After two years of planning, delayed by the conflict in Iraq, Major Julian Millard kindly consented to undertake a survey of the battlefield, despite challenging operational commitments. I spent a fascinating time in the fields of Belgium in the care of Sergeant Dave Mills. My thanks to WO2 Kev Brixton, Sergeants Jon McCurry and Phil Wagh, Corporal Neil Fassam and Lance-Corporals Dougie McDougall, Andy Grubb, Lee Leighton, Jim Norton and Karl Reid; Lieutenant-Colonel James Carmichael Smyth, Wellington's Engineer-in-Chief, would have been proud of them. Of course none of this would have been possible without the active support of Majors Tony Crook and J. P. Smith, Lieutenant-Colonel John Kedar and, finally, General J. D. Moore-Blick, CBE. I must convey my thanks to Raf Muylaert, Commercial Director, and the staff of the Institut Géographique National, Brussels, who were most generous in providing much of the data on which the survey was based. I owe a debt of gratitude also to Hubert Lardinois of the Institute, who was of great assistance in locating rare maps by Ferraris and Capitaine, the series produced for de Bas and Jackowick's contemporary street plan of Brussels. Martin Brown, my cartographer, has made a splendid interpretation of all this information in the excellent maps he has created.

Understanding how this topography has changed over time enabled me to examine certain aspects of the battle in a new light. Mention must be made of my own 'family' archaeologist, Chris Jones, who offered his own opinions and put me in touch with several useful experts in his field. Principal amongst these was Dr John Carman of the University of Cambridge, who provided me with his expert observations. Despite his new-found celebrity status, Tony Pollard of Glasgow University did not hesitate to correspond with me on a number of issues. In Belgium itself, I was fortunate to meet Daniel Dehon trudging up the heights of Bati-Saint-Bernard one snowy morning in February. In sharing with me details of the artefacts he has recovered from the field,

I gained fresh insights into the movements of various corps, in particular how close the French came to seizing the crossroads.

The difference between dream and reality has most notably been made by a small number of individuals, characterised by their unquestioning support, generosity and friendship. George Caldwell's knowledge of the 95th Regiment of Foot is encyclopaedic. Barbara Chambers shared with me her knowledge of the 1st Regiment of Foot Guards. André Dellevoet passed on his insights into the Netherlands' cavalry and van Bijlandt's Brigade and provided me with rare eye-witness accounts. I am indebted to the implacable Karin Desczka, who tracked down the whereabouts of the painting of the Death of the Duke of Brunswick that graces the dust jacket of this book. Carole and John Divall shared their expertise on the 30th Regiment of Foot and spent many hours at the National Archives in Kew, on my account. My thanks are due to Lieutenant-Colonel (Retd) John Downham of the Queen's Lancashire Regiment, for sharing his research on Ensign Edward Macready and for his hospitality during my several visits to the regimental archives. I am indebted to Alan Lagden, a continued source of support and encouragement and to his co-author, John Sly, who was kind enough to take a day off to educate me in the ways of the National Archives.

Much of the material contained within this book would have remained inaccessible without the skills of Beatrice Capelle, Julia Kriz, Martin Kroon and Jo McLennan, who all provided me with priceless assistance in French, German and Dutch translation.

A special word must go to the late David Chandler. An iconic Napoleonic historian, his passing marked the end of an era. I was privileged to meet him on a number of occasions in his later life. He was generous enough to provide me with access to his extensive collection, provided much valuable advice and, along with his wife Gill, was a source of inspiration.

In a similar vein, I have been privileged to make the acquaintance of Pierre de Wit, possibly the most knowledgeable Waterloo specialist that I have ever met. He has saved me countless hours in archives by generously providing me with rare material and I extend my grateful thanks to him.

I also owe an immense debt to John Franklin, without whose help much obscure and hitherto unpublished material would have lain undiscovered. Despite the enormous pressure of writing his own book, he has proven an invaluable adviser, source of encouragement and very good friend.

The difficulty of obtaining primary accounts from all the participating nations is well documented. In many cases the time, effort and cost required to locate, transcribe and translate documents leads to historians simply ignoring this material and perpetuating the errors of earlier historians; Waterloo literature is infinitely the worse for this. I have been incredibly fortunate that, in the course of my own research, I have benefited from the scholarship of Erwin Muilwijk, whose study of the part played by the Army of the Netherlands has been so extensive. He has been generous enough to share his manuscript with me, to provide me with translations of primary material, to answer

Foreword

my questions and to correct my faults. In permitting me to quote directly from the material he has researched, he has allowed me, in many cases for the first time, to tell the story of the Netherlands' and Nassau soldiers. In particular, the accounts contained in the family archive of Ernst van Löben-Sels, would never have graced the pages of this book. Words are inadequate to express my gratitude.

After many months of searching for a publisher, I am indebted to Jamie Wilson for giving me the opportunity to realise my dream in print. Jamie was prepared to take a risk on what will always be a specialised project and, throughout, has been unfailingly supportive. My thanks also extend to his team.

Finally, I must acknowledge the loving support of my wife, Alison and my children, Christian and Roxy. They have borne the brunt of the late nights, lost weekends and ruined holidays and have done so without complaint. Theirs is the Kingdom of Heaven.

This book is dedicated, with my love, to my parents, Peter and Hilary, who started the whole thing in the first place.

Mike Robinson
Newark, Nottinghamshire

ACKNOWLEDGEMENTS

This journey began eight years ago and its completion has only been possible with the most generous help from others. Words of encouragement, guiding hands, expert knowledge, help with translation, all have been generously provided by many people and organisations, without whose involvement the burden would have proved impossible. Some I have already mentioned in the foreword.

Thanks are due to Colin Ablett, Mark Adkin, Alain Arcq, Gary Ashby, Sean Bisset-Powell, Peter Blom, Franjo Bogdanowicz, Pieter-Jan Borsch, Jean-Claude Boyron, David and Janet Bromley, Ian Castle, Peter Catley, Robert Chenier, Thierry Choffat, Adrie le Clercq, Peter van der Coelen, Dick Collins, Graeme Cooper, Bernard Coppens, Jean Defranceschi, Derrick Dorn, Commandant Jean-Luc Dubrunfaut, Captain Jörg Duppler, Albert van Ee, Paul Elliott, Emma Fletcher, Lieutenant Tom Florizoon, Jeremy Freeston, Lieutenant-Colonel Eduard Gerckens, Prof. Mordechai Gichon, Dave Gower, Eric Graver, Clive Hamilton, Philip Haythornthwaite, Jens Henkel, Peter Hofschröer, Dr. Johanna Jacobs, Hugo Janssens, Colonel Pierre Kohn, Yolande Kortlever, Dr. Jürgen Krauss, Prof. Vijay Kumar, Colonel Daniel Laude-Bazan, Lionel Leventhal, John Lichfield, Patrick Maes, Els van der Meer, Wies van Meurs, René van Mierlo, David Miller, Els van Nieuwenhuizen, Jan Nuis, Keith Oliver, Dr. Wolfgang Petter, Jean Pezard, Ad van Pinxteren, Jan-Piet Puype, Commandant Jean-Pierre van Puyvelde, Georgina Pye, Stuart Reid, Arie Rens, Wim van Riemsdijk, Cees van Romburgh, Louise Say, Sergeant Daniel Simbrey, Eveline Sint Nicolaas, Dr Frits Snapper, Bob Snibbe, Pete Starling, Michael Stratford, Karel Thönissen, Debbie and Lucio Tozzi, Andrew Uffindell, Jan Vanhoucke, Annemarie Vels Heijn, Sergeant Daniel Verdonck, Elisabeth Verheij, Jean Verhulst, Prof. Dr. Hans-Erich Volkmann, Ben Weider, Lina van der Wolde and Vaughn Wrenn.

I was fortunate to receive much assistance from a number of institutions. My thanks go also to Colonel Jean-Claude Aumoine and Samuel Gibiat (Service Historique de l'Armée de Terre, Vincennes), Dr. Gerhard Bauer (Militärhistorische Museum der Bundeswehr), Richard Boijen and Piet de Gryse (Musée Royale de l'Armée, Brussels), Brigadier-General Hans Bosch (Koninklijke Militaire Academie, Breda), Matthew Buck (Royal Artillery Museum), Stephen Bull (Museum of Lancashire), V. van den Burgh (Algemeen Rijksarchief), Gilles Chabrière (Musée de l'Emperi), Lieutenant-Colonels Chaduc and Riccioli (Musée de l'Armée, Paris),

Acknowledgements

Major R. Courage (Royal Hospital, Chelsea), Françoise Dupriez (Musée Wellington, Waterloo), Britta Edelmann (Braunschweig Landesmuseum, Brunswick), Dr. Andreas Fahl (Historisches Museum, Hanover), Lieutenant-Colonel (Retd) Angus Fairrie (Queen's Own Highlanders Museum, Fort Augustus), Major (Retd) David Gilchrist (RHQ Royal Anglian Regiment, Warley), Major (Retd) D. Harrap and Bill Norman (Duke of Wellington's Regiment Museum, Halifax), Mark van Hattem and Sjak Draak (Koninklijk Leger en Wapen Museum, Delft), Ian Hook (The Essex Regiment Museum, Chelmsford), Captain (Retd) David Horn (Guards Museum, London), Colonel (Retd) I. McCausland (Royal Green Jackets Museum, Winchester), Lieve de Mecheleer (Archives Générales du Royaume, Brussels), Major (Retd) Dick Mason (Museum of the Royal Scots, Edinburgh), Sarah McKay, Malcolm Ross and Bob Smith (Gordon Highlanders Museum, Aberdeen), Gilbert Menne (Musée Provincial du Caillou), Edith Philip (National War Museum of Scotland, Edinburgh), Major (Retd) C. Rebbeck and George Streatfield (Soldiers of Gloucester Museum, Gloucester), John Rees (The Welch Regiment Museum, Cardiff), Sigrid Schieber (Hessisches Hauptstaatsarchiv, Wiesbaden), Dr. W. Smit and Liesbeth Brama (Instituut voor Militaire Geschiedenis, The Hague), Tommy Smyth (The Black Watch Museum, Perth), John Spencer (Bankfield Museum, Halifax), Norbert Steinau (Bomann Museum, Celle), Major (Retd) R. Swift (Royal Military School of Music), Jeremy Taylor (Berkshire Records Office, Reading), Dr. Peter Thwaites and Andrew Orgill (Royal Military Academy, Sandhurst), Prof. L. deVos (École Royale Militaire, Brussels), Major (Retd) Hugo Whyte (Duke of Cornwall's Light Infantry Museum, Bodmin) and Dr. B. Woelderink (Dienst van het Koninklijk Huis, The Hague). Without exception, they assisted me in locating valuable information and in many cases introduced me to people with specialised knowledge. A special mention must be made of the staff of the Reading Rooms at both the British Library and the National Army Museum; to George Brown, Keith Oliver and Ed Parker of the Napoleonic Association, who published a request for assistance in the Association's Journal; and to John White of the Association of Friends of the Waterloo Committee, who was unfailingly supportive.

PROLOGUE

Violets were blooming across Europe.

The spring of 1815 heralded a fresh beginning. After twenty-three years of almost continuous conflict between the forces of revolutionary, consular and imperial France and a series of coalitions between the greater and lesser powers of the Continent at a cost of some £54 million and some 3½ million military and civilian casualties, Napoleon Bonaparte, the lieutenant of artillery who had become the conqueror of Europe, was brought to bay before the walls of Paris and forced to abdicate the throne. The victorious Allies chained 'The Monster' to the rock of Elba and set about dismantling the might of the Napoleonic machine. From his long exile in England, the brother of the beheaded French king supplanted the 'Corsican Ogre' on the throne of France as Louis XVIII and immediately set about attempting to recreate the 'Ancien Régime', though he was prevented from exercising his divine right by a constitutional charter and bicameral assembly. The Allies were uncharacteristically lenient. There were to be no financial reparations for the misery caused by France's exported wars, her colonial possessions were to be largely left intact and her borders maintained as they had been in 1791.[1]

The winter had, however, been an unhappy and uncertain one. Peasants who had benefited from the sequestration of lands from the clergy and nobility were suspicious of the returning aristocrats and priests. The middle classes, who had profited from the war, viewed the new regime with distrust and worried over the precarious nature of state finances and the volatility of the Bourse. The meritocracy of generals, ministers and civil servants was snubbed as 'parvenu' by the returning émigrés; their presence at court not welcomed. Though they had benefited the most under the Consulate and Empire, they felt compelled to exile themselves to their châteaux, whilst Royalists were favoured with appointments to grand office.

By far the most disaffected, however, was France's military. Proud regiments, with long traditions, were obliged to wear royal devices and bear royal titles, their crosses of the *Légion d'Honneur* debased by its indiscriminate award to all and sundry. With the army reduced to 200,000 men, thousands of officers were replaced by the appointees of the new Minister for War, General Count Pierre Dupont de l'Étang. The man whose defeat and disgrace at the battle of Bailén had resulted in over 18,000 Frenchmen being incarcerated in the hulks at Cadiz and then left to rot on

Prologue

the barren island of Cabrera. Those officers dismissed from the service, or left to the penury of half-pay festered in the cafés and chop-houses of towns and cities across France, reminiscing over past glories and present slights. Elsewhere, French soldiers returned from the fortresses of Poland, Germany and the Netherlands, undefeated by their enemies, to be joined in the ranks of the unemployed by those released from the British hulks and the wreckage of the Grande Armée, the bulk of which had been lost forever in the icy steppes of Russia. All simmered with a desire for vengeance. Had not the Emperor promised he would return in time to see the violets bloom?[2]

From his confinement on Elba, Napoleon sensed the mood. Spies and agents reported to him on the state of public opinion. Secret reports arrived, detailing rifts at the Congress of Vienna, the assembly called to redraw the map of Europe. Austria, Britain and Royalist France were in dispute with Prussia and Russia and the façade of Allied unity seemed on the verge of collapse. Napoleon spent the winter watching and waiting, until his restless spirit could bear no more. Slighted, belittled and paranoid that he was about to be assassinated, the 'Grand Disturber' chose to risk all on a final throw of the dice. Taking advantage of the absence of Colonel Sir Neil Campbell, his British gaoler, the Emperor and his household, with their escort of just over a thousand soldiers, set sail from Portoferraio on the evening of 26 February 1815; France was about to suffer its smallest ever invasion. The news of his subsequent landing at Golfe Juan on 1 March electrified Europe. Louis XVIII was informed the following day, but it would take until 7 March before the tidings reached Vienna.[3]

At the town of Ypres in western Belgium, Fanny Watson, daughter of Major Lewis Watson of the 69th Regiment of Foot, heard the news unofficially and found it hard to credit:

> It is strange, and in vain attempts have been made to explain, how rumours precede intelligence of actual events with a rapidity most wonderful, and yet in so mysterious a manner that it has proved impossible to trace it; thus in the army the expected arrival of 'the Route,' or order of removal, is frequently known amongst the men before the commanding officer even has had an expectation of it. So it was in this instance; one afternoon when the sergeant brought the Orderly Book with the 'Orders' to my father, he told the servants in the kitchen, 'That the men had it that Bonaparte had escaped from Elba and invaded France.' The information was laughed at, and the sergeant asked, 'How could he possibly believe so absurd and improbable, nay, impossible an event?' Two days afterwards, news arrived to confirm that report.[4]

Word reached Brussels on 9 March and spread like wildfire across Belgium and through the remnants of Lieutenant-General Sir Thomas Graham's British expeditionary force that had helped to liberate the Netherlands the previous year. James Elkington, surgeon of the 30th Regiment of Foot for the past two years, was less sceptical:

> In the midst of our pleasure, with the idea of the regiment being reduced, we were on this day astonished to hear of the escape of Buonaparte from Elba, and his landing at Cannes. Consternation was the order of the day, there were some who thought he would be immediately captured having so small a force ... I laid two wagers of £5 each, one with Colonel Bailey and one with Captain Howard; that Napoleon would reach Paris without firing a shot and secondly, that in six months the Allied Armies would be in Paris.[5]

At first, the probability of a bloodless coup seemed wholly unrealistic, but on 7 March, troops sent to arrest Napoleon at Laffrey went over to the Emperor, followed by the city of Lyons, two days later. His growing entourage received a cautious and inconsistent reception. The populace were amazed at the boldness of his actions, but the acclamations were half-hearted in many towns and villages, or limited to ex-soldiers in others. Elsewhere, veterans rushed to rejoin the colours, 'habit-vestes' and accoutrements were taken from chests and tricolour cockades fixed to shakos that bore the marks of the Spanish sun and sabre cuts from Austrian dragoons. The generals, however, sat on the fence, awaiting the outcome of this imperial gamble, wrestling with conscience over their oaths to Louis, while recollecting their former glories under the '*Petit Caporal*'.[6]

The moment he had landed once again on French soil, the Emperor had opened a correspondence with the crowned heads of Europe, pledging himself committed to peace. His appeals fell on stony ground. On 13 March, the delegates to the Congress of Vienna, having suspended their wrangling, signed a declaration.

> Napoleon Buonaparte, by again appearing in France with projects of confusion and disorder, has deprived himself of the protection of the law and has manifested to the universe that there can be neither peace nor truce with him. The powers consequently declare, that Napoleon Buonaparte has placed himself without the pale of civil and social relations; and that, as an enemy and disturber of the tranquillity of the world, he has rendered himself subject to public vengeance.[7]

If his reception abroad was a hostile one, his progress through eastern France was met by a more equivocal response. In the end, Elkington's prediction turned out to be correct and Napoleon reached Paris on 20 March, less than twenty-four hours after Louis XVIII had fled the city, bound for Lille and Ghent, where Prince Willem van Oranje-Nassau reluctantly offered him sanctuary and exile.[8]

Even while the Emperor was being carried up the stairs of the Tuileries by his delirious supporters, the diplomats and their sovereigns were busy putting the finishing touches to the agreement that would bind the Allies together until they had finally beheaded the Napoleonic hydra. The seventh and final coalition of the wars came into being on 25 March 1815, a renewal of the Treaty of Chaumont, signed in March the previous year. Each of the four great powers pledged to put an army of 150,000 men into the field, until such time as 'Buonaparte shall have been rendered absolutely unable to create disturbance, and to renew his attempts for possessing himself of the supreme power in France'. With its modest army already heavily committed in North America, Great Britain was exempt from this requirement and agreed instead to provide financial subsidies to her allies, to the tune of £5 million. Once again, British gold would feed, clothe and arm the warring nations of Europe.[9]

Realising that conflict was inevitable, Napoleon set about cementing his domestic position through the creation of a liberal constitution by means of the *Acte Additionel aux Constitutions de l'Empire*. His political opponents appeased for the time being, he then embarked on the task of putting France once again on a war footing. '*La Patrie est en danger!*' was the rallying cry, as it had been in the heady days of 1792. The Bourbon appointees to the regular army had fled into exile with their master, or into rebellion in the Vendée and were replaced by retired officers and those on half pay. Hundreds of thousands of men were raised from recalled veterans, volunteers, returned deserters, the 'Marie-Louises' of 1814 and the conscripts of the 'Class of 1815'. These were supplemented by the auxiliary troops of the Garde Nationale, who garrisoned the fortresses and kept order in the towns and cities. In the space of a mere ten weeks, the Emperor hoped to have as many as half a million men under arms. Though imposing in number, the troops were badly equipped. Many of the arsenals had been emptied the previous year and the foundries, smithies, workshops and factories hummed with intensity as they churned out muskets, bayonets, uniforms, harness and cannon. The countryside was scoured for suitable horseflesh, with those of the mounted *Gendarmerie* requisitioned for the use of the heavy cavalry. By every ingenious device, an army was forged to defend the nation, but it was a brittle one; distrustful of its generals; loyal to 'Le Tondu' alone.

In the meantime, the Allies had set to work with equal vigour. The long columns of Russians and Austrians who had occupied France and were returning home were halted and faced about, though it would be some time before they found themselves on the Rhine. The Allies drew up a simple plan. They would descend upon France with three quarters of a million men, in a concentric attack that would leave Bonaparte unable to repeat his brilliant campaign of the previous year. To the north, an Anglo-Netherlands army of 100,000 men under the Prince van Oranje-Nassau and 130,000 Prussians under Field-Marshal Prince Gebhard von Blücher would march on Paris. The main thrust would come across the Rhine and Meuse, where Field-Marshal Prince Karl von Schwarzenberg, with over 200,000 Austrians, Bavarians and Hessians would drive into eastern France. He would be supported by Field-Marshals Mikhail Barclay de Tolly and Ferdinand Winzingerode, with a similar number of Russians. Farther to the south, 40,000 Swiss, 50,000 Austrians and Piedmontese and 20,000 Neapolitans would pour across the borders, whilst a force of 50,000 Spanish troops would mass at the foot of the Pyrenees. Such was the plan, but until the arrival of these vast legions, the Allies would be thin on the ground and vulnerable to a pre-emptive strike.[10]

If Bonaparte was to launch an offensive, the most likely target would be the newly created Kingdom of the Netherlands, which comprised lands which, until recently, had been ruled as part of Metropolitan France. A quick victory for the French could be devastating in its outcome, potentially knocking Britain and Prussia out of the war, providing Bonaparte with manpower and matériel and having far reaching propaganda value among the less committed of the Allied nations. The Low Countries, therefore, were the point of danger and accordingly it was here that Field-Marshal Arthur Wellesley, the Duke of Wellington, arrived on 4 April to take up his new appointment as commander-in-chief of the British and Netherlands forces.[11]

Just short of his 46th birthday, Wellington possessed a formidable military reputation and was seemingly at the summit of his martial career, lionised across Europe for his five-year campaign in the Peninsula and France. The third surviving son of Garret Wesley, first Earl of Mornington, educated at Eton and Angers, the young Arthur was not an outstanding academic and was accordingly found an ensigncy in the 73rd Regiment of Foot. During the course of the next nine years, through purchase and exchange, he became colonel of the 33rd Regiment of Foot. Having already served in Flanders, where he, 'learned what not to do', he spent the next eight years campaigning in India, where he was schooled in the use of terrain, the management of allies, the value of intelligence and the realities of military administration. Sent to Portugal in April 1809 with the advanced party of a British army, he put this knowledge to excellent use; in the years that followed, he defeated a succession of French generals, culminating in his invasion of France in 1814. Made Viscount Wellington of Talavera in 1809, Earl of Wellington in 1812 and Marquess of Wellington later that year, victory after victory had accelerated his ascent of the aristocracy, until he was created the first Duke of Wellington in 1814.[12]

Wellington would need all his personal attributes to be successful in his new role. A stern, aloof and aristocratic figure, he despised every facet of the French Revolution and what it stood for, becoming in time the champion of the established order. He was inured to hard service and dedicated to simple living, a man of great energy and courage and possessing the highest level of integrity. His dealings in India, the Peninsula and at the Congress of Vienna had honed his skills and forged him into a highly able soldier, administrator and diplomat; an all-rounder with the kudos, contacts and qualities that made him an obvious choice for the job.

From the moment that he arrived in Brussels, Wellington was beset by difficulties. Strident demands from Louis XVIII's court in exile at Ghent; the failure of King Willem I of the Netherlands to deliver much in the way of promised troops and supplies; the conflicting priorities of the Prussian army and the machinations of its Anglophobic chief-of-staff, General Baron August Niedhardt von Gneisenau. He was further exasperated by the quality and quantity of troops and equipment allocated to the army by Horse Guards and the Master-General of the Ordnance. As early as the day after his arrival, he was writing to Earl Bathurst, the Secretary of State for War and the Colonies concerning the forces he commanded:

> I cannot help thinking, from all accounts, that they are not what they ought to be to enable us to maintain our military position in Europe. It appears to me that you have

not taken in England a clear view of your situation, that you do not think war certain, and that a great effort must be made, if it is to be hoped that it shall be short. You have not called out the militia, or announced any intention in your message to Parliament, by which measure troops of the line in Ireland or elsewhere might become disposable; and how we are to make out 150,000 men, or even the 60,000 of the defensive part of the treaty of Chaumont, appears not to have been considered. If you could let me have 40,000 good British infantry, besides those you insist on having in garrisons, the proportion settled by the treaty you are to furnish of cavalry, that is to say, the eighth of 150,000 men, including in both the old German Legion, and 150 pieces of British field artillery fully horsed, I should be satisfied, and take my chance for the rest, and engage that we would play our part in the game. But as it is, we are in a bad way.[13]

The army he had inherited was a polyglot one, comprised of contingents from several powers and bringing with them the complexity of political expediency, sensitivity over chains of command and acrimony over whom exactly would pay for what. Lieutenant-Colonel Sir Henry Hardinge, Wellington's liaison officer with the Prussians commented, 'This army is not unlike a French pack of hounds: pointers, poodles, turnspits, all mixed up together and running in sad confusion.' By far the greatest proportion of the hounds were those drawn from German nations and secured for the Duke's command despite the objections of the Prussians, who strongly believed that German troops should serve alongside their Prussian brothers.[14]

Within the ranks of Wellington's army were 7,000 men of the King's German Legion, first raised in 1803 after the French occupied the Electorate of Hanover, a possession of the British crown. Volunteers had flooded aboard British warships and the men were evacuated to England and formed into infantry battalions, cavalry regiments and artillery batteries. With extensive service in the Peninsula, these formed a valuable body of veteran troops, but their contract of engagement with the British was due to expire six months after 'The ratification of a definitive treaty of peace', and the men were on the point of being discharged and sent back to their homes. Fortunately, the senior officers of the Legion voluntarily offered a new six-month engagement, which was accepted by the British government and those elements of the Legion not already in the Netherlands were shipped there forthwith. By the time the campaign opened, two infantry brigades would be present on active service, comprising two light infantry and six line infantry battalions. Two horse batteries and one of foot artillery were also available and were attached to Anglo-German infantry divisions, although cadres of officers and men from the 1st and 2nd companies under Lieutenant-Colonel Heinrich Brückmann, which had arrived in the Netherlands without horses or matériel, were seconded to newly raised Hanoverian artillery formations. Finally, two regiments of light dragoons and three of hussars, stationed in Flanders since the previous year, were brigaded with British cavalry as part of the Cavalry Reserve. The only troops of the KGL to see action at Les Quatre Bras, however, would be Major Heinrich Kuhlmann's 2nd Horse Artillery Troop and Captain

Andreas Cleeves' 2nd Foot Artillery Troop, both of which were equipped with five 9-pounder guns and one 5½-inch howitzer.[15]

The liberation of Hanover in 1813 provided the opportunity to raise a new Hanoverian army and King George III of Britain, who was also Elector of Hanover, immediately authorised three infantry battalions to be raised at Bremen-Verden, Lüneburg and Lauenburg, supplemented by a *Feld-Jäger-Korps* of light infantry, which ultimately comprised four companies. During the course of 1813 and 1814, further Field Battalions were raised, along with thirty battalions of *Landwehr* (militia), three hussar regiments and three companies of foot artillery. During the course of the winter of 1814–1815, a Hanoverian 'Subsidiary' Corps was stationed in the Netherlands. From this formation and from subsequent drafts, a field force comprising a brigade of cavalry and five of infantry was eventually formed, totalling 16,000 officers and men, three brigades of which were composed entirely of Landwehr troops. Two of these brigades would see action at Les Quatre Bras. The 1st (Hanoverian) Infantry Brigade, under Major-General Count Friedrich von Kielmansegge, was entirely formed of regulars, while the 4th (Hanoverian) Infantry Brigade, under Colonel Carl Best, was composed of four Landwehr battalions. Captain Georg Wiering's battery had been broken up in early May 1815 and its men and equipment re-distributed to the remaining two batteries under Captain Wilhelm Braun and Captain Carl von Rettberg. Only this latter company, equipped with British 9-pounder guns, would fight at Les Quatre Bras. On the whole, the Hanoverian army was untried; although some units had been raised in 1813 and had fought in the War of Liberation, the majority were newly raised Landwehr, their ranks filled with young, inexperienced and in some cases reluctant soldiers, peppered with a cadre of experienced KGL officers and NCOs.[16]

Another German contingent in the ranks of Wellington's army was that of Duke Friedrich Wilhelm von Braunschweig-Lüneburg, an inveterate enemy of the French. His father, a field-marshal in the Prussian army, had been mortally wounded at the battle of Auerstädt on 14 October 1806, following which the duchy had been dissolved and the young Duke forced to flee to Austria. Here, he set about raising a corps of infantry and cavalry to fight against the French in the campaign of 1809, which the Austrians provided with weapons and clothing. As an ancient German symbol of mourning and vengeance, their uniforms were black and the corps became known as the 'Schwarzer Schar', or the Black Band. After the defeat of the Austrians at Wagram, the Duke led his troops across a swathe of French occupied northern Germany, before being evacuated by the Royal Navy to England where, after a period of reorganisation, an infantry battalion styled the Braunschweig-Oels Jagers and a regiment of hussars comprising two squadrons, entered British service and fought throughout the Peninsular War. The advance of the Allied armies across Germany in 1813 resulted in the liberation of the Duchy of Braunschweig-Lüneburg and the Duke returned home to reclaim his territories and to raise more troops with which to take the fight to the French. Starting with a company of *Gelernte Jäger*, or light infantry raised from professional gamekeepers and foresters, this force quickly grew, such that by the end of the year the Duke's infantry comprised an *Avantgarde-Battalion*, a *Leib-Battalion* or bodyguard, three light and three line infantry battalions. A further five reserve battalions were also raised, as well as a body of Landwehr. In addition, a new Hussar Regiment and a squadron of Uhlans was created, together with a single battery each of foot and horse artillery, the former equipped with 9-pounder and the latter 6-pounder guns, all supplied by Britain. On Christmas Day 1814, the infantry of the original Black Band left British service and returned to Germany, to be incorporated into the new army. Difficulties were experienced integrating the two formations and British and Prussian battalion structures and drill regulations had to be reconciled. Despite being fiercely patriotic and with ranks stiffened by a cadre of veteran officers and NCOs, the battalions and squadrons were, in the main, untested troops and many would receive their baptism of fire in the coming campaign. Following Napoleon's return, and true to his character, the Duke agreed to provide a division of troops to serve under Wellington; the first of which left Germany on 15 April, the final elements arriving in early June, where they took up cantonments to the north of Brussels, as part of Wellington's reserve. Here, under the complex arrangements made for supplying the Allied forces, they received British musket ammunition, food and fodder, although these latter provisions were paid for by the Kingdom of the United Netherlands.[17]

The United Netherlands was itself a fledgling kingdom. Landing at Scheveningen on 30 November 1813, Prince Willem Frederik van Oranje-Nassau, son of the last *Stadhouder*, or head of state, was proclaimed Prince-Sovereign the following day and immediately set about raising an army. As the Prussians and British drove French garrisons from the country, the nucleus of this army was formed on eleven infantry battalions which had been raised in Holland, Prussia and Britain. With progress slow, the nation was called to arms in December 1813, but despite some volunteers coming forward, the appeal was unsuccessful and Willem was forced to introduce conscription in order to raise a militia to support the small regular army. On the back of this move, the government announced the creation of a regular army of some 30,000 men and a National Militia composed of a further 23,000 reservists. As well as Dutch forces, the Prince also recruited in his hereditary territories of Oranje-Nassau and formed the two-battalion Regiment Oranje-Nassau from these troops, while separately, the state of Nassau-Usingen provided a further two regiments for Netherlands service. Under the terms of the Treaty of Paris of 30 May 1814, it was agreed that Willem's territories would be expanded to incorporate modern-day Belgium, which had formerly been ruled as part of Metropolitan France and before that, as a province of the Austro-Hungarian Empire. It was agreed that Willem's eldest son, Prince Willem Frederik – who held the rank of general in the British army and who had served as aide-de-camp to the Duke of Wellington in Spain – would take command of the Anglo-Hanoverian army that occupied these possessions. In the meantime and over the course of the following autumn and winter, the Netherlands army was expanded and reorganised, incorporating returning Dutch and Belgian troops who had served Napoleon. The Kingdom of the United Netherlands was created on 16 March 1815 and Prince Willem was elevated to the throne as King Willem I, by which time the Netherlands forces in Belgium comprised three infantry divisions and a cavalry division of three brigades.[18]

The understandable nationalist tensions between the Dutch and Belgian elements of the new army and between those officers and men who had served Napoleon and those returning from exile were problematic. Mistrust of the Belgians in particular was a source of concern to many, including Wellington himself. In a letter to Earl Bathurst, he counselled against concentrating, 'All the youth and treason of the Army' and care was taken that troops from Belgium, or the 'South Netherlands' were brigaded with those from Holland, now styled the 'North Netherlands' and not in homogeneous formations. Nor was Wellington averse to sharing such views with his allies. Writing in subtle phrases to the Prince van Oranje-Nassau on 17 April 1815, he advised that:

> His Majesty should, in my opinion, consider that he has but a small, and very young army to oppose possibly a numerous and well disciplined one; that he has a large extent of country to cover but lately brought under His Majesty's government, whose inhabitants are supposed by some to be not very well disposed towards it.

The senior officers of the Netherlands army were a similarly diverse set. Lieutenant-General Baron David Chassé and Major-General Baron Jean-Baptiste van Merlen had both been general officers in Napoleon's army, while Lieutenant-General Baron Henri-Georges de Perponcher-Sedlenitzky and Major-Generals Baron Jean-Victor de Constant-Rebecque and Count Willem van Bijlandt had shared the exile of their prince and fought with the British. The situation was mirrored at regimental level, the 5th (South Netherlands) Light Dragoons boasted twelve officers who were holders of the *Légion d'Honneur* and 117 other ranks who had seen service in the French army.[19]

Despite these tensions and their recent mobilisation, the quality of the troops in most cases was reasonable, as Lieutenant Chrétien Scheltens of the 7th (South Netherlands) Line Battalion described:

> The battalion was well-composed; nearly all the officers had served on campaign. The cadre of non-commissioned officers and corporals was passable, but needed, like the soldiers, practical instruction. All were volunteers.[20]

Hurriedly clothed with the assistance of the British treasury and armed from the arsenals of the fortresses seized at length from the French, the towns and villages of the Low Countries echoed with the sound of these young troops being drilled in manoeuvre and musketry and taught the rudiments of military life. For many, the period of training would be all too short, before they were flung into the horrors of combat itself.

As for Wellington's British army, despite its mongrel nature and even having scraped the manpower barrel a number of times, it never quite reached the numbers that he had demanded. Writing to Lieutenant-General Lord Charles Stewart on 18 May 1815, he vented his frustrations:

> I have got an infamous army, very weak and ill equipped, and a very inexperienced staff. In my opinion, they are doing nothing in England. They have not raised a man; they have not called out the militia either in England or Ireland and are unable to send me any thing; and they have not sent a message to Parliament about the money. The war spirit is therefore evaporating as I am informed.[21]

Wellington's criticism was not altogether fair, and within a short space of time troops began arriving from England and Ireland, followed in May and June by more battalions returning from North America. The backbone of this small British field army was its infantry and at Les Quatre Bras, sixteen battalions would be engaged, although the quality of the troops was variable. At the end of the war, much of Wellington's Peninsula army was shipped to North America, while over 47,000 experienced soldiers were discharged, their terms of service expired. Despite his general laments to the contrary, the Duke was fortunate at Les Quatre Bras, as of the dozen line infantry battalions, nine had seen extensive service and could rightly be described as veteran. For example, the first battalion of the 28th Regiment of Foot, under Colonel Sir Charles Belson had seen action in Egypt, northern Germany and Denmark, before being shipped to the Peninsula, where they fought at Corunna, Douro, Busaco, Talavera, Barrosa, Arroyo de Molinos, Burgos, Vitoria, Maya, Sorauren, the Pyrenees, Nivelle, Nive, Orthes and Toulouse. Even in those veteran battalions where casualties and time-expired men had necessitated recruitment, the bulk of the soldiers were experienced; almost half of the first battalion of the 92nd Regiment of Foot (the Gordon Highlanders) for example, had served for eight years or more. Other first battalions, however, were unproven, such as the 33rd Regiment of Foot, which had spent the majority of the Napoleonic Wars in India, until it was thrown into the fray at Bergen-op-Zoom in March 1814.

Among the remainder of Wellington's line infantry were many second battalions, which had also seen little or no active service. The second battalion of the 73rd Regiment of Foot for example, had only been raised on Christmas Eve in 1808 and its only experience of action had been at Ghörde in 1813 and Merxem in 1814. The majority of the men in its ranks had enlisted in 1812 and 1813 and therefore had but a short regular service record although most had volunteered from the Militia and were at least well trained. By far the strongest battalions numerically, but somewhat lacking in battle experience, were the four Guards battalions, which had spent the bulk of the War on home and ceremonial duties. Despite Wellington having eight Anglo-German cavalry brigades at his disposal, none were destined to arrive in time to fight at Les Quatre Bras, though he did have the benefit of three experienced brigades of foot artillery, equipped with the highly effective 9-pounder cannon. If some of his troops were mediocre in quality, he was more fortunate concerning the availability of experienced senior commanders. Despite the interference of the Duke of York, the commander-in-chief, he managed to secure the services of divisional and brigade commanders who had almost all served extensively under him in the Peninsula.[22]

Although obliged by King Willem to maintain the integrity of the Netherlands infantry divisions and to allow its cavalry division to operate as an autonomous formation, Wellington formed his British, Hanoverian and KGL infantry brigades into composite divisions, of which it was hoped there would eventually be seven. In the event, however, only five were fully formed, the remainder operating as independent brigades held in reserve, or forming garrisons for the fortresses. Each formed division contained three brigades, with the exception of the 1st (British) Infantry Division, which was composed of four large guards battalions, formed in two brigades. Wellington took care to mix his veteran infantry with the inexperienced Hanoverian Landwehr, creating divisions that had a balanced fighting capability. Lieutenant-General Baron Carl von Alten's 3rd (British) Infantry Division, for example, contained a veteran KGL brigade, supplemented by an inexperienced British brigade and one of Hanoverian regulars, who had seen little action. Each division was supported by two batteries, mainly companies of foot artillery. Although not a proponent of the army corps as a strategic or tactical formation, Wellington's appointment to supreme command of Netherlands troops as well as his Anglo-Hanoverian force, came with the condition that the Prince van Oranje-Nassau retain nominal command of the Netherlands troops in addition to that of an Anglo-Netherlands army corps. Consequently, under his supreme command the 1st and 3rd (British) Infantry Divisions were grouped under Major-General George Cooke and General von Alten. Together with the 2nd (Netherlands) Infantry Division under General de Perponcher-Sedlnitzky and General Chassé's 3rd (Netherlands) Infantry Division. These divisions constituted I Corps. Similarly, two further Anglo-German divisions were combined with the 1st (Netherlands) Infantry Division and the Netherlands Indian Brigade to form II Corps under Lieutenant-General Lord Rowland Hill. The Reserve was still forming when hostilities commenced, but comprised the fully formed 5th (British) Infantry Division, the partially assembled 6th and 7th (British) Infantry Divisions, the Brunswick Division, the Hanoverian Reserve Division and Major-General Baron August von Kruse's 1st Nassau-Usingen Regiment. Other than the three brigades of Netherlands cavalry, attached to I Corps, the cavalry were grouped in brigades under the command of Lieutenant-General Henry Paget, Earl of Uxbridge.

The responsibility of maintaining communications with the Prussians along the axis of the chemin Brunhaut, the old Roman road running through Binche that divided the frontier between the Allied sector to the west and that guarded by the Prussians to the east, was given to I Corps. The Prince van Oranje-Nassau established his headquarters at Braine-le-Comte, with divisions in the vicinity of Enghien, Soignies, Nivelles and Fayt and a cavalry screen between Mons and Binche. Farther to the west, four Anglo-Hanoverian cavalry brigades maintained an outpost line as far as the River Lys at Courtrai, while in their rear, Hill concentrated the divisions of II Corps in the region of Ath, Leuze, Renaix, Grammont, Alost and Sotteghem. The remainder of Uxbridge's cavalry went into cantonments in the valley of the Dender, with his headquarters at Ninove. The reserve, under Wellington's personal control was stationed in and around Brussels. In addition to his field army, Wellington established garrisons in the fortresses and towns of Antwerp, Ath, Ghent, Mons, Nieuport, Ostend, Tournai and Ypres and civilian and military resources were allocated to make these places ready to withstand a French assault.

If Wellington's preparations were characterised by tensions in his relationships with Horse Guards and King Willem, he was to experience more problems in his dealings with the Prussians. Initially concerned that the French might invade before he had time to organise an effective resistance, he had been reassured to receive a letter from General von Gneisenau, stating that he could count, 'On the support of all our available forces in the event of your being attacked. We are firmly determined to share the lot of the army which is under Your Excellency's command.' The forces to which von Gneisenau referred were a field army of four corps, each comprised of four infantry brigades and two or three of cavalry, under the leadership of Field-Marshal von Blücher, the 72-year-old hero of the War of Liberation and an implacable enemy of the French. Initially an admirer of Wellington, relations were somewhat soured between the two allies and their senior officers, following the capture of a French official bearing a copy of a secret treaty, whereby Britain would side with France and Austria against Russia and Prussia, in the event that a territorial dispute over Saxony resulted in a war. Nevertheless, during the spring, the Prussian army finally entered Belgium, the four corps being cantoned in the vicinity of Charleroi, Namur, Ciney and Liège, where von Blücher also established his headquarters.[23]

Unlike Wellington, whose meticulous administration had ensured that his supply arrangements were adequate, the Prussians were stationed in a region that had been devastated the previous year. Even though Wellington had managed to establish an arrangement whereby British gold would pay the Netherlands government to supply the Prussians, the logistical situation that von Blücher found himself in strengthened his already aggressive instincts and led him to conclude that the sooner he could export the cost of his army to enemy territory, the better. As well as these issues, von Blücher also had other problems with which to contend. On 2 May, Saxon grenadiers had come to blows with Prussian staff officers when they arrived at his headquarters to protest their enforced transfer to Prussian service as new subjects of the Prussian king, a consequence of the dismemberment of their own country. The commander-in-chief refused to meet them and threatened to, 'Restore order by force, even if I be compelled to shoot down the entire Saxon army'. The resulting mutiny was quelled by the troops being separated and disarmed, selective executions and the eventual repatriation to Germany of the disaffected division, some 14,000 strong.

Amid this atmosphere of tension, division and hardship, Wellington and von Blücher met at Tirlemont on 3 May 1815. Although Wellington and von Gneisenau had both previously developed strategies in isolation, they had not had the opportunity to exchange ideas on Napoleon's intentions, nor to agree a joint plan of operations. Whilst no official record exists that describes the agenda and agreement at this meeting, it is reasonable to assume from their subsequent actions that the two allies concluded that Napoleon's most likely course of action would be to fight a campaign in the style of his defence of France the previous year. Despite von Blücher's eagerness to invade enemy territory, both men were constrained by the timetable imposed by Prince von Schwarzenburg's Council of War at Vienna, which had informed Wellington that such an advance would only begin some time around 20 June and no sooner. The second, less likely, scenario that was discussed was the possibility of Napoleon invading the Netherlands and Wellington persuaded von Blücher that, in this eventuality, they should unite their armies and offer battle.[24]

Such was the situation in mid-June – rumours abounded of Napoleon having left Paris; of enormous bodies of French troops gathering; of defensive works being erected about the French border towns; of invasion. While the spies flitted across the frontier and the generals wrestled with supply problems, government interference and dry diplomacy, the troops endured the boredom of waiting for a war that it seemed would never begin. This boredom was punctuated by route marches, reviews and training exercises across the fields and in the dirty, isolated villages of southern Belgium.

A short distance to the south, however, the enemy was on the move.

Endnotes

1. Lachouque, p. 12.
2. Lachouque, p. 44.
3. Barnett, p. 200. Chandler (II) pp. 13–14.
4. Myddleton, p. 66.
5. Chandler (II), p. 27. Elkington (I), pp. 11–12.
6. Barnett, p. 201. Chandler (II), pp. 11,18.
7. C. Kelly, p. 3.
8. Chandler (II), p. 18. Longford, p. 395.
9. Barnett, pp. 196, 201. Chandler (II), p. 20. C. Kelly, pp. 4–5. Lachouque, p. 12.
10. Lachouque, p. 19.
11. Chandler (II), p. 29.
12. M. Glover, pp. 33-6. Longford, pp. xix, xxi-xxii. P. Stanhope, p. 136.
13. Gurwood, pp. 291–2.
14. Brett-James, p. 20.
15. Beamish, pp. 319, 322, 350–1.
16. Hofschröer (II), pp. 74-7. Hofschröer (III), pp. 37–40.
17. Adkin, p. 284. Haythornthwaite (III), p. 332. Hofschröer (I), pp. 77, 79–80. von Pivka (III), pp. 8, 14, 17
18. Pawly (III), pp. 6–7, 9–11.
19. Gurwood, p. 312. Pawly (III), p. 20. Rens, pp. 96–7. Wellesley, pp. 167–8.
20. Scheltens, p. 195.
21. Gurwood, p. 312.
22. Lagden and Sly, pp. xi-xii. Sutherland, p. 57.
23. Henderson, p. 1. Hofschröer (I), p. 104. von Ollech, pp. 19–23.
24. Henderson, p. 279. Hofschröer (I), p. 48.

CHAPTER 1

The sentries snapped to attention and presented their carbines as the Prince van Oranje-Nassau rode into the sleepy village of Saint-Symphorien, shortly after 7.00 a.m. on 15 June 1815. As he passed the cottages, barns and stables, he observed that some men of the green-jacketed 5th Regiment of Light Dragoons were still busy mucking out the stables or feeding and grooming their horses, while others were preparing to go out on yet another patrol towards the frontier. In compliance with standing orders, the troops had been paraded by Lieutenant-Colonel Edouard de Mercx de Corbais at 5.00 a.m., the same time that the Prince had left his quarters in the house belonging to Monsieur Mary, the Mayor of Braine-le-Comte.[1]

Although this was one of his routine inspections of the cavalry outposts that formed his eyes, ears and first line of defence, the Prince had become increasingly anxious over the past few days and tensions had been rising among his senior officers. On 10 June, these very troopers had fought a brief skirmish with the French 6th Chasseurs à Cheval at Goegnies-Chaussée, twelve kilometres south of Mons, on the Roman road from Bavay to Binche. As the days passed, more reports, rumours and sightings had heightened the sense of expectation at the Prince's headquarters. His chief-of-staff, General de Constant-Rebecque, had noted in his diary on 11 June that Napoleon was expected to leave Paris the following day. On 13 June the Prince had passed a report to the Duke of Wellington which confirmed that the Emperor's headquarters had been established at Avesnes, a mere 38 kilometres from Mons. For several nights, the skies had reflected thousands of camp fires to the south of the River Sambre, from which a trickle of deserters had slipped away, handing themselves over to the patrols of the Prussian or Netherlands cavalry and warning of an attack on either 14 or 15 June. As recently as the day before, General van Merlen, whose headquarters the Prince was approaching, had seized a letter from a French cavalry officer Captain Baron Niel, and forwarded it to the Prince's headquarters at Braine-le-Comte. The French, it seemed, were on the highest state of alert, had been issued with eight days' worth of rations and were on the move.[2]

There was a flurry of activity as the Prince reined in his horse at van Merlen's headquarters and the General and his staff hurriedly assembled to greet their chief. The dialogue was, however, brief. There were no new developments to report, the vedettes had not been attacked and all had remained quiet overnight. Colonel de Mercx de Corbais had earlier reported to Lieutenant-General Baron Jean-Marie de Collaert that

The Battle of Quatre Bras

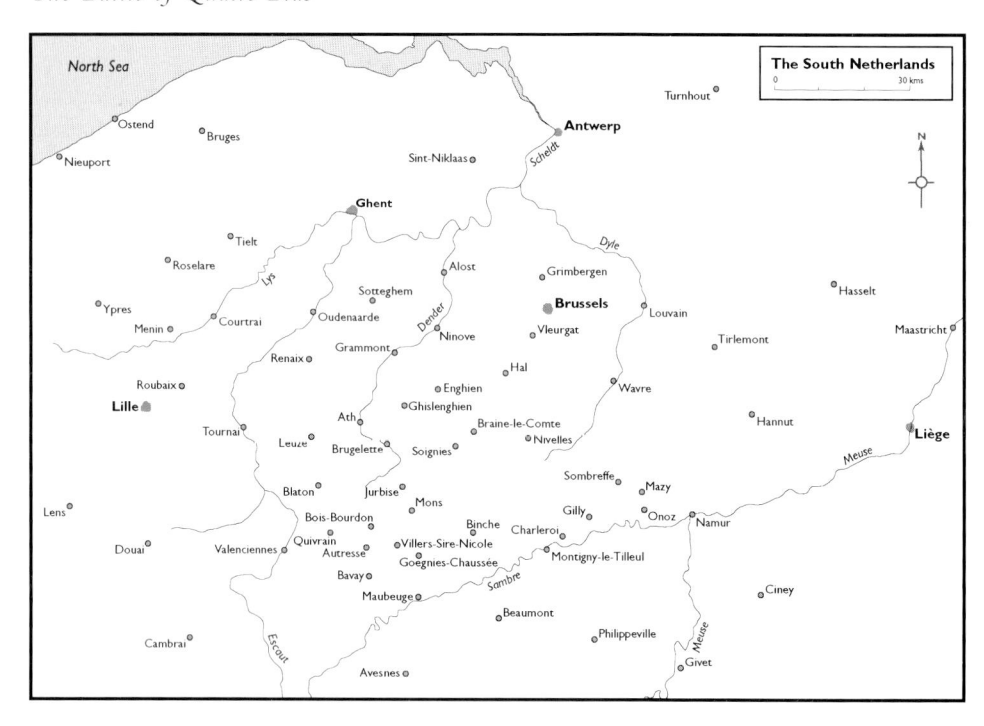

the French advance posts seemed to have disappeared during the night. The occasional French patrol had been seen in the direction of Bois-Bourdon and Villers-Sire-Nicole, but between Mons and Binche, it seemed that 'perfect tranquillity' reigned. Perhaps today would bring more intelligence of the French. As the Prince and the General discussed the correspondence between Baron Niel and Lieutenant de Bourgoing of the 6th Chasseurs à Cheval, a messenger arrived from the 7th Company of the 6th (North Netherlands) Regiment of Hussars, the second regiment of van Merlen's brigade. He brought word of heavy gunfire in the direction of Lobbes and Thuin, less than ten kilometres from the company's cantonment at the Abbaye de Bonne Espérance; perhaps it was yet another rumour, the air had been full of them for weeks.[3]

Given the heightened probability of the French taking the offensive, the Prince deemed it prudent to order van Merlen to take up new positions, somewhat closer to the boundary he shared with Major-General Carl von Steinmetz, commanding the 1st (Prussian) Infantry Brigade. The 5th Regiment of Light Dragoons would move from Harveng, Harmignies, Spiennes, Bougnies and Asquillies and take up new positions, with one squadron at Bray, where van Merlen was to establish his new headquarters and the other in reserve at Saint-Symphorien. Although outposts would be retained at Harmignies and Spiennes to keep watch to the south-east, it was evident to van Merlen that the Prince, in redeploying this regiment, was shifting the focus of his brigade from the south to the east. A second order was to be sent to Lieutenant-Colonel Lord Willem Boreel, commanding the 6th Hussar Regiment. He was to vacate Estinnes-au-Mont and to use the companies at Saint-Symphorien and Villers-Saint-Ghislain to create a line along the Estinnes stream, with a squadron at Estinnes-au-Val and a company each at Bray and Maurage, where two of the four pieces of horse artillery under Captain Adrianus Geij van Pittius would also be stationed. In advance of this line, a squadron would be stationed at Péronnes, from where it would be able to maintain contact with the Prussians in and around Binche.[4]

There was also time to pen a quick note to General Chassé, commanding the 3rd (Netherlands) Infantry Division at Haine-Saint-Pierre:

My dear General,

The Prussians have been attacked. I bid you to assemble your division, without losing time, at the assembly point on the heights behind Haine St. Pierre, where you will await my further orders.

Willem van Oranje-Nassau.[5]

His business at Saint-Symphorien concluded and conscious that he had a dinner engagement in Brussels at 3.00 p.m. and an invitation to the Duchess of Richmond's ball later that evening, the Prince remounted his horse shortly after 8.00 a.m. and headed back up the dusty road towards Havré, Roeulx and Soignies.[6]

Unknown to the Prince, General Chassé had already received information at about 8.30 a.m., that the French had crossed the frontier and there had been fighting at Thuin and Lobbes. For the time being, he thought, it appeared that he was not under immediate threat. The most advanced Netherlands infantry division, his troops occupied cantonments north of Binche, stretching from Chapelle-lez-Herlaimont in the east, to Thieu in the west, with the advanced troops occupying Péronnes. The bulk of his division was cantoned within a short march of its alarm post, the village of Fayt, halfway between Mons and Nivelles. However an order received on 18 May had instructed him – in the event of hostilities commencing – to leave two battalions of Colonel Hendrik Detmers' brigade at the villages where they were billeted. The 6th National Militia Battalion was to remain at Trivières and Strépy, whilst the 17th National Militia Battalion would continue to occupy Thieu; both were important crossing points over the River Haine. A subsequent order of 9 June stated that the 4th National Militia Battalion would remain at Haine-Saint-Pierre, with the 19th National Militia Battalion a short distance downstream at Saint-Vaast, Captain Rochell's company being posted at a windmill to the east of the village. The 35th Jager Battalion would remain at Haine-Saint Paul, where it would be joined by the 10th National Militia Battalion of Major-General Count Alexandre d'Aubremé's brigade, marching north from Péronnes. The only remaining infantry of Detmers' brigade, Lieutenant-Colonel Speelman's 2nd Line Battalion, was already quartered at Fayt. In this manner, Chassé surmised, he would not only hold all the key crossings over the River Haine, thereby guaranteeing van Merlen's line of retreat, his disposition would also buy time for d'Aubremé's brigade to mass on the high ground to the north of Haine-Saint-Pierre.[7]

An experienced soldier with forty years' service – much of it fighting alongside or in the ranks of the Grande Armée – Chassé had been very active during the preceding months, ensuring his inexperienced battalions were drilled, marched and mustered relentlessly, until they had reached an acceptable degree of proficiency. Orders had been received from the Prince van Oranje-Nassau on 9 June that the division was to be prepared to march at a moment's notice. In order to effect this, the battalions were to assemble each day at their cantonments and remain under arms until nightfall. Chassé had not only implemented this order, but had conducted several exercises at divisional level to rehearse an assembly, some of which had been undertaken at night in order to prepare the commanders for all eventualities. As luck would have it, Chassé had conducted just such an exercise the previous day; in the fields around Fayt, the 2nd, 3rd, 12th and 13th Line and the 36th Jager Battalions were mustered, having been joined during the night by the artillery batteries of Captains Carel Krahmer de Bichin and Johannes Lux, marching in from their cantonments at La Hestre and Seneffe respectively.[8]

The men had eaten breakfast and finished cleaning their arms and were on the point of marching back to their cantonments, when the Prince van Oranje-Nassau's messenger arrived, towards 9.30 a.m. Chassé, perhaps blessing his good fortune, ordered General d'Aubremé to keep his brigade assembled for the time being. Towards 11.00 a.m., Major Nahuys arrived at headquarters, having taken it upon himself to reconnoitre towards Binche, the closest town occupied by the Prussians and the cantonment of the Fusilier Battalion of the 12th (Brandenburg) Infantry Regiment. The news was not promising: Binche had been evacuated. Without further hesitation, Chassé sent an order for General d'Aubremé to advance to the high ground at Baume, overlooking the Haine crossings. Colonel Speelman was instructed to detail an officer to oversee the safe removal of the division's baggage to Seneffe. Couriers were then sent to Baume, in order to alert the 3rd National Militia Battalion and to Haine-Saint-Paul, with orders for the 35th Jager and 10th National Militia Battalions to join them there. The 4th National Militia Battalion at Haine-Saint-Pierre was instructed to prepare to defend the crossings, as were the 6th and 17th National Militia Battalions at Trivières, Strépy and Thieu. Lieutenant Holle of the former recalled the order:

> On the 15th, our commander was ordered that we were no longer part of the division we belonged to and that from now on we would serve as cover for the light cavalry. Therefore we received during the night the order to position our forward posts in skirmish order up to an hour's distance of Morage [Maurage].

Having complied with his prince's order to assemble the men on the heights behind Haine-Saint-Pierre, Chassé sat down and penned a note for General de Constant-Rebecque at Braine-le-Comte.[9]

Farther to the west at Mons, Major-General Sir Wilhelm von Dörnberg, the general officer commanding the 3rd (British) Cavalry Brigade, but unofficially Wellington's chief border guard, had also received intelligence and was penning the latest in a series of reports to the Duke of Wellington:

'The Prussians have been attacked'

Mons, 15th June, ½ past 9 o'clock in the morning.

My Lord,

A picket of French lancers has been placed again at Autresse, on the Bavay road; but at Quivrain there are only National Guards, with a few gendarmes. A man who was yesterday at Maubeuge says that all the troops march towards Beaumont and Philippeville, and that no other troops but National Guards remained at Maubeuge. He thinks that near 40,000 men have passed that place. I have sent towards Pont-sur-Sambre, where, I believe, a corps remains. I just heard the Prussians were attacked.
I have the honour to be, my Lord,

Your most obedient, humble servant,
Dörnberg.[10]

Recognising the potential gravity of his report, von Dörnberg decided to go and see the situation for himself and made his way towards Binche. Some five kilometres to the east, Second Lieutenant Willem Wassenar van Sint-Pancras was busy preparing to move his section of guns to Maurage, as were the other officers and men of Captain Geij van Pittius' half battery. Teams of horses were led in from the fields and stables and harnessed to the limbers, to which the three 6-pounder guns and single 5½-inch howitzer of the troop were hitched. Ammunition caissons were checked and checked again, straps tightened and tools stowed. Not knowing whether they would be returning, the gunners gathered up their possessions and stuffed them into portmanteaux already bulging with all the necessaries that a soldier requires. Amid the clamour of preparations, someone pointed out to him the irregular booming of distant cannon fire, but this was put down to the Prussians and their habit of target practice. No one for a moment considered that these could be alarm cannon, still less that it could be French horse artillery, firing on General von Steinmetz's brigade, a short distance away.[11]

Shortly after 9.30 a.m., the Prince van Oranje-Nassau and his party were approaching the relay station at Naast, where Major van Gorkum of the Quartermaster-General's department was waiting to see him. As they rode along the chaussée together, the Prince mentioned the strong rumours that there had been fighting between the Prussians and the French, but that while he had been at Saint-Symphorien, no firing had been heard. Perhaps the fighting was a long way off? Whatever might be the case, the Prince was clearly not troubled and advised van Gorkum that within an hour he would leave for Brussels and remain there for the night. Should anything special occur, van Gorkum was to let him know through one of his adjutants that would remain behind. It was 10.15 a.m. before the group of officers reached Braine-le-Comte, where they called in at the Hôtel de Miroir – the headquarters both of the Netherlands Army and of I Corps – in order to update General de Constant-Rebecque on their inspection.[12]

By the time the Prince sat down he had been awake for the best part of six hours and having ridden over fifty kilometres, he was famished and ordered breakfast. He briefed de Constant-Rebecque and his officers of the situation on the frontier and the precautionary orders he had seen fit to issue to van Merlen and Chassé. He asked de Constant-Rebecque to ensure that if any further intelligence was received that indicated serious developments, he was to order General de Perponcher-Sedlnitzky and General de Collaert to assemble at their alarm posts. For the time being, he reiterated, there seemed no immediate cause for alarm, and he informed them that he would still dine with the Duke of Wellington that afternoon and remain at Brussels for the Duchess of Richmond's ball, probably staying there overnight. Another man in the room expecting to attend the ball was Captain Charles Lennox, the Earl of March, serving with the Prince as an extra aide-de-camp; after all, it was his mother's ball. Perhaps with this in mind, the Prince suggested that:

> Lord March should keep himself ready with a fast-running horse, that whenever news arrived that the enemy had attacked, one of ours was to bring the message with all haste to His Royal Highness at Brussels, and another adjutant was to go to the place of the attack to gather the reports and return to the headquarters as soon as possible and let His Royal Highness know the situation.

Captains Lord John Somerset and Hon. Francis Russell were also planning to attend the dance, as were Colonel du Caylar, the Prince's First Adjutant and Colonel Baron de Knijff, one of his aides-de-camp. In contrast, Lieutenant-Colonel Baron Ernst Trip, though invited, possibly felt it would be unseemly to attend an event where he would be likely to once again meet the Hon. John Capel, with whom he had been obliged to fight a duel over his relationship with Capel's daughter, Harriet; indeed the Duke of Richmond had been his opponent's second. His breakfast briefing complete and with the social whirl to come, the Prince took his leave and rode back to his residence for a wash and change of clothes, before climbing into his cabriolet at about 11.30 a.m. and heading for Brussels, not knowing as the wheels of his coach started turning, that the enemy was at the gates.[13]

Breakfast was also being served at the Hôtel d'Angleterre, on the rue de la Madeleine in Brussels. Among the guests, and fresh from his arrival in the city that morning, was Lieutenant-General Sir Thomas Picton, the old warhorse who had been recalled from his estates in Pembrokeshire. Despite his gritty character and dogged reputation, his health had suffered much in the Peninsula and, though he had indicated that he would serve with the army, he insisted that it be under the orders of no general officer but the Duke of Wellington himself. Perhaps the General was tired of campaigning or perhaps he felt that his number was up. Only a few days before, he had been walking with friends:

> They came to a churchyard, in which a grave had been dug for the reception of some humble individual. The party was induced to ascend the newly thrown-up earth and look down. Sir Thomas Picton, after commenting upon the neatness with which it had been dug, observed, 'Why, I think this would do for me;' at the same time

jumping in and laying himself at full length along the bottom, he observed that it was an exact fit.[14]

Breakfasting with Picton were Captain John Tyler, his principal aide-de-camp and Ensign Rees Gronow, an officer of the first battalion of the 1st Regiment of Foot Guards, whose connections, persuasive tongue and good fortune had resulted in the General agreeing to take him to Belgium as an extra aide-de-camp. While they were still at table, Lieutenant-Colonel Charles Canning, one of Wellington's aides-de-camp, arrived and informed him that the Duke, who was walking in the park with Lieutenant-Colonel Lord Fitzroy Somerset and Charles Lennox, the Duke of Richmond, wished to see him immediately.

> Picton's manner was always more familiar than the Duke liked in his lieutenants, and on this occasion he approached him in a careless sort of way, just as he might have met an equal. The Duke bowed coldly to him, and said, 'I am glad you are come, Sir Thomas'... Picton did not appear to like the Duke's manner; for when he bowed and left, he muttered a few words which convinced those who were with him that he was not much pleased with his interview.[15]

At about the same time that the Prince van Oranje-Nassau was departing Braine-le-Comte and General Picton tasted his latest dose of Wellingtonian bile, a man on a lathered horse galloped up to the vedettes posted on the road at Saint-Symphorien, towards 11.30 a.m. It was a Prussian staff officer with a message for General van Merlen. Without delay, he was conducted to the headquarters where he introduced himself as Major von Arnauld, serving on General von Steinmetz's staff. Hurriedly, he outlined the situation. The 2nd (Prussian) Infantry Brigade had been attacked by the French and a lively infantry fire had erupted as the latter headed towards Charleroi. Had they not heard the alarm cannon firing or the bombardment of Lobbes, Thuin and Maladrie? There were blank looks and shrugs amongst the Netherlands cavalrymen. It had been the same, explained Major von Arnauld, with the Prussian forces at Binche, who had also heard nothing, despite being a mere eight kilometres away from the nearest firing. Continuing his account, he passed on the significant news that von Steinmetz had decided to evacuate Binche, an order that Major von Arnauld had delivered less than an hour ago. The villages around Binche, in which the Prussian 4th (1st Silesian) Hussar Regiment and elements of the 12th (2nd Brandenburg) and 24th (4th Brandenburg) Infantry Regiments had been cantoned, were also being evacuated. General von Steinmetz's intention, said von Arnauld, was to withdraw behind the River Piéton and if possible take up a position at Gosselies, but if they were seriously attacked, they were to retire on Fleurus in compliance with orders that Field-Marshal von Blücher had issued in early May.[16]

The importance of this information was not lost on General van Merlen, who immediately called forward his Major of Brigade, Major de Paravicini di Capelli, and dictated a letter to General de Constant-Rebecque, at Braine-le-Comte. Thinking that it would also be advisable to inform the Governor of Mons of these developments, van Merlen ordered that a second note be written and dispatched to Major-General Johann Behr. It was approaching 11.15 a.m.[17]

The bustle around headquarters and the departure of Major de Paravicini di Capelli's messenger led Captain Geij van Pittius to suspect that hostilities had commenced and the news spread quickly through the village. Taking up his pen, he composed a brief note to his brother:

> This morning at four o'clock, the big dance has begun. Two hours' distance from here, the French have attacked the Prussian army, which stands on our left flank. We are saddled and expect to march at any moment, but as the bulk of our army is behind us, we shall certainly make a movement to the rear. It gives me pleasure that the game has finally started, as we were very bored in these miserable villages and had to be saddled all the time. Bonaparte has come opposite us since the day before yesterday. My company is well-equipped and so I think will not be the worse for it.[18]

Towards noon, the courier from General von Dörnberg clattered through the Grand'Place at Braine-le-Comte, past the Hôtel du Miroir, before turning into the rue des Folles where the residence of the Prince van Oranje-Nassau was located. He was informed that the Prince was not at home, but with his message delivered the orderly dragoon believed his duty was completed and he headed back towards the relay station at Naast.[19]

Twenty-four kilometres to the south, General von Dörnberg finally arrived back at the fortress of Mons towards 12.45 p.m., having completed his reconnaissance. He had passed through Saint-Symphorien and learned of the visit of the Prince van Oranje-Nassau and the orders given to van Merlen and Chassé. On leaving Saint-Symphorien, he had encountered detachments of the 5th Regiment of Light Dragoons accompanied by horse artillery. As he had proceeded through Bray, he was challenged by picquets from the 6th Regiment of Hussars, before being recognised and allowed to proceed to Binche. On his arrival, he found the town deserted. The Brandenburgers had left some two hours earlier and most of the civilians, expecting the imminent arrival of the French, had boarded up their houses and shops, or locked themselves into their homes. Aside from the information that Thuin and Lobbes had been lost and that the French had advanced on Marchienne-au-Pont, von Dörnberg's visit had yielded little positive intelligence. Although he could assume from the Prussian evacuation of Binche and what he knew of their own assembly plans, that von Steinmetz was probably pulling his troops back to avoid them being outflanked by way of Marchienne or Charleroi.

As soon as he arrived back at Mons, von Dörnberg hurried to call on General Behr, who briefed him on the earlier news that he had received from van Merlen and had relayed to the Prince van Oranje-Nassau. Given that his efforts had procured no more information than had already been received and relayed, there seemed little sense in any further communication being sent for the time being. After ensuring that all

'The Prussians have been attacked'

remained quiet at Mons and having given instructions that any additional intelligence was to be brought to him immediately, von Dörnberg returned to his headquarters.[20]

While the villagers along the frontier cowered behind bolted doors, the inhabitants of Braine-le-Comte were going about their everyday business and the shouts of the traders in the *marché* barely penetrated to the *salle communale* of the Hôtel du Miroir, overlooking the Grand'Place. Inside, General de Constant-Rebecque and the officers of the headquarters staff were attending to routine matters. The clock was striking 1.15 p.m. when the messenger arrived from General Chassé. Major van Gorkum noted the receipt of the message in the Headquarters' Register of Incoming Correspondence, whilst de Constant-Rebecque opened the document and absorbed its contents:[21]

> Haine-Sainte-Pierre, 15 June 1815,
> 11 o'clock.
>
> We have come to receive certain news that the enemy has crossed our frontier. Binche is evacuated by the Prussians. The division is assembled at Fayt and I await the further orders of His Royal Highness.
>
> The Lieutenant-General Commanding,
> Baron Chassé.[22]

The chief-of-staff was considering the news when a second messenger, carrying Major de Paravicini di Capelli's letter, entered the room and handed over his own document. Though it lacked a time, it included some additional information about Prussian intentions. The General eagerly read of the developing situation along the frontier:

> Saint-Symphorien, the 15th of June.
>
> General,
>
> I have the honour to report that General Steinmetz has sent me an officer to give notice that the 2nd (Prussian) Infantry Brigade has been attacked this morning. He had not yet received a report. The alarm cannon have been firing along the length of the line. The infantry fire appears very lively and is directed towards Charleroi. The intention of the Prussians is to evacuate Binche and the neighbouring villages immediately, in order to take up a position behind the River Piéton at Gosselies and, in case of a determined attack being made on it, the position of their Army Corps is fixed close to Fleurus.
>
> By order of Major-General van Merlen,
> J. de Paravicini, Major.[23]

Less than fifteen minutes later, one of the couriers from the relay station at Naast reported to Captain Baron van Heinecken, the commander of the Headquarters

Guides; he handed over General Behr's letter, which was addressed to the Prince van Oranje-Nassau. Hurriedly entering the *salle communale*, van Heinecken saluted the Quartermaster-General and handed him the letter, which de Constant-Rebecque opened and read in the absence of his chief.

> My Prince,
>
> I have the honour to make your Royal Highness aware of a report which has been dispatched to me by Major-General van Merlen. It results from General von Steinmetz, commanding at Fontaine-l'Evêque, having just sent an officer to him with notice that the 2nd Prussian brigade was attacked this morning and that the alarm cannon have been firing all along the line. It appears that the attack is directed on Charleroi, where the infantry fire is very sharp. At General van Merlen's outposts, all is tranquil.
>
> I have the honour to be, with a profound respect,
> The Major-General Superior Commandant,
> Baron Behr.
>
> P.S. The outposts in front of Mons are also very quiet.[24]

Aware of the importance of the documents he had just received, de Constant-Rebecque's usually precise mind omitted to note down the receipt of Behr's letter. The French were across the border and had attacked the 2nd (Prussian) Brigade, whose alarm cannon had been firing. French infantry were approaching Charleroi, while von Steinmetz had already evacuated Binche and was taking up a position behind the River Piéton at Gosselies, though he might perhaps be forced back on Fleurus. The news of General Chassé's concentration was welcome, as was van Merlen's move to the east, thereby providing a screen across his front. The most critical news, however, was that all was quiet at Mons.[25]

While de Constant-Rebecque was considering the implications of the newly-arrived intelligence at the Hôtel du Miroir, at the Prince's private residence, Lieutenant-Colonel Sir George Berkeley, his British Assistant Adjutant-General was wondering what to do with the message that had earlier arrived from Mons. Not having been present when the Prince had returned from Saint-Symphorien, he was unaware that his chief had already departed for Brussels. Taking the letter with him, he walked to the Hôtel du Miroir towards 1.45 p.m., with a view to asking General de Constant-Rebecque or one of his staff the time at which the Prince was expected. When he arrived the atmosphere inside the office was electric. Glancing up from his paperwork, de Constant-Rebecque beckoned him over and showed him the letters from Chassé, van Merlen and Behr. Berkeley pulled the letter from Mons from his pocket, now realising that this too, could contain critical information. With de Constant-Rebecque looking on, he broke the seal and quickly read the contents. He soon realised that the letter was a precis of that contained in van Merlen's note and contained little else of value. The senior Netherlands and British officers of the Prince's general staff now resolved to forward all four documents to Colonel Somerset, Military Secretary and right-hand man to the Duke of Wellington. Taking a sheet of paper and a pen, Berkeley hastily scribbled a covering note. The clock ticked towards 2.00 p.m.[26]

Captain Lennox had been waiting at de Constant-Rebecque's headquarters since late morning, anticipating just such a mission to Brussels. He hurriedly gave orders for his horse to be saddled and made ready. Having shared the dangers of a storming party at the siege of Ciudad Rodrigo, in which his companions had been none other than the Prince van Oranje-Nassau and Lord Fitzroy Somerset, the young officer was exceedingly well connected and could be relied upon to ensure the message reached its recipient safely. With the documents hastily bound together and handed to him, Lennox galloped off towards Tubize, Hal and Brussels. News of the invasion safely dispatched, Colonel Berkeley started penning brief messages for the attention of Generals Cooke, commanding the 1st (British) Infantry Division at Enghien and von Alten, at the headquarters of the 3rd (British) Infantry Division at Soignies. As the Anglo-Hanoverian element of the army corps, it was important that he warn them of developments and of the possibility that hostilities had commenced.[27]

Another prince who had been on a tour of inspection that morning was Colonel Prince Bernhard von Sachsen-Weimar, the commanding officer of the Regiment Oranien-Nassau. Formed during the summer of 1814 from troops originally raised the previous winter by the Prince van Oranje-Nassau in his hereditary territories, the first battalion – under Lieutenant-Colonel Wilhelm von Dressel – had left for the Netherlands on 29 August 1814, provoking a storm of protest at home. On 5 September, the Rheinische Merkur had declared that:

> Our government has continued the conscription of the French and has raised the quota to two per cent. In this way, two thousand young people are taken away from their parents and sold to Holland. Nobody has objections to a reasonable conscription to defend our homeland, but now they have to serve in the army of a foreign country!

Regardless of the furore, the battalion had been incorporated into the Royal Netherlands Army on 15 January 1815 and had, since April, been cantoned in southern Belgium, initially in the neighbourhood of Sombreffe, but more recently at Genappe on the River Dyle and the village of Ways, a kilometre downstream. Three days earlier, von Dressel's men had been joined by the second battalion, commanded by Major Christian Schleyer. Despite emptying the depot and pressing Landwehr troops into the ranks, the battalion had only been able to muster 22 officers and 666 men, who had been marched into Belgium and put into quarters in the surrounding villages of Glabais, Thy and Bousval.[28]

Earlier that morning, von Sachsen-Weimar and his adjutant Major Ludwig Vigelius, had visited Thines, where Captain Emilius Bergmann occupied cantonments with his Volunteer Jager Company, a body of troops that had accompanied the second battalion to the Netherlands and which had since remained attached to it. During their ride back, along the dappled road through the Bois du Haroy and between the swaying fields of ripening wheat, the two men had discussed the strength of the company. Though its return – at 5 officers and 172 men – remained the same as that of 12 June 1815, only 153 men were present and fit for duty, the remainder being detached, on command or sick.

Perhaps more concerning had been the discovery that the men were equipped with four different calibres of rifle, a situation that compounded von Sachsen-Weimar's already profound anxieties in respect of his regiment's firearms. The first battalion, though issued with British 'Brown Bess' muskets, had found these to be old and worn out, while the second battalion had been issued with French muskets. Somehow, the quartermasters would have to procure six different calibres of ammunition.[29]

When von Sachsen-Weimar returned to his headquarters at Genappe, towards 11.00 a.m., he found a note waiting for him from Colonel Friedrich von Gödecke, his brigade commander at Houtain-le-Val. That morning, it transpired, von Gödecke had been on the drill ground inspecting the first battalion of the 2nd Nassau-Usingen Regiment, when the horse of Lieutenant Friedrich von Steprodt, his Adjutant, had kicked him painfully in the shin and broken the bone. Carried off the parade in agony and confined to his bed, von Gödecke realised that he could not continue to perform his duties and had written to General de Perponcher-Sedlnitzky at Nivelles, requesting that command of the brigade be temporarily handed to von Sachsen-Weimar. As the next most senior officer of the brigade, this made eminent sense, but von Sachsen-Weimar perhaps wondered when the appointment would be confirmed.[30]

Colonel von Dressel had also been on parade that morning. On 9 June, an order had been issued by corps headquarters at Braine-le-Comte, requiring each battalion to muster under arms on the drill ground at its alarm post at 5.00 a.m. each morning and remain assembled until the evening when if all was quiet, they could return to their separate quarters. He had paraded the first battalion of the Regiment Oranien-Nassau and having taken roll call, was satisfied with the 774 men present for duty. After being given the order to fall out, the men had occupied themselves with military routine. Some men were cooking the provisions they had been instructed to bring with them, while others practised drill, or became accustomed to the much heavier British muskets that had recently replaced their elegant French Charlevilles. For three hours, officers and men had gone about their business, undisturbed by the sound of gunfire to the south. Doubtless, the officers speculated, it was the Prussian artillery at practise along the frontier, something they had engaged in several days previously without deeming it necessary to send warning to their allies farther north.[31]

Eight kilometres to the south, the young soldiers of the second battalion of the 2nd Nassau-Usingen Regiment had also been listening to the rumbling sound, as it drifted across the still air towards their outposts at Frasnes. Despite all the rumours of previous weeks, no news of the commencement of hostilities had yet been heard from Genappe, Houtain-le-Val or Nivelles. For Captain Ludwig Wirths, the day had passed routinely, as had all the days since he had arrived in these remote, dirty villages. The battalion had been paraded before daybreak on its drill ground, which was to the south of the village and close to the Charleroi road. As was usual, patrols had been sent out into the surrounding countryside, which returned with reports of nothing more threatening than agricultural labourers and pigs and cattle. Although his standing orders only obliged him to keep his battalion assembled until the day had fully dawned, the commanding officer, Major Philipp von Normann, had decided to drill them for what seemed to the men, an unconscionably long time. The 800-strong battalion had subsequently stood at attention, marched and sweated in their tight-fitting green coats, as von Normann put them through their paces; the grenadiers suffering especially beneath their cumbersome bearskin headgear. At last, with the morning sun continuing to beat down, the Major ordered the men to fall out and return to their cantonments, and it was as they were marching off that they first heard the sound of distant gunfire, which seemingly came from the direction of Charleroi. The officers initially assumed the noise was caused by the Prussians, who had regularly practiced musketry and artillery fire, but as the sound moved closer, suspicions were aroused and Major von Normann was persuaded to recall the battalion to its assembly area. Muttering oaths under their breath and hurriedly donning cartridge belts and knapsacks, the men streamed out of the Ferme de la Cense de l'Encloître, the Ferme du Try and the buildings around the great courtyards and hurriedly took their places in the ranks and files.[32]

Shortly afterwards, towards noon, the soldiers on sentry duty next to the chaussée from Charleroi to Brussels noticed some people and vehicles approaching from a distance. Puzzled, they took up their muskets and stood to arms in the shimmering heat. A short while later, they could make out wagons and carts approaching, drawn by heavy plough horses and filled with women, children, furniture, poultry and provisions. As they trundled, groaned and squeaked past the baffled Germans, youngsters in wooden sabots herded cattle, goats and pigs along behind. On being questioned, it turned out they were local townspeople and villagers who had heard that the French had attacked Charleroi and were pushing the Prussians back; the refugees were heading for the sanctuary of Genappe and Nivelles. As the troops fidgeted with muskets and equipment, they speculated on the clouds of dust in the south, in the direction of Gosselies, Jumet and Charleroi.[33]

Far to the north, others were also on the move. For Charlotte Waldie and her siblings, the day had started more promisingly than the 36 hour crossing of the English Channel from Ramsgate to Ostend that they had just endured. They were rattling along the broad, flat and tree-lined chaussée from Ghent to Brussels, absorbing the sights and sounds of the unfamiliar countryside.

> The peasants almost all wore sabots; but the cottage children, bare-footed and bare-headed, frequently pursued the carriage for miles, keeping pace with the horses, tumbling as they went along, singing Flemish patriotic songs, the burden of which was invariably, 'Success to the English, and destruction to the French;' and crying with unwearied perseverance, 'Vivé les Anglaises!' 'Dat for Napoleon!' expressing at the same time, by an emphatic gesture, cutting off his head. They threw bouquets of flowers into the carriage,

twisted their little sun-burned faces into the most extraordinary grimaces, and kept whirling round on their hands and feet, in imitation of the rotary motion of a wheel.

Towards 1.00 p.m. the carriage reached Alost, just over 26 kilometres north-west of Brussels, where a violent shower of rain obliged them to seek shelter. As they sipped coffee with the mistress of the house, she lectured them on her views of the French, much to the surprise of the visitors, who had supposed the Belgians to be Francophiles.

> 'Ah, madame! Before they came among us,' she said, 'this was a very different country. Then we were rich, and good, and happy.' She lamented over the trade, the manufactories, the commerce they had destroyed; the contributions they had exacted; the fine young men they had seized as conscripts; the convents they had ruined, the priests and 'les bonnes religieuses' they had turned to the door.

To Miss Waldie, these sentiments seemed to burst out

> … spontaneously, as if they could not suppress it; their whole countenances change; their eyes sparkle with indignation; their very gestures are eloquent, and they seem at a loss for words strong enough to express the bitterness of their detestation.

It seemed as though their stay in Belgium would prove to be an interesting education in the ways of the Continent.[34]

For the time being completely oblivious to the events unfolding to the south, the Duke of Wellington was at his desk at No. 54 rue Royale in the heart of the elegant upper city of Brussels. A letter from Lieutenant-General Sir Lowry Cole at the beginning of June had sparked a debate on the composition and numbering of the British infantry divisions. Cole had been assigned command of the 6th (British) Infantry Division, which was still forming and had expressed a desire to have it renumbered as the 4th, the division he had commanded in the Peninsula, but now the number allocated to Lieutenant-General Sir Charles Colville's division. Writing shortly after midday to Lieutenant-General Sir Henry Clinton, Wellington outlined his intentions on the subject:

> Some of the General Officers would wish very much to have the divisions numbered over again, and have their old numbers, which appears a very natural wish; and I should be very much obliged to you if you would let me know as soon as you can if you participate in it.

General Cooke's would remain the 1st Division, Clinton's second would become the 6th; General von Alten's third the 5th; Colville's fourth the 2nd; the 5th, to the command of which General Picton had been appointed, the 3rd; and Cole's 6th the 4th. Despite the great soldier and statesman's best diplomacy, developments elsewhere would result in these divisions marching to battle numbered as they were. Checking his watch, the Duke decided that there was still plenty of time to write to the Tsar of Russia, offering his observations on the intended operations of the Allied armies massing on France's eastern borders. Little did he suspect the storm that was about to break.[35]

A couple of minutes' walk away, the Prince van Oranje-Nassau and his companions arrived at their hotel on the rue de la Loi, towards 2.30 p.m., having made good time on the road through Tubize and Hal. This allowed the Prince time for a leisurely toilet, following which he walked across the park to the Duke of Wellington's residence, where he arrived shortly before 3.00 p.m.[36]

The footman greeted the Prince with a low bow and ushered him into the drawing room, where he joined a small party of fellow diners and exchanged pleasantries. Always hungry for intelligence from the frontier, Wellington greeted him by asking if there was any news. The Prince, without any sense of undue alarm, replied, 'No! Nothing but that the French have crossed the Sambre and had a brush with the Prussians. Have you heard of it?' The Duke certainly had not, but it soon became evident as the Prince outlined the sketchy rumours that had wafted along the Sambre valley that morning, that little of note could be gleaned from such a vague statement. Since the French had begun massing along the border, clashes had been expected and, as May turned into June, skirmishes between outposts and cross-border incursions had been part of everyday life. On 12 June, the Bremen and Verden Hussars had clashed with French cavalry near Warquenies. Even the day before, as the Prince no doubt reminded him, French and Netherlands cavalry had crossed sabres at Goeignies-Chaussée, to the south of Mons. Satisfied with the Prince's decision to rely on the network of spies, cavalry patrols and outposts to perform its function and to gather, sift and transmit intelligence, Wellington invited his guests to take their seats in the dining room.[37]

Meanwhile, at Braine-le-Comte, General de Constant-Rebecque was busy writing the orders that would put the corps on the move. With Chassé already alerted and assembled at Fayt there was, for the time being, no need to send him further instructions. Priority must be given to assembling General de Perponcher-Sedlnitzky's 2nd (Netherlands) Infantry Division and General de Collaert's cavalry at their respective alarm positions. He sat down and wrote a letter to the former, taking care to log it in the Register of Outgoing Correspondence as number 178; it would not do to abandon correct procedure, no matter how urgent the situation was becoming. As soon as he had completed the brief letter, he took a second sheet of paper and, registering it as number 179 in the Register of Outgoing Correspondence, penned a similar brief note for General de Collaert. Once completed, de Constant-Rebecque folded both letters, sealed them and handed them to separate staff officers for transmission. Glancing up at the clock, he inscribed their time of departure in the register. It was 3.00 p.m.[38]

Despite the appearance of the refugees earlier in the day, nothing more had been seen on the road from Charleroi to Brussels and at the same time de Constant-Rebecque was issuing his orders, the hungry Nassauers at Frasnes had been given permission to fall out and cook their main meal of the day. The sound of gunfire had gradually increased during the early afternoon and by the time the camp kettles were simmering, the rattle of musketry could be heard blending with the throatier booming of cannon in the direction of Jumet. The men exchanged glances. Was their dinner about to be rudely interrupted? As the troops busied themselves at the fires, Captain Adriaan Bijleveld listened to the sound of the gunfire with a practised ear. The 28-year-old was no stranger to combat, having fought at Ulm, the siege of Kolberg, Friedland and the Katzbach, where he had been stabbed by uhlans in his left hand and shoulder and taken prisoner. Even at this distance, he could make out that the sound was coming from 6-pounder guns, which suggested that a sizeable confrontation was taking place somewhere to the south. Shortly afterwards, the arrival of wounded Prussian infantry in coats with green and red facings, along with uhlans in black, each with his own tale of alarm, confirmed his suspicions and left his nominal superior, Major von Normann in no doubt that this was more serious than anticipated. These men, of the 1st Westphalian Landwehr Infantry, the 29th Infantry and the 6th Uhlan Regiments, had been attacked by at least two French battalions at Jumet, a mere ten kilometres away and then forced back on Gosselies, even closer. After some quick calculations, the Allied officers realised that the same French infantry could be at Frasnes within three hours.[39]

Having questioned the fugitives for some minutes, von Normann consulted with Captain Bijleveld, whose brigade of Netherlands horse artillery was dispersed between the villages of Frasnes and Villers-Perwin, two and a half kilometres to the south-east. As the two officers discussed the situation, von Normann reminded Bijleveld that the last set of standing orders, issued by General de Perponcher on 7 May, dictated he assemble his battalion at Frasnes in the event of an alarm being raised, before pulling back to Les Quatre Bras. They additionally charged him with responsibility for the artillery, which was on no account to be abandoned and for which he was instructed to wait, before evacuating Frasnes. He was therefore only obliged to hold Frasnes for as long as it took him to assemble his infantry and artillery and pull them back to Les Quatre Bras.[40]

In light of these instructions, the two men agreed to assemble the main body of the battalion on the chaussée, adjacent to a fenced-off area on the ridge to the north of the village, which had served Bijleveld as his artillery park. A small picquet of a sergeant, a corporal and twelve men would be placed in the village itself. Realising the importance of keeping his commanding officer informed of his actions, von Normann requested the loan of a horse artilleryman, whom he briefed on the situation and the steps that he intended to take in order to cover the withdrawal from Frasnes, before sending the gunner to Colonel von Gödecke, at Houtain-le-Val. In the meantime, Bijleveld rode away and ordered his limbers to be harnessed and the guns to be made ready to move off along the road, before also instructing the men to harness the wagons and other vehicles. Having directed that the battalion assemble under arms, von Normann detailed additional men to reinforce the picquets on the roads to Charleroi, Rèves and Liberchies and ordered Captain Franz Müller to take up a position in Frasnes itself, with his 2nd Flanquer Company. By now, the remainder of the battalion was drawn up and as Bijleveld's teams moved off with the battery, they were followed up the road by the five remaining companies of infantry, as far as the Balcan Inn. Here they were deployed on the plateau, facing south, with the

Grenadier Company's right flank close to the road. As von Normann's soldiers dressed their ranks, Bijleveld and his officers sited their artillery pieces to take every advantage of the field of fire; the position dominated the road and the village. Lieutenant Alfred Wasseroth de Vincy saw to the positioning of two howitzers on the roadway itself, while the six guns commanded by Second Lieutenants Frederik Dibbetz and Wijnand Koopman were placed in the fields to either side, ensuring that the village and its approaches were well covered. Shortly after 3.15 p.m., all was in place and the troops awaited, with anxiety, the arrival of the cloud of dust to the south.[41]

At Nivelles, some eleven kilometres to the north-west, the newly promoted General de Perponcher-Sedlnitzky was at his headquarters, reading through Colonel von Gödecke's report of the accident that had befallen him earlier that morning. Such an injury would take time to heal and would leave him with a command dilemma in the short term. With the clouds of war gathering, a suitable officer would need to be appointed to command the brigade in his place. The logical choice was Colonel von Sachsen-Weimar, the man on the spot and the ranking officer, but he was only 23 years old. Then again, the General mused, he was surrounded by experienced and able officers who would exercise judgment and provide sound advice. Setting aside von Gödecke's letter, de Perponcher-Sedlnitzky decided there was no hurry. He would make his decision later, perhaps he might even sleep on it.[42]

The importance of having good officers was about to be demonstrated at Houtain-le-Val. Fatigue parties of the first battalion of the 2nd Nassau-Usingen Regiment were engaged in routine tasks when Bijleveld's gunner galloped down the road towards 3.30 p.m., searching for the headquarters of the regiment. He eventually found Major Johann Sattler, who had temporarily assumed command of the regiment in the absence of Lieutenant-Colonel Baron Ernst von Umbusch. Immediately realising the importance of the intelligence, he summoned Captain von Mühlmann, the regimental Adjutant and instructed him to report personally to General de Perponcher-Sedlnitzky at Nivelles. Given that the senior officer of the brigade was now Colonel von Sachsen-Weimar, he asked Captain Alexander van Coustoll, the Major of Brigade, to send a messenger with the same news to Genappe. Summoning Captain Moritz Büsgen, he invested him with command of the first battalion and gave instructions for it to be immediately paraded and marched on Les Quatre Bras, the designated alarm post. Finally, another courier was sent to Major Gottfried Hegmann at Sart-Dame-Avelines, ordering him to also march the third battalion on Les Quatre Bras. The orders dispatched, the Major hurried to make his own preparations for departure.[43]

Endnotes

1. de Bas &c, p. 382. de Constant-Rebecque (I). van Gorkum. Gurwood, p. 480. van Limburg-Stirum. Mathieu, p. 4. Wellesley, p. 480.
2. de Bas, pp. 517, 1158. de Bas &c., pp. 349-51. de Constant-Rebecque (I). van Gorkum. van Limburg-Stirum.

The Battle of Quatre Bras

3. de Bas &c., p. 382. de Constant-Rebecque (I). Manchot, p. 76.
4. de Bas &c., pp. 367, 382-3. Boulger, pp. 67-8. Bowden, p. 268. de Constant-Rebecque (I). Hoynck van Papendrecht, pp. 67–8.
5. Bosscha. del Campo. Koolemans-Beijnen.
6. de Bas &c., pp. 383–4. de Constant-Rebecque (I). van Gorkum.
7. Anonymous (Letterbook). de Bas, p. 1333. de Bas &c., p. 361. Bunsen (I). van Deelen, p. 43. Hofschröer (I), pp. 170–1. van Omphal.
8. de Bas &c., p. 361. van Bentinck tot 't Nyenhuis. van Deelen, p. 43. van Omphal.
9. Anonymous (Letterbook). de Bas &c., pp. 379–80. Chassé. van Deelen, p. 43. Holle. van Omphal.
10. von Dörnberg. von Pflugk-Harttung (I), pp. 204-5. C. Robinson, p. 516. Wellesley, pp. 480–1.
11. von Dörnberg. Hofschröer (I), p. 169. von Ollech, p. 96. Wassenaar van Sint-Pancras.
12. de Constant-Rebecque (I). van Gorkum. C. Robinson, p. 515.
13. de Bas &c., pp. 384-5. de Constant-Rebecque (I). Koolemans-Beijnen. van Limburg-Stirum. Miller (II), pp. 84, 118. van Uythoven. Young, pp. 100–1.
14. Anonymous (Journal), p. 377. Dalton, p. 14. Gronow, pp. 125–6. Leach, p. 373. von Rettberg (III). H. Robinson, pp. 361–2. F. Somerset, p. 7. Stephens.
15. Gronow, pp. 125–7.
16. de Bas &c., pp. 379–80, 394. Bunsen (I). Hofschröer (I), pp. 118, 171, 176, 195. von Lettow-Vorbeck, p. 174. van Löben-Sels, p. 449. von Ollech, p. 45. von Pflugk-Harttung (I), p. 51.
17. de Bas &c., pp. 380, 388–9.
18. Geij van Pittius.
19. de Bas &c., p. 391. Gurwood, p. 363.
20. de Bas &c., p. 380. von Dörnberg. Hussey (I).
21. Anonymous (Incoming Register). de Bas &c., p. 388. Matthieu, pp. 4, 6.
22. Anonymous (Incoming Register). de Bas &c., p. 393. Bosscha. del Campo. van Gorkum. Koolemans-Beijnen.
23. Anonymous (Incoming Register). de Bas &c., pp. 393–4.
24. Anonymous (Incoming Register). de Bas &c., pp. 380, 388-90, 393–4. de Constant-Rebecque (I). von Pflugk-Harttung (I), p. 203–4. C. Robinson, p. 518.
25. de Bas &c., pp. 389–390.
26. de Bas &c., p. 392. de Constant-Rebecque (I). von Dörnberg.
27. de Bas &c., pp. 391, 393. Dalton, p. 11. Miller (II), p. 62. C. Robinson, p. 516.
28. de Bas, p. 1332. Hofschröer (I), p. 202. van Löben-Sels, p. 457. von Pflugk-Harttung (I), p. 294. Starklof, p. 130. van Uythoven.
29. de Bas p. 1332. Bowden, p. 239. Jonxis, p. 138. von Morenhoffen. von Sachsen-Weimar (I). Starklof, p. 131. van Uythoven. Wüppermann, p. 88.
30. Anonymous (Namenslisten). Hofschröer (I), p. 82. Leonhard (I). von Morenhoffen. von Sachsen-Weimar (II). Starklof, pp. 129–30. van Uythoven. Peter Wakker, p. 510.
31. de Bas &c., p. 363. Bowden, p. 239. von Kruse. Starklof, p. 131. van Uythoven. van Zuylen van Nyevelt (I), p. 49.

'The Prussians have been attacked'

32. de Bas &c., pp. 398-9. Hofschröer (I), p. 201. von Pivka (II), p. 20. Sattler. van Zuylen van Nyeveld (I), p. 49. van Uythoven. Wirths.
33. de Bas &c., p. 399. Hofschröer (I), pp. 170–6, 201. Starklof, p. 131.
34. Eaton, pp. 1, 7–9.
35. de Bas &c., p. 384. Brett-James, p. 37. Sutherland, p. 86. Wellesley, pp. 435–6, 469–72.
36. de Bas &c., pp. 384, 389. Eaton, p. 15. Miller (I), p. 105. G. Paget (I), pp. 49–50. F. Somerset. Wellesley, p. 524. Young, p. 99.
37. de Bas &c., pp. 347–8, 384, 389. Wellesley, pp. 455, 524.
38. de Bas &c., pp. 383, 389–90, 395–6. van Limburg-Stirum. van Löben-Sels, p. 455. Wellesley, pp. 523–4.
39. de Bas &c., p. 399. Bijleveld. Haythornthwaite (I), p. 162. Hofschröer (I), pp. 176–81, 201. von Kruse. van Opstall. G. Paget (I), pp. 49–50. Miller (II), p. 134. von Pivka (II), p. 20. von Sachsen-Weimar (II). Sattler. van Zuylen van Nyeveld (I), p. 49.
40. de Bas, pp. 1147–8. de Bas &c. pp. 316–20, 398. Bijleveld. Hofschröer (I), p. 202. von Kruse. von Pflugk-Harttung (I), p. 294. von Sachsen-Weimar (I). Wirths. van Zuylen van Nyeveld (I), pp. 49–50.
41. de Bas &c., p. 399–400. Bijleveld. Hofschröer (I), p. 201. Houssaye, pp. 70–1. von Kruse. van Opstall. de Perponcher-Sedlnitzky. von Pivka (II), p. 19. Sattler. van Uythoven. Wirths. van Zuylen van Nyeveld (I), pp. 49–50.
42. de Bas &c., p. 398. von Sachsen-Weimar (II). von Sachsen-Weimar (III).
43. de Bas &c., pp. 318, 400. Hofschröer (I), p. 201. von Kruse. de Perponcher-Sedlnitzky. Sattler. Wirths. van Zuylen van Nyeveld (I), p. 49.

The former Hôtel du Miroir at Braine-le-Comte, headquarters of the Prince van Oranje-Nassau's I Corps. The original building comprised the left-hand side of the 'Point Video' shop and the building to its immediate left. (Author's collection.)

CHAPTER 2

Away to the west, hundreds of red-coated infantrymen were resting in the shade of the Church of Saint-Nicolas de Myre at Enghien when, towards 3.30 p.m., an orderly dragoon arrived from Braine-le-Comte with word that the French were crossing the frontier and that in consequence, orders to assemble the division in readiness should be expected at any moment. General Cooke, who commanded the division was, however, absent. Along with his aide-de-camp, Captain George Disbrowe, he had ridden to Brussels in order to attend the Duchess of Richmond's ball, leaving behind his second aide-de-camp, the less well-connected 18-year-old Ensign Augustus Cuyler. Perhaps even more perplexing for the courier, was that neither brigade commander was present, both having departed for Brussels with the same intention. Major-General Peregrine Maitland, in particular, had been eager to renew his acquaintance with Lady Sarah Lennox, the 22-year-old daughter of the Duchess, and had taken his young aide-de-camp, the dashing Ensign James Lord Hay, as company. Major-General Sir John Byng had likewise departed with his own aides, Captain Henry Dumaresq and Ensign the Hon. William Stopford; they were joined by Ensign the Hon. Henry Montague of the second battalion of the 3rd Regiment of Foot Guards, who had also been fortunate enough because of his connections to have received an invitation in his own right. It must have seemed to the orderly that the Guards were living up to their reputation as the most fashionable regiments in the British Army. The division, as well as the officers of the three Guards regiments seconded to staff duties elsewhere would account for over a third of the invitations sent by the Duchess to Wellington's army.[1]

Although the Assistant Quartermaster-General, Lieutenant-Colonel Sir Henry Bradford and some 24 other officers of the division had gone to Brussels, many had not been invited and so, fortunately, a skeleton staff remained on duty at the divisional headquarters. The senior of these was the Assistant Adjutant-General, Lieutenant-Colonel Henry Rooke, who listened with interest as the dragoon passed on his message to the Deputy-Assistant Quartermaster-General, Captain Edward Fitzgerald. As the staff officer responsible for transmitting orders and organising troop movements, Fitzgerald sent word to Captains William Stothert and James Gunthorpe, Majors of Brigade to Maitland and Byng respectively. As the permanent staff officers of each brigade, it would be their responsibility to put the four battalions on alert and to ensure

'The French are on the Nivelles road'

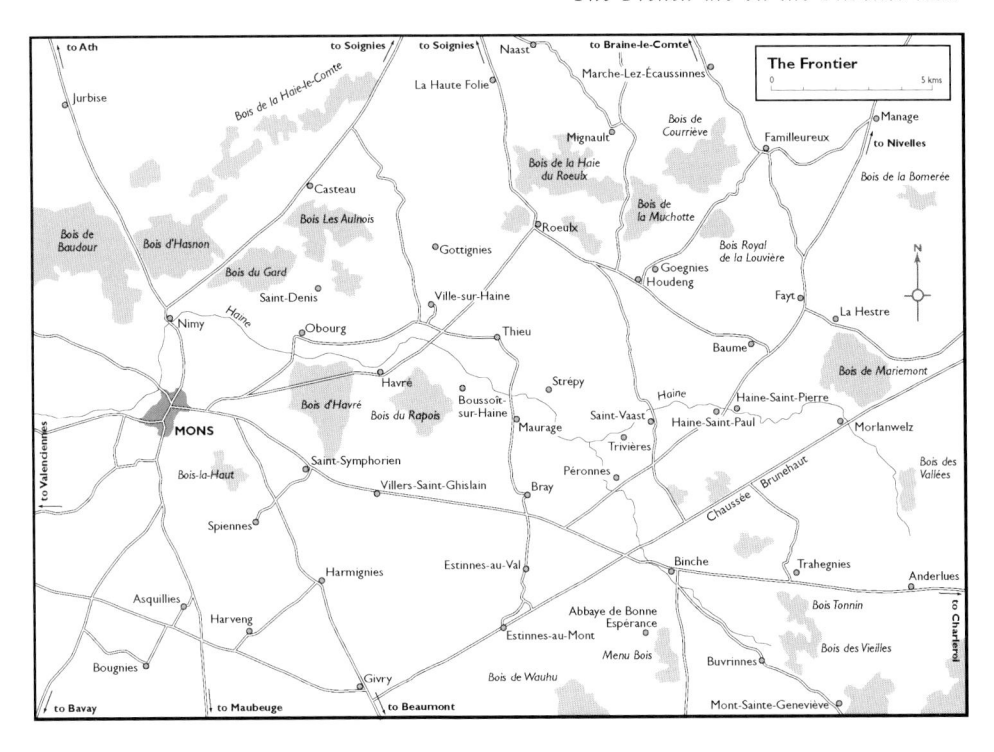

that every one of the 4,000-strong division that was not sick, guarding ammunition and baggage, or on other command duties was ready to march, with a haversack full of rations, a pouch full of cartridges and a serviceable musket. After weeks of drill, exhausting route marches to nowhere and false alarms, it looked like the troops would be going into action very shortly; the officers set to work with zeal.[2]

It did not take long for the news to spread through the town; most of the division's officers were billeted at the Château d'Enghien. Colonel Henry Askew's second battalion of the 1st Regiment of Foot Guards had its quarters in the town itself and he speedily passed on Captain Gunthorpe's message; it was a good job he had declined to attend the Duchess of Richmond's ball. Not all, however, had such convenient arrangements. When the message reached Colonel Hon. William Stuart, he knew that the dispersal of his command, the third battalion of the 1st Regiment of Foot Guards, would result in it taking longer to assemble in the event of an alarm. The left wing of the battalion was cantoned at Hoves, a village some four kilometres to the south of Enghien, the battalion assembly point, whilst the right wing was at Marcq, a pretty village clustered around the church of Saint-Martin, about an hour's march away. He sent word immediately to the duty officers and senior non-commissioned officers with each wing, to be prepared to assemble the five companies in heavy marching order and to direct them on Hoves.[3]

Elsewhere in the town, other officers were receiving information from more senior sources. Ensign Charles Lake of the second battalion of the 3rd Regiment of Foot Guards was enjoying a late dinner with Colonel Francis Hepburn, his commanding officer and witnessed one such exchange:

> While we were at our dessert, Major Hesketh of our regiment came into the room and said, 'Colonel, I have just left the Prince of Orange's and have galloped over to tell you that the French have suddenly moved towards us on the Nivelle road,' on which Colonel Hepburn said, 'Hesketh, may I depend upon this news being correct?' 'You may, Colonel.' 'Will you then tell the Adjutant to immediately come to me, as it will enable me to have the Regiment in readiness to move as soon as orders arrive from headquarters.'[4]

Despite his conviction, Captain Robert Hesketh was confused. At the Hôtel de Miroir at Braine-le-Comte, the news of the French invasion had indeed been received, from four separate sources: General Chassé at Haine-Saint-Pierre, General van Merlen at Saint-Symphorien and Generals von Dörnberg and Behr at Mons. The French were not, however, on the Nivelles road, but the debate amongst the British and Netherlands staff officers concerning the defence of the roads to Nivelles, as well as the dispatch of an order at 3.00 p.m. to General de Peponcher-Sedlnitzky, which instructed him to keep one of his brigades on the chaussée, close to Nivelles, had perhaps caused this name to stick in Hesketh's mind. When he returned shortly afterwards with Ensign Barclay Drummond, Hepburn warned the acting adjutant to have the regiment prepared to move.[5]

Some eight kilometres to the south of Enghien, in the small village of Horrues, Lieutenant-Colonel Charles Morice of the 69th Regiment of Foot had given most of his officers the day off. Consequently, Ensign George Ainslie had enjoyed a peaceful morning. In particular, he had relished the respite from brigade or divisional field days at Casteau and the fatiguing marches which they generally entailed; the battalion usually marching off at 3.00 a.m and returning, bone-weary, to their cantonments at 6.00 p.m. He had toyed with the idea of making one of his occasional rides to Mons, but chose instead to spend the day quietly. Life in the army had not been unlike Eton, where he had never been flogged for lessons, despite being rather idle in the four years he had spent there. Joining the battalion at the end of February, he had found that military life suited him perfectly:

> The novelty of the scene, the partiality of our commanding officer, Colonel Morris [sic], and the friendship of my brother officers, caused the three following months to pass most agreeably; during which time we shifted quarters frequently from place to place, occupying Menin, Courtray, Tournay, Ath, or cantonments in small villages and detached farm houses – where we trifled away our time, ignorant of the impending storm. During this period, I was instructed in the rudiments of my profession; while the lenient command of Colonel Morris and the friendship of Hobhouse and Barlow, captains in the regiment, served to render my situation extremely pleasant. The tranquillity of our lives in those rustic quarters, was strangely contrasted with the confusion of the scenes which followed.

There had been no intimation of a move that day and the officers had amused themselves by riding to each others' quarters, catching up on correspondence and pleasant conversation. Towards 3.15 p.m., a messenger arrived from headquarters at Soignies, four kilometres away, with a despatch for the Colonel. The officers speculated. This was clearly too late for a field day. Had the alarm been given? It seemed that it had, but the order seemed to convey no sense of urgency and Ainslie and his servant leisurely packed up his baggage horse and saddled his charger.[6]

At the château belonging to Monsieur de Villagude Saint-Pierre at Horrues, which had formerly been the quarters of Major-General Sir Colin Halkett – commanding the 5th (British) Infantry Brigade – another soldier of the 69th Regiment of Foot was making ready to move off. Major Watson had been spending time with his family, who had arrived in Belgium almost a year previously, on 18 June 1814. As well as his wife Maria, he had been joined by his 16-year-old daughter Fanny, whose engagement to an officer of the 7th Light Dragoons had just been broken. Perhaps, he wondered, something would come of the numerous visits paid to her by young Ensign Edward Macready of the 30th Regiment of Foot, stationed in nearby Soignies. Fanny herself had learned of the fighting earlier that day from some workmen at the house:

> During the forenoon, I chanced to be in the court of the château, where there were some masons at work building a wall, and observed to them that it was thundering; they laughed at my ignorance – 'Tonnere, Mademoiselle; ce n'est pas tonnere, ce sont coup de canons;' they further informed me that the cannonade had been going on all morning.

Perhaps the sound of the gunfire from the east had frightened the family's terrier, Fan, because it was nowhere to be seen. Since being wounded in the back by a musket ball at the assault on Bergen-op-Zoom the previous year, the dog: 'was always frightened, and trembled, and hid herself when she heard the sound of fire-arms'.[7]

Young Macready, Fanny Watson's supposed new suitor was, in fact, standing with a number of his brother officers in the Grand'Place at Soignies, a town which was the headquarters and rallying point of the 3rd (British) Infantry Division, commanded by General von Alten. The junior officers of the 30th Regiment of Foot were idly discussing the probable events of the approaching campaign. Their well-respected surgeon, James Elkington, had heard a report that morning 'that the French had driven in the Prussian advanced posts'. Rumours had been circulating for days that hostilities were imminent and Lieutenant Frederick Pattison of the 33rd Regiment of Foot, also quartered at Soignies, had heard similar reports during the morning of intelligence being received at headquarters that Napoleon himself was advancing with his army on the frontiers of Belgium. As the afternoon wore on, supposition increased in proportion to the arrival of couriers from numerous points. Someone mentioned that they had seen 'Slender Billy', the troops' nickname for the Prince van Oranje-Nassau, on his way to Brussels. Whatever the truth, thought Macready, at least the Prince's absence had temporarily put a stop to the detestable drills that he insisted the troops carry out:

> He prepared for a campaign by filling the hospitals. Twice a week we marched ten miles to the heath of Casteau, near Mons, and were drilled in corps or division. These parades, with our return to quarters, often lasted from three in the morning to six in the afternoon. Our men sometimes fainted, and more frequently pretended to faint, from heat and fatigue; so much so that it became a standing trick, if I may be allowed the expression, for some old hand to drop as the Prince passed the line. This always had a good effect, and we soon marched home.

No doubt Lieutenant-Colonel Morris Bailey, who commanded a wing of the same regiment, had seen much of this behaviour during his time in the Peninsula and elsewhere and found it faintly amusing. Was not initiative, after all, what one expected from a British infantryman?[8]

At about 4.00 p.m. a rumour reached Macready's group that the French had crossed the frontier, provoking a degree of incredulity and apprehension. Almost immediately afterwards, General Halkett, the brigade commander, rode up and asked: 'Are any Light Infantry officers among you?' Stepping forward, Macready saluted and replied in the affirmative. 'Parade your company in ten minutes on this spot,' Halkett instructed and Macready dashed off to assemble the men and to notify Lieutenant John Rumley, his company commander. Having done this, Macready ordered his servant to put his baggage and a recently arrived box of light infantry appointments on his pony. If he was going to war, it would be as a newly-assigned light infantry officer.[9]

At Horrues, Major Watson was already packing all the incidentals that an officer would need on campaign; clean shirts, socks, washing and shaving kit, with the help of Paget, his regimental servant and his daughter, Fanny:

> In the course of the afternoon, an order arrived for the brigade to assemble at the rendezvous at Soignies. Great were the speculations amongst those so deeply interested, whether this order was preparatory to the army moving to the front to meet the enemy, or merely to try how soon they could be got together under arms when wanted. Everything was anxiety and commotion; we were busily employed preparing my father's campaigning baggage, and packing his bât horse. The buglers went across the country sounding, 'Turn out the whole,' the import of which is so well known to military ears, summoning the men from the detached billets in the farmhouses; and the brave fellows were seen hastening with the utmost celerity to join the ranks of death.

A short while later, word came from Colonel Morice, Watson's commanding officer, to dine with him, thus saving him an afternoon of prolonged leave-taking. In his absence, his wife and daughter strolled through the lanes of the surrounding countryside, where they chanced upon Lieutenant Edmund Wightwick, who was marching his men in from their rural billets. Removing his shako, he extracted some newspapers that Mrs Watson had earlier lent him and returned them to her with thanks. True to his belief that the Major's wife must know everything, he asked, 'Are these really the orders to move forward or not?' Shaking her head mournfully, Mrs Watson replied that she felt sure they were going into action.[10]

'The French are on the Nivelles road'

If rumours were starting to circulate in the cantonments in Nivelles, Soignies and Enghien, then Brussels, which hosted the reserve of Wellington's army and also his headquarters, had become a veritable hotbed of speculation. Commercial travellers, tourists, spies and soldiers rubbed shoulders in the cafes and hotels of the upper and lower towns. Lieutenant Basil Jackson, serving on the Quartermaster-General's staff, had learned during the course of the morning that the French were crossing the frontier at Charleroi. If such intelligence or rumour was the privilege of staff officers, it seems Captain William Burney of the 44th Regiment of Foot was more fortunate than most in that he was sharing a billet with an officer of the Quartermaster-General's Department. Towards 4.00 p.m., he noticed this officer and his solitary escort ride in from a reconnaissance of the frontier around Mons, Binche and Charleroi and proceed straight to Wellington's residence at rue Royale to deliver his report.

> On arriving at his billet, all was bustle. I found he had ordered his servants to look well to his horses and prepare everything for a sudden move to the front. I took the hint, packed my baggage and went early to bed.[11]

At Genappe, refugees and rumour had been flowing steadily through since the morning, the more recent fugitives bringing with them accounts that the French were across the border and had approached Charleroi. During the course of the afternoon, an officer of the Marechaussée called Lieutenant Basslé arrived. Stationed at Charleroi, he confirmed the news and added that he had left the place as the French were passing his house. Hurriedly making his escape with a number of important documents, he had ridden to Fleurus, where he reported the Prussian artillery had formed up in expectation of supporting its withdrawing infantry. Continuing his journey north, he claimed to have witnessed fighting at Gosselies towards 5.00 p.m. and reported that Allied artillery had taken up a position well in advance of Genappe. Colonel von Sachsen-Weimar pondered this intelligence. He knew that Frasnes was occupied by the second battalion of the 2nd Nassau-Usingen Regiment and Bijleveld's artillery and, assuming that Major von Normann would be keeping the brigade headquarters informed, decided against writing a report himself. Shortly after the departure of the police officer, the warm afternoon breeze had once again brought with it the sound of distant artillery fire, though both von Sachsen-Weimar and Vigelius, despite the fact that they knew there were enemy to the south, had sometimes found it difficult to tell from exactly which direction the thunder was coming. Nervousness grew into concern, which in turn changed to anxiety. In the absence of definite intelligence and, above all, of orders, the two officers were reduced to a combination of tension and impotence. Should he take the initiative? Should he be bold and seize the command?[12]

Finally, at about 4.00 p.m., they received the message sent by Captain van Coustoll from Houtain-le-Val, stating that artillery fire had been heard close to Gosselies and that musketry could also be distinctly heard. The implication was that the enemy was moving in force on Major von Normann's modest command at Frasnes. In von Sachsen-Weimar's mind, circumstances required that he take the initiative, so the

The Battle of Quatre Bras

Prince decided to assemble the two battalions of his regiment and the Volunteer Jager Company at Les Quatre Bras, the assembly point of the brigade in the event of an alarm. Word was sent to gather the officers present and, once they were assembled, von Sachsen-Weimar addressed them. 'Gentlemen,' he began, 'I am totally without orders; however, I have never heard that they start a battle with a retreat. Therefore we will stand here at Quatre Bras.'[13]

For von Sachsen-Weimar, it was advantageous that in early May, de Perponcher-Sedlnitzky had designated Les Quatre Bras as the place of alarm for the entire brigade. His task was further aided by the standing order of 9 June 1815 to assemble each battalion daily in its cantonment, and the officers had long since become accustomed to the exercise of assembling the troops, feeding them and dispersing them back to their billets. Word was sent by courier to Major Schleyer of the second battalion at Bousval. Colonel von Dressel, commanding officer of the first battalion of the Regiment Oranien-Nassau at Genappe immediately sent officers to rouse his own men. Private Holighausen was gathered with his comrades when one of these officers came up to them. Drawing his sabre, he yelled for the drummer and within seconds, the hollow thump of the 'General' had the infantry hurriedly forming up with loaded muskets.[14]

If the 2nd Nassau-Usingen Regiment were similarly assembled at their respective cantonments and if orders had already been given for the assembly of the brigade, von Sachsen-Weimar calculated that the five battalions could be mustered at Les Quatre Bras sometime between 6.00 and 7.00 p.m. Although the greater distance that the second battalion of his regiment had to march and their dispersal over a wide area at Glabais, Thy and Bousval, might delay the arrival of these troops.[15]

Sitting down with pen and paper, he composed a letter to General de Perponcher-Sedlnitzky at Nivelles, describing the intelligence situation, outlining his orders to assemble at Les Quatre Bras and stating his intention to resist the French if necessary. A short distance away at Vieux-Genappe, the 1769 bell donated by the Abbaye de Villers-la-Ville to the new church of Saint-Géry was striking 4.30 p.m. The previous three bells had all been stolen by the French. Perhaps it was an omen.[16]

In common with the Nassauers, the sixty-strong Light Company of the 30th Regiment of Foot paraded in the square at Soignies. Lieutenant-Colonel Charles Vigoreux, commanding the combined light companies of the brigade, ordered it march off in the direction of Naast, four kilometres to the south-east, in order to stand picket. As the company left the town, the outlying elements of its parent battalion were arriving, along with the ten companies of the 69th Regiment of Foot. Marching briskly along the banks of the Senne, through Les Carrières, Macready could see other troops of the division hurriedly marching towards Soignies in response to the orders to assemble. The game, he thought, was most definitely afoot.[17]

It had been a pleasant day in Brussels and in the late afternoon sun many had taken to the Royal Park, enjoying the opportunity to stroll among the fountains and statues, or along the formal gravel walks that separated parched grass plots from colourful parterres. The scene was

'The French are on the Nivelles road'

… crowded with officers in every variety of military uniform, with elegant women, and with lively parties and gay groups of British and Belgic people, loitering, walking, talking, and sitting under the trees! There could not be a more animated, a more holiday scene; everything looked gay and festive, and everything spoke of hope, confidence and busy expectation.[18]

General Picton was in the park for the second time that day, strolling with Captain Tyler, when he met Colonel Belson of the 28th Regiment of Foot, who was taking the air with Lieutenant-Colonel Robert Nixon and Captain Charles Cadell. Although all three were veterans of the Peninsular War and Belson sported the Gold Cross with two clasps to prove it, they had never served in Picton's famous 'Fighting Third Division'. Respondng to their desire to be introduced, Picton gruffly acknowledged that he was pleased to have them in his division.[19]

Another Peninsular veteran, who had arrived over a month previously, was First Lieutenant George Simmons, whose lodgings were in the lower town, across the street from the Hôtel de Ville at rue de l'Étoile 119, with Monsieur Overmann and ten members of his family and household. Though comfortable in his lodgings, he was distinctly uncomfortable with his finances, finding himself in the oft-quoted straitened circumstances. His cares had been added to by the expensive necessity of procuring a riding horse, a baggage horse and other equipment. With no income due until the following month and with the prize money for the Peninsular War still unpaid, he was fretting over how his parents would manage and how he could help with his sister's tuition fees. A quick campaign and a substantial prize fund would make the world of difference to his situation.[20]

At about 4.00 p.m. General de Constant-Rebecque's courier arrived at Bornival, a short distance to the west of Nivelles. Both rider and mount were hot and tired after the long journey across the steep valley of the Sennette and he welcomed the opportunity to rest briefly and inform Lieutenant-Colonel Wijbrandus de Jongh that, according to the orders he was carrying to de Perponcher-Sedlnitzky, the Netherlanders of the 8th National Militia Battalion would shortly be directed to take up their brigade alarm post at the Porte de Soignies at Nivelles. Showing not a moment's hesitation, de Jongh decided to march to Nivelles and asked de Constant-Rebecque's courier to advise his brigade commander, General van Bijlandt, of his intentions. He then sent word to the outlying detachments of the battalion at Monstreux to meet him en route and within minutes the battalion was paraded, under arms and on its way.[21]

At his headquarters in Nivelles, General de Perponcher-Sedlnitzky was being briefed by Captain von Mühlmann, who had arrived shortly after 4.00 p.m. from Houtain-le-Val. The Nassau officer described the situation faced by Major von Normann and Captain Bijleveld at Frasnes, the reports of the fugitives from Charleroi, Jumet and Gosselies and the defensive measures that had so far been taken by both Major von Normann and Major Sattler. Firing from Gosselies rapidly approaching Frasnes? Discharges from firearms distinctly audible? Summoning Captain Baron Friedrich von Gagern, de Perponcher-Sedlnitzky briefed him on von Mühlmann's

Lieutenant-General Baron Henri de Perponcher-Sedlnitzky (after Hoffmeister). *Musée Royal de l'Armee, Brussels*

report and instructed him to ride for Houtain-le-Val, Genappe, Les Quatre Bras and Frasnes, assess the situation for himself and report back with further news.[22]

The General was still considering the importance of the intelligence that von Mühlmann had brought, when, shortly after the departure of the two officers, he received the courier from General de Constant-Rebecque, dated from Braine-le-Comte at 3.00 p.m:

No. 178.

Main Headquarters of the Royal Netherlands Army
at Braine-le-Comte
15 June 1815.

His Royal Highness has charged me to write to you that on the receipt of this present you must gather your division as quickly as possible. You will keep a brigade ready for action on the main road, close to Nivelles, the other to place itself at Les Quatre Bras. These dispositions will be maintained until new orders are received from His Royal Highness. In case Your Excellency has already put the troops under arms since this morning, it will perhaps be necessary that they prepare meals and eat at the place of assembly.

Baron de Constant-Rebecque.[23]

The headquarters was immediately put on alert. Fighting to the south of Frasnes? Reports from Prussian wounded and stragglers of engagements with the French? Orders from Braine-le-Comte to assemble the division at their alarm posts? Clearly something serious was unfolding. What remained unanswered so far in de Perponcher-Sedlnitzky's mind, however, were the key questions of how far the French advance had reached and what had become of the Prussians; especially the corps of Lieutenant-General Count Hans von Zieten, covering the frontier to the south of his division. If the French had smashed through the Prussians and were moving on Frasnes, his left flank would be seriously threatened. Enclosing a copy of the note from von Normann, he wrote von Sachsen-Weimar a letter instructing him to assemble the brigade at Les Quatre Bras and handed the packet to a courier.[24]

Having dealt with his left wing, de Perponcher-Sedlnitzky instructed General van Bijlandt to assemble the right wing at Nivelles. Within minutes, messengers were heading off to the respective headquarters of every battalion and battery at Nivelles, Buzet, Baulers and Bornival. For the time being, the 7th Line Battalion at Feluy, Arquennes and Petit-Roeulx was left in place, covering the approaches to the town from the south, although orders were sent to Lieutenant-Colonel François van den Sanden not to allow the detachments cantoned at Arquennes and Petit-Roeulx to return to their billets. Since it was already quartered in the town of Nivelles, van Bijlandt judged that there would be plenty of time to notify the 27th Jager Battalion; so the 23 officers and 791 green-jacketed light infantrymen continued to enjoy the late afternoon sunshine, beneath the imposing Romanesque edifice of the collegiate church of Sainte-Gertrude, blissfully unaware that war was rapidly approaching.[25]

At Brussels, Wellington was still dining with his guests. Shortly after 5.00 p.m., as dessert was served, Colonel Somerset arrived. He had just received Captain Lennox, who had passed on the packet of letters from the frontier, under cover of the 2.00 p.m. note from Colonel Berkeley:

> Braine-le-Comte, the 15th of June, at 2 o'clock p.m.
>
> My dear Lord,
>
> HRH the Prince of Orange, having set out at 5 o'clock this morning for the advanced posts, and not being returned, I forward the enclosed letter from General Dörnberg. General Constant desires I would inform you that the reports just arrived from different quarters state that the Prussians have been attacked upon their line in front of Charleroi; that they have evacuated Binche, and mean to collect first at Gosselies. Everything is quiet upon our front and the 3rd Division of the Netherlands is collected at Fayt. He sends you also the copy of a letter from the commandant of Mons.
>
> I remain, my dear Lord, very faithfully yours,
> G. H. Berkeley.[26]

Wellington's guests no doubt speculated on the contents of the packet forwarded from the advanced posts between Mons and Fontaine-l'Evêque, but the Duke chose not to reveal the contents of the dispatch to those officers present. Towards 6.00 p.m., Colonel Baron Friedrich von Müffling, his Prussian liaison officer, arrived, with the news that he had received a dispatch sent from Charleroi at about 9.00 a.m. by General von Zieten. The enemy had attacked the Prussian positions on the Sambre and, at the time of writing, had taken Thuin, pushing the advanced posts back as far as Montigny-le-Tilleul. The two Prussian brigades in this sector were withdrawing to a new position between Gosselies and Gilly, falling back if necessary on Fleurus. Napoleon was present in person, with his Imperial Guard and a large force of cavalry. Consistent with a commitment made by von Müffling only the previous day, General von Zieten requested that the Duke concentrate his troops without delay at Nivelles. Wellington received all this news with his usual calmness. After a short debate, he expressed an opinion that these opening encounters posed no immediate danger. Although Binche had been abandoned, he trusted the Prussians to cover the route from Charleroi to Brussels. General Chassé's infantry at Fayt and that of de Perponcher-Sedlnitzky, farther to the rear at Nivelles, would continue to cover the approaches to Brussels from Mons; in addition, General de Collaert's cavalry would provide him with early warning of any other developments on his stretch of the frontier. Upon further reflection, he decided it would be beneficial to concentrate his respective divisions at their alarm points and gave instructions that the staff officers make the necessary arrangements.[27]

Unaware that the commander-in-chief was pondering the intelligence that General van Merlen, among others, had forwarded to Braine-le-Comte, General de Collaert received de Constant-Rebecque's orders at his headquarters in the hamlet of Boissoît-sur-Haine. It was approaching 5.00 p.m.

No. 179

                              Headquarters at Braine-le-Comte, 15 June.

HRH the Prince of Orange charges me to ask you to collect at once General de Ghigny's 1st Light Cavalry Brigade close to Havré and General Trip's Carabinier Brigade in rear of Strépy and to hold them assembled there until further notice. His Royal Highness has himself, this morning, given orders to General van Merlen, concerning his own brigade.

Baron de Constant-Rebecque[28]

Though possibly puzzled by the order, it contained nothing to suggest that de Collaert faced any form of threat; nor did it contain any instructions to undertake any reconnaissance activities. Within minutes, couriers were dispatched to Major-General Lord Albert Trip at Roeulx, and in the villages of Houdeng, Goegnies and farther to the north, at Mignault. The trumpets were soon sounding the assembly

'The French are on the Nivelles road'

and the blue-coated carabiniers with their burnished helmets were quickly saddled up and on the move. Just along the road from Boussoît-sur-Haine, at Havré, was the headquarters of Major-General Baron Charles de Ghigny, commanding de Collaert's 1st (Netherlands) Light Cavalry Brigade, the remainder of which was dispersed in small garrisons to the north of the river, at Obourg, Gottignies and Saint-Denis. At Boussoît-sur-Haine itself, and across the river at Thieu and Ville-sur-Haine, the two sections of the depleted 3rd Company of Horse Artillery, with three bronze 6-pounder guns and a short, sinister looking 24-pounder iron howitzer, made preparations to join the heavy cavalry at Strépy, under the watchful eye of their commander, Captain Abraham Petter. Petter had served in every rank from gunner upwards, in a career that had so far spanned twenty years.[29]

At the same time as de Collaert's sabres were rattling in their scabbards, Colonel von Sachsen-Weimar had completed his report and sent it to General de Perponcher-Sedlnitzky at Nivelles. At about 5.00 p.m. he mounted his horse and set off from Genappe for Les Quatre Bras. As his horse climbed the steep gradient of the Chaussée de Charleroi, he met Captain von Gagern, arriving from Nivelles, by way of Houtain-le-Val and Les Quatre Bras. Perhaps he was bearing instructions from the headquarters directing the concentration of the brigade. Instead, von Gagern informed him that his mission was confined to reconnoitring the area and making a report of the situation to General de Perponcher-Sedlnitzky. Perhaps somewhat concerned that the divisional commander had not found von Normann's warning a sufficiently strong case for assembling the brigade, the Prince summarised the intelligence situation concerning Charleroi and the threat to Frasnes and informed the staff officer that he had ordered both battalions of the Regiment Oranien-Nassau, as well as the Volunteer Jager Company, to concentrate at Les Quatre Bras. He did, however, take some from comfort from von Gagern's confirmation that Major Sattler had marched for Les Quatre Bras with the first battalion of the 2nd Nassau-Usingen Regiment, and that Sattler had also sent orders to the third battalion at Sart-Dame-Avelines to do likewise. Satisfied that there was no further information to be gathered, von Gagern rode off in the direction of Nivelles, eager to report back to his chief on the situation.[30]

After the brief downpour earlier in the afternoon, Charlotte Waldie and her family had continued their journey and were on the road between Asse and Kobbegem, where their progress became even more ponderous; their carriage was caught behind a body of the Duke von Braunschweig-Lüneburg's Hussars; 'sombre, ominous looking men'. Everything about them seemed to be black, the uniform; the horses; the nodding horsehair plumes. To Charlotte, their whole aspect 'gave them a most sombre and funereal appearance' and as they moved slowly along the road, 'they looked like an immense moving hearse'. Jokingly, she turned to her sister and suggested this might be a bad omen. Absent from the cortège in front of them was Sergeant Wilhelm Langenstrasse of the 4th Company. He and some others had been given the day off by their commanding officer and far from the dismal aspect of the men on the chaussée, he and his comrades were 'cheerfully engaged at a party given by our

The Battle of Quatre Bras

departed major, where with music and songs, we shot at a target', little knowing that within 24 hours their carbines would be put to more lethal use.[31]

The sound of musketry was not confined to Langenstrasse's party, however. Just over 32 kilometres to the south, outside Baulers, to the north-east of Nivelles, the Dutch recruits of the 7th National Militia Battalion were busy rehearsing the routine of priming, loading and ramming their muskets, before firing volleys at targets that had been set up on the other side of the field. Since being raised at Amsterdam the previous year, their commanding officer, Lieutenant-Colonel Henry Singendonck had taken every opportunity to practise musketry, though initially weapons had been in short supply and ammunition was – even at this stage – scarce. Among the men was Jan Rem, a 22-year-old from Wormer, a village some fifteen kilometres to the north of Amsterdam. Under the peak of his British manufactured stovepipe shako, the sweat was running into his eyes and the bitter taste of the powder around his mouth and the dryness of his throat made him long for a cooling drink of water and the shade of the trees. Suddenly a messenger rode up and Colonel Singendonck immediately ordered the alarm to be sounded. As the drummers pounded out the rhythmic message, the firing ceased, targets were dismantled and the men fell in. Within the space of a few minutes, 22 officers and 622 men were paraded and marched off towards the Namur road. To the west of Nivelles, other militiamen were already on the move. At 5.00 p.m. the column of Colonel de Jongh's 8th National Militia Battalion appeared on the dusty road from Bornival and came to a halt at the Porte de Soignies, before falling out and preparing to bivouac in the open. The first of General van Bijlandt's battalions had safely reached its alarm post.[32]

In the sleepy neighbouring hamlets of Obaix and Buzet, some seven or eight kilometres south-west of Les Quatre Bras, the sentries of the 5th National Militia Battalion had been listening to the sound of artillery fire to the south-east and had reported the discovery to Lieutenant-Colonel Jan Westenbergh, their commanding officer. As the afternoon wore on, the low rumbling of cannon had been embellished by the distinct rattle of musketry, which meant that whatever was happening, it was not happening very far away. Towards 4.00 p.m., some of the officers had been standing with Colonel Westenbergh, when several of the outposts reported that local inhabitants were fleeing with all their possessions. Captain Dirk van Toll and First Lieutenant Barre were ordered to undertake a reconnaissance and, as their horses climbed the heights to the south of Liberchies, the sound of musketry had become increasingly distinct. Gosselies had come into view, just over a kilometre distant, when they realised that the noise emanated from a rearguard action by the Prussians, as they evacuated their positions on the Sambre and Piéton rivers. The two Netherlands officers had remained for some time, observing the ebb and flow of the combat, until they noticed the Prussians disengaging and retreating towards the east, following which the French began a tentative advance up the Charleroi road. Undetected by either side, van Toll and Barre hastened back to their battalion. When they arrived at Buzet, at about 5.15 p.m., they reported their observations to Westenbergh, who was concerned by the severity and proximity of the fighting. He concluded that the brigade and divisional headquarters must be unaware of it, otherwise they would have alerted the battalion, or summoned it to the assembly point at Nivelles. The nearness of the enemy meant that French cavalry patrols could be at Obaix or Buzet within the hour. Calling forward Lieutenant-Adjutant Vos, he ordered him to ride to General van Bijlandt's headquarters at Nivelles, brief him on what van Toll and Barre had seen at Gosselies, update him on the situation of the battalion and, above all, to request orders. In the meantime, the Colonel assembled the company commanders and gave orders that the men be prepared to march at a moment's notice. As luck would have it, less than half an hour after Lieutenant Vos had departed, a courier arrived from General van Bijlandt, carrying the order for the battalion to assemble at Nivelles. Having already been placed on alert, the young militiamen were soon underway, doubtless grateful to be putting some distance between themselves and the French.[33]

At Frasnes, meanwhile, Captain Wirths was standing with the main body of the second battalion of the 2nd Nassau-Usingen Regiment, when a lone horseman was spotted approaching their positions shortly before 6.00 p.m. He turned out to belong to the Prussian 4th (1st Silesian) Hussars, separated from his regiment during the retreat from Gosselies.

> An unarmed Prussian Hussar broke through the fence of the place where the battalion was standing, covered in wounds and blood and told us that the French were very close and would probably break through to where the picquet of the battalion was standing.[34]

To the south of the village, Commissioner-General Vrijthoff arrived from Charleroi with a convoy of wagons, accompanied by a small escort of Prussian uhlans. Having had been ordered to remove the Commissariat's cash to Brussels, his journey had been uneventful until the party had been ambushed a few moments before by a patrol of lancers in red jackets. They explained to the picquet of the Flanquer company at the Ferme du Gros Caillou that their escort had managed to drive the small patrol away, but it was clear to the Nassauers that the enemy were now very close. Not long after Vrijthoff left them, the men soon observed isolated parties of red-coated cavalry approaching from the direction of Gosselies. Were they British? Prussians? Some of the keener-sighted Nassauers could make out red and white pennons. Uhlans? Captain Müller, the company commander, was alerted. As the horsemen came nearer and failed to satisfy the challenge of the sentries, they were peppered with musket shots from the marksmen, hidden behind the hedgerows and walls and firing from the open windows of the houses. Some lancers hurried back down the road, whilst others dismounted and returned fire with their musketoons, their horses being hurriedly led into cover by other troopers. To the north, a rhythmic booming trembled through the still air, as Bijleveld's battery, opening fire at long range, attempted to dissuade the enemy from pressing the point. The French, however, were having none of it and reinforced their efforts with additional squadrons. It soon became clear to von Normann

The Battle of Quatre Bras

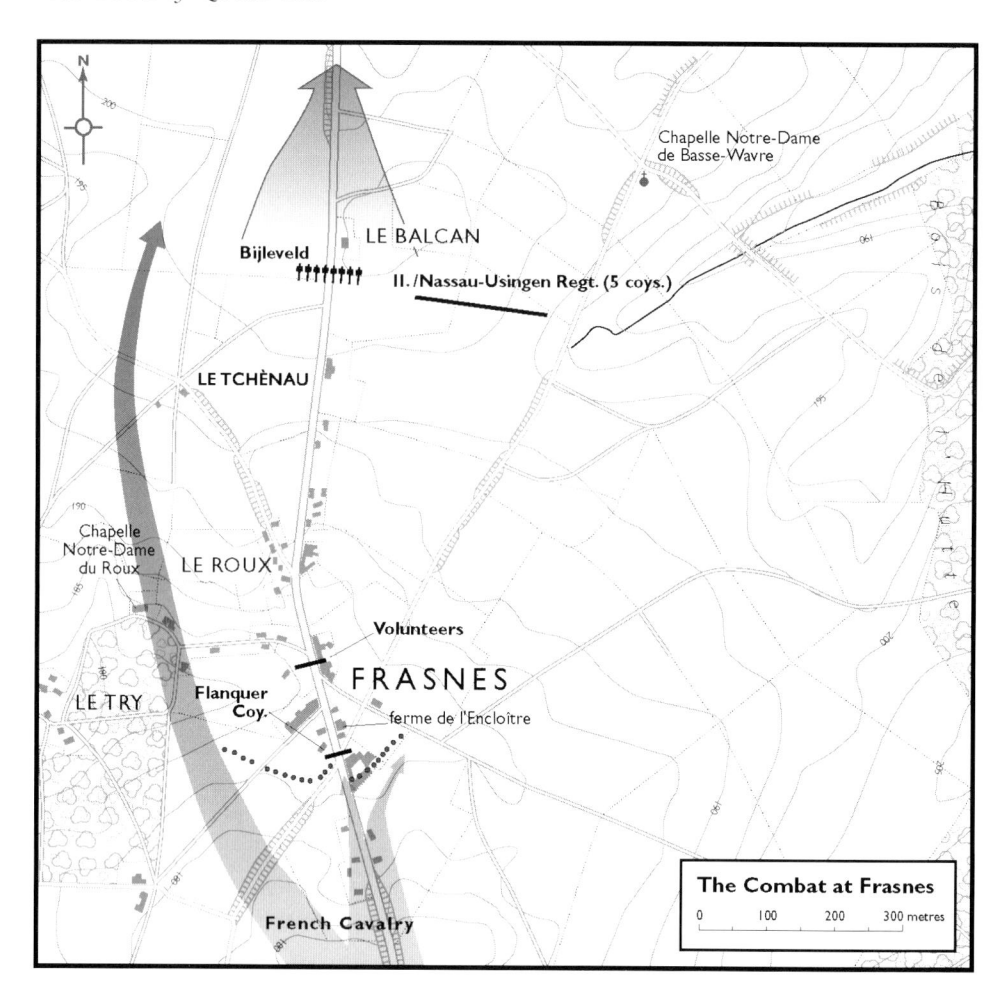

that what had first appeared to be a probing attack by a small patrol, now bore the hallmarks of a fully-fledged assault conducted by a sizeable body of cavalry.[35]

Suddenly, the French dashed up the road, dispersing the soldiers of the Nassau picquet and forcing them to take cover behind the hedges and fences of the nearby gardens, from where several successfully made their way back to their parent battalion. Pushing forward sections of dismounted troopers equipped with firearms, the French slowly gained ground. Recognising the need to bolster the skirmishers, Major von Normann ordered Captain Müller to move forward with the remainder of the company, reinforce his outposts and arrest the progress of the lancers through the village and to the east. Gathering together eighty volunteers from the four Jäger companies posted on the Balcan plateau, Lieutenant Johann Hölschen led them into Frasnes in support, whilst Bijleveld's guns and the remainder of the battalion continued to occupy the heights, for the time being discouraging any further advance on the part of the French.[36]

The skirmish was now half an hour old and all the efforts of the French to progress through the village itself and along the chaussée had so far been frus-

'The French are on the Nivelles road'

A 20th-century photograph of Quatre Bras from the south-east angle of the cross-roads showing buildings that have since been demolished.

trated. Before long, however, von Normann noticed the main body of the lancers preparing to make an attempt to bypass the village completely, across the open fields to the west of the Charleroi road. Arriving within a few hundred metres of von Normann's position, the cavalry were now exchanging fire from horseback with the main body of the Nassau battalion but, stung by the heavy and accurate musketry and flailed by the rounds of canister with which Bijleveld's sweating gunners obliged them, the French pulled back some distance in order to avoid the worst of the fire. Finding the direct route blocked, the attack eddied around the obstacle, extending towards the Ferme du Grand-Pierrepont and the dark mass of the wood of the same name. Those on the right of the Nassau line could see a richly-costumed French general, leading the blue-jacketed Poles of the Elba Squadron in person towards the gap between the Charleroi road and the wood itself, little knowing that this was *Général de Division* Count Édouard de Colbert-Chabanais, the general officer commanding the light cavalry division of Napoleon's Imperial Guard.[37]

At Nivelles, the divisional staff was unaware that its troops were already engaged. Indeed, when Captain von Gagern arrived at headquarters towards 6.00 p.m. and reported his observations, the intelligence he had collected and Colonel von Sachsen-Weimar's intentions, General de Perponcher-Sedlnitzky must have felt a sensation close to relief. The Prince, it seemed, had taken the initiative in assembling his regiment at Les Quatre Bras and this, combined with Major Sattler's resourcefulness meant that his own orders had been pre-empted; a fragile defensive cordon had been created, which if unable to stop the French completely, might at least slow them down. As soon as von Gagern had briefed him on the preparations that Major von Normann had made at Frasnes, the General asked him to return there, attach himself to the brigade and keep him informed of developments.[38]

The Battle of Quatre Bras

At Frasnes, meanwhile, the situation had taken a turn for the worse. Observing the French outflanking movement with a growing sense of unease, and fearful of being cut off from the position he hoped was being taken up by the remainder of the brigade at Les Quatre Bras. Major Von Normann and Bijleveld held a brief conference, following which they decided that it was time to pull back in the direction of the Ferme de Saint-Pierre at Gemioncourt, a little in advance of the crossroads. Here, the right flank of the infantry would be protected by the Bois de Bossu, whilst Bijleveld's guns could take up positions from which they could cover both the Charleroi and Namur roads. In the hope that his message to Houtain-le-Val had mobilised some support, von Normann sent a non-commissioned officer of Bijleveld's artillery train to his brigade commander, whom he assumed would by now be at Les Quatre Bras with a request that Colonel von Gödecke bring up troops to help cover the retreat. Shortly afterwards, the vehicles of the artillery park were successfully removed, the teams of horses clattering up the road towards Les Quatre Bras, hauling the precious equipment. Having lost thirty horses already to the fire of the French cavalry, some vehicles had insufficient animals to move them and the drivers were consequently ordered by Bijleveld to return to Frasnes as soon as possible in order to remove the remaining matériel.[39]

Immediately afterwards, von Normann drew in the remaining picquets and recalled Captain Müller's Flanquer Company and Lieutenant Hölschen's volunteer Jager detachment from the village. As soon as they saw these detachments withdrawing from the buildings and gardens, the French made an impetuous charge, which Bijleveld's guns stopped in its tracks, firing round after round of canister into the closest enemy horsemen. Heads down, the green-coated infantry laboured up the long slope from Frasnes, covered by fire from the four companies posted to the east of the road. The two remaining companies took up posts from which they could protect the flanks of the position. As soon as the battalion was reunited, von Normann made arrangements for the recovery and evacuation of the wounded. Amongst the 39 men killed, wounded or missing, was Captain von Müller, who had been injured during the fighting for the village. There was little that could be done for the dead and von Normann ordered their bodies to be left behind. The wounded begged their comrades not to abandon them also. Those that had served in the Peninsular War were well aware of the atrocities of which the *fantassins* were capable and those who had fought in the ranks of the 1st Nassau-Usingen Regiment – which had been disarmed by the French at Barcelona in 1813 – could testify to the French contempt for their erstwhile allies. Though most of the uninjured had managed to make it back as far as the Balcan plateau and were taking up positions in the ranks and files of the battalion, any missing were to be left to fend for themselves.[40]

The withdrawal of the guns and vehicles was somewhat improvised, but despite the loss in horses, von Normann and Bijleveld were determined that having successfully evacuated the majority of the park in the first instance, nothing would be abandoned to the enemy. Teams of horses gradually started returning from the Ferme de Gemioncourt and Bijleveld and his officers set about the task of bringing the ordnance off the field. By reducing the size of the teams and using spare horses from the artillery park, the young officer managed to extricate his pieces and to remove all his ammunition wagons and other vehicles to the safety of a position in rear of Les Quatre Bras. The moment the last gun had moved off, the second battalion of the 2nd Nassau-Usingen Regiment commenced its withdrawal in good order and took up a new position on the southern edge of the Bois de Bossu, in the buildings and enclosures of the Ferme de Gemioncourt and on the highway itself. Though the lancers pursued them energetically and attempted repeatedly to close with them, regular volleys of musketry served to keep them at a distance.[41]

Captain Wirths was in the thick of the action:

> The battalion, together with the artillery, now marched from this place [Frasnes] . . . retreating to Quatre Bras in such a way that the artillery remained on the road, which just outside Frasnes was in a deep cutting, whilst the battalion, in two halves, on both sides of the road, slowly went to Quatre Bras in closed columns. We had hardly marched a little distance on this road, when from all around us, swarms of French Guard Lancers came dashing forward, encircled us and executed many charges upon us, whereupon the battalion each time made 'Halt!', lowered the muskets and so, every time, held off the attacks. In this way, the half-hour journey from Frasnes to Quatre Bras was covered very slowly, but without accidents or losses.[42]

For their part, the artillery conducted a withdrawal by sections. Periodically, Captain Bijleveld halted his sweating teams and, smoothly unlimbering, they brought the guns into action, discharging a few rounds apiece at those French horsemen who had been bold enough to pursue them too closely. Once they arrived at the Ferme de Gemioncourt at about 7.30 p.m., Bijleveld's guns unlimbered for a final time and fired a number of canister rounds, which must have suggested to the officers leading the French advance that these Netherlanders and Germans did not intend to cede further ground. Suddenly, the attacks ceased, as though the enemy had finally lost heart and settled for the occupation of Frasnes. As the French withdrew and the firing died away, Major von Normann sent picquets into the Bois de Bossu and the remainder of the battalion set about establishing itself in what Captain Wirths described as a 'comfortable position', the officers and men perhaps reassured that they had done enough to dissuade the French from any further advance that evening. It was 8.00 p.m.[43]

Endnotes

1. Dalton, pp. 18, 20, 25. Master. Miller (II), pp. 17, 43, 62–6, 88, 111, 187–91. Powell. Swinton, pp. 132–3.
2. Dalton, pp. 20, 25, 30–1, 35–7. Miller (II), p. 63. Rooke (I).
3. Dalton, p. 97. Fraser &c., p. 11. F. Hamilton, pp. 13, 15. Maurice, p. 8. Powell.
4. Lake.

5. Anonymous (Outgoing Register). Dalton, p. 112. Lake.
6. Ainslie, pp. 12–13. Macready (I).
7. Myddleton, pp. 4–5, 37, 42–3, 77. Macready (I).
8. Elkington (I), p. 12. Macready (I). Morris, p. 64. Pattison (II), p. 2.
9. Macready (I). Pattison (II), p. 2.
10. Myddleton, p. 77.
11. Burney, p. 82. Jackson, p. 12.
12. Basslé. Houssaye, p. 71. von Sachsen-Weimar (III). Starklof, p. 131.
13. de Bas &c., p. 400. Hofschröer (I), p. 201. Houssaye, pp. 71, 342. van Löben-Sels, pp. 130–2. 29. von Sachsen-Weimar (III). Starklof, pp. 131–2. van Zuylen van Nyeveld (I), p. 49.
14. de Bas &c., pp. 316–20, 463. Holighausen.
15. Hofschröer (I), p. 201. Starklof, p. 132.
16. de Bas &c., p. 400. von Sachsen-Weimar (III). Starklof, p. 132.
17. Bannatyne, pp. 319–20. Brett-James, p. 52. Elkington (I), p. 12. Macready (I). Morris, p. 64. Pattison (II), p. 2
18. Eaton, pp. 13–14.
19. Cadell (I), pp. 232–3. Dalton, p. 137.
20. Dalton, p. 16. Simmons (I), pp. 359–61.
21. de Bas &c., p. 447. Dellevoet, p. 20. de Jongh. de Perponcher-Sedlnitzky.
22. de Bas, p. 1332. de Bas &c., pp. 400–1, 405, Hofschröer (I), pp. 201, 206. von Sachsen-Weimar (III). Sattler. Starklof, p. 132. Wüppermann, p. 88. Wirths. van Zuylen van Nyeveld (I), pp. 49–51.
23. Anonymous (Outgoing Register). de Bas &c., pp. 395, 400.
24. Hofschröer (I), p. 206. van Zuylen van Nyeveld (I), p. 49.
25. de Bas, pp. 96, 1332. de Bas &c., p. 318. van Bijlandt. Dellevoet, p. 20. Grunenbosch. Hofschröer (I), p. 202. van Löben-Sels, p. 457. von Pflugk-Harttung (I), p. 294. Scheltens, p. 197. Wüppermann, p. 83. van Zuylen van Nyeveld (I), p. 49.
26. Anonymous (Outgoing Register). de Bas &c., 392. de Constant-Rebecque (I). Hofschröer (I), p. 196. Miller (I), pp. 66, 106. C. Robinson, p. 516. F. Somerset, pp. 6–7. Wellesley, p. 480.
27. de Bas &c., p. 390. Anonymous (Letters), p. 220. Carter, p. 92. Eaton, p. 15. Alexander Forbes (II). Gomm (I), p. 5. Hofschröer (I), p. 193. Hussey (III). von Lettow-Vorbeck, p. 253. MacKinnon, pp. 210–11. Maurice, p. 7. Miller (II), p. 134. von Müffling (I), p. 1. von Müffling (II) p. 228. von Ollech, p. 96. Young, pp. 99–100.
28. Anonymous (Outgoing Register). de Bas &c., pp. 395–6.
29. de Bas &c., p. 396. van Uythoven.
30. de Bas &c., pp. 401. Muilwijk, p. 29. von Sachsen-Weimar (III). van Zuylen van Nyeveld (I), p. 49.
31. Eaton, pp. 11–12. Langenstrasse.
32. Bowden, p. 238. de Jongh. van Löben-Sels, p. 457. Rem. van Zuylen van Nyeveld (I), pp. 49, 51.
33. de Bas &c., pp. 447–8. Barre. Hofschröer (I), p. 179. Knoop (II), p. 190. Mollinger. de Perponcher-Sedlnitzy. de Roo van Alderwelt. van Toll.
34. Wirths.

35. de Bas &c., p. 401. Bijleveld. Hofschröer (I), pp. 129, 201. Houssaye, p. 70. von Kruse. van Oranje-Nassau (II). Pawly (I), p. 104. de Perponcher-Sedlnitzky. von Sachsen-Weimar (I). Sattler. Starklof, p. 131. van Zuylen van Nyeveld (I), pp. 49–50.
36. de Bas &c., p. 401. Hofschröer (I), pp. 201–3. Wirths. van Zuylen van Nyeveld (I), p. 50.
37. de Bas &c., pp. 401–2. Bijleveld. Hofschröer (I), p. 203. Houssaye, pp. 71, 341–2. von Kruse. Lemonnier-Delafosse, p. 204. Ney. Pawly (I), p. 104. de Perponcher-Sedlnitzky. von Sachsen-Weimar (I). Starklof, p. 133. van Zuylen van Nyeveld (I), pp. 49–50.
38. de Bas &c., p. 401. van Zuylen van Nyeveld (I), p. 50.
39. Bijlandt. von Sachsen-Weimar (III). van Zuylen van Nyeveld (I), p. 50.
40. de Bas &c., p. 403. Bijleveld. Wirths. Wüppermann, p. 109 van Zuylen van Nyeveld (I), p. 50.
41. de Bas &c., pp. 402–3. Bijleveld. Dellevoet, p. 20. Hofschröer (I), p. 203. Houssaye, p. 71. von Kruse. Maurice, p. 8. Pawly (I), p. 104. de Perponcher-Sedlnitzky. Ross-Lewin, p. 255. von Sachsen-Weimar (I). von Sachsen-Weimar (II). Sattler. Starklof, p. 133. van Zuylen van Nyeveld (I), p. 50
42. Wirths.
43. Bijleveld. van Oranje-Nassau. (II). de Perponcher-Sedlnitzky. Sattler. Starklof, p. 133. van Zuylen van Nyeveld (I), p. 50.

The crossroads at Les Quatre Bras, viewed from the south-west. (Author's collection.)

CHAPTER 3

A short distance away at the edge of the Bois de Bossu, Colonel von Sachsen-Weimar had witnessed the struggle. Captain von Gagern was once more at his side, having returned from Nivelles towards 7.30 p.m., with orders to continue to monitor the situation. The Prince ruefully contemplated what could have been achieved, had he been supported by cavalry; it was a handicap that the Allies would feel keenly in the coming 24 hours. To von Sachsen-Weimar, the signs seemed otherwise promising. Having ridden ahead of the first battalion of the Regiment Oranien-Nassau, he had arrived at the crossroads of Les Quatre Bras, towards 5.20 p.m. and was delighted to find Major Hegmann, who, 'with a martial instinct', was already present with the third battalion of the 2nd Nassau-Usingen Regiment. These troops were drawn up in column in the pasture to the south-east of the crossroads, the alarm post it had been given by an order of 7 May. The Prince's satisfaction had, however, been tempered by the ominous booming of cannon towards the south. Were they Bijleveld's guns? French? Both? He and Major Hegmann waited impatiently for reinforcements, unable to abandon the crossroads and move forward in support of von Normann until more troops arrived. Help was not long in coming. At around 6.00 p.m., four companies of the first battalion of the 2nd Nassau-Usingen Regiment, with Major Sattler at their head, marched up the dusty road from Houtain-le-Val and formed in line, the left wing at Les Quatre Bras and the right wing behind the Bois de Bossu, to the north of the Nivelles road. En route, Sattler informed the Prince, he had detached two companies down the western side of the Bois de Bossu, with orders to occupy its southernmost point as close to Frasnes as possible, where it was to establish communications with the second battalion. Almost simultaneously, the first battalion of the Regiment Oranien-Nassau arrived and took up its alarm post along the Namur road, its right flank resting on the Ferme des Quatre Bras. Their march from Genappe had been eventful. They left the town in buoyant mood and singing lustily, but soon came across several wagons full of Prussian wounded, whose sutlers gloomily warned them that, 'you will soon have no desire to sing;' the men became gloomy and despondent. Their sister battalion was also on the move, marching from distant Bousval, but would probably not arrive much before 7.30 p.m.[1]

With the best part of three battalions present, von Sachsen-Weimar convened the senior officers at the farmhouse. Tackling the sensitive issue of seniority, he observed

'Be ready to march in the morning'

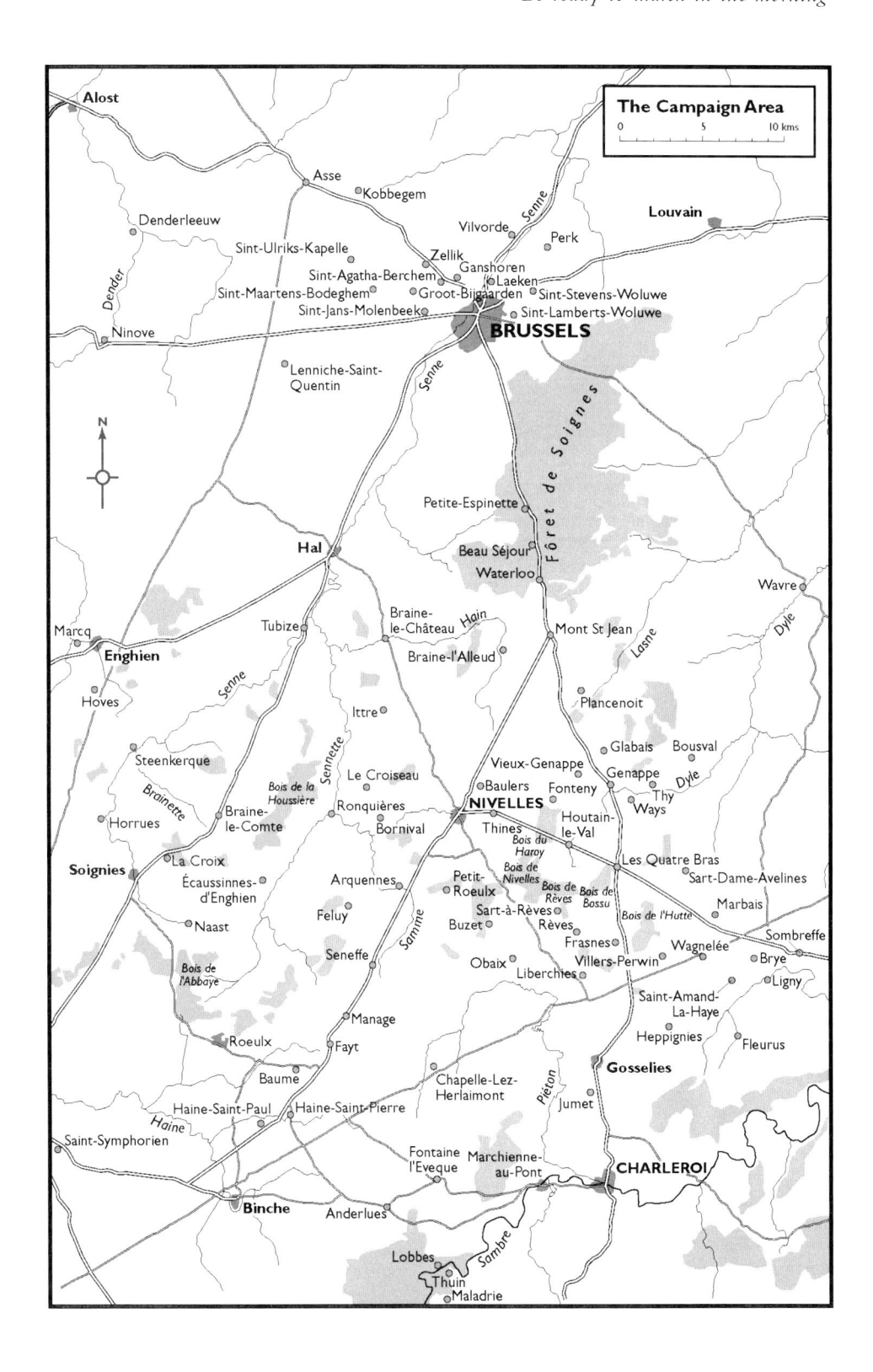

The Battle of Quatre Bras

that since Sattler and Hegmann were majors and von Dressel a lieutenant-colonel, he would, as colonel and ranking officer, take command of the brigade in the absence of Colonel von Gödecke. From now on, von Dressel would replace him in command of both battalions of the Regiment Oranien-Nassau.[2]

As these troops were arriving, so did the courier carrying de Perponcher-Sedlnitzky's instructions for their assembly; having completed a circuitous journey to the crossroads by way of Genappe, on the assumption that the Prince would be found at his headquarters there. As he read the letter, von Sachsen-Weimar must have felt a sense of relief that his actions and those of Major Sattler, taken on their own responsibility, were consistent with the intentions of their superiors. The prompt action of a few Nassau officers had ensured that Les Quatre Bras would be occupied at brigade strength three hours earlier than would otherwise have been possible. Despite the boost these orders gave to his confidence, he still feared that the French juggernaut might yet roll on towards the crossroads and overwhelm his modest command.[3]

Shortly before 7.00 p.m. Captain Bergmann's Volunteer Jäger Company arrived at Croix-Gilbert. Colonel von Sachsen-Weimar instructed Adjutant Steprodt to ride across and escort Bergmann's skilled riflemen to a position in the Bois de Bossu. Learning that he was to fight in woodland, Bergmann decided to issue the supply of cartridges recently delivered from Dillenburg before moving off and to keep the ammunition wagon well to the rear. The two officers then led the men south from Croix-Gilbert, across the Champ du Sarti and cut through the Bois de Bossu, by way of the road from Sart-à-Rêves and Wattimez to Frasnes; before taking up a position in four sections, to the north of the two detached companies of the first battalion of the 2nd Nassau-Usingen Regiment.[4] Whilst Bergmann's sweating troops quick-marched to their positions, the messenger from Major von Normann galloped up to the small knot of officers at Les Quatre Bras with word that French cavalry had now entered Frasnes. The second battalion of the 2nd Nassau Regiment intended to retreat in column towards the woods between the Charleroi and Nivelles roads but, in compliance with standing orders, the courier confirmed that the infantry would first cover the safe retreat of Bijleveld's artillery. Without delay, von Sachsen-Weimar instructed Major Hegmann to form the third battalion of the 2nd Nassau-Usingen Regiment into column and to march it some 300 paces south of the crossroads, where it halted in the vicinity of a small sheep farm called Ferme de la Bergerie. Here, it would provide support for von Normann's retiring troops.

A short while after Hegmann's men had taken up their new position, the second battalion of the Regiment Oranie-Nassau arrived and von Sachsen-Weimar immediately detached two companies, leaving the remainder to take up positions behind their sister battalion. Marching them forward to the position occupied by the third battalion of the 2nd Nassau-Usingen Regiment, the Prince led all eight companies in person down the Charleroi road, until they reached the junction with the chemin Bati-Saint-Bernard. Here von Sachsen-Weimar deployed the reinforcements. Major Hegmann was ordered to detach his Grenadier Company and two of the fusilier companies and take up a position in support of the second battalion, to the east of the Ferme de Gemioncourt.

Early 20th-century photograph of the Ferme de Piraumont.

The two companies of the second battalion of the Regiment Oranien-Nassau were to occupy the Ferme de Gemioncourt and its enclosures, whilst the second battalion of the 2nd Nassau-Usingen Regiment extended between that farm and the Ferme de Piraumont. They were supported in their rear by the Volunteer Jager Company, drawn up in four platoons along the southern edge of the Bois de Bossu. Some three hours since he had set his own regiment in motion, von Sachsen-Weimar had his new command assembled. As the tired infantry settled themselves down for the evening, Captain von Gagern hurriedly left for Nivelles a second time, bearing news of the outcome of the opening engagement at Frasnes to General de Perponcher-Sedlnitzky.[5]

Whilst their allies were marching, the British were dining. At the house of the Count de Lannoy in the Impasse du Parc, Colonel Sir William Howe De Lancey and Lady Magdalene, his bride of 72 days, were about to be separated for the first time since their arrival in Brussels a week earlier. Accustomed to walking out at 3.00 p.m., when most people were dining, and dining at 6.00 p.m., when most people were walking out, the couple had shunned social occasions, with Magdalene fearing that they might soon be separated.

> Sir William had to dine at the Spanish Ambassador's, the first invitation he had accepted; he was unwilling to go, and delayed and still delayed, till at last when near six o'clock, I fastened all his crosses and medals on his coat, helped him to put it on, and he went off. I watched at the window till he was out of sight, and then I continued to muse upon my happy fate. I thought over all that had passed, how grateful I felt, I had no wish but that this might continue; I saw my husband loved and respected by everyone. My life gliding on, like a gay dream.[6]

Elsewhere, Sir Hew and Lady Jane Dalrymple-Hamilton were taking a gentle postprandial stroll about the semi-derelict ramparts of the city, unaware of any fighting.

Arriving back at their house, they found two French friends, Count de Chabot and Count Maynard and invited the émigrés to join them in a cup of tea:

> Chabot remarked that he would not be surprised if Bonaparte commenced his advance that very day, since it was the anniversary of two of his most famous battles – Marengo, in 1800 and Friedland in 1807 – and as the Emperor was known to be superstitious he could consider this a fortunate omen.[7]

Chabot was, however, in error. Both these victories had been fought fifteen and eight years previously, but on 14 June.

Shortly afterwards, between 5.00 and 6.00 p.m., Lord Henry Apsley, the eldest son of Earl Bathurst, called on them with news: 'Wellington had received credible intelligence that the French had been at Charleroi the previous night and that it seemed probable that the British troops would march the following morning.' Where had he heard this news? From the very top, it seemed. Apsley added: 'Wellington had announced his intention to go to the ball and was passing the word around that he hoped other officers would do the same'.[8]

Ensign Macready did not quite move in the same circles as Apsley and as one was preparing to dance the quadrille, the other was busy completing his rounds. Nearing 6.00 p.m., the Light Company of the 30th Regiment of Foot had arrived at Naast, occupied a large barn and established picquets at the crossroads of La Haute Folie in the direction of Nivelles and on the road to Écaussinnes d'Enghien and Nivelles, where contact was also made with patrols furnished by two companies of the Hanoverian Feld-Jager-Korps.[9]

As the junior officers went about their business, the generals deliberated. Towards 7.00 p.m., Lieutenant Vos brought the news of fighting at Gosselies to General de Perponcher-Sedlnitzky at Nivelles, which helped to explain the source of Major von Normann's earlier accounts of firing to the south of Frasnes. The Prussians must have evacuated their positions on the Sambre and Piéton rivers, but aside from Vos mentioning that they had withdrawn towards Heppignies, he was at a loss to divine their intentions. Were the Prussians concentrating their army? And if so, where? On a more practical note, the implication was that if the French had taken Gosselies, Frasnes would be their next objective and after that, the crossroads at Les Quatre Bras – the point to which he hoped Colonel von Sachsen-Weimar was hurrying with his troops. Lieutenant Vos requested orders for the 5th National Militia Battalion and, turning his thoughts back to the matter in hand, de Perponcher-Sedlnitzky explained that these had left Nivelles at 4.30 p.m. and that the courier must therefore have passed him somewhere on the road. Reassuring Vos that his commanding officer would almost certainly by now have received the orders he was seeking, he suggested that it would be pointless for him to return to Buzet himself and in so doing to tire his horse; he may as well await the arrival of the battalion at Nivelles and rejoin it there. As Vos left his office, the General moved on to other matters.

'Be ready to march in the morning'

Word was slowly starting to filter through the command structure. Towards 7.00 p.m. Magdalene De Lancey was still at her fourth storey window, when she saw an aide-de-camp ride under the gateway below. Discovering that Sir William was not at home, he asked his wife for the address of the place where the Deputy Quartermaster-General was dining. On receiving her note, the officer clattered back out into the street and made for the residence of Lieutenant-General Miguel de Alava. A few minutes later, having commandeered the aide's horse, De Lancey galloped along the street himself to the Duke of Wellington's residence, dismounted and ran into the house. Once inside, Wellington briefed him on the situation at the frontier, the evacuation of Binche and the intentions of the Prussians to withdraw on Gosselies. De Lancey was instructed to make arrangements for the divisions to assemble at their respective headquarters and to be in readiness to march at a moment's notice. Still uncertain of the direction of the main attack and concerned that the fighting around Charleroi might prove to be a feint, Wellington would continue to await reports from Mons concerning any advance of the enemy's columns in that quarter. In the meantime, he hoped that the Prussians would be as implacable in the face of the French advance as they had proven throughout the Wars of Liberation in 1813 and 1814. Drinking a final toast, Wellington ordered his officers to prepare for their departure and the convivial group left for their respective quarters.[10]

The city was teeming with elegantly attired soldiers and civilians enjoying the early evening air. Having dined himself, Lieutenant James Hope and two or three fellow officers of the 92nd Regiment of Foot had proceeded to the park at about 6.00 p.m. for their usual stroll and found that subsequent reports from the frontier had greatly strengthened the rumours that had circulated earlier in the day. The snippets of intelligence from Wellington's dinner table were being eagerly devoured by an army hungry for action. Having strolled in the park for an hour, Hope and his friends met 'an officer of our acquaintance, who possessed the means of knowing what credit was due to the floating rumours of the day'. This officer passed on some intriguing news:

> [He] candidly told us that the Prussian hero had been attacked that morning – that advices to that effect had been received by the Duke of Wellington, during dinner, and that his Grace (without communicating the contents of the dispatch to any one), on the cloth being removed, desired those at table to fill a bumper to 'Prince Marshal Blücher and his gallant army'. He advised us to pack our baggage and prepare for a sudden movement, as it was extremely probable that we would leave Brussels during the night.[11]

Hastening back to his billet, Hope was joined in his apartment by his host, who asked him if he needed anything. Seeing that the young officer was already packed and prepared, the Belgian instead sat down and mused on the situation:

> Well, well, Bonaparte is once more advancing towards Brussels, with a terrible army. The Duke of Wellington's military talents, we are all convinced, are of the highest order. The spirit and enterprise of Prince Blücher is well known even to Napoleon himself. In

both of those generals we have implicit confidence but, when we compare the numbers of the hostile armies, the quality of the troops of which each are composed, we cannot but look forward to the issue of the approaching conflict with considerable anxiety.

Hope was about to ask why the quality of the troops was of such concern to the man, when the Belgian continued:

The French troops are all veterans: men of desperate character, who will undertake to execute the most daring and hazardous enterprises. To them, danger has long been familiar; robbery and plunder their daily occupation. The Prussians are brave, hardy, and inveterate enemies of France, but there is a considerable portion of them only militia, from whom much cannot be expected for some time. The allied army, in point of numbers, is, no doubt, respectable but, when we look to the quality of the troops, we have much to fear. The British contingent, I have been told, does not exceed 33,000. The Hanoverians are very young men, and their officers, many of them, mere children. The Dutch are good soldiers; so are the Belgians but they have served one or more campaigns under Napoleon.

Having thus expressed his opinions, with much sighing, the Belgian took Hope by the hand, and with considerable emotion, said: 'Farewell. Remember that our sole dependence is on the British troops, and their unconquered leader.'[12]

The unconquered leader was still awaiting information.

First Lieutenant John Kincaid of the first battalion of the 95th Regiment of Foot, the celebrated 'Rifles' of Peninsular War fame, was more fortunate. He had also been anxious for news all day, but since time drifted by without further word being received, he too wandered into the park at about 7.00 p.m. and met another staff officer, who asked him whether his pack-saddles were ready. Replying that they were, Kincaid suggested that they would not be wanted, 'at all events, before tomorrow?' As he took his leave, the staff officer hinted strongly to him: 'if you have any preparation to make, I would recommend you do not delay so long'. Kincaid took the hint and immediately returned to his quarters in the expectation that, at any time, his battalion would receive a movement order. Other officers of the regiment exchanged news and views; indeed, Major Jonathan Leach had heard confirmation that Napoleon had driven back the Prussian outposts and was anticipating that 'affairs would, in all probability, be speedily brought to a crisis'.[13]

At Nivelles, General de Perponcher-Sedlnitzky was himself starting to learn more of the fighting on the Sambre and across a swathe of southern Belgium. He was increasingly concerned. Shortly after the departure of Lieutenant Vos, a report arrived that Prussian stragglers, picked up by his patrols, had confirmed the evacuation of Charleroi and its occupation by the French as early as 11.00 a.m. Though the reports from Major von Normann and Lieutenant Vos had advised him of the fighting around Gosselies, he was still not clear who had been involved and what the outcome had been; nor was he aware whether the French had attacked Frasnes and Les Quatre Bras. Now, stragglers from Thuin and Lobbes, who had been involved in the fighting withdrawal earlier that afternoon, confirmed that the Prussians had crossed the River Piéton, engaged the French at Jumet and Gosselies and finally withdrawn towards Fleurus. As to the strength of the enemy and the direction in which it was advancing, de Perponcher-Sedlnitzky remained ignorant. The key information here had been the Prussian intention to concentrate at Fleurus. A dangerous ten kilometre gap had opened up between Gosselies and that place, into which the French could be pouring any number of troops. His left wing had lost touch with the right of the Prussian army. It was clear to him what he must do. The brigade at Les Quatre Bras would have to be reinforced substantially and, in the absence of orders he would have to take this decision on his own initiative. If he did not make the most energetic efforts, the enemy could be pushing on for Brussels before nightfall.[14]

Not everyone was as well-informed as de Perponcher-Sedlnitzky. It had taken longer for Halkett's order to reach the second battalion of the 73rd Regiment of Foot, which had remained ignorant of events until 4.00 p.m. that afternoon. Private Thomas Morris later recalled the moment the news broke:

> Some of the officers and men were playing at ball, against the gable end of a house in the village when an orderly dragoon brought dispatches from General Halkett, who commanded a brigade, ordering us to fall in immediately and proceed to the town of Soignies. The men were scattered about, variously engaged, but they soon understood, from the roll of the drums and the tones of the bugles, that their attendance was immediately necessary, in marching order.[15]

By 6.00 p.m. the battalion had finally departed and was the last unit of Halkett's brigade to arrive at Soignies, near 7.30 p.m. As it marched in, the town was fast filling with the troops of General von Kielmansegge's Hanoverian brigade, coming up in its turn. Each arriving battalion was besieged by swarms of semi-naked beggar children shouting: '*Vivent les Anglais! Vive le Roi de France! Donnez-moi un sou, Monsieur! Vive le Prince d'Orange! Vive les Hanovriens!*' The grinding and clanking noise of the carts, the neighing of horses and shouts of the wagon masters filled the narrow streets of Soignies, as the incredulous inhabitants watched the troops assemble, the population of the town growing with each passing hour.[16]

In the ranks of the British battalion, there was a sense that something extraordinary had provoked this sudden movement, but no one, least of all Morris, knew the cause. Private George Hemingway of the 33rd Regiment of Foot had heard that the French were within a few miles of the town. The Adjutant of his regiment, Ensign William Thain, had only been told that the French had crossed the frontier and had driven in the Prussian advanced posts. Paraded in the evening, his battalion was ordered to exchange its comfortable quarters in the town for the collegiate church of Saint-Vincent, which it was to share with the Bremen Field Battalion, recently arrived from Neuville and the Verden Field Battalion, another of General von

Kielmansegge's Hanoverian battalions. In total, almost 9,000 Allied troops choked the square and the Grand'Place, piling arms and building fires on the cobbles. Inside the church, the nave, aisles and transepts echoed with a babble of voices – every pew, confessional and side-chapel buzzed with animation, the sound of voices mixing with the odour of incense and stale sweat. Here and there, infantrymen admired the carved wooden panel work, perhaps wondering if in the coming days and hours, they would mirror the exploits of the medieval knights, amongst whose stone effigies they sat. From his plinth, the statue of Christ in Chains gazed with a melancholy look on those about to undergo their own passion. Aware that his light company was still detached, Lieutenant-Colonel Alexander Hamilton of the 30th Regiment of Foot summoned a corporal and ordered him to go to Naast and inform the officers there that the whole of von Alten's division had entered Soignies and occupied the church and other buildings. As the soldier left, the noise of the men gradually lessened as more and more decided to try and get some rest, not knowing what the morning would bring.[17]

Troops were gathering in other villages, towns and cities across the ancient provinces of Brabant, Hainaut and Wallon. By 5.00 p.m., the two companies of the 7th National Militia Battalion cantoned in Nivelles had assembled at their alarm post, the Porte de Namur. Unknown to them, the remainder of the battalion was resting at the roadside chapel of Notre-Dame-des-Sept-Douleurs, on the road leading to Houtain-le-Val and Les Quatre Bras. As they clustered around the curious Catholic effigy, perhaps the young protestant Dutchmen had a presentiment of the wounds they too would suffer in the coming days. A few kilometres away, the 8th National Militia Battalion had been halted outside the Porte de Soignies and was busy cleaning its weapons and cooking. Everywhere one looked, Nivelles resembled an armed camp, ringed by the assembling battalions of the brigade. At the heart of the town, the 27th Jager Battalion, having received van Bijlandt's order at 7.00 p.m., packed the Marché Saint-Paul on the northern side of the Grand'Place, along with Captain Emmanuel Stevenaar's brigade of guns. The commanding officers of each battalion were reminded by staff officers to maintain regular patrols to guard against any surprise attack on the part of the French. The night passed without the troops being disturbed and a fragile peace reigned in the respective camps.[18]

At Brussels, the convivial evening progressed. Having ridden over from Ninove earlier in the day, the Earl of Uxbridge was dining at the Hôtel Bellevue, with Major-General Sir Hussey Vivian, commander of the 6th (British) Cavalry Brigade and three of his aides; Captains James Fraser and Thomas Wildman of his beloved 7th Regiment of Hussars, and Captain Horace Seymour of the 60th Regiment of Foot, reputedly the strongest man in the British Army. Just after they had finished dressing for the ball, they were joined by Rear Admiral Sir Pulteney Malcolm, the commander of the Royal Naval squadron in the Scheldt, who had earlier dined with Wellington. He communicated the startling news that the French had advanced that morning, driven in the Prussians outposts and had taken Binche and Charleroi.[19]

'Be ready to march in the morning'

Unlike Sir Pulteney, Colonel Somerset had not been invited to dinner by his chief and was instead at his own quarters with Lady Emily, his wife of less than a year and their daughter, Charlotte, whose arrival on 16 May had somewhat curtailed their social life. On receiving word from the Duke of Wellington of the news from Braine-le-Comte, he had gone directly to headquarters, discovered the Duke was not there and found him instead in the park, giving the necessary instructions to those around him. The tone of the orders was clear. He wished everything to be in readiness to move in a moment, but had not yet determined on where.[20]

Many staff and regimental officers were strolling around the park in ignorance of developments. Amongst them was Lieutenant Jackson, who was taking the air with Lieutenant-Colonel Robert Torrens. Instantly recognisable in the uniform of the Royal Staff Corps, they were stopped by a soldier of the Guards and requested to go immediately to the Quartermaster-General's office, where they arrived at 7.00 p.m. Colonel De Lancey had just received a memorandum from Wellington, detailing his instructions to collect the army. He had already pressed Major De Lacy Evans, another newly-arrived staff officer, into service. Along with Evans, Jackson, Torrens and a number of other officers were instructed to begin the laborious process of writing out orders, based on this memorandum, to set the several divisions in motion.[21]

MEMORANDUM

FOR THE DEPUTY QUARTER MASTER GENERAL.

MOVEMENTS OF THE ARMY.

BRUXELLES, 15 June 1815.

General Dornberg's brigade of cavalry, and the Cumberland Hussars, to march this night upon Vilvorde, and to bivouac on the high road near to that town.

The Earl of Uxbridge will be pleased to collect the cavalry this night at Ninhove [sic], leaving the 2d Hussars looking out between the Scheldt and the Lys.

The 1st division of infantry to remain as they are at Enghien, and in all readiness to march at a moment's notice.

The 2nd division to collect this night at Ath and adjacent, and to be in readiness to march at a moment's notice.

The 3rd division to collect this night at Braine le Comte, and to be in readiness to move at a moment's [the shortest] notice.

The 4th division to be collected this night at Grammont, with the exception of the troops beyond the Scheldt, which are to be moved to Audenarde [Oudenaarde].

The 5th division, the 81st Regiment, and the Hanoverian brigade of the 6th division, to be in readiness to march from Bruxelles at a moment's notice.

The Duke of Brunswick's corps to collect this night on the high road between Bruxelles and Vilvorde.

The Battle of Quatre Bras

> The Nassau troops to collect at daylight tomorrow morning on the Louvain road, and to be in readiness to move at a moment's notice.
>
> The Hanoverian brigade of the 5th Division to collect this night at Hal, and to be in readiness at daylight tomorrow [morning] to move towards Brussels, and to halt on the high road between Alost and Assche [Asse] for further orders.
>
> The Prince of Orange is requested to collect at Nivelles the 2d and 3d divisions of the army of the Low Countries; and, should that point have been attacked this day, to move the 3d division of British Infantry upon Nivelles as soon as collected.
>
> This movement is not to take place until it is quite certain that the enemy's attack is upon the right of the Prussian army, and the left of the British Army.
>
> Lord Hill will be so good as to order Prince Frederick of Orange to occupy Audenarde [Oudenaarde] with 500 men, and to collect the 1st division of the army of the Low Countries and the Indian Brigade at Sotteghem, so as to be ready to march in the morning at daylight.
>
> The reserve artillery to be in readiness to move at daylight.
>
> Wellington.[22]

As each 'route' was finished, pen set aside and envelope sealed, it was handed to one of several troopers, resplendent in their white-braided blue dolmans and pelisses. Each man had been seconded from the 3rd Hussar Regiment of the King's German Legion, selected for their reliability and their fluency in both English and German, a valuable commodity in a polyglot army. Each messenger was told the rate at which to proceed and the time that he would be expected to reach his destination. He was also instructed to return with the cover of the dispatch, providing confirmation by the recipient of the time at which it had been received. In addition, cards were prepared for the senior officers, intended for distribution, after supper, at the Duchess of Richmond's ball. In the glow of candlelight and with aching fingers, this task would not be complete until 10.00 p.m.[23]

Though serving on the staff as an Assistant Adjutant-General, Major Alexander Wylly of the 7th Regiment of Foot, had no responsibility for the issue of orders or putting the army on the move and was therefore thankfully spared the tedium of copying out the Duke's intentions. He had arrived in Belgium four days earlier, in the company of the Waldie family and standing in the Place Royale amongst a crowd of officers, he happened to glance up at the third floor of the Hôtel de Flandre and recognised Charlotte Waldie. Doffing his hat, he darted into the hotel and was soon breathlessly articulating that hostilities had commenced.

> Our amazement may be conceived: at first we could scarcely believe him to be in earnest. 'Upon my honour,' exclaimed Major Wylie [sic], still panting, and scarcely able to speak, from the haste with which he had flown up the hundred steps, 'It is quite true; and the troops are ordered to be in readiness to march at a moment's notice; and we shall probably leave Brussels tomorrow morning.'

Sensing and then seeing that he had alarmed the ladies, Wylly sought to reassure them by saying that, although the fighting was hot, it seemed to be von Blücher's opinion that it would most probably turn out to be nothing more than a mere skirmish.[24]

Other officers, their spirits buoyed by the prospect of glory, promotion and bounties, were already on the move. Towards 8.00 p.m., Captain Hon. Francis Russell, aide-de-camp to the Prince van Oranje-Nassau, was clattering through the Porte de Hal, bearing the assembly order from his chief, who was to stay in Brussels for the remainder of the evening. Riding hard, he would arrive at the Prince's headquarters at 10.30 p.m.[25]

Elsewhere, news was thin on the ground. Six long hours had passed since word had first reached Captain Fitzgerald of the invasion, but since then no further tidings had been received at Enghien. Perhaps it was a false alarm after all. The arrival of a second dragoon towards 8.00 p.m., however, disabused him of that notion. The Prussians had been forced across the Sambre. Once again, Fitzgerald forwarded the intelligence to Gunthorpe and Stothert, requesting in particular that Colonel Stuart and the third battalion remain at Hoves and Marcq until more specific orders for movement were forthcoming.[26]

Whilst many of his colleagues were dining or dancing, Lieutenant-Colonel Sir William Gomm, the Assistant Quartermaster-General attached to the 5th (British) Infantry Division at Brussels, received the order at 8.30 p.m. to assemble the troops, but to await further directions concerning movement. Perhaps he noted the curious instruction for the Hanoverian brigade of the division to collect at Hal, to be in readiness at daylight to move towards Brussels and to halt on the high road between Alost and Asse for further orders. What was the purpose behind such a move? These orders would prevent the division assembling fully and would result in Colonel Ernst von Vincke's men moving from the south-west to the north-west of Brussels, away from the likely source of any French attack. Perhaps the Duke was concerned for his communications with Ostend, Ghent and Antwerp? Setting aside his opinions, he sent word for Captain Charles Eeles and Major Charles Smyth to join him. Both men were officers of the 95th Regiment of Foot, but for the duration of the campaign, they would serve as the Majors of Brigade to Major-General Sir James Kempt's and Major-General Sir Denis Pack's brigades respectively. After explaining the orders he had received, the three men prepared to rouse the battalions and batteries. The sun was setting.[27]

Throughout the course of the afternoon and evening, rumours spread by Prussian stragglers and civilian refugees had contributed to an increasing atmosphere of uncertainty and disquiet at the headquarters of the 2nd (Netherlands) Infantry Division at Nivelles. Colonel Baron Pieter van Zuylen van Nyeveld and his chief, General de Perponcher-Sedlnitzky, were both anxious for information. Was it true that Charleroi had been evacuated? Were the reports of the Prussians retreating on Fleurus correct? Towards 8.30 p.m., a French deserter who had been apprehended by a patrol was brought to his headquarters. Delighted with this development and keen to know more, the General busied himself by interrogating the prisoner.[28]

Though dressed as a peasant, he claimed to be a '*Capitaine-Adjoint*', or a staff officer named Adjudant-Commandant Chevalier Gordon, serving as the chief-of-staff to *Général de Division* Count Pierre Durutte's 4th (French) Infantry Division. If this was true, thought de Perponcher-Sedlnitzky, he might prove to be a very useful acquisition. When questioned, the Frenchman confirmed that Charleroi had fallen and that Napoleon was marching on Brussels with between 130,000 and 150,000 men, of which 6,000 were cavalry. No mention was made of the strength of the artillery, but if it was in the usual Napoleonic proportion, the General concluded that it must be immense. The left wing of this army was under the orders of Maréchal de l'Empire Michel Ney, the fabled Duke d'Elchingen and Prince de la Moscowa, the man dubbed 'The bravest of the brave.' His command comprised four infantry divisions of the 1st Corps d'Armée under *Général de Division* Jean-Baptiste Drouet Count d'Erlon and four of the 2nd under *Général de Division* Count Honoré Reille. Support was provided by two divisions of heavy cavalry under *Général de Division* Count François Kellermann, together with a light cavalry division under *Général de Division* Count Hippolyte de Piré and a division of Imperial Guard light cavalry. Of this last, the lancers were commanded by the celebrated General Colbert and the Chasseurs à Cheval by *Général de Division* Baron François Lallemand, both under the orders of *Général de Division* Count Charles Léfèbvre-Desnoëttes, the man who had been a prisoner of war in England, but who had broken his parole in 1812 and had daringly escaped to the Continent.[29]

If, as had previously been reported, General von Steinmetz had withdrawn from Thuin, Binche and Fontaine l'Evêque towards Gosselies and if Major-General Otto von Pirch had been forced to evacuate Charleroi, this news confirmed afresh that a significant gap had opened up in front of his division. He was still digesting the consequences of these events when Captain von Gagern reined in outside the building and hurried inside to brief him. The General sat quietly as he was told that French troops were indeed driving north through this gap and had forced von Normann to evacuate Frasnes. Though the news confirmed his earlier fears, de Perponcher-Sedlnitzky was somewhat reassured in the knowledge that, according to standing orders, von Sachsen-Weimar had been successful in assembling the brigade at Les Quatre Bras, but concerned at the same time, that the true strength of the French forces to the south was still unknown. He was more than ever convinced that Les Quatre Bras was the point of real danger and despite the concentration of one brigade, he would, 'Have to, whilst awaiting orders and reinforcements, deploy at this point the most energetic efforts in order to prevent the enemy from pushing on Brussels.' The question uppermost in his mind was whether to reinforce Colonel von Sachsen-Weimar's brigade with General van Bijlandt's? For that, he would need a second opinion. Though he had heard nothing from Generals Chassé or de Collaert on the frontier, it was feasible that the French had smashed through their positions and, even now, were advancing on Nivelles. The 3.00 p.m. order from de Constant-Rebecque had not revealed why it had been felt necessary to assemble his division in the first place and it was unlikely that de Constant-Rebecque had become aware of the French attack on Frasnes before he had himself.[30]

His only option was to send someone to Braine-le-Comte and as he mulled over how best to present his case at headquarters, an idea slowly started to form in his mind; who better to convey the news of this attack on Frasnes and the intelligence provided by the deserter than von Gagern himself? An eyewitness to the opening engagement with the French, the recipient of briefings from the principal players: von Normann, Sattler and von Sachsen-Weimar, he was perfectly equipped to throw light on the situation and to secure definitive orders on the deployment of the division. Though his horse was now starting to tire, von Gagern agreed and left immediately for Braine-le-Comte, whilst de Perponcher-Sedlnitzky sent an order to von Sachsen-Weimar to maintain himself in the position at Les Quatre Bras for as long as he could. He also instructed that the heavy baggage train, superfluous artillery stores, the court-martial, clothing depot, staff and equipment of the hospital and all other non-combatants of the division be sent to Waterloo, where they were to await his further orders. Nothing could be chanced that might impede the movement of the army. As the officers of his staff carried out these instructions, the General could not escape from the recurring thought that, unwilling as he was to denude Nivelles of van Bijlandt's brigade without the proper authority, it all depended on von Sachsen-Weimar doing the right thing. At the same time, he dispatched an officer to Feluy, with orders for Colonel van den Sanden to assemble his 7th Line Battalion and march it to its alarm post at Nivelles, the Porte de Mons. Word was also passed to Captain de Crassier's 6th Flanker Company of the 27th Jager Battalion, along with a company from the 7th National Militia Battalion. They were to establish posts along the chaussée between Nivelles and Les Quatre Bras. It was approaching 9.00 p.m.[31]

Meanwhile, at Brussels Major Henry Ross-Lewin of the 32nd Regiment of Foot was enjoying dinner with General Kempt, his brigade commander, when news from Wellington arrived:

> Coffee and a young aide-de-camp from the Duke of Wellington came in together. This officer was the bearer of a note from the Duke and while Sir James was reading it, said, 'Old Blücher has been hard at it. A Prussian officer has just come to the Beau, all covered with sweat and dirt and says they have had much fighting.' Our host then rose and, addressing the regimental officers at the table, said, 'Gentlemen, you will proceed without delay to your respective regiments and let them get under arms immediately.'[32]

Ross-Lewin immediately rose and hurried off to spread the word. As he passed a coffee shop, he found several officers of his regiment sitting at the door and told them Sir James' orders:

> They seemed at first to think that I was jesting, being hardly able to credit the tidings of so near and so unexpected an approach of the French; but they soon perceived that I spoke seriously and dispersed each to his own quarters. In a few minutes, however, the

most incredulous would have been thoroughly undeceived, for then drums began to beat, bugles to sound and Highland pipes to squeal in all quarters of the city. The scene that ensued was of the most animated kind: such was the excitement of the inhabitants, the buzz of tongues, the repeated words of command, the hurrying of the soldiers through the streets, the clattering of horses' hoofs, the clash of arms, the rattling of the wheels of wagons and gun-carriages, and the sounds of warlike music.[33]

At the same time as Ross-Lewin's brother officers were finishing their coffee in Brussels, the representatives of the Commissariat Department at Soignies – working closely with the quartermasters of each battalion – were already distributing provisions for the following day to fatigue parties. As these groups returned to their battalions and batteries, the men were roused from their slumbers in turn and fell in for the ration issue. Hastily packing away biscuit, bread or rice, most of the men of the 73rd Regiment of Foot chose to cook the raw meat immediately and as they boiled and roasted in the streets, they partook liberally in the wine and gin on offer and animatedly discussed what the morning would bring. Ensign Ainslie of the 69th Regiment of Foot had still heard no confirmed report of any action having taken place, but the commotion and confusion in the streets, as well as the noise of the divisional artillery and ammunition columns passing through the town, prevented him from sleeping and he passed the night fitfully with his friends Captains Benjamin Hobhouse and George Barlow.[34]

Meanwhile, at Braine-le-Comte a courier from the Prince van Oranje-Nassau arrived at the Hôtel de Miroir at 9.00 p.m. At last, thought de Constant-Rebecque, these must be orders to concentrate the army. After signing for the letter, he opened it eagerly.

My dear Constant,

Unless you have had news since this morning which makes you believe it necessary to hold the troops outside all night, please send the order on my behalf to them to go to their cantonments, but to be gathered again tomorrow morning at four o'clock at the fixed points. Please tell Abercromby, on my behalf, to do the same with the English troops. The Duke of Wellington wishes that I remain here this evening. I will thus leave only at midnight or one o'clock.[35]

This order was tantamount to a stand-down. Had the Prince sent this message before the arrival of the dispatches borne by Captain Lennox? If not, did his chief and the Duke of Wellington attach such little credence to the intelligence from the frontier that they felt it appropriate to call off the assembly of I Corps? Surely the Prince must be unaware of the seriousness of the situation? Faced with such a conundrum, de Constant-Rebecque felt he ought not to implement this order and in so doing, modify any of the instructions already sent to de Perponcher-Sedlnitzky and de Collaert. In his mind, the level of military threat outweighed the well-being of the troops. Aware that he was disregarding a direct order however, and feeling a need to

'Be ready to march in the morning'

account for this decision, he took a pen and added a footnote to the Prince's letter: 'It has been judged appropriate, in view of the circumstances, to leave the divisions in bivouac, the present notice having arrived too late.'[36]

In comparison to the anxious Swiss general, the heavily pregnant Lady Caroline Capel had few concerns. At the large and airy Château de Walcheuse three kilometres to the north of Brussels, she was resting and admiring the twilight view of the Palace and leafy grounds of Laeken in the company of her eldest daughter, Harriet. With her new child expected in early July and having only moved into the house the previous Saturday, there was still much to do, though she was grateful that the accommodation had been provided free of charge until the end of August. Any chance to economise would reduce the financial impact of her husband's gambling debts.[37]

She had decided that the Duchess of Richmond's ball was not a sufficiently brilliant event for her to stir from the comfort of her temporary home. Instead, she put the finishing touches to the picnic dinner party planned for the following day, grateful at last for the services of an English cook. The invitation list comprised Lady Isabella Seymour and her daughter Lady Isabella Horatia, Lady Charlotte Greville, the Smyths, Captain Lord Arthur Hill, Captain Seymour, Lieutenant-Colonel Hon. Sir Alexander Gordon, Major Hon. George Dawson and a few others. Also invited was Major-General Sir Edward Barnes whose proposal of marriage had been declined by her daughter Maria, much to the astonishment of her doting sisters and the sadness of her parents. Barnes remained a firm family friend and had accepted the invitation to stand as godfather to Caroline's new baby.[38]

Not all the expatriate civilians in Belgium were as tranquil. In contrast to Lady Capel, Magdalene De Lancey's courage had failed her upon seeing her husband so suddenly summoned to his duties:

> About nine o'clock, Sir William came and seeing my wretched face bid me not be foolish, for it would soon be all over. They expected a great battle on the morrow; he would send me to Antwerp in the morning, and desired I would be ready next morning at six o'clock. He said that though he expected the battle would be a decisive one and a conclusion of the business, he thought it best I should keep the plan of going to Antwerp, to avoid the alarms he knew would seize everyone the moment the troops were gone – and he said he would probably join me there, or send for me to return the same evening. He said he would be writing all night, and wished me to prepare some strong green tea in case he came in, as the violent exertion of setting the whole army in motion quite stupefied him sometimes.[39]

Another man writing by candlelight was the Duke of Wellington. As his staff officers busied themselves with dispatching his assembly orders, the Duke was writing to Charles d'Artois, the 37-year-old Duke de Berri and the nephew of the exiled King Louis XVIII, at Ghent:

The Battle of Quatre Bras

At Brussels, the 15th of June, 1815. 9½ p.m.

My Lord,

I have the honour to make known to Your Royal Highness that the enemy attacked the Prussian posts at Thuin this morning, and appears to be menacing Charleroi. I have ordered our troops to prepare themselves to march at daybreak, and I beg Your Royal Highness to concentrate yours on Alost.
I have the honour to be, etc.

Wellington.[40]

In keeping the exiled King's commander-in-chief apprised of the military situation, it was more of a case of Wellington going through the diplomatic motions. Berri's command was the rump of the Royal French Army, the majority of which had gone over to the returning Emperor in the spring. Comprising a mere 4,000 infantry and 800 cavalry, many of its formations boasted more officers than men, with some cavalry squadrons commanded by generals. Its deployment in an active role during the campaign would have been farcical, though Wellington perhaps thought he might need all the help he could get.

At Enghien, the messenger carrying Wellington's assembly order arrived at the headquarters of the 1st (British) Infantry Division at about 10.00 p.m. Having signed for its receipt and entering it into the ledger, Captain Fitzgerald requested Captains Gunthorpe and Stothert to inform the battalion commanders to be in readiness to march at a moment's notice. Within a short time, the Majors of Brigade had completed their tasks and the commanding officers, summoning their respective adjutants, passed the order along without too much fuss. Quartermasters broke open the stores of ammunition and provisions and distributed their contents; the spirits issue was particularly welcome. For Colonel Hepburn of the 3rd Regiment of Foot Guards, the advanced warning from Braine-le-Comte had gained him an hour's grace, his officers were already well prepared and his men in full marching order and ready to depart.[41]

The servants started packing away plate, glassware, provisions and the other comforts to which the young officers of the Guards were accustomed, even whilst on campaign. The talk was of the French and of the likely route of their advance.

Some felt that they would cross the frontier between the fortresses of Tournai and Mons and that consequently, the brigade would be sent to Ath, to which some suggested the Duke had already given the division the order to move. Others, recalling the punishing route marches to Casteau, near Mons, speculated by implication that the Duke would concentrate them farther to the east; whilst others predicted that they would remain as they were, defending the Duke's lines of communication with Ostend and Antwerp. Whatever proved to be reality, the debate would only end when further orders were received. As the servants and bâtmen made preparations to

'Be ready to march in the morning'

depart, the soldiers were turned out of their billets by noisy corporals and sergeants, their weapons and accoutrements inspected. The men were dismissed, but warned not to stray too far from the parade ground, on pain of a flogging.[42]

Endnotes

1. de Bas &c., pp. 319, 401. Döring. Hofschröer (I), p. 201. von Kruse. von Sachsen-Weimar (III). Sattler. Starklof, p. 133. van Zuylen van Nyeveld (I), p. 50.
2. von Sachsen-Weimar (III). Starklof, p. 132.
3. Starklof, p. 132.
4. de Bas &c., p. 404. Bergmann. Hofschröer (I), p. 206. von Sachsen-Weimar (III). Starklof, p. 133. van Zuylen van Nyeveld (I), p. 50.
5. de Bas &c., p. 404. Bergmann. Hofschröer (I), pp. 203, 206. von Sachsen-Weimar (III). Starklof, p. 133. van Zuylen van Nyeveld (I), p. 50.
6. Dalton, p. 33. G. Paget (I), p. 50. Miller (I), pp. 106–7. Miller (II), p. xvii.
7. Miller (II), p. 135.
8. Miller (II), p. 135.
9. Macready (I).
10. Anonymous (Letters), p. 220. von Müffling (I), p. 2. J. Ross (II). F. Somerset, pp. 6–7.
11. Anonymous (Letters), p. 220. Hope (I) J. Ross (II).
12. Anonymous (Letters), p. 221–2. Hope (I).
13. Kincaid (I), pp. 308–9. Leach, p. 373.
14. de Bas &c., pp. 405–6, Hofschröer (I), p. 206. de Perponcher-Sedlnitzky. van Zuylen van Nyeveld (I), p. 51.
15. Morris, p. 66.
16. Ainslie, pp. 13–14. Hemingway. Morris, p. 66. Thain (II).
17. Bannatyne, p. 320. Bowden, p. 242. von Bülow. Finlayson. Hemingway. Hofschröer (III), pp. 37–8. Macready (I). Müller, Pattison (II), p. 2. C. von Scriba (II), pp. 80–1. Thain (II).
18. Bowden, p. 239. Dellevoet, p. 20. Grunenbosch. de Jongh. Meijer. von Pivka (II), p. 20. Rem. Starklof, p. 145. van Zuylen van Nyeveld (I), p. 51.
19. Vivian. Wildman. Miller (II), p. 118.
20. F. Somerset, p. 7. Miller (II), p. 134.
21. Gurwood (1852 edition), pp. 142–3. Jackson (I), p. 542. Jackson (III), pp. 12–13. Mackenzie &c., p. 54. Young, p. 100.
22. Anonymous (Incoming Register). Gurwood, pp. 472–3. Gurwood (1852 edition), pp. 142–3. Hamilton-Williams, pp. 374–5.
23. Jackson (II), p. 3. Jackson (III), pp. 12–13. Young, p. 100.
24. Dalton, p. 31. Eaton, pp. 1, 14–15.
25. de Bas &c., p. 437.
26. Anonymous (Near Observer), p. 56. Powell. Whitworth, p. 45.
27. Anonymous (Letters), p. 220. Gomm (I), p. 5. Gomm (IV). Gurwood, p. 472.
28. de Perponcher-Sedlnitzky. van Zuylen van Nyeveld (I), p. 51.

29. de Bas &c., pp. 406, 491. Bowden, p. 93. Frazer, p. 545. Hofschröer (I), p. 206. Kellermann. Léfebvre-Desnoëttes. van Zuylen van Nyeveld (I), pp. 51, 54.
30. de Bas &c., pp. 404–6. Hofschröer (I), p. 206. van Zuylen van Nyeveld (I), p. 50.
31. de Bas &c., pp. 406–7. Grunenbosch. Scheltens, p. 197. van Zuylen van Nyeveld (I), pp. 50–1.
32. Ross-Lewin, p. 253.
33. Ross-Lewin, p. 253.
34. Ainslie, p. 14. Morris, pp. 66–7.
35. Anonymous (Incoming). de Bas &c., pp. 396–7.
36. de Bas &c., p. 396.
37. G. Paget (I), pp. 105–7.
38. Dalton, p. 21. Miller (II), pp. 116–17. G. Paget (I), pp. 88–9, 104–7.
39. Miller (I), p. 107.
40. Gurwood, pp. 473–4.
41. Anonymous (Order Book). Gurwood, p. 472. Lake. Powell. Rooke (II).
42. Hamilton, pp. 13, 15. J. Paget (I), p. 84. Whitworth, p. 45.

The Ferme de la Bergerie, occupied by French infantry late in the afternoon and carried by assault by the 92nd Regiment of Foot. Picton's Division occupied the fields in its rear. (Author's collection.)

CHAPTER 4

All had remained quiet at Les Quatre Bras. Despite the arrival of an enemy infantry battalion, it seemed that the French were unwilling to dispute the possession of the Ferme de Gemioncourt in the failing light and appeared content to bivouac in the northern outskirts of Frasnes.

Colonel von Sachsen-Weimar reviewed his own dispositions. The Grenadier Company and two fusilier companies of the third battalion of the 2nd Nassau-Usingen Regiment had been reinforced by the remaining three companies of the regiment and held the heights of Gemioncourt to the east of the Charleroi road, its picquet line extending from Piraumont in the east to the Charleroi road at Delsot. Two detached companies from the second battalion of the Regiment Oranien-Nassau formed the garrison for the Ferme de Gemioncourt and its enclosures. The second battalion of the 2nd Nassau-Usingen Regiment occupied the high ground on the opposite side of the road, in the space between the chaussée and the Ferme du Grand-Pierrepont, continuing the picquet line from Delsot to the Bois du Pierrepont. They were supported in this position by the four platoons of Bergmann's Volunteer Jager Company and by the two companies of the first battalion of their parent regiment, drawn up on their right. To the north, the remainder of the first battalion of the 2nd Nassau-Usingen Regiment was posted between Croix-Gilbert and Les Quatre Bras, guarding the Nivelles road. Around the crossroads itself, the first battalion of the Regiment Oranien-Nassau occupied the garden and orchard of the Ferme des Quatre Bras, feasting on supplies brought in from Genappe by its Quartermaster. Four companies of the second battalion were bivouacked in the fields to the northeast. The artillery was dispersed to cover all eventualities. Captain Bijleveld parked his train vehicles behind the Ferme des Quatre Bras and detached Lieutenant Koopman, with three 6-pounder pieces, to the point where the chemin Bati-Saint-Bernard crosses the Namur road, north of the étang Materne. Here, they were protected by a picquet drawn from the third battalion of the 2nd Nassau-Usingen Regiment. A single 6-pounder was placed to the north-east – on the Nivelles road – protected by Sattler's infantry. The remainder of Bijleveld's guns, were posted facing the French, where he established a 6-pounder gun and two howitzers on the Charleroi road and in the fields on either side, to the south of the Ferme de Gemioncourt. The final 6-pounder alarm gun was placed on the highway towards Delsot, as part of the picquet line. Each gun team was kept occupied. The artificers were busy with running repairs to the pieces, whilst the gunners cleaned the bores and scrubbed the touch-holes free of powder residue. Others replenished the ammunition supplies or fetched water from the Gemioncourt stream to refill the sponge buckets.[1]

Though concerned that he might still be forced to relinquish his hold on Les Quatre Bras and fearful of reports that French cavalry had been seen in the vicinity of Marbais, von Sachsen-Weimar had established a defensive perimeter with the resources at hand. Satisfied overall with his disposition, he moved his field headquarters from the high ground at the south-eastern tip of the Bois de Bossu to Les Quatre Bras itself, from where he penned a brief report for General de Perponcher-Sedlnitzky at Nivelles.

Quatre Bras, the 15th of June, 9 o'clock at night.

I have the honour to inform Your Excellency that the enemy, at about half-past five this evening, attacked my outpost at Frasnes with infantry and cavalry. Because of this, the 2nd Nassau battalion and the Bijleveld Battery had to draw back, half-way to Les Quatre Bras. The Brigade united at Les Quatre Bras. I moved the 3rd Nassau battalion, in column, forward on the road to Frasnes and threw the first battalion into the Bossu wood for its defence, giving them the second battalion for support. The rest of the brigade, I concentrated around Les Quatre Bras and on the road to Marbais. The artillery, which behaved very bravely, prevented the enemy gaining any ground on this side of Frasnes. The enemy at this time stands in the first outer houses of Frasnes. Enemy cavalry in the direction of Sart-Dame-Avelines has been moved forward and is threatening my left flank. Of the Prussian troops, none have joined my ranks. I do not know what sort of position I am in with respect to the other troops, or if there is any danger of being cut off from Brussels. To give you the strength of the enemy is not possible since the Bossu Woods, the hilly terrain, and the high grain make it very difficult to get an accurate estimation. I cannot detect any enemy artillery. All the measures are taken for our security during the night. I must confess to Your Excellency that I am too feeble to be able to remain here for long. The second battalion of Orange-Nassau has French muskets and only ten rounds per man. The Volunteer Jägers have carbines of four different calibres and ten rounds per carbine. I will defend the post confided in me as well as and as long as I can. I await an attack at daybreak. The troops are animated by the best spirit. As password and battle cry, I have taken the words Wilhelm Wiesbaden.

Colonel Bernhard zu Saxe-Weimar.

There are no reserves of musket ammunition at the battery.

The lack of ammunition was the cause of some concern for the Prince. For some reason, eight ammunition wagons had been left behind at the vehicle park at Nivelles. The courier was instructed to ask the General to send, if possible, some infantry ammunition caissons and to detach some cavalry so that von Sachsen-Weimar could reconnoitre his threatened left flank.[2]

At length, von Sachsen-Weimar's anxieties were lightened by the excitement of his officers. The second battalion of the 2nd Nassau-Usingen Regiment felt it had been singularly privileged to have been the first troops of Wellington's army to engage the French. Their enthusiasm was increased when a corporal and four men, who had been seized by the enemy as they withdrew from Frasnes, rejoined the battalion having managed to give their captors the slip; it seemed their gaolers were more interested in plunder than prisoners. Reports from other battalions suggested that the spirits of the men were high, jealous that they too had not had the opportunity to fight; but such bravado was always the official line. Around the camp fires, under the trees and in the barns, there were doubtless those of a more despondent nature, writing to loved ones, discussing prospects with their friends and perhaps holding private conversations with their God. For the young Prince however, anxiety turned to excitement. Had it not been he – rather than his superiors – who had taken the initiative, understood the state of affairs and been decisive in stopping the French? Of course it had been, suggested his companions; it would never do to argue with one's brigade commander, even if he were not a Prince. As they discussed the successful outcome of the combat at Frasnes, his delight was palpable and his eyes gleamed as he congratulated Major Vigelius and Captain von Coustoll on their own contributions.[3]

As von Sachsen-Weimar's mood lifted, his earlier dispatch, laden with foreboding, had arrived at de Perponcher-Sedlnitzky's headquarters. It added little to the verbal report delivered by von Gagern, other than confirmation of the positions in which the brigade had been deployed. There was minimal intelligence on the strength or activities of the enemy. What did, however, come across in the tenor of the report, was the anxiety of the Prince. His words suggested a sense of isolation, a concern over the strength of the enemy, a fear of being outflanked and anxiety over ammunition. Though doing his best to put on a brave face, von Sachsen-Weimar was clearly rattled, and in the mind of de Perponcher-Sedlnitzky, liable to do something impulsive. A steadying hand was required. After some consideration, he decided to send his own chief-of-staff, Colonel van Zuylen van Nyeveldt, to Les Quatre Bras, in order to reinforce the importance of the crossroads in the mind of von Sachsen-Weimar.[4]

Seven kilometres to the south-west, Colonel van den Sanden was similarly engaged in a reinforcing movement. On the receipt of the 8.30 p.m. order, he had immediately assembled the 7th Line Battalion and had been joined by the detachments from Arquennes and Petit-Roeulx. Within minutes, the battalion was mustered on the drill ground and the tally recorded. At 9.00 p.m. 23 officers and 666 men from the city of Bruges marched off along the tree-lined chaussée towards Nivelles.[5]

At Braine-le-Comte, night had fallen and the candles were flickering in the Prince van Oranje-Nassau's headquarters. A tired Captain von Gagern arrived from Nivelles at 10.00 p.m., on an equally tired horse and was immediately introduced to General de Constant-Rebecque, who had some difficulty in believing his report concerning the events at Frasnes and the intelligence provided by the French deserter and other fugitives. The enemy had attacked the detachment of infantry and artillery at Frasnes and driven it back on Les Quatre Bras, with a loss of several men and some artillery horses? The Prince van Oranje-Nassau must be informed immediately. Though his opinions were strong that the road from Brussels to Charleroi should not be given up under any circumstances, de Constant-Rebecque was still swayed, to some extent, by Wellington's view that the French would invade by way of Binche and Mons and therefore dare not advise de Perponcher-Sedlnitzky to completely evacuate Nivelles. After reflecting for some minutes, he decided to write to the General in person, advising him to reinforce the crossroads with van Bijlandt's brigade. Since Captain von Gagern's mount was tired and would take a considerably longer time to make the return journey, de Constant-Rebecque called for Major Count Otto van Limburg-Stirum, one of the Prince van Oranje-Nassau's adjutants, and entrusted the letter to him.[6]

Having taken the significant step of recommending the reinforcement of Les Quatre Bras at the expense of Nivelles, it was time for de Constant-Rebecque to write to his chief and explain his actions and the motivations that had prompted them. Taking paper and pen, he immediately sat down and began writing:

> Braine-le-Comte, 15 June 1815
> At 10½ hours in the evening.
>
> Monseigneur,
>
> A moment ago, Captain Baron von Gagern arrived from Nivelles with the report that the enemy has already pushed as far as Les Quatre Bras. I have thought it necessary to take it upon myself to tell General de Perponcher to support the 2nd Brigade with the 1st and to evacuate the hospital and Council of War to Brussels. I have sent an officer to Nivelles and Fayt in order to firstly assess the state of things at this first place and secondly to inform Generals Chassé and de Collaert in order that they are to unite and support the 2nd Division in case of need.
>
> The Chief-of-Staff
> Baron de Constant-Rebecque.
>
> To H. R. H. the Prince of Orange.[7]

Having spent most of the day at the Hôtel de Miroir and having no invitation to the ball, Lieutenant Henry Webster had observed this flurry of activity amongst the Netherlands staff with interest, though he had not been able to fully comprehend the chattering of staff officers in Dutch and French. He had, however, worked out that the advanced guard of the Prussian army had been driven in and at about 10.30 p.m., he was handed de Constant-Rebecque's dispatch – for the eyes of the Prince only – and was urged to leave without a moment's delay: 'A horse, ready-saddled awaits you at the door and another has been sent on, half an hour ago, to a half-way house, to help you the faster. Gallop every yard! Stand on no ceremony, but insist on seeing the Prince at once!' Webster needed no second invitation. As an officer in the 9th Regiment of Light Dragoons, galloping was his speciality and mounted on a thoroughbred, he sped off into the darkening countryside.[8]

Scarcely had Webster left, when Captain Russell arrived at Braine-le-Comte. He had made good time from Brussels, though his horse was flecked with sweat and he himself was tired. Drawing rein in front of the Hôtel de Miroir, he hurried inside and handed his packet over to a staff officer, who dutifully noted down the time of its arrival in the Register of Incoming Correspondence; 10.30 p.m. Shortly afterwards, de Constant-Rebecque opened the documents and read through the order with an increasingly perplexed expression on his face.[9]

> The 1st division of infantry to remain as they are at Enghien, and all in readiness to move at a moment's notice…
> …The 3rd division to collect this night at Braine le Comte, and to be in readiness to move at a moment's notice…
> …The Prince of Orange is requested to collect at Nivelles the 2nd and 3rd divisions of the Army of the Low Countries; and, should that point have been attacked this day, to move the 3rd Division of British infantry upon Nivelles as soon as collected. This movement not to take place until it is quite certain that the enemy's attack is upon the right of the Prussian army, and the left of the British army…[10]

These orders seemed to suggest a partial movement towards the east, focused on a concentration of three Netherlands divisions of I Corps at Nivelles. The content and tenor of the order suggested that headquarters in Brussels was still either unclear whether the attack on the Prussians was the main offensive or reasoned that it was somehow unimportant. The reference to an attack on Nivelles seemed to indicate that Wellington himself was expecting an invasion farther to the west of the area where fighting had been raging all day. They were also clearly unaware that Frasnes had been attacked, or if they were, considered it of little consequence; otherwise, why the Duke's order to concentrate at Nivelles and not Les Quatre Bras, the point of danger? Finally, and perhaps the most troubling point of all, was why instead of moving von-Sachsen-Weimar's brigade to Nivelles – in accordance with Wellington's order – had he just sent van Limburg-Stirum with a message to do quite the opposite and reinforce Les Quatre Bras with van Bijlandt's brigade. Not only that, he had indicated that he would reinforce it with Chassé's infantry and de Collaert's cavalry divisions, should this become necessary. Perhaps feeling his inexperience as a chief-of-staff, de Constant-Rebecque was torn. The Prince would not return for some hours. In the meantime, he was unsure of what to do.

As de Constant-Rebecque vacillated, Brussels waltzed. Though Captain Burney had abandoned his plans to attend the Duchess of Richmond's ball that evening and his invitation remained on the mantelpiece, the other guests were either preparing themselves, or were already arriving at the converted coach showroom at rue de la Blanchisserie. Wellington was to be an understandably late arrival. It was 10.00 p.m. and he had just

The Battle of Quatre Bras

completed a letter to Henri-Jacques-Guillaume Clarke, Count d'Hunebourg and Duke de Feltre, who had served for seven years as Napoleon's Minister for War and having helped persuade the Emperor to abdicate in 1814, now found himself as Minister for War to the exiled King Louis XVIII. It was curious how some 'blues' had become and remained 'whites', whilst others had reverted to 'blue'. As he had to the Duke de Berri earlier, Wellington passed on news of the French invasion:

> I received the news that the enemy attacked the Prussian posts this morning at Thuin on the Sambre, and he appears to be menacing Charleroi. I have received nothing since nine o'clock this morning from Charleroi. I have written to the Duke de Berri, in order to beg him to assemble his forces at Alost, and I beg you to make report of this event to His Majesty; and to have the goodness to advise him to make preparations to leave Ghent in case this movement renders it necessary. I will write as soon as I have more news.[11]

Having placed the letter in the hands of a courier, he was engaged in conversation by Colonel Somerset on the subject of the French invasion and the prospects of the Allies being successful in the forthcoming campaign. Somerset, with the confidence of the professional soldier, laconically observed that, 'No doubt we shall be able to manage these fellows.' Though Wellington shared his confidence and agreed with his sentiments, he qualified himself with the proviso that, 'He did not make a false movement'. Still unwilling to set the army in motion, he again sent word to De Lancey to remind him that, 'The troops were not to be ordered to march till further information was received.'[12]

They were interrupted by the arrival of Colonel von Müffling, who had just received a message sent towards noon by General von Gneisenau at Prussian headquarters at Namur.

> The enemy opened hostilities this morning at 4.30 a.m. and is advancing strongly along both banks of the Sambre. It is said that Bonaparte and the Guard are there, the latter certainly. General Ziethen has been ordered to watch the enemy closely and if possible not to retreat beyond Fleurus. The army will concentrate tomorrow on the Sombreffe position where the Prince intends to accept battle. Overnight, the three Army Corps received orders to concentrate today. II towards Onoz and Mazy, III at Namur, IV near Hannut. If necessary II Corps could even be at Sombreffe today and III at Onoz. In two hours time headquarters are moving to Sombreffe, to which place I desire that you inform us as soon as possible when and where the Duke of Wellington intends concentrating his forces and what he has decided to do. It will be best to adapt the relay line via Genappe.

Wellington now had considerable intelligence from his own advanced posts that the French had not attacked his sector of the front, but here was yet further evidence of a serious incursion on the right of the Prussian army. If von Zieten was at risk of being pushed back on Fleurus, Wellington would have to take measures to concentrate his own army farther to the east. He immediately gave instructions that the necessary order be dispatched.[13]

The Prince van Oranje-Nassau was one of the first to receive a copy of the movement order.

MOVEMENT OF THE ARMY.
After Orders, 10 o'clock P.M.

Brussels, 15 June 1815.

> The troops in Bruxelles (5th and 6th Divisions, Duke of Brunswick's and Nassau troops) to march when assembled from Bruxelles by the road of Namur to the point where the road to Nivelles separates; to be followed by Gen. Dornberg's brigade and the Cumberland Hussars.
>
> 3rd division of infantry to continue its movement from Braine le Comte upon Nivelles.
>
> The 1st division to move from Enghien upon Braine le Comte.
>
> The 2nd and 4th divisions of infantry to move from Ath and Grammont, also from Audenarde [Oudenaarde], and to continue their movements upon Enghien.
>
> The cavalry to continue its movement from Ninove upon Enghien.
>
> The above movements to take place with as little delay as possible.

Wellington.

As he prepared to attend the ball, the Prince hastily penned an additional instruction at the foot of the order:

> The Netherlands Cavalry Division will move from Haine-Saint-Pierre on Arquennes and will place itself behind that village. The headquarters must move tomorrow from Braine [Braine-le-Comte] to Nivelles.

The Prince was drawing in his horns. Since the earlier order for the 3rd (Netherlands) Infantry Division to withdraw to Nivelles, General de Collaert's cavalry had been left in an isolated position on the frontier. Even now, Wellington's staff seemed to have forgotten its existence.[14]

At the rue de la Blanchisserie, in the lower part of the town, guests had been steadily arriving at the Duchess of Richmond's ball, their carriages soon creating a tangle among the shrubs and trees of the courtyard, jamming the narrow streets that surrounded the 'Palace', the three-storey mansion that the Duke of Richmond had let from the impecunious Michel-Jean Simons; coach-builder and stationery supplier. The 'Suisse' had been instructed to expect almost 230 guests and as they entered the hallway of the house to be greeted by their hosts, they were directed down a passageway to the left, the chandeliers picking out the rich Renaissance-style gilded ornamental ceilings. As they passed through a crowded ante-room into the long and narrow ballroom, its improvised nature became obvious. Despite the lengths to which the Duchess had gone, the ground floor room was a former carriage showroom, more usually used by the Lennox children as a schoolroom, or to play shuttlecock and battledore on rainy days. The glow from the lamps picked out the trellis and rose-patterned wallpaper, 'The saloons of the Duchess were filled with a brilliant company of distinguished guests, the officers in their magnificent uniforms threading the dance with the most lovely and beautiful women.'[15]

The blind Duke Prosper-Louis d'Arenberg exchanged pleasantries with Baron Joseph van der Linden d'Hoogvoorst, the Mayor of Brussels, but was not fully on speaking terms with Duke Frédéric-Auguste-Alexandre de Beaufort-Spontin, the other 'great man' of Brussels, with whom he had disagreed over the former's lamentation on the, 'new order of things'. Count Auguste de Liederkerque-Beaufort made small talk with his mother-in-law, Countess de la Tour Dupin, the wife of Louis XVIII's minister at The Hague. Lord Apsley, stood with his younger brother, Ensign Hon. Seymour Bathurst and glanced longingly across at his cousin, Lady Sarah Lennox; Vice-Admiral Sidney Smith discussed naval affairs with Rear-Admiral Malcolm; and Thomas Legh flirted with Lady Elizabeth Conyngham. At least, thought Lady Georgiana Lennox, her mother had not invited young Beaumont Lord Hotham of the Guards, whom she considered to be a potential suitor for her daughter. Despite the allure of his annual income of £20,000, Hotham was considered hideously ugly and had a reputation for being averse to spending his money. In every corner of the small room diplomatists mingled with aristocrats, retired generals bowed to emigrés, while children scampered throughout; it was even rumoured that one of Napoleon's generals was in attendance. The hum of a hundred conversations, in Dutch, English, Flemish, French and German wafted into the night.[16]

As the orchestra played, the more energetic guests danced the risqué waltzes, four-couple quadrilles and the occasional *colonne*, or country dance. The floor became a promenade of scarlet and a whirlwind of taffeta and gauze. Having become accustomed to yielding the palm to the Bruxellois, where dancing was concerned, many of the officers had taken lessons and could now perform respectably. The training ground of the Concert Noble had done the rest. Towards 10.00 p.m, Lieutenant-Colonel Sir Andrew Barnard heard rumours of an engagement having taken place between the French and the Prussians circulating through the room in whispers, but few believed them and the dancing continued.[17]

Whilst Barnard drank, danced and exchanged gossip, the adjutants and orderly non-commissioned officers were busy setting the army in motion. Across the city, Lieutenant John Kynock, Adjutant of the 79th Regiment of Foot, received the order at 10.00 p.m. that his regiment was to hold itself in readiness to march at a moment's notice; it was said that Napoleon had crossed the Sambre and that the attack was imminent. Amongst those men of his regiment that tumbled from their beds was Private Dixon Vallence. Sharing a billet at a public house, he and three of his comrades from No. 6 Company had 'experienced as much kindness as we could have received at home', during their brief stay at Brussels. Having responded by being as 'civil, grateful and obliging as possible', they had formed a close bond with their landlord, who had treated them as if they had been his own relatives. Hearing the news, they made haste to pack their possessions. One, however, realising that two of his shirts were with the washer woman, dashed off to get them from her and found them steeping in water. Hurriedly wringing them, he stuffed the still wet clothing inside his bulging knapsack. Finally, they were ready. The tight cross-belt of the knapsack was digging into Vallence's chest and the shoulder straps bit into his underarms, but he was accoutred. Festooned with haversacks, cartridge boxes and canteens and not able to sit comfortably, the four soldiers found it easier to lie back down again, where they impatiently awaited the order to turn out.[18]

Elsewhere in the city, another Highland regiment was still largely ignorant of developments and was lacking in orders. Although rumours had started circulating in Brussels that the French army was in motion, few officers of the 92nd Regiment of Foot gave the reports much credit. Despite having heard as early as 7.00 p.m. that the troops were to move that night in consequence of the enemy being in motion, Lieutenant James Ross, had not seen fit to pass on this news. In the meantime, the regiment's duty sergeants had been in the orderly room all evening, smoking their pipes. Each was equipped with a list of the streets and house numbers where the men were quartered, with great care having been taken to arrange that 'Every company and regiment should be billeted in the same, or adjacent streets, to prevent confusion if called out at a moment's notice.' Amongst them was one of Ross's men, Sergeant David Robertson, a veteran of Egypt, Walcheren, Denmark, the Peninsula and France. As the evening slowly slipped away, he and his fellow sergeants concluded that no orders would be issued that night and dispersed to their quarters shortly before 10.00 p.m., not knowing that the orders, amongst the latest to leave the divisional headquarters, were on their way through the darkened streets.[19]

Ignorance had no respect for rank on this occasion and Lieutenant-Colonel Sir Augustus Frazer, commanding the Royal Horse Artillery, had spent most of the evening in the dark, in both a literal and figurative sense. He had eschewed the amusements of the various patrons of the table d'hôte at the Café Bellevue and had foregone the companionship of Baron Drièses, an elderly Russian general. Tonight had been a special occasion and he had instead attended a dinner party hosted by James Hawker, who was celebrating his promotion to Lieutenant-Colonel. Since Hawker commanded the artillery of General Colville's 4th (British) Infantry Division, Frazer had been obliged to ride to the small village of Lenniche-Saint-Quentin, where he joined a jolly party of about a dozen guests at Hawker's large and comfortable house. Though the company had been good, the roads had been detestable and he was glad to once more find himself back in Brussels. As he entered his quarters, however, he found Lieutenant-Colonel Sir Hew Ross, commanding one of the reserve batteries of horse artillery.[20]

> He had dined at General Kempt's, and had learned in the course of the evening that the enemy had moved upon Mons, and that in consequence we are to move during the

The Battle of Quatre Bras

night. Sir George Wood has just been here to say the same thing. He was one of the party at Hawker's, and has gone to headquarters to learn the news. I never suffer myself to be disturbed by these alerts: there is nothing new in looking the enemy in the face, and tomorrow may be as good a day as any other; not that I think we shall move; however, Wood will soon return from the Duke's, and then we shall know what is to be done. I find on my table an invitation to dine with Delancey [sic] tomorrow; his lady is here; this will be a pleasanter way of passing the day than marching to Mons. Of course I have accepted the invitation. The day before yesterday I dined at headquarters.[21]

Unknown to him, his host for the following evening was already deeply involved in issuing the orders that would ruin the social occasion that they had planned and although Mons still loomed large in Wellington's thinking, it was a hamlet, 37½ kilometres to the north-east, which would prove to be his eventual destination.

In contrast to Frazer's imperturbable attitude, another gunner was feeling distinctly agitated. Major Percy Drummond, who commanded the reserve artillery, had earlier notified Colonel Ross and Major George Bean at Brussels and Captain William Morrison at Vilvorde, of the order to be ready to move at daylight and was pondering the lack of subsequent orders. Had they been forgotten? What were his orders in respect of Captain Courtenay Ibert's and Captain Thomas Hutchesson's brigades at Ostend? Thirty guns remained motionless.[22]

In her room at the Hôtel de Flandre, Charlotte Waldie was alone. Her brother and sister had gone out, intending to call upon a family friend. Shortly after they had left, there was a tap at the door. Colonel Campbell of the 54th Regiment of Foot presented his compliments and asked if she would admit him? Sir Neil Campbell? 'The man who let Boney go'? The man who had shared their packet from Ramsgate to Ostend? She glanced at the clock. It was 10.00 p.m. How could she refuse, despite her unease over receiving such a, 'Splendid beau', alone, at such a late hour, and in her bedroom of all places. The conqueror of Countess Miniacci, no less. What would they have said in England?

Sir Neil made an impressive entrance and looked, 'Magnificent in a full dress uniform, covered with crosses, clasps, orders and medals'. He was, 'A handsome man, with a rather solemn face, framed by heavy whiskers'. Over his left eye, the white outline of a scar, the consequence of a blow from a wayward Russian sabre at the battle of La Fère-Champenoise the previous year, served only to add to his dashing appearance. She ordered tea. Having also dined with Wellington, Sir Neil corroborated Major Wylie's account, but alarmingly added that the French were said to be upwards of 100,000 strong, and that Napoleon himself was at the head of the army. Surely, asked Charlotte, these numbers must be exaggerated? How had this intelligence not been known?

They spent the next hour debating whether Napoleon's attack on Blücher was a ruse and whether 'The Monster' would attack Brussels and destroy Wellington's army. Sir Neil, having been Military Attaché to the headquarters of the Tsar and having met many of Europe's crowned heads, was well connected in diplomatic circles. He expressed a view that Napoleon was hoping to destroy Wellington by rapid and unexpected movements before the Russians, who had crossed the Rhine, could intervene.

Despite the ominous nature of their conversation, Charlotte felt reassured by the presence of this Mars and felt confident that the French

> … would meet with a very different reception from that which they expected; and that Napoleon, with every advantage on his side, would not find the defeat of an English army quite so easy a thing in practice, as he had always seemed to consider it in theory. Having settled this point much to our mutual satisfaction, Sir Neil Campbell went away.[23]

At about the same time as Sir Neil was taking his leave of Miss Waldie, the beleaguered officers of De Lancey's staff continued at their work a short distance away on the rue Royale, oblivious to their errors, their eyes smarting from the candles and the gloom. As Lieutenant Jackson put his pen down for what he thought was the final time, Colonel Torrens whispered to him that he had, 'Put him in for a ride'. A few moments later, De Lancey approached and handed him a packet, saying, 'I am told you know the road to Ninove; here is a letter for Lord Greenock; be as speedy as possible.' Within minutes, Jackson was in the saddle, wending his way by a cross road, one of many with which he had become familiar during the course of May and June, whilst on missions to locate suitable cantonments for the army.[24]

Across the darkened countryside, couriers were handing over messages to the polyglot components of Wellington's infamous army. At the Brunswick headquarters at Laeken, to the north of Brussels, Colonel Elias Olfermann and Lieutenant-Colonel von Heinemann had just received the assembly order and signed for its receipt, noting that the time was 10.00 p.m. Their chief was at the Duchess of Richmond's ball, but these instructions required immediate action. The division was to be mustered on the Allée Verte, the tree-lined high road between Brussels and Vilvorde, alongside the Canal du Petit Willebroek. To assemble them there by daybreak – as the order required – would prove a challenge. Having arrived only about a month before, the division was quartered over a large area, in a semicircle to the north of Brussels. From the easternmost elements to the westernmost was a four hour march. It would be especially difficult for the artillery in and around Asse, the hussars at Kobbegem and the 3rd Light Battalion at Grimbergen to keep to the timetable. The 1st Light Battalion faced a ten kilometre march from its distant cantonments around the villages of Sint-Ulriks-Kapelle, Sint-Martens-Bodegem, Zellik and Groot-Bijgarden, to the west of Brussels. Anticipating that it might take as much as two or three hours to reach the outlying cantonments, all the available staff officers were pressed into service and immediately started drafting orders for the respective battalions, squadrons and batteries. Towards 11.00 p.m. the Polizeihusaren of the Brunswick Division would leave Laeken with the first dispatches, but the night was dark, the roads bad and the terrain very broken.[25]

Colonel van Zuylen van Nyeveld could testify to the difficulties of riding by night over unfamiliar ground. Towards 10.45 p.m., he approached Les Quatre Bras and was challenged by the sentries of the first battalion of the 2nd Nassau-Usingen Regiment, who manned a picquet line close to the alarm cannon that Bijleveld had earlier sited on the road to Houtain-le-Val. 'Wilhelm!' came the challenge. 'Wiesbaden!' shouted the Dutchman; it would be foolish for him to be shot by a jumpy young lad from Villmar. At the Ferme des Quatre Bras, von Sachsen-Weimar welcomed the arrival of a senior officer from the divisional headquarters' staff and, after the two men had sat down, they discussed de Perponcher-Sedlnitzky's concerns over the loss of Charleroi, the withdrawal of the Prussians to the east and the events at Frasnes, which suggested that the French might be present in force on the road from Charleroi to Brussels. It was imperative, the visitor urged, that the Prince defend Les Quatre Bras '*À l'outrance*' and to only retire if he were attacked by very superior forces. In this eventuality, he was to withdraw in the direction of Mont-Saint-Jean, where he would be joined by van Bijlandt's brigade. Sensing the nervousness of the young man, aware of the burden of responsibility on his shoulders and cognisant of the fragility of the situation, van Zuylen van Nyeveld sought to reassure him by announcing de Perponcher-Sedlnitzky's intention to reinforce him with two further battalions during the night and to assume the command in person. If Binche were not threatened, then Chassé could ensure the continued protection of Nivelles and in so doing, relieve the remainder of the division. In this eventuality, the Colonel explained, an even greater reinforcement might be possible.[26]

At Brussels, Private Vallence and his three comrades of the 79th Regiment of Foot were still lying fully-equipped on their beds, when the sound of bugles, drums and bagpipes was heard coming from all directions. They clearly heard the distinctive notes of 'The gathering of the Camerons' and 'The War-Note of Lochiel' and sprang to their feet. The door burst open.

> Our host came running to the room where we were, to tell us to get ready, but he found us all prepared, upon which he told us that the French army was on the road to Brussels, but that he was not in the least afraid of their coming to the town. Our host kindly treated us to a flowing bumper of gin and a loaf of bread and, as is the custom of the place when friends part, he kissed and shook hands with each of us.[27]

Elsewhere, Private Edward Costello of the 95th Regiment of Foot was one of the green-jacketed riflemen dispersed over the most distant parts of Brussels and had been about to retire to bed at 11.00 p.m., when the buglers of the regiment blew the assembly and the men were turned out of their billets in full marching order by jostling corporals and sergeants. Drafted into a party formed by the orderly non-commissioned officers, Costello drew three days' rations and distributed them to the troops of Major Leach's company, though the company commander himself was unaccountably absent. Whilst the old soldiers squirrelled away as much as possible, the majority of the younger men simply left them behind, being disinclined to carry them and assuming that further supplies would be forthcoming. For many, this would be a mistake they would later regret. Lieutenant Simmons was roused by his servant and immediately dressed himself and reported to his alarm post. His commanding officer, Colonel Barnard, was determined that his 'Light Bobs' would be the first to muster and by 11.00 p.m. they were formed up in quarter distance columns in the Grand'Place. Officers were few and far between in No. 2 Company. Major Leach was still missing, as was First Lieutenant John Cox, who was undergoing the exfoliation of a wound he had received at the battle of Ciudad Rodrigo, three years earlier. With the next most senior officer – Lieutenant James Gairdner – detailed to remain behind and bring up the odds and sods, it would be left to Lieutenant John Fitzmaurice to command, assisted by Sergeant-Major William Shine. With no further orders forthcoming however, Lieutenant-Colonel Alexander Cameron, Barnard's second-in-command, gave the order for the men to fall out and pile arms amongst the tangle of the division's baggage wagons and the pack animals belonging to officers of the staff. There, in the great infantry tradition, with no orders forthcoming, they went to sleep.

> Waiting for the arrival of the other regiments, we endeavoured to snatch an hour's repose on the pavement, but we were every instant disturbed, by ladies as well as gentlemen, some stumbling over us in the dark – some shaking us out of our sleep, to be told the news – and not a few, conceiving their immediate safety depending upon our standing instead of lying. All those who applied for the benefit of my advice, I recommended to go home to bed, to keep themselves perfectly cool, and to rest assured that, if their departure from the city became necessary (which I very much doubted), they would have at least one whole day to prepare for it, as we were leaving some beef and potatoes behind us, for which, I was sure, we would fight, rather than abandon!

It would be 2.00 a.m. before the remaining regiments of the brigade assembled.[28]

As the infantry made its preparations, Colonel Frazer had once again taken up his pen and was in the middle of writing another long letter to his wife, Emma, at home in England with their two sons. Since hearing the news from Ross, his letter had moved away from martial matters to his love of fine arts, but during the last hour, more information had arrived. Towards 11.30 p.m., he went to rouse Colonel Ross and ordered him to return immediately to his 'Chestnut Troop' at Perk, some fifteen kilometres to the north-east of the city. It appeared that there was every probability that the army would move in the morning. Returning to his letter, he picked up his pen and, in the candlelight, resumed writing.

> It seems that Bonaparte is at Maubeuge, that he has about 120,000 men there, that he has advanced in the direction of Binch [sic], leaving Mons to his left and rear; that Blucher with 80,000 Prussians has moved from Namur to Sombreffe (on the road from Namur to Nivelle), that we shall concentrate our force in front of Braine l'Aleud [sic] (near Hal). Admitting all this to be true, we may have a battle the day after tomorrow.

The Battle of Quatre Bras

> The Duke has gone to a ball at the Duchess of Richmond's, but all is ready to move at daybreak. Of course all depends on the news which may arrive in the night. By way of being ready, I shall go to bed, and get a few hours' sleep. It is now half-past 11. I hope you and the dear boys are enjoying peaceful slumbers in our happy England, safe from all the alarms and confusions which tomorrow may see here.[29]

Though late in the evening, General de Constant-Rebecque was still at his headquarters, holding the earlier order from Wellington in his hands, but perplexed at its content:

> The Prince of Orange is requested to collect at Nivelles the 2d and 3d divisions of the army of the Low Countries; and, should that point have been attacked this day, to move the 3d division of British Infantry upon Nivelles as soon as collected.
> This movement is not to take place until it is quite certain that the enemy's attack is upon the right of the Prussian army, and the left of the British Army.

He knew that Colonel Berkeley had alerted Generals Cooke and von Alten and that consequently, the two British divisions would be assembling overnight at Enghien and Braine-le-Comte respectively, in accordance with Wellington's earlier wishes. Since the arrival of this order, however, he had delayed taking action in respect of the Netherlands troops, fearing that moving von Sachsen-Weimar's brigade from Les Quatre Bras to Nivelles would leave the road open for the French to march on Brussels. At the same time, moving Chassé from his positions behind the Haine would leave de Collaert's cavalry isolated. Since the order in respect of Chassé was entirely consistent with his thoughts on how best to deal with the threat to Les Quatre Bras and Nivelles, he decided to write to 'Général Baïonette' as Chassé had been known in the ranks of the French army. Before he did, however, he sat down and drafted an order for de Collaert, whose cavalry would have to cover this movement:

> No. 183
>
> Headquarters at Braine-le-Comte
> 15 June 1815, 11.30 p.m.
>
> To Lieutenant-General Collaert, commanding the cavalry at Boussoît-sur-Haine.
>
> On receipt of this present order, Your Excellency will place the division of cavalry under his orders in motion and will go to occupy the heights behind Haine-Saint-Pierre, detaching a brigade with the necessary artillery to cover the passage of the Haine, close to Saint-Paul [Haine-Saint-Paul].
>
> The Quartermaster-General, etc.[30]

Next, he drafted an order for General Chassé:

No. 184

> Headquarters at Braine-le-Comte
> 15 June 1815, 11.30 p.m.
>
> To Lieutenant-General Chassé, commanding the 3rd Division, at Fayt.
>
> Your division must march immediately to Nivelles, to support the 2nd Division there, in case of need. You are warned that General Collaert is taking position behind the Haine.
>
> The Quartermaster-General, etc.[31]

Once complete, he handed the order for de Collaert to the commander of the Mounted Guides, Captain Baron van Heinecken; and that for Chassé to his personal aide-de-camp, Captain Baron Charles Nepveu, both of whom left immediately. His dilemma concerning de Perponcher-Sedlnitzky, however, continued to occupy his mind, almost two hours after the receipt of Wellington's order. There would be no word from Brussels for some time; nor was the Prince expected back until the early hours. Having considered seemingly every avenue, de Constant-Rebecque concluded that he had no choice but to forward the Prince's orders to de Perponcher-Sedlnitzky, who was his senior in both rank and length of service. Despite the fact that they were most likely based on faulty intelligence, it was his duty to forward the direct orders of his superior. That said, it was perfectly legitimate for him, as chief-of-staff, to provide advice and hope that de Perponcher-Sedlnitzky would take it. In this manner, the responsibility would pass from him to the commander on the spot. He wrote out the necessary order:

No. 185

> Headquarters at Braine-le-Comte
> 15 June 1815, 12.15 a.m.
>
> After having sent to you the Count of Stirum, I have received the order of HRH the Prince van Oranje-Nassau, from Brussels, telling you to assemble your division at Nivelles. General Chassé's division has received orders to move to Nivelles, in order to join itself to you and to support you. General Collaert has received orders to take position on the heights behind Haine-Saint-Pierre.
>
> The Quartermaster-General, etc.

By 12.15 a.m., a third staff officer, this time Captain Willem Schröder of the Netherlands Quartermaster-General's Department, was on his way to de Perponcher-Sedlnitzky, the message securely tucked into his coat pocket.[32]

Far away in Brussels, the clocks in the churches and public buildings across the city were chiming midnight. Colonel Frazer had by now received directions from

The Battle of Quatre Bras

Colonel Sir George Wood, the commander of Wellington's artillery and had despatched messengers to Colonel Charles Gold at Antwerp and his recent dinner host, Colonel Hawker, who commanded the artillery of the 2nd and 4th (British) Infantry Divisions respectively. A courier was also dispatched to order Major Bean to march on Vilvorde and to establish his reserve troop of 6-pounders in any village thereabouts where he could find accommodation. Shortly after, Lieutenant-Colonel Stephen Adye, the officer commanding Major-General Cooke's two artillery batteries, arrived from Ghent. A soldier of almost 27 years' experience, Adye had been sitting on a court of enquiry into the misconduct of part of the Corps of Royal Artillery Drivers, whose grievance was that they had embarked from Bordeaux for America the previous year and since returned, without once receiving their pay. The warriors were slowly starting to gather. Turning back to his letter, Frazer wished his wife a good night and blew out the candle.[33]

Though still alight, the candles had burned low in de Perponcher-Sedlnitzky's office by the time Major van Limburg-Stirum arrived at about midnight. His appearance was a tonic for the tired General. Anxiously, he opened the letter and perused its contents:

> His Royal Highness is at Brussels at the moment, but is expected back at any time. I believe that it would be important to support the Second Brigade with the First, and that, if it is necessary, General de Perponcher-Sedlnitzky be supported by the Third Division, which is at Fayt, and also the cavalry of General Collaert, which is in the vicinity of Roeulx. The hospital and the Council of War will fall back on Brussels. In any case, General de Perponcher-Sedlnitzky will wish to send an officer to General Chassé at Fayt in order to make him aware of the state of things and to beg him to communicate with General de Collaert.[34]

As the General absorbed the meaning of the formal letter, von Gagern passed on the verbal instructions that would help de Perponcher-Sedlnitzky to read between the lines. The Chief-of-Staff believed that if the report von Gagern had made to him was correct, the Duke of Wellington must already have been informed of these events by Marshal Blücher. General de Constant-Rebecque believed accordingly that the Duke would not delay in taking measures in consequence. He therefore considered it vital to persist at Les Quatre Bras and at Nivelles for the longest time possible, but that if he had to yield to a superior force, he was to withdraw on Braine-le-Comte. Although he was not in a position formally to urge General de Perponcher-Sedlnitzky to abandon Nivelles and march with the whole of van Bijlandt's brigade to Les Quatre Bras, the Chief-of-Staff felt that if that General judged the moment to be right, he should send a reinforcement of a few battalions there. The position was clear to de Perponcher-Sedlnitzky. He understood that de Constant-Rebecque was not able formally to issue orders in place of the Prince van Oranje-Nassau, but it was reassuring that someone closer to the Prince than he – and no doubt more intimately acquainted with the strategic intentions of his chief and of Wellington himself – seemed to consider his proposed action legitimate.[35]

'I am too feeble to remain here long'

Far away at Brussels, oblivious to these finer points, Colonel von Müffling, resplendent in his full dress uniform and displaying his glittering orders, was drafting a dispatch to Marshal von Blücher that would detail the movements of the Anglo-Allied army. He had, however, left the names of the rendezvous points blank, ready to be added as soon as he had been briefed by Wellington. A courier and post-chaise waited outside his door, so that the message could be transmitted with the minimum of delay. Towards midnight, Wellington, who had been preparing for the Duchess of Richmond's ball, hurried in, still wearing his dressing-gown and slippers and clutching a map, which he unrolled.

> I have got news from Mons, from General von Dörnberg, who reports that Napoleon has turned towards Charleroi with all his forces and that there is no longer any enemy in front of him. Therefore, orders for the concentration of my army at Nivelles and Les Quatre Bras have already been dispatched. The numerous friends of Napoleon who are here, will raise their heads. The well-disposed must be tranquilised. Let us therefore go, all the same, to the ball of the Duchess of Richmond.

In the Duke's mind, if the reports he had received were true, now was not the time to panic. He determined to show a bold front to his opponents, encourage the military and civilian population and steady the nerves of his allies. Even though he could have sent word to the Duchess to cancel proceedings, he realised that considerable numbers of his generals, senior staff and regimental officers would be attending, many from distant cantonments. Far better to gather his officers to him, communicate his wishes and send them back to their parent units informed. Colonel von Müffling, however, was confused. Concentrate at Les Quatre Bras? Surely – he thought – the orders that Wellington had dispatched earlier, assembled his army no farther east than Nivelles? Had Wellington really determined to move on Les Quatre Bras, or was he mistaken? There was a knock at the door. It was De Lancey, arrived to update the Duke on progress in mobilising the army and to receive any further instructions. As the two talked, von Müffling hurriedly completed and dispatched his letter.[36]

Endnotes

1. de Bas &c., p. 404. Hofschröer (I), pp. 203, 206. von Kruse. van Opstall. de Perponcher-Sedlnitzky. Starklof, p. 133. van Zuylen van Nyeveld (I), p. 50.
2. de Bas &c., p. 405. Hofschröer (I), p. 206. van Löben-Sels, p. 461. von Sachsen-Weimar (I). von Sachsen-Weimar (III). Sachsen-Weimar (IV). Starklof, pp. 134–5. van Zuylen van Nyeveld (I), p. 51.
3. Starklof, p. 134.
4. Starklof, p. 136.
5. Scheltens, p. 197.
6. de Bas &c., pp. 407–8. de Constant-Rebecque (I). Hofschröer (I), p. 207. F. von Gagern.

The Battle of Quatre Bras

van Limburg-Stirum. van Zuylen van Nyeveld (I), p. 52.

7. Anonymous (Outgoing Register). de Bas &c., pp. 409–10. de Constant-Rebecque (I). F. von Gagern. Hofschröer (I), p. 207.
8. Young, p. 100.
9. de Bas &c., p. 410.
10. Anonymous (Incoming Register). Gurwood, p. 472.
11. Carter, pp. 98–9. Gurwood, pp. 473–4.
12. F. Somerset, p. 7.
13. de Bas &c., p. 418. Hofschröer (I), pp. 197–8. Hussey (III), pp. 98–9. Hussey (IV), pp. 464–7, 479–80. von Ollech, p. 99.
14. Anonymous (Incoming Register). de Bas &c., pp. 444–5. Gurwood, p. 474. Hofschröer (I), pp. 166–7.
15. Anonymous (Near Observer), p. 46. Cotton, p. 108. W. Fraser, pp. 216–7, 223–4. Maurice, p. 7. Miller (II), pp. 69, 127–32. Swinton, pp. 122–3.
16. Miller (II), pp. 73–8, 88, 93. G. Paget (I), pp. 51, 78–9. Swinton, p. 125.
17. Jackson (II), pp. 8–9.
18. J. Allan. Anonymous (Cameron), pp. 87–8. Anonymous (Near Observer), p. 46. Dalton, p. 189. Vallence.
19. Anonymous (Letters), p. 220. Mackenzie &c., p. 54. Miller (II), p. 111. Robertson, p. 143. J. Ross (II). Winchester (II).
20. Frazer, pp. 533–4.
21. Frazer, p. 534.
22. Asquith, p. 26a. Dalton, pp. 248–9.
23. Dalton, pp. 240–1. Eaton, pp. 1, 16–17. N. Mackenzie, pp. 39–41, 114, 167.
24. Dalton, pp. 34–35. Jackson (II), p. 13.
25. Anonymous (Near Observer), pp. 76–7. von Herzberg. Hofschröer (I), p. 79. Olfermann. F. Somerset, p. 7.
26. de Bas &c., p. 407 Hofschröer (I), p. 207. Sachsen-Weimar (I). von Sachsen-Weimar (III). Starklof, p. 136. van Zuylen van Nyeveld (I), p. 51.
27. J. Allan. Vallence.
28. Anonymous (Letters), p. 222–3. Anonymous (Near Observer), p. 46. Costello, p. 150. Dalton, p. 199. Kincaid (I), pp. 309–11. Miller (II), p. 138. Simmons (II), pp. 362–3.
29. Frazer, pp. 535–6.
30. Anonymous (Incoming Register). Anonymous (Outgoing Register). de Bas &c., p. 437.
31. Anonymous (Outgoing Register). de Bas &c., p. 437.
32. de Bas &c., pp. 438–9.
33. Adkin, p. 42. Adye. Dalton, pp. 209–211. Frazer, pp. 535–6.
34. Anonymous (Outgoing Register). de Bas &c., p. 408. Hofschröer (I), p. 207. van Limburg-Stirum. van Zuylen van Nyeveld (I), p. 52.
35. de Bas &c., pp. 408–9. Hofschröer (I), p. 207. van Limburg-Stirum. van Zuylen van Nyeveld (I), p. 52.
36. Arthur, p. 591. Brett-James, pp. 40–1. Cotton, p. 108. Miller (I), pp. 107, 143. Houssaye, p. 82. von Müffling (I), p. 2. von Müffling (II), pp. 229–30. Napier. Owen, p. 7. F. Somerset, p. 7.

CHAPTER 5

The Grand'Place in the centre of Brussels' Old Town was swarming with men, and the inhabitants watched in astonishment from the Golden Tree, the Swan, the King of Spain and the magnificent Guild Houses. Even by midnight, the 44th Regiment of Foot was still not mustered at its alarm post, despite the insistence of the drums and bugles. Lieutenant Alexander Riddock had learned from those returning from the Duchess of Richmond's ball that 'The work of death was begun' and likened the scene to that of sinners being called to judgement. Amongst the sinners were forty men who had recently arrived in a draft from England, to whom the nickname 'The Forty Thieves' had gleefully been attached. By the light of candles wedged in the barrel of each man's musket, or by the flickering glare of torchlight, Quartermaster-Sergeant John Rossiter and Armourer Sergeant Henry Boyd issued each man with 120 rounds of ball cartridge tied in bundles, which were hastily stowed in the camp kettles on top of the men's rolled blankets. Among the throng of people galloping about in all directions, Captain Burney and Quartermaster Henry Jones were endeavouring to oversee the issue of three days' provisions, including three pounds of meat per man, which Lieutenant-Colonel John Hamerton had ordered to be cooked 'on the spot if time would admit before advancing'. The men were also issued with a pound of bread or 1½ pounds of rice and either three pints of wine or a pint of spirits. Unfortunately, there were insufficient supplies to go round and Corporal John Conway was possibly one of those complaining, when Captain George Crozier's company was only issued with a pound of bread and a third of a pint of Dutch courage. Perhaps it was providence. He would be killed later that day.[1]

Others were more fortunate. Quartermaster Donald McIntosh of the 42nd Regiment of Foot was busy issuing four days' rations of beef and perhaps to more popular acclaim, spirits, to the fatigue parties. The battalion was paraded in the street and the muskets rang on the cobbles as the command was given: 'Order arms!' The roll was called and, as he waited his turn in the ranks of Captain Stirling's Company, it seemed to Private James Gunn that 'Everything that could make a noise in the way of a drum or bugle', was sounding throughout the city, though the regiment's pipers were adding to the din considerably with their rendition of the pibroch 'Come to me and I will give you flesh'. He must have felt a long way from the remote beaches of Dornoch in Sutherland, but if the 'Gineva' was as good here as that he had tasted

The Battle of Quatre Bras

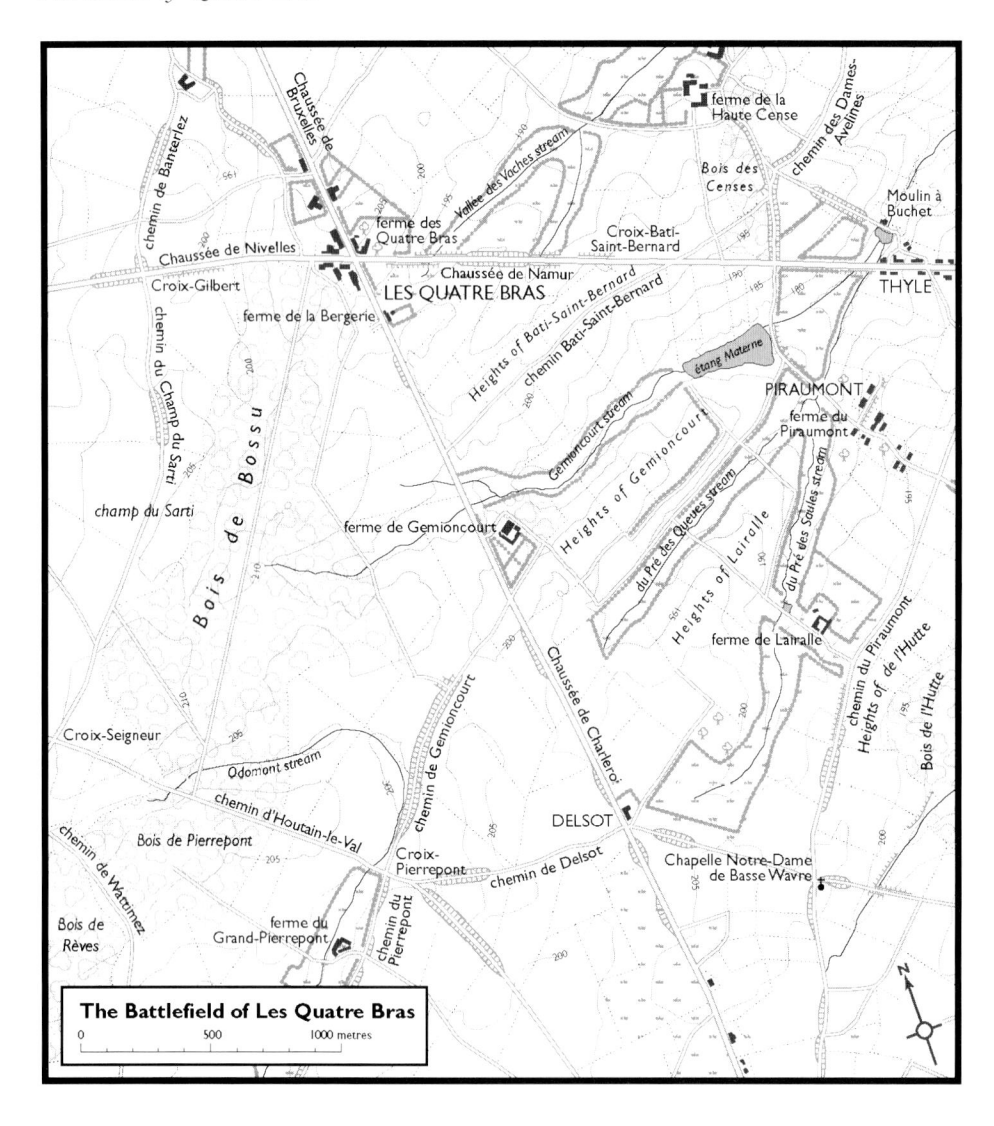

The Battlefield of Les Quatre Bras

at Ghent, then his unexpected early rising might well be worth it. The inhabitants looked on as the men with whom they had shared their lives for some considerable time made their final preparations and came outside to bid farewell.[2]

Shortly after retiring to bed, a drowsy Sergeant Robertson was roused by the alarm and hastily buckled on his kilt. Along with the other sergeants and corporals of the 92nd Regiment of Foot, they ignored the commotion outside and hurried to the quarters of their respective sections, dragging the reluctant men from their beds. Having assembled the company on private parade for the inspection of Captain Archibald Ferrier, Robertson then reported with a fatigue party to Quartermaster Sergeants Robert Bryce and John McCombie and received four days' rations for each man. Some of the companies were a little more fortunate or favoured, and received six days' worth of soft bread and biscuit, which they tried in vain to stuff into their bulging haversacks, but without much success. What would not fit was devoured, presented as a parting gift to their hospitable landlords and landladies, tossed to urchins, or simply left in the streets.[3]

Corporal John Douglas of the 1st Regiment of Foot, the Royal Scots, had very much enjoyed the ease of his time in Brussels. Indeed, that particular evening had been even more comfortable for the men, several officers of the division having been invited to the Duchess of Richmond's ball. His enjoyment had, however, been interrupted when word circulated that a few wagon-loads of Prussian wounded had been bought in. Was this a sign that hostilities had commenced? The raucous blare of bugles, the shouts from officers and sergeants to assemble at the alarm post and the distribution of rations could mean anything.[4]

In the upper town, Charlotte Waldie had briefly chatted to her brother and sister on their return from visiting friends and was enjoying the comforts of the Hôtel de Flandre:

> Scarcely had I laid my weary head on the pillow, when the bugle's loud and commanding call sounded from the Place Royale. 'Is that the call to arms?' I exclaimed, starting up in the bed. My sister laughed at the idea; but it was repeated, and we listened with eager and anxious suspense. For a few moments a pause of doubt ensued. Hark! Again! It sounded through the silence of the night, and from every quarter of the town it was now repeated, at short and regular intervals. 'It is the call to arms!' I exclaimed. Instantly the drums beat; the Highland pibroch sounded, – It was the call to arms! Oh! Never shall I forget the feelings of that moment! Immediately the utmost tumult and confusion succeeded the silence in which the city had previously been buried.[5]

Lieutenant Edward Stephens of the 32nd Regiment of Foot had also heard the insistent note of the bugler of the Light Company. Together with other officers of his battalion, he hurriedly dressed and, finding that an order for the army to assemble had arrived at the Colonel's house, hastened to his post. Despite reports earlier in the day that the French were advancing and that von Blücher's outposts had been driven in, no-one had gave them any credence, but now it was openly suggested that Wellington had been keeping a profound secret from the troops; that the French had attacked the Prussians![6]

Less concerned with Boney and Nosey was Sergeant James Battersby of the same regiment, who was quartered nearby. As he hurriedly prepared to depart, he also tried to reassure his wife, who was to give birth at any time. Things would turn out for the best, he said. This was probably no more than a false alarm or a practice drill. The lot of the soldier's wife was a harsh one and all those who followed the drum were inured to its rigours. Resignedly accepting her abandonment, she begged him to take care, not wishing her child to be born an orphan.[7]

Such notions were alien to the well-born, but mostly impecunious families that had taken up temporary residence in Brussels. Accustomed to reading about distant hostilities and hardship in newspapers, ensconced in their own homes and safe behind

The Battle of Quatre Bras

The 92nd Regiment of Foot leave Brussels in the early hours of 16 June 1815. Print after James Thiriar. (Author's collection)

the wooden walls of the Royal Navy, their sojourn on the continent somehow now seemed less secure:

> Never dreaming of danger, in streets crowded with the gay uniforms of their countrymen. It was not until their defenders were summoned to the field, that they were fully sensible of their changed circumstances, and the suddenness of the danger multiplying its horrors, many of them were seen running about in the wildest state of distraction.[8]

At last, Wellington arrived at 'The Wash-House', as he called the residence of the Duke and Duchess of Richmond. It was rather late but he had, after all, promised the Duchess earlier that month that she may give her ball 'with the greatest safety, without fear of interruption'. Lady Georgiana Lennox was dancing, but on the arrival of the Duke, whom she had known since 1807, she immediately approached him and asked him about the rumours. In a grave tone – and conscious that the eyes and ears of the company were all trained on him – Wellington turned to his 'Dearest Georgy' and said, 'Yes they are true. We are off tomorrow.'[9]

Hearing confirmation from the mouth of the Duke himself shocked the young woman and the news spread through the building. John Capel, chaperoning his daughters Georgiana and Maria, perhaps recalled the view that his wife, Caroline, had expressed earlier in the week:

> 'The suddenness of the danger multiplying its horrors'

> I should suppose the commencement of hostilities (if they ever do begin) cannot be far distant, but nobody can guess Lord Wellington's intentions and I dare say nobody will know he is going till he is actually gone. In the meantime he amuses himself with humbugging the ladies, particularly the Duchess of Richmond.[10]

Some officers hurriedly departed, while others remained. The news seemed to have a deep effect on Wellington himself, as Lady Jane Dalrymple-Hamilton noticed:

> Although the Duke affected great gaiety, and cheerfulness, it struck me that I had never seen him have such an expression of care and anxiety on his countenance. I sat next to him on a sopha a long time, but his mind seemed quite pre-occupied and, although he spoke to me in the kindest manner possible, yet frequently in the middle of a sentence, he stopped abruptly and called to some officer, giving him directions, in particular to the Duke of Brunswick and the Prince of Orange.[11]

Wellington approached General Hill, in command of II Corps and told him 'The Prussians had suffered severely that same evening … The Belgian outposts had given notice that the enemy was in sight of them.' It was consequently necessary to 'Start immediately and join as quickly as possible our several Corps.' To Captain Sir Digby Mackworth, Hill's aide-de-camp, this was thrilling news.

> In our ball costumes, brilliant with gold lace and embroidery, exulting in the assurance that our long tiresome days of inactivity were at an end, and that we were on the point of meeting this celebrated lou-garou Bonaparte, so long our anxious wish, we spurred our chargers.[12]

The commander-in-chief was taking the opportunity to call together the generals commanding divisions and brigades and to warn them to be prepared to move in the morning. To General Vivian, it appeared that the Duke must have been aware that the French were concentrating, though he seemed uncertain as to which part of his front they would attack.[13]

Lady Georgiana Lennox had hurriedly left the ball room with her eldest brother, Charles, the 23-year-old Earl of March. As an aide-de-camp to the Prince van Oranje-Nassau, he would need to accompany his chief whenever he chose to leave, so it had seemed sensible to pack some necessaries whilst the 'Young Frog' continued to enjoy Brussels' society. In delivering the first news of the French invasion to Wellington, the young officer had already secured his place for posterity, but the history of this campaign would be written by the victor and there was consequently much more to be done. Together, they crossed the garden and entered the Dower-House in which he lodged and packed up his uniform and equipment, ready for the coming campaign.[14]

The strains of the orchestra died away. Suddenly, there was a skirl of pipes and heads craned to detect the source. Into the glittering assembly marched Lieutenant

Claude Alexander, Adjutant of the 92nd Regiment of Foot, followed by Pipe-Major Alexander Cameron and four sergeants bearing broadswords. A centrepiece of the evening – as far as the Duchess was concerned – would be a display of Highland sword dancing and reels by her father's regiment, the Gordon Highlanders. The Belgians, especially, were expected to be impressed by the skill and grace of the dancers. The group came to a halt and Lieutenant Alexander saluted his commander-in-chief. His colonel, the newly-knighted Sir John Cameron of Fassiefern, was watching them intently.[15]

The four men crossed the swords and, inflating the bag that had been shot through by a French sniper at the battle of Fuentes d'Oñoro, Pipe Major Cameron introduced the dance 'Ghillie Callum', reputedly first danced by King Malcolm Canmore after his defeat of one of Macbeth's chieftains at the battle of Dunsinane in 1054. The first steps were danced outside the weapons, as the men 'addressed' the swords, following which they moved across them, picking their way delicately through the steps on the points of their feet, careful not to disturb the blades and bring bad luck. As the dance progressed, the heavy wool of their kilts swayed in rhythm and, arms held aloft, the men clapped their hands to increase the tempo before a final, mesmerising, flutter of steps brought the dance to an end, to the resounding applause of the assembled guests. Perhaps there was also time for 'Lady Charlotte Gordon's Reel', composed in honour of the hostess by William Marshall, steward of the household of the Duchess's father?[16]

Elsewhere in the ballroom, the Duke von Braunschweig-Lüneburg was sitting with the 10-year-old Prince Eugene Lamoral de Ligne on his knee, when news that the French were advancing reached him. He leapt to his feet, dropping the unfortunate child on the floor. As his mother, Countess Louise d'Oultremont picked the child up, the Duke seemed to stand still for a moment and turned pale, as if he had a pre-sentiment of his imminent death. Making his apologies, he headed for the entrance hall passing through the ante room, at the door of which he spoke briefly to Lady Georgiana Lennox, who had just returned with her brother. Having invited her to accompany the Duke of Wellington at a review of his troops on 22 May at Vilvorde, he was at pains to assure her that his men would repay the honour by distinguishing themselves in the coming conflict. Having bid his hosts good night, he left for Laeken.[17]

Despite the glittering assembly at the rue de la Blanchisserie, Captain George Bowles of the Coldstream Guards was unhappy. Notwithstanding the prospect of a campaign, he was piqued at the prospect of having to serve it out in a regimental capacity. He had harboured aspirations to serve as aide-de-camp to the Duke of Richmond whom, it had been suggested, would command the reserve if both the 5th and 6th (British) Infantry Divisions had formed. The continued absence of Sir Lowry Cole, who was newly-wed, seemed to have put paid to this ambition.

Captain Bowles was further embittered by the appointment of Lieutenant-Colonel Henry Wyndham to the command of the battalion's Light Company at his expense, though he had been unfair to that officer in describing him to friends as being his junior by two years and having served abroad for about as many months as Bowles had years; Wyndham was his senior by over four years and had survived eight general actions in the Peninsular War.[18]

More optimistic about the campaign was 17-year-old Ensign Lord Hay of the 1st Regiment of Foot Guards, the son of the Earl of Errol and a 'dashing, merry youth, full of military ardour'. Looking very grand in his full dress uniform, silk hose and silver-buckled shoes, he was talking to Lady Maria Capel. Since he was about to embark on his first campaign, perhaps she reminded him of a promise he had made, half in jest, a short time before.

Ensign Lord Hay had named his favourite mare Muzzy, after Maria, and promised, should he fall in the first action but still have breath to speak, the horse would be hers to keep. Not everyone shared his high spirits. As Hay expressed his 'delight at the idea of going into action and of all the honours he was to gain', Lady Georgiana Lennox, who had joined the party, was 'quite provoked'. Her evening was becoming progressively more dreadful, having to take leave of friends and acquaintances that she feared she might never see again.[19]

Another officer at the ball was perhaps more keen than others to take his leave; Colonel Cameron of the 92nd Regiment of Foot. Three days earlier, he had written to his father:

> This is a fine, gay place at present. Besides the military around, there are crowds of English of all descriptions here at present, but I was never much calculated for a gay life and am now still less than ever so. I would therefore be much more amused shooting moor-fowl in the Highlands than attending at levées here.

At least, his health had improved sufficiently to enable him to meet the rigours of the campaign in far better spirits than had been the case a few weeks before, when he had even found it difficult to put pen to paper. That said, the news that 'Nap has come to our neighbourhood', a few days previously, had made him nervous for Wellington, whose forces he wished were a little stronger.[20]

Starting imperceptibly, the trickle of departing officers became a stream, leading the dancers to falter and gradually stop. The music of the orchestra died away mid-note. Faces, which moments ago had been flushed with pleasure, suddenly expressed anxiety. Several women were in tears. The unfortunate Duchess of Richmond barred the doorway, imploring the departing officers to 'Wait one hour more', and not 'spoil her ball'. Her efforts were fruitless.[21]

The 92nd Regiment of Foot marched into the rue Royale at about 12.30 a.m. and was ordered to halt at its northern end, where it was rejoined by Colonel Cameron. In the rue Royale, the Parc, the Place Royale and in the numerous side-streets, especially those leading to the lower town, the red and green-coated masses of the 5th (British) Infantry Division were inexorably forming up, until the whole of the fashionable upper town began to resemble a citadel. From her window in the Hôtel de Flandre, Charlotte Waldie had a panoramic view of the influx of infantry and artillery:

As the dawn broke, the soldiers were seen assembling from all parts of the town, in marching order, with their knapsacks on their backs, loaded with three days' provision. Unconcerned in the midst of the din of war, many a soldier laid himself down on a truss of straw and soundly slept, with his hands still grasping his firelock. Others were sitting contentedly on the pavement, waiting the arrival of their comrades.[22]

Shortly afterwards, the 79th Regiment of Foot marched into the Place Royale under the critical eye of Sergeant-Major Masterton McIntosh. Their kilts swayed with the cadence of the march, but as yet it was too dark to see the Cameron overstripe that transformed the Macdonald sett into Cameron of Erracht. As they halted between the 28th and 32nd Regiments of Foot, Lieutenant-Colonel Neil Douglas gave orders for the issue of three days' provisions and gin.[23]

By the iron railings of the Parc, General Pack consulted his watch with an irritated scowl. Around him were the men of the 1st, 44th and 92nd Regiments of Foot, formed in column of battalions. The space between the Royals and the 44th should have been occupied by the 42nd Regiment of Foot, which was only now arriving. As Lieutenant-Colonel Sir Robert Macara came up, Sergeant James Anton – marching past with the rest of Captain Murdoch McLaine's company – was witness to his commanding officer being 'chidden severely for being so dilatory'. The battalion rushed to take up its position in the column. Colonel Cameron of the 92nd, standing nearby, perhaps suppressed a wry grin. At the end of May, in a letter to his father he had written: 'Major-General Sir Denis Pack is our immediate commander of the brigade and we are, of course, sure of being much tormented.'[24]

Lieutenant Webster had arrived at Brussels from Braine-le-Comte shortly after midnight and had gone firstly to the Prince van Oranje-Nassau's hotel. There, he discovered that his chief had already departed for the Duchess of Richmond's ball and conducted by a valet, he trotted down to the lower town and arrived at the rue de la Blanchisserie at about 12.30 a.m..

> The Place at Brussels was ablaze with light; and such was the crowd of carriages, that I could not well make my way through them on horseback: so I abandoned my steed to the first man I could get hold of and made my way to the porter's lodge. On my telling the Suisse I had despatches of moment for the Prince, he civilly asked me if I would wait five minutes; 'For,' he said, 'The Duchess has just given orders for the band to go upstairs, and the party are now about to rise. If you were to burst in suddenly, it might alarm the ladies.' On that consideration, I consented to wait.

Webster had misinterpreted the man's broken English. The band had gone upstairs to the first floor in order to provide continued entertainment during supper, which would commence shortly. The company were about to follow them. As Webster hid behind the folding doors, the Duchess of Richmond took the arm of the Prince van Oranje-Nassau, followed by the Duke of Wellington and Lady Charlotte Greville. As soon as they had reached the foot of the stairs, Webster boldly hastened to the

Prince's side and handed him the despatch. Recognising Webster and understanding that it contained information for Wellington, the Prince simply handed it behind him to the Duke, who quietly deposited it in his coat pocket; yet another dispatch to add to the several he had received during the course of the evening. Before continuing, the Prince signalled Webster to remain in the hall. Fearing awkward questions from other guests, the young officer hid in a recess. The last couple having been seated, Wellington read the dispatch; it contained news of the combat at Frasnes, late that afternoon.

Coming back downstairs, Wellington beckoned Webster over and quietly instructed him to order the Prince's four horses and carriage. Returning upstairs, the Duke whispered to the Prince van Oranje-Nassau who, having thanked his hosts, declined supper and made his exit. A short time later, he returned briefly to Wellington's side, but after whispering for some minutes in his ear, the Duke tersely told him that he had no fresh orders to give and recommended him to go back to his quarters and go to bed. The Prince finally left the house just after 1.00 a.m. Wellington resumed his seat and turning to Lady Georgiana Lennox and reaching into a pocket, presented her with a miniature portrait of himself, painted by a Belgian artist.[25]

Word circulated that the Duke had received an account of the Prussians being pushed back and that the French were a mere 22 kilometres from Brussels. Officers instinctively gathered around their generals. Were the French across the Dyle already? Lady Jane Lennox, a young woman merely seventeen years of age, became aware of the changed mood:

> I know I was in a state of wild delight – the scene itself was so stirring, and the company so brilliant. I recollect, on reaching the ball-room after supper, I was scanning over my tablets, which were filled from top to bottom with the names of the partners to whom I was engaged; when, on raising my eyes, I became aware of a great preponderance of ladies in the room. White muslins and tarlatans abounded; but the gallant uniforms had sensibly diminished. The enigma was soon solved. Without fuss or parade, or tender adieux, the officers, anxious not to alarm the ladies, had quietly stolen out; and before they had time to guess the nature of the news which had robbed them of their partners, and changed the festive aspect of the scene, they found themselves, instead of asking questions, holding their breath.[26]

The generals whose troops were most in advance started to depart and many of those who had hitherto been unconvinced awoke to the realisation that circumstances had taken a significant turn for the worse. In twenty minutes, the room was virtually devoid of dancers. There remained, however, those of a more confident disposition, among them Captain Bowles. The day before, he had written to his friend Lord Fitzharris:

> The Army of the Moselle, about 25,000 strong, has lately been moved forward, and including garrisons the enemy probably muster 110,000 effective troops in our front.

> The united forces under Marshals Blücher and Wellington are nearly double, and we are quite ready. One day's march would concentrate us on the centre, and two on either flank of our present line, and we must always have sufficient notice to enable this to be done with ease.[27]

His confidence was misplaced and was certainly not shared by his commander-in-chief. The day required to concentrate on the centre had almost disappeared and the Prussian withdrawal to Fleurus had shifted their right wing a further ten kilometres east. Shortly after 1.30 a.m., Wellington approached the Duke of Richmond and indicating to the departing guests, suggested 'It is time for me to go to bed likewise.' Whilst wishing his host goodnight, Wellington asked if he had a good map in the house. The two men disappeared into Richmond's study on the ground floor, opposite the entrance to the ballroom.[28]

Whilst his chief was in conference with his father, Lieutenant Lord George Lennox, Wellington's 21-year-old aide-de-camp, was hurriedly making for the courtyard when he encountered Captains William Verner and Standish O'Grady of the 7th Regiment of Hussars. They had arrived in Brussels by cabriolet, in time to use the facilities of the Hôtel de la Reine de Suède to dine and to change from their dusty uniforms into the splendour of evening dress. Taking Verner in to his confidence – they had both serve as aides-de-camp to the Duke of Richmond – Lennox informed him 'The Prussians have been attacked and defeated and I am going to order the Duke's horses, who is going off immediately.' Startled by the news, Verner turned to O'Grady, saying 'Let us go into the room, to have it to say we were in the ball room.'

> It is scarcely necessary to say that the room was in the greatest confusion and had the appearance of anything but a ball room. The officers were hurrying away as fast as possible, in order that nothing might prevent them joining their regiments. At this point, Lord Uxbridge came to the door and said 'You gentlemen who have engaged partners had better finish your dance and get to your quarters as soon as you can.'

Turning to his companion, Verner observed, 'Standish, this is no time for dancing. Let us secure a cabriolet without loss of time and be off as soon as we can.' Lord Uxbridge, having conversed at length with Wellington, was not far behind.[29]

Behind the closed door of the Duke of Richmond's study, Wellington exclaimed: 'Napoleon has humbugged me by God, he has gained twenty-four hours' march on me.' Studying the map, Wellington mused over concentration points, distances and intelligence reports and realised that his dispositions would be insufficient to stop the French juggernaut. He must buy himself time to fight another day. Bidding his friend goodnight and avoiding the main entrance Wellington took his leave. It was 2.00 a.m.[30]

The night had been full of drama at Nivelles. The arrival of Major van Limburg-Stirum at midnight had confirmed in de Perponcher-Sedlnitzky's mind the need to reinforce von Sachsen-Weimar at Les Quatre Bras, with elements of General van Bijlandt's brigade. With the Namur road secured by Colonel Jan Grunenbosch's

Jagers, he prepared to set the troops on the march. Towards 1.00 a.m., the Belgians of the 7th Line Battalion, the only unit of the division to recruit in the South Netherlands as it was now styled, passed through the Porte de Mons and reached the Grand'Place, where they piled their arms. Here they found the 27th Jager Battalion formed in closed columns, but also with their arms piled, as well as Stevenaar's artillery, his guns, wagons, horses and men occupying virtually every remaining part of the square. Shortly after this battalion arrived, de Perponcher-Sedlnitzky sent one of van Bijlandt's staff officers, Captain Count van Hogendorp, to summon Colonel de Jongh of the 8th National Militia Battalion, whose command was still bivouacked at the Porte de Soignies. Another aide was sent to the 27th Jager Battalion, with orders to prepare themselves for an immediate departure. As these preparations were being made, an officer arrived from Colonel van Zuylen van Nyeveld, informing him of the discovery of a party of Prussian cavalry whom he had persuaded to place themselves under de Perponcher-Sedlnitzky's orders.[31]

By 1.30 a.m. Colonel de Jongh was back at the Porte de Soignies, having been ordered by General de Perponcher-Sedlnitzky to march his troops through the streets of Nivelles in silence and to join the 27th Jager Battalion. These two battalions, under de Jongh's overall command, were then to proceed to Les Quatre Bras, where they were to be placed under the orders of Prince Bernhard von Sachsen-Weimar. Quietly, the sleeping troops were roused, burdening themselves once more with packs, cartridge pouches, haversacks, bayonets and other accoutrements, before taking up arms and falling into the ranks of the long column. The rue de Mons, Grand'Place and rue de Namur echoed with the sound of tramping feet as the silent troops snaked through sleeping Nivelles and emerged at the Porte de Namur.[32]

Here they found General de Perponcher-Sedlnitzky, who had decided after all to ride for Les Quatre Bras, accompanied by his divisional staff and Major Jan van de Poll and Captain Baron Frederik de Smeth van Duerne, his aides-de-camp. General van Bijlandt would remain, together with the 7th Line Battalion, the 5th and 7th National Militia Battalions and Captain Stevenaar's foot battery of eight 6-pounder guns, guarding Nivelles from any enemy movement by Binche; they would await the head of General Chassé's division, which was expected sometime in the morning. Before he left, de Perponcher-Sedlnitzky had relayed to van Bijlandt his concern that the whole area south of Nivelles might now be unoccupied by Allied forces; should this prove true and the French engage him at Nivelles, van Bijlandt was to defend this point vigorously, but if forced to cede, he was to make for Mont-Saint-Jean, where de Perponcher-Sedlnitzky would join him with the second brigade. As the column of troops moved off, the men of the 7th Line Battalion occupied the former bivouac of the 27th Jager Battalion on the Grand'Place.[33]

As soon as the troops were assembled, de Perponcher-Sedlnitzky assigned the 8th National Militia and 27th Jager Battalions to the care of Colonel de Jongh. The General, with the draft companies of both battalions doubling beside him as his escort, rode off to Les Quatre Bras, where the first faint signs of dawn were starting to appear on the horizon. Close by Hermitage-les-Sept-Douleurs, he encountered

The Battle of Quatre Bras

Colonel Singendonck and the main body of the 7th National Militia Battalion. Mistakenly, the Colonel had believed he was to march from Baulers only as far as the Namur road and there to await further orders. Warning him to be ready to move during the night, de Perponcher-Sedlnitzky directed Singendonck to join the rest of his battalion at the Porte de Namur. At Houtain-le-Val, he encountered a body of fifty Prussian horsemen, belonging to the 4th Regiment of Hussars (1st Silesian) and under the command of Lieutenant Zehelin, who had become detached from Lieutenant-Colonel von Lützow's brigade of reserve cavalry during the withdrawal from Gosselies the previous afternoon. These same cavalry had been provided with food and drink by Colonel van Zuylen van Nyeveld, en route from Nivelles to Les Quatre Bras, who proposed that they take up positions at Houtain-le-Val and place themselves at the disposal of his chief. In the absence of General de Collaert's cavalry, de Perponcher-Sedlnitzky requested Lieutenant Zehelin to accompany him to the crossroads, a proposal that the young officer eagerly accepted. As they progressed down the Namur road, the General gathered in the outlying companies of the 27th Jagers.[34]

At the very hour that Wellington was complaining to the Duke of Richmond of having lost the initiative, General von Alten was working hard to regain it. Towards 1.45 a.m., a courier had clattered into Soignies, bearing the assembly order to the 3rd (British) Infantry Division, which had been immediately forwarded to General Halkett, General von Kielmansegge and Colonel Baron Christian von Ompteda. Shortly before 2.00 a.m., the cavernous vaulted ceiling of the collegiate church of Saint-Vincent at Soignies echoed with the pounding of drums as the 'General' was beaten, preparatory to marching.

In the guttering light of torches and votive candles, the men stirred as sergeants and corporals made their way along the rows of men and roused them from their slumber. As the soldiers buttoned up their coats, shouldered their knapsacks and checked their weapons, Lieutenant Pattison could not help but take a moment to admire their 'Buoyant spirit and earnest desire to meet the enemy'. The men tumbled from the pews, confessionals and choir stalls, gathering up weapons, accoutrements and food, and word was passed to fall in. The 'route' was for Braine-le-Comte.[35]

Halkett's brigade packed the Grand'Place, over 2,300 officers and men being present and fit for duty. At the end of May, the 33rd Regiment of Foot had returned 33 officers and 472 other ranks but was still short of a major, Major John Guthrie having been absent without leave since the 24th of April. Captain William McIntyre would have to oblige in the interim.

The commanding officer, Lieutenant-Colonel William Elphinstone had, however, persuaded Ensign Thain to assume the duties of Adjutant and as he stood on parade, the young man sniffed the air and commented on the fineness of the weather. In common with the other battalions of the brigade, the Colonel had ordered the hospital scoured for malingerers. With almost seventy men in the hospital at Soignies alone, it was imperative that the idle and those of a nervous disposition were not permitted to shirk their duty.[36]

'The suddenness of the danger multiplying its horrors'

To the left of the men from West Yorkshire, Colonel Morice watched the scene from the back of his half-Arab grey mare, whilst his officers were busy inspecting the weapons, ensuring that the flints were secure, that each man had sufficient ammunition and that every frog held a serviceable socket bayonet. Captain Barlow paid particular attention to the state of his men's boots. He had heard that they were to march on Fleurus, which those with maps said must be all of fourteen hours' march away. Sat astride his horse, Ensign Ainslie was grateful that despite being the junior officer and therefore entrusted with the King's Colour, he would at least have a sergeant to carry it for him whilst he rode his horse to the battlefield. In front of the battalion, the commanding officer perhaps reflected on the letter he had written to his father the previous Sunday, whom he had informed 'We are all looking forward to stars and ribbon, some of us perhaps may succeed.' Others, their thoughts far from glory and honours, were in a more reflective mood. Major Watson contemplated the matter-of-fact way in which his daughter had earlier taken leave of him with a handshake and a simple 'Good-bye.'[37]

In the ranks of the 73rd Regiment of Foot was Ensign Thomas Deacon; he had been sharing his quarters with his three young children and his wife, Martha, who was a matter of days from giving birth. He had made arrangements for them to travel with the baggage guard and they had no doubt parted full of anxieties, the husband off to war and the wife abandoned to face her own dangers, alone and in unfamiliar company. The parade came to attention and Captain Walter Crofton, the Major of Brigade, gave the order, 'Right turn!' and against all custom and practice, the brigade arched off the square with its senior regiment – the 30th Regiment of Foot – at the rear of the column. This decision was to have some consequences on the march, which became apparent even as the brigade was filing through the narrow streets. Though Lieutenant-Colonel William Harris of the 73rd Regiment of Foot had received some 'hasty and ill-defined instructions' from General Halkett, concerning the march to Braine-le-Comte, the pace he set was proving to be a slow one.[38]

Almost thirteen kilometres to the north, the candles had burned low in the headquarters of the 1st (British) Infantry Division at Enghien and Colonel Rooke, Captain Fitzgerald and Ensign Cuyler dozed whilst awaiting further developments. The generals had still not returned from Brussels. Perhaps, they surmised, the situation was not as serious as had first been believed. Reality was about to wake them with a start as, shortly after 1.00 a.m., a second orderly arrived. This was it! The division was ordered to move on Braine-le-Comte. Within minutes, the drums were beating to arms, sending officers and men scurrying in all directions, in varying states of undress.[39]

Shortly after the assembly had been beaten, thousands of red-coated soldiers thronged the narrow rue des Capucins, rue d'Argent and rue d'Herinnes. The second battalion of the 2nd Regiment of Foot Guards was the first to assemble and was ready to leave by 2.00 a.m., though no one was keen to march until the officers had returned and first light had started to illuminate the dark sky. The sound of creaking wheels echoed in the dark streets as the drivers of the heavy stores wagons

The Battle of Quatre Bras

and those transporting the patients and equipment of the hospital assembled prior to their departure for Brussels. The second battalion of the 1st Regiment of Foot Guards alone had forty patients in its hospital. Each of these convoys was accompanied by an officer, an assistant surgeon, a senior non-commissioned officer and anywhere between four and ten private soldiers. Everywhere was the sound of activity, the startled inhabitants peering from their windows, as men jostled each other to squeeze into the ranks. As they parted from the people on whom they had been billeted, the soldiers expressed their gratitude and the civilians responded with tears and prayers. Colonel Rooke was completing arrangements for his wife, Selina, to depart for Brussels. In the event that things went badly, she was to head for Antwerp and if necessary, take ship for England. By now, officers had started to return from Brussels in caleches, cabriolets and on horseback, bursting with rumour, romance and recollections of a glittering evening. They were a grand lot, thought Ensign Charles Short of the Coldstream Guards, who was particularly impressed by the ball uniform of Colonel Alexander Woodford, his commanding officer.[40]

In the meantime, at Hoves Colonel Stuart impatiently awaited the arrival of the right wing of his third battalion, which marched into the village towards 3.00 a.m. and halted in the broad square opposite the church. It had taken but a short while to muster the men at Marcq and for them to gather together their meagre possessions. Each had then been issued with ammunition and provisions before being paraded in full marching order. They were led by Lieutenant-Colonel Hon. Horatio Townshend, a twenty-year veteran of the regiment, who had survived the retreat to Corunna in 1809, after a short but disastrous campaign in Portugal and Spain. Under the critical eye of this seasoned campaigner, the five companies had marched for an hour across the dusty byways, crossing the chaussée d'Ath and continuing south-east to Hoves. Arriving to find the remainder of the battalion already assembled, the young soldiers welcomed the order to fall out. Largely ignorant of the events transpiring elsewhere, they must have feared that this was the start of another punishing route march, of the kind that left their feet blistered and bloody inside their ill-fitting shoes.[41]

One officer of the third battalion had more reason than most to be pleased. Marching with Lieutenant-Colonel Henry d'Oyly's company was Ensign Edward Pardoe, who had rejoined the battalion only the previous day. Severely wounded in both arms and taken prisoner at the assault on Bergen-op-Zoom in March of the previous year, he had been found, lying on the floor of the entrance to a French hospital in the fortress, by Ensign Richard Master, who had then kicked up such a fuss among their captors that he was found a bed, treated and later evacuated. Reunited at Hoves, the former messmates would regrettably serve in the campaign in different companies, Master being charged with carrying the battalion's King's Colour. Despite this inconvenience, they agreed immediately that they would mess together, albeit without the services of their former servant, Bowman. As they waited for further orders to arrive, Master chaffed Pardoe over his renowned bad luck. Laughing, they sat in the cool of the dawn, reminisced about their experiences together and exchanged news of the Guards for news of England.[42]

'The suddenness of the danger multiplying its horrors'

As the Guards completed their assembly, another packet arrived at Braine-le-Comte from Brussels. Rubbing his eyes, a weary General de Constant-Rebecque looked at the time; it was nearing 2.30 a.m. He broke the seals, unfolded the stiff paper and skimmed through the contents. The 3rd (British) Infantry Division, already on the march from Soignies to Braine-le-Comte, would subsequently march on Nivelles, whilst the 1st (British) Infantry Division, was to move from Enghien on Braine-le-Comte. Colonel Berkeley and his officers immediately drew up the necessary instructions and within minutes, couriers were heading for Soignies and Enghien, with instructions to intercept the marching infantry and brief their leaders on the change in destination. The Prince had even summarized the new destinations for the 1st, 2nd and 3rd (British) Infantry Divisions; to Braine-le-Comte, Enghien and Nivelles respectively. From the nature of this and the other orders, it was apparent to de Constant-Rebecque that further Allied divisions and the cavalry reserve were also shifting eastwards. There was, however, no further reference to Chassé's and de Perponcher-Sedlnitzky's divisions, both of which were supposed to be at Nivelles and his anxiety remained over this contravention of Wellington's earlier orders. The Prince van Oranje-Nassau had added a note, requiring de Constant-Rebecque to move the Netherlands cavalry division from Haine-Saint-Pierre to the high ground on the northern bank of the Brussels-Charleroi canal at Arquennes. He was also instructed to be prepared to move the headquarters the following day to Nivelles. By 3.00 a.m., he had drafted a letter to de Collaert, requesting him to march with the cavalry on Arquennes and entered it into the Register of Outgoing Correspondence as No. 186, not knowing it was to be the last written order he would issue for four days. With no available staff officers, de Constant-Rebecque entrusted this dispatch to Lieutenant van Kaps of the engineers and turned to the considerable task of making preparations to move the headquarters.[43]

As at Braine-le-Comte, sleep eluded many of those at Brussels. Charlotte Waldie and her sister were roused by a loud knocking on their door at 2.30 in the morning. It was her brother, calling them to rise instantly. Fearing that the French had arrived, Charlotte panicked, her head full of confusion. In seconds, her brother had reassured her, confirming that the troops were under arms and were about to march out against the French. Amongst them was an old family friend, Major Richard Llewellyn of the 28th Regiment of Foot, whose battalion was gathering in the square below.

> We got up with the greatest alacrity and, hastily throwing some clothes about us, flew to see Llewellyn, who was waiting on the stairs. Short and agitated indeed was our meeting under such circumstances. By the light of a candle in my brother's room, we sat down for a few minutes on some boxes, scarcely able to believe our senses, that all this was real and almost inclined to doubt whether it was not a dream, but the din of war which resounded in our ears too painfully convinced us that it was no illusion of phantasy [sic]. We could scarcely even 'Snatch a fearful joy', for not a single moment could we banish from our minds the impression that in a few moments we must part, perhaps for ever, and that this hurried interview might prove our last. We could only

The Battle of Quatre Bras

The 28th Regiment of Foot in square under attack by French lancers. Print after Lady Butler. *Melbourne City Art Gallery, Australia*

gaze intently upon each other, as if to retain a lasting remembrance of the well-known countenance, should we indeed be destined to meet no more. We could only utter incoherent words or disjointed speeches. While he still lingered, we heard his charger, which his servant held in the courtyard below, neighing and pawing the ground, as if impatient of his master's delay and eager to bear him to the field. We bade him farewell and saw him go to battle.[44]

The sky was perceptibly lighter over the treetops of the Bois de Bossu as de Perponcher-Sedlnitzky and his party, escorted by von Zehelin's hussars arrived at Croix-Gilbert towards 3.00 a.m. Passing through the picquet lines and the flickering watch fires of the first battalion of the 2nd Nassau-Usingen Regiment, the General was directed to Colonel von Sachsen-Weimar, who had remained awake at the Ferme des Quatre Bras throughout the night. Relieved at last, that his superior had arrived and would no doubt assume the command, the tired young officer briefed his chief on the arrangements of his brigade. As the two officers toured the outposts, de Perponcher-Sedlnitzky warmly complimented him on the merit of his dispositions, much to von Sachsen-Weimar's pleasure; however, the weakness of the position was evident. Observing the potential of the Bois de Bossu, which he considered to be the key to the position, de Perponcher-Sedlnitzky asked how many troops were assigned to its defence. On hearing that Bergmann's Volunteer Jager Company was occupying the southern end, only supported by two companies from the first battalion of the 2nd Nassau-Usingen Regiment, he suggested that these might be augmented by the remainder of the battalion. Though aware that the strength of the division was limited, he also recommended that von Sachsen-Weimar reinforce and extend his front towards Piraumont, in order to establish a complete chain of outposts between the Bois de Bossu in the west and the Bois de l'Hutte in the east. He suggested that this task might be best suited to the 27th Jager Battalion, which he estimated would arrive at the crossroads shortly.[45]

In contrast to the stillness of the outposts at Les Quatre Bras, the rolling of drums, the sound of muskets on the cobbles and the cacophony of voices in the town of Enghien and the nearby château and park ensured that none of the inhabitants could sleep, but instead leaned from the windows or stood by the roadside, watching the men prepare to depart. Companies were marched from the massive stables of the château and drawn up in the Grand'Place, whilst others poured from their billets and formed up on the Vieux-Marché. Colonel Woodford of the Coldstream Regiment of Foot Guards arrived back at Enghien towards 3.00 a.m., to find that Lieutenant-Colonel James Macdonell, his second-in-command, had taken measures to ensure that his second battalion was ready to march. His fellow ball guests, Lieutenant-Colonels the Hon. Edward Acheson and Henry Wyndham were resplendent in ball dress. Ensign Hon. James Forbes parted from his 17-year-old brother Walter and along with Ensign Hon. John Montagu, rejoined his company. Captain Bowles, lately so sullen and resentful, was still missing and it would be 5.00 a.m. before he rejoined the battalion.[46]

Allowing time for the officers to change, General Byng got his 2nd (British) Infantry Brigade underway a short time afterwards. His column was also preceded by a detachment formed of its light companies and under the orders of Colonel Macdonell of the Coldstream Guards. As well as being a Peninsula veteran, the Colonel had also been present at the battle of Maida on 4 July 1806, where for the first time in the Napoleonic Wars, the British two-deep line formation had proven its superiority over the hitherto-successful French column. As he watched the troops move off, Byng's excitement was surely tempered by anxiety. The brigade comprised the second battalions of the Coldstream and the 3rd Regiments of Foot Guards, both regiments rich in history, but lacking in fighting experience. The ranks had been leavened by drafts of several hundred soldiers from the militia shortly before they were shipped overseas. Though well-trained, these men were less well-equipped and had, as yet, seen little action. Since the brigade was cantoned in the substantial park of the château of Enghien, Byng chose to avoid the congestion of the town itself and had instead marched the brigade south-east, before picking up the chemin Brunehaut, the ancient Roman road to Mons.[47]

By 4.00 a.m., the three battalions of the division quartered in the town had come to attention and formed in column of route, they marched out, ready at last to go to war. In the vanguard were the light companies of the 1st Regiment of Foot Guards, formed into a composite 'Light Battalion', under the command of Lieutenant-Colonel Alexander Fraser, Lord Saltoun. It was a service he had undertaken at Bayonne in 1814, with great success. Following them were the second battalion of the 1st Regiment of Foot Guards, led by Colonel Askew. A short distance beyond the defensive moat, the regiment wheeled to the south, along the chaussée de Soignies and towards the cantonments of its sister battalion at Hoves.[48]

The Battle of Quatre Bras

Whilst Wellington slept undisturbed at Brussels, the Prince van Oranje-Nassau's carriage rattled down the broad chaussée towards Braine-le-Comte, where it arrived at 3.30 a.m. As soon as de Constant-Rebecque heard that his chief had returned, he hurried over to rue Père Damien to see him. The Prince changed his attire for something more practical and his chief-of-staff summarised the intelligence position, briefed him on the orders received and issued in his absence and explained how he had felt obliged to advise General de Perponcher-Sedlnitzky in particular on the disposition of his division. Major van Limburg-Stirum, who had earlier arrived back from Nivelles, confirmed the situation. The Prince's front, de Constant-Rebecque described, was still screened by de Collaert's cavalry, though it would not receive the order to withdraw on Arquennes for about another hour. Chassé was hopefully already on the march for Nivelles, which would release the remaining elements of de Perponcher-Sedlnitzky's division to rejoin their parent formation at Les Quatre Bras. Help was on its way from the west, but the leading British division, von Alten's 3rd, was still some way off. The Prince rapidly realised the importance of the situation and nodded his approval of the action de Constant-Rebecque had taken, especially his efforts to ensure that Les Quatre Bras was reinforced. The news that the French had attacked Frasnes, brought to him earlier by Webster, had reassured him to some extent, that the attack that had caused de Constant-Rebecque such concern was indeed something considerably more than a demonstration; but the Prince still seemed to be labouring under the misapprehension, shared by the Duke of Wellington, that the enemy might make an attempt on Nivelles. Now, it seemed the future of the entire campaign depended on de Perponcher-Sedlnitzky – and on the French.[49]

It was time for action. The Prince instructed de Constant-Rebecque to leave immediately for Les Quatre Bras. As he passed through Nivelles, however, he was to ensure that all the troops remaining there were warned to prepare themselves to march immediately on Les Quatre Bras. The Prince himself would follow closely behind. The Chief-of-Staff spent a few minutes gathering up his papers, before giving instructions to the orderlies concerning the packing and removal of the headquarters, as well as the directions to be given to staff officers returning from the delivery of dispatches. These matters attended to and with all his officers absent, *en mission*, de Constant-Rebecque left alone for Nivelles at 3.45 a.m.[50]

Endnotes

1. Anonymous (Cameron), p. 88. Anonymous (Letters), p. 222. Anonymous (Waterloo Medal Roll), p. 244. Bluth, p. 59. Carter, p. 99. Dalton, pp. 161–2. Mudie (I). Riddock.
2. Anonymous (42nd Regiment), p. 141. Anonymous (Near Observer), pp. 61–2. Anton, p. 186. Cornford and Walker, p. 103. Dalton, p. 158. Alexander Forbes (II), p. 263. Gunn. Wauchope, p. 48.
3. Anonymous (Letters), p. 222–3. Anonymous (Waterloo Medal Roll), p. 311. Robertson, p. 143. Winchester (II).

'The suddenness of the danger multiplying its horrors'

4. Douglas, p. 97.
5. Eaton, p. 19.
6. Stephens. Swiney, pp. 115–6.
7. Clayton.
8. Kincaid (I), p. 311.
9. Richardson, p. 373. Swinton, p. 123.
10. G. Paget (I), pp. 107, 111.
11. Maxwell, p. 13. Miller (II), pp. 138-9. Swinton, p. 123.
12. Mackworth, p. 324. Traupe, p. 15.
13. Vivian.
14. Gardyne, p. 345. Miller (II), p. 138. Swinton, pp. 119, 123–4.
15. Miller (II), pp. 67–8, 139. Robertson, p. 143.
16. Anton, p. 186. Gardyne, pp. 210, 349. Gunn. Robertson, p. 143. Sinclair-Stevenson, p. 39.
17. Cotton, p. 108. Maxwell, p. 13. Miller (II), p. 140. Swinton, p. 122. Traupe, p. 15.
18. J. Harris, p. 439. J. Paget (II), p. 28.
19. Brett-James, p. 41. Miller (II), p. 141. G. Paget (I), p. 112. Swinton, pp. 132–3.
20. Cameron (II).
21. Mackworth p. 324. Miller (II), p. 140. G. Paget (I), p. 112. Young, p. 102.
22. Anonymous (Cameron), p. 88. Anonymous (42nd Regiment), p. 141. Anonymous (Letters), pp. 220, 222-3. Anton, p. 186. Cadell (I), p. 232. Eaton, p. 21. Archibald Forbes, p. 263. Robertson, p. 143. J. Ross (II). Ross-Lewin, p. 253. Simmons (I), pp. 362–3.
23. J. Allan. Anonymous (Cameron), p. 88. Vallence, p. 5.
24. Anton, p. 188. Cameron (I).
25. Arthur, pp. 591-2. de Bas, p. 563. de Bas &c., pp. 410–411, 446. de Constant-Rebecque (I). Dalton, p. 12. Maurice, p. 7. Maxwell, p. 13. von Müffling (II), p. 229. Neumann, p. 415. J. Paget (I), p. 85. Riddock. F. Somerset, p. 7. Swinton, pp. 122, 133. Traupe, p. 15. Young, pp. 100–102, 222.
26. G. Paget (I), p. 112. Young, p. 102.
27. Anonymous (Near Observer) p. 46. J. Harris, p. 440. G. Paget (I), p. 112.
28. J. Harris, p. 445. Swinton, p. 134.
29. Richardson, p. 373. F. Somerset, p. 7. Wildman.
30. Arthur, pp. 591–2. J. Harris, pp. 441, 445–6. Maurice, p. 7. Maxwell, p. 13. G. Paget (I), p. 110. Daniell, p. 132. Stanhope (II), p. 109. Swinton, p. 134. Vivian.
31. de Constant Rebecque (II). de Bas, &c., p.447. de Jongh. Meijer. Scheltens, p. 197. van Zuylen van Nyeveld (II).
32. Grunenbosch. de Jongh. de Perponcher-Sedlnitzky. Starklof, p. 136. van Zuylen van Nyeveld (I), p. 52.
33. de Bas, p. 1332. de Bas &c., p. 447. North, p. 40. de Perponcher-Sedlnitzky. Starklof, p. 136. Wüppermann, p. 89. van Zuylen van Nyeveld (I), pp. 51–2.
34. de Bas &c., p. 447. Hofschröer (I), pp. 179, 370. Hofschröer (II), p. 345. Rem. Starklof, pp. 133–4. van Zuylen van Nyeveld (I), p. 52. van Zuylen van Nyeveld (II).
35. Ainslie, p. 14. Butler, p. 77. Elkington (I), p. 12. Hemingway. Gurwood, p. 472. Lee, p. 226. Morris, p. 67. Myddleton, p. 79. Pattison (II), p. 2. Thain (I). Thain (II).

36. Hemingway. Lee, p. 226. Thain (I). Thain (II).
37. Ainslie, p. 14. Morice, p. 31.
38. Dalton, p. 187. Elkington, p. 12. Lagden and Sly, pp. 52–4. Morris, pp. 69-70.
39. Anonymous (Small Order Book). Aubrey-Fletcher, p. 370. Gurwood, p. 474. Hamilton, p. 15. J. Paget (I), p. 85. Powell. Short. Whitworth, p. 45.
40. Anonymous (Near Observer), p. 56. Hamilton, p. 15. Powell. Rooke (II). Short. Wheeler, p. 168.
41. Anonymous (Outgoing Register). de Bas &c., pp. 444–5. de Constant-Rebecque (I).
42. Eaton, pp. 18–19.
43. de Bas &c., p. 448. de Perponcher-Sedlnitzky. von Sachsen-Weimar (II). Starklof, p. 136. van Zuylen van Nyeveld (I), p. 52.
44. Dalton, p. 107. Miller (II), pp. 62–6. Short.
45. Clay. Dalton, p. 108. Haythornthwaite (III), p. 37. Maurice, p. 8.
46. Anonymous (Britain Triumphant). Anonymous (Near Observer), p. 49. Anonymous (Near Observer), p. 56. Aubrey-Fletcher, pp. 370–1. Dalton, p. 100. Goodinge, p. 44. Hamilton, p. 15. Maurice, p. 8. Saint-John. Short. Whitworth, p. 45.
47. Dalton, pp. 97, 99. F. Hamilton, pp. 13, 15. Powell.
48. Chambers, p. 583. Dalton, pp. 98, 103-4. Master.
49. de Bas, p. 563. de Bas &c., p. 446. de Constant-Rebecque (I). van Limburg-Stirum. Rens, p. 106.
50. de Bas &c., pp. 446–7. de Constant-Rebecque (I).

CHAPTER 6

At Laeken, Lady Caroline Capel and her children had long since gone to bed, when at 3.00 a.m., there came a commotion from the stables and outhouses behind their château, which had been occupied by 300 men of the Brunswick Leib-Battalion. They normally paraded in the courtyard at 6.00 a.m., the drumming causing a considerable nuisance to their civilian neighbours. Rumour had it, however, that the troops were to be moved elsewhere. On hearing the loud roll of the drum and the young Germans breaking into a hymn, Lady Caroline and her eldest daughter Harriet – who had been sleeping in her room – happily concluded that the promised day had arrived and that the Brunswickers were about to march.[1]

Just over eleven kilometres to the west, the earlier assembly order had taken a considerable time to reach the headquarters of the Brunswick artillery at Asse and Major Carl von Moll was still busy turning out the teams for his eight guns and assembling their wagons, limbers, equipment, food and ammunition. Along with Second Captain August Venturini, First Lieutenant Georg Orges and Second Lieutenants Friedrich Bredenschey, Philipp Lemme and Christian Schult, he was trying to rouse, equip, feed and assemble 218 gunners, non-commissioned officers, bombardiers, hornists, farriers, smiths, wheel makers and drivers. A short distance away, it had seemed to Sergeant Langenstrasse that he had hardly laid down when the alarm was sounded. The news spread quickly, orders had arrived for the Brunswick cavalry to assemble near Brussels at daybreak. As he hastily saddled his horse and gathered his kit, the first faint flecks of dawn were illuminating the sky.[2]

From her window in the Hôtel de Flandre, overlooking the Place Royale, Charlotte Waldie could see, by the faint twilight of the same dawn, the confusion and tumult of the scene below. The city was alive with soldiers:

All was 'hurry skurry for the field.' Officers were looking in vain for their servants. Servants running in pursuit of their masters. Baggage wagons were loading, bât horses preparing, trains of artillery harnessing. And amidst the clanking of horses' hoofs, the rolling of heavy carriages, the clang of arms, the sounding of bugles and the neighing of chargers, we distinctly heard, from time to time, the loud, deep-toned word of command, while the incessant din of hammers nailing 'gave dreadful note of preparation'.[3]

The Battle of Quatre Bras

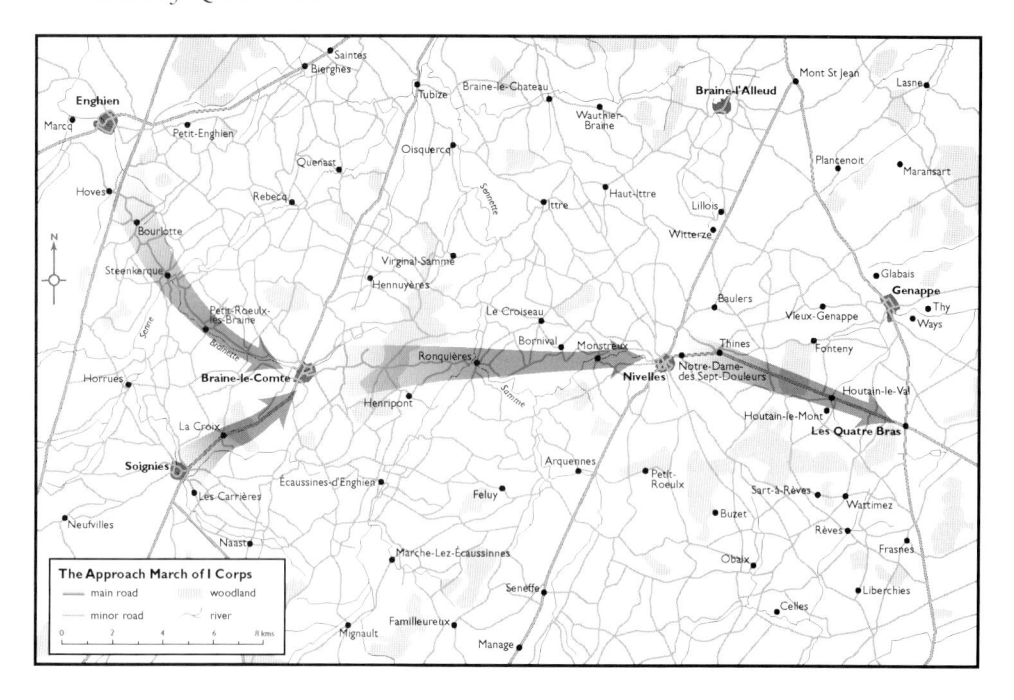

Lieutenant Hope of the 92nd Regiment of Foot was with his battalion at the northern end of the rue Royale. They seemed to be an island of calm, discipline and order in a sea of panic. On hearing the news of Napoleon's approach and the impending departure of the garrison, the inhabitants

> ... became greatly alarmed; and although many of them expressed themselves satisfied with regard to their safety, whilst a Wellington and a Blücher were between them and the enemy; still they could not banish from their countenances the look of despair.[4]

Major Thomas Rogers was overseeing the assembly of his brigade of 9-pounders. 'Boot and saddle' had turned the men out and with the help of Lieutenant Henry Dunnicliffe, recently attached from the reserve artillery, provisions were issued and stuffed into the haversacks and rolled hay strapped to the horses. Officers inspected their divisions, bât horses were packed and made ready and the shoes and harness of the horses were checked and adjusted and checked again. All was bustle. The commissary was off somewhere, trying to sort out the wagons.[5]

It was approaching 4.00 a.m. when another staff officer, Lieutenant Jackson, entered Brussels after a leisurely ride back from Ninove, during which he had been gainfully occupied in directing officers returning from the ball, to their parent units. He trotted through the rue Marché aux Herbes and rue de la Madeleine, before climbing the steep rue Montagne de la Cour and entering the Louis XVI splendour of the Place Royale. He arrived to find a large number of troops from the 5th (British) Infantry Division in line, stretching from the Place Royale, along rue Royale, as far as the rue de la Loi and beyond. The park itself and the rue de Belle-Vue were clogged with baggage vehicles, artillery pieces, caissons and horses.[6]

From her third floor window, Charlotte Waldie studied the scene below:

> Numbers were taking leave of their wives and children, perhaps for the last time and many a veteran's rough cheek was wet with the tears of sorrow. One poor fellow, immediately under our windows, turned back again and again, to bid his wife farewell and to take his baby once more in his arms and I saw him hastily brush away a tear with the sleeve of his coat, as he gave her back the child for the last time, wrung her hand and ran off to join his company, which was drawn up on the other side of the Place Royale.[7]

General Kempt inspected both brigades of the division. Despite Wellington's desire that General Picton should assume the command as soon as possible, it made sense that Kempt organise its departure from Brussels. Picton would join it later in the morning. In the Place Royale, facing the Hôtel de Flandre, was the 95th Regiment of Foot, followed on its left by the 28th, 79th and 32nd Regiments of his own 8th (British) Infantry Brigade. As he progressed into the rue Royale, he joined General Pack and his 9th (British) Infantry Brigade. Passing the 44th, 42nd and

Lieutenant-General Sir Thomas Picton. Sir William Beechey.
Wellington Museum, Apsley House, London

1st Regiments of Foot, he eventually came to the Gordon Highlanders – the 92nd Regiment of Foot – at the head of which, Colonel Cameron saluted as his battalion presented arms.[8]

Lieutenant Jackson was stirred by the sight of the splendid division and reined in his horse at the Hôtel Bellevue at No. 9, Place Royale, to await the termination of the ceremony. Above him, the guests of Monsieur Louis de Proft were lining the windows and balconies. Business had not been so brisk since Prince Louis-Joseph de Bourbon-Condé had taken rooms, accompanied by his son Louis-Henri, Duke de Bourbon and grandson, the ill-fated Louis-Antoine, Duke d'Enghien. They had been accompanied by King Louis XVI's brother, Charles-Philippe, Count d'Artois, Marie-Antoinette's First Lady-in-Waiting, Princess de Lamballe, the dashing Swedish Count Axel Fersen and a host of French aristocrats, all fleeing from the terror of 1789. To the right, the Hôtel de Grande-Bretagne, the property of Baron de Aguilar was equally crowded by military and civilian onlookers, surveying the spectacle from this magnificent amphitheatre.[9]

When Kempt gave the signal, the commanding officers in turn barked the order to form sub-divisions. In the ranks of the Gordons, the officers were mindful of the regimental order issued by Colonel Cameron exactly a week earlier:

> It is to be perfectly understood that when any word of command or other caution is given, which is intended should be passed along the line, that if it is not done by a mounted officer, it is to be done solely by the officers or non-commissioned officers commanding companies, sub-divisions or sections, and never upon any account or under any pretence is it to be done by the men in the ranks.[10]

As the order was passed to No. 6 Company of the 79th Regiment of Foot, it was drummed by Thomas McDonald. The first sub-division pivoted on Ensign Archibald Cameron, whilst Captain James Campbell brought up the right of the second. Lieutenants John Thompson and Donald Cameron took up their positions behind the centre of each sub-division respectively. The column halted, eighteen men abreast, the remaining companies filling the breadth of the rue Royale.[11]

Somewhere close to the church of St. Jacques, the command 'Quick March' set the green-jacketed and black-accoutred Rifles in motion at 4.00 a.m., with Colonel Barnard in the van. As they moved off they were followed by the 28th Regiment of Foot, proudly sporting their 'stovepipe' shakos, ornamented at the rear with a small diamond-shaped badge to commemorate their glorious resistance at Alexandria, fourteen years earlier. Mistaking the 79th for the 42nd Regiment of Foot, Lieutenant Jackson observed them, 'Marching so steadily that the sable plumes of their bonnets scarcely vibrated', and was impressed with the theatrical aspect of the full kilted dress. As he watched the troops file past, Jackson noted the contrast between those wearing, 'The garb of old Gaul', and the 32nd Regiment of Foot, following behind, who had something of a mean appearance in their low, 'Belgic' shakos, ill-fitting red coatees and tattered grey trousers. Though not the most glamorous of soldiers, the ranks of the regiment from Cornwall contained some very tough old warriors, such as Corporal James Jennett, who in the space of seven years, had fought at Roliça, Vimeiro, Corunna, Salamanca, the Pyrenees, Nivelle, Nive, Orthes and Toulouse.[12]

Lieutenant Simmons, marching with 95th Regiment of Foot, was surprised at the number of people who had come to see the army leave, but for many Bruxellois, the tranquillity of the preceding weeks and months had brought them close to the soldiers. The troops passed through the Porte de Namur and marched towards the Forêt de Soignies; it was a beautiful summer's morning and as the sun slowly rose above the horizon to the east, it peeped through the trees and dappled the roadway. Private Costello and his comrades:

> Were merry as crickets, laughing and joking with each other, and at times pondered in their minds what all this fuss, as they called it, could be about; for even the old soldiers could not believe the enemy was so near.[13]

As the Rifles disappeared through the gates of the city, Colonel Nixon ordered the fife and drum band of the 28th Regiment of Foot to strike up 'The Young May Moon' and as the men sang, the words seemed prophetic:

> Then awake! The heavens look bright, my dear,
> 'tis never too late for delight, my dear;
> and the best of all ways
> to lengthen our days
> is to steal a few hours from the night, my dear!

Close behind, the men of the Cameron Highlanders were in similar high spirits, chattering away to each other as they followed the regimental band, which was playing 'Loudon's bonnie woods and braes'.[14]

Unable to sleep, Lady Dalrymple-Hamilton rose at 4.00 a.m. and went to the window of the house overlooking the park that she and her husband had leased. It was a fine morning. The men of the 44th Regiment of Foot in the street below, 'Looked pretty well fagged, having been accoutred since twelve'; they had only just completed drawing rations and ammunition. In contrast, the men of the 42nd Regiment of Foot were in high spirits. They marched past her window with their pipes skirling jaunty flourishes and the drummers pounding out the cadence of 'Hieland laddie', to the rapturous shouts of the surrounding multitude. As they passed the city's walls, few would have imagined the horror that lay ahead. At the tail of the column, the 92nd Regiment of Foot eventually moved off, following the remainder of the brigade. Sergeant Robertson and the other men of the regiment gave the inhabitants three farewell cheers, which the civilian population returned, 'Very sorrowful, thinking that many of us would never return'.[15]

Captain von Rettberg's 2nd (Hanoverian) Brigade of Foot Artillery was also off to war in place of Captain von Braun's company. Having been at Ostend with the artillery of the King's German Legion until the end of February, von Rettberg had been given command of the newly raised battery which was destined to join General Colville's 4th (British) Infantry Division. He had subsequently marched the battery from Namur to Brussels a few days before, but instead of receiving a route for Oudenaarde, orders had arrived during the night for him to join the 5th (British) Infantry Division which was due to march south in the early hours of 16 June. A vastly experienced soldier, von Rettberg had joined the Legion in 1804 and served in Hanover, the Baltic and throughout the Peninsular War; he was looking forward to putting his new command through its paces.[16]

The noise of the division moving off did not disturb Wellington, who slept on, to be awoken at 4.30 a.m. by a visitor from the frontier. It was General von Dörnberg, who had left Mons at 7.00 p.m. the evening before, faithful to Wellington's instruction not to allow himself to be encircled and taken prisoner. Rumour had it that von Dörnberg's erstwhile employer, Prince Jérôme Bonaparte, was with the enemy army and it was therefore safe to assume that there was still a price on von Dörnberg's head. The news from the frontier was reassuring; the Mons road remained secure. Wellington confided to the General that he thought there would probably be a battle that day, briefed him on the order he had issued the night before and asked him to join Picton's division at Waterloo. The Duke himself would follow on behind.[17]

To the south-west, the third battalion of the 1st Regiment of Foot Guards was assembled in the square at Hoves, when its Light Company and that of the second battalion arrived, followed closely behind by the remainder of its sister battalion. Colonel Stuart immediately had his men brought to attention and, as General Maitland passed with the remainder of the brigade, his battalion followed on behind, taking the road towards Bourlotte. The clear sky, illuminated by the rising sun, promised more fine weather, which hopefully would not be wasted on a punishing field day.[18]

Farther to the south, on the sector of the frontier guarded by Chassé's division, all had been quiet until 1.15 a.m., when Captain Nepveu arrived at Chassé's headquarters, bearing de Constant-Rebecque's note of 11.30 p.m. Rising immediately, Chassé had sent a messenger to recall the 6th National Militia Battalion from Trivières and Strépy and another to the 17th National Militia Battalion at Thieu; they were to march on Baume. Another courier was sent to Colonel Detmers and General d'Aubremé at Baume, to inform them of these orders and instruct them to assemble their respective brigades with immediate effect. The division would not move off until it was complete and the crossings over the Haine destroyed. Towards 3.45 a.m. the last men had marched into the encampment and the thirteen battalions set off. It would be a long march of twenty kilometres and already, despite the cool of the early morning, the clear skies warned of hot weather – and perhaps hot work – to come.[19]

Towards 5.00 a.m., the two battalions that de Perponcher-Sedlnitzky had set in motion from Nivelles in the early hours reached the crossroads at Les Quatre Bras. On his arrival, Colonel de Jongh learned from the officers commanding the picquets that General de Perponcher-Sedlnitzky had ridden in over an hour earlier. Having halted his own troops, he sent forward an officer to find the General and request orders for their deployment. Shortly afterwards, de Jongh's messenger returned, with instructions from von Sachsen-Weimar, to march the 27th Jager Battalion into the front line, which he was informed was in the direction of the Ferme de Gemioncourt, an imposing cluster of brick and stone buildings and walls, a little distance from the chaussée. Here, it was to take up a position to the left of the Charleroi road. The mood in Colonel Grunenbosch's battalion was enthusiastic; a sense not shared by the men of Major von Normann's second battalion, posted on the high ground on the opposite side of the highway. Perhaps as these Germans watched their young Dutch allies march up, the veterans of Mesa de Ibor, Medellin and Talavera pitied their exuberance. No doubt the next 24 hours would temper it somewhat. The Nassauers had been on the alert for much of the previous day, a tension which had firstly been replaced by the rush of adrenalin that combat brings, followed by the sense of fatigue when the danger passes. Nor was the mood any better in the third battalion of the 2nd Nassau-Usingen Regiment, which Grunenbosch was to relieve. The excitement of the previous day and the boredom of a long and irksome night in the picquet lines and outposts had left the men exhausted. The relieving battalion deployed along the heights of Gemioncourt – to the east of Bijleveld's guns – with picquets posted on the heights of Lairalle to the south, from where they could observe the Bois de l'Hutte.[20]

Hardly had Grunenbosch completed these arrangements when another order arrived, this time from de Perponcher-Sedlnitzky, instructing him to extend his lines farther east. Bearing in mind the nature of the task and that it required adaptability and initiative, Grunenbosch decided to detach his two flanquer companies, comprising his most experienced and best-trained troops. The first company, the Carabiniers, was commanded by his senior company commander, Captain Eichholtz, whilst the sixth, led by Captain de Crassier, was highly proficient in skirmishing. Eichholtz was instructed to keep a careful watch on the French and if necessary, to use musketry to drive off any hostile patrols or incursions. The light infantrymen moved off towards the growing daylight and took up a position in the fields farther to the east, with picquets thrown forward towards the hamlet of Piraumont. Back at the crossroads, Colonel de Jongh discovered he was not to play an immediate part in the defence, but was to remain in reserve to the north of the crossroads, where he marched the grateful men of the 8th National Militia Battalion into a temporary bivouac in a clover field to the north of the hamlet. At seemingly every point of the compass around Les Quatre Bras, horses and men were stirring, yawning and stretching and the pungent smell of dung, stale sweat and woodsmoke lingered in the still morning air.[21]

Across the whole of southern Belgium, troops were on the march. Shortly before 5.00 a.m., the long column of the 3rd (British) Infantry Division was approaching Braine-le-Comte and its commander took the opportunity to visit the corps headquarters; though to his mild disappointment, he had found only junior officers and orderlies making arrangements for its removal. The Prince van Oranje-Nassau and his Netherlands and British staff had all, it seemed, ridden for Nivelles. General von Alten was, however, largely unconcerned. His column had been intercepted by a courier from Brussels shortly after 2.00 a.m., bearing Wellington's supplementary dispatch; the troops were to follow their chief and move on Nivelles.[22]

When the division arrived at Braine-le-Comte, orders were given for the regimental baggage and heavy stores to continue north to Hal, while the 73rd Regiment of Foot – still in the vanguard – left the Grand'Place and town behind by way of the rue du Pont and passed through Croix Huard and Long Jour; both tiny hamlets, well shuttered for the night. Not knowing how close the French might be, Colonel Harris decided to deploy a party in advance to guard against unexpected encounters. The cadence, already slow, became a crawl and the long column proceeded like a human accordion, bunching and stretching along the chaussée. It had taken three hours to march nine kilometres. As they entered the Bois de La Houssière, the light was not yet strong enough to fully illuminate the tangle of tracks and minor roads, which proved sufficient to lead the battalion astray, taking a more circuitous route than intended. The soldiers cursed the day that officers had been given maps. The wood seemed to stretch on forever, with the only consolation being that all around them, scarlet and green-coated bodies of men were flowing steadily in the same direction; east.[23]

Despite the anxiety of the commanding officers, the subalterns were in much better humour. In the ranks of the 33rd Regiment of Foot, Lieutenant Pattison was very excited, enjoying jokes which he felt only soldiers in similar circumstances would have indulged in and speculating widely on what might happen during the forthcoming battle. In a display of spectacular distaste, Lieutenant James Hart, his brother officer in the Grenadier Company, turned to him and said, 'Pat, you will be going to ground with your teeth uppermost before night!' Hart had been with him at the storming of Bergen-op-Zoom, the previous year, when he had shouted, 'Well Jamie, this is a glorious achievement. We shall all have medals.' The medals had not come and perhaps warfare had not proven so glamorous after all. Whether surprised by the comment or sobered by the prospect, Pattison quietly replied, 'Take care of yourself Jamie.'[24]

Towards 5.00 a.m., Lieutenant van Kaps of the Engineer Staff arrived at the hamlet of Haine-Saint-Pierre, now filled with 3,400 carabiniers, light dragoons and hussars. He had ridden in the wake of Captain van Heinecken, who, at 2.00 a.m. had passed on de Constant-Rebecque's 11.15 p.m. order for the cavalry to assemble in rear of Haine-Saint-Pierre. Roused for the second time that morning, General de Collaert immediately ordered 'boots and saddles'. Hurriedly dressing, he sent for his chief-of-staff, Lieutenant-Colonel Arend-Johann Hoynck van Papendrecht and instructed him to send word to his three brigade commanders: Major-Generals Trip, de Ghigny and van Merlen to move on Baume. Additional couriers were sent to Captains Petter and Geij van Pittius, to assemble their respective half-batteries of horse artillery and to ensure that all equipment, ammunition wagons, horses and men were ready to move at a moment's notice. His division would, over the following hours, be the fragile screen covering the slow withdrawal to Arquennes.[25]

Awaiting the arrival of Chassé's division, General van Bijlandt was still at Nivelles with the 7th Line Battalion, the 5th and 7th National Militia Battalions and Stevenaar's artillery, anxiously awaiting instructions and reinforcements. General Chassé, even if he was marching his men as hard as he had in the defence of France in 1814, would not arrive for some considerable time. At 4.45 a.m., he was joined by de Constant-Rebecque, who had ridden hard along the winding lanes that traversed the steep valley of the river Sennette. Halting briefly, the Swiss chief-of-staff passed on the verbal order of the Prince and instructed him to have the troops assembled in readiness to leave for Les Quatre Bras.[26]

General van Bijlandt immediately sent word to Major Cornelius van Opstall, commanding the division's artillery, to prepare Stevenaar's brigade of foot artillery, most of which was already gathered in the Grand'Place. They were to be put in marching order, which required all superfluous vehicles and stores to be sent off, under guard, to the rear. In the meantime, the 5th National Militia Battalion, assembled at the Porte de Namur and the 7th National Militia Battalion, guarding the Porte de Charleroi, were also assembled and the tired young infantrymen busied themselves with packs, haversacks, cartridge pouches, bayonets and other accoutrements. Fires were doused and cooking pots overturned; breakfast would have to wait. As the two generals discussed the situation, Captain Nepveu entered the market place and threaded his way through the bivouac of the 7th Line Battalion, whose men were already being roused by their drummers. The staff officer was on his way back from delivering de Constant-Rebecque's earlier message to General Chassé and was able to reassure both the Chief-of-Staff and van Bijlandt that the instructions for Chassé to relieve his remaining troops at Nivelles had been safely delivered and that even as he was leaving, the bivouac at Baume was being broken up and the first troops set on the march.[27]

Having satisfied himself that all was in motion, de Constant-Rebecque ordered Nepveu to accompany him, and having remounted his horse, the two men galloped out of the town on the chaussée de Namur. Djan-Djan, the gilded Jacquemart in the south tower of the collegiate church of Sainte-Gertrude was striking 5.00 a.m., when the Prince van Oranje-Nassau, mounted his favourite grey horse, Vexy, clattered up the chemin de Braine-le-Comte accompanied by his glittering entourage, which included no less than fourteen adjutants and aides-de-camp. The Prince himself was resplendent in a dark blue pelisse, trimmed with black fur and heavily decorated with gold bullion embroidery and braid. Even by his usual standards, this excitable young man was brimming with confidence and energy. The cavalcade came to a halt and General van Bijlandt hurried across to pay his compliments. The young Prince listened as the General briefed him on the steps that he and de Constant-Rebecque had taken. Concerned, however, at the prospect of completely abandoning Nivelles, the Prince changed his mind and decided that the 7th Line Battalion would be left behind, to occupy the town until reinforcements arrived. The drummers accordingly stopped beating the assembly and the muttering infantry slumped back into their places. The Prince instructed van Bijlandt to get the two militia battalions and the artillery underway and eager to press on for Les Quatre Bras, departed shortly afterwards.[28]

The Battle of Quatre Bras

Within minutes, Stevenaar's brigade was assembled in column, the vehicles and their teams snaking along the edge of the large square, the non-commissioned officers barking instructions to the drivers and gunners. The Captain would take his six 6-pounder guns, two howitzers, eight artillery caissons and two spare gun carriages to Les Quatre Bras. In addition – and further to the request received the previous evening from Prince Bernhard – eight additional caissons, each packed with infantry ammunition, were attached to the column. The remaining vehicles, including the mobile forge, the tool wagons and supply fourgons were assembled under Second Lieutenant Friquelwat, who was directed to remove them to Mont-Saint-Jean, where he was to await further orders. A short distance away, another young officer, Lieutenant Barre of the 5th National Militia Battalion, was formed up on the chaussée, along with his men. This battalion would lead the column, whilst Colonel Singendonck's 7th National Militia Battalion would provide the escort for the artillery. General van Bijlandt spoke briefly to Colonel van den Sanden, commanding the 7th Line Battalion, explaining that he was not to leave Nivelles until the arrival of the vanguard of Chassé's division relieved him, or he was driven from it by the French. Satisfied that everything was in order, van Bijlandt and his men started the long climb out of the town, shortly after 5.30 a.m.[29]

Twenty-five kilometres to the west, the early morning sun was shining on the 1st (British) Infantry Division, as it passed through shuttered and sleepy hamlets on the winding, dusty roads, before descending the gentle hill into the valley of the River Senne and passing through the village of Steenkerque. Though probably of no significance to the vast majority of the men in the ranks, those officers who had studied military history or those with an interest in the origins of the Guards Regiments, might have realised its importance. Here, almost 123 years ago, a British army, under the command of another William of Orange, had been narrowly defeated by a French army under Maréchal the Duke de Luxembourg. Some of the staff officers, riding ahead of the column to identify and mark the route may even have noticed the crossed swords symbol on their Ferraris and Capitaine maps. Who would be favoured by Fate today?[30]

Whilst the Guards enjoyed the history lessons in the sunshine, by 5.30 a.m., Picton's division had been consumed within the Forêt de Soignies, with the 92nd Regiment of Foot bringing up the rear. Sergeant Robertson was impressed by the remarkable height of the trees and the width of the road, but less so by the going underfoot. The beginning of the month had been rather rainy and there had been a thunderstorm on 12 June that had saturated the ground; shaded by the trees, the sun had not yet been able to dry it out. The road had also been churned up by the tramping feet of the seven preceding battalions, to the extent that his battalion had to diverge to its right and left several times to avoid the worst of the quagmire; but mud was shortly to become the last of their concerns. As the regiment approached Petite Espinette, towards 7.00 a.m., for the first time they encountered evidence that this was no mere brigade day:

'We suspected treachery on the part of the foreigners'

We met a number of wagons conveying Prussian soldiers who had been wounded the day before, who told us that the French were driving all before them and that we were greatly needed. As we are too apt to entertain bad opinions, we suspected treachery on the part of the foreigners and that we should have to retreat, for we did not credit much what the Prussians told us of the affair.[31]

Meanwhile, at Laeken, Lady Capel and her daughters had slept on, undisturbed. The regular 6.00 a.m. reveille of the small Brunswick detachment had not sounded. Along with the remainder of the Leib-Battalion, they had been roused from their billets in Ganshoren, Sint-Agatha-Berchem and Sint-Jans-Molenbeek, small villages to the west of Brussels. After a short march of less than five kilometres, they had assembled on the Allée Verte, with the Hussar Regiment, the Avantgarde-Battalion, the 1st Line, the 2nd Light and the 3rd Line Battalions. In some cases, however, the order to assemble had arrived after the time at which the troops were supposed to be in Brussels; 5.00 a.m. had come and gone. Sergeant Langenstrasse and the 4th Company of the Hussar Regiment was present, as was Andreas Möreke, originally from the village of Ölper, north-west of Brunswick. He had been stood to arms since midnight. Where, though, was the artillery? Had the 1st and 3rd Light Battalions become lost? What of the 2nd Line Battalion? Was it still at Sint-Stevens-Woluwe and Sint-Lamberts-Woluwe? How had the Uhlan squadron become detached? As the staff officers marshalled the battalions and sent out orderlies to locate the missing troops and accelerate their march, the Duke von Braunschweig-Lüneburg pondered his options. His instructions were to move through Brussels and to march to Waterloo, where he was to await further orders. Burning to be at the French, he decided to leave a few officers to direct the absent detachments and to press on with the troops at hand. At 6.00 a.m., at the head of his infantry, he had given orders to move off. Now, half an hour later, the Allée Verte was jammed by the marching Brunswick battalions and squadrons. Normally one of the most fashionable promenades of Brussels, the mile-long broad walks on either side of the carriageway were devoid of the beaux and belles of the post-prandial hour. Instead, the road and its verges were filled with the soldiers of the Brunswick Division. Though the sun was not yet high in the sky, the shade provided by the double avenue of trees was most welcome. On the opposite side of the road, the peasants watched their progress laconically, their animals grazing quietly in the lush meadows.[32]

Farther south, General de Constant-Rebecque and Captain Nepveu had enjoyed an uneventful ride along a similar, wide chaussée; that from Nivelles to Les Quatre Bras. As they entered Houtain-le-Val, they passed the newly-built Ferme de Pontaille, its whitewashed buildings still occupied by a handful of men from the first battalion of the 2nd Nassau-Usingen Regiment, along with their wives and camp followers. The pretty village was dominated by the sandstone château, set in pasture, with the imposing red-brick church tower rising behind it. Pressing on, they reached Les Quatre Bras shortly before 6.00 a.m.[33]

Hard on their heels, the Prince van Oranje-Nassau and his staff arrived shortly afterwards and, for the second time that morning, control of the modest forces and all

The Battle of Quatre Bras

the anxieties that went with that command, passed to a superior officer. For the first time in the campaign, the four senior Netherlands and Nassau officers were united. Turning to de Constant-Rebecque, de Perponcher-Sedlnitzky and von Sachsen-Weimar, the Prince asked them to accompany him in an inspection of the division's positions. As they trotted down the Charleroi road, he congratulated von Sachsen-Weimar on the steps he had taken to defend the position and on his personal conduct during the previous day. As the divisional commander, de Perponcher-Sedlnitzky assumed responsibility for briefing the Prince on the intelligence of the enemy and the disposition of the troops. Those present who had spent the night worrying about the isolated position they were taking measures to defend, were no doubt greatly reassured when the Prince, shortly afterwards, announced that they were 'soon to be supported by a part of the English army'. The mood of the group brightened by this revelation, they arrived at the summit of the heights of Gemioncourt, where they drew rein. For the first time, de Constant-Rebecque and the Prince van Oranje-Nassau had a clear view of the enemy position and the corresponding disposition that his own officers had made. General de Constant-Rebecque noted that:

> The enemy was with his right at the Bois de l'Hutte and his left at the Ferme du Grand-Pierrepont. The small Netherlands posts had their right at the Bois de Bossu, passed the road in front of the Ferme de Gemioncourt and extended east, as far as the hamlet of Piraumont and the étang Materne.'[34]

The earlier firing had largely died down, though to the west of the road, some of the skirmishers popped away at each other when the picquets got edgy or when the patrols strayed too close to the opposing lines. The Prince van Oranje-Nassau insisted on riding the length of the picquet line, beyond which enemy foragers were a short distance away busy kindling fires for their breakfast, unaware of the scrutiny of the royal observer. It was clear to him that for the time being at least, soup was a priority over skirmishing on the part of the French. Beyond these scattered groups of men, substantial bodies of lancers and chasseurs à cheval could be seen amongst the high crops, though if a significant mass of infantry was present, it could not be distinguished in and amongst the houses and neighbouring woods. Discussing the situation with de Perponcher-Sedlnitzky, he stated emphatically that the position was to be not only held but, perhaps sensing that there was an opportunity to regain some of the ground that had been lost the previous evening, it was to be extended once again towards the south. As long as they took care not to provoke the French into a full-blooded counter-attack, a lively skirmish would perhaps create the impression amongst the enemy that Wellington's main army was now in the vicinity.[35]

Colonel Grunenbosch was ordered to push two companies of the 27th Jager Battalion forward and to make an attempt to seize the heights to the south of the Ferme de Lairalle. If successful, this manoeuvre would secure a position from which any attempt on the part of the enemy to drive up the road towards Piraumont and outflank the Prince's position by the east, could be blocked. Deploying in extended order, the line of light infantrymen slowly passed over the low ground between the two ridges and crossed the small du Pré des Queues stream. As they moved through the fields of high wheat and rye, they flushed out startled pheasants, partridges and the occasional French soldier. Isolated outposts were driven back at bayonet point, their picquets firing shots to alert their sleeping comrades. Before the French had the opportunity to establish a line of resistance, the Jagers had reached the crest of the heights of Lairalle, below which they could see French soldiers pouring out of the barns and sheds of the farm of the same name and forming up in companies in the pasture.[36]

The Netherlands Jagers had continued their advance and the distance between the two opposing bodies of infantry closed rapidly, until their lines disappeared in a cloud of smoke and flame as they engaged in a lively fire fight. The momentum was with the Jagers and they drove the French back over chemin du Piraumont. Whilst the infantry continued to fire at each other, Lieutenant von Zehelin's Silesian hussars executed several effective charges on bodies of French cavalry, who were thrown back in exchange for the loss of four men and thirteen horses.[37]

Meanwhile, in the centre and to the west, Colonel von Sachsen-Weimar judged that the second battalion of the 2nd Nassau-Usingen Regiment was the most familiar with the terrain on account of its engagement the previous evening. Sending Major van Limburg Stirum to Major von Normann, he ordered forward two companies of skirmishers, followed shortly afterwards by the remainder of the battalion. He was to push south, extending the front along the edge of the Bois de Bossu and if possible, advance as far as Petit-Pierrepont, just over a kilometre from Frasnes. After a brief exchange of musketry and a few rounds from Bijleveld's troop, the Nassauers succeeded in forcing the enemy cavalry vedettes to give ground and eventually the battalion found itself back at the position it had occupied the previous evening. Major von Normann detailed one company to establish itself at the Balcan, whilst three more occupied the open ground between this plateau and the Ferme du Grand-Pierrepont. The remaining two companies occupied the edge of the Bois de Bossu, with picquets posted at the Ferme du Petit-Pierrepont.[38]

Towards 6.30 a.m., the Prince van Oranje-Nassau rode up to the position occupied by the horse battery and on being presented to Captain Bijleveld, expressed his 'Special contentment with his performance of the previous day and of the measures taken, which had prevented the enemy from taking control of Les Quatre Bras'. In light of the new positions occupied by the infantry, he ordered the redeployment of the battery. Flushed with pride, the gunners hurriedly stowed all the rammers, sponges, buckets, ammunition and trail spikes, before limbering up. Word was sent for the alarm guns to return and when they had, Lieutenant Wasseroth de Vincy brought the three 6-pounders forward to the high ground of the Balcan plateau and unlimbered them to the east of the Charleroi road, where they commanded an excellent field of fire over Frasnes. Following closely behind, Lieutenant Dibbetz directed his teams to drag the two howitzers into the field to the west of the road, where they rapidly made them ready for action. A short while later, the Prince van Oranje-

Nassau ordered that the whole battery be moved to the west of the road, the right of the gun line linking with the left of the second battalion of the 2nd Nassau-Usingen Regiment. Lieutenant Koopman's three 6-pounders would take ground on the chemin Bati-Saint-Bernard, in the angle between the Namur and Charleroi roads. From here they would be able to counter any frontal attack, or any flanking movement from the east. While the train teams and '*pourvoyeurs*' hauled the ammunition vehicles into the lee of the ridge, some two hunded metres in the rear, the gunners busied themselves with preparing their pieces and stockpiling sufficient round shot and canister cartridges. Elsewhere, First Lieutenant Jacobus van der Hoeven and the men of the artillery withdrew all the superfluous vehicles and brought them off safely to the park in rear of the Ferme des Quatre Bras. As the infantry, cavalry and artillery settled into their new positions, the small skirmishes gradually diminished into an uneasy ceasefire.[39]

The gunfire had not disturbed the repose of Colonel Frazer, who awoke to the early sunshine of what promised to be, 'A beautiful morning', having slept very soundly during the remainder of the night. He washed, dressed and breakfasted, following which, he sent his Staff Adjutant, Lieutenant William Bell, over to Colonel Wood's quarters to check whether the army was to move. A short while later, the messenger returned and Frazer wrote down the news in a continuation of the letter to his wife:

> I have just learned that the Duke moves in half an hour. Wood thinks to Waterloo, which we cannot find on the map: this is the old story over again. I have sent Bell to Delancey's office, where we shall learn the real name, &c. The whole place is in a bustle. Such a jostling of baggage, of guns, and of wagons. It is very useful to acquire a quietness and composure about all these matters; one does not mend things by being in a hurry. Adieu! I almost wonder I can write so quietly. But nothing can be done today. My horse is ready when the signal for mounting shall be given.[40]

Unlike Frazer, many soldiers on both sides had been mounted for several hours. At Frasnes, the French had at first seemed content to remain in the positions to which they had been forced by the Prince van Oranje-Nassau's earlier offensive reconnaissance, but their skirmishers had become progressively more adventurous and were proving to be an increasing threat for the Prince and his staff, who remained in the front line. Parties of patrolling lancers, their eyes drawn to the gleam of bullion and braid, had galloped forward in turn, fired off their carbines and galloped away to reload beyond pistol range. Concerned for the safety of the Prince, de Constant-Rebecque pleaded with him not to uselessly expose himself to the danger of death or wounding and contrary to his natural instincts, the Prince eventually consented to this request and pulled back a short distance to the rear and dismounted. Giving the order to de Perponcher that the troops were to avoid provoking the French further and were to cease firing, he sat down on a patch of grass and rested.[41]

'We suspected treachery on the part of the foreigners'

The Prince van Oranje-Nassau leads the 5th National Militia Battalion into action. Print after Hoynck van Papendrecht. See page 202. (Author's collection)

Shortly afterwards, Major von Brunneck, a Prussian staff officer attached to Field Marshal von Blücher, was presented to him. Concerned by the noise of fighting from Frasnes the previous evening, von Blücher had sent him to Les Quatre Bras for news. As soon as the Prince had obliged with a verbal briefing, von Brunneck took some small squares of paper from his coat and composed a letter to Major-General Carl von Grolmann, at his own headquarters, timed at 6.30 a.m.

> I have the honour to make known to you that I have found here the Prince van Oranje-Nassau with seven battalions. The noise of the combat which was heard by our right yesterday evening came from the village of Frasnes, which was first occupied by Belgian troops. The enemy still occupies Frasnes and, in the night, he has pushed patrols as far as Sart-Dame-Avelines and beyond the road to Nivelles, so that the communication between the two armies was cut during the night. Currently, this communication is only assured by a post with the strength of an officer and thirty horsemen, placed at Marbais. Quatre Bras and the woods which are to be found in its proximity were held during yesterday's combat and are still today in the hands of Belgian troops. The musket and cannon shots that you hear from time to time are exchanged near Frasnes between the French and Belgian troops. Since yesterday evening, the enemy has hardly moved

The Battle of Quatre Bras

and, still at this time, I report no movement amongst them. The Prince van Oranje-Nassau believes that, in three hours, all the Belgian Army and the greater part of the English army can be concentrated close to Nivelles. Seventeen English battalions have been put on the march from Brussels in order to reinforce the troops at Quatre Bras. I will remain at the outposts, close to the Prince van Oranje-Nassau, in order to observe the enemy and report to you on his actions.[42]

Having learned from Major von Brunneck the whereabouts of their brigade, Lieutenant von Zehelin requested permission to rejoin it. Though reluctant to surrender even this meagre handful of cavalry, permission was granted and the Silesians left for Sombreffe.[43]

The brief discussion with von Brunneck had set the Prince thinking. The Bois de l'Hutte and the road to Gosselies could potentially be masking large numbers of troops, but an almost total lack of activity on the part of the enemy led him to believe that the forces present before him served only to cover another attack, most probably farther to the west. General Cooke had only been ordered as far as Braine-le-Comte and once General von Alten, presumably on his way between there and Nivelles, arrived at the latter, there would be no further orders awaiting him. He needed to issue clear instructions concerning the defence of the town. Shortly before 7.00 a.m., two headquarters guides were accordingly dispatched; the first to Braine-le-Comte, to instruct General Cooke to continue the march of his Guards Division on Nivelles; the second, to General von Alten, to pass through Nivelles and take up a position to its east. Perhaps as he issued these instructions, his thoughts turned to the reconnaissances he had undertaken with the Duke of Wellington. During the spring, they had evaluated a number of defensive positions. These were at Arquennes, behind Nivelles, at Blaton on the road from Valenciennes to Ath, at Mont-Saint-Jean and at Vleurgat, almost before the walls of Brussels itself. All had been assessed with a view to their suitability as places where the French could be stopped, but it seemed for now, that the area around Nivelles and Arquennes would prove the most likely battlefield.[44]

Having briefed Major von Brunneck and in turn being apprised of the measures the Prussians had taken, the Prince van Oranje-Nassau thought it might prove useful, despite the absence of notable activity, to update the Duke of Wellington on the situation. Towards 7.00 a.m., he asked for a sheet of notepaper and wrote a single-sided message in English to the commander-in-chief:

Near Frasnes, June 16, 1815. 7 o'clock.

My Lord Duke,

I am just arrived. The French are in possession of Frasnes, near <u>3 Bras</u> [sic], with infantry and cavalry, but not as yet in force. Our troops are near the village and a sharpish tirailleur fire was going on when I came, but I ordered all firing to cease and the French fire has diminished. I ordered a cavalry brigade over here, the other two are to remain at Arquennes. A brigade of the British 3rd Division is to occupy the height behind Arquennes, the rest to be in position on the ridge behind Nivelles, and that town to be occupied. I ordered the First Division to Nivelles from Braine-le-Comte.

Most sincerely yours.
(Signed) William of Orange.[45]

Even before his letter had passed the crossroads on its way to Brussels, a body of French cavalry tentatively made its way forward on both sides of the chaussée, provoking the second battalion of the 2nd Nassau-Usingen Regiment, along with a company of the 27th Jager Battalion, into a brief fire fight. Under the protection of the infantry, von Sachsen-Weimar ordered forward Bijleveld to engage them and shortly afterwards, the five guns were pelting the French with iron. The cavalry made a few half-hearted charges but, having little stomach for this treatment, retired to the sanctuary of Frasnes. Shortly afterwards, two companies of the 2nd Nassau-Usingen Regiment attempted a further push forward, probing towards Frasnes, but were brought up short by some pieces of artillery, which suggested to the Nassau officers that the French had been reinforced. Stalemate ensued and both sides desisted from further manoeuvring, being content to maintain some desultory skirmishing as the morning wore on.[46]

Cavalry was also preying on the mind of General van Bijlandt. As brigade commander, he was responsible for the safe arrival at Les Quatre Bras of the 5th and 7th Militia Battalions and Captain Stevenaar's eight guns of the foot artillery. As they progressed along the road from Nivelles towards Les Quatre Bras, he had felt increasingly vulnerable. Neither with the main body of the division at Les Quatre Bras, nor sheltered behind the walls of Nivelles, the rolling fields and luxuriant forests of Brabant suddenly took on a somewhat sinister aspect. Though the day had long since dawned, his anxiety about being intercepted increased as the road passed between the Bois de Haroy and the Bois de Nivelles. Some way off to the right, the scouts had observed a body of cavalry in the direction of Rèves. Judging that discretion was the better part of valour, van Bijlandt concealed his command in the woods until, having allowed sufficient time for what he assumed was the enemy to pass, he gave orders for the march to be resumed.[47]

Endnotes

1. G. Paget (I), pp. 108–9, 112.
2. Adkin, p. 45. Hellemann.
3. Eaton, pp. 19-20.
4. Anonymous (Letters), p. 221. Hope (III), p. 221.
5. Anonymous (Waterloo Medal Roll), p. 97. Dalton, p. 227.

The Battle of Quatre Bras

6. Anonymous (Letters), p. 222–3. Jackson (II), pp. 14–15.
7. Eaton, p. 21.
8. Gronow. Jackson (II), pp. 14–15. Riddock. Stephens.
9. Brett-James, p. 48.
10. Anonymous (Regimental Order Book).
11. J. Allan. Anonymous (42nd Regiment), p. 141. Anonymous (Journal), p. 377. Anonymous (Letters), p. 223. Anonymous (Near Observer), pp. 61–2. Cadell (I), p. 232. Calvert (II). Carter, pp. 93, 99. Daniell, p. 132. Eaton, p. 18. Alexander Forbes (II). Gomm (I), p. 5. Grant and Youens, p. 21. Gunn. P. Howard, p. 52. Jackson (II), p. 14. Kincaid (I), p. 311. Mackenzie &c., p. 54. Nafziger, pp. 24–5. Riddock. Robertson, p. 143. J. Ross (II). Ross-Lewin, p. 254. Simmons (II), pp. 363, 366. F. Somerset, p. 7. Stephens. Swiney, pp. 115-6. Vallence. Wauchope, p. 48. Winchester II.
12. Anonymous (42nd Regiment), p. 141. Daniell, p. 132. Archibald Forbes, pp. 263–4. Jackson (II), pp. 14–15.
13. Anonymous (42nd Regiment), p. 141. Anonymous (Letters), p. 223. Cadell (I), p. 232. Caldwell and Cooper, p. 3. Costello, p. 150. Robertson, p. 143. Simmons (II), pp. 363, 366.
14. J. Allan. Anonymous (Cameron), p. 88. Vallence, p. 5.
15. Anton, p. 188. Carter, p. 99. Grant and Youens, p. 21. Maxwell, p. 13. Miller (II), pp. 59, 90. Robertson, p. 143. Sinclair-Stevenson, p. 39.
16. de Bas &c., p. 499. Beamish, p. 533. Braun. Delhaize and Aerts, p. 455. Heise (I). Heise (II). May. von Rettberg (II). von Rettberg (III). Rogers (II).
17. Arthur, p. 592. Daniell, p. 132. von Dörnberg.
18. Aubrey-Fletcher, p. 371. Hamilton, p. 15. Master. J. Paget (I), p. 85. Powell. C. Wood.
19. de Bas &c., pp. 437–8.
20. de Bas &c., p. 453. Grunenbosch. de Jongh. von Pivka (II), pp. 14–15. van Zuylen van Nyeveld (I), p. 52. van Zuylen van Nyeveld (II).
21. de Bas &c., p. 453. Grunenbosch. van Zuylen van Nyeveld (I), p. 52. van Zuylen van Nyeveld (II).
22. de Bas &c., p. 445. Gurwood, p. 474.
23. Elkington (I), p. 12. Morris, p. 67. Thain (II).
24. Pattison (II), p. 2.
25. de Bas &c., pp. 438, 445–6. Bowden, pp. 267-8. de Constant-Rebecque (I). Hoynck van Papendrecht, p. 68.
26. de Bas &c., pp. 446–7. van Zuylen van Nyeveld (I), p. 52.
27. de Bas &c., p. 446. Meijer. van Opstal.
28. Bowden, p. 231. Haythornthwaite (I), pp. 55, 128. Hourtoulle and Jirbal, p. 191. Lachouque, p. 30. van Limburg-Stirum. de Wilde, p. 19. van Zuylen van Nyeveld (I), p. 52.
29. Barre. de Bas &c., p. 447. Meijer. van Opstall. van Zuylen van Nyeveld (I), p. 53.
30. Aubrey-Fletcher, p. 371. Hamilton, p. 15. Maurice, p. 8.
31. Robertson, p. 144.
32. Anonymous (Near Oberserver), pp. 76–7. Frazer, pp. 503–4. von Herzberg. Traupe, p. 17.
33. de Bas &c., p. 447. de Constant-Rebecque (I). de Constant-Rebecque (II).

'We suspected treachery on the part of the foreigners'

34. Arthur, p. 592. Aubrey-Fletcher, p. 362. de Bas &c., p. 455. de Constant-Rebecque (I). de Constant-Rebecque (II). van Oranje-Nassau (II). Rens, p. 106. von Sachsen-Weimar (I). von Sachsen-Weimar (III). Starklof, p. 136.
35. de Bas &c., p. 453–6. Batty, p. 48. van Limburg-Stirum. Ross-Lewin, p. 255. von Sachsen-Weimar (II). von Sachsen-Weimar (III). Starklof, p. 136–7. van Zuylen van Nyeveld (I), p. 53.
36. de Bas &c., pp. 454–6. Grunenbosch. van Limburg-Stirum. van Zuylen van Nyeveld (I), pp. 52–3. van Zuylen van Nyeveld (II).
37. de Bas &c., p. 454. Grunenbosch. van Zuylen van Nyeveld (I), pp. 52–3. van Zuylen van Nyeveld (II).
38. de Bas &c., p. 454. Bijleveld. van Zuylen van Nyeveld (I), p. 52. van Zuylen van Nyeveld (II).
39. Bijleveld. Koopman. van Opstall. van Zuylen van Nyeveld (I), p. 53.
40. Dalton, p. 209. Frazer, pp. 536–7.
41. de Bas &c., p. 457.
42. von Pflugk-Harttung (I), p. 143.
43. de Bas &c., pp. 457–60. Hofschröer (I), pp. 224–5. von Lettow-Vorbeck, p. 298. von Pflugk-Harttung (I), p. 143. van Zuylen van Nyeveld (I), p. 52.
44. de Bas &c., pp. 458–9. de Constant-Rebecque (I). van Zuylen van Nyeveld (II).
45. de Bas, p. 565. de Bas &c., pp. 460–1. von Ompteda, p. 275. van Oranje-Nassau (I).
46. de Bas &c., p. 456. Sachsen-Weimar (II). Starklof, p. 137. van Zuylen van Nyeveld (I), p. 53.
47. Meijer. van Zuylen van Nyeveld (I), p. 53. van Zuylen van Nyeveld (II).

CHAPTER 7

The head of the Brunswick column had now arrived at the walls of Brussels, having marched along the banks of the Willebroeck Canal under the cooling shade of the plane trees. As they reached the end of the road, they crossed a bridge and passed an area where 'Seats and benches in the German style' were situated. Those engaged in more social pursuits could quaff wine and beer to the sound of the organ and the tabor. Passing the boatyards, they passed through a handsome triumphal arch of painted wood, designed to celebrate the entrance into the city of its new sovereign, King Willem I. The gate had been more commonly known until the previous year as the 'Porte Napoléon'; indeed in the minds of many Bonapartist sympathisers, it still was.[1]

Elsewhere in Brussels, Colonel Frazer was continuing his correspondence and had embarked upon a new epistle, this time to Major Moor, his brother-in-law, who lived at Great Bealings in Suffolk.

> My journal is apparently on the point of commencing with something more interesting, or at least less peaceable, than has hitherto filled its pages. Bonaparte has moved; and in consequence we are moving too. It may hardly be worth while to describe what I hardly yet understand, but today will unravel the mystery; tomorrow we may try the fate of arms. Our troops are concentrating. I suspect the scene of the struggle will be in the vicinity of Braine l'Alleud near Hal.[2]

Even as he wrote, his servant brought in a letter from Moor and Frazer took a short while to read it, before continuing with his response.

> Whilst I write I receive your letters; shall I continue to describe movements and battles, or shall I read the delicious pages of affection? Can I hesitate?
>
> I accept your challenge at Dutch billiards, and care not how soon I play with balls amusing and harmless: can one avoid making the contrast with those here? You say your travelling days are over; no, no, they are not, I hope. I trust you will yet travel, and in company with a brother. Ought a man who should think nothing but Braine l'Alleud [sic] and Bonaparte to bestow one thought on Bealings and billiards? Methinks he ought, and without doubt he will. Fancy will turn; the heart, you know, untravelled will turn.

'I know who expects to be killed today'

A flower girl has just bought me a parting bouquet of roses: was it possible to receive it and not think of the dear boys, and the flowers which may, nay which must wither? And to what, and to how many reflections does not the idea lead? I have written you a shabby return for your letter; but when I wrote this late last night, I little thought of having so much time as I now expect to have today. I have never less to do than previous to an action; there are then no difficulties, no littlenesses to be plagued with; in truth, at present every preparation in my power has already been made, and I never felt lighter or easier. Now for Bonaparte, the disturber of all the great as well as of all the little folks of this lower world. He has advanced from Maubeuge, had passed Binche, leaving Mons to his left and rear. His line (of 120,000) last night extended from Roeulx towards Charleroi. Blücher with 82,000 had quitted Namur, and, moving in the direction of Genappe, had reached Sombreffe. Our army (84,000) is concentrating near Braine l'Alleud. Today Bonaparte attacks the Prussians, or we join our forces; this seems the alternative. But a day or two are easily passed, one may say lost, in manoeuvring, before two masses meet; and perhaps after all movement may be but a demonstration. 'When Greek meets Greek,' &c.; now have we the two great captains fairly met. – Adieu. Say what you know I feel to you and yours, and let me hear that my boys and their mother are happy.[3]

The Brunswick Avantgarde-Battalion was marching up the rue de Laeken at Brussels when, towards 7.30 a.m., Wellington emerged from 54 rue Royale. His charger, Copenhagen, was pawing the ground. Awaiting him were his staff and the representatives of the foreign powers. The splash of scarlet, the sheen of the horses and the clacking of hooves on cobbles was reminiscent of a hunting party, though the absence of a stirrup cup suggested otherwise. Today's 'fox' might prove a more resilient animal than those that the officers had abortively hunted in the Forêt de Soignes. The Duke appeared, wearing a costume that resembled in part uniform and in part gentleman rider; his habitual campaign dress. The blue riding coat contrasted with that of his suite, whilst his simple white breeches and hat belied his status. Colonel Somerset pulled out his pocket watch and flicked open the case. It was 8.00 a.m. The cavalcade moved off. As they approached the Place Royale, they halted to watch the Brunswick infantry march past and were joined by the 'Black Duke' himself, to whom Wellington showed a letter, perhaps a disposition. After a moment's pause, the Commander-in-Chief of the army clattered off towards the south.[4]

The streets of Arquennes were also echoing to the sound of horses' hooves. The leading elements of the Netherlands Cavalry Division had just entered the village and found it occupied by some of their infantry. During the early hours, General Chassé had met Lieutenant van Kaps, carrying the 3.00 a.m. order for the cavalry to pull back to Arquennes and the General had subsequently ordered d'Aubremé to detach some infantry to secure the village. Three companies of Lieutenant-Colonel Bagelaar's 12th Line Battalion were halted by the roadside and formed a picquet line to guard the chaussée until relieved by the light dragoons, hussars and carabiniers. Shortly after the arrival of the horsemen, towards 8.00 a.m., the Prince van Oranje-Nassau's messenger arrived. After signing for the receipt of the order, de Collaert briefed General van Merlen that his cavalry brigade was required at Les Quatre Bras and, having enjoyed the briefest of halts, the 5th Regiment of Light Dragoons and 6th Regiment of Hussars moved off and de Collaert busied himself with making his dispositions for the defence of the village.[5]

Some fourteen kilometres to the west, Ensign Macready was also setting out 'en mission', albeit on a less impressive mount. Lieutenant John Pratt and his company commander, Lieutenant Rumley had agreed shortly before 8.00 a.m. that he should ride over to Soignies and order some necessaries from the Regiment.

> I cantered on without thinking and pulled up in the marketplace. I was thunderstruck. Not a soul was stirring. The silence of the tomb reigned here, where I had expected to have met 10,000 men. The breath left my body as if extracted by an air pump. I ran into a house and asked, 'Where are the troops?' 'They marched at two this morning,' was the chilling reply. 'By what road?' 'Towards Braine-le-Comte,' was all I said or heard, when, jumping on my pony's back, I endeavoured, by sympathetic heel, to convey the rapidity of my ideas into his carcass. But vain were my efforts – Gil Blas' ass was lightning compared to him. Soignies was his home and his obstinacy invincible. So, getting off, I thrashed him in the face till my knuckles ran blood and made the best of my way on foot, lugging him by the bridle.[6]

Elsewhere, troops on the move were also starting to think about breakfast. The vanguard of the 5th (British) Infantry Division had made good time. At around 8.00 a.m., the 95th Regiment of Foot arrived at the small village of Waterloo and halted on the left of the road, in a field by the edge of the wood. Despite having purchased a horse for £10 some weeks previously, Lieutenant Simmons was still exhausted and lay down on the verge for an hour. Having been up for most of the night and being unused to fifteen kilometre marches, the recruits followed his example. The older soldiers, such as Private Costello, were more concerned with the business of eating. Breaking out their camp kettles and mess tins, they started on breakfast, listening to, 'The birds in full chorus straining their little throats as if to arouse the spirits of the men to fresh vigour for the bloody conflict they were about to engage in'. Others exchanged, 'A multiplicity of rumours, reports, speculations and calculations, most of them vague, contradictory and unfounded'. It had ever been thus in the Army.[7]

Seeing that the men were gainfully occupied, Lieutenant Kincaid, walked a short distance to the centre of the village of Waterloo and succeeded in procuring breakfast at a small inn, before the remainder of the brigade came up. Perhaps, had he looked at the sign above the door, he might have noticed whether this was the inn of Jean de Nivelles, whose proprietor, Catherine Bodenghien was to profit handsomely from the trade of allied officers over the coming days; not least from Wellington himself, who would establish his headquarters there.[8]

Just under two kilometres to the north, Private Gunn of the 42nd Regiment of Foot had at last realised that the battalion had travelled rather too far for this to be a mere exercise. 'Then the truth began to come out, that we were on the road to meet

'I know who expects to be killed today'

Bonaparte'. The mood changed. The deeper the soldiers penetrated into the forest, the more they noticed how its 'dark foliage in some parts excludes the rays of the sun, casting an awful gloom over the road'. The Duke of Wellington and his staff caught up with the battalion and, as he passed along its ranks, he returned their salute.[9]

Whilst Kincaid tucked into his repast, the 28th Regiment of Foot marched into the village, was halted and the men ordered to fall out. Close behind, the Cameron Highlanders halted shortly after 8.00 a.m., grateful for some water to drink and for some respite from the sun. As far as the eye could see, the verges of the road from Brussels were littered with tired men, cooking, sleeping, smoking and chattering, but for some reason, the commanding officer of the Highland battalion had not given his men permission to cook. Perhaps the halt was to be only a brief one? Nonetheless, Private Vallence took the opportunity to unbuckle his knapsack and remove his shirts, laying them out in the sunshine to dry. As he did so, he uncovered his seldom-used bible, which in the rush to pack, was not tucked away in its usual place at the bottom.

> I took up my best, but much-neglected companion and, retiring a little into the wood, in order to avoid the taunts and scoffs of some of my profligate colleagues, who throw into ridicule everything of a serious nature, I there, unmolested, read some of the psalms most suited to our situation. I had always a firm conviction that we would come off victorious, and that God would spare my life on the day of battle; and after reading the psalms this feeling became stronger than ever.[10]

Perhaps his eyes passed over Psalm 25. 'Unto thee, O Lord, do I lift up my soul. O my God, I trust in thee: let me not be ashamed, let not mine enemies triumph over me'.

The 32nd Regiment of Foot had been slightly delayed on the road and were given the order to halt at about 8.30 a.m. As they wandered through the crowds of men, Lieutenant Stephens and the other officers of the Grenadier Company heard a rumour that the French were less than three leagues away, but could not bring themselves to believe it. Major Ross-Lewin was in a dreamier mood. Stretched out under the canopy of trees, he imagined himself in a small part of the immense Ardennes. Would this day emulate the 'deeds and adventures of which that forest had been the scene since classical times'? All about him, however, others of a more practical nature viewed the forest in the same way as the Bruxellois; it provided excellent firewood.[11]

Shortly after 8.30 a.m., some of the troops blocking the chaussée, were forced to make way, as the Duke of Wellington and his numerous staff arrived. So 'Hookey' was on the move? But to where? Someone told Lieutenant Robert Winchester that the Commander-in-Chief was on his way to Marshal Blücher's headquarters at Ligny. Riding alongside Wellington was the Duke von Braunschweig-Lüneburg. Mounted on a light brown horse, he cut an impressive figure, wearing a round cap of Morocco leather, a short black overcoat with a tasselled and corded yellow and silver sash, wide black ankle-length trousers with light blue piping and spur-less boots. As Wellington rode off to consult with the officers of the division, the Black Duke dismounted and

The Battle of Quatre Bras

sat down at the roadside together with his Adjutant-General, Colonel Olfermann. Shortly afterwards, the Duke sent Olfermann on an errand and Lieutenant Kincaid, observing the scene nearby, was amused to see

> … the vacated place immediately filled by an old beggar man who, seeing nothing in the black hussar uniform beside him denoting the high rank of the wearer, began to grunt and scratch himself most luxuriously! The Duke showed a degree of courage which few would, under such circumstances, for he maintained his post until the return of his officer, when he very jocularly said, 'Well Olfermann, you see that your place was not long unoccupied!'[12]

Perhaps the peasant reminded the Duke of the story of the colourful General von Dörnberg, whose acquaintance he renewed at Waterloo. They were kindred spirits; implacable enemies of the French; immensely patriotic Germans; and staunch allies of the British, in whose service both had placed themselves. Adjutant to King Jérôme Bonaparte, von Dörnberg had also been the commanding officer of his Westphalian Guards when he staged an abortive coup in Hesse; like the Duke von Braunschweig-Lüneburg, he had been forced to flee to Bohemia, disguised as a peasant much like this man. Whilst there, the two men had met and von Dörnberg had joined the 'March for the sea', when Brunswick had led a substantial body of troops to the mouth of the Elbe, from where they had been evacuated by British warships. He had then gone on to command the Brunswick Hussars, before fighting the French in Russia, Germany and France, between 1812 and 1814.[13]

Riding up to Colonel Barnard of the 95th Regiment of Foot, Wellington gave 'very particular orders, to see that the roads were kept clear of baggage and everything likely to impede the movements of the troops'. Given the lack of wheeled transport, however, it was difficult to see how the slightest confusion might arise. Perhaps Wellington wished to ensure his line of retreat on Brussels and Antwerp was unimpeded? Whatever the case, the Duke's orders were precise on the point. Keep the roads clear, but do not, as yet, march.[14] Pausing briefly to allow the Duke von Braunschweig-Lüneburg to remount and give orders for his young troops to fall into column of route once again, the two Dukes and their staffs galloped on towards the front at about 8.45 a.m. Colonel Douglas of the 79th Regiment of Foot, seeing Wellington depart without having ordered a continuation of the march, relented and issued orders for the troops to cook. The men gathered kindling, fetched water and began the slow process of boiling their beef amongst the trees.[15]

Towards 9.00 a.m., the footsore battalions of Pack's brigade approached the village. The 44th Regiment of Foot halted, piled arms and rested under the shade of the trees. Lieutenant Riddock had heard they were marching on Nivelles, Braine-le-Comte or Enghien, depending on the movements of the French. Did anyone know where the enemy was? The 92nd Regiment of Foot had also marched in and Colonel Cameron ordered some companies to bivouac in the open, outside the tree line, whilst others were to occupy the wood itself. He gave the men strict instructions, however, not to

'I know who expects to be killed today'

Friedrich Wilhelm, Herzog von Braunchweig-Lüneburg. Sir George Hayter. *Victoria and Albert Museum, London*

kindle any fires and on no account to move out of their places. With little else to do, the men lay down and the majority slept for some considerable time.[16]

A short distance away, the 42nd Regiment of Foot arrived at Beau Sejour, a small hamlet, centred upon an inn, to the right of the chaussée. The 'dilatory' Colonel Macara halted the column and ordered it to fall out, upon which the men immediately took to the verges.

> Some were stretched under the shade to rest; others sat in groups, draining the cup, and we always loved a large one and it was now almost emptied of three days' allowance of spirits, a greater quantity than was usually served out at once to us on a campaign.[17]

Whilst Sergeant Anton and others supped their gin, the more industrious men set about gathering wood and lighting fires. Others were occupied fetching water and preparing the camp kettles; all assumed that the march was over for the day. If the majority of the rank and file were unaware of any alarm, most of the officers were none the wiser. As the British rested on the roadside, Major August von Pröstler and over six hundred men of the Brunswick Leib-Battalion passed to the front, marching at a blistering pace. Private Gunn, watching keenly from the roadside, thought they looked

The Battle of Quatre Bras

… as proud as a Spaniard on sentry, or like a turkey cock in a farm yard, dressed in dark uniform, something like a horse's tail in their helmets, with the shape of a scalped face and a man's shin-bone.

Shortly afterwards, more Brunswick troops and Best's 4th (Hanoverian) Infantry Brigade arrived and were formed up in the wood.[18]

Just over eighteen kilometres to the south, the firing had long since died down and the French did not appear to be aggressively inclined. At about 8.00 a.m., after the outposts had been quiet for about an hour, the Prince gave instructions for the troops to cook breakfast on the spot with whatever rations they had to hand. The starving soldiery settled down in the fields and shared their meagre rations. The Netherlands generals were uneasy and the Prince van Oranje-Nassau discussed the situation with his senior officers, expressing his own surprise that having gained such a significant advantage the previous day, the French had so far done so little to exploit the situation to their benefit. The enemy at Frasnes seemed to be in no great strength, having so far revealed only a small number of line infantry, which the prisoners had revealed to be part of the corps of General Reille; as well as lancers, chasseurs à cheval and horse artillery of the Imperial Guard. What if these were only a detachment or a reconnaissance force and the mass of the French army was about to descend upon another part of the front line? Other officers, gesturing to the curtain of trees, suggested that the Bois de l'Hutte, which itself was part of the larger Fôret de Villers-Perwin, could be hiding a far greater body of troops, as could the town of Gosselies, farther to the south. Without cavalry, there had been no opportunity to discover more of the whereabouts of the French.[19]

As well as the location of the enemy, the discussion extended to their probable intentions. Up to now, there had been only a weak attempt at pushing ahead on the Brussels road, which Major von Normann and Captain Bijleveld had successfully contained the previous evening. A serious outflanking movement by way of Nivelles or Marbais had yet to materialise and, in any case, the defence of the former would be adequately protected by Chassé and de Collaert in the short-term. Perhaps, said the Prince, thinking aloud and mirroring the Duke of Wellington's own philosophy, the combat at Frasnes was merely a demonstration? Was the main body of the French about to fall elsewhere? In any case, he mused, the Duke would shortly arrive at Les Quatre Bras himself and assume the responsibility for making the necessary decisions. For the time being, he would take steps to ensure that the remainder of I Corps continued to collect nearby, whilst remaining in the position secured by his subordinates, maintaining communications with the Prussians and enjoying the tranquillity of the summer morning. General de Constant-Rebecque was instructed to return to Nivelles, in order to oversee the deployment of Chassé's division. The Prince van Oranje-Nassau furthermore suggested that Colonel Abercromby, his British Assistant Quartermaster-General accompany the Chief-of-Staff, in order to assist von Alten in deploying Halklett's and von Kielmansegge's brigades in such a manner that they provided a link between Chassé's division at Nivelles and de

Perponcher-Sedlnitzky's division at Les Quatre Bras. Colonel von Ompteda's brigade would meanwhile support General de Collaert's cavalry from the high ground to the north of Arquennes. Should the French not drive home an attack on Frasnes, but fall upon Nivelles instead, at least he would have concentrated one cavalry and three infantry divisions about that town.[20]

Perhaps it was the talk of de Collaert's cavalry; perhaps it had been the sight of the French lancers earlier that morning, but the Prince van Oranje-Nassau's thoughts now turned to cavalry. Alhough von Zehelin's small detachment had proved of great value in the outposts, he was very conscious of the complete absence of his own cavalry and concerned over the superiority of the enemy in that arm, both in terms of quality and quantity. Towards 9.00 a.m., he decided to send an aide-de-camp to General de Collaert, with instructions for him to detach General van Merlen's light cavalry brigade and send it to Les Quatre Bras. As a former officer of the Chevau-légers-Lanciers of the Imperial Guard, van Merlen would know how to handle these fellows.[21]

Elsewhere, soldiers continued to march. Having been on the road for five hours and on alert for even longer, the men of the 7th National Militia Battalion were weary. Along with Captain Stevenaar's brigade of artillery and the 5th National Militia Battalion, it arrived at Les Quatre Bras towards 9.00 a.m., where it found the 8th National Militia Battalion and the bulk of the Regiment Oranien-Nassau already assembled and enjoying their breakfast. The two infantry battalions were ordered to bivouac in a clover field, to the north-west of Les Quatre Bras and to cook, an order which was especially well-received by the 5th National Militia Battalion, the men of which had only managed a little meat and some badly cooked rice in the previous 24 hours. It was rumoured that the 27th Jager Battalion was farther in advance and that the Prince van Oranje-Nassau himself was in command of these 4,000 men. Having been cantoned at Baulers and Nivelles for almost two months, the 7th National Militia Battalion had been quite settled. Now, it appeared, they were to bivouac at this place. In the ranks of the battalion was Militiaman Sebastiaan Allebrandi:

> I arrived with my corps (being one of the militia battalions), at the wood lying close to Les Quatre Bras, after a very tiring march, which I nevertheless made with the greatest pleasure, since I, despite only being seventeen years old, burned with the same desire as my comrades in arms to try our strength with the enemy. A stretch of clover field was considered good enough to serve us as a bivouac and we immediately took possession of it. Our immediate need, which we tried to satisfy, was to regain our strength through a meal, which in bivouac has to be gathered from all over with pain and danger. We succeeded in our efforts, spurred on by a large appetite and the few things that our mobile kitchen supplied were enjoyed with much taste, as if an exquisite party had been held for us.

Whilst Allebrandi busied himself with foraging and food, others pitched tents or were detailed to form platoon patrols. Perhaps this would prove to be nothing more than a training exercise after all and the battalion would be back in its billets at Baulers by the weekend?[22]

The clanking carriages and limbers of Captain Stevenaar's brigade rumbled slowly past and turned down the Charleroi road, where they took up a position in the fields, on the high ground between the south-eastern tip of the Bois de Bossu and the Charleroi road. Not long afterwards, Captain Jean van Osten, an officer attached to the Chief-of-Staff of the Artillery rode up; four 6-pounders and two howitzers were needed to reinforce Bijleveld's position, whilst the remaining two guns were to be positioned on the right flank. Any artillery vehicles not required for action, as well as superfluous stores and matériel, were to be removed to the rear of Les Quatre Bras and parked alongside Captain Bijleveld's vehicles. Calling over Second Lieutenant Leopold Winsinger, Stevenaar instructed him to take the two guns of his No. 4 Section to the southern end of the Bois de Bossu. Having previously served with the Corps Impériale d'Artillerie de la Marine, perhaps Winsinger had mixed feelings at the prospect of engaging his former comrades in arms. Detecting no sense of urgency on the part of van Osten, Stevenaar delayed in giving orders to the remainder of his brigade and it remained in column, the left flank facing the enemy positions. Shortly afterwards, Captain van Osten returned, this time accompanied by Major James de la Sarraz. Major-General Carel van Gunkel, the general officer commanding the artillery, was sick and confined to bed at Nivelles and de la Sarraz had subsequently assumed responsibility for the operations of the artillery. He proceeded to berate Stevenaar for the delay in deploying the remainder of his brigade in battery. No doubt bristling with indignation, Stevenaar immediately summoned First Lieutenants von Gahlen and Charles van de Wall and Second Lieutenant George Ruysch van Coevorden and ordered them to have the guns unlimbered immediately and formed up.[23]

With tempers fraying at Les Quatre Bras, General Cooke was also becoming exasperated. He had successfully assembled the two brigades of his division a short distance to the west of Braine-le-Comte, where they had been joined by Major Kuhlmann's artillery from Ghislenghien. As soon as his troops entered the town, he had sent Lieutenant Disbrowe to the Hôtel du Miroir, in search of the headquarters and further orders. The place was deserted. The staff, he was told, including the Prince van Oranje-Nassau and his chief-of-staff had all departed for Nivelles in the early hours, since which time, British and German troops had been passing through the town, headed in the same direction. Confusion reigned everywhere. No orders appeared to have been left for the division. When Disbrowe reported back, Cooke found himself on the horns of a dilemma. Was he expected to remain at Braine-le-Comte? Should he march for Nivelles? To him, it must have seemed like an echo of his first campaign in Flanders, over twenty years before under the 'Grand Old Duke of York'. Back then he had been a young officer in the 1st Regiment of Foot Guards, but serving as an aide-de-camp to Major-General Samuel Hulse. Now he was the Major-General and his own aide was looking expectantly at him for orders. Turning to Disbrowe and to Ensign Cuyler, he told them to pass the word that the division was to move through the town and halt on the eastern side. They would rest here until noon, before continuing the march on Nivelles.[24]

Passing through the town proved easier said than done. Braine-le-Comte was thronged with people, vehicles and animals. The baggage wagons of the 3rd (British) Infantry Division, on their way to Brussels, had still not all passed through and countless caissons, carts and carriages choked the streets and blocked the lanes. The chaussée from Brussels to Mons was a continuous traffic jam, the civilian carters cursing in a choice blend of Flemish and Walloon, whilst urchins scampered around, begging for food or money. Parties of Guards officers, non-commissioned officers and men pushed through the crowded streets, manhandling broken-down vehicles. Through a combination of shouting, threats and where necessary, a few well-judged blows from the flats of swords, butts of muskets or the staffs of the sergeants' spontoons, sufficient space was created for the column of men and their artillery to pass through.[25]

Outside Braine-le Comte, the third battalion of the 1st Regiment of Foot Guards was halted. Lieutenant-Colonels Edward Stables, Charles Thomas and William Miller, along with Captain Edward Grose, Lieutenant Robert Adair and Ensign Pardoe were on their way to breakfast. Towards 10.00 a.m., some of them spotted the arrival of Lieutenant William Hay of the 12th Regiment of Light Dragoons, an old friend who was instructing his servant to feed his horse with corn. Within moments he had been invited to join them and, as they sat on the grass, chattering about the prospects of the day, one of the Guards looked at Hay and jokingly said, 'I know who expects to be killed today.' On asking him what he meant, the officer pointed to a rip in Hay's trousers. Little did they know, as they laughed at the young cavalryman's misfortune, that one of them of them would be dead by nightfall and two more would sustain horrific wounds before they too succumbed to death's embrace.[26]

Another man anxiously awaiting orders was Chief Medical Officer Mergell of the Netherlands Staff. At 3.00 a.m., he had been given instructions by Colonel Reuther, the Administrative Inspector, to be ready to leave immediately. It was expected that he would be given the order to move towards 5.00 a.m. The hours dragged by and still no orders came. Mergell watched as Netherlands staff officers and British troops passed through the town. At about 10.00 a.m., General Hermann van der Wijk, the Netherlands Adjutant-General rode up and from him, Mergell heard that the Prince van Oranje-Nassau had already left in the small hours. Learning also that General de Constant-Rebecque had departed for Nivelles, as had General van der Wijk, he determined to head for Nivelles himself. Since his own ambulance vehicles, two caissons for the cavalry and the invalid carriages would be delayed for some time making repairs and would be further delayed by the congestion on the roads, he hoped he would be able to utilise the equipment of the 2nd (Netherlands) Infantry Division ambulance instead. Leaving his own vehicles in the care of Surgeon-Major Scharten, with instructions to move as soon as possible, he departed for Nivelles.[27]

At Naast, nearly eight kilometres south, Lieutenants Rumley and Pratt were deep in conversation with the Mayor, when Ensign Macready dragged his sullen pony into

The Battle of Quatre Bras

the village. Recounting the astonishing news from Soignies, he listened as in turn he was told that the French had crossed the Sambre and occupied Charleroi, some thirty kilometres to the south-east. The Prussians had fallen back and the absence of troops in Soignies was the direct result of Wellington's army hastening to support its allies. The company's patrols had not encountered a single soldier in the surrounding area; even the Hanoverian Jagers had disappeared.

> We were most unpleasantly situated, ignorant whether we were left here by mistake or design and dreading equally the consequences of quitting our post without orders, or the Division being engaged in our absence. Our commissions were safe by remaining where we were, but – as Egan said, 'Ireland for ever and damn Kilmainham,' – we determined to risk them and all the hopes of young ambition, rather than be absent from the field of glory.

Lieutenant Rumley ordered the assembly and by 10.00 a.m., the little band of warriors marched off in the direction of Braine-le-Comte.[28]

Farther to the east, the men of the 73rd Regiment of Foot sweated up the steep slope out of the valley of the Sennette. At about 9.30 a.m., they reached the small hamlet of Le Croiseau and halted. Somewhere to the east, hidden by the woods, was the town of Nivelles. The countryside was luxuriant. Colonel Harris had the men fall out, whilst General Halkett paced up and down, anxiously awaiting more definite instructions from General von Alten. The men must have hoped that their march for the day was done and that this would be their bivouac; they were soon to be disappointed. The word to resume the march having come in, Colonel Harris had the drummers beat the 'General' and once again, packs were hoisted onto aching shoulders, muskets were slung and the men took up their positions in the shuffling ranks. The march resumed.[29]

Some distance ahead, Lieutenant Pattison was admiring the beauty of the well-cultivated countryside, as the rising sun bathed it in warm light. His spirits had lifted since the gloom of the Bois de la Houssière:

> Everything inspired the troops with life and animation and the songs of the men, caught up by one company after another, expressed more the feelings of a party going to a banquet, than of soldiers marching to a field of blood.[30]

Unknown to Pattison, his commander-in-chief had just arrived at the field of blood. At 10.00 a.m., Wellington and his party reached the crossroads at Les Quatre Bras. They had left Waterloo at about 8.45 a.m. and halted briefly at the crossroads at Mont-Saint-Jean a short while later. The Duke had made extensive enquiries as to where the various roads led and was told that the road from Brussels divided at this point into two chaussées: the first, leading to Genappe and Les Quatre Bras; the second, leading to Nivelles. Choosing the road to Genappe, Wellington's entourage had arrived there at 9.40 a.m. and with a practised eye, the Duke had quickly assessed the position. The prominent ridge and the narrow defile over the River Dyle, by a single bridge, might prove to be useful in blocking an advance on Brussels and, perhaps as important, there was a reasonable lateral road to Nivelles, ten kilometres distant, by way of Fonteny and Thines. The Genappe option gave him a strong defensive position, should the French have already passed Les Quatre Bras; but it also afforded him the opportunity to shift the axis of his advance, were the fighting at Frasnes to prove to be a feint for a more serious attack, farther to the west. Deciding that such a position would meet both eventualities, Wellington sent officers back up the Brussels road with orders for the reserve troops to continue their march on Genappe.[31]

Wellington was accompanied by a host of dignitaries, though some, such as Colonel von Müffling and General von Dörnberg performed sensitive duties not necessarily reflected in their rank. As the cavalcade arrived, some seemed keener than others to get their first glimpse of the French. Colonel Somerset was perhaps disappointed not to see many of the enemy in front, though the occasional popping of musketry signified that the second battalion of the 2nd Nassau-Usingen Regiment was still skirmishing with the opposing tirailleurs. General von Dörnberg chose to ride forward in order to observe, though he stayed a safe distance from the skirmishers as some of the Prince's troops exchanged fire with the French. There was little to see amongst the swaying wheat, save the occasional puff of smoke and the glint of gunmetal. Some more adventurous Brunswick staff officers rode much closer to the front, to the crest of a ridge, from where they were able to observe the approach of the French, rumoured to be in considerable force. No sooner had they become visible to the enemy, than they were subjected to canister fire; at such a close range, this only narrowly failed to kill or wound them and, 'Persuaded them to leave the spot immediately'. Farther to the rear, Wellington looked about him and concluded that there was, 'Only a small body of Belgian troops, two or three battalions of infantry, a squadron of Belgian dragoons and two or three cannon which had been at Les Quatre Bras – the four roads – since the preceding evening', which illustrated perfectly the nature of the ground and the difficulties of reconnaissance. There were nine battalions present, with sixteen guns.[32]

Word that the commander-in-chief had arrived travelled very fast through the bivouacs and shortly afterwards, the Duke was joined by the Prince van Oranje-Nassau and General de Perponcher-Sedlnitzky. With good grace, he congratulated them both on the initiative they had shown in concentrating troops of the 2nd (Netherlands) Infantry Division at Les Quatre Bras and diplomatically omitted to mention his order for it to assemble at Nivelles. The Prince realised to whose credit the decision should be attributed, but no doubt appreciated the manner in which Wellington had tackled the sensitive issue. As they rode down the Charleroi road, inspecting the troops and their positions, Wellington was briefed on the situation. Though not yet visible from the heights of Frasnes, French prisoners had reported that their main body was advancing very fast and that it was very large in number. To meet the threat, de Perponcher-Sedlnitzky had so far assembled nine battalions, totalling 6,500 men and sixteen guns on the field. A further 700 men of the 7th Line Battalion were still at Nivelles. Ammunition, especially some calibres of small-arms ammunition, was scarce. Perhaps most importantly, the Prince advised Wellington of the orders he had issued for de Collaert, Chassé, von Alten and Cooke to concentrate in the vicinity of Nivelles. In his turn, Major von Brunneck was introduced to Wellington and von Müffling and summarised the situation of the Prussian army, which had occupied a position at Sombreffe, with considerable masses of French drawn up against it. Glancing at his map, Wellington noted that Sombreffe was about thirteen kilometres to the south-east, linked to Les Quatre Bras by the chaussée running from Namur to Nivelles. He would, it seemed, have to fight with his back to this same road in order successfully to maintain contact with his ally. He would also, however, have to defend the road to Brussels, but whether here at Les Quatre Bras, or in the neighbourhood of Nivelles, it was yet to be seen. What was readily apparent, however, was that the Prussians were going to offer battle to the French.[33]

As the senior officers rode through the positions of the Nassau troops, Colonel von Sachsen-Weimar joined them, saluted and was presented to the Duke by the Prince van Oranje-Nassau. Rather than congratulating the young Colonel for his industry and steadiness the previous evening, Wellington said nothing. Without praising his conduct or that of the troops under his temporary command, Wellington merely looked him up and down for a long time. Eventually, to the embarrassment of the Netherlands officers, he turned his back on the young Prince and continued his inspection, a snub which von Sachsen-Weimar would never forgive.[34]

Shortly afterwards, the party arrived at Marianne Brelon's inn on the Balcan plateau. From this vantage point, Wellington could see the village of Frasnes. To the west, on the road to Rèves, the sails of the Moulin Druet could be seen, but to the east, the area about Villers-Perwin and the distant battlefield between Fleurus and Sombreffe was hidden by the Bois de l'Hutte. Though it had been rumoured that the heads of the French columns were visible, little could be seen of the enemy, shielded by the undulating ground and clumps of trees. Wellington would have to resort to assumptions and guesswork. If the French were not here and there was no word from Nivelles and beyond, then they must all be to the east, moving on the Prussians. With everything quiet in his sector, the Duke felt that his time would be better spent gauging von Blücher's intentions and sharing his own; things here would do as they were, for now. Turning to the Prince van Oranje-Nassau and without making any changes, the Duke approved his dispositions.[35]

Dismounting, Wellington took a sheet of paper from his saddle and consulting a 'disposition' that De Lancey had prepared for him earlier, composed a letter to von Blücher:

> On the heights behind Frasnes,
> 16th of June 1815, at 10½ o'clock.
>
> My dear Prince,
>
> My army is situated as follows. The Prince of Orange's corps has a division here at Les Quatre Bras and the rest at Nivelles. The Reserve is on the march from Waterloo to

Genappe, where it will arrive at noon. The English cavalry will, at the same time, be at Nivelles. The corps of Lord Hill is at Braine-le-Comte. I do not see very much of the enemy before us and I await the news of your Highness and the arrival of the troops in order to decide my operations for the day. Nothing has appeared from the direction of Binche, nor on our right.

Your very obedient servant, Wellington.[36]

This letter was misleading in just about every respect. The remainder of the Prince van Oranje-Nassau's Corps was not at Nivelles, with the exception of the 7th Belgian Line, though Chassé's 3rd (Netherlands) Infantry Division was close by. General von Alten's 3rd (British) Infantry Division was on the march between Braine-le-Comte and Nivelles, whilst Cooke's 1st (British) Infantry Division was still halted at Braine-le-Comte, for lack of orders. Having only sent the Reserve the order to march on Genappe towards 9.45 a.m., there was simply no way it would be able to cover the fourteen kilometres by noon; it would only arrive there towards 2.00 p.m. Uxbridge and the cavalry were somewhere between Ninove and Enghien and Lord Hill's Corps was still dispersed, with Clinton's 2nd (British) Infantry Division at Ath, Colville's 4th (British) Infantry Division on the march for Enghien and the Netherlands troops of Stedman and Anthing still at Sotteghem. In fact, only the disposition given for the 2nd (Netherlands) Infantry Division towards 12.00 p.m. would prove correct.[37]

Wellington was still obsessed with the prospect of an attack farther to the west of Les Quatre Bras, though if necessary, the reserve could block the road from Charleroi

Major-General George Cooke.
Jan Willem Pienemann.
Wellington Museum, Apsley House, London

to Brussels at Genappe. The remainder of the army would concentrate to cover the two other likely routes. The easternmost of these would be Nivelles, where Chassé's, Cooke's and von Alten's infantry, along with de Collaert's Netherlands Cavalry Division, would cover the road from Binche to Brussels. Farther to the west, the two British infantry divisions of Clinton and Colville would occupy Braine-le-Comte, in order to guard against any attempt through Mons. The cavalry would remain at Enghien, covering the Tournai road.[38]

As he rode back up the chaussée towards Les Quatre Bras, Wellington carefully noted the features of the ground around him, especially the Bois de Bossu. If pushed back from the positions that his troops now occupied, this wood acted as a natural funnel, limiting the enemy frontage significantly, compared to the open, undulating plain to the south. The solid farm buildings of Gemioncourt and its enclosures would form an additional strongpoint, capable of checking the enemy cavalry's advance completely and of bogging down the enemy infantry by threatening both of its flanks. He made a mental note that, at the first opportunity, the house should be garrisoned by a British battalion.[39]

The closest of these was, however, still at Waterloo, over eighteen kilometres away, though they would soon be on the move. Towards 10.30 a.m., the men of 79th Regiment of Foot had just started boiling their beef, when the order was given to resume the march at once and Private Vallence had just finished packing his dry shirts away when the bugle sounded for the men to fall in. Perhaps, speculated Lieutenant Alexander Forbes, the information received by the Duke about the enemy's forces had been incorrect? Had, after all, his plans had been frustrated by the Prussians and Belgians? Throughout the battalion, the expectation was that the 'about face' would soon be ordered and they would be back in their comfortable billets in Brussels by evening.[40]

The men of the 28th Regiment of Foot were in high spirits, having just managed to complete their breakfasts by the time the order was given. The bugle was also sounding for the 32nd Regiment of Foot and as the men scurried into their positions, Captain Edward Whitty prophetically exclaimed, 'That is my death warrant!' Similar orders were being passed to the other regiments. Lieutenant Winchester's company had just finished its breakfast: gin and biscuit, but many other meals were left unfinished. Partly-cooked beef was hurriedly fished out of the pots, wrapped in cloth and stuffed into haversacks and knapsacks. The Flanders kettles were hastily overturned and hoisted onto the back of the unfortunate eighth man of the section. Captain Cadell could hear a distant cannonade, or was he imagining things? Hastily falling into column of route, the men were soon underway. When the 42nd Regiment of Foot arrived at Waterloo, it was briefly halted whilst the fidgety, irascible General Pack spoke with Colonel Macara. Private Gunn overheard Pack say, 'Well, if there is anything to be done the day I will try and get this brigade in.' As Gunn pondered the meaning of this, an orderly galloped up with dispatches.[41]

Even as the reserve was snaking south from Waterloo, the Brunswick artillery was still far away to the north-west. It had not left Asse until 8.00 a.m. and Chief Gunner

August Hellemann yawned as he marched alongside his gun, carriage, limber and team, having been at pains to check that his crew had remembered to stow all their equipment as instructed. The lads were young and there had been emotional scenes on taking leave of their landlady. Captain von Heinemann's Brunswick horse artillery trotted through the Porte de Flandre and passed through the city quickly, accompanied for some distance by crowds of Bruxellois, offering them their best wishes. The silver skull and crossbones plate on their shakos and their drooping horse-hair plumes gave them a sombre appearance, matching the mood of the men.[42]

Thirty-eight kilometres to the south, Ensign Thain of the 33rd Regiment of Foot could feel the strain on his horse as he and the rest of his regiment negotiated the steep descent into Nivelles. The men were tired, having marched over twenty kilometres in just over eight hours, across rolling terrain. As they entered the Grand'Place, at about 10.30 a.m., they collided with a stream of troops belonging to Chassé's division, which had started to arrive shortly before and was moving ponderously along the rue de Mons. The British battalion was brought to a halt.[43]

Groaning gun carriages and ponderous caissons belonging to Captain Krahmer de Bichin's horse battery rumbled across the cobbles, more vehicles to add to the tangle of baggage wagons, forges, ambulances, bât horses and carriages left behind by the 2nd (Netherlands) Infantry Division in its scramble to reach Les Quatre Bras. Green-jacketed Belgian Jagers sat about in groups, whilst ruddy-cheeked Dutch militiamen went for water. The more entrepreneurial traders moved steadily from group to group, offering food and drink for sale, whilst the scene was observed keenly by the inhabitants, looking down from shuttered windows and balconies into the square below. It was a memorable day for the wide-eyed urchins of the town. The tired redcoats were grateful for the respite and only too happy to rest for a moment; let the officers sort it out. Adjutants sent by the Netherlands divisional chief-of-staff, Major Baron Leonard van Delen, directed units to their rendezvous points and argued with the British and Hanoverians.[44]

At this moment, General de Constant-Rebecque arrived at Nivelles, accompanied by Colonel Abercromby, the Prince van Oranje-Nassau's British Assistant Quartermaster-General. Seeing that Chassé's and von Alten's divisions were deadlocked, someone had to determine the priorities. Since Chassé's orders were to occupy Nivelles and von Alten's to move on, de Constant-Rebecque persuaded the former to halt his troops and allow von Alten to pass. Whilst the two men consulted, Colonel Abercomby rode up to his own countrymen and urged them to move off as quickly as possible. It would take some time. Not everyone had received or understood the earlier order to send the baggage to Hal, and the road between Nivelles and Braine-le-Comte was choked with heavy fourgons, herds of cattle, wagons belonging to the Netherlands headquarters and the personal equipment of the Prince van Oranje-Nassau himself.[45]

With traffic starting to move again, de Constant-Rebecque gave Colonel van den Sanden permission to march for Les Quatre Bras with the 7th Line Battalion and rejoin his division. It had earlier mustered for the Colonel's inspection and, on his

The Battle of Quatre Bras

orders, loaded its weapons. Very shortly after having received the order to march, van den Sanden drew up the battalion in column at full distance and, with everything organised to his satisfaction, the men from Namur marched off towards their home town. Mounted on his tall Ardennes horse and riding alongside his men in Captain Mathon's company, Lieutenant Scheltens felt a strong sense of pride in his battalion. To his mind, it was well-composed, with nearly all the officers having been on campaign before. The non-commissioned officers, he judged passable and the rank and file were volunteers to a man. All they had lacked, when he had joined them the previous year, was practical training in manoeuvring and the theory of regulations, which Scheltens and the other experienced officers had busied themselves in supervising whilst the battalion had been stationed at Ghent.[46]

Not all the Allied soldiers had been so fortunate. The Belgians of the 5th Light Dragoon Regiment had not had the opportunity to cook at Arquennes, but had continued their march, passed through Nivelles at about 12.20 p.m. and were now watering their horses at Notre-Dame-des-Sept-Douleurs. Among them was Lieutenant Chevalier Adolphe de Cléty de Witterzee. He had earlier received permission from Colonel de Mercx de Corbais to visit his mother, who lived in the town.

> In leaving our cantonments to take ourselves to Les Quatre Bras, we passed by Nivelles where I preceded the regiment by a quarter of an hour in order to embrace my mother. Thus, duty complete, I rejoined the corps at the moment it entered the town, which it traversed without stopping . . . The halt was only made at the barrier of Sept Douleurs, half a league outside Nivelles. My mother's domestics rejoined with two great panniers of excellent wine, which I offered to my colonel, who accepted them and distributed them not just to the officers, but to all the troops, without distinction of rank. Our part was each, doubtless, very small but the moral effect which resulted from this cup of wine was great.

The thirsty troopers were delighted by the sacrifice of Madame de Cléty de Witterzee and many a toast was proposed in her honour.[47]

By now, other troops had begun passing through the town. Following Abercromby's intervention, Colonel Elphinstone had immediately marched the 33rd Regiment of Foot up the rue de Namur and beyond the hamlet of Thines, before turning off the road into an extensive field of clover. On his orders, the regiment halted and the officers passed word for the men to pile arms and remove their knapsacks. The sun continued to beat down and the throats of the troops were parched. Soldiers were told off into watering parties, each collecting dozens of canteens from their comrades, before setting off in search of streams, wells or ponds, whilst others prepared to cook.[48]

Already resting in the field were Colonel Morice and the 69th Regiment of Foot. Though the countryside seemed peaceful, Captain Barlow had heard it rumoured that Marshal Ney, at the head of the French, was less than a league from here. Long before the regiment's arrival at Nivelles, occasional distant concussions had been heard, which seemed to add credence to his theory, though others scoffed at him, claiming the sound was far-off thunder. Heedless of the doings of generals and captains, the men had slumped down immediately; French or no French, they were going to get some rest.[49]

Also pulled off the roadway were Major William Lloyd's brigade of 9-pounders and Captain Cleeves' Hanoverian brigade. Whilst some drivers took the buckets from beneath the axles of the guns and went to fetch water, others strapped on nosebags filled with oats or pulled hay from the nets for the ravenous horses. Elsewhere, the men checked them for sores, examined the hooves, wiped away the sweat and adjusted the harness. Where necessary, the farriers and smiths made running repairs. Passing through Nivelles, an hour's march behind the remainder of the brigade, the men of the 73rd Regiment of Foot were, for the first time, 'made acquainted with the service on which [they] were going'. Word passed quickly through the ranks; Boney himself, at the head of a large army, had been hard at it with the Prussians the day before.[50]

Endnotes

1. Frazer, p. 504.
2. Frazer, p. 504.
3. Frazer, pp. 538–9.
4. Anonymous (Near Observer), pp. 76–7. de Bas &c., p. 464. J. Harris, p. 446. Maxwell, p. 13. G. Paget (I), p. 110. von Herzberg. van Limburg-Stirum. F. Somerset, pp. 7–8. Swinton, p. 142. Young, p. 251.
5. Anonymous (Outgoing Register). de Bas &c., pp. 437–8. van Delen, p. 43. Hoynck van Papendrecht, p. 68. Wüppermann, p. 84.
6. Macready (I).
7. Bluth, p. 59. Costello, pp. 105–6. Kincaid (I), p. 311. Leach, pp. 373–4. Mackenzie &c., p. 8. Simmons (II), p. 363.
8. Kincaid (I), p. 311. Lachouque, p. 116. Sutherland, p. 165.
9. Anonymous (Journal of an Officer), p. 392. Cornford and Walker, p. 104. Gunn.
10. J. Allan. Anonymous (Cameron), p. 88. Cadell (I), p. 232. Mackenzie &c., p. 54. Ross-Lewin, p. 254. Stephens. Vallence, p. 5.
11. Ross-Lewin, p. 254.
12. Anonymous (Cameron), p. 88. Anonymous (Journal), p. 392. Bowden, p. 256. Costello, p. 151. von Dörnberg. von Herzberg. Kincaid (I), pp. 311–13. Mackenzie &c., p. 54. Maxwell, p. 13. Simmons (II), p. 363. F. Somerset, pp. 7–8.
13. Hofschröer (I), p. 77. Hussey (I).
14. Kincaid (I), pp. 311–12.
15. Anonymous (Cameron), p. 88. Anonymous (Journal), p. 392. Anonymous (Near Observer), pp. 76–7. von Herzberg. Kincaid (I), pp. 311–12. Mackenzie &c., p. 54. Ross-Lewin, p. 254.

The Battle of Quatre Bras

16. Anonymous (Letters), p. 223. Riddock. Robertson, pp. 144–5. J. Ross (II).
17. Anton, pp. 188–9
18. Anton, pp. 188–9. Bowden, p. 256. Gunn. Haythornthwaite (I), pp. 125–6. von Herzberg. Kincaid (I), pp. 311–12. Leach, pp. 373–4. von Pivka (II), pp. 39–40. von Müffling (I), p. 2. Robertson.
19. de Bas &c., pp. 457–8. van Zuylen van Nyeveld (I), p. 53.
20. de Bas &c., pp. 457–9. de Constant-Rebecque (I). von Ompteda, p. 275. van Zuylen van Nyeveld (I), p. 53.
21. de Bas &c., p. 458. Hoynck van Papendrecht, p. 68.
22. Allebrandi, p. 4. Beets. Meijer. Rem. Starklof, p. 136. van Zuylen van Nyeveld (I), p. 53.
23. Meijer. van Opstall. van Osten. van Zuylen van Nyeveld (I), p. 54.
24. Aubrey-Fletcher, p. 371. de Bas &c., pp. 461–2. Clay. Hamilton, p. 15. Maurice, pp. 8, 11. J. Paget (I), p. 85. Powell. Whitworth, p. 45.
25. Powell.
26. Chambers, pp. 79, 363, 531. Dalton, pp. 97–9. Hay, pp. 161–2.
27. Mergell.
28. Macready (I).
29. Morris, p. 67. Thain (II).
30. Pattison (II), p. 2. Hemingway. Thain (II).
31. Arthur, p. 593. de Bas &c., p. 464. Costello, p.151. Daniell, p. 133. von Dörnberg. von Herzberg. Hofschröer (I), p. 225. Jennings, p. 175. Kincaid (I), pp. 311–12. van Limburg-Stirum. Maurice (p. 11). von Müffling (I), p. 3. von Pflugk-Harttung (I), p. 292. Rens, p. 107. Sichart (I). F. Somerset, pp. 7–8. Traupe, p. 15. van Zuylen van Nyeveld (I), p. 54. van Zuylen van Nyeveld (II).
32. Anonymous (Near Observer), p. 77. de Bas &c., p. 464. Hofschröer (I), p. 225. Jennings, p. 175. von Pflugk-Harttung (I), p. 292. F. Somerset, p. 8. van Zuylen van Nyeveld (II).
33. Anonymous (Near Observer), p. 77. de Bas &c., pp. 459–60, 465. van Limburg-Stirum. Maurice, p. 11. von Müffling (I), p. 3. F. Somerset, p. 8. Traupe, p. 14. van Zuylen van Nyeveld (I), p. 54. van Zuylen van Nyeveld (II).
34. de Bas &c., p. 464.
35. de Bas &c., pp. 465–6. Dellevoet, p. 21. Maurice, p. 11. Rens, p. 106. van Zuylen van Nyeveld (I), p. 54. van Zuylen van Nyeveld (II).
36. de Bas &c., p. 466. Hofschröer (I), p. 232. von Ollech, p. 125.
37. de Bas &c., pp. 467–8, 474.
38. de Bas &c., p. 467.
39. Gomm (IV).
40. J. Allan. Gomm (I), p. 56. Gomm (IV). Kincaid (I), pp. 313–14. Leach, pp. 374–5. Riddock. F. Somerset, p. 8. Vallence, p. 5.
41. Cadell (I), p. 232. Calvert (II). Crummer (II). Gunn. Houssaye, p. 71. Leask and McCance, pp. 332–3. Mackenzie &c., p. 54. Robertson. J. Ross (II). Ross-Lewin, pp. 254, 261. Winchester (II).
42. Hellemann.
43. de Bas &c., p. 462. van Delen, p. 44. Hemingway. Thain (II).

44. Hemingway. Thain (II).
45. de Bas &c., p. 462. Dalton, p. 33. van Delen, p. 44. F. Somerset, p. 9. Thain (II).
46. de Bas &c., pp. 463, 482. Scheltens, pp. 195, 198. van Zuylen van Nyeveld (I), p. 54.
47. Bowden, p. 268. Manchot, p. 76. Rens, p. 110. Wüppermann, p.84.
48. Ainslie, p. 14. Hemingway. Lee, p. 226. Morris, p. 67. Pattison (II), p. 3. Thain (II).
49. Ainslie, p. 14. Barlow. Pattison (II), p. 3.
50. Morris, p. 67. Rudyerd. Wells.

CHAPTER 8

At 10.45 a.m., Major von Brunneck penned another brief note from Les Quatre Bras for General von Grolman:

> From the forward posts between Quatre Bras and Frasne
> Morning, ¾11 o'clock.

> The enemy still stands near Frasne, as he did earlier this morning. His strength is difficult to estimate, due to the high crops and the terrain being intersected with woods. Three battalions, about two lancer regiments and a half-battery are all that is visible of him so far and these maintain the fight at the outposts. How far his left wing stretches and in what direction this runs, is also unknown. It seems that Rèves in the meantime, is not occupied by him.[1]

The skirmishing between Major von Normann's battalion and the French had continued in a desultory fashion, with both sides occasionally peppering the others' picquets and patrols with musket fire, each seeking to force the other to disclose intentions and strengths, but in reality, causing little more than annoyance, frayed nerves and the odd casualty. The heavy expenditure in ammunition, added to that consumed the previous evening, became more and more noticeable as the men fished inside their cartridge pouches for rounds. One by one, they started declaring to the sergeants and corporals that their pouches were empty. The reserve supplies for the brigade were still at Nivelles with the remainder of the artillery park, so Major von Normann sent back a request to be relieved.[2]

General de Perponcher-Sedlnitzky agreed to von Normann's appeal and detailed Major Hegmann to assemble the third battalion of the 2nd Nassau-Usingen Regiment at its bivouac and to march it down the Charleroi road and into the front line. As these troops arrived at Delsot, shortly after 12.00 p.m., von Normann began withdrawing his skirmishers and pulled back from the advanced position he had taken up at the Ferme du Petit-Pierrepont. Deploying two companies in the outpost line, Hegmann formed the remaining four in column, hidden from the view of the French by the rising ground to the south. As he, in turn, marched his battalion north along the chaussée, perhaps Major von Normann reflected on the events of the morning. Though the engagement had not escalated into full-scale fighting, his battalion had managed to recover and retain much of the ground that it had been obliged to cede the previous evening. The French cavalry and infantry, persuaded it seemed, that their enemy had been heavily reinforced in the course of the night, had been content to give ground. The troops deserved a well-earned breakfast.[3]

In another bivouac, fifteen kilometres to the west at Braine-le-Comte, General Cooke was restless. From the time of his arrival that morning, there had been no further word since the orders he had received in the early hours, which instructed him to march to Braine-le-Comte, but no further. What next, he pondered? Having just returned from a reconnaissance towards Ronquières and Écaussinnes, during which he questioned stragglers, baggage masters and civilians, he decided that considering the rest of the army seemed to be headed for Nivelles, he too should follow this line of march. Shortly before noon, orders were given for the assembly and within the space of a few minutes the division resumed its march.[4]

A short time later at Les Quatre Bras, Colonel von Müffling rode up to Wellington. He had been questioning some stray soldiers from General von Steinmetz's 1st (Prussian) Infantry Brigade, who had borne the brunt of the previous day's fighting. From them, he had learned that General von Ziethen had abandoned the line of the Sambre, and that two French columns had passed, one by Charleroi and one by Marchienne-au-Pont. They had been involved in heavy fighting around Gosselies, whilst other Prussian brigades had been engaged near Fleurus. The soldiers believed that enemy spearheads had cut the road between Sombreffe and Les Quatre Bras. General von Dörnberg, meeting a body of Prussian hussars patrolling the gap between the allied armies, had confirmed that von Blücher was still at Sombreffe. None of this added much to the intelligence received by Wellington the day before, nor to that provided by von Brunneck earlier in the morning.[5]

Had von Blücher managed to concentrate all his forces at Sombreffe, and if so, did he still intend to fight? Certainly the occasional gun had been heard away to the east. After thinking for some minutes, the Duke turned to Generals von Müffling and von Dörnberg and expressed the opinion that it would be best, in the circumstances, to ride over to von Blücher's headquarters and to agree what measures needed to be taken to unite their forces prior to a decisive battle. He asked them both to accompany him.[6]

Some fifteen kilometres to the north, the 95th Regiment of Foot tramped along the road from Waterloo to Genappe, not knowing that the whitewashed farmhouse to the right of the highway and the sandpit and knoll to the west would prove – two days later – to be the scene of their final and perhaps most sanguinary, struggle of the Napoleonic Wars. As they progressed south, it became more obvious that the French were not too far away. A cart, groaning with wounded Nassau and Prussian soldiers passed them. One of the officers, questioning the wagon drivers and the casualties, discovered that 'The French and Prussians had been fighting the day before and that another battle was expected when they had left the advanced posts.'[7]

As these same wounded soldiers passed the 79th Regiment of Foot, a short distance behind the Rifles, they passed on news from the front. Imperceptibly, the pace quickened. The sun burned high in the sky and the men, no longer protected by the shade of the leafy forest, choked in the clouds of dust disturbed by the thousands of marching feet. Vision was reduced to the swaying pack and sweaty neck of the man in front. Those whose throats were parched from the raw Dutch gin suffered the most and Private Vallence, for one, was grateful to the villagers.

> As we advanced, the day became very warm and many of us suffered much from thirst; but the inhabitants of the villages which we passed through evinced their sympathy with us in the best possible manner – having a row of tubs filled with water on each side of the road, in front of their houses, with wooden cups floating in them, for us to drink along the way.[8]

The Brunswick Division arrived at Genappe shortly before 12.30 p.m., where the order was given for it to rest. Sergeant Langenstrasse and the hussars had arrived over an hour before and were watering their horses in the Dyle. Having gathered during the night on the road between Brussels and Vilvorde, they had trotted without a break through Brussels and along the verges of the chaussée, though still under the misapprehension that they were only moving quarters. The horses were tired. Around them, the men of the Leib-Battalion, Avantgarde-Battalion, 2nd Light Battalion and 1st Line and 3rd Line Battalions sat on the roadside and under the shade of trees in the small square. By now, Lieutenant-Colonel Carl Pott's 258-strong Uhlan squadron and Major Johann von Strombeck's 2nd Line Battalion, had rejoined, after a blistering march.[9]

As the Brunswickers were entering Genappe, the Duke of Wellington, with General von Dörnberg, Colonel von Müffling, Colonel Somerset and one of his aides-de-camp, Colonel Gordon, had finished inspecting the troops at Les Quatre Bras. It was approaching 12.45 p.m. His modest escort of light dragoons was ready and having given his orders to the columns marching on Genappe, there was not much else he could do. At the moment he was about to move off, Wellington turned to the Prince van Oranje-Nassau, fixed his eye upon him and said: 'If you are attacked, I count that you will hold the position until the arrival of reinforcements.' Wellington did not think this likely to happen, his mind was already elsewhere; the young Prince saluted gravely. As he turned his bridle and led his party off down the road towards Marbais and Sombreffe, Wellington turned to von Müffling:

> If, as it seems, what the enemy has standing at Frasnes, opposite Les Quatre Bras, is so insignificant, and should only mask the English army, then I can use my entire strength to support the Field Marshal, and everything he wishes as a joint operation, I will gladly carry out.

The Prussian, convinced of the Duke's integrity, possibly assumed that Wellington was thinking aloud, or perhaps somehow expressing concern over the coming

'The first booming of distant guns'

discussions, especially with General von Gneisenau, whom he knew to have a distrust of his intentions.[10]

With the Duke of Wellington gone and the firing having more or less stopped, an exhausted von Sachsen-Weimar requested that he be relieved for a short while to rest. He had been awake since early the previous morning, on horseback for much of the day before and fully occupied directing the defence of Frasnes and Les Quatre Bras the preceding evening. Receiving permission from de Perponcher-Sedlntizky, he rode wearily back to Les Quatre Bras and throwing himself on a straw mattress, was instantly asleep.[11]

A short time after the Duke of Wellington had left, towards 1.00 p.m., word reached the Prince van Oranje-Nassau of the arrival of a substantial body of French troops. Riding up to the outposts with his staff, it soon became obvious to all that the growing dust clouds to the south concealed at least one, perhaps two infantry brigades. Now, he surmised, would be a sensible time to strengthen the front line between the Ferme du Grand-Pierrepont and Piraumont and he discussed the situation briefly with General de Perponcher-Sedlnitzky, before the latter issued several orders.[12]

Captain Bijleveld was directed to limber up his five pieces and withdraw them to the original position of the battery on the heights of Gemioncourt. Here, they were joined shortly afterwards by the six pieces of Captain Stevenaar's brigade, which took up ground to the right of the horse artillery. In preparing for action, he too had ordered all superfluous vehicles to be drawn off to a holding area some 300 metres to the rear of Les Quatre Bras and his gunners had wasted little time in ensuring that the pieces were made ready and were busy hacking with their 'sabre briquets' at the nearly ripe wheat and rye, which would make excellent wadding for the guns.[13]

At each piece, a 6-pounder cartridge was pushed into the muzzle and rammed home with a satisfying thud. Stepping forward with a wire 'pricker' the chargeman drove it into the vent, piercing the powder bag, before removing a cut reed primer filled with fine-grain powder from his waist pouch, which he pushed down the vent and into the bag. Now loaded, the Gunner First Class, aimed the gun, passing instructions to the men heaving on the levers shoved through the rings on the transom, whilst the ventsman adjusted the elevating screw to ensure, by dead reckoning, that the ball would strike the ground a mere six hundred metres away, on the high ground near Delsot. The linstocks were driven into the ground at the side of each piece, waiting to provide the spark that would ignite the fighting. To the south-east, Lieutenant Winsinger's section of two 6-pounder guns was similarly cleared for action, drawn up on the slopes to the north of the Ferme du Petit-Pierrepont, where the Bois de Bossu was separated from the Bois du Pierrepont by the chemin d'Houtain-le-Val. Its new position was calculated primarily to support the infantry protecting the Bois de Bossu, but if needs be, an enfilade fire could be brought to bear towards the Charleroi road, some 1,700 metres distant.[14]

With the artillery positioned, a staff officer was dispatched to find Colonel von Dressel, who was ordered to break up the overnight bivouac of the first battalion of the Regiment Oranien-Nassau in the garden and orchard of the Ferme des Quatre Bras. The insistent rolling of the drums as they beat the 'General' quickly roused the men. As soon as the battalion was assembled, von Dressel marched it off to the south, along the Charleroi road. Arriving at a junction of tracks to the south of the Ferme de Gemioncourt, it was directed by another staff officer to wheel to the right and the men marched along the dusty chemin de Gemioncourt, their view to the south obscured by the rising ground and the height of the crops. Arriving at the Ferme du Grand-Pierrepont, von Dressel halted the battalion and sent a detachment to occupy the farm, as well as another to press on to the south and put the Ferme du Petit-Pierrepont into a state of defence. The remainder of the battalion then moved off the road and through the wheat, labouring up the slope until it reached a position half-way between the farm and the Bois du Pierrepont, where it deployed into line. Here they were joined by the Volunteer Jager Company under Captain Bergmann, who had just received orders to attach himself to the battalion. Judging that these men would be best utilised as sharpshooters, von Dressel posted them in four sections on his open right flank, covering the chemin de Wattimez, at the point where it passed between the Bois du Pierrepont and the Bois de Rèves.[15]

General de Perponcher-Sedlnitzky also sent Major Baron Taets van Amerongen to Colonel de Jongh an order, in turn, to muster the 8th National Militia Battalion and follow von Dressel's men. As the troops arrived at Croix-Pierrepont, they were marched into a position to the north of the farm of the same name, where they formed a line a little forward of the hollow way on the edge of the woodland, extending from the chemin d'Houtain-le-Val, as far as the left flank of the first battalion of the Regiment Oranien-Nassau.[16]

At Croix-Gilbert, orders were similarly received by Major Sattler for the remaining four companies of the first battalion of the 2nd Nassau-Usingen Regiment to move forward. As soon as the men had fallen into column, a staff officer conducted them down the chemin du Champ du Sarti, to the west of the Bois de Bossu, where they were reunited with the two companies that had been detached the evening before. Emerging from the wood, the reassembled battalion was assigned the defence of the area to the north of Croix-Pierrepont and the column wheeled to the left and took up a position in the open ground between the chemin de Gemioncourt and the Bois de Bossu. Once the battalion had formed into line, Captains Christian Werneck and Peter Trittler were ordered to take their companies forward in skirmish order and occupy the lane itself, much of which formed a natural entrenchment as it cut through the rising ground.[17]

At the crossroads of Les Quatre Bras, the 5th and 7th National Militia Battalions continued to occupy positions behind the Bois de Bossu, in the fields to the north of the Nivelles road. Close by were Major von Normann's men, who had earlier been withdrawn as far as the crossroads, where in the shade of the farm buildings, garden and orchards, his troops had fallen out and prepared soup. While the men were cooking, officers were dispatched with fatigue parties to scour the artillery caissons for British cartridges, without which the battalion would be utterly ineffective.

To the east of von Normann's men, the four companies of the second battalion of the Regiment Oranien-Nassau were in a similar predicament. Without sufficient ammunition to sustain a prolonged fire, it was judged prudent to hold them in reserve for the time being.[18]

The remaining two companies of this battalion continued to occupy the Ferme de Gemioncourt, the strongpoint in the centre of the Allied line. The buildings themselves were solidly constructed of brick and stone, linked together by a high wall. The barns and farmhouse had limited points of entry which could be easily barricaded but no one, it seemed, had decided whether it should be fortified. In any case, there were no pioneers with the two Oranien-Nassau companies and Captain Esau's company of Netherlands engineers was still at Braine-le-Comte with the picks and other tools. Even if the manpower and equipment had been available, it would still have proven difficult, in the time available, to make loopholes and construct fire steps, dig ditches and prepare other defensive measures necessary to transform it into a fortress.[19]

In contrast to the ground in front of the Bois de Bossu, which bristled with bayonets, nowhere was the general shortage of infantry more apparent than the area to the east of the Ferme de Gemioncourt, defended by a mere 762 officers and men of the 27th Jager Battalion. Newly raised and inexperienced in light infantry tactics, only 182 of them had fought before, either for Napoleon or against him. For 580 men, the coming few hours would see the commencement – and in some cases the termination – of their military careers. These raw troops were tasked with the occupation of almost three kilometres of front between the Charleroi and Namur roads. So lightly defended was it, that an approaching enemy could easily surmise that this area was not intended to be vigorously defended, but was designed more as an early warning system. Colonel Grunenbosch, however, was determined to make the best use of his limited resources. Shortly after 1.00 p.m., he detailed Captain de Burleux and No. 3 Company to cover the eastern flank of Bijleveld's guns. Captain Eichholtz, First Lieutenant de Croes and Captain de Crassier occupied the heights of Gemioncourt farther to the east with Nos. 1, 2 and 6 Companies respectively, two of them defending the crossing over the du Pré des Queues stream, to the north of the Ferme de Lairalle, with the third posted overlooking Piraumont. All three companies maintained a line of picquets several hundred metres in advance. The remaining two companies of the battalion; No. 4 under Captain de Nave and No. 5, commanded by Captain Baron van Heekeren van Waliën, were kept in reserve, close to the étang Materne, under the control of Colonel Grunenbosch.[20]

Shortly after the artillery had withdrawn to the heights of Gemioncourt, Major Hegmann had been ordered to pull back most of his third battalion of the 2nd Nassau-Usingen Regiment and now occupied a new position to the west of the gun-line. Whilst the main body sat down in the tall crops, formed up in battalion column, the two companies he had left in advance, fanned out in open order, establishing a screen of skirmishers which would not only provide the gunners with some protection from French tirailleurs, but would also sound the alarm in the event that the French advanced. As the troops hurried into position, de Perponcher-Sedlnitzky

The Battle of Quatre Bras

was probably all too aware of the frailty of his situation. His division occupied a position that would not have been crowded had it been held by four. Stretched in an arc that measured four kilometres from tip to tip, the two brigades formed an extended line that had little depth and negligible reserves; it would have to do.[21]

As the Netherlanders and Nassauers settled down to await the enemy, some of General Halkett's men were still on the march, several kilometres to the west. Finally catching up with the remainder of the brigade, the 73rd Regiment of Foot arrived at the halting place, towards 1.00 p.m., followed about half an hour later by the weary 30th Regiment of Foot. Digging the straps of their packs from aching shoulders and with throats parched by the dust and the heat, the spirits of the men were lifted by the arrival of some commissariat wagons, whose enterprising drivers had somehow managed to find a way through the congestion at Nivelles. The order to issue three days' provisions was given and the soldiers were duly served with salt beef and ship's biscuit, it proving impossible to provide fresh food for so many. The old soldiers bore the news with equanimity. It was typical of the army. Fatigue parties filled camp kettles with water from distant streams, whilst others gathered kindling for the fires.[22]

Some ten kilometres behind them, their stray Light Infantry Company was marching at a punishing pace. Passing through Braine-le-Comte, its officers had learned that the division had struck off from that place in the direction of Nivelles. The town and its exits were clogged with vehicles of all descriptions. Servants, bâtmen and grooms guarded the horses and baggage of the officers. Commissaries officers tried to drive their convoys of biscuit, ball and bandages along the thronged byways, shouting at the camp followers and families to make way. Negotiating the obstacles with shouts and threats, the 'Light Bobs' cleared the town and entered the shade of the Bois de la Houssière.[23]

Some 26 kilometres away, the Duke von Braunschweig-Lüneburg returned to Genappe from Les Quatre Bras at about 1.30 p.m. and was delighted to discover that his troops had arrived at the town. Burning with a desire for retribution, he turned to his staff officers and 'Strongly expressed his wish of having an opportunity of meeting the French in equal force with his troops', little knowing that the Prince van Oranje-Nassau, five kilometres to the south, was about to send him just such an express. Having briefed his senior officers on the developing situation at Les Quatre Bras, he dismounted and lay back against a mound of earth, dozing peacefully on the bed of heather for fifteen minutes, as the leading elements of Kempt's brigade moved through the village.[24]

The march south, albeit, 'at the quick', had not troubled Major Ross-Lewin, though he did have the advantage of being mounted. The lush, rolling countryside had passed by without event, until his battalion gently descended into the village of Genappe just before 2.00 p.m., passing the Ferme de la Posterie, where the relay horses were stabled. Riding along the rue de Bruxelles, he admired the large and comfortable houses that lined its solitary street, perhaps in particular, the Hôtel du Roi d'Espagne, destined to house Wellington, Prince Jérôme Bonaparte, Field Marshal von Blücher and a dying *Général de Division* Count Philibert Duhesme, over the course of the following two days. In consequence of the improvements made to the national network of stage-coaches, Genappe had prospered from the regular arrivals of diligences and malles-postes and numerous coaching inns had sprung up along the main road to serve this passing trade. Lieutenant Stephens had little time for such sightseeing, or the developments in local commerce. He was sure that for the past four or five miles, he had heard the sound of a distant cannonade. Perhaps it was the Prussians?[25]

A short while later the 92nd Regiment of Foot arrived, not having left Waterloo until 11.00 a.m. The day was oppressively warm and Sergeant Robertson was sweating under his thick serge coatee and heavy woollen kilt. Bonnets had long since come off, collars and coats were opened and stocks loosened. The heavy muskets were moved from one aching arm to the other. Two hours after leaving Waterloo, the grateful battalion had received an order to halt on the roadway, as it breasted a rise to the west of the Ferme de Tout-lui-Faut; but after a short rest of fifteen minutes, it set off once again down the hill and into Genappe, where the considerate inhabitants had placed large tubs of water at the doors. As his men gulped down precious mouthfuls and poured the refreshing water over their heads, Robertson learned from a villager that a French patrol had been there that morning.[26]

The Duke von Braunschweig-Lüneburg was woken by the young soldiers of Best's Landwehr battalions tramping past and 'tired and hungry as they were, they sang as they passed the Duke, abusing and swearing against Buonaparté, wishing that they might soon meet him, and have an opportunity of setting the soldiers of the Grande Nation to rights.' Shortly afterwards, the Duke received the welcome order to move urgently to Les Quatre Bras and in no time, his own troops were following Kempt and Best's brigades towards the field of battle.[27]

The situation at Frasnes was rapidly deteriorating. The picquets had reported the steady arrival of large numbers of enemy infantry, cavalry and artillery, which were massing to the east of Frasnes and along the chaussée for as far as the eye could see. Having earlier abandoned the Balcan plateau, the Prince van Oranje-Nassau and his staff observed the arrival of these troops from the heights of Gemioncourt. The tiraillade between the opposing skirmishers had become far more vigorous and it seemed to both the Prince and General de Perponcher-Sedlnitzky that the mood had changed; the French were on the move.[28]

Amongst those carefully watching the French deployment were Major van Opstall, commanding the artillery of the 2nd (Netherlands) Infantry Division and Major de la Sarraz, the Chief of the Artillery Staff. Judging from the positions the enemy were taking up, they concluded that the decisive action would most likely occur close to the main road. Even if the French were to attempt an outflanking manoeuvre, the presence of Koopman's three guns on the high ground of the heights of Bati-Saint-Bernard was sufficient to command the area around Piraumont. The artillery would remain as it was.[29]

A little to the south, the French masses continued to gather and the Nassau and Netherlands officers, posted with their men in the picquet line, watched the build up through their telescopes and relayed their findings to the battalion commanders, who in turn passed the word to the generals and their staffs. An increasing number of enemy battalions had now taken up positions in the fields to the east of the Charleroi road, with long columns of artillery halted in their intervals. Though difficult to make out the precise number in view of the high crops and the screen provided by the Bois de l'Hutte, the observers estimated that the French had more than a brigade present, perhaps even an entire division of eight or more battalions. With the passing of time, however, even more infantry and artillery had arrived. At about 1.30 p.m., word had been sent back of this reinforcement. It was now believed that the enemy had assembled two infantry divisions, two cavalry divisions and two or three batteries of artillery. As soon as this news reached the Prince van Oranje-Nassau and General de Perponcher-Sedlnitzky, messengers had been sent to the Duke von Braunschweig-Lüneburg at Genappe and to Generals Kempt and Pack, requesting them to continue their march on Les Quatre Bras. Even as this order was being sent, the French started moving troops forward, through the 600-metre gap between the Charleroi road and the Bois de l'Hutte. In the vanguard, teams of foot artillery could be seen moving off the road and forming a gun line to the east of the Balcan, the batteries occupying the ground between Delsot and the roadside chapel of Notre-Dame-de-Basse-Wavre. The men of Bijleveld's troop watched the French gunners perform the drills common to all artillerymen, as they brought their pieces into action, perhaps whiling away the time in speculating on the calibre and model of the French equipment. Standing silently by their own cannon, Gunners Frankhuizen, Glas and de Wit probably contemplated the coming minutes with a mixture of apprehension and a strong sense of duty. The ordeal, when it finally came, would be by iron.[30]

Through the intelligence gleaned from refugees, prisoners and deserters the day before, the Prince and his officers knew that these formations were probably only the leading elements of a far greater body of troops. Despite the anxiety that this caused the young man, at least he now knew with a reasonable degree of confidence that Les Quatre Bras and not Nivelles was the real axis of the enemy attack. The quiet of the morning, he surmised, could only have been the consequence of the French needing time to bring their troops forward from their overnight bivouacs. The Prince and Wellington used this time to bring forward several divisions of infantry and cavalry to Nivelles, Les Quatre Bras and Genappe. Aware that Wellington's infantry reserve – though on the move – was still some way off, he reflected on the fact that none of his remaining divisions had orders to move farther east than Nivelles. After a quick conference with General de Perponcher-Sedlnitzky, the Prince decided that Les Quatre Bras was sufficiently threatened to warrant him reinforcing the position still further and he dictated orders for Generals von Alten and Cooke to continue their march from Nivelles to the crossroads. Colonel Felton Hervey, his Assistant Quartermaster-General, was handed the message for von Alten, whilst Major van Gorkum was given the message for Cooke and briefed that this officer would be found at Nivelles or somewhere on the road between Braine-le-Comte and that town. In addition to delivering the orders to Cooke, the same messenger was to inform Colonel Abercromby of his intentions, as well as General de Constant-Rebecque, should the officer still be at Nivelles. Though the Prince's concern for his right flank was waning, he remained sufficiently cautious to retain the bulk of de Collaert's cavalry, and von Ompteda's infantry brigade at Arquennes, with Chassé's infantry division at Nivelles. It was close to 2.00 p.m.[31]

As the staff officers dashed along the Nivelles road, they passed a body of blue-jacketed infantrymen, coated in dust. It was Colonel van den Sanden and the 7th Line Battalion, the final formation of de Perponcher-Sedlnitzky's division, hurrying to rejoin its corps. Having signalled his arrival to General van Bijlandt, van den Sanden was told to halt to the west of the Bois de Bossu, in the open ground to the north of the Champ du Sarti. For the time being, and until the intentions of the French were better understood, they would form a reserve, whilst also guarding against an outflanking manoeuvre towards Houtain-le-Val. Happy not to have any more marching to do for the time being, the soldiers rested their muskets on the ground and turned their attention to the myriad of minor tasks that occupy an infantryman about to go into action. As the men fell out, perhaps Flanker Dominique Soudan and Fusilier Daniel Leary suddenly felt themselves a long way from their homes in the United States of America.[32]

As van den Sanden's men settled down to the west, to the east of the Bois de Bossu, the troops of de Perponcher-Sedlnitzky's division stood to arms, ignorant of the strategies and plans of their generals, but aware that the next few hours would see their survival or extinction. Those of a more nervous disposition slipped away to relieve themselves, huddled in the rye, away from prying eyes; having nothing inside your bladder and bowels made it less likely that you would embarrass yourself when the moments of pure fear arrived.

Suddenly, the air was rent by a metallic bang as the first of the French guns disgorged its 6-pound iron ball. The sky darkened for an instant, as birds were flushed from the fields, hedges and trees. Each piece in the battery successively followed until the enemy gun line was shrouded in acrid smoke. As the crews hauled the guns back into position, barrels were swabbed and cartridges rammed home and the metronomic routine of serving the cannon took over. Observing the fall of shot by telescope, the French officers could be seen issuing corrections; elevations were adjusted and handspikes raised the heavy trails sufficiently for the barrel to be aligned once more with the green and blue-clad soldiers in the open fields to the north. Before long, the horizon in the direction of Frasnes was obliterated by smoke, from which emerged flashes of igniting powder and for those with the keenest eyesight, the small black specks that carried death and destruction to those in their path. It was shortly after 2.00 p.m.[33]

Some way to the north, the 79th Regiment of Foot was halted and the men had gratefully fallen out on the roadside to rest their weary legs. Private Vallence was tired, stiff and hot. Loaded down with knapsack, blanket, camp kettle, sixty rounds of ball cartridge, musket and bayonet and three days' bread, his burden seemed infinitely heavier than when he had left Brussels. The road from that city was choked

The Battle of Quatre Bras

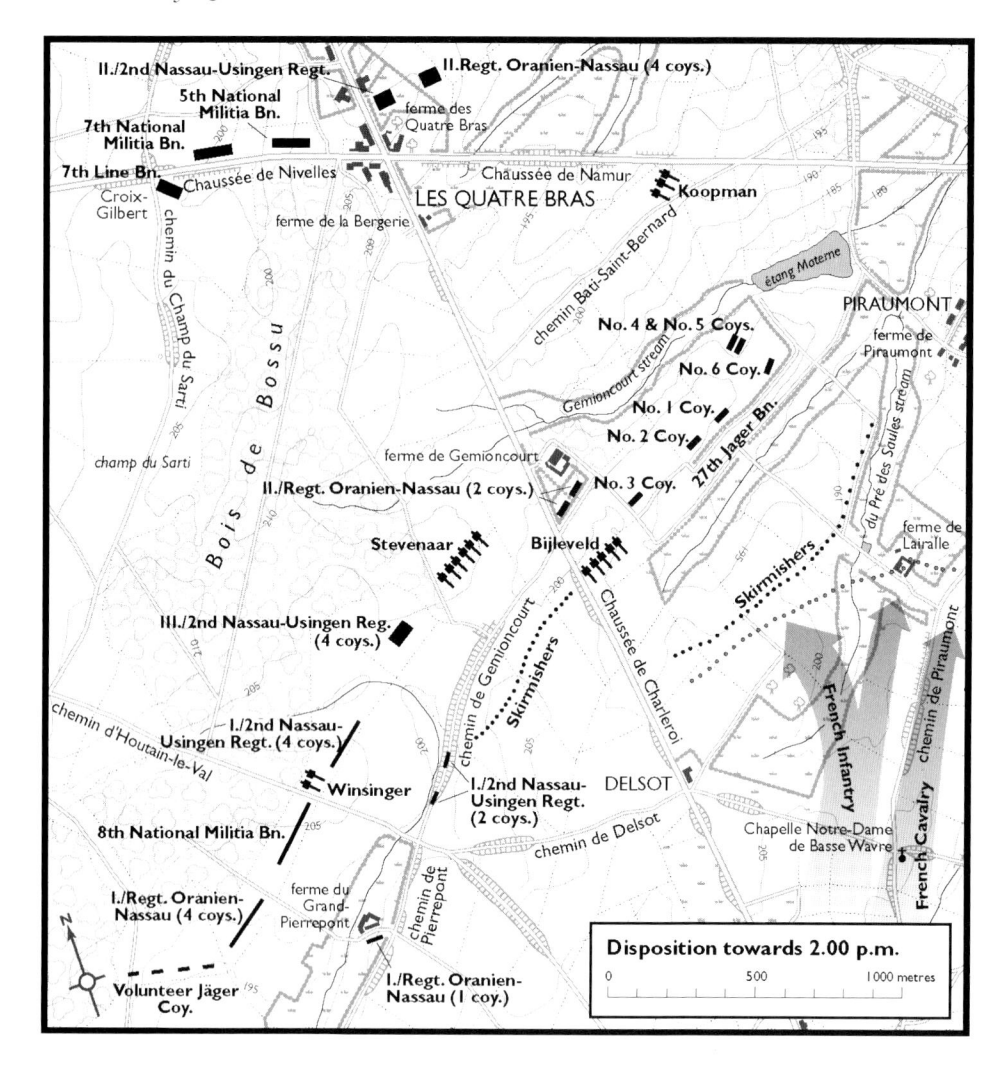

with the red-coated battalions of Kempt's, Pack's and Best's brigades, mixed with the sombre black of the Brunswick division and the dusty blue of the artillery. It took some minutes for the sound of the cannonade to be heard over the chattering of thousands of voices, but slowly the conversation died away, as ears were turned to the south, from where the distinct crack of the big guns came trembling through the air.[34]

The opening salvos of the French artillery could also be heard in Brussels, over thirty kilometres to the north, where anxious foreign visitors lined the walls, straining their ears to catch the sound. In their midst was Lieutenant Jackson:

> The first booming of distant guns; and then began the cry of 'Sauve qui peut' among the numerous English families residing there. All the post horses were soon engaged in transporting them to Antwerp or to Ghent; but numbers were forced to remain, at least for the present. As to the inhabitants, they had seen so much of armies traversing

their city in the preceding year, that the aspect of things seemed little more in their eyes than the threatening of a whirlwind, which might or might not seriously and injuriously affect them. Besides, half of the inhabitants were French at heart, and if Napoleon should prevail, they would only be welcoming friends. The cannonade had become almost continuous, seeming very near; and as I knew that the Duke and headquarters staff had gone in the direction of Waterloo, I felt it to be my only proper course to endeavour to join headquarters; the roar of the cannon, moreover, aroused my boyish ardour, and I was speedily mounted and on my way.[35]

At Laeken, five kilometres to the north of Brussels, the anxious Capel family could hear the guns, sometimes swelling in sound as if approaching; at other times diminishing. They hushed their breath to hear better.[36]

Though the same cannon could be heard at Nivelles, the troops there were far too busy to waste time in speculation. Once the tail of von Kielmansegge's Hanoverians had moved off to the east, followed closely by Halkett's brigade, Chassé's division had once again been set in motion, passing through the narrow and congested streets of the town, until it gained the Faubourg de Bruxelles and continued its march north. Climbing the dusty road out of the town, staff officers directed the first of its twelve battalions to wheel into the meadows and orchards that lined the great highway. As successive troops arrived, they occupied a position facing south, overlooking the town. The champ du Merly was steadily filled with troops; artillery were posted on the higher ground, at the Ferme de Bon-Aire. To the east, patrols were despatched to establish a link with von Alten's division, still bivouacked on the road to Houtain-le-Val. His role of traffic policeman fulfilled, General de Constant-Rebecque had in the meantime ridden south and inspected General de Collaert's deployment. The vedettes of de Ghigny's brigade were well-placed, observing the roads to Arquennes, Buzet and Rèves, while General Trip's three regiments of carabiniers rested their horses. Nothing had been seen of the French.[37]

To the south, Colonel von Ompteda's 2nd (King's German Legion) Infantry Brigade approached Arquennes and fell in with elements of de Collaert's cavalry, guarding the road from Binche. Having initially marched on Nivelles, he had been ordered by von Alten to cover the right flank of the division. The men were exhausted. They had marched for upwards of fifteen hours along rutted farm tracks that had been baked hard in the sun, from the remote cantonments of Jurbise and Brugelette, over forty kilometres away. Piling arms and drinking thirstily from their canteens, they could hear the distinct noise of combat towards the east.[38]

The cannonade had served as a timely wake-up call for others. Colonel von Sachsen-Weimar had managed very little rest, but despite the inadequacy of his surroundings, it had served to refresh him somewhat, having remained awake the whole of the previous night on a blend of anxiety and adrenalin. He awoke with a start as the orchestra of enemy guns commenced their symphony of cracks, booms, whooshes and bangs. By the time he had pulled on his boots, buttoned up his coat and fastened his sword belt, the sound had merged into a more constant rumbling noise. Seizing his hat, he dashed outside, mounted his horse and galloped back to his station in the Bois de Bossu.[39]

To the east of the Charleroi road, Colonel Grunenbosch remained with his reserve companies, to the south-west of the étang Materne. It was almost as if he had deployed his battalion as an illustration of the light infantry regulations. A line of sharpshooters, operating in file pairs, had been deployed on the heights of Lairalle at five metre intervals, with instructions to watch for any enemy movement. The young men had a grandstand view as the French infantry deployed on the heights of de l'Hutte, just over a kilometre distant. Not more than 500 metres to their rear, No. 1, No. 2 and No. 6 Companies had been drawn up in platoons along the crest of the heights of Gemioncourt; doubtless, Jager Hubert Hendeloo, Corporal Gerhardus Gerritsen and Sergeant Abraham de Beer were experiencing a combination of excitement and dread as the minutes ticked slowly by. Eventually, through the shimmering heat, the skirmishers of Captain Eichholtz's No. 1 Company observed a single, immense column emerge from the clouds of dust, its frontage seemingly four or five hundred metres broad. The mass was preceded by a swarm of skirmishers, amounting to an entire battalion; perhaps even more. The pounding of drums was mixed with wild cheering and shouts of, '*Vive l'Empereur,*' an alloy of sound that was enough to chill the blood of even the most resolute soldier. The swaying, glittering mass advanced closer and perspective was restored. Two distinct columns emerged into view, advancing alongside each other in the direction of Lairalle and Piraumont; whilst along the chemin du Piraumont itself, green-coated cavalry moved into the ground between the road and the Bois de l'Hutte. Colonel Grunenbosch had ridden forward as the cannonade commenced and was keenly observing these developments. Though it was still difficult to make out detail, he surmised that each column must comprise at least five or six battalion columns; possibly even more. The column to the left appeared to be making for the Namur road to the east, whilst the troops on the right seemed to have pivoted as they approached Lairalle and were now headed straight for Lieutenant de Croes' No. 2 Company.[40]

With the distance rapidly closing and the head of the column marching into range of the skirmish line, Grunenbosch ordered his bugler to sound 'vuren', the order to open fire; as the half-moon bugle blared out the repetitive five-note call, musketry crackled from the line of jagers, wreathing the position in billowing white smoke. The men had been ordered to fire at the column and to ignore the enemy skirmishers, but it was virtually impossible to see what damage, if any, the fusillade had inflicted on the French. As the smoke cleared somewhat, it became obvious that it had been insufficient to arrest the enemy's progress. Maintaining a brisk independent fire, Colonel Grunenbosch's skirmishers slowly fell back towards the crossings over the du Pré des Queues stream. As they withdrew, the men recalled their drill routine and methodically bit through the ball-end of the cartridge and primed the pan. Ramming the powder, ball and cartridge paper wadding down the barrels and pulling back the cock, the weapon was once more made ready to fire. The moment that each man's covering file had completed reloading his own musket, the jager levelled his piece and pulled the trigger. A shower of sparks and smoke flew from both the pan and the muzzle, spewing lead balls and scraps of smouldering cartridge paper into the faces of the advancing enemy infantry. The skirmishers maintained their fire for some considerable time, musket balls slapping past, as the two-man teams alternately fired and loaded. The height of the crops made it difficult to pick out individuals, but the experienced French tirailleurs managed to keep Grubenbosch's men sufficiently distant from their column that the Dutch were unable to make many telling shots on the French officers, non-commissioned officers and 'têtes-de-colonne'.[41]

Gradually, it became obvious that the right-hand column had closed up and changed the direction of its advance, inclining more directly towards the right flank company of Captain Eichholtz and Captain de Burleux's No. 3 Company, posted to the east of the Charleroi road in support of Bijleveld's guns. It seemed that the French intended to drive this part of their attack directly across the du Pré des Queues stream, whilst to the east, the enemy masses continued their advance on Piraumont. As they keenly observed the progress of the approaching French column, Eichholtz's jagers noticed it seemed to lose a degree of cohesion. The boggy ground around the stream, churned up by the feet of cattle, goats, sheep and pigs, was sucking the boots from the feet of the 'fantassins' and causing others to slip and lose their footing, disrupting the succeeding ranks. As the infantry slithered in the mire, Captain Bijleveld's battery, just over eight hundred metres away on the firmer ground of the road and its verge, took the opportunity to pound the stationary mass with canister. Leaving the leading battalion to extricate itself and re-form, the remaining battalions fanned out closer to the road, seeking a more solid footing. To the nervous jagers awaiting their baptism of fire, every delay, no matter how minor, must have been welcomed with relief, but must also have served to increase their anxiety. In the meantime, the enemy column to the east had bypassed the Ferme de Lairalle and was nearing Piraumont, under the watchful gaze of Captain de Crassier's No. 6 Company, drawn up on the high ground to the north of the hamlet. The French were now advancing obliquely across the fields and down the lane and for a short while, their advance seemed tentative, as if uncertain whether the scattered farm buildings and cottages were occupied by the green-coated jagers. Within minutes, however, the French skirmishers were dashing down the lane and through the enclosures, breaking open the doors of each building and searching for enemy soldiers; there was no rattle of musketry in response. The village was empty.[42]

The advance of the infantry columns eventually cleared sufficient room on the heights of de l'Hutte for the French to bring up more artillery and Captain Bijleveld watched anxiously as more guns appeared and took up a position to the east of the road, under the direction of various staff officers. At a range of six hundred metres, two companies of French artillery opened fire in a cacophony of concussive blasts. Within seconds, Bijleveld's beloved troop was being pounded. Horses were pulverised into inanimate heaps of mangled flesh, whilst others kicked in the traces, as ball after stinging ball ploughed into the line of vehicles. As quickly as teams were decimated, their industrious drivers sought to unbuckle the harnesses from the still-twitching horsemeat, move the vehicles into clear ground and to fill the gaps with horses from the ammunition wagons, or those of the gunners themselves. At all costs, the troop must be capable of movement. The sweating soldiers, many of whom were being cannonaded for the first time, attempted to return fire, but the odds weighed heavily against them and Bijleveld decided that he risked the complete destruction of his command if he remained where he was. Under pressure from the advancing infantry and parties of light cavalry closer to the chaussée, he reluctantly ordered the troop to limber up and withdraw eight hundred metres to the north, where he would be at a more extreme range from the enemy's 6-pounders. The gunners frantically stowed sponges, rammers, buckets and ammunition on the carriages and limbers and by a combination of drag rope, hand spike and brute force, managed to reverse the cannon and lift the trails onto the limber pintles. One by one, the straining teams of horses pulled the guns from the rutted fields and dragged them back up the Charleroi road, away from their baptism of fire, followed closely by the men of Captain de Burleux's company of the 27th Jager Battalion.[43]

On the opposite side of the road, Stevenaar's brigade took up the struggle in turn and made valiant efforts to match the French for effort, accuracy and rate of fire. Under the eye of their officers and following the barked instructions of the gun commanders, the crews discarded shakos, stocks and coats and served the guns in their waistcoats and shirtsleeves. Once Bijleveld's troop had withdrawn, however, the full weight of the enemy fire shifted to Stevenaar's six crews and it was to prove a short-lived and unequal contest. The company was being methodically and relentlessly destroyed. As the enemy ordnance tore through the gun line, men and animals were reduced to unrecognisable heaps of mutilated leather, cloth and gore. Ammunition wagons that had been brought forward to replenish the guns were wrecked, great fragments of metal and splinters of wood tearing into the men. In the centre of the violence, two of the cannon were disabled and an anxious Stevenaar gave orders for both pieces to be evacuated to the north of Les Quatre Bras, hoping that the attentions of his carriage-smith and wheelwright might render them serviceable once more.

Just as the Captain was making preparations for the damaged cannon to be moved, a message arrived from the Prince van Oranje-Nassau, carried by one of his British aides. Sensible of the futility of remaining in such a perilous position and concerned over the loss of two valuable guns in the centre of the position, the Prince directed Stevenaar to retire and take up a new position adjacent to that which had been occupied by Captain Bijleveld, who had just resumed firing from the chemin Bati-Saint-Bernard, to the north of the Ferme de Gemioncourt. He was also to send word to Lieutenant Winsinger, to pull back through the Bois de Bossu and rejoin the battery with his section of two guns.[44]

Colonel Grunenbosch had just seen Bijleveld's guns move off, when he decided to bring forward the battalion reserve. As the sweating soldiers took up ground along the top of the ridge, they saw for the first time the enormity of the task ahead of them. Grunenbosch directed Captains de Nave and van Heekeren van Waliën to deploy in skirmish order and bolster the thin line of resistance being offered by the two companies of Captains Eichholtz and de Croes. With the French already in possession of Piraumont and with several battalions of infantry already advancing up the southern slope of the heights of Gemioncourt, the scattered companies of his battalion were in danger of being isolated and cut off from the remainder of the division. Sending an order to Captain de Crassier to rejoin the main body with No. 6 Company, the jagers prepared for the impending struggle.[45]

The French advance was inexorable and heavy fighting erupted as Grunenbosch's men engaged the advancing columns. A short distance to the west, the withdrawal of No. 3 Company had exposed the flank of Captain Eichholtz's company to a body of French infantry advancing closer to the Charleroi road. Though Grunenbosch had hoped to slow the French advance by firepower alone, the sheer numbers of the French infantry, the weight of fire laid down by their artillery and skirmishers and the increasingly isolated nature of his position, prompted him to decide upon a withdrawal to the vicinity of the Ferme de Gemioncourt. As soon as de Crassier's company had rejoined, instructions were quickly given. Leaving behind those too seriously wounded to move, the five companies disengaged and quickly formed into a column. Within minutes, the battalion's intervals were established, so as to be able to swiftly form a defensive square, should the need arise. Slowly, the men moved off in the direction of the farm.[46]

Endnotes

1. C. White. G. Glover, pp. 300–2.
2. de Bas &c., p. 456. Batty, p. 48. Dellevoet, p. 21. von Kruse.
3. de Bas &c., p. 456. Dellevoet, p. 22. von Kruse. von Morenhoffen. Sattler. van Zuylen van Nyeveld (I), p. 54.
4. Aubrey-Fletcher, p. 371. de Bas &c., p. 461. Hamilton, p. 15. Maurice, pp. 8–11. J. Paget (I), p. 85. Powell. Whitworth, p. 45.
5. de Bas &c., p. 465. Hofschröer (I), pp. 233–4. von Pflugk-Harttung (I), p. 293. von Scriba (Bemerkungen), pp. 293–4.
6. de Bas &c., pp. 474–5. Daniell, p. 133. Hofschröer (I), p. 234. von Müffling (II), p. 230. von Pflugk-Harttung (I), p. 293. van Zuylen van Nyeveld (I), p. 54.
7. Anonymous (Near Observer), p. 46. Kincaid (I), pp. 313–14. Leach, pp. 374–5.
8. Allan. Anonymous (Cameron), p. 88. Alexander Forbes (II). Leask and McCance, p. 333. Robertson, p. 145. Mackenzie &c., pp. 54–5. Vallence, p. 6.
9. Anonymous (Das braunschweigische Korps). Bowden, p. 257. von Herzberg. Hofschröer (I), p. 234. Sichart (I), p. 7.
10. Arthur, p. 594. de Bas &c., p. 475. Daniell, p. 133. Archibald Forbes, pp. 264–5. Hofschröer (I), p. 234. van Limburg-Stirum. Maurice, p. 11. von Müffling (II), p. 230. Rens, p. 107. F. Somerset, pp. 8–9. P. Stanhope, p. 81. Starklof, p., 138.
11. Starklof, p. 138.

The Battle of Quatre Bras

12. Girod de l'Ain, pp. 270–4.
13. Bijleveld. Koopman. van Opstall. van de Wall. van Zuylen van Nyeveld (I), p. 53.
14. de Bas &c., pp. 479–80. Dellevoet, p. 22. Meijer. Starklof, p. 138. van Zuylen van Nyeveld (I), p. 54.
15. de Bas &c., p. 481. de Jongh. van Uythoven. van Zuylen van Nyeveld (I), p. 54.
16. de Jongh. Starklof, p. 138.
17. de Bas &c., p. 481. Dellevoet, p. 22. Leonhard. Starklof, p. 138. van Uythoven. van Zuylen van Nyeveld (I), p. 55.
18. Dellevoet, p. 22. de Jongh. Starklof, p. 138. van Uythoven.
19. de Bas &c., p. 404. Hofschröer (I), pp. 203, 206. Wüppermann, p. 85. van Zuylen van Nyeveld (I), p. 50.
20. de Bas &c., p. 480. van Bijlandt. Grunenbosch. Welter. van Zuylen van Nyeveld (I), p. 54.
21. de Bas &c., p. 480. Starklof, pp. 137–8.
22. Elkington (I), p. 12. Morris, p. 67.
23. Bannatyne, p. 320. Brett-James, p. 53. Macready (I).
24. Anonymous (Near Observer), pp. 76–7. Gomm (IV). von Herzberg.
25. Ross-Lewin, p. 254. Stephens. Verhulst, p. 35.
26. Anonymous (Letters), p. 223. Robertson.
27. Anonymous (Das braunschweigische Korps). Anonymous (Near Observer), pp. 76–7. von Herzberg. Kubel.
28. de Bas &c., p. 492. van Zuylen van Nyeveld (I), p. 54.
29. Bijleveld. Dellevoet, p. 22. van Opstall. van Osten. Starklof, p. 137. van Zuylen van Nyeveld (I), p. 55.
30. Aubrey-Fletcher, p. 367. de Bas &c., pp. 490, 493. Bowden, pp. 102–3. Archibald Forbes, p. 266. Girod de l'Ain, pp. 270–4. Grunenbosch. Kellermann. Houssaye, pp. 112–13. van Löben-Sels, p. 519. Reille. W. Siborne (V), p. 68.
31. de Bas &c., p. 491. Batty, pp. 47–8. van Gorkum. van Limburg-Stirum. Rooke (II).
32. de Bas &c., p. 482. van Limburg-Stirum. Scheltema, pp. 106–7. Scheltens, p. 198. van Zuylen van Nyeveld (I), p. 54.
33. Bowden, p. 103. Brett-James, p. 54. de Constant-Rebecque (I). Dellevoet, p. 22. Archibald Forbes, p. 266. F. von Gagern. Grunenbosch. Henckens, p. 225. von Herzberg. Heymès. Knoop (II), p. 144. van Limburg-Stirum. Ney, p. 8. van Oranje-Nassau (II). Reille. Rens, p. 107. von Sachsen-Weimar (I). Sichart (I). Starklof, p. 139. van Toll. Welter. van Zuylen van Nyeveld (I), p. 54.
34. Allan. Anonymous (Das braunschweigische Korps). Vallence, p. 8.
35. Jackson (II), pp. 16–17.
36. G. Paget (I), p. 112.
37. de Bas &c., pp. 462–3. van Delen. Hoynck van Papendrecht, p. 68.
38. de Bas &c., p. 463. Dehnel, p. 282. von Ompteda, p. 276. Wheatley, p. 59.
39. Starklof, p. 139.
40. Delhaize and Aerts, p. 432. Girod de l'Ain, p. 271. Grunenbosch. Henckens, p. 225. Ney, p. 58. Puvis, pp. 115–16. Reille. Trefcon, p. 181.
41. de Bas &c., p. 494. Grunenbosch. Welter.

42. Arthur, p. 596. de Bas &c., p. 494. Brett-James, p. 54. Foy. Grunenbosch. Houssaye, p. 113. van Löben-Sels, p. 519. Reille. W. Siborne (V), pp. 68–9. Trefcon, p. 181. van Zuylen van Nyeveld (I), p. 54.
43. de Bas &c., p. 494. Delhaize and Aerts, p. 433. Grunenbosch. Nafziger, p. 252. van Opstall. W. Siborne (V), p. 69.
44. de Bas &c., pp. 494–5, 508. Dellevoet, p. 22. van Opstall. W. Siborne (V), p. 69. van Uythoven. van Zuylen van Nyeveld (I), pp. 55–6, 58. Meijer. van de Wall.
45. de Bas &c., p. 494. Grunenbosch. Welter. van Zuylen van Nyeveld (I), p. 54.
46. de Bas &c., p. 494. Dellevoet, pp. 22–3. Grunenbosch.

CHAPTER 9

To the west of the Charleroi road, the men of the first and third battalions of the 2nd Nassau-Usingen Regiment had not yet been threatened by infantry. Though drawn up in line on the exposed slopes to the north of the chemin de Gemioncourt, they were also shielded from the French artillery at Delsot by the rising ground to the south. The French, however, we not content to leave them in this enviable position. Suddenly, the two skirmish companies under Captains Werneck and Trittler hurriedly withdrew to the main body of the first battalion. Moments later, over 600 horsemen in scarlet jackets and tall 'czapkas' poured over the crest of the ridge to the south, the pennons of the leading rank of each squadron fluttering at the end of the deadly lances. Those men that had served in the ranks of the Grande Armée recognised them instantly as the Chevau-Légers-Lanciers of Napoleon's Imperial Guard; the same men that von Normann's second battalion had frustrated during the course of the previous evening. As well as its skirmishers, the battalion was joined by the Prince van Oranje-Nassau and under the direction of the imperturbable Captain Büsgen, it formed square and drove off the cavalry with musketry. Dissuaded from pressing the attack by Lieutenant Winsinger's two guns, the lancers withdrew along the strip of open ground between the Ferme du Grand-Pierrepont and the Bois du Pierrepont, forcing the 8th National Militia Battalion and the first battalion of the Regiment Oranien-Nassau to seek sanctuary in the trees. Dutchman fired on Dutchman as the horsemen rushed past and passing the southern end of the woods, they received a lively farewell from the rifles of Captain Bergmann's Volunteer Jager Company. As soon as the threat receded, the Prince van Oranje-Nassau directed Büsgen to pull back into the Bois de Bossu and to take up a position to the north of the chemin d'Houtain-le-Val. An adjutant was also directed to take the same order to the third battalion, which was to occupy the south-eastern tip of the wood.[1]

Captain Bijleveld, established in his new position, continued to engage the French with his three 6-pounders and remaining howitzer and was joined shortly afterwards by Captain Stevenaar with a further three guns. Lieutenant van de Wall's howitzer had been separated but as Stevenaar took up ground to the west of Bijleveld's line, the lieutenant rejoined with his piece, having withdrawn through the wood along a track which had brought him out at the crossroads. Realising his error, he hurriedly brought his howitzer forward once again. Stevenaar's guns now came into action one

'We had the wood to retreat into'

by one, but in less than a minute, they were showered with such a quantity of shot and shell that the gunners and horses were soon falling in great numbers. A limber was destroyed, rendering its piece immobile. Captain Stevenaar was himself killed instantly by a 6-pounder ball and Major-General Herman van der Wijck, the Prince van Oranje-Nassau's Adjutant-General, fell heavily to the ground as his horse was killed beneath him. Miraculously, the young Prince remained unscathed and calmly dispatched one of his British aides-de-camp to bring forward the recently arrived 7th Line Battalion, which had halted to the west of the Bois de Bossu. The division was now complete on the field of battle, with almost 8,000 men and 16 guns assembled; but not before time.[2]

The men of the 5th National Militia Battalion were suffering from the same cannonade. A short time after the French had opened fire, the battalion had been roused from its bivouac at Les Quatre Bras and Colonel Westenbergh was given orders to march it to a new position to the north of the Ferme de Gemioncourt. As soon as it emerged on the Charleroi road, the column attracted the long-range attentions of several French guns, firing from the Balcan plateau and numerous projectiles were soon ploughing through the packed ranks of the column. With the exception of 19 soldiers, none of the 454 men from Arnhem had been in action before and this unnerving barrage was as unfamiliar as it was unpleasant. Conscious of their inexperience and knowing that even the most seasoned troops would have found their exposure to such a bombardment unsettling, Colonel Westenbergh and his officers made strenuous efforts to encourage and steady them. Having been an officer of the Pupilles de la Garde Impériale, he had plenty of experience of leading boy soldiers. Another officer marching in the column was Captain van Toll:

> When the battalion had left the crossroads a little behind it, a cannonball greeted us obliquely, to the left of the road, and wounded Lieutenant Klein and some men, which caused some consternation, whereupon the brave Westenberg shouted, 'Long live the King!' which was answered with enthusiasm by our young militiamen, who marched forward at the double.

Hunched under their packs and stumbling over the writhing bodies of the less fortunate men as they jostled their way forward. The battalion finally halted about four hundred metres to the north of the Ferme de Gemioncourt, just behind the chemin Bati-Saint-Bernard; where they continued to suffer losses not only from the cannonade directed at them, but from the rounds that were overshooting Bijleveld's troop, drawn up in a battery a short distance to the south. The 7th National Militia Battalion was more fortunate than its sister formation. It had received orders at the same time as Westenbergh's men, to move onto the chaussée to the north of the Bois de Bossu, whence it would be able to provide support either to the east or west, dependent upon the development of the French attack. Formed in column, the battalion was sheltered from the stray round shot by the protection of the trees.[3] Whilst the 5th National Militia Battalion was undergoing its baptism of fire and the

181

7th National Militia Battalion was resting on the highway, the 7th Line Battalion had remained drawn up in column to the west of the wood. The Adjutant, Lieutenant Scheltens, recollected the instructions carried by an English officer from the Prince van Oranje-Nassau's staff:

> March forward, wheel the head of the column to the right and deploy into line, traverse the wood and to flank it on the other side in skirmish order. The movement was made with regularity. We left the 12th Platoon in reserve. My battalion commander gave me the order to follow the movement. The line was well-formed. We had the wood to retreat into.

As the battalion advanced through the wood, it suffered several casualties from cannonballs that crashed through the trees, having carried a considerable distance from the high ground at Delsot. For those in the ranks with no experience of a cannonade, this was an unpleasant sensation. As it emerged into the open, to the north-west of the Ferme de Gemioncourt, it could see the 5th National Militia Battalion, several hundred metres away, but precious little else on account of the height of the crops. To the south, the smoke and noise suggested that it would not be long before they too were engaged.[4]

To the north of the Ferme de Gemioncourt, General de Perponcher-Sedlnitzky watched the withdrawal of the 27th Jager Battalion towards the Ferme de Gemioncourt and ordered Colonel Westenbergh to lead the 5th National Militia Battalion forward in support. No doubt glad to be on the move, rather than standing motionless under fire, the young militiamen descended the gentle slope and marched steadily towards the farm. Captain van Toll felt proud of his No. 3 Company and how it had withstood the attentions of the French artillery; now that the enemy was approaching musket range, its examination was about to become infinitely more testing.[5]

The moment that the 27th Jager Battalion started moving across the slope, it lost sight of the enemy, now hidden by the rise of the ground. Every now and then, the jagers paused to close up, the sergeants urging the men to maintain their ranks and files. As the battalion approached the enclosures of the Ferme de Gemioncourt, Colonel Grunenbosch, on General de Perponcher-Sedlnitzky's orders, detached the Carabinier and Flanquer companies under Captains Eichholtz and de Crassier. He instructed them to occupy the buildings, whilst the remainder of the battalion was to take up positions between the enclosure and the étang Materne, along the line of the stream. All the while, the battalion was engaged in a running fire with the pursuing French infantry and the air was thick with musket balls, one of which hit and wounded Captain van Heekeren van Waliën. Captain de Crassier hurried his men towards the buildings, a short distance to the east of which the main body of the 5th National Militia Battalion had arrived. Drawn up on the Charleroi road, it too was already under heavy musketry fire from nearby French infantry.[6]

Assuming that the jagers were headed for the buildings, Colonel Westenbergh detached both his flanquer companies, to occupy the garden and orchard to the south of the farm. Turning his attention to the remaining four companies, he quickly realised the difficulties he would face in this exposed position. Three companies under Captain Mollinger were posted in advance, close to the chaussée and on the road itself, but even as these troops took up their positions, the Colonel suddenly realised the threat posed by the masses of French skirmishers descending the heights to the south and south-east. Riding up to Captain van Toll, Westenbergh ordered him to lead his No. 3 Company up the slope and to drive the French back.[7]

The results were catastrophic. After van Toll had led his men some distance forward, the attack rapidly bogged down. Untrained in skirmish tactics and confronted by hundreds of veteran French tirailleurs, the young Dutchmen huddled together for protection in the tall crops, desperate to avoid the shower of musket balls that smashed into the heads, arms, chests and legs of their less fortunate comrades. In an instant, dozens of men were rendered hors de combat, their screams mingling with the cheers of the relentlessly advancing French columns. Everywhere, parties of bayonet-wielding French infantry dashed forward, seeking to outflank and cut off the Dutchmen. Second Lieutenant Wijnoldie, trying to cut his way through to safety with a small party of men was killed, his body trampled beneath the onrushing enemy. A ball smashed into the leg of Captain van Toll himself and he collapsed to the ground, perhaps fully expecting to share the fate of his subordinate. More fortunately for him, however, he was dragged to safety by a few of his men and saw little of the debacle as the remnants of his company streamed back towards the Ferme de Gemioncourt.[8]

The remaining three companies of the 5th National Militia Battalion lined the chemin de Gemioncourt and were defending themselves as best they could. Swarms of French skirmishers advanced to within a very close range of the position and were exploiting the cover afforded by the tall crops to pick off officers, senior non-commissioned officers and horses, raking the ranks and files with musketry; Captain Mollinger was hit. Powerless to counter this galling fire for the present, the men stood nervously in line, trying not to flinch as, here and there, lifeless bodies slumped from the ranks or the screams of wounded soldiers filled their ears. The smell of burnt powder filled the air. Men tried to focus on anything but death, muttering invocations to their God, repeatedly checking their weapons and listening for the words of command. At least the enemy artillery, with its own infantry in such close proximity to the enemy, had turned its attentions once more to Bijleveld's and Stevenaar's batteries; and the slow progress of the enemy columns seemed to have ground to a halt. For some, time had long since ceased to be relevant; events that flashed by in moments seemed to take minutes; the passage of hours was compressed into seconds.[9]

General de Perponcher-Sedlnitzky realised that Grunenbosch and Westenbergh's commands were insufficient to hold the centre of the line by themselves. The 5th National Militia Battalion alone could scarcely occupy 200 metres of ground, even if deployed in a thin two-deep line. Without substantial reinforcement, it could not possibly hope to defend the frontage of five hundred metres between the Bois de Bossu and the Ferme de Gemioncourt. To the east of the road, the situation of the 27th Jager Battalion was even more precarious. Fresh troops were needed to shore up the position, which was crumbling under the weight of the French assault. At that moment, the 7th Line Battalion emerged into the open, its 689 officers and men extended in a long line. Sensing that the French were about to punch a huge hole through the centre, de Perponcher-Sedlnitzky hurriedly sent orders to Colonel van den Sanden to commit his men to the support of the 5th National Militia Battalion. The 7th National Militia Battalion would remain on the chaussée, acting as a reserve.[10]

To the east of the farm, Grunenbosch's remaining companies had completed their fighting withdrawal. Their platoons were deployed behind the low, scrubby hedges that bordered the Gemioncourt stream, partially concealed by the thickets and brambles. To the south, in the fields of tall wheat and rye, the skirmish line continued to contest the ground with the French. The sweating marksmen groped through the vegetation, catching the occasional glimpse of an adversary as he stood to fire off a round. It was virtually impossible to see anything else, given the slope of the ground, the nature of the crops and the glare of the sun. The heat was intense.[11]

On the opposite side of the chaussée, Colonel Westenbergh was busy trying to restore order in Captain van Toll's company, which had taken shelter behind the three companies of the battalion that lined the chemin de Gemioncourt. Harrassed by enemy skirmishers, the troops in the open had been pressed back slightly to the north of the farm, but the fire of his men, combined with that of the companies of the 27th Jager Battalion in the farm complex, had dissuaded the French skirmishers from approaching too closely until formed infantry support arrived. With the skirmish line in tatters, the battalion was bereft of its eyes and ears; suddenly, a shout went up that enemy cavalry were approaching. Realising that it would prove impossible to reach the safety of the Ferme de Gemioncourt in time, Westenbergh calmly gave instructions for the men to form square. Now less than 200 metres away, the French horsemen charged over the crest, partly on the chaussée and partly in the fields to the west. Unable in some cases to see or avoid their own skirmishers, the cavalry bowled them over and the leading squadron cut a wide swathe through the crops as it descended the slope towards the waiting infantry. The militiamen ran to their posts instinctively, the long weeks of training at last paying off, and with a degree of shouting and pushing on the part of the sergeants, a ragged square was completed in sufficient time.

> After we had formed square, we noticed that some men from one company or platoon were mixed with those of other companies and wanted to restore the proper order; then Lieutenant-Colonel Westenbergh told us we did not have to be so precise.[12]

The humour broke the tension and must have encouraged the troops. As the French horsemen, frustrated at being deprived of their prize milled about, unable to press home their charge, the young infantrymen learned a valuable lesson about the impotence of cavalry against properly formed and steady infantry. Squadron after squadron launched themselves at the battalion, without result. Horsemen passed through the gap between the Ferme de Gemioncourt and the infantry, but sustained a flanking fire from the jagers posted in the buildings. Others, unable to force their horses onto the bayonets, had no option but to pass the battalion to the west, several saddles being emptied by canister fire from Stevenaar's remaining guns. The cohesion of the charge had disappeared, yet the cavalry lingered for some minutes, close to the farm, perhaps hoping that their temporary gain could be made permanent by the arrival of infantry. With no support forthcoming, the horsemen wheeled about and cantered off to towards the south to reform. They were followed by jeers from the ranks of the 5th National Militia Battalion. Men turned to those beside them and shook hands, cheering, congratulating each other and relishing their new-found immortality.[13]

The conduct of the battalion in the face of repeated attacks by superior numbers of French infantry and cavalry had impressed the nearby Prince van Oranje-Nassau, who shouted his satisfaction to them. Their performance had a similar effect on the chief-of-staff of the division, Colonel van Zuylen van Nyeveld. Perhaps, he thought, it was the close proximity of the Prince himself, along with his staff, which had inspired the young militiamen to perform so steadily in their first hostile action. No one, however, was as proud as Colonel Westenbergh. Bustling with energy, he deployed his battalion into line and chased off the more adventurous French skirmishers at bayonet-point, supported all the while by Bijleveld's and Stevenaar's guns. Arriving once more at the chemin de Gemioncourt, Westenbergh deployed his own skirmishers, who managed to secure the release of some men who had been captured earlier by the French and who had been stripped of weapons and equipment. These were sent to the rear in the charge of non-commissioned officers in the hope that spare muskets might be found in the supply wagons. For the time being, it seemed that the centre would hold.[14]

While the 5th National Militia Battalion had been obliged to receive the cavalry in square, Colonel van den Sanden's position, closer to the wood, had given him the option to withdraw the 7th Line Battalion into the shelter of the trees, a movement which was completed before the French cavalry could cross the intervening ground. As soon as its front was clear of the enemy, the battalion emerged from the eastern edge of the wood and took up a position on the right flank of the 5th National Militia Battalion, in the space between the Charleroi road and the Bois de Bossu. In the ranks were officers who had fought with seven different French infantry regiments and it must have been a curious feeling to be opposing the very men with whom they had served at Lützen, Bautzen, Dresden and Leipzig.[15]

Not far away, Colonel von Sachsen-Weimar was stationed in the Bois du Pierrepont alongside the first battalion of the Regiment Oranien-Nassau, but could see little of the French assault to the east. The rise of the plateau to the south-east, around Delsot and the Balcan effectively concealed the dispositions of the French from this part of the field and the noise of the artillery and the crackle of musketry in the distance must have made the Nassau and Netherlands troops anxious for news. Were the French seeking to outflank them to the north? Was the quietness an indication that the enemy had somehow turned their position by the south? The minutes slowly ticked by with no discernable threat materialising. Though it was stiflingly hot, the Nassau troops in

The Battle of Quatre Bras

the wood benefited from the shade of the trees and the proximity of the Gemioncourt stream, which had replenished many canteens as the troops had taken up their positions earlier in the day. The eastern edge of the wood was bounded by a narrow lane, occasionally bordered by a ditch or hedge, and was lined with troops, from the vicinity of the Ferme de Gemioncourt to the open ground where the road from Frasnes to Wattimez separated the Bois du Pierrepont from the Bois de Rêves.[16]

In front of the Bois du Pierrepont, the first battalion of the Regiment Oranien-Nassau and the 8th National Militia Battalion were once again deployed in line, in the open ground between the wood and the chemin du Pierrepont. The French had placed artillery on the high ground between the farm and Delsot and were bombarding the infantry with regularity. This, combined with the earlier probing charges by the lancers of the French Imperial Guard had made the soldiers edgy. Colonel de Jongh was on horseback in front of his militiamen.

> Having been here for a short while 'en bataille', under the fire of an enemy battery of three pieces, I saw the Oranien-Nassau battalion, amongst which a panic occurred, move backwards. I was in front of the centre of my battalion and the right flanquer company was disrupted by the Nassau battalion. I spurred my horse and, aided by the brave Captain Sijbers, acting Adjutant-Major, I immediately brought my company back into the line of battle. I discovered that the Nassauers had become frightened by His Royal Highness, the Prince of Orange, accompanied by staff and dispatch riders, who rode in front of our line of battle, under the fire of the enemy battery.[17]

If the mere sight of the Prince van Oranje-Nassau, his numerous staff and the presence of a number of mounted guides of the Netherlands headquarters had proven enough to spook the Nassauers, von Sachsen-Weimar must have been alarmed by his prospects of repulsing any serious attempt that the French might make to seize the wood. Though the enemy still seemed to have no interest in making any assault upon it. Deciding to protect the two battalions from the artillery, he moved them into the chemin du Pierrepont. Here, to some extent, they were sheltered from the worst effects of the French cannonade by the cuttings and embankments. It was 2.30 p.m.

The artillery firing on the Netherlanders was being heard elsewhere. Some distance to the north, toiling up the slope out of Genappe, Lieutenant Kincaid recollected that the 'distant sound of a solitary gun struck the ear'. In the column behind his battalion, Lieutenant Forbes of the 79th Regiment of Foot could also hear the distinct thunder of the enemy's artillery, as it echoed back and forth across the shallow valley of the Dyle. As far as the eye could see, sweating infantrymen filled the road and fields. Somewhere amongst the masses, Lieutenant Riddock and the 44th Regiment of Foot marched into Genappe, where they halted and piled arms under the shade of the trees, away from the scorching sun. As they rested, they listened to the random booming of the guns and imagined what they were doing to the Belgians, Dutch and Brunswickers. A short distance behind, the 42nd Regiment of Foot had also halted briefly. Suddenly, someone exclaimed, 'Hark! a gun!' The entire battalion strained to listen. 'Every ear is set to catch the sound and every mouth seems half-opened, as if to supersede the faithless ear that doubts of hearing'. With the gunfire becoming more pronounced:

> Every ear now catches the sound and every man grabs his musket. No pensive looks are seen. Our Generals' weather-beaten, war-worn countenances are all well known to the old soldiers and no throb of fear palpitates in a single breast.[18]

In an instant, the column was re-assembled and the regiment moved off, the march being urged on with greater speed than before. To Private Vallence, marching in the ranks of the Cameron Highlanders 'The sound of the cannon and the thunder of war', became louder and louder and he and his comrades 'Met more and more wounded soldiers, some of whom were sitting on the roadside with their wounds bleeding, some fainting from loss of blood, while others went limping past us.'[19] Where possible, the surgeon of the battalion, George Ridesdale, offered assistance, but his priority was to remain with his own men and he had to abandon the piteously injured casualties, who begged for water, for relief and in some cases, for death. Far to the rear, the Gordon Highlanders passed through Genappe in the wake of the Royal Scots and also heard the sound of cannon at no great distance, assuming that it originated from the scene of the fighting between the French and the 'Belgians'. Sergeant Robertson's blood was up, and he was not alone:

> This sound had a stimulating effect upon us, for so eager were we to enter the field of action, that we felt as fresh as if we had newly started. In fact, we were all anxious to assist the poor Belgians, who were but young soldiers and consequently but little experienced in military affairs. 'Forward,' was the word that ran through all the ranks, but the colonel had more discretion and would not allow us to run, lest we exhaust ourselves before the time. He issued peremptory orders that every man should keep his rank as if on parade and not to march above three miles an hour.[20]

In contrast, the Light Company of the 30th Regiment of Foot, some distance to the west of Nivelles, had also noticed a noise that sounded like distant peals of thunder and was breathlessly jogging along the highway:

> 'The Dutch artillery are practising,' said a young soldier in a tremulously inquisitive tone. 'They've redder targets than your cheeks, my boy, that fire those guns,' replied a swarthy veteran, who had learned this music in Spain.[21]

Meanwhile, at Thines, Captain Rudyerd noticed Colonel Hervey ride up to General Halkett, as his brigade rested in the open fields. The Assistant Quartermaster-General was easily recognisable, having lost an arm during the assault on Oporto. Hervey had passed through the Hanoverian brigade of the division, where he had been told that Generals von Alten and von Kielmansegge had already ridden on ahead, to establish the situation at Les Quatre Bras. General Halkett, commanding the 5th (British)

The Battle of Quatre Bras

Infantry Brigade was therefore the ranking officer and Hervey passed on the Prince van Oranje-Nassau's orders; the division was to continue its march on Les Quatre Bras. Halkett immediately sent a messenger to pass the word to von Kielmansegge's Major of Brigade, whilst Hervey – keen to return to the battlefield – spurred his horse in the direction of the fighting.[22]

A short distance from the business of generals, Private Hemingway of the 33rd Regiment of Foot was still listening to the gunfire, which had started barely an hour after the battalion had bivouacked. The rumble was now continuous, suggesting the presence of a great number of cannon. As the men went about their routines, oblivious to any change in the situation, Lieutenant Pattison and the nine other company commanders of the regiment were summoned by Colonel Elphinstone. Word had quickly filtered down from Halkett. The battalion would shortly be going into action and Elphinstone instructed them to assemble their companies and say something to inspire and encourage the soldiers. The young subaltern, immensely proud of his temporary position in command of the Grenadier Company hurried back to his men and delivered an oration that 'had an electric effect, awakening great enthusiasm' among men who seemed 'evinced by an earnest desire to get into battle'. For every eager face, however, there were others who pondered the prospect of the impending struggle with anxiety and even dread, though this was not the place to reveal either. Having completed his address and ensuring that the men were formed up and stood at ease, Pattison was on his way back to Elphinstone to report the completion of his task and to receive further orders, when he encountered his friend, Lieutenant John Boyce

> … whose countenance wore an unusual expression of anxiety. He addressed me in his ordinary, friendly manner, saying, 'Pat, I feel certain I shall be killed.' I rebuked him for indulging in such a feeling, saying, 'Banish such thoughts from your mind. No doubt some of us will be killed, but you have the same chances as the others.'

Pattison was surprised to hear such a premonition from someone who had always shown himself to be a brave soldier, but had little time to reflect on the episode. Shortly afterwards, he and the other officers were ordered to rejoin their companies and the battalion prepared to march.[23] Elsewhere in the brigade, the officers and men reacted to the news in different ways. Ensign James Howard and Surgeon Elkington of the 30th Regiment of Foot had both been listening to the increasing ferocity of the cannonade. Elkington had the welfare of the men uppermost in his mind and felt sorry for the soldiers, as they were again obliged to abandon their attempts to cook. In contrast, Howard's reaction was one of surprise; like many others, he had assumed that this field would be his bivouac for the night. The insistent beating of the drums flooded his body with adrenalin and with the sense of adventure so often present in young men, he looked forward to the prospect of some 'sport'.

Colonel Morice of the 69th Regiment of Foot immediately got down to business and ordered the baggage and women to the rear. Small knots of wives, husbands and children tearfully separated, amid reassurances that everything would turn out for the best; women kissed their menfolk as though for the last time. Ensign Ainslie reluctantly surrendered his horse to his servant, as did the other subaltern officers. It was inappropriate for any but field officers and the Adjutant to be mounted in a battle; his place was in the ranks. In any case, as the junior officer, he was appointed to carry the regimental colour and as he unfurled the 6½ foot green standard, with the small Union flag in the upper canton, there was barely a flutter of breeze to ripple the heavy, painted silk. Next to him, Ensign Henry Keith, the next most junior officer, wrestled with the King's colour. All about them, the men of the battalion busied themselves by ensuring that their muskets were well flinted. While the infantry prepared to move off, Major Lloyd's brigade of 9-pounder guns had already passed to the front, with the gunners marching in double-quick time.[24]

Along the length of the column, the bugles sounded the advance and to the tune of the band of the 33rd Regiment of Foot playing 'The British Grenadiers', the brigade resumed its march along the dusty road. It did not take long before they came across the 'broken faces, legs and arms' of the less fortunate men of de Perponcher-Sedlnitzky's division; 'bloody proofs' that the fighting was in earnest. The intact and the mutilated passed each other in silence; these were the lucky ones. Numbers of men sat helpless on the verges, their crippling wounds rendering them unable to crawl any farther. Elsewhere, the corpses of those who had bled to death before reaching the sanctuary of Nivelles, littered the roadside. For those in action for the first time and the volunteers from the Militia, the sight was sobering. For the old sweats, this was a time to be anything but sober and swilling gin around their mouths, they checked flints, pricked the vents of their muskets and unbundled their ammunition.[25]

If the sound of artillery fire was disconcerting to the young recruits in the British army, it was deeply troubling for Wellington. Two hours earlier, there had seemed to be nothing at Frasnes to be concerned over. Now he was hearing artillery. He knew that the Prince van Oranje-Nassau had a horse battery to the south of the Ferme de Gemioncourt, but if this was the source of the gunfire, it indicated that Les Quatre Bras might in some way be threatened. He had just left von Blücher's headquarters at the windmill of Brye, a short distance to the north of Fleurus. As he had approached the village, towards 1.00 p.m., he had been met by his liaison officer, Colonel Hardinge, who quickly briefed him on the dispositions that the Prussians had adopted to oppose what appeared to be a significant French army. Wellington was far from impressed by the nature of the ground and by the way in which von Blücher had deployed his three corps. The Prussians, on the other hand, were confident. Reassured by Major von Brunneck's earlier messages, they were also hopeful that Wellington might afford them assistance by either outflanking the French position by the west, or providing support by marching his troops down the Namur road to take up positions around Sombreffe itself. With General von Dörnberg the only officer able to speak both English and German, an inconclusive conversation had followed, conducted largely in French, the outcome of which was a vague assurance from Wellington that he would come to his ally's aid, if he were not attacked himself. As he left Brye, towards 2.00 p.m., he had first heard the low rumble of artillery to the west. He bumped Copenhagen with his spurs and the horse responded instinctively, the less equestrian members of his entourage struggling to keep pace.[26]

On the battlefield itself, the struggle intensified. The first battalion of the Regiment Oranien-Nassau and the 8th National Militia Battalion were still occupying the chemin du Pierrepont, sheltered to some degree from the effects of French artillery, firing from the high ground to the south-east. Shortly after 2.30 p.m., the Prince van Oranje-Nassau sent an aide-de-camp to Colonel de Jongh, ordering him to withdraw his battalion towards the Bois de Bossu, where it took up a position in the open ground to the north of the Odomont stream. He later recollected the events,

> The cannon balls of the enemy artillery, against which the battalion had been covered in the hollow road, now fell amongst it, leading to the colour-sergeant-major and two subaltern officers of the colour platoon being severely wounded and one corporal and several men killed or badly wounded. Some confusion arose in the battalion. I made it march forward in line to the right, under the fire of three enemy guns; gave the officers and men a short and businesslike speech; reminded them of their duty to king and country; aroused their sense of honour; and soon the most beautiful tranquility reigned.[27]

With his fidgety battalion back in some form of order, de Jongh awaited further instructions, which were not long in coming. An ongoing concern for the fragility of the centre had presented the Prince van Oranje-Nassau with a dilemma. Not being able to defend the entire line in depth, how could he shore up the centre of his position, whilst not exposing another part of the line? Could he, at the same time, also safeguard against being outflanked to the west of the Bois de Bossu and cut off from the remainder of the corps? At present, two battalions, the first battalion of the Regiment Oranien-Nassau and the 8th National Militia Battalion, were posted in front of the Bois du Pierrepont. A further two, the first and third battalions of the 2nd Nassau-Usingen Regiment were deployed in the southern portion of the Bois de Bossu, whilst the 7th National Militia Battalion was on the chaussée, to the north of the same wood. Finally, stood in reserve at the crossroads of Les Quatre Bras were the second battalions of both the Regiment Oranien-Nassau and the 2nd Nassau-Usingen Regiment, though neither battalion had much in the way of small arms ammunition.

Discussing the situation with de Perponcher-Sedlnitzky, he sent orders to Colonel von Dressel to march the first battalion of the Regiment Oranien-Nassau through the Bois du Pierrepont and, by way of the chemin d'Houtain-le-Val, to take up a defensive position to the west of the woods, at Croix-Seigneur. As soon as this battalion had passed, Captain Büsgen was ordered to follow it with the first battalion of the 2nd Nassau-Usingen Regiment, which was to take up a position along the chemin d'Houtain-le-Val, where it divided the Bois du Pierrepont from the Bois de Bossu. Major Hegmann's third battalion of this same regiment, still occupying the south-eastern tip of the Bois de Bossu, was now given responsibility for lining the entire southern edge of the wood and began extending its six companies towards the west. This shortened line would require fewer defenders and therefore release some much-needed manpower elsewhere. Finally, the Prince van Oranje-Nassau sent one

'We had the wood to retreat into'

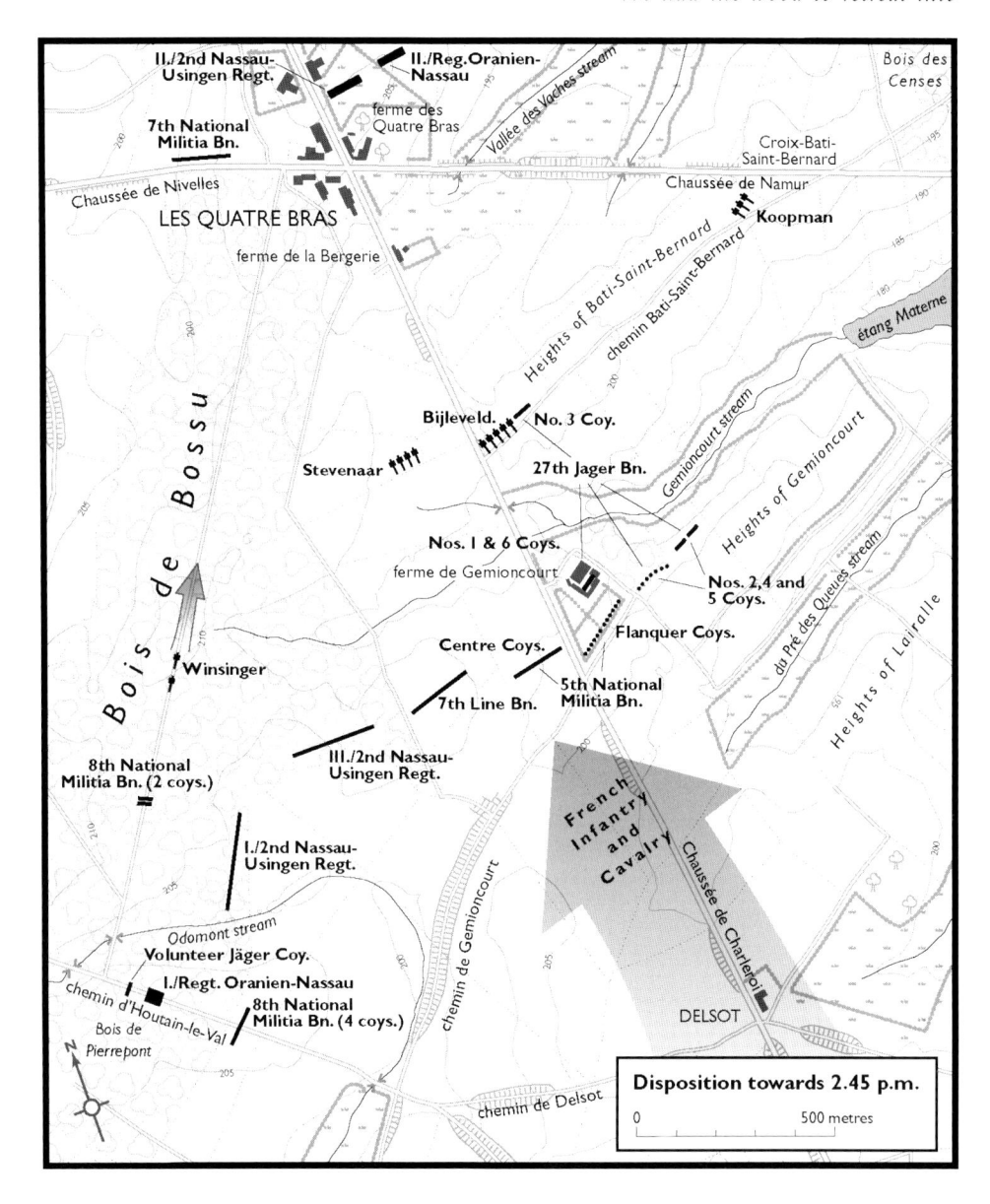

of his own aides, Major van Limburg-Stirum, to Colonel de Jongh. The 8th National Militia Battalion was to cover the establishment of this new defensive line, whilst detaching two companies to the left of the woods. Assigning this task to the 5th and 6th Companies, de Jongh had no choice but to keep the remainder of the battalion in its exposed position, lashed by round shot and canister from the French guns, which caused numerous killed and wounded.[28]

Arriving back to report to the Prince van Oranje-Nassau, van Limburg-Stirum briefed his chief on Colonel de Jongh's situation and the havoc being caused in the ranks of the 8th National Militia Battalion by the French artillery. Reconsidering his deployment, the Prince sent him back to de Jongh, with the order for the remaining

The Battle of Quatre Bras

four companies to withdraw to the shelter of the wood. Almost as soon as he received it, the commanding officer of the militia battalion protested the order,

> I earnestly made my objections to this, asking his Honour to consider that this was a waste for the battalion, composed of young men, to fight dispersed as skirmishers in a wood, and that I would rather prefer to advance to remove the three enemy guns that were firing at me.

The response was not long in coming. Probably considering that van Limburg-Stirum had been insufficiently forceful in delivering his earlier order, the Prince now sent Captain Somerset, the brother of Wellington's military secretary. This time, the order was unequivocal. The Colonel was to advance into the wood without further ado, traverse it and oppose the enemy attacks in the centre. With the 5th and 6th Companies still detached by order of the Prince, the remaining four company commanders were ordered to march their men through a gap in the hedge to the north of the meadow that bordered the Odomont stream at Grand-Pierrepont and to form up on the other side. When this had been successfully completed, the battalion marched to the point where the chemin d'Houtain-le-Val entered the woods. Under the watchful eyes of its commanding officer and of Captain Sijbers, the battalion defiled. As soon as the last troops had entered, Colonel de Jongh dismounted, abandoned his horse, and took up his position at the head of the column, guiding it to the eastern edge of the wood, where it emerged a short time later in rear of the 7th Line Battalion. The Prince had successfully re-oriented his front line, but everywhere along it, the tiring troops were inexorably being forced back.[29]

The guns had been firing for some 45 minutes by the time Wellington and his party passed through the hamlet of Thyle on their way back from their conference with the Prussians. The speed of the ride had made conversation difficult, but each of the horsemen was no doubt mulling over the consequences of the delays in assembling Wellington's forces. Though it was clear that von Blücher was opposed by a significant element of the French army, no news had reached the Duke concerning the situation at Les Quatre Bras. Where were the rest of the French? Instead of Nivelles, Braine-le-Comte or Ath, could it be Les Quatre Bras that was threatened; and, if so, by what force?

As they reached the crossroads formed by the junction of the chemin du Piraumont and the Namur road, they could see smoke from the French artillery to the southwest and could discern blue-coated soldiers in the buildings of the village and in the valley below it. Were these Dutch infantry or French? The rattle of musketry as they ran the gauntlet towards the safety of Les Quatre Bras answered Wellington's question for him. How had the French managed to press forward, almost severing the Namur road? Had the Netherlands outposts been overrun already? Approaching the crossroads, he sent Colonel Somerset off to find the Prince van Oranje-Nassau and to obtain his report on the events of the past hour. From now on, he would assume command. It was approaching 3.00 p.m.[30]

Arthur Wellesley, Duke of Wellington. Francisco Goya. (*National Gallery, London*)

Willem Frederik, Prince van Oranje-Nassau. (*Netherlands Army Museum, Delft*)

Major General Baron Jan-Victor de Constant-Rebecque. Jan-Baptist van der Hulst. (*Netherlands Army Museum, Delft*)

The Ferme de la Cense de l'Encloître, Frasnes, in which men of the 2nd Nassau-Usingen Regiment were billeted until 15 June 1815. (*Author's collection*)

The collegiate church of Saint-Vincent at Soignies, which was used to accommodate the men of Halkett's brigade on the night of 15 June 1815. (*Author's collection*)

The church and market place at Hoves where the third battalion of the 1st Regiment of Foot Guards assembled prior to marching on Quatre Bras. (*Author's collection*)

The Hôtel de Bellevue, Brussels, from which residents watched the assembly of Picton's Division in the Place Royale on the night of 15 June 1815. (*Author's collection*)

A coloured aquatint of Quatre Bras viewed from the south. Publisher Bowyer, 1816. (*Author's collection*)

A contemporary print of Quatre Bras with the farm to the right. (*Author's collection*)

An aerial view of the Ferme de Gemioncourt from the south. This farm was defended by the 27th Jager and 5th National Militia Battalions on 16 June 1815. (*Author's collection*)

The Ferme de Gemioncourt, secured at the close of the action by the 30th Regiment of Foot. (*Author's collection*)

The Ferme de Grand-Pierrepoint from the south-west. The trees of the copse at Gemioncourt can be seen in the top right hand corner. (*Author's collection*)

The heights of Bati-Saint-Bernard. The trees in the centre follow the line of the Gemioncourt stream, with the farm itself obscured by the copse to the right. (*Author's collection*)

The southern slope of the heights of Bati-Saint-Bernard, down which Picton's two brigades counter-attacked. (*Author's collection*)

Piraumont from the south-east. The chaussée de Namur can be seen in the top right-hand corner. The farm itself is easily identifiable by its large red barn roof. (*Author's collection*)

The courtyard of the Ferme de Piraumont, recaptured late in the day by British Brunswick and Hanoverian light infantry. (*Author's collection*)

Monument to the Duke von Braunschweig-Lüneburg. (*Author's collection*)

Monument to the British and Hanoverian forces. (*Author's collection*)

Monument to the Netherlands cavalry. (*Author's collection*)

Monument to the Belgian soldiers killed at Quatre Bras. (*Author's collection*)

Monument to the Netherlands forces and their allies. (*Author's collection*)

Prince Bernhard von Sachsen-Weimar (second right) briefs the officers of his brigade on his decision to hold the position of Quatre Bras. Print after Hoynck van Papendrecht. (*Author's collection*)

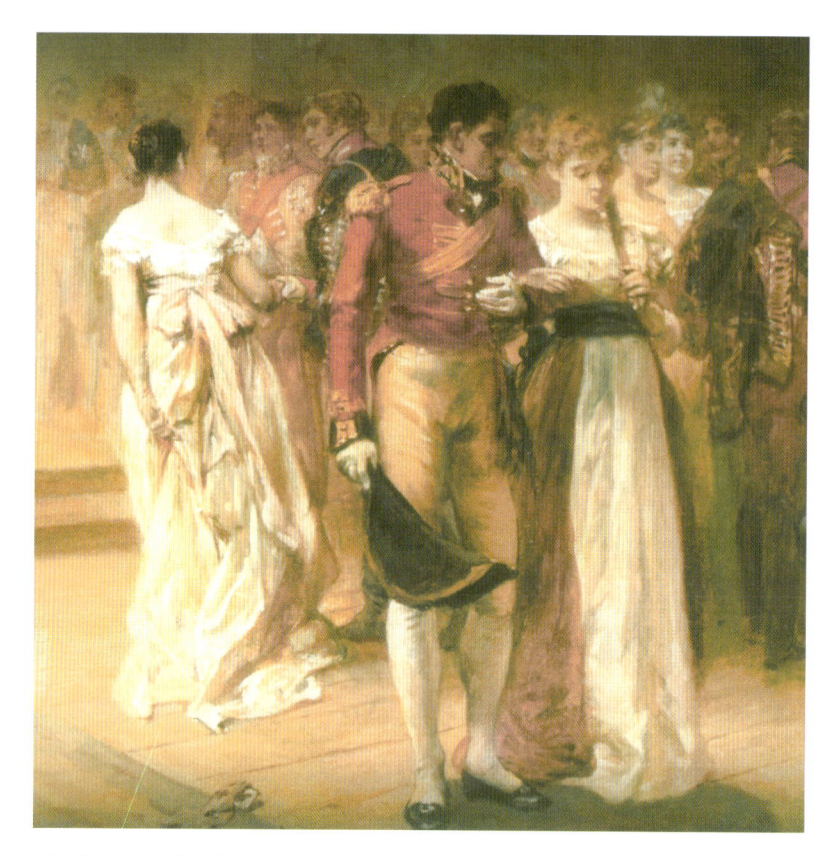

The Duchess of Richmond's Ball. Print after Robert Hillingford.
(*Author's collection*)

The 44th Regiment of Foot under attack by French light cavalry. Print after Vereker Hamilton.
(*Author's collection*)

The death of Lieutenant-Colonel Sir Robert Macara. Print after Richard Simkin. (*Author's collection*)

Major-General Sir Edward Barnes forms up the 92nd Regiment of Foot prior to its assault on La Bergerie. Print after J. Jirbal. (*Author's collection*)

The Battle of Les Quatre Bras. Watercolour by Jean-Baptiste Madou. (*Private collection*)

A wounded Highlander is dressed by a wealthy Belgian lady in this anonymous oil on canvas 'After Waterloo'. The real horror of the conflict is better captured by Sir Charles Bell's watercolour opposite, above. (*Courtesy Musée Wellington, Waterloo*)

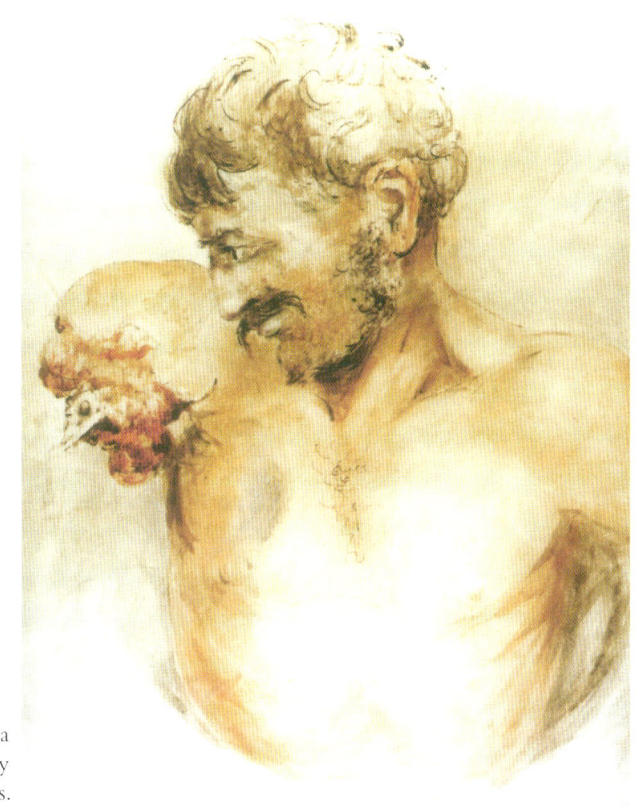

Watercolour by Sir Charles Bell of a Brunswick hussar whose arm was severed by a cannon ball at Quatre Bras. (*Courtesy Mick Crumplin*)

The remains of a soldier of the 1st Regiment of Foot, discovered on the southern slope of the heights of Bati-Saint-Bernard, one of twenty officers and men who met their deaths at Les Quatre Bras. (*Courtesy Daniel Dehon*)

Prince Frederick-Willem van Oranje-Nassau at Les Quatre Bras, at the head of the 5th (South Netherlands) Regiment of Light Dragoons. Print after J. Jirbal. (*Author's collection*)

'The death of Duke Friedrich-Wilhelm von Braunshweig near Quatre Bras 1815'. Heinrich-Maria Monten. (*Courtesy Braunschweigishes Landesmuseum*)

'We had the wood to retreat into'

A short distance to the north-west, the weary men of the 95th Regiment of Foot had reached the brow of a modest rise, about halfway between Dernier Patard and Les Quatre Bras and had halted for a brief rest. The sound of firing from the front was very distinct and it was rumoured that the Belgians were 'playing at long shot' with the enemy. Lieutenant Gairdner had rejoined the battalion at Genappe and was still busy reuniting the stragglers with their companies. Lieutenant Fitzmaurice was therefore sent forward with Captain Leach's company to occupy some high ground, a little to the south, in order to establish an alarm post in the event of an enemy advance. Stretching before him was a wide plain filled with high crops and bounded by woodland to the left and right, though the signs of fighting were concealed in the lee of a gentle rise to the south, above which a pall of smoke hung in the still air.

Shortly after taking up this position, Fitzmaurice noticed a small party of horsemen trotting up the Namur road. It was the Duke of Wellington and his party. Recognising the unmistakable dark green uniform of the Rifles, the Duke shouted: 'Where is Barnard?' and Fitzmaurice, saluting, replied that he would send word for his commanding officer to come forward. Minutes later, the breathless runner arrived back at the main body of the battalion and passed on the message to the Colonel, who immediately asked Lieutenant Kincaid to accompany him to Les Quatre Bras. As Adjutant of the battalion, he might be needed to convey Wellington's orders back to Colonel Cameron if the Duke detained his chief. The two officers cantered off down the road, to a point just beyond the crossroads where the Duke of Wellington and his staff were stood in a field overlooking the Ferme de Gemioncourt, nervously watching the advance of the French and under fire from artillery.[31]

> The moment we approached, Lord Fitzroy Somerset, separating himself from the Duke said, 'Barnard, you are wanted instantly. Take your battalion and get possession of that village,' pointing to one on the face of the rising ground, down which the enemy were moving, 'but if you cannot do that, secure the wood on the left, and keep the road open for communications with the Prussians.'[32]

Wellington was understandably concerned for his left flank. He had seen for himself the extent of the French gains. He knew from his inspection earlier that morning that the weight of the Netherlands defence had been positioned towards the west, designed to preserve the line of communication and potential retreat, on Nivelles and the bulk of the Allied army. If the French succeeded in establishing and maintaining themselves on the Namur road, they could possibly separate Wellington from von Blücher and even gain the Brussels road by a flanking movement, turning Wellington's position at Les Quatre Bras.[33]

Having received their instructions, Barnard and Kincaid joined Fitzmaurice and his men. From this elevated viewpoint, enemy troops could be seen clearly, emerging from a wood to the south-east and it soon became apparent that their force comprised several battalions. The French were already in possession of Piraumont and it was unlikely that an attempt to retake it with Barnard's own modest means would be successful. Furthermore, a substantial body of hostile infantry had already passed the village and was approaching the Bois des Censes, the secondary objective that Somerset had assigned to them. Barnard turned to his officers and said: 'These fellows are coming on.' Pointing to the trees, he looked at Fitzmaurice and continued: 'You must stop them by throwing yourself into that wood.' With his vanguard on the move, Barnard could concentrate on bringing forward the remainder of the battalion. As Fitzmaurice moved off, he again encountered the Duke of Wellington, who advised him to pass to the north of a knoll, close to where the chemin Bati-Saint-Bernard crossed the Namur road. It would shield his men from the effects of French artillery fire.[34]

Barnard and Kincaid hurriedly rode back to the battalion, which was instantly formed up in column and led into the fields of high wheat and rye, to the north-east of Les Quatre Bras. As they marched, double-quick, over the gentle rises and waded through the shallow Vallée des Vaches stream, speculation was rife as to the battalion's objective. Some said the woods, others a village beyond. The sound of artillery could be heard close by; it was Lieutenant Koopman's three 6-pounders, engaging the French infantry. A short while afterwards, the head of the column arrived on a low ridge, just to the north of the chaussée, to the west of the Bois des Censes, which comprised a narrow band of trees between the farms of the same name and the Namur road. Though less conspicuous in their dark green coats and black accoutrements, Barnard's battalion had been observed by the French artillery on the heights of Gemioncourt, six hundred metres to the south and a bombardment commenced, round shot bounding across the Namur road and into the fields beyond.[35]

Despite the fire, the battalion continued to advance through the fields until it came up to a dense, thorny hedge. For the first time, the soldiers came under direct fire from French infantry, whose skirmishers had advanced sufficiently close to the chaussée, that they could pepper the riflemen as they approached the wood. Despite their exposure to the fire, the men of the leading company seemed disinclined to push through the hedge, merely poking their rifles through in a half-hearted attempt to clear a path. No one seemed prepared to be the first to force a gap, on account of the sharpness of the thorns.

Frustrated, Lieutenant Simmons decided to take matters into his own hands. Allowing himself a short run-up, he crashed into Sergeant Daniel Underwood's knapsack and butted him through the other side. As the two men tumbled through the hedge, they realised that the ground on the far side was somewhat lower and rolled down the slope in a tangle of arms, legs, weapons and accoutrements. The breach having been made, the remainder of the company now poured through in turn and within minutes, the battalion was once more advancing towards its objective. The troops had hardly got under way, however, when there was a commotion in the ranks and Lieutenant Kincaid noticed a soldier – doubtless exhausted by the heat – suffer some kind of seizure: 'The poor fellow cut a few extraordinary capers and died in the course of a few minutes.' The regiment had just suffered its first fatality.[36]

Meanwhile, at the crossroads, Wellington was joined by the Prince van Oranje-Nassau and General de Perponcher-Sedlnitzky, who immediately informed him that the enemy had been greatly reinforced at Frasnes. The Duke received the news with equanimity. The Prince also informed him that his advanced troops were being driven back and that his artillery had retired from the vicinity of the Ferme de Gemioncourt, with the loss of three guns. As yet, there had been no attempt made on the Bois de Bossu. Glancing at the second battalions of the Regiment Oranien-Nassau and the 2nd Nassau-Usingen Regiment, perhaps Wellington questioned why these had not been committed. The Duke satisfied himself with thanking the Prince, who rode off towards the Ferme de Gemioncourt. By this time, the reinforcements that the Prince van Oranje-Nassau had summoned were beginning to arrive from the north and Wellington and his staff focused their efforts on quickening the pace of those lagging behind and placing the first arrivals in position in and around the crossroads. It seemed that help had arrived in the nick of time.[37]

Endnotes

1. de Bas &c., p. 481. Bowden, p. 80. van Opstall. van Uythoven. van Zuylen van Nyeveld (I), p. 55. van de Wall. van Zuylen van Nyeveld (II).
2. de Bas &c., pp. 482, 495. Dellevoet, p. 22. Meijer. van Opstall. Scheltens, p. 198. Starklof, p. 136. van de Wall. van Zuylen van Nyeveld (I), pp. 54, 56.
3. de Bas &c., pp. 496–7, 501. van Bronkhorst. de Jongh. Knoop (II), p. 145. Rentenaar. van Toll. Westenbergh. Wüppermann, p. 107. van Zuylen van Nyeveld (I), p. 54.
4. de Bas &c., p. 482. Scheltens, p. 198. van Toll. van Zuylen van Nyeveld (I), p. 54.
5. van Toll. Westenbergh. van Zuylen van Nyeveld (I), p. 54.
6. de Bas &c., pp. 494, 497. van Bijlandt. Dellevoet, p. 23. Grunenbosch. Mollinger. van Toll. Westenbergh.
7. Barre. de Bas &c., p. 494, 497. van Bijlandt. Dellevoet, p. 23. Knoop (II), p. 145. Mollinger. van Toll. Westenbergh.
8. Dellevoet, p. 23. Knoop (II), p. 191. van Toll.
9. de Bas &c., p. 497. Barre. van Bijlandt. Dellevoet, p. 23. Knoop (II), p. 145. Mollinger.
10. Dellevoet, p. 23. Scheltens, p. 198. van Toll.
11. de Bas &c., p. 497. van Bijlandt. Dellevoet, p. 23.
12. Barre. de Bas &c., p. 497. Dellevoet, p. 24. Henckens, p. 225. Houssaye, p. 113. Knoop (II), pp. 145, 191–2. Mollinger. van Toll. Westenbergh.
13. de Bas &c., p. 497. Dellevoet, p. 24. Henckens, p. 225. Houssaye, p. 145. Knoop (II), pp. 145, 192–3. Meijer. van Toll. Westenbergh.
14. de Bas &c., p. 500. Dellevoet, p. 24. Knoop (II), pp. 192–3. van Toll. van Zuylen van Nyeveld (I), p. 56.
15. Dellevoet, p. 24. Knoop (II), p. 192. Haythornthwaite (II), pp. 27–32.
16. Houssaye, p. 113. van Löben-Sels, p. 516; W. Siborne (V), pp. 63, 68–9.
17. de Jongh, p. 11. von Sachsen-Weimar (III).
18. Anonymous (Letters), p. 223. Anonymous (Near Observer), p. 46. Costello, p. 151. Houssaye, p. 93. Kincaid (I), pp. 313–14. Leach, pp. 374–5. Riddock.
19. Allan. Anonymous (Cameron), pp. 88–9. Anton, p. 189. Alexander Forbes (II). Vallence, p. 6.

20. Mudie (I). Robertson.
21. Bannatyne, p. 320. Brett-James, p. 53. Macready (I).
22. de Bas &c., p. 491. Halkett (I). Halkett (IV). Pattison (II), p. 3. Rudyerd.
23. Hemingway. Pattison (II), pp. 2–3.
24. Ainslie, p. 14. Elkington (I), p. 12. J. Howard. Rudyerd.
25. Ainslie, p. 14. Hemingway. Pattison (II), p. 2.
26. Arthur, pp. 593–4. de Bas &c., pp. 458, 475–6. Cathcart. Clausewitz, p. 67. von Damitz, pp. 117–18. Daniell, p. 133. von Dörnberg. Hofschröer (I), pp. 233–42. Maurice, p. 11. Maxwell, pp. 19–20. von Müffling (I), pp. 3–4. von Ollech, pp. 278, 292. Rens, p. 107. Reuter, p. 277. F. Somerset, pp. 8–9. P. Stanhope, pp. 81–2.
27. de Jongh, p. 12.
28. Dellevoet, p. 25. de Jongh, p. 12. van Zuylen van Nyeveld (I), p. 55.
29. Dellevoet, p. 25. de Jongh, p. 12.
30. Arthur, p. 594. Aubrey-Fletcher, pp. 365–7. Croker, p. 175. Houssaye, p. 113. Jennings, p. 185. von Müffling (I), p. 4. W. Siborne (V), p. 70. J. Somerset. F. Somerset, p. 9. Starklof, p. 139. Wellesley, p. 525.
31. Anonymous (Near Observer), p. 46. Caldwell and Cooper, p. 7. Cope, p. 197. Costello, p. 150–1. Kincaid (I), pp. 313–15.
32. Caldwell and Cooper, p. 7. Cope, p. 198. Costello, p. 151. Gomm (V). Kincaid (I), p. 315. Leach, p. 375.
33. Houssaye, p. 114.
34. Aubrey-Fletcher, p. 368. de Bas &c., p. 513. Caldwell and Cooper, pp. 7–9. Cope, p. 198. Costello, p. 151. Archibald Forbes, p. 266. Gomm (V). Houssaye, p. 114. Kincaid (I), pp. 314–16. W. Siborne (V), p. 70.
35. Aubrey-Fletcher, p. 368. de Bas &c., p. 513. Caldwell and Cooper, p. 6. Cope, p. 197. Simmons (II), p. 363.
36. Anonymous (Waterloo Medal Roll), pp. 322–3. Caldwell and Cooper, pp. 6–9. Cope, p. 197. Kincaid (I), pp. 315–16.
37. Alexander Forbes (I) and (II). Maurice, p. 12. von Müffling (I), p. 4.

CHAPTER 10

To the north of Les Quatre Bras, the battalions of Picton's division stretched out in the fields and along the verges of the chaussée. In their habitual place in the vanguard of Kempt's brigade had been the 95th Regiment of Foot, followed by the 28th and 79th, with the 32nd Regiment of Foot bringing up the rear. Behind them was Pack's brigade, led by the 1st Regiment of Foot, followed by the 42nd, 44th and 92nd Regiments of Foot. In the distance, the black and red masses of the Brunswick division and Best's brigade could be made out on the shimmering horizon.[1]

Though the majority of the men of the 79th Regiment of Foot had piled arms and were resting, the more curious and adventurous soldiers had walked a short distance farther south, to a knoll, behind which the 28th Regiment of Foot had halted. This provided an excellent vantage point from which to obtain a view of the enemy, who appeared to be advancing obliquely to the left, seemingly a mere kilometre distant. To the east, a brisk cannonade was going on in what the soldiers assumed was the direction of the Prussian army. One of these casual tourists, Private Vallence, caught an occasional glimpse of the French, slowly driving the Prince van Oranje-Nassau's troops back over the gentle heights and hollows and through the occasional thicket. The fields however, some enclosed by hedges – in places decayed and broken down – were covered with crops of clover or rye, so tall that he could see little more than the heads of the French skirmishers in the distance. Another observer from his battalion, Lieutenant Forbes, was little better informed, but he watched with interest as what seemed to be two companies of the 95th Regiment of Foot deployed in support of what he thought was some Belgian infantry.[2]

Colonel Gomm, on his fidgety horse, George, had ridden forward a little more than the sightseers and was at Les Quatre Bras itself with General Picton, who had arrived on the battlefield in a costume of not altogether regulation description:

> Sir Thomas Picton was a stern-looking, strong-built man, about the middle height. He generally wore a blue frock-coat, very tightly buttoned up to the throat, a very large black silk neckcloth, showing little or no shirt-collar; dark trousers, boots, and a round hat; it was in this very dress that he was attired at Quatre Bras, as he had hurried off to the scene of the action before his uniform arrived.[3]

The Battle of Quatre Bras

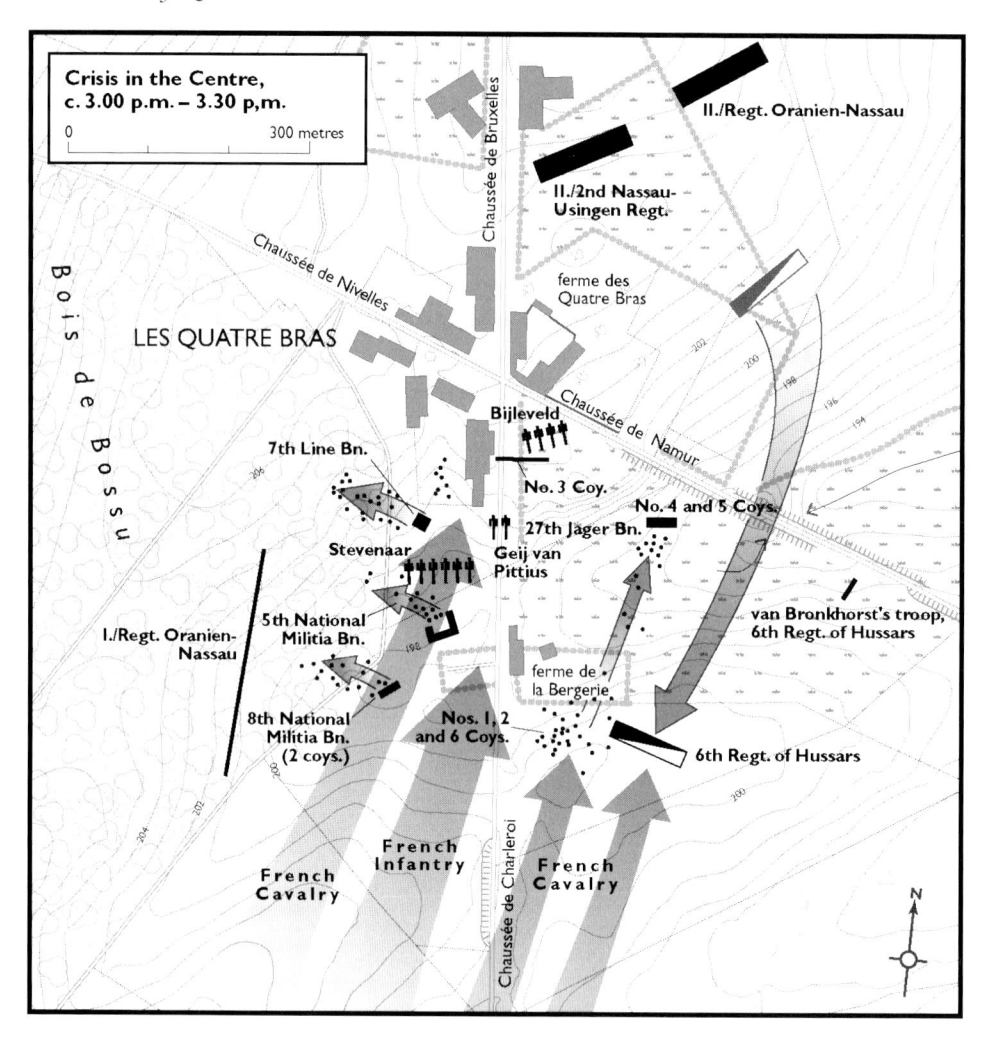

Looking at the confusion all about him, it seemed to Gomm that the only troops in the vicinity were foreign, mainly those of the second battalion of the Regiment Oranien-Nassau and some Belgians under the command, he was told, of the Prince von Sachsen-Weimar. Chatting with several officers of Wellington's staff, he learned that the French had supposedly occupied this very spot the previous day, but that de Perponcher-Sedlnitzky's men had driven them back during the course of the morning. Looking across the swaying fields of wheat and rye to the south, amongst which several battalions could just about be discerned, he was convinced that they could not withstand the French.

Wellington, it seemed, had now decided that there was no threat from Mons and had ordered the remainder of the Prince van Oranje-Nassau's corps and the whole of Lord Hill's corps to move on Les Quatre Bras. Rumours, however, continued to abound; French cavalry was said to be operating far to the west, perhaps with the intention of outflanking the Duke's position. To counter this threat, Wellington had apparently ordered General Colville's 4th (British) Infantry Division to reinforce Colonel von Vincke's 5th (Hanoverian) Infantry Brigade. Gomm's conversation was curtailed by

Picton, who ordered him to ride into the Bois de Bossu and to make a report back on the nature of the ground and the state of its defence. Spurring his horse, Gomm probably tried to second-guess his chief's motives; was the division to garrison the forest?[4]

Shortly after 3.00 p.m., General van Merlen finally arrived at Croix-Gilbert, with his two regiments of light cavalry, totalling almost 1,000. Still only 42 years old, van Merlen had spent 26 of those as a soldier. Holder of the *Légion d'Honneur*, Baron of the Empire, former officer in Napoleon's 'Red Lancers', he was a cavalryman of great experience and loyal to his new sovereign. Galloping forward between the Bois de Bossu and the chaussée de Charleroi, he made an initial assessment of the situation. Deploying his leading regiment, van Merlen established Colonel Boreel and the 6th (North Netherlands) Hussar Regiment to the south of the Namur road, in front of the Ferme des Quatre Bras. Immediately behind them were two pieces of the half-battery commanded by Captain Geij van Pittius, the remaining 6-pounder and howitzer having been left at Arquennes in the care of Lieutenant Reijntjes, attached to General Trip's heavy cavalry brigade.

In reserve at Croix-Gilbert, was Colonel de Mercx de Corbais' 5th Regiment of Light Dragoons, the green-clad troopers of the former 'van den Burch Chevau-Légers' of the Belgian Legion. Despite the horses having been saddled for nine hours and having been on the march since the early hours, Colonel Boreel considered it unwise to unsaddle the horses of the hussar regiment, given the proximity of the enemy. The men, equally weary and sweating in the oppressive heat, dismounted to give the animals some respite. The troopers had drained their canteens whilst on the march and the horses were thirsty, so permission was given for fatigue parties to go and fetch water, but these returned empty-handed and the horses could only eat the dry oats very slowly. Though his own horse might have been thirsty, Captain Jan van Bronkhorst of the 6th Hussar Regiment had been more fortunate. When his regiment had passed the 7th National Militia Battalion, stationed to the north of the Bois de Bossu, he had been spotted by his brother, Captain Abraham van Bronkhorst, who hurried across to give him something to eat and drink. The two men stood talking between the lines of horses, whilst to the south, the rattle of musketry and the booming of the guns continued to mark the ebb and flow of the struggle.[5]

On the extreme left of the line, the 95th Regiment of Foot had drawn first blood. Seeing large numbers of enemy infantry making for the wood, Fitzmaurice had ordered his men to double forward and they had arrived at the wood, breathless, shortly before the enemy. As they were taking up their position among the trees, some of the men noticed a cavalryman in a burnished helmet, whom they took to be a cuirassier but who was, in fact, a chevau-léger-lancier. Assuming him to be a vedette, scouting ahead of the French troops and seeking to ascertain the strength and dispositions of the riflemen, the British soldiers immediately opened fire and succeeded in shooting his horse from beneath him. The agile Frenchman, however, was not so easily discouraged; disentangling himself from his stirrups as the horse fell, he waved his sword in a gesture of defiance which would have probably gone unpunished by musket-wielding infantry, but not by those armed with the relatively accurate Baker

The Battle of Quatre Bras

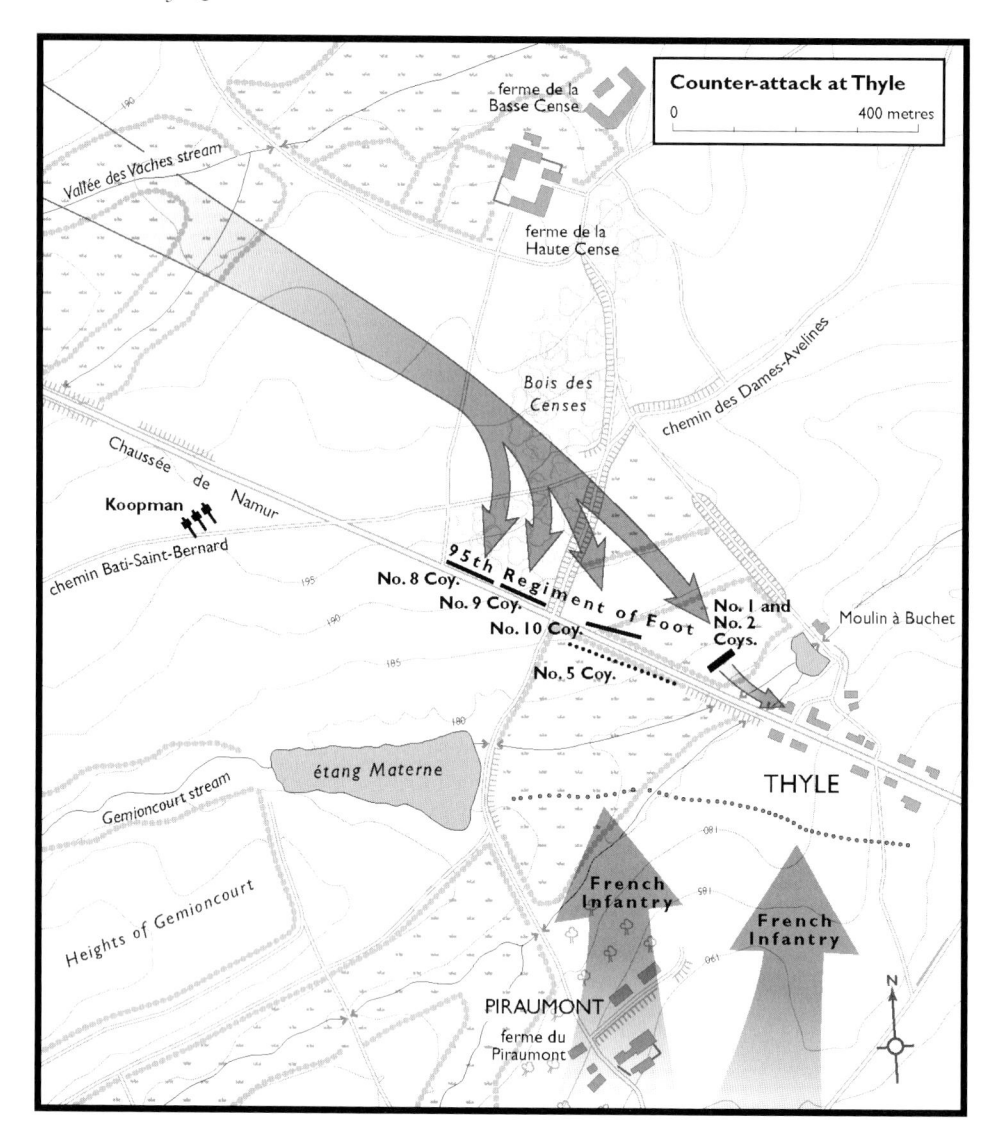

rifle; he was immediately shot dead. Within minutes, the entire line crackled with fire as the British riflemen came into action against the advancing French tirailleurs.[6]

As soon as Colonel Barnard reached the wood himself, he gave orders for the battalion reserve, comprising Captain Henry Lee's No. 8 and Captain Glasse's No. 9 Companies, to occupy the south face of the wood and to fire on the French to the south of the road. The remainder of the battalion lined the verge and Lieutenant Kincaid, feeling very conspicuous on horseback amid the shower of balls that were flying crossing it, thought wryly that only a desperate traveller would have undertaken a journey on it in order to maintain communications with the Prussians. The superior accuracy of the British infantry gradually drove the French off; it appeared that their prompt action had prevented the French from outflanking and overrunning the ground that 'Arthur' had selected for the deployment of Picton's division.[7]

'Many found their deaths beneath the hooves'

Towards 3.15 p.m. a sizeable body of French troops in extended order began to move down the slope to the north of the Ferme de Piraumont in the direction of the area occupied by Barnard's regiment. The Colonel, intending to counter this move and to extend his own flank, edged his battalion farther to the east, along the northern side of the Namur road. In the vanguard, was Captain Leach's No. 2 Company, followed by Captain Edward Chawner's No. 1 Company. As the riflemen hurried into position, the French infantry opened up a brisk fire until the British managed to pass the du Prés des Saules stream and take cover in some roadside houses, where the chaussée climbed out of the shallow valley towards the crossroads at Thyle. Captain William Johnston, his No. 5 Company deployed in skirmish order on the Namur road, immediately engaged the French, supported by the men of Major Charles Beckwith's No. 10 Company, under the command of Lieutenant Jonathan Layton; these lined an embankment and ditch on the southern side of the chaussée, from which they exchanged a heated fire with the French. Amongst the first victims of the fusillade was Layton himself, wounded in the wrist and side. As he pulled out of the line and made his way to the rear, command of the company devolved upon Lieutenant Simmons, who urged his men to stay closer together than usual, for fear of being surprised by enemy cavalry. By the sound of the cannonade farther to the west, the remainder of Picton's division was already deploying. For the time being, the left wing of Wellington's position was secure.[8]

In the centre of the battlefield, the situation was considerably less stable. Shortly after having taken position on the chemin de Gemioncourt, the 5th National Militia Battalion once again observed French cavalry advancing upon it, having been concealed in a dip of ground behind the heights to the south. As Westenbergh gave orders to form square, the horsemen gathered momentum in a jangling, jostling line. Stevenaar's brigade had been reinforced by the arrival of Lieutenant Winsinger's two pieces and the battery of six guns, supplemented by the four remaining guns of Bijleveld's troop, opened fire on the French, bringing horses and riders tumbling down in a tangle of limbs and harness.

Heedless of loss, however, the horsemen gathered speed and before long, those infantry closest to the French could hear the pounding hooves, the snorting of the horses and the rasp of steel as sabres were drawn. The surprisingly rapid pace of the advance meant that not all of the companies managed to reach their posts in time. Lieutenant Boltjes was killed before he could reach the bristling ranks and many men of his No. 5 Company were caught in the open and killed or wounded by the vengeful horsemen. Ignoring the frenzied efforts to close ranks, Westenbergh bided his time as he sat on his horse behind the centre of the south face. He ordered the troops to shoulder arms. Seconds passed yet still their commanding officer kept his silence. Finally, when the French were an alarmingly short distance away, the order to present was shouted, followed almost immediately thereafter, by that to give fire. As the volley crashed out, the horsemen were obliterated by a cloud of smoke. Nervous hands fumbled for cartridges and ramrods, but the smoke cleared to reveal the French making off in considerable disorder, pursued by rounds from the artillery and sporadic firing from the militiamen themselves. In front of the battalion, the débris of the charge remained;

men and horses writhing or motionless amongst the grain, supplicant voices pleading for water, medical attention or their mothers. The wave of relief that had swept through the battalion was dissipated by the sight of the enemy's reserve squadrons, who made a further charge, only to be repulsed in a similar manner.

Whilst the men in the south face of the square busied themselves with driving off the cavalry, the men in the northern and western faces of the square cast envious glances at their comrades in the 7th Line Battalion, whose position close to the wood had once again enabled Colonel van den Sanden to withdraw them to its shelter. The men in the wood continued to pepper the French with musket shots as the remnants of the cavalry made off to the south.[9]

As soon as he deemed it safe to do so, Colonel Westenbergh deployed his battalion in a two-deep line, with the 7th Line Battalion in its right rear in the same formation. They had been joined by the two detached companies of the 8th National Militia Battalion, which plugged the gap between Westenbergh's men and the edge of the wood, still being held by the third battalion of the 2nd Nassau-Usingen Regiment. As the French skirmishers once again advanced, covering the withdrawal of their cavalry, the Dutch infantry opened fire on them, following which they sent out skirmishers of their own to counter the repeated advances of the enemy.[10]

Impressed with the steadiness of the men, the Prince van Oranje-Nassau galloped up to the 5th National Militia Battalion with his staff, shouting, 'Bravo!' and waving his hat in salute. Joining the commanding officer, he vigorously shook Westenbergh's hand and congratulated him on his intrepid behaviour. Remaining in this advanced position, amid the shot and shell of the French bombardment, the men were encouraged by the presence of their young Prince, proud that he was sharing their dangers. Frequent cheers of '*Altijd Oranje boven!*' and '*Leve de Prinsen van Oranje*' signalled to the French that the battalion was not finished yet. The gradual advance of heavy columns, however, preceded by swarms of skirmishers, forced the 5th National Militia Battalion to give ground slowly, retiring towards the gun line. The 27th Jager battalion was similarly pressed back up the southern slope of the heights of Bati-Saint-Bernard. With the high ground of the heights of Gemioncourt now securely in their hands, the French had brought artillery forward and, at a range of just over 500 metres, opened a powerful fire against the 27th Jager Battalion, the 5th National Militia Battalion, the two companies of the 8th National Militia Battalion and the 7th Line Battalion somewhat to their rear. Under cover of this fire, further French infantry advanced up the Charleroi road and in the fields to the west. The French cannonade was also causing mayhem amongst the Netherlands artillery. One round shot, bounding across the road, shattered the limber of one of Lieutenant Dibbetz's howitzers, causing an explosion amongst the rounds stored within it which wounded the officer himself.[11]

Shorn of his infantry support, Major de la Sarraz ordered Captain Bijleveld to withdraw his guns to the south-east angle of the crossroads. The movement was safely executed, but with no means of moving Lieutenant Dibbetz's 5½-inch howitzer, Bijleveld reluctantly gave the order that the piece be abandoned. Supported on his horse by some of his men, the wounded Lieutenant Dibbetz was hurriedly evacuated. Major van Opstall similarly oversaw the removal of the remaining serviceable guns and caissons of Stevenaar's depleted brigade, now under the command of Lieutenant van de Wall, but the damage caused by the French artillery to the limbers and the high losses in draught horses made executing the order difficult and dangerous. Nonetheless, by the exertions of the officers and men, the guns were brought to a new position just to the south-west of Les Quatre Bras.

With the 5th National Militia Battalion and the 7th Line Battalion pushed back beyond the Ferme de la Bergerie and almost as far as the crossroads, the Prince van Oranje-Nassau decided that desperate measures were required and called for volunteers to launch a counter-attack to drive the French back down the chaussée; the 5th National Militia Battalion volunteered to a man. At the same time, orders were sent to Colonel Grunenbosch to advance in support with the 1st, 2nd and 6th Companies of the 27th Jager Battalion, the 4th and 5th companies being held in reserve. Major de la Sarraz ordered Major van Opstall to advance in support with Stevenaar's remaining guns and passing the order to Lieutenant van de Wall, the gunners formed a battery some two hundred paces to the south of the crossroads. With the Prince at their head, urging them on and waving his hat, the militia charged once again down the Charleroi road towards the French infantry, supported by the 27th Jager battalion, who launched an assault on the Ferme de la Bergerie, now occupied by French troops. The Netherlanders made a spirited attack on the enemy infantry and gun teams, but in turn suffered severely. Colonel Grunenbosch recollected events:

> Shouting 'Long live the King!' both officers and men were driven by the best will to repel the French skirmishers from the surrounding hedges there, but the murderous fire at short distance was very disadvantageous for these companies and the attack was not crowned with success, even though many of the men had already reached the hedges, as well as some officers. Among these, Captain Eichholtz, First Lieutenant de Croes of the second company and many men were severely wounded, others lightly and some killed. Although our men had reached the foot of these hedges, the attack did not result in a positive outcome because of strong pressure from the enemy cavalry.[12]

The screams of the wounded, the crash of small arms fire and the smell of blood, mingled with the scent of the crops assaulted the senses. In the dense, grey smoke, each man's world was compressed to a few metres of field, which was desperately contested by the apparitions looming through the fog. Despite the Jagers pouring volley after well-directed volley into the head of the French column, the odds were too great and the ragged line of men was slowly forced to retire, pressed ever more closely by the advancing French skirmishers. Hostile horsemen suddenly appeared and the shadow of panic spread across the greatly outnumbered infantry. Isolated on the bare slopes and weighed down by musket, rations, ammunition and accoutrements, the breathless soldiers struggled to reach a place of safety, hampered by the high crops. Captain de Nave tumbled to the ground, wounded, and fell into the hands of the enemy. Cadet Sergeant Welter was wounded in the neck. Colonel Grunebosch, fighting on foot after his horse had been killed by a round shot, was hacked about his head and arm by a French sabreur and fell, grievously wounded, whereupon Captain de Crassier immediately assumed the command. Second Lieutenant Henric van Heerdt was also wounded and command of his company devolved upon Second Lieutenant Hylckema, who was wounded shortly afterwards by a musket ball in his left leg and captured by the enemy horsemen:

> The yielding skirmish line hurried in confusion to the ground in advance, hoping to find cover. Before it could be reached, they were overrun by the cavalry; many were sabred and found their deaths beneath the hooves of the horses. The wounded were soon easy prey for the foragers who roamed behind the columns. Those who could still walk were assembled by them into small groups and driven back to the main body of their army.[13]

Whilst many of the Jagers were run down by *chasseurs à cheval* and sabred, those who begged for quarter and were fortunate enough to be spared by the horsemen, were taken prisoner and handed over to the infantry. Here the disarmed men were greeted with punches and blows from musket butts, before being robbed and dispatched under escort to the rear. Other soldiers, not in the direct line of the French charge, simply dropped out of sight, hidden by the dense vegetation, gradually crawling back to the northern edge of the fields, where they fell in with other fugitives, some of whom had lost their weapons and equipment in their scramble to safety. Still more dashed headlong for the buildings at Les Quatre Bras, or for the sanctuary of the Bois de Bossu. By the exertions of the officers, the bulk of the battalion was collected to the north-west of the crossroads; but it had now virtually ceased to exist as a fighting force, with the exception of the 3rd Company, which remained in contact with the 5th National Militia Battalion. As he sought to rally his troops around the reserve companies, de Crassier probably realised that they would play no further part in the engagement for the time being.[14]

An eyewitness to the slaughter, the Prince van Oranje-Nassau realised that if he were unable to counter the threat posed by the French cavalry and infantry, his remaining troops in the centre would be overwhelmed and the crossroads lost. He sent an aide to General van Merlen with the order to charge the enemy. The men of 6th (North Netherlands) Hussar Regiment had only just finished feeding the horses behind the Ferme des Quatre Bras, where they had moved to shelter from the artillery fire. Though Colonel Boreel had raised the regiment two years previously, the men were lacking in military experience, as was their leader. Captain Geij van Pittius of the horse artillery had sent word to Colonel Boreel that he had observed some French cavalry to the east, seemingly attempting to outflank the position at the crossroads; a platoon under the command of Captain van Bronkhorst had been dispatched to investigate. Boreel's trumpeter had just sounded the call to mount and the remaining men were busy removing and stowing the nosebags. Boreel had been ordered to clear the ground for the approaching Allied infantry by moving his regiment and as he remounted his own horse, he issued the command, 'Platoons, left, head of column half-right.' This order was in the process of being relayed when an officer sent by

General van Merlen rode past the horsemen, shouting, 'Hussars charge!' and gesturing excitedly towards the area around the Ferme de la Bergerie.[15]

The hussars were in a wholly unsuitable formation in which to deliver a charge. The order to mount had not yet reached every squadron; others were formed in column of route and still more were already moving off. The expectation of action, the urgency of the staff officer's instructions and the assumption that the Colonel had given the order led to each squadron's officers wheeling their troops this way and that, so that a considerable part of the regiment was unformed. Despite the obvious confusion, the inexperienced commanding officer made a catastrophic error. He decided to attempt a deployment whilst on the move, rather than halting the horsemen and then carrying out the regulation manoeuvre to form up. The close succession of different orders and the confusion of trumpet calls led to jostling and curses as the troops and squadrons sought the space in which to form line. Anxiety and exasperation reigned in equal measure as the leading squadron trotted away, the remaining squadrons colliding and becoming detached from the vanguard as they sought to follow.[16]

The ragged lines of hussars cantered across the shallow bowl of ground to the south-east of the crossroads, gaps appearing as the troopers tried and failed to maintain the dressing of the ranks. Following on behind, the fragmented squadrons tired their mounts in a vain attempt to maintain the correct intervals. As the sweating horses swept across the fields, Colonel Boreel at last had a sight of the enemy and a clear view of the terrain ahead of him. The main body of the enemy infantry was drawn up in two squares, supported by cavalry. Realising that the bulk of these forces were to his right, Boreel ordered the regiment to wheel. The insistent notes of the trumpet blaring in their ears, the men attempted to execute this manoeuvre, further gaps opening up as those on the left struggled to increase their speed and maintain contact; the charge started to disintegrate. Officers were exerting themselves to no avail in an effort to remedy the situation, when the first squadron encountered French *chasseurs à cheval* and lancers, counter-charging to check their advance.

The Netherlands hussars splintered as the opposing horsemen rode at them, the veteran French sabreurs inflicting heavy losses. Captain van Wijnbergen fell dead from his horse, as did thirteen other ranks. Somewhere in the mêlée, Second Lieutenant Wolff received his mortal wound. Amongst the more fortunate, Major Frederik de Jacobi, First Lieutenants Zwannebeek and Paauw, Second Lieutenants Looft, Rendorp, Bar van Utenhoven and 31 men were wounded. Though fighting with animation and courage, the hussars had lost what little cohesion they had possessed at the outset and in the ensuing contest were overwhelmed by their more numerous, disciplined and organised adversaries. Dispersed and unsupported, the blue-coated novices fled back towards the crossroads, their confidence shattered; they would play no further part in the combat.[17]

Having overwhelmed the Netherlands hussars, the French regrouped, leaving it to supporting cavalry to pursue the beaten enemy. As these fresh lancers and *chasseurs à cheval* trotted forward, they caught sight of the wholly unprotected guns of Stevenaar's artillery to their left, which had advanced in support of the Netherlands cavalry and were still limbered up in the fields to the west of the Charleroi road. The gunners watched in apprehension as their own cavalry swept past their flank, galloping for the sanctuary of the crossroads, hotly pursued by the French. The 7th Line Battalion, a short distance to the rear, had also noticed the threat and was preparing to receive cavalry. Several of the artillery crews scrambled back through the tangled crops, hoping to take cover in its ranks.

The battery had advanced too quickly and the gun teams were halted too close together for the drivers to be able to turn properly. Confusion ensued as teams became entangled and collided with each other. Some of the artillerymen employed to guard the vehicles and replenish ammunition had the foresight to unhitch the limber and wagon teams and escape to the Ferme de la Bergerie or the crossroads, but the remainder of Stevenaar's gunners, realising the danger too late, saw that there was nowhere to run for safety and prepared to defend themselves and their pieces as best they could. Drawing their short swords or arming themselves with *écouvillons*, ramming staves and trail spikes, they attempted to ward off the blows of the horsemen as they dashed amongst the guns, limbers and ammunition wagons. The contest was wholly uneven, though some gunners managed to save themselves by sheltering under the carriages and caissons. The horsemen were initially exultant over the capture of the four cannon, but soon realised that they possessed neither the tools nor the skills to destroy them and that the bulk of the means to bring them off had already been removed by those wishing to escape the butchery. Instead, they redoubled their assault on the gunners. Lieutenant Ruysch van Coeverden fell with fourteen wounds and Lieutenant van Gahlen of the Artillery Train with two. Lieutenant van de Wall received four wounds and was briefly taken prisoner, before managing to escape. Also wounded was Major van Opstall, General de Perponcher-Sedlnitzky's artillery commander, who had remained with Stevenaar's brigade since the death of its commander. Physically unable to continue the struggle, he reluctantly sent a messenger to Captain Bijleveld, requesting him to assume command of the wreckage of the division's artillery.[18]

Whilst the leading French squadron consumed the artillery, the succeeding waves of lancers poured across the fields to the east and west of the chaussée, the axis of their charge directed towards the infantry scurrying for cover in their immediate front. Closing with dramatic speed, the cavalry fell on the remnants of the 5th National Militia Battalion, the 27th Jager Battalion and the two detached companies of the 8th National Militia Battalion, which were still retiring through the fields towards the crossroads. Captain van Toll, the only company commander of the 5th National Militia Battalion to remain unwounded, recollected the impact they had:

> A great mischief followed; namely that after the unsuccessful charge of the Hussars of Boreel, which took place at that moment, the disorderly retreat of these hussars, as well as the great number of officers of the 5th Militia who were out of action, amongst which were five company commanders, caused confusion with this battalion.[19]

Shrouded by gunsmoke, the small, dense column of infantry was making its way towards safety along the chaussée de Charleroi and had reached a point just to the north of the Ferme de la Bergerie. Realising that cavalry were close by, Westenbergh ordered the battalion to form square, but several platoons were not yet in formation when the French, spurred on by the success of their comrades and ignoring the faltering musketry from the depleted and largely leaderless ranks, smashed into the hapless men and drove the fragments into the wood, stabbing at the scurrying infantrymen as they strove to effect their escape. As they poured across the rutted tracks and through the hedgerows protecting the edge of the Bois de Bossu, the once jubilant expressions of the infantrymen were replaced by the shocked demeanour of beaten men.[20]

Witnessing the devastation being wreaked amongst the artillery and the 5th National Militia Battalion, the nerve of the 7th Line Battalion collectively disintegrated and it abandoned its attempts to form a square. With the exception of two companies, which possessed enough presence of mind to form a rallying square in the space between the chaussée de Charleroi road and the Bois de Bossu, the remainder of the battalion broke ranks, cast aside their muskets and ran helter-skelter. Hunted down by the lancers, which on account of their burnished helmets many of the young soldiers mistook for cuirassiers, the panicked infantry fled across the fields for the refuge of the wood. Here amongst the trees, they mingled with hundreds of men from other battalions and arms of service, in differing states of exhaustion, discipline and morale. Isolated and abandoned in the field, Lieutenant Scheltens realised that he could not possibly reach the wood or the rallying square in time and he survived the butchery only by throwing himself beneath the wheels of one of Stevenaar's abandoned caissons. Lieutenant Gérards was less fortunate and was taken prisoner during the rout. Scheltens tried to make himself as inconspicuous as possible as he squatted amongst the crushed rye, beneath the belly of the ammunition wagon. Biding his time and judging that the threat had passed, he eventually emerged from his hiding place and reached the shelter of the wood, where he rejoined his men.

The battalion, he discovered to his horror, was a wreck. A combination of musketry, round shot, canister and cold steel had caused heavy losses but, more importantly, had totally destroyed its morale. Lieutenant Carondal was reported killed; indeed, Scheltens' own shako was perforated by a musket ball which, had it been a centimetre lower, would have done for him also. Dozens of men were missing in the wood and the fields, some possibly never to be seen alive again. So much damage had been done in such a short space of time that Scheltens was convinced that all that was required by the French to win the day was for them to form up in column and march resolutely forward. There seemed to be absolutely nothing left in front to arrest their advance on Brussels, his home town. Along with Captain Henri l'Olivier, Captain Édouard de Bast and Lieutenant Count Édouard de Nieulant, he set about the task of rallying the crippled battalion.[21]

At the same time that the French cavalry was sabring Stevenaar's battery and the remnants of van Bijlandt's infantry – the élite company of the *chasseurs à cheval*, recognisable by their red epaulettes and fur colpacks – noticed a group of officers with no discernable troops under their command. It was the Prince van Oranje-Nassau and his staff, together with the artillery staff of the 2nd (Netherlands) Infantry Division.

The Battle of Quatre Bras

As the enemy cavalry approached, the Netherlands generals, aides and orderlies realised their peril and dug their spurs into the horses to make off. In their midst, the Prince was very nearly seized, hemmed in by horsemen so tightly that some thought he was surrounded. The knot of men and horses dashed pell-mell towards the sanctuary of the rallying square formed by the two companies of the 7th Line Battalion, the Prince and his officers only escaping thanks to the speed of their horses. Less fortunate was Major van Limburg-Stirum, his aide-de-camp. His own horse being exhausted, he had mounted a replacement, which shortly afterwards was hit by an unidentified projectile. He had dismounted to examine the wound, only to discover with great surprise, the French at such a short distance He had insufficient time to remount and was therefore compelled to fight his assailants on foot. Surrounded by a number of chasseurs, shouting: 'Kill him! He's the Prince!' the Major attempted to defend himself with his sword, but suffered two sabre cuts to his head and one to his left hand in the attempt. On the point of being made prisoner, he was extricated from his predicament by the courage and selflessness of Colonel du Caylar, the Prince's First Adjutant, who rode into the knot of struggling men, accompanied by a number of Boreel's hussars, and managed to drag him away from his assailants. As du Caylar and the virtually insensible van Limburg-Stirum approached the square of infantry, a number of men from the 7th Line Battalion ran out to their assistance and dragged the injured officer into the refuge of its ranks.[22]

Seizing van Limburg-Stirum's wounded horse as a trophy, the *chasseurs* swept past the infantry, secure in their makeshift formation and protected by a hedge. As they did so, the Belgians opened a fusillade, which prompted the French commanding officer to sound the recall. Within the square itself, the Prince van Oranje-Nassau was almost beside himself with excitement and adrenalin. Tearing the elaborately embroidered star of the Military Order of Willem from the breast of his coat, he pressed it into the hands of the Colour-bearer, declaring: 'My brave Belgians, take it, you have won it fairly! You have all deserved it!' His remark was met by cheers from, amongst others Sergeant Winsinger, who might have wondered how his brother, an artillery officer, was faring. Fastening the device to their colour and shouting 'Long live the Prince!' the Belgians swore to defend it till death.[23]

Charging in support, yet more French cavalry fell on the two guns of Captain Geij van Pittius' battery that had advanced in the wake of the hussars. The section commander, Lieutenant Wassenaar van Sint-Pancras vividly remembered the confusion that followed:

> The cavalry of General van Merlen rushed to assist, but soon we saw these brave men return in the direction of our position. My captain [Geij van Pittius] threw himself . . . from his horse and the gunners crowded together beneath the pieces. Judging the danger not to be so great, I remained in doubt for a moment, when . . . I found myself in the midst of the mêlée, packed together like sardines. How I got out is still a dream and I was lucky, too, that not one or the other *Chasseur* of the Guard tried his sabre on me.[24]

'Many found their deaths beneath the hooves'

The area to the south of Les Quatre Bras was shrouded in smoke, through which isolated figures and small groups of infantry and cavalry could be seen milling about in confusion. As Boreel's cavalry had passed by at the charge, parties of men had been able to rejoin Captain de Crassier and the rump of the 27th Jager Battalion. Those companies that had been less severely engaged managed to make their way to the rear. Sergeant Welter had managed to evacuate Colonel Grunenbosch into the Bois de Bossu, but others had not been as fortunate. Somewhere in the tall rye lay the body of 60-year-old Captain de Nave. Having earlier fallen victim to a lancer, who wounded him with a thrust from his weapon, the unfortunate man had been taken prisoner and herded towards the rear. Alarmed by the charge of the Netherlands cavalry, many of the French had abandoned their prisoners, but de Nave amongst others, was not so lucky. Rather than permit the captives to return to their ranks, the French horsemen callously sabred them. Lieutenant Hylckema was more fortunate. Captured as he tried to flee the butchery, he had been staggering into captivity, holding the stirrup of his escort, as Boreel's men collided with the French. More concerned for his own safety than for his prisoners, his captor had dashed off, only to be brought down a short distance away by a well-aimed musket shot. His prisoners remained unharmed and Hylckema, astonished at his good fortune, made his way slowly back up the slope. He later recalled the experience.

> We fired a few well-aimed volleys, which was followed by a cavalry charge that our brave hussars attempted to counter in vain; the yielding skirmish line hurried to the ground in front for more cover, with a loss of cohesion. Before it was reached, we were overrun by the cavalry, many were sabred and found their deaths under the hooves of the horses. The wounded were soon easy prey for the foragers who roamed behind the columns; those who could still walk were assembled by them in small troops and driven away.[25]

The slaughter of the 5th National Militia Battalion had been witnessed by the men of the first battalion of the Regiment Oranien-Nassau, whom Colonel von Sachsen-Weimar had ordered to move from Croix-Seigneur a short while earlier. They had only just taken up a new position on the eastern side of the Bois de Bossu, when the French cavalry had struck. As the horsemen receded, fresh columns of French infantry attempted to pass through the gap between the wood and the Charleroi road, in order to launch an assault on the crossroads itself and to finally break the resistance of the Netherlanders and Germans. In the ranks of the Grenadier Company of the Oranien-Nassau battalion was Sergeant Heinrich Döring:

> A Dutch battalion was overrun almost immediately, and as it was positioned on the high road in the centre of our line, a terrible danger arose to our corps. This was increased by the fact that the Dutch suffered from the cannon fire. They lost their courage altogether and left their position, throwing away their muskets. In order to counter the threat and repulse the French, who were advancing with all their might, our colonel, Prince

The Battle of Quatre Bras

Bernhard of Weimar, ordered our battalion, which was posted next to the Dutch, to attack the enemy and drive him from the said position ... He had called for volunteers; but the whole of our battalion, with the drummers in the front and with fixed bayonets, marched against the French in the position they had conquered without having fired a shot. The enemy were beaten and the centre was restored at once. During the advance, a cannon ball hit the sabre scabbard of our sergeant-major, Geiss (who comes from Dillenburg), the impact of which threw him unconscious to the ground, although he was unhurt, apart from the shock.[26]

Even as Döring's battalion advanced into action, some of the French infantry entered the eastern edge of the wood, threatening to outflank the first and third battalions of the 2nd Nassau-Usingen Regiment, as well as the 8th National Militia Battalion in the open ground to the west. With the sound of thousands of Frenchmen shouting '*Vive l'Empereur!*' filling his ears, General de Perponcher-Sedlnitzky directed Colonel Singendonck and his 7th National Militia Battalion, which had earlier moved into the northern end of the Bois de Bossu, to counter-attack. Militiaman Allebrandi later recalled the moment:[27]

We received orders to advance and deploy ourselves as skirmishers in the wood, bcause the French, who had advanced in force, were not more than a hundred paces removed from us with their advanced guard. We nevertheless bravely advanced whilst skirmishing, without being in the least deterred by the warm welcome that we received from the enemy voltigeurs. We kept on advancing through the wood in the direction of Houtain [sic] and made many Frenchmen tumble in the sand, whilst on our side also, more than one brave soldier sealed his loyalty and love for his country with his death, or was put out of action because of his wounds. The first fight would have been even bloodier for both sides, had it not been for the dispersed trees and branches that often made firing so uncertain.

After driving the French from the eastern edge of the Bois de Bossu, the 7th National Militia Battalion emerged into an open field of rye, to the right of the first battalion of the Regiment Oranien-Nassau. Captain van der Bruggen van Croy and First Lieutenant van Zante urged their men on and Militiamen Rem, Bindt and Pruimpje stumbled through the tangled crops as the battalion advanced. Militiaman Allebrandi had hardly advanced a few paces into the open, when he noticed the dead body of a Nassau officer some distance away, close to a road. Motivated by curiosity, he hurried across to examine the corpse, but was struck across the shoulder by the sabre of his company commander. Perhaps mistaking Allebrandi's intentions for looting or cowardice, the Captain was not about to tolerate such indiscipline and forced the hapless soldier back into the ranks.[28]

Having earlier led the first battalion of the Regiment Oranien-Nassau, von Sachsen-Weimar had returned to the Bois de Bossu and found that the first and third battalions of the 2nd Nassau-Usingen Regiment had withdrawn into the open

'Many found their deaths beneath the hooves'

ground of the Champ du Sarti, to the west of the wood, where they took up ground to the north of the 8th National Militia Battalion. As he passed through the wood, he came across the two detached companies of this latter battalion that had been heavily engaged in the centre of the battlefield. As the French moved through the trees and applied pressure to his left flank, the Prince called for volunteers from the Nassau battalion and led the composite force forward in a bayonet charge against the leading French troops. Mounted on his horse – a large black Arab stallion that had been a gift from the Tsar of Russia – he led the attack from the front, swinging his sabre in encouragement. The cheering Dutch militiamen poured into the wood behind him, but as the Prince passed into the trees, his enthusiasm got the better of him and he inadvertently managed to wound himself in the right leg with his own blade. Considering the injury to be slight, he continued to advance and in his wake, the men from The Hague drove the French back some considerable distance.[29]

From his position at the crossroads, Wellington watched this sequence of events with concern. He had an uninterrupted view of the ground to the south of Les Quatre Bras and was alarmed at the progress the French seemed to be making in the centre. To the east of the Charleroi road, only No. 3 Company of the 27th Jager Battalion remained, continuing to protect the four guns of Bijleveld's troop, drawn up in the south-east angle of the crossroads. The counter-attack by the first battalion of the Regiment Oranien-Nassau and the 7th National Militia Battalion had, for the time being, stopped the French advance beyond the Ferme de la Bergerie in its tracks, but two of van Bijland's infantry battalions and the 6th Hussar Regiment would play no further part in the action. Through the smoke and haze, further large bodies of enemy infantry could be seen advancing towards the crossroads, evidently intent on seizing the position and supported to the east by further substantial infantry formations that were crossing the Gemioncourt stream to the south of the heights of Bati-Saint-Bernard.[30]

With measures already taken to safeguard the extreme left flank and the centre temporarily stabilised, Wellington was able to focus his attention on the problem. Discussing the matter with Picton, the Duke decided that support was needed immediately in the centre, in the form of what the two deemed to be 'reliable' infantry. Firstly, Picton was to launch an immediate attack on the Ferme de la Bergerie in order to prevent it falling into the hands of the French; he was then directed to place his two brigades along the Namur road. The Welshman immediately hurried off to confer with Generals Kempt and Pack, who were to bring their remaining battalions up the Brussels road and to deploy them in positions to the east of the chaussée.[31]

The next available troops were the first battalion of the 28th Regiment of Foot, under the orders of Colonel Nixon, its commanding officer being absent. The 'Slashers' were one of Nosey's battle-hardened Peninsular War battalions, having fought in fifteen major actions in the course of the campaigns in Portugal, Spain and France. Whilst Picton was organising the deployment of Kempt's and Pack's brigades, Colonel Gomm returned from the Bois de Bossu to report that the wood, though in some parts intricate, was passable everywhere for light infantry. Having fulfilled his reconnaissance, Picton sent him back to bring up the 28th Regiment of Foot. Riding up to Colonel

The Battle of Quatre Bras

Nixon, Gomm explained the urgency of the situation and the tired infantrymen were rapidly formed up and doubled down the Charleroi road towards the Ferme de la Bergerie. The column advanced in the teeth of a brisk cannonade from French horse artillery, brought forward to the heights of Bati-Saint-Bernard and through the débris of van Bijlandt's brigade. They had only advanced a short distance from the crossroads when they saw that the French were already swarming through the building and its enclosures. The battalion remained halted briefly, checking flints and bayonets were secure, but before Nixon could give the order to charge, one of Wellington's staff officers galloped up to Gomm and ordered him to cancel the attack and withdraw the battalion; the French were already in possession of the farm in numbers too great to risk its destruction. Instead, the battalion was to file off to the right and take up its post with the other regiments of Kempt's brigade along the Namur road. No doubt grateful not to have to storm the farm buildings, the men doubled back, pelted by musketry and canister shot, their backs hunched as though moving through a storm.[32]

Endnotes

1. Arthur, p. 596. Batty, p. 48. Swiney, p. 116.
2. Allan. Alexander Forbes (II). Anonymous (Cameron). Mackenzie &c., pp. 54–5. Vallence, p. 6.
3. Gronow, p. 126.
4. Gomm (I), pp. 5–6. Gomm (IV).
5. Anonymous (V. d. W.). van Balveren. de Bas &c., pp. 497–8. Bowden, p. 268. van Bronkhorst. Deebetz. Delhaize and Aerts, p. 435. van Doren, p. 48. Eenens, pp. 74–5. Gomm (IV). Houssaye, p. 114. Hoynck van Papendrecht, p. 68. van Löben-Sels, pp. 196–7, 526. Manchot, p. 76. van Oranje-Nassau (II). Pawly (I), p. 139. Pawly (III), p. 37. Rens, p. 110. Roijen. J. Ross (II). W. Siborne (V), p. 71. Storm de Grave. Wassenaar van Sint-Pancras. van Zuylen van Nyeveld (I), p. 56.
6. Anonymous (Near Observer), p. 46. Aubrey-Fletcher, p. 368. Caldwell and Cooper, p. 9. Cope, p. 198. Costello, p. 151.
7. Aubrey-Flecher, p. 368. Caldwell and Cooper, pp. 9–10. Kincaid (I), p. 316.
8. Anonymous (Waterloo Medal Roll), p. 322. Caldwell and Cooper, p. 10. Cope, p. 198. Costello, p. 151. Dalton, pp. 197–9, Kincaid (I), p. 316. Simmons (I), p. 363.
9. de Bas &c., p. 500. Dellevoet, p. 24. Alexander Forbes (II). Knoop (II), p. 192. van Toll.
10. de Bas &c., pp. 499–500. Dellevoet, p. 23. Grunenbosch. van Löben-Sels, p. 529. de Perponcher-Sedlnitzky. van Toll.
11. de Bas &c., pp. 499–500. Dellevoet, p. 24. Knoop (II), pp. 192, 145. van Limburg-Stirum. van Opstall. de Perponcher-Sedlnitzky. Starklof, p. 139. van Zuylen van Nyeveld, p. 56.
12. de Bas &c., pp. 499–500. Dellevoet, p. 24. Knoop (II), pp. 145, 192. van Limburg-Stirum. van Löben-Sels, p. 523. van Limburg-Stirum. van Opstall. van Osten. de Perponcher-Sedlnitzky. W. Siborne (V), p. 70. Starklof, p. 139. van de Wall. van Zuylen van Nyeveld (I), p. 56. van Zuylen van Nyeveld (II).

13. de Bas &c., p. 497. van Bijlandt. de Crassier. Dellevoet, p. 24. Grunenbosch. Hylckema. Henckens, pp. 224–5. de Perponcher-Sedlnitzky. Wassenaar van Sint-Pancras. Welter. van Zuylen van Nyeveld (I), p. 56.
14. de Bas &c., p. 497. van Bijlandt. de Crassier. Dellevoet, p. 24. Hylckema. Grunenbosch. de Perponcher-Sedlnitzky. W. Siborne (V), p. 70. van Zuylen van Nyeveld (I), p. 56.
15. Anonymous (VdW). Arthur, p. 596. van Balveren. de Bas &c., pp. 500, 505–6. Deebetz. Delhaize and Aerts, p. 436. van Doren. Henckens, p. 225. Houssaye, p. 114. Koopman. Pawly (II), pp. 34. Pawly (III), p. 23. Rens, pp. 108–9. Roijen. W. Siborne (V), p. 71. van de Wall. Wassenaar van Sint-Pancras.
16. Anonymous (V. d. W.). van Balveren. de Bas &c., p. 506. Deebetz. Delhaize and Aerts, p. 436. van Doren. Koopman. van Löben-Sels, pp. 526–7. Pawly (II), p. 34. Rens, pp. 108–9. Roijen. W. Siborne (V), p. 71. van de Wall.
17. Arthur, p. 596. van Balveren. de Bas &c., pp. 506–7. Brett-James, p. 55. Delhaize and Aerts, p. 436. Dellevoet, p. 26. van Doren. Eenens, pp. 74–5. Henckens, p. 225. Houssaye, p. 114. Koopman. de Mercx de Corbais. von Müffling (I), p. 5. Norden, p. 391. Pawly (II), p. 34. Rens, pp. 108–10. Roijen. W. Siborne (V), p. 71. Wüppermann, p. 110.
18. Arthur, p. 596. de Bas &c., pp. 506–7. Bijleveld. Brett-James, p. 55. Delhaize and Aerts, p. 436. Henckens, pp. 228–9. Houssaye, p. 114. Koopman. van Löben-Sels, pp. 527–8. Meijer. van Opstall. van Osten. de Perponcher-Sedlnitzky. van de Wall. van Zuylen van Nyeveld (I), p. 57.
19. Barre. van Bijlandt. Grunenbosch. Henckens, p. 225. Houssaye, p. 114. Knoop (II), p. 192. Mollinger. van Toll.
20. Allebrandi. Arthur, p. 596. Barre. van Bijlandt. Damitz, p. 197. Dellevoet, p. 26. Girod de l'Ain. Grunenbosch. Henckens, p. 225. Houssaye, pp. 113–4. van Löben-Sels, pp. 190–8. Mollinger. Scheltens, p. 198. W. Siborne (V), p. 71. Starklof, p. 139. van Toll.
21. Houssaye, p. 114. Scheltens, p. 205.
22. de Bas &c., p. 507. de Constant-Rebecque (I). Delhaize and Aerts, p. 436. Dellevoet, p. 26. Foy. Henckens, pp. 225–6. Houssaye, p. 113. van Limburg-Stirum. van Löben-Sels, p. 524. van Osten. Reille. Ross-Lewin, p. 259. W. Siborne (V), p. 71. Starklof, p. 139. Swiney, pp. 117–8. van Toll.
23. de Bas &c., pp. 507–8. Henckens, pp. 225–6. Scheltens, p. 198. F. Somerset, p. 9. Swiney, pp. 117–8.
24. Wassenaar van Sint-Pancras.
25. de Crassier. Grunenbosch. Hylckema. Welter.
26. Döring. Muilwijk, p. 80. van Zuylen van Nyeveld (I), p. 55.
27. Allebrandi, pp. 5–6. Muilwijk, pp. 80–1. van Zuylen van Nyeveld (I), p. 54.
28. Allebrandi, pp. 5–6. Knoop (II), pp. 193–4. Muilwijk, pp. 80–1. Rem.
29. Döring. von Sachsen-Weimar (I). Muilwijk, pp. 80–1.
30. de Bas &c., p. 498. van Opstall. van Zuylen van Nyeveld (I), pp. 55–6.
31. Gomm (IV). J. Ross (II).
32. Aubrey-Fletcher, p. 368. Dalton, pp. 135–6. Fosten, pp. 26–7. Glazebrook, pp. 10, 14–15. Gomm (I), p. 6. Gomm (IV). Gomm (V). von Müffling (I), pp. 4–5. Reille. Seale, p. 7. W. Siborne (V), p. 71.

CHAPTER 11

In the meantime, Colonel Gomm lost no time in riding back towards La Baracque to carry out the second part of his mission. As he passed on Picton's instructions, he warned the commanding officers of each battalion that the enemy looked likely to launch an attack at any moment, stressing the urgency of their moving into position without delay. General Kempt was ordered to line the Namur road, his left flank covered by the étang Materne and the 95th Regiment of Foot, already engaged in the Bois des Censes and in the fields towards Piraumont. The 1st Regiment of Foot, nominally a part of Pack's brigade, was temporarily placed under his orders. General Pack, with the remainder of his command, was directed to form up on the roadway to Kempt's right, with his own right flank at the crossroads of Les Quatre Bras. Colonel Best and his four Hanoverian Landwehr battalions was to form the second line behind the two British brigades, in the rolling ground to the north of the Namur road, his troops taking cover in the marshy but sheltered rye fields.[1]

The third of Kempt's four battalions to be committed to the fray was the 79th Regiment of Foot, which received orders to move off in the same direction as the Rifles had taken. As they reached the rising ground to the north-west of Les Quatre Bras, Lieutenant Forbes could see this battalion ahead of them. Glancing to the south, across the swaying fields of grain, he noticed a battalion of Belgians exchanging shots with the French and withdrawing slowly.[2]

Hard on the heels of the Cameron Highlanders were the veterans of the 32nd Regiment of Foot, which had arrived and halted to the north of the crossroads a short while earlier. Having passed the Brunswick cavalry in rear of Les Quatre Bras, observing the remainder of the 5th (British) Infantry Division deploying and noticing the arrival of the Hanoverians in their rear, some of the officers of the regiment thought that these forces, along with the small numbers of Dutch troops that were visible in front, would prove altogether too weak a force with which to withstand the enemy. It was rumoured that across the shallow valley, hidden somewhere in the rolling fields and dense woods, were 70,000 Frenchmen, led by Bonaparte himself. Major Ross-Lewin in particular was concerned about the uneven numbers of the protagonists; in his estimation, Wellington had only some 19,000 men at his disposal and as far as he could make out, no artillery whatever. When the battalion had passed the Brunswick Hussars and Uhlans, he had been impressed with the men, but not

'A field of rye as tall as our Grenadiers'

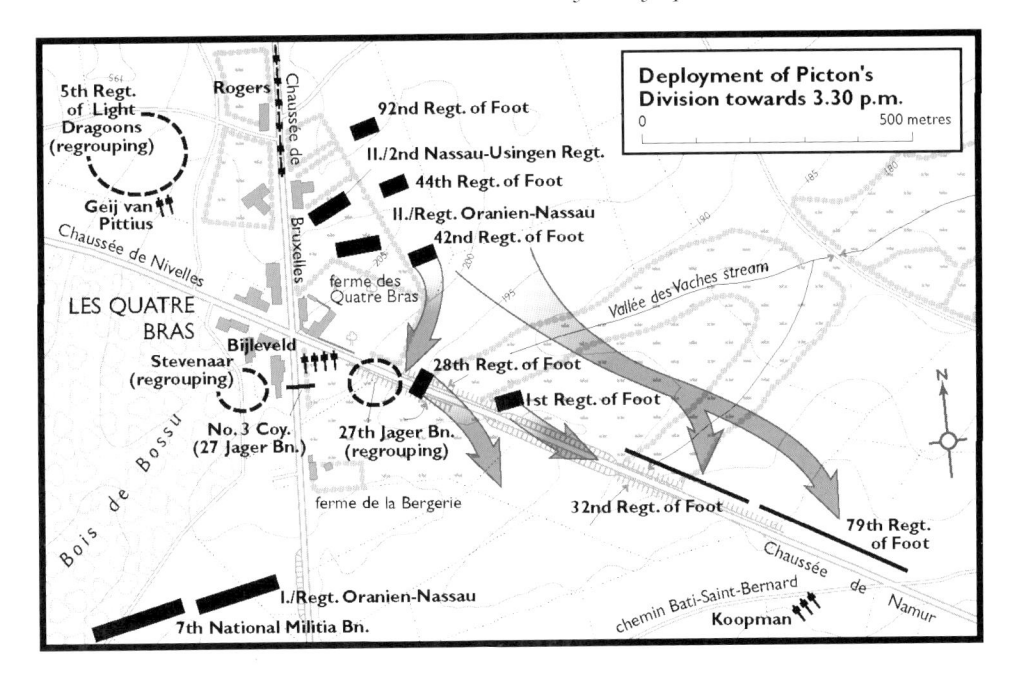

Deployment of Picton's Division towards 3.30 p.m.

by the quality of their mounts. Nor was he impressed with the position, which to his mind was of no strength at all. From the point upon which he stood, the ground swelled into gentle slopes, stretching from the Namur road on his left, across the whole front, bisected by the Charleroi road and eventually concealed by the Bois de Bossu on the right. To the immediate front of the battalion, there were some fields of 'Amazingly tall rye'. With the sang-froid of an experienced soldier, he concluded that they would have to rely on the skill and presence of mind of the generals, the courage and discipline of what few troops there were and, above all, the favour of the God of battles.[3]

Another officer of the regiment who had gone forward with Ross-Lewin was Ensign Charles Dallas, who had only joined the battalion in March.

> I went forward with some other officers to view the French position and got close to Lord Wellington whom I heard say, 'I am sure we shall have an attack tonight,' and immediately afterwards we saw them moving in columns towards our position. Ours was the only division up, and after such a march, you may conceive we were in want of a little rest – but as soon as the enemy was seen coming on, fatigue seemed to be forgotten – the mere thought of nothing but advancing and giving them another licking.[4]

Farther to the north, Corporal Douglas estimated that his legs had already marched over thirty kilometres and he was enjoying the rest, along with the remainder of the third battalion of the 1st Regiment of Foot. The troops had halted between La Baracque and Les Quatre Bras for the purpose of cooking, but as the pots bubbled away, their idyll was interrupted by an unwanted visitor:

A straggling shell coming over the camp told us in language not to be mistaken that the enemy were not far off. In a few minutes the cooking was settled and the utensils packed up and the guests preparing for another kind of entertainment. We were ordered 'Stand to your arms,' fall in, the ammunition examined, flints fast, all's right. Here we moved forward a little, filed to the right into a field of rye as tall as our grenadiers and the day began.

Corporal John Olday, sat nearby, probably cursed as the order to fall in was given. He had received a ball in the knee during the fighting in the Peninsula, which had never been removed. The voyage from Cobh to the Downs had somehow inflamed the injury and he had subjected himself to the tender mercies of a 'Drunken old file' named Frazer, who in between his drinking sessions, acted as the hospital orderly. Though the surgery was a complete success, his knee would not cope with many more route marches like this one.[5]

The battalion was separated from the remainder of Pack's brigade and formed into a column at quarter distance intervals in the fields to the left of the chaussée. Captain Robert Macdonald was on foot at the head of his Light Company, which brought up the rear of the column. Once all the divisions had taken up their appointed places, the battalion was marched across the fields that covered the rising ground to the north-east of Les Quatre Bras. Descending the slope to the Namur road, some four hundred metres from the crossroads, the officers were able to assess the seriousness of the situation for the first time. General van Bijlandt's wrecked brigade was in the greatest of disorder. Captain Macdonald was unable to see much, but as the command was given to deploy into line, he caught sight of Generals Picton and Kempt and soon gained a clearer impression of their efforts to establish a line of defence. To the left of his battalion, Macdonald could see the 32nd Regiment of Foot and beyond them the 79th Regiment of Foot in their own positions behind the tree-lined Namur road, partially protected by the embankments. A short while later, his battalion was joined by the 28th Regiment of Foot, breathless from its abortive advance on the Ferme de la Bergerie. Owing to some confusion, it took up ground to the right of the Royals instead of the left, behind the shallow reverse slope of the heights of Bati-Saint-Bernard.[6]

The Royal Highlanders of the 42nd Regiment of Foot had been resting by the side of the chaussée de Bruxelles, fatigued after the long march of over thirty kilometres in the stifling heat, without so much as a thimbleful of water. Knapsacks, haversacks and cartridge boxes had been removed and the heavy Brown Bess muskets laid aside by weary arms. Those of the battalion not dozing on the verges may have noticed some houses to the left of the road, but were oblivious as to their whereabouts. The local inhabitants, had any remained behind, could have told them that they had reached Dernier Patard, a village less than two kilometres north of Les Quatre Bras.

After the briefest of halts, the order came to 'Stand to your arms,' and the tired men once more roused themselves and formed up in column. Having marched a short distance, the troops were wheeled off the road to the left into a cornfield and deployed

'A field of rye as tall as our Grenadiers'

into line, under the cover of some rising ground. A short distance to their right, Major John Campbell's grenadiers could see the small clump of houses called La Baracque on the officer's maps, around which were gathered scores of wounded soldiers in unfamiliar uniforms. Sergeant Anton could now smell the powder. Advancing in the wake of the Royals, the 42nd was halted behind a gently rising eminence. The men were ordered into column of companies, an evolution which proved awkward in the tall, thick grain. Once formed up, the battalion toiled up a steep slope covered in ripening rye. As they breasted the rise, they could see Kempt's brigade ahead of them, moving forward to engage the enemy. To the right, Sergeant Anton admired the beautiful plain, surrounded by belts of wood and with the main road from Brussels driving through it, straight as far as the eye could see. Between this road, however, and the isolated troops of Kempt's brigade, was an inviting gap, into which the battalion seemed directed. Though the rattle of musketry was now very clear, nothing could be seen of the skirmishers evidently at work in the high crops. Colonel Macara ordered his battalion to execute an intricate echelon movement to the right and one by one, the companies negotiated the descent. Finally arriving on the Namur road after a short march that had been characterised by confusing changes in direction, Sergeant Anton found that he had lost his bearings. Was this the road to Charleroi? Either way, it had a nice solid bank on one side of it, opposite which the Highlanders formed up in two ranks.[7]

Some distance behind them, the 44th Regiment of Foot was also on the move. Captain Burney's company had been cooking their dinners by the roadside, opposite the Brunswick Hussars, who had mounted up and moved off a short while before. A steady stream of fugitives and wounded, which many of the men took to be Prussians, passed by, saying that 'It would be warm work in front' and that 'They had had enough of it the day before'. The crackle of musketry and the faint sound of cheering drifted back across the fields in rear of Les Quatre Bras, to where Lieutenant Riddock was resting, having witnessed the departure of the 1st and 42nd Regiments of Foot. Suddenly, an aide-de-camp came dashing along the chaussée with orders for the battalion to advance. Colonel Hamerton gave the order to 'Stand to' and Sergeant-Major James Corcoran immediately shouted 'Fall in 44th.' Cooking was stopped immediately, the men scrambling to douse fires, retrieve food from the pot and hastily re-stow knapsacks and haversacks. Within minutes, the battalion was formed up in a quarter-distance column, in regular order of battle, bayonets glittering in the afternoon sunshine as the men chewed the salty beef or hurriedly crammed a final piece of biscuit or bread into mouths already dry with anticipation. 'This is it', thought many of the men. Messmates wished each other well and shared a final swig of gin, the raw spirit burning in the back of the throat. Sergeants prowled the ranks, muttering words of encouragement and reproach. Suddenly, they were underway, General Pack at their head, the rhythmic pounding of the drums filling the ears as the column snaked up the low hill that separated their rest area from the scene of the fighting. As the head of the column reached the knoll immediately to the rear of Les Quatre Bras, they had a clear view of the enemy for the first time, reputedly 50,000 strong and all chosen men. They seemed to be in possession of the wood on the right of the road and were engaged at a distance with some troops in unfamiliar uniforms which were taken to be Prussians. Farther along the Charleroi road, the plain seemed covered by solid masses of French troops between the Ferme de Gemioncourt and the enclosures of the Ferme de la Bergerie. The air was heavy with the smell of burnt powder. As they came down the slope on the other side, they were met with a panorama of dense formations of soldiers, booming artillery and lines of skirmishers, their muskets popping amongst the dense fields of rye. The sweet smell of crushed wheat blended with the unmistakable odour of unwashed bodies and stale sweat. After several minutes, the leading files encountered a thick hedge, which took some time to negotiate, before they found themselves crossing the cobbled Namur road and entering a field where the crop was so tall, it was as high as the shoulders of the tallest men. The combination of the low ground and the tall crop gave many men a feeling of security, yet filled others with a sense of vulnerability and foreboding. What was on the other side of the ridge?[8]

Behind Hamerton's battalion, the footsore men of the 92nd Regiment of Foot toiled up the gentle slope towards the buildings on the crest of the ridge, beyond which, the roar of artillery and the crackle of musketry could be heard. They were the last of Pack's regiment to arrive and Lieutenant Winchester was puzzling over how it had lost its natural order in the brigade. Perhaps it had been decided by Wellington? Perhaps the large farm and what looked to Sergeant Robertson like a public house had some special significance? A pall of smoke hung in the air. It was shortly after 3.30 p.m.[9]

The booming of the guns filled the ears of the young Brunswick infantrymen as they too marched along the Brussels road, to the north of Les Quatre Bras, in the wake of Picton's infantry. There were chaotic scenes as they approached the crossroads, with the rear areas strewn with dead and wounded men and horses, the wreckage of wagons, cannons and caissons. Here and there, small groups of Dutch and Nassau infantry were being gathered in, many without arms, having escaped their French captors. Ahead of them, they could see several squadrons of light cavalry moving off towards the south. Casualties, some alert and others unconscious, were hauled back to the aid stations and field hospitals that had been hastily set up in the buildings around the crossroads and to the north. Elsewhere, the less fortunate wounded dragged their shattered limbs back up the cobbles, begging for water and help in languages that the young Brunswickers did not understand. The fields to the rear of Les Quatre Bras were crowded with blue-coated cavalry and foreign-looking battalions of infantry, into whose ranks stray round shot came bounding at regular intervals. Staff officers clustered around their generals, including the Duke of Wellington himself, who was urgently sending off orderlies to 'Collect all the troops as quick as possible and to prepare for battle.' To the left of the road, filling the gardens, orchards and fields behind the Ferme des Quatre Bras were vehicles of all descriptions. This then, was the battlefield.

A short distance in front, the Duke von Braunschweig-Lüneburg and the Prince van Oranje-Nassau were deep in conference. The conversation was a serious one:

'A field of rye as tall as our Grenadiers'

the French attack on the eastern flank of Wellington's position had been substantially reinforced, seemed to have succeeded in penetrating past Piraumont and was in danger of severing the road to Namur. Though Wellington had dispatched the 95th Regiment of Foot some forty minutes earlier, further support was needed to shore up the position. The Black Duke directed Major Heinrich von Brandenstein to move the leading troops, his 2nd Light Battalion, down the road, to the Bois des Censes, to aid the British in holding their ground there and to occupy it until further notice. The young soldiers, their braided black tunics covered in grey dust, sweat staining their collars a darker shade of yellow, moved off at the 'Geschwind', or quick march, their blue and yellow pom-poms nodding in unison as they proceeded.[10]

As the orders for the deployment of Kempt's brigade filtered through its constituent formations, Major Rogers' artillery was directed to follow the infantry. Given the difficult nature of the ground to the north-east of Les Quatre Bras, in particular the thick hedges, small streams and marshy areas, he had determined to take his five 9-pounder guns and single 5½-inch howitzer down the Namur road instead. As the heavy guns, limbers and ammunition caissons rumbled down the chausseé, the French artillery posted along the crest of the heights of Gemioncourt took every opportunity to pound the slow-moving convoy, though by luck rather than judgement, the bulk of the battery arrived unscathed at Croix-Bati-Saint-Bernard. Here it was directed to halt and unlimber in the open fields to the south of the road, taking up a position between the 95th Regiment of Foot, already skirmishing away to the left, and the 79th Regiment of Foot, drawn up on the Namur road to its right. Immediately it halted, the French guns posted on the lower part of the heights of Gemioncourt, to the south-west of the étang Materne opened up at a range of five hundred metres. Rogers' sweating crews brought their own pieces into action under canister fire, the rough-cast iron balls tearing into men and horses; the gun carriages, limbers and ammunition vehicles were fortunately unscathed by the round shot that came bounding across the fields. Overhead, a canopy of shells exploded in a hail of shattered casing, filling the air with the acrid stench of gunpowder. Down went Second Captain Thomas Scott, though fortunately it was the horse and not the rider that had been killed. Rogers himself could not clearly make out the number of enemy pieces and was convinced that the line of trees he could see were partly concealing some of the enemy battery. A combination of the smoke and the shimmering heat was playing tricks with his eyesight; the trees were the Bois de l'Hutte, some six hundred metres behind the French gun line. A short time after having taken up his position, Rogers was joined by Lieutenant Koopman of Bijleveld's troop and the three six-pounders of his section soon came into action on the right of the British gunners. Not content with counter-battery fire, the French hurried a swarm of tirailleurs into the area between the Namur road and the étang Materne, whilst others peppered the gun crews from the concealment of the tall crops to the west of the pond.[11]

Lieutenant Forbes of the 79th Regiment of Foot was in an altogether more fortunate position; he was stood with Captain William Bruce and the men of No. 1

Company in the relative shelter of an embankment on the north side of the Namur road, close to Croix-Bati-Saint-Bernard. The young officer was grateful for its protection, since French artillery some six hundred metres away had raked the battalion as it had followed the 95th Regiment of Foot into position. To the west, in the more exposed positions occupied by the 28th and 32nd Regiments of Foot, French skirmishers had advanced through the crops until they were a very short distance away and were causing heavy casualties as they methodically targeted the officers. To the east, Forbes could see two of Major Rogers' guns similarly suffering at the hands of French sharpshooters, who being unopposed, were taking every opportunity to snipe at the gunners.[12]

It was a problem of which Wellington himself was keenly aware, having ridden up a short while earlier. Concerned that the French marksmen had seemingly picked off nearly all the artillerymen of one section and conscious of the progress that considerable numbers of French light troops had made in ascending the slopes at the eastern end of the heights of Bati-Saint-Bernard, he ordered Picton to bring up some infantry to arrest their progress and cover the guns. After a brief conference, Sir James Kempt galloped over to Colonel Douglas and informed him that 'The honour of executing His Grace's orders would devolve upon the Cameron Highlanders.'[13]

Word was passed for the Light Company and No. 8 Company, as well as the battalion's marksmen, to form up. Under the command of Captain William Marshall, they were ordered to deploy into the fields to the south of the road and to form a skirmish line. Recognising that two companies in extended order might prove difficult to control, Colonel Douglas detailed Lieutenant William Riach of No. 5 Company and Lieutenant Thompson of No. 6 Company to join the detachment. The men quickly formed up, checked their flints and moved off.[14]

Once the marksmen had advanced into the open, the main body of the regiment was ordered to occupy a field to the north of the étang Materne in support; it was an exposed position, within a short distance of French infantry and artillery. Private Vallence was stood in the centre of the battalion:

> We entered the field, and, under a dreadful and destructive cross-fire of artillery and musketry, took up our station and formed line. A great number of killed and wounded lay scattered around us. An old soldier who stood next to me was struck on the head by a musket ball which knocked off his bonnet. I inquired whether he was hurt; to which he humorously replied, 'I have had many a one of that sort.' While he spoke a cannon ball struck the canteen that hung by my side and smashed it to pieces and killed a man behind me. A soldier lay on his back severely wounded. We burned with impatience to be at the enemy, but a great number of our comrades were killed or wounded before we were ordered to fire.[15]

Having galloped farther along the line, General Kempt came to the 32nd Regiment of Foot, drawn up on the chaussée itself. Tugging at his bridle, he swung his horse off the road and into the fields to the south of the battalion and reined in on a slope, from which he could be seen and heard by the waiting soldiers. On the General calling out for marksmen, Captain John Crowe immediately led his Light Company up the slope to where Kempt was waiting and hurried forward for instructions. Kempt pointed behind him, towards a body of French tirailleurs, and said: 'Here they are, sir. Extend your company as fast as you can and drive them back.' Losing no time, Crowe deployed the men in open order and the line dashed forward through the high crops, flushing out the more adventurous Frenchmen and chasing them back down the slope as far as the thick hedge that separated the boggy and overgrown banks of the Gemioncourt stream from the well-tended fields to the north. Here, Crowe's men encountered a solid line of French infantry, firmly established behind the hedge and were brought up short by a heavy fire of musketry. Pausing to regroup, the intrepid officer and his men again dashed forward and drove the remaining French through the gaps in the hedge; but on pressing forward themselves, they were unable to make any impression on the swarms of French light infantry. With several columns drawn up a short distance away on the northern slope of the heights of Gemioncourt, Captain Crowe judged that it was too risky to continue the unequal contest and withdrew his men and rallied them in a field halfway up the slope, all the time being peppered with musketry from the numerous enemy marksmen. As he effected his withdrawal, Crowe noticed that his parent battalion had advanced in column of quarter distance, as far as the chemin Bati-Saint-Bernard, as had other battalions of the brigade to the east and west. He was joined soon afterwards by a number of sections that had been ordered out by Lieutenant-Colonel John Hicks to reinforce him and to hold the numerous French skirmishers in check. Just as he was deploying these men to shore up his precarious position, Crowe himself fell victim to a French sharpshooter and was obliged to leave the field.[16]

The main body of his battalion was in a similarly exposed position, posted as it was on the very crest of the ridge. It was consequently suffering severely from a combination of close-range artillery fire and musketry, particularly from the same French skirmishers who had driven the Light Company up the lower slopes of the heights of Bati-Saint-Bernard. Lieutenant Stephens did not believe he had ever witnessed so galling a fire, except perhaps the carnage at Salamanca, when the regiment had attacked the ridge held by Bonnet's and Ferey's divisions. With officers and men falling at an alarming rate, Colonel Hicks ordered the battalion to deploy into a less dense line formation and immediately after this was complete, had the battalion lie down just in the lee of the ridge, where it suffered less severely from the shower of projectiles scything through the fields.[17]

Despite this intense fire, Major Felix Calvert had somehow remained unharmed, in spite of being mounted. Benefiting from his elevated position, he shortly afterwards observed the advance of a powerful French column down the northern slope of the heights of Gemioncourt. Slowly but surely, the infantry passed through the hedges that separated the fields on either side of the Gemioncourt stream from the tangled ground about its banks and began to ascend the slope towards his position. Through the intervening smoke caused by the musketry of the opposing skirmishers, Major

Ross-Lewin, standing on the right of No. 6 Company, could distinctly make out the enemy officers, marching at the head of the column and encouraging their men by flourishing their swords. The enemy drums pounded out 'Old Trousers', the rhythmic beat familiar to those who had campaigned in the Peninsula, but with the rye almost up to the tops of their shakos, the dismounted officers and men of the battalion could see little and waited nervously for the order to come.[18]

As the French exerted pressure to the east, its infantry in the centre were held in check by the fragile presence of the first battalion of the Regiment Oranien-Nassau and the 7th National Militia Battalion. Concerned that one more French cavalry charge might suffice to bring them victory, the Prince van Oranje-Nassau decided to commit his only remaining cavalry, the 5th Regiment of Light Dragoons. Its commander, Colonel de Mercx de Corbais had arrived at the crossroads at Les Quatre Bras in the immediate aftermath of the French cavalry charge. Bringing his regiment forward, he watched as the remnants of the 6th Regiment of Hussars streamed past along the Brussels road and into the fields to the north and west of the crossroads. The encounter had emphasised their inexperience and though the French cavalry had pursued them vigorously, the near proximity of fresh Allied cavalry and infantry had discouraged any pursuit beyond the crossroads. Despite the temptation to engage, de Mercx de Corbais was not about to commit his three squadrons without express instructions.[19]

He was not to wait long. Shortly afterwards, General van Merlen rode up to him and ordered him to move his regiment down the Charleroi road and to effect a charge on the French cavalry that had caused so much destruction and was now in some degree of disorder itself. Time must be bought; the enemy must be somehow delayed. A supreme effort was necessary, one which would embroil the French sufficiently to allow the defences to be shored up by the arriving British, Brunswickers and Hanoverians. Conscious as he was of the importance of his next move, de Mercx de Corbais was highly experienced and too old a soldier to rashly charge forward. He therefore sent out a patrol to assess the situation, which galloped to within sight of the Ferme de Gemioncourt, before returning and briefing him on the terrain and the positions of enemy and friendly troops. Turning to his senior officers, he gave them their instructions in his usual resounding voice.[20]

With his front largely clear of retiring infantry and cavalry, de Mercx de Corbais ordered the trumpeter to sound 'fours right' and the 400 men of the regiment clattered onto the chaussée and its verges. Progressing down the road in an orderly fashion, the light dragoons passed the Ferme de la Bergerie and wheeled off the highway, the head of the column crossing the fields in the direction of the Bois de Bossu.[21]

As they passed the last position of Stevenaar's brigade, they could see a number of energetic officers working hard to make good the damage. By cutting free the dead horses from the teams and replacing them with those of the gunners, Major de La Sarraz, Captain van Osten and the acting battery commander, Lieutenant van de Wall managed to assemble sufficient horses to remove some of his remaining pieces.

Realising that additional help was required, de La Sarraz sent van Osten to Captain Geij van Pittius, commanding General van Merlen's horse artillery nearby. Co-opting Lieutenant Clements and Sergeant Wanders of the Artillery Train, Geij van Pittius assembled a team of gunners and drivers from Lieutenant Wassenaar van Sint Pancras' section. Leading these men forward in person, he was escorted by Lieutenant van Bronkhorst's recently-returned troop of the 6th Regiment of Hussars and managed to bring off Stevenaar's stranded guns. Advancing in the wake of the Belgian light dragoons, another team of artillery drivers, escorted by men from van Bronkhorst's troop, braved the fire of the French skirmishers and ventured to recover the howitzer of the wounded Lieutenant Dibbetz, which had been abandoned close to the chemin Bati-Saint-Bernard. Despite the attentions of the French infantry, the team managed to get the piece on the move and to convey it in safety back to the crossroads. Here, it rejoined the three guns and caissons of Lieutenant Wasseroth de Vincij, the second of Lieutenant Dibbetz's howitzers and both his caissons.[22]

Negotiating his way around isolated parties of infantry and approaching the woods, de Mercx de Corbais judged that he had gained sufficient frontage and halted the regiment, deploying it into line by facing left. Satisfied that the dressing and intervals were correct, the call was made for the regiment to march and the dragoons slowly advanced. Major Count Jean-Joseph-Benjamin de Looz-Corswarem was instructed to form the vanguard with his squadron, the two other squadrons forming the reserve. There was a rasping sound as almost 400 steel sabres were drawn. No doubt Dragoon Augustini grasped his weapon firmly; surely Staff-Sergeant Brandt was keeping a professional eye on the dressing of his men; Lieutenant Louis de Brunfaut was perhaps reminded of the six years he had served in the French 8th Regiment of Dragoons in Spain, Russia and Germany; he was one of twelve chevaliers of the legion d'honneur in the regiment's ranks.[23]

The thrill of the advance trembled through the lines of horsemen. To the east, French skirmishers peppered the cavalry with musketry but as the regiment rounded the shoulder of ground to the south-west of the Ferme de la Bergerie, they caught sight of a swarm of French cavalry sheltering in the slight dip beyond. Distinctive in their green coats and yellow collars, a uniform almost identical to that of the Belgians, the French were immediately identified as the 6th Regiment of *Chasseurs à Cheval*, many of de Mercx de Corbais' men having served in the ranks of the French regiment until the peace had been signed the previous year. Regardless of their mixed emotions, they advanced without hesitation and closed with their former comrades. There was no charge; no tremendous clash of horseflesh. The two bodies of horsemen simply rode up to each other at a canter and as the ranks opened and horsemen passed through each other's lines, the combat degenerated into a mêlée of individual duels. Sergeant Beauce wounded, captured and disarmed a sergeant-major from his former squadron in the French regiment, but was then wounded himself as he attempted to disengage with his prisoner. Captain Delenne struggled with Captain Devielle, his erstwhile French brother-in-arms.

Somewhere in the press was Lieutenant de Bourgoing, fighting in the ranks of the *chasseurs à cheval*. Amongst the carbine and pistol fire, he affably called out to his former Belgian comrades, some of whom he had last seen eighteen months beforehand at the Hôtel of the Imperial Pages. Other Frenchmen called the Belgians by name, shouting that they were fighting under the wrong colours and should rejoin the tricolour; the *chasseurs* themselves counted eleven Belgians in their ranks. Elsewhere, there was less bonhomie. Captain van Remoortere was accidentally stabbed in the stomach by his sergeant, who had formerly served with him in the 19th Regiment of *Chasseurs à Cheval* and had his horse shot from beneath him for good measure. Lieutenant Henckens, a Belgian fighting in the French ranks inflicted a deep sabre wound across the face of an enemy officer. Here was no place for sentiment. Sergeant-Major Courtin, who had served in the *Chasseurs à Cheval* of Napoleon's Garde Imperiale could not recollect a single melée in which he had fought for so long; his tired sabre-arm was swinging rhythmically; Dragoon Gerate was trying to remember all his training and experience; Trumpeter Jansen's mouth was almost devoid of saliva. Amongst the grunting, the sweat and the ringing of steel, minds were focused on the work of death.[24]

With the French regiment enjoying a considerable advantage in men, the experience and courage of de Looz-Corswarem's troopers was insufficient to maintain the combat. Successive charges were made in support by the remaining two squadrons under Colonel de Mercx de Corbais in person, but the French had also been reinforced by a body of lancers and quickly gained the upper hand. Major de Looz-Corswarem was captured by the French, only to be liberated by Dragoon Rassonet. In the crush, Colonel de Mercx de Corbais was shot through the arm in two places by pistol bullets and wounded in the kidneys by a canister ball. Grievously injured, he was knocked to the ground unconscious by a sabre blow and his horse being killed, he lay trapped beneath it, surrounded by stamping hooves. Seemingly alone in the press, his misfortune had thankfully been witnessed by Trumpeter Jansen and Second Lieutenant Pierre Henkart, who later recalled the circumstances:

> I met my colonel in the melée, wounded and covered in blood and spread out beneath his horse, from which he could not extricate himself. Pulling up, I gave him my horse in order that he could go and have his wounds dressed at the ambulance.

On hearing that his commanding officer was wounded and aware of the presence of further French cavalry nearby, Major Baron du Val de Beaulieu ordered the recall to be sounded. The shrill notes were blasted out and the regiment conducted a fighting withdrawal, during which they were rejoined by a couple of troops that had outflanked the French cavalry and charged other enemy units. Some boastfully but untruthfully claiming to have gone as far as Frasnes. The main body of the regiment then commenced a long and dangerous fighting withdrawal across the fields towards Les Quatre Bras, whilst other troopers were detached to escort some twenty prisoners into captivity behind the crossroads. It became apparent as the regiment withdrew, that Captain Mertens had failed to obey the order to charge, citing the death of one of his sergeants by round shot as his excuse; the inquest would have to come later.[25]

'A field of rye as tall as our Grenadiers'

Even as the Belgian cavalry were engaged with the enemy, Wellington sent word to the Duke von Braunschweig-Lüneburg, requesting that he move his troops to the south of the Nivelles and Namur roads. The threat of cavalry, the firepower of the French artillery and the persistent attentions of hundreds of skirmishers had forced the first battalion of the Regiment Oranien-Nassau and the 7th National Militia to once again withdraw inside the Bois de Bossu. The open ground in the centre of Wellington's position was therefore completely bereft of organised troops. Eager to oblige and have his chance with the hated French, the Black Duke needed no second invitation and immediately set about deploying his five available infantry battalions.[26]

Major Adolf von Rauschenplatt was ordered to detach the two companies of Gelernte Jager of the Avantgarde-Battalion to the assistance of the Allied troops engaged in the wood itself. As the gamekeepers approached the tree line, they were halted by the sudden exit of a body of Netherlands and Nassau troops, being closely pursued by the French. The grey-coated riflemen deployed in skirmish order to the north of the wood and engaged the leading French companies, enabling the retiring Allied soldiers to fall back towards the second battalion of the 2nd Nassau-Usingen Regiment, which was drawn up behind the Nivelles road, immediately in their rear.

The Prince van Oranje-Nassau ordered Major von Normann to counter-attack, but his men were unable to make any headway and were rapidly driven back, the second battalion of the Regiment Oranien-Nassau also pulling back a short distance on the opposite side of the east of the chaussée de Bruxelles. The progress of the French was checked by the arrival of the Light Infantry companies of the Brunswick Avantgarde-Battalion, together with the Leib-Battalion and Lieutenant-Colonel Friedrich von Specht's three Line battalions, which moved forward onto the high ground just north of the Nivelles road. Intimidated by these new arrivals, a rapid advance by von Rauschenplatt's two Gelernte-Jager companies, accompanied by some Nassau volunteers was sufficient to push the French back some distance into the wood. The Leib-Battalion and 1st Line Battalion were now formed up in close column and moved forward a short distance to the south of the Ferme de la Bergerie, the Leib-Battalion taking up its position closest to the chaussée. Having witnessed the hurried withdrawal of the Netherlands hussars, the Duke felt it prudent to hold his troops in a formation that would facilitate deployment into defensive squares, should the French threaten further cavalry attacks.

From the moment they entered the field of battle, the densely-packed black columns became the target of a vicious cannonade. Round shot and canister tearing through their ranks and bowling the men over like skittles, the infantry no doubt cursed the absence of their own artillery, which was only now passing Maison du Roi, an unimpressive building that was destined to host Bonaparte himself the following evening.[27]

Suddenly, in a manner almost fulfilling the prophecy, a body of cavalry swept up the Charleroi road and across the fields to the west. Were they French? Allied? Not having the luxury of time to make enquiries and establish their identity, the cry went up to form square and within minutes, the two battalions were in formation, ready to receive the horsemen. Fortunately, however, the cavalry was recognised as Colonel de Mercx de Corbais' 5th Regiment of Light Dragoons, who made their way through the intervals between the squares into the fields to the north-west of the crossroads, where they re-grouped. As they withdrew, the Brunswick Hussar Regiment clattered up the Brussels road to Les Quatre Bras. The Duke immediately ordered Major Friedrich von Cramm to press on ahead and throw back the pursuing enemy cavalry, but the French, seeing Les Quatre Bras occupied by infantry in good order, had already commenced their withdrawal. As the danger receded, the squares were disbanded. Several parties of Hussars were sent off to the south-west, in rear of the Bois de Bossu, to patrol the western flank of the position and to bolster von Sachsen-Weimar's brigade.[28]

Between the 1st Line Battalion and the Bois de Bossu, Major von Rauschenplatt extended the two Light Infantry companies of his Avantgarde-Bataillon, linking up with his two Gelernte-Jäger companies, which had pressed forward through the wood itself. Under the command of Captain Berner, they deployed into groups of four at six-pace intervals, lining a ditch along one of the field boundaries. Major von Cramm posted three squadrons of the Hussar Regiment in rear of the two infantry battalions, with Colonel Pott's squadron of Uhlans drawn up behind the skirmish line. Major von Strombeck was ordered to remain in reserve at Les Quatre Bras with the 2nd Line Battalion, as was Major Gustav von Normann with the 3rd Line Battalion, from where they were both to support the advanced troops and keep watch for any French attacks through the Bois de Bossu. As their soldiers took up positions in the houses, barns, sheds and gardens, it was emphasised to the two officers that this important post was to be held with the utmost determination; they were now the final line of defence between the French and Brussels. Conscious that he still had no artillery support, the Duke hurriedly detached Captain Lübeck, his aide-de-camp, in search of the two missing batteries.[29]

The arrival of these reinforcements had an immediate impact on the young men of the 7th National Militia Battalion. Militiaman Jan Rem was particularly relieved:

> We received reinforcements of English, Hanoverian, Bergschots [Highlanders], Brunswickers, some squadrons of Hussars and a battalion of Belgian troops. When we saw them arrive on the battlefield, we were once again encouraged, because the battle had been very heavy.[30]

As soon as the Brunswick troops deployed in the Bois de Bossu, they came in to contact with the first battalion of the Regiment Oranien-Nassau, which had charged the flank of the French infantry as it was driven back through the wood by the advancing Brunswickers. Sergeant Döring came across an unfortunate man of von Rauschenplatt's command:

> When I was advancing through the wood, which the enemy had vacated again, I noticed a Brunswick Jäger leaning against a fir tree. A musket ball had lodged in his

'A field of rye as tall as our Grenadiers'

stomach. He looked as pale as death and complained of terrible pain and asked for a surgeon. Our battalion surgeon . . . Neuendorf . . . who was walking beside, removed the ball and probably saved his life.[31]

With the gap in the centre temporarily plugged, the final battalion of Pack's brigade, the 92nd Regiment, at last arrived at the crossroads at Les Quatre Bras, after what had seemed to some, a route march of almost fifty kilometres. Covering the final few hundred metres towards the road junction, they passed through the rear areas of de Perponcher-Sedlnitzky's division, choked with vehicles, casualties, fugitives and shocked groups of men in the process of being organised once more into a semblance of a fighting formation. To the right of the road, they noticed some Brunswick infantry, whilst to the left was the remnant of van Opstall's artillery, now effectively hors de combat for want of horses and ammunition. Immediately Colonel Cameron arrived behind the Ferme des Quatre Bras, he was met by a staff officer and directed to move his battalion off the road, to the left of the houses. The column mounted the slight incline to the north-east of the buildings, from where they could see other British battalions to the east; the officers found it mildly curious that, being the junior regiment, it should be holding the right of the line. The column passed the second battalion of the Regiment Oranien-Nassau, skirted the vehicles of the Netherlands artillery park, and moved through the orchard and gardens that had been the bivouac of the Nassau troops the previous evening. Upon reaching their intended position, the column halted and closed up on the leading division. From this vantage point, they could distinctly make out French skirmishers and formed battalions advancing in column a short distance away. Indeed, the plain that stretched away before them was littered with troops; some in groups, some in formation, individual horsemen galloping here and there, and troops advancing, retiring or standing motionless in the tall crops. Lieutenant Hope had heard that the French were attacking the army's wing; that the Duke of Wellington's orders to Picton were for him to hold the French to the east of the Charleroi road, with the Prince van Oranje-Nassau and Duke von Braunschweig-Lüneburg endeavouring to do likewise to the west of the chaussée, until further reinforcements arrived from Nivelles and beyond. Almost as soon as the Highlanders had reached their position, the French artillery opened up a galling fire from the heights of Gemioncourt, which annoyed Sergeant Robertson, since there appeared to be no Allied artillery on the field with which this fire could be opposed. Others perhaps wondered whether it was the presence nearby of the Duke of Wellington and his conspicuous entourage that was attracting the attention of 'Johnny'.[32]

Lieutenant Winchester took a moment to glance about him. To the left of the regiment and a short distance to its rear, several battalions of Hanoverians had been posted in a field intersected by hedges. Though he did not know it, this was Colonel Best's 4th (Hanoverian) Infantry Brigade, comprising four Landwehr battalions, drawn up in line. On the right was the Lüneburg Battalion, followed by the Verden and Osterode Battalions, with the Münden Battalion taking up position on the

The Battle of Quatre Bras

extreme left, in the direction of the Bois des Censes. Though nominally a part of the 6th (British) Infantry Division, its parent formation was not yet complete and being cantoned in the vicinity of Brussels, they had been brigaded in Picton's 5th (British) Infantry Division instead. Also to Winchester's left were some of the Brunswick infantry, but they were too distant for him to determine which battalions.[33]

Shortly after the Gordon Highlanders arrived in this position, the Duke of Wellington sent Colonel Sir John Elley, the Deputy Adjutant-General, across to Cameron and ordered him to move his battalion to the front of the Ferme des Quatre Bras. There, he was to deploy into line and shelter the men in the ditch and behind the bank that lined the southern side of the chaussée, with the right flank of his right-hand company, Captain Dugald Campbell's grenadiers, in front of the buildings at the crossroads. Despite the cover of the bank and ditch, the projectiles flew thick and fast across the highway, in some cases bouncing back off the walls of the farm in the rear of the battalion, such that Cameron passed the word that the men were to prime, load and then lie down. Sergeant Robertson sat down, grasping his firelock in both hands, noticing that Wellington had followed his own advice, dismounted and now occupied the ditch along with his staff. Whether they were in the centre of the line, the most important position on the battlefield or the place with the best view, it seemed to Robertson as though the Duke had chosen to station himself in person with the regiment. Even as his men were trying to keep their heads down, Lieutenant Hope was attempting to get his bearings. The position he occupied, it seemed, was slightly elevated from the ground around it. Having marched down the road from Brussels to Charleroi, he surmised that the road they were now lining must be that from Nivelles to Namur. To the right of the Charleroi road, he could see a thick wood, extending a considerable way towards the smoke in the distance. Some Brunswick troops could be made out on the edge of the wood; perhaps inside it as well. Everywhere else, the fields contained a lush expanse of wheat and rye, through which it was difficult to follow the movements of enemy and allied forces. Either the musketry and artillery fire must be at very short range, he thought, or both sides were firing blindly into the crops. Very shortly afterwards, he was distracted by a predicament much closer to hand:[34]

> On the left side of the road leading from Quatre Bras to Ligny a bank rose eight or ten feet above the crown of the highway, which trifling circumstance was occasionally the means of placing a few of our men in jeopardy. For on hitting the bank, the shells frequently came dancing across the road to their own music, till they arrived in the ditch among the Highlanders.[35]

The shells were courtesy of French 5½-inch howitzers, the crews of which were trying to plot the trajectory and fuse length that would enable them to lob the powder-filled iron balls across the valley, arriving directly overhead the chaussée, before exploding into dozens of razor-sharp iron fragments. It seemed that the trajectory had been judged perfectly and as the fizzing shells bounced off the bank and skidded into the ditch, the alert Highlanders were obliged to hurriedly pick them up and attempt to throw them over the opposite bank, where their blast would be absorbed by the earth. Whenever the French got it right and the Scots got it wrong, carnage ensued.

Although the Highlanders had some chance against the shells – as long as they were alert – the round shot that came bounding across the bank did not announce themselves until the whooshing noise had come and gone. In the expert hands of the French gunners, the pieces were trained and elevated such that the fall of shot hit precisely on the parapet of the ditch. Private Milne was sat on the right of Lieutenant Hope, when a French round shot tore off his bonnet. Though it caused him no apparent injury, it threw him into a state of shock, leading to a deep depression that would remain with him for some days; at least he was alive.[36]

At the same time that the 92nd Regiment of Foot was moving onto the Namur road in front of the Ferme des Quatre Bras, the five 9-pounder guns and single 5½-inch howitzer of Captain von Rettberg's 2nd (Hanoverian) Brigade of Foot Artillery creaked as they trundled up the chaussée towards the crossroads. The tired gunners marching alongside each piece could see the wreckage of the Netherlands artillery and the jam of waggons, ammunition caissons, forges and spare limbers in the fields to their left; clearly the Dutch artillery had suffered severely at the hands of the French. The young gunners felt their throats tighten and their bodies course with adrenalin as they prepared to endure their own baptism of fire. A staff officer rode up to Captain von Rettberg and ordered him to drive his guns and vehicles through the orchard and to take up a position overlooking the Namur road, several hundred metres from the crossroads. At this point, the ground to the north of the road rose more steeply than to the south, creating a natural firing platform, onto which he ordered the drivers and teams to haul the guns and form up in battery. To the rear of the position, the ground sloped gently away towards the Vallée des Vaches, affording slight cover for the limbers and ammunition wagons, which were drawn off a short distance to the north. Within minutes, von Rettberg's gunners were achieving an impressive rate of fire in support of Pack's brigade, the Brunswick division and the remnants of van Bijlandt's brigade. Reassuring as this was to the new drafts, the old sweats in the ranks of the battalions closest to them could not help but think it would result in the Germans being cannonaded in return.[37]

Endnotes

1. Anonymous (Near Observer), pp. 67–8. Arthur, p. 596. de Bas &c., pp. 498–9, 513. Batty, p. 48. Brett-James, pp. 54–5. Cathcart. Gomm (III). Gomm (IV). Houssaye, p. 114. Leask and McCance, p. 334. von Müffling (I). von Pflugk-Harttung (II), p. 20. van Zuylen van Nyeveld (I), p. 56.
2. Anonymous (Cameron), p. 89. Alexander Forbes (II). Mackenzie &c., p. 55.
3. Calvert (III). Crowe. Ross-Lewin, pp. 254–6. Stephens. Swiney, pp. 115–6.

4. Dallas.
5. J. Douglas, p. 96.
6. Cathcart. Dewar. Alexander Forbes (II). Gomm (I), p. 6. Gomm (IV), Gomm (V). Leask and McCance, pp. 332–3. Macdonald.
7. Anonymous (Near Observer), pp. 61–2. Anton, pp. 189–90. Brett-James, p. 58. Campbell. P. Fitchett, pp. 290–1. Howard, p. 52. Malcolm.
8. Carter, pp. 93, 99. Riddock.
9. Calvert (I). de Constant-Rebecque (I). Gomm (I), pp. 6–7. Gurwood, p. 479. Heise (I). Heise (II). Hope (III), p. 225. Leach, p. 375. Macdonald (I). D. Mackenzie. Mudie (II). Robertson, p. 145. J. Ross (II). Ross-Lewin, pp. 255–6. Vallence. Winchester (II). van Zuylen van Nyeveld (I), p. 57.
10. Anonymous (Das braunschweigische Korps). Anonymous (Journal), pp. 380–1. Anonymous (Near Observer), pp. 72, 76–7. Brett-James, p. 55. Gairdner. von Herzberg. Hofschröer (I), p. 294. Kincaid (I), pp. 316–7. Simmons (I). von Wachholtz, pp. 24–5.
11. de Bas &c., pp. 499, 513. Dalton, p. 226. Koopman. Rogers (I). Rudyerd.
12. Allan. Anonymous (Cameron), p. 89. Arthur, p. 596. Alexander Forbes (II). Mackenzie &c., p. 55. Vallence.
13. Anonymous (Cameron), p. 89. Mackenzie &c., p. 55.
14. Allan. Anonymous (Cameron), p. 89. Dewar. Alexander Forbes (II). Mackenzie &c., p. 55. Riach (I). Vallence.
15. Allan. Anonymous (Cameron), p. 89. Riach (I). Vallence.
16. de Bas &c., p. 514. Crowe. Stephens. Swiney, p. 116.
17. Calvert (III). Ross-Lewin, p. 184. Stephens. Swiney, p. 116.
18. de Bas &c., p. 514. Calvert (III). Ross-Lewin, pp. 256–7.
19. de Bas &c., p. 508. van Balveren. Dellevoet, pp. 26–7. de Mercx de Corbais. Pawly (II), pp. 34–6. Renard, p. 58. Roijen.
20. de Bas &c., p. 508. Delhaize and Aerts, p. 434. van Doren, p. 49–50. Manchot, pp. 74, 78. de Mercx de Corbais. Pawly (II), pp. 34–6. Renard, p. 58. Rens, pp. 110, 114. Roijen.
21. Bowden, p. 268. van Doren, pp. 49–50. de Mercx de Corbais. Pawly (II), pp. 34–6. Rens, p. 110. Roijen.
22. de Bas, pp. 507–8. Henckens, pp. 228–9. Koopman. von Müffling (I), p. 6. van Osten. Pawly (II), pp. 34–6. Rens, pp. 108–9. Roijen. W. Siborne (V), p. 71. Wassenaar van Sint-Pancras. van Zuylen van Nyeveld (I), p. 58.
23. de Bas &c., pp. 508–9. Bikar. van Doren, pp. 49–50. de Mercx de Corbais. Pattyn, p. 20. Pawly (II), pp. 34–6. Renard, p. 58. Rens, pp. 93, 111–4. Roijen.
24. de Bas &c., pp. 508–9. Bikar. van Doren, pp. 49–50. de Mercx de Corbais. Pattyn, p. 20. Pawly (II), pp. 34–6. Renard, pp. 58–9. Rens, pp. 111–4. Roijen.
25. de Bas &c., p. 509. van Doren, pp. 49–50. Eenens, pp. 74–5. de Mercx de Corbais. Manchot, p. 81. Pawly (II), pp. 34–6. Renard, pp. 58–9 Rens, p. 114. W. Siborne (V), p. 71.
26. Anonymous (Near Observer), p. 77. Dellevoet, p. 27. von Herzberg. Langenstrasse. von Wachholtz, p. 24.
27. de Bas &c., p. 511. Cathcart. Gomm. Hellemann. von Herzberg. Hope (III), p. 225. von Wachholtz, p. 25. van Zuylen van Nyeveld (I), p. 56.

28. Anonymous (Das braunschweigische Korps). van Balveren. Best (I). Best (II). Brett-James, p. 55. Deebetz. Delhaize and Aerts, pp. 446–7. von Herzberg. von Müffing (I), p. 5. de Mercx de Corbais. Oppermann. Rens, p. 114. Roijen. von Wachholtz, pp. 25–7. Wassenaar van Sint-Pancras.
29. Anonymous (Das braunschweigische Korps). de Bas &c., pp. 511–3. Bowden, p. 257. Delhaize and Aerts, pp. 446–7. Gomm (IV). von Herzberg. Hofschröer (I), p. 284. von Kortzfleisch, pp. 63–5. Kubel. von Müffling (I), p. 5. Rem. von Wachholtz, pp. 26–7. C. Wood, p. 78.
30. Rem.
31. Döring.
32. Anonymous (Letters). Anonymous (Near Explorer), pp. 62–3. Hope (III), pp. 224–5. Robertson, pp. 145–6. Winchester (II). Winchester (III).
33. Anonymous (Letters), p. 225. Best (I). Best (II). Archibald Forbes, p. 266, Gomm (III). Hope (III), pp. 224–5. Houssaye, p. 114. Kannicht, p. 203. Robertson. Winchester (III). Winchester (IV).
34. Anonymous (Letters), pp. 224–5. Anonymous (Near Explorer), pp. 62–3, 68. Batty. Campbell. Gomm (V). Hope (I). Hope (III), pp. 224–5. Robertson. J. Ross (II). Winchester (I). Winchester (II).
35. Hope (I).
36. Anonymous (Letters), pp. 274–5.
37. Braun. Campbell. Heise (I). Heise (II). May. von Pflugk-Harttung (II), pp. 11–12. von Rettberg (I). von Rettberg (III). Rogers (II). Winchester (III). Winchester (IV).

CHAPTER 12

It was approaching 3.15 p.m. when General Cooke and his footsore division pulled off the road, turned into a field and halted. Their rest area bordered an elevated and wooded area, just to the west of the town of Nivelles. The men had suffered excessively from the heat, the flies and the weight of their packs and were grateful for the respite. Few knew where they were, or for that matter, cared. The optimists cherished the hope that the day's work was done. Had not Nivelles been the place to which the General had ordered them? Private Matthew Clay of the Light Company of the 3rd Regiment of Foot Guards was certainly of this opinion and his comrades wasted no time in throwing off their knapsacks and sending out watering parties, in the full expectation of remaining there for the night. Others in the regiment were of the same opinion and Ensign Lake's men also started to prepare a meal. The second battalion of the 1st Regiment of Foot Guards busied itself in a similar fashion, dressing the rations they had been issued at Enghien, trimming off the rotten portions, picking out the weevils and washing the meat to get rid of the worst of the salt. Ensign Master was in charge of a party detailed to collect and bring in wood and although he heard the noise, he did not stop to consider the significance of the distinct and constant roar of cannon-fire in the distance.[1]

Shortly afterwards, a horseman rode up. The men of the second battalion of the 1st Regiment of Foot Guards resting nearby, wondered if he was a messenger from Wellington. Others felt he was too 'Foreign-looking'. It was Major van Gorkum of the Prince van Oranje-Nassau's General Staff, looking for General Cooke. Having handed over his packet, the major waited whilst the General read the dispatch from his chief. If Cooke felt any relief, it remained invisible to his staff officers. His instructions were to continue his march from Nivelles upon Les Quatre Bras. They implied he was in the right place by being at Nivelles, but not having received any orders to advance beyond Braine-le-Comte, the General could only surmise that another dispatch had somehow gone astray. But how could a messenger have failed to locate the 4,000 marching soldiers? Perhaps for some reason he had not gone by way of Petit Roeulx and Steenkerque and had instead taken one of the many roads that traversed the valleys of the Rivers Senne and Sennette. Nevertheless, the receipt of the Prince van Oranje-Nassau's latest order confirmed the correctness of his decision to take the initiative.[2]

The urgent tone of the message galvanised Cooke into action. Relieved and reinvigorated, he was eager to come to blows with the enemy. Shoulders slumped as once more the drums beat, the bugles called and word was passed to fall in. 'No dinner today!' thought Ensign Master, calling on his men to rejoin the battalion at the double. Word circulated the short-lived bivouac that the order was to move immediately to the left, to a place called Nivelles, though others heard mention of a different place; Les Quatre Bras. Fires were doused, tepid water poured over sweat-caked faces and kettles stowed away on aching backs.[3]

Private Clay witnessed the touching scenes of separation between the married men of the Light Company of the 3rd Regiment of Foot Guards and the few wives that had accompanied them thus far:

> They were ordered to the rear and, going a short distance from the throng in the open field, were joined by others who delivered to them for security their watches and various other small articles which they held in esteem. Others, whose families were absent, desired that their expressions of affection might be communicated to their absent wives and families. The parting embrace, although short, was sincere, affectionate and expressed with deep emotions of grief as though the state of widowhood had suddenly come upon them, while the loud thunder of the destructive cannon was sounding in their ears.[4]

As this painful separation was taking place, most of the foraging parties returned, with the exception of those that had been sent off by Lieutenant-Colonel Charles Dashwood, to whom messages were sent instructing them to rejoin on the march. In the interim, the men of all four battalions had packed everything away and the column was soon re-assembled and ready to march off. At the rear of the column, Colonel Adye ensured that his two batteries of artillery were equally ready to march. Supervising his sweating gunners as they once more brought the teams into position on the road was Major Kuhlmann. Exactly fourteen years ago to the day, he had first been commissioned into the King's German Legion, but the celebrations would have to be postponed until another time. When the word of command was given, the battalions marched off at the double-quick down the hill, the urgency of the march leading Captain Henry Powell to believe that the French must be entering the town at the other side.[5]

As the four battalions passed through the streets of Nivelles, the soldiers looked about with amazement. The town was teeming with people, as Braine-le-Comte had been earlier; though General Chassé's 3rd (Netherlands) Infantry Division had by now largely taken up defensive positions outside the walls. The débris left in its wake, as well as the congestion caused by the numerous vehicles of the 2nd (Netherlands) Infantry Division and von Alten's 3rd (British) Infantry Division, slowed progress and frustrated the officers. Once free of the crowds of stragglers, civilians and reserve troops, Cooke's column emerged from the Porte de Namur and with the noise of the battle sounding so close, the officers were ordered to double the men forward. A short distance beyond the town, the Light Company of the 3rd Regiment of Foot Guards was rejoined by its watering parties. Whilst many canteens of water were handed back to the parched 'Light Bobs', Private Clay noticed that his contained table beer which his enterprising messmate had somehow contrived to procure, much to the delight of his comrades. Exhausted, sweating and covered in dust, a few mouthfuls of the brew somehow made his condition and immediate prospects a touch more bearable.[6]

Despite the dryness of their throats and the punishing pace of the march, the men were encouraged to sing, with the most enthusiastic singing the verses, whilst the remainder belted out the chorus. Riding alongside the men of Lieutenant-Colonel George Fead's company of the third battalion of the 1st Regiment of Foot Guards, Ensign Master joined in as the men roared out the refrain: 'London is out of town; all the world's in Paris', the pronunciation of which, to Master's ear, sounded like the men were singing 'Pairess'.[7]

Despite the forced gaiety, the baking heat was starting to take its toll. Except where the trees that lined the chaussée cast their lengthening shadows across the cobbles, the men were constantly subjected to the powerful sun. Coats were saturated in sweat, but woe betide the man who to unbuttoned or removed them. The endless exercises in the preceding months had done much to build up the stamina of the men and even though the more physically fit probably pitied their weaker comrades, such pity did not translate into carrying their pack, cartridge box or musket. Some encouraged their comrades with words and water. Others numbed the pain of blistered feet with generous swigs of gin. Boots were torn to tatters by the unforgiving surface. Ahead, the road shimmered in the distance, the glare of the sun causing black spots to dance before eyes. The air was thick with dust.[8]

The seemingly endless torment continued and the booming of the cannon increased. There was a faint tang of burnt powder in the still air. Scattered on the side of the road were the wounded; mute Belgians, Germans and Netherlanders. Some had crawled into the ditches in search of stagnant water, others had finally slumped down on the verge and waited for death. Clouds of flies plagued the congealing scabs of those with sabre or bullet wounds, many now too weak to brush them away. Now and then, the battalions made way for the slow, rumbling farm carts, laden with human wreckage on their way to the hospitals or the burial pits. From time to time, other foreign soldiers, some with no discernible injuries passed on prophecies of doom in broken English or accented French. Bonaparte's advance, it seemed, had been far more rapid than anyone had foreseen and if the rumours were true, the 'Grand Disturber of Europe' himself was waiting for them on the battlefield. The mood became sombre.[9]

A short while after the Guards had passed Nivelles, towards 4.00 p.m., the footsore Light Company of the 30th Regiment of Foot reached the town, having redoubled its efforts. At last, they seemed to be closing on their division. They forced their way through the crowds of baggage animals, commissaries, quartermasters and women, who thronged the streets:

Some of our regimental wives came up, blessed us and kissed their husbands, many for the last time. Such memories agitate the hearts even of soldiers' wives, the most callous and insensitive creatures in existence. They told us the battalion had halted at Nivelles and marched again about an hour before, towards Quatre Bras, where the enemy was said to be. We met our stores and, seizing them, took out an allowance of spirits for every man. The repeated, 'God in Heaven bless you, my dear child,' of a poor woman who was choking in a ditch and who shared my gin, was a better renovator than the spirits. Thus re-inspired, we started double quick, for the firing increased.[10]

For the Guards, however, exhaustion was now exacting its toll. Unable to maintain the pace, some of the men were close to collapse. Despite the sergeants cajoling the men, the columns were opening up as those able to maintain the pace became detached from those whose energy was spent. Stragglers fell away; men fainted in the ranks and were stumbled over by others too tired to notice. Sergeant Charles Wood, in the ranks of Colonel Miller's company of the third battalion of the 1st Regiment of Foot Guards, was drawing deeply on his Methodist faith and was ever after convinced that: 'The Lord gave us strength, both of body and of mind, on that day and through the whole of our labours.' Recognising the need for rest, Generals Maitland and Byng agreed to call a short halt to collect the stragglers and give the men a breather. In unison, the men tore off their accoutrements and collapsed on the verges of the road, their strength utterly spent, whilst Colonel Adye took the opportunity to bring his two batteries and their ammunition wagons to the front of the column.[11]

The Guards were not the only soldiers being pushed to their physical limits. As they lined the road, resting, they were passed by the Light Company of the 30th Regiment of Foot, following in the wake of their brigade. Ensign Macready had never seen 'Such numbers of men knocked-up', in his life. As the wiry, robust light infantrymen passed the tall, muscular men of the King's personal bodyguard, they were subjected to jeers about their hurry. Not about to suffer such taunts without response, the men of the line infantry in their turn began to tease the Guards:

'Shall I carry your honour on my pack?' said one of ours to a Grenadier Guardsman, as he was sitting down. 'Haven't you some gruel for that young gentleman?' shouted another and continued, 'It's a cruel shame to send gentlemen's sons on such business. You see they don't like it. They've had quite enough at Bergy-my-Zoon.' High words arose, but we stopped our men, who, however, took leave of them, saying 'Good-bye to ye, young gentlemen. Pray don't hurry yourselves. We'll do your work, never fear.'[12]

Having enjoyed its repartee with His Majesty's Guards, Macready's company cut across the road through the interval between two of their battalions and provoked the ire of a senior officer for doing so. In truth, his men were in almost as poor a condition as those that they had jeered, though they had marched some five kilometres less. Lieutenant Rumley, deciding that the highway was too congested, left the road and struck off through the fields to its south. As they waded through the clover and rye, many of the men tumbled over, simply too exhausted to retain their footing as the crops tangled in their gaiters or their feet stumbled in the deep furrows. Suddenly, without any word of command being issued, but as if one had, every knapsack was removed, except for those few who still felt strong enough to carry them. In their wake, the officers of the four Guards battalions, stung by the insults, roused the men and resumed the march. The column was once again formed in order of seniority. Maitland's brigade would lead, with the second and third battalions of the 1st Regiment of Foot Guards. Byng would then follow with the Coldstream and the 3rd Regiment of Foot Guards. Before long, the steady tramp of 4,000 infantrymen could be heard once again on the pavé.[13]

Elsewhere, other tired reinforcements were closing on the battlefield. The firing from Les Quatre Bras had reached a crescendo as Captain Heinemann's edgy troop of gunners arrived at Genappe. Baggage wagons moving north had caused some delays and their progress had been impeded by numbers of wounded men from von Sachsen-Weimar's and van Bijlandt's brigades, making their way through the town towards Brussels. Offering water and tobacco, the Brunswickers questioned the blood-stained, blackened, vacant-looking men from Nassau. Those who had been involved in the fighting claimed that the Brunswick Hussars had been in action since 10.00 a.m. Time was playing tricks with them. They also recounted how Major von Pröstler's Leib-Battalion, along with the three line battalions and two of the light battalions had also been under fire and had so far managed to repulse the enemy several times. Just as the column of guns was about to resume its march, Lieutenant Bredenschey received a report that one of the powder wagons had broken down and he and Chief Gunner Hellemann organised a party of men to repair it, following which they were to rejoin the battery as soon as possible. As the men unloaded tools and took the opportunity to water the horses, Major von Lubecq's valuable ordnance continued its journey.[14]

Some 25 kilometres to the north, two staff officers, oblivious to the severity of the fighting to the south, were enjoying a leisurely ride through the Forêt de Soignies. Having left Brussels shortly after 2.15 p.m., Lieutenant Jackson had been riding for some time when he came up with Colonel William Nicolay of the Royal Staff Corps, his titular superior. Perhaps from politeness, perhaps from ambition, Jackson decided to slow down and join him:

> As he did not suggest my pushing on, I felt bound to remain with him, and accommodate myself to his sober pace; so we jogged on together at a far more gentle rate than that at which I had been riding. While traversing the forest of Soignies, the cannonade was so loud as to lead us to believe that the battle was raging within a very few miles of us, probably near Waterloo. On emerging, however, from its glades, the firing seemed to be more distant than we had supposed.[15]

At the same time that General Cooke's division was passing Nivelles, the French received a substantial reinforcement, which observing Allied officers estimated at divisional strength. While the original French forces had drawn up between the Bois de Bossu and Thyle, these new arrivals took up ground between the Ferme du Grand-Pierrepont and the Ferme de Gemioncourt. It rapidly became apparent that they had been given the objective of seizing the Bois de Bossu, perhaps with the aim of cutting Wellington's army off from its line of communication with Nivelles. Fresh artillery opened up at short range from the chemin de Gemioncourt, sending round after round into the trees, where the men of the first and third battalions of the 2nd Nassau-Usingen Regiment nervously awaited them, along with Captain Bergmann's Volunteer Jager Company. Stationed some distance inside the wood, the men could see little of the enemy, but the cheering of the assailants as they climbed the slope towards the wood could be heard distinctly. As the French closed in, Major Hegmann repeatedly urged his men to retain their fire. The noisy shouts of '*Vive l'Empereur*' and the relentless thumping of the *pas de charge* filled the ears of the Nassauers. French musket balls pinged through the air as the enemy skirmishers approached the thickets. Still Hegmann reserved his fire. Finally, when the French were almost upon them, the order was given.

The fusillade tore into the head of the French infantry, smashing into the first wave and bringing down several soldiers. Their view obscured by the acrid smoke from their muskets, the first rank of the Nassau-Usingen battalion stepped back to reload and was replaced by the second rank, which poured another volley into the mass. The French, however, were not to be resisted and continued advancing over the writhing bodies of the wounded, extending their attack to the west, where Captain Büsgen now engaged them with first battalion of the 2nd Nassau-Usingen Regiment. Flanker Johann Pinstock quietly mumbled a prayer to God and to Jesus for his safety and gripped his musket tightly. With a shout, the French rushed through the wood, bayonets levelled, screaming curses and jabbing at the defenders as they fumbled for cartridges and ramrods. Shoulder-to-shoulder, the Nassauers lowered their own bayonets and the fighting degenerated into a mêlée in the thick, tangled undergrowth, with Germans and Frenchmen grappling with each other, bayoneting, shooting and clubbing anyone in an unfamiliar uniform. Though managing to preserve order in their ranks, the two defending battalions were inexorably forced back, as the French secured the edge of the wood, but managed to create and maintain a new line of battle, some two hundred metres into the interior.[16]

Entire French battalions were deployed in skirmish order amongst the trees. The air was thick with smoke from the musket discharges and it soon became difficult to differentiate friend from foe in the acrid fog. Taking position behind trunks and piles of logs, the Nassauers fired on the vague shapes moving about in the undergrowth. Shouts and shrieks in French and German mingled as each side tried to maintain order and momentum. Here and there, men stumbled over the wounded, maimed and disfigured. Countless corpses lay concealed in the bracken, stripped of possessions and dignity; their identities already lost to humanity. Green-coated men fired on both green and blue-coated men as silhouettes, colours and nationalities blurred. Soldiers became disoriented with the direction of advance or retreat. Parties of French infantry outflanked the Nassauers, or were they Nassau troops retiring? Young infantrymen nervously stuck closely to their wiser, more experienced comrades, desperate not to fall into the hands of the enemy. Popping and rattling, the sounds of the firing gradually moved north-west. In the midst of the fray, Colonel von Sachsen-Weimar had come to the end of his tether. French troops poured forward in every direction, almost surrounding the remnants of the two battalions, as they desperately sought to hold their positions. He had sent repeated messengers to General de Perponcher-Sedlnitzky, but had received no word as to how he should act. Finally, he dispatched Major von Ampt in one last attempt to obtain instructions, but this officer did not return. All around, men expended their final rounds of ammunition and having exhausted that of the dead and dying, pulled back towards the western edge of the wood. Unable to maintain a line of resistance any longer and bereft of orders, von Sachsen-Weimar gave the order to fall back on Houtain-le-Val.[17]

As the Nassauers streamed back across the Champ du Sarti, so too did the wounded Colonel de Jongh and four companies of the 8th National Militia Battalion which had advanced in support of the two Nassau-Usingen battalions:

> It was impossible for me to maintain proper order amongst my troops whilst in the wood. The French, protected by a strong artillery fire on both sides of the wood, advanced into it. I retired, whilst fighting, through the wood, up to the chaussée between Houtain-le-Val and Les Quatre Bras, close to Les Quatre Bras and there formed four companies and let myself be dressed. My Adjutant-Major took a cavalry horse, which was led by an officer of the Jagers . . . I was helped on to it and marched to Les Quatre Bras.[18]

The first battalion of the Regiment Oranien-Nassau and the 7th National Militia Battalion had been forced back through the northern end of the Bois de Bossu at the same time as the first and third battalions of the 2nd Nassau-Usingen Regiment and had taken up positions in the Champ du Sarti. Colonel Singendock was ordered to take up a position in reserve, to the north of the chaussée de Nivelles. For Militiaman Allebrandi, this was marvellous news:

> We once again took possession of our earlier bivouac, while our small force was gradually strengthened by the different troops of the Allies, among whom were English, Hanoverians, Brunswickers . . . they in their turn had to go into battle, whilst we for the moment could stretch out on our green army beds.[19]

To the north of the crossroads, the Duke of Wellington was engaged in a hurried roadside conference with the Prince van Oranje-Nassau, during which he asked what troops were in the Bois de Bossu. The Prince replied: 'Those of Nassau,' which was confirmed to Colonel Somerset by Colonel Abercromby. Almost as soon as they had asked this question, French troops began pouring from the edge of the wood, though from the blue of their uniforms, the staff officers at first simply assumed these were Belgians or Nassauers.[20]

'Sir Andrew pointed out which was the French'

In an attempt to stem the onrushing French, the Prince van Oranje-Nassau was obliged to commit his only remaining reserves:

> His Royal Highness also ordered the 2nd Battalion Nassau to advance, flanked by the 2nd Battalion of Regiment No. 28; but the enemy, by superior numbers, a well-sustained artillery and rifle fire, and uninterrupted cavalry charges, drove back the troops of the first line. They retreated without hurry and in the best of possible order, headed by the Prince of Orange and General Perponcher, whilst on both sides a heavy fire was being kept up. These troops, with both the 6-pounders of the foot battery, for the greater part made their way in an oblique line through the wood, and so reached the chaussé of Hautain Leval [Houtain-le-Val].[21]

The first and third battalions of the 2nd Nassau Regiment linked up with Bergmann's Volunteer Jager Company and pulled back in some semblance of order towards the chaussée de Nivelles. But the bulk of van Bijlandt's and von Sachsen-Weimar's brigade was by now incapable of further resistance and was scattered across a wide area to the north and west of the Bois de Bossu and in the rear areas about the crossroads. The artillery too had been roughly handled. Bijleveld's troop had managed to effect its withdrawal on Les Quatre Bras relatively unscathed, having been accompanied by No. 3 Company of the 5th National Militia Battalion throughout, and remained in position to the north of the crossroads. The detached section of three guns under Lieutenant Koopman had continued to hold its position on the right of Rogers' brigade of guns, from where it had fired on the French cavalry as it counter-charged the 6th (North Netherlands) Hussar Regiment. Suffering from the effects of the French cannonade, he removed his five caissons to the dip in the ground to the north of the chaussée, through which ran the southern tributary of the Vallée des Vaches stream.

As Kempt's brigade was pushed back up the slopes of the heights of Bati-Saint-Bernard, some as far as the Namur road, so too had Koopman withdrawn, taking up a position on the highway itself. After maintaining himself here for some time, he withdrew to Les Quatre Bras. On the way, he encountered Major de la Sarraz, who seemed dazed and unable to offer him advice or given any instructions. Koopman finally took up ground in a field to the north-west of the crossroads, where he formed in battery opposite the northern edge of the Bois de Bossu. No one seemed to know the whereabouts of Captain Geij van Pittius' section of horse artillery. Across the front of the position, individuals and small groups of men from the 27th Jager battalion steadily made their way back towards the crossroads; the charge of the light dragoons had given them the chance to bid for freedom.[22]

As de Perponcher-Sedlnitzky's division disintegrated and Picton's division deployed, Major von Brandenstein led the four companies of the 2nd Brunswick Light Battalion down the Namur road in support of the hard-pressed 95th Regiment. When he saw them arriving at the southern end of the Bois des Censes, Lieutenant Kincaid was delighted at the prospect of so timely a reinforcement, feeling that with the assistance of these 700 men, his regiment would be able to drive the enemy back a greater distance from the Namur road and thereby stabilise the left flank of the Allied position.[23]

> But they were a raw body of men, who had never before been under fire; and, as they could not be prevailed upon to join our skirmishers, we could make no use of them whatever. Their conduct, in fact, was an exact representation of Mathew's ludicrous one of the American militia, for Sir Andrew Barnard repeatedly pointed out to them which was the French, and which our side; and, after explaining that they were not to fire a shot until they joined our skirmishers, the word 'March!' was given; but march, to them, was always the signal to fire, for they stood fast, and began blazing away, chiefly at our skirmishers too; the officers commanding whom were every time sending back to say that we were shooting them; until we were, at last, obliged to be satisfied with whatever advantages their appearance could give, as even that was of some consequence, where troops were so scarce.[24]

In the centre of the line, the remainder of the Brunswick troops were enduring a different ordeal. Almost as soon as they had moved into the open, the French brought artillery up to the shoulder of high ground to the west of the Ferme de Gemioncourt, from where they opened a terrific cannonade, sweeping the fields to the north with round shot, canister and shells. Parties of French tirailleurs moved forward, concealed by the folds of the ground and the high crops, until they were a short musket shot away. The air filled with the crackle of musketry as these skirmishers began picking off officers, non-commissioned officers and drummers. For Sergeant Langenstrasse, this was perhaps the most unpleasant situation for a cavalryman to be in:

> We were the only cavalry present on our side and therefore were ordered to cover two batteries, the worst possible task I can think of, because you stand with your sword in your hand without being able to defend yourself against the missiles and shells, let alone parry them.[25]

The regiment quickly started to take casualties and officers and men fell to the ground at regular intervals. Major von Cramm, commanding the Brunswick cavalry, was prominent at the head of the Hussar Regiment on his White Russian horse. Suddenly, his leg was smashed by a round shot and he fell heavily to the ground. Despite calls for a surgeon, none could be found nearby and, within a few short minutes, he bled to death amongst the rye. Major von Braun took command and handed the Hussar Regiment to Major von Oeynhausen, but the casualties continued to mount. Despite being in line, the horsemen were exposed to canister fire from eight guns at a rate of two or three rounds a minute. Great gaps were being torn in the ranks as men and horses crumpled to the ground. It seemed to Sergeant Langenstrasse that men were falling all about him. Captain von Pavel was killed; in rapid succession, Lieutenant Rudolphi severely wounded and Lieutenant Clauditz, at Langenstrasse's side, was slightly wounded.[26]

The situation was no better for the infantry. At a range of little more than five hundred metres, the French gun teams were firing round after round into their densely packed columns. Major von Rauschenplatt of the Avantgarde-Battalion was wounded and compelled to hand over command of the battalion to Major von Bülow. Dozens of other officers and men were killed or wounded to varying degrees. Though the battalions had been built around a cadre of experienced commissioned and non-commissioned officers, the majority of those in the ranks were raw recruits and this was their first time under fire. The Duke von Braunschweig-Lüneburg was highly conscious of the impact that such a cannonade could have on brittle morale and set his troops a fine example by calmly sitting on horseback in front of the battalions, smoking his pipe and giving orders as he would have done at a field day. His staff officers, more concerned for his personal safety than he was himself, argued in vain for him to move to a less exposed position. They were doubtless concerned not only for the well-being of the Duke himself, but also cognisant of the crushing effect on morale that his being killed or wounded would have upon the troop that witnessed it. Pressing their arguments forcefully and bordering on the insolent, they were unsuccessful in pleading their case. Like his father before, this Duke would lead from the front.[27]

To the east of the Charleroi road, Picton's division was enduring similar treatment. On horseback between the 79th and 32nd Regiments of Foot, the General calmly assessed the situation. The French artillery visible on the ridge to the south was pounding his position with round shot and canister, ploughing up the ground on which the struggle would be won or lost. At about 4.00 p.m., numerous columns of French infantry were observed, preparing to ascend the heights of Bati-Saint-Bernard, the majority in compact battalion columns. Other than the hedges, thorns and brambles of the Gemioncourt stream at the foot of the shallow valley, there was no physical obstacle to impede its progress. The attack would go in between the Ferme de Gemioncourt and the étang Materne. Picton did, however, have some advantages. The majority of his men were invisible to the French and were posted in the dead ground behind the Namur road, protected by its embankments. Others, on the road itself, took shelter in the cuttings, where the chaussée passed through the gently rolling folds of ground; even those in the open were lying down for protection. The French would come in for an unpleasant surprise when reached the top of the slope. The nature of the ground would, however, define the method of attack. The eastern end of the position was much closer to the French than the ground further to the west, a circumstance that would necessitate a counter-attack 'en echelon'; timing would be everything. He hurriedly sent word to Kempt to hold the commanding officers in readiness to execute this manoeuvre.[28]

Close to Picton, in the ranks of the 79th Regiment of Foot, Private Vallence was tired and stiff, weighed down by knapsack, cartridge pouch, haversack, belts, blankets and weaponry. Suddenly the word was passed down the line to load and every man recovered his arms, and went through the familiar routine of: 'handle the cartridge'; 'prime'; 'cast about' and 'ram'; before returning to shouldered arms. Nothing could be seen to the front, the view obscured by the gently swaying crops. Now, however, the pounding of the artillery was supplemented by the muffled roll of drums beating the '*pas de charge*', the shouted commands of the French officers and the enthusiastic cheers of the enemy. Through the din came the command, 'Make ready!' and over seven hundred muskets pointed towards the sky, gripped tightly by sweating hands. Was the priming pan completely closed? Did the flint look worn? Was the lock fouled? The men gripped the muskets tighter, prayed to the Lord of Misfires and glanced nervously at Colonel Douglas. Eventually, at the command, 'Present,' the barrels came down and almost immediately, as the Colonel shouted, 'Fire!' the ripple of flashes down the line, followed by the belching of the muzzles, poured a hail of lead into the unseen French column. Suddenly, the cheers were replaced by screams. This was the signal that Douglas had been waiting for; the sign that the volley had done its job. Raising his hat, he shouted for the battalion to, 'Charge!':[29]

> No sooner said than done. A great number were killed or wounded while those who could fled from our bayonets. As we charged we gave them three Highland hurrays and put them to flight as fast as their legs could carry them, yelling out the most opprobrious epithets against the 'men without breeches.' Guns, knapsacks and all were abandoned to facilitate their escape.[30]

As Vallence charged down the slope, yelling at the top of his voice, he could not feel his feet touch the ground. In complete contrast to his sensations only a few moments earlier, his musket and bayonet seemed as light in his hands as a feather; adrenalin coursed through his veins. Arriving back at the hedge in the bottom of the shallow valley, the French continued in flight but, had they not, Vallence was convinced that he and his comrades would have thrown them over the hedge on the point of their bayonets, like sheaves of corn.[31]

Another body of French infantry began to ascend the slope towards the position occupied by the 32nd Regiment of Foot. When it was a little over forty metres from the skirmish line, the British battalion's light infantry and marksmen ran in again to take up their position on the left of the main body. With the distance closing by the second, Colonel Hicks ordered his men to their feet. Each weapon was loaded and, an instant after his roared command, the air was rent by a deafening explosion as the battalion's muskets erupted in a jagged line of fire and smoke. The thunderous sound was still ringing in Lieutenant Stephens' ears, when the welcome command was received:

> Sir Thomas Picton immediately ordered us to charge (which we were very happy to hear, as we had been under a very galling fire and not able to return it in consequence of the skirmishers being in our front and our men were falling in every direction) but we no sooner set up the usual shout and moved on, than the cowardly rascals ran in every direction. Our poor fellows were so fagged (not having any sleep the night before and marching that day twenty miles under a broiling hot sun), that we were not able to

get up to them and we were wading up to our middle in corn. However, we peppered them pretty well as they were getting through the gaps in the hedges.[32]

A short distance from Stephens, Ensign Dallas was experiencing his first taste of combat:

We were now in the thick of it. Such a fire of shells, cannon and musketry, I was told by the oldest officers had never before been witnessed. You may ask me how I felt – why rather queerish, I believe, but I had no time to analyse my feelings. I had something else to do. We were driving at them like so many devils. Finding that they advanced rapidly we prepared to charge as soon as they entered the field before us. The corn was breast-high, so that they got pretty close before they came in sight. The word was given and we advanced with shouts that drowned the fire to the charge. Nothing could have withstood us. They had already turned and we were following them down the hill, when I was desired to stay where I was by a piece of shell.[33]

Driving his men on, Major Calvert dashed forward against the French, who evidently were not intending to make a stand. If they were closely enough pursued, he thought, the hedges close to the stream would impede their flight and give his men an opportunity to either shoot down a good number, or to seize a considerable body of prisoners. It was an opinion shared by Major Ross-Lewin:

They [the French] had to cross a long, narrow field and a second hedge before they could get under cover from our fire and an admirable opportunity of taking a number of prisoners was lost here, while they were making their way through a small opening. Indeed, numbers of them had ordered their arms in the expectation of being pursued and taken, but they escaped with inconsiderable loss, as our troops were halted at the first hedge.[34]

Who had reined in the battalion on the point of such a glorious victory? Colonel Hicks? No one seemed to know. Surprised at their good fortune, the French now passed through and into the fields to the south of the stream. Some had abandoned all notion of retiring and formed a solid line behind the southern hedge from where they commenced a fusillade at short distance on the exposed British battalion.[35]

Shortly after the 32nd Regiment of Foot had moved off, the men of the Royals had received similar orders from Picton. Encouraged by their officers and the shrill whistles of the sergeants, the soldiers scrambled up the banks of the Namur road and formed up in a field of wheat to the south. Corporal Douglas was pleased, having felt that the battalion was 'awkwardly placed, not being able to destroy the enemy until close at hand'. Rather than attacking perpendicular to the Namur road, however, the right wing was wheeled forward and the angle of the advance was realigned towards the crest of the ridge. Within minutes, round shot were ploughing through the ranks, bowling men over, severing limbs and tearing ragged holes in the files, which the

The Battle of Quatre Bras

covering sergeants hurried to close with much pushing and shoving. As the long line of redcoats toiled up the slope and passed the chemin Bati-Saint-Bernard, they could suddenly see the swarms of French skirmishers advancing across the fields of tall rye below, followed by a column of hostile infantry. As the distance closed, a terrific crackle of musketry erupted from the French tirailleurs:[36]

> Their fine, long, light firelocks, with a smaller bore, are far more efficient for skirmishing than our abominably clumsy machine. The French soldiers whipping in the cartridge, give the butt of the piece a jerk or two on the ground, which supersedes the use of the ramrod; and thus they fire two for our one.[37]

The pace of the drums seemed to quicken and the battalion gained momentum as it descended the slope, through crops that were planted with 'Corn that took the tallest men up to the shoulders'. From the advantage of the heights opposite, the enemy artillery had a much clearer view than their own infantry did in the bottom of the shallow valley. At a range of less than five hundred metres, round shot after round shot smashed into the British ranks, 'Which did astonishing execution'. Suddenly, Colonel Campbell gave the order to charge and in a long, glittering sweep, the bayonets came down; the needle points directed towards the French, now less than a hundred metres distant. With loud cheers, the Royals dashed forward towards the column; it was too much for the enemy to take. Skirmishers scattered in every direction before the battalion's onset and the French column immediately wheeled about and rushed for the openings in the hedge that bordered the Gemioncourt stream. The British were astonished; the manoeuvre had succeeded beyond their wildest expectations. The officers in particular were impressed by the character that the men had shown – remarkable for the young soldiers of a third battalion. On the opposite side of the stream, the routed enemy column appeared to be reforming under the protection of some cavalry and within a few short minutes, it had deployed into line and advanced to the southern hedge, from where it 'Commenced a most galling fire' on the British battalion, which was 'Returned with the utmost steadiness and precision'. As volley succeeded volley, the two assailing forces lost sight of each other in the billowing clouds of acrid smoke, illuminated briefly by spluttering fire as yet more muskets poured forth their deadly contents. Within a short time of the fire fight commencing, the ground was littered with dead and wounded.[38]

Like their sister battalions, the charge of the 79th Regiment of Foot had met with some resistance as it crossed the shallow stream and approached the hedge on its southern side. The French had chosen to make a stand, receiving the British infantry with a shower of musketry into which the Highlanders ran headlong, not having had time to reload their pieces. In some places, the irresistible wave of yelling Scotsmen swept forward and drove the French from the southern hedge, pursuing them up the heights of Gemioncourt, towards another body of French troops drawn up on the slopes. In other places, the French line held firm and a bloody fire fight ensued. The momentum of the attack was slowly diminishing and despite being joined by

'Sir Andrew pointed out which was the French'

The counter-attack of the 79th Regiment of Foot, part of Kempt's brigade. Print after Henri Dupray. (Author's collection)

the men of No. 8 Company, the British line had become ragged and broken. In the very teeth of the French position, the charge petered out. Private Vallence was one of those blazing away at the enemy, separated only by a few yards and some broken hedgerow:

> While the bloody combat was going on at the hedge, the French seeing our regiment alone and at a considerable distance in front of our main body, advanced against us in great numbers, and made an attempt to surround us, to make us prisoners, shouting to us, 'Prisoners! Prisoners!' Our commanding officer, seeing this, called to us to, 'Run like devils – the French shall not make us prisoners.' We soon got clear of the French; they were afraid of coming near us, numerous as they were. We had to pass through a fence in our retreat from the French, which hindered us greatly, as we could only get through it at openings and slaps. The French directed their fire at us as we were crowding to get through the hedge and killed and wounded many of us in our retreat to our station in a field of rye.

By this time, many men of the regiment had exhausted their ammunition; such had been the prodigious expenditure during the fire fight with the French. A short distance away, unseen by some in the smoke and confusion, the 32nd Regiment of Foot, still posted behind the northern hedgerow to the west of the Camerons, covered their withdrawal with some judicious volleys.[39]

The Duke of Wellington and his staff had ascended the heights of Bati-Saint-Bernard in the wake of Kempt's counter-attack. Though the charge appeared to have met with success for the time being, he had been concerned to see Colonel Douglas' men ascending the slopes of the French position and sent his military secretary to ride down the line of the brigade, passing the order that the troops were to be kept in hand. Colonel Somerset galloped off and shortly afterwards encountered General Kempt, who agreed that his troops were certainly not in hand, but that he would ensure that order was restored as soon as possible. His task completed, Somerset spurred his horse back towards the Duke's entourage, whilst Kempt sent Captain Hon. Charles Gore to pass the word.[40]

At the crossroads of Les Quatre Bras, the senior officers of the 92nd Regiment of Foot were watching the advance of Kempt's brigade with a degree of professional interest. Though an excellent point from which to observe the steady advance of the French columns down the northern slopes of the heights of Gemioncourt, it brought home to them the numerical superiority of the French. Whilst their battalions were invariably smaller than their British counterparts, they seemed to be four times as numerous. The opposing forces closed and within minutes were hidden from view as they entered the dead ground to each side of the Gemioncourt stream. Exchanging apprehensive looks, many of the field officers and senior subalterns 'looked forward with uneasiness to the issue of the conflict'.[41]

The Gordons need not have been so concerned for the welfare of the Camerons. In the pit of the valley, towards the right of the line formed by the 79th of Foot, Lieutenant Forbes' company received the order to disengage and to pull back towards its former position on the road. Officers and men were relieved to regain some cover, their exposed position during the advance having led to numerous casualties. Slowly, maintaining good order, the Highlanders toiled back up the slope, amongst them Private Vallence:

> We lost a great number of our men by the fire of the French musketry. Two men that were next to me in the ranks fell, one on my right hand and the other on my left, and at the same time a musket ball struck the camp kettle which I carried on top of my knapsack. One of the men that fell cried most piteously to me to help him forward; I knew if I had attempted to help him the French bullets would have soon laid me beside him. Our passion of rage and fury had risen to such a height that we were like madmen all the time we were engaged; yet we always kept our rage and fury within proper bounds; none of us were ever so base and cruel as to hurt or insult our fallen foes. The French, on the other hand, cruelly tortured and stabbed to death our wounded men whenever they found them.

When it had arrived at a point some fifty metres short of its original position behind the Namur road, the battalion was ordered to halt, the commanding officer's orders apparently being to remain between the French and the chaussée. The troops had been pounded without respite by the French artillery the whole time they had been retiring up the slope and by a cruel coincidence, the nature of the heights of Bati-Saint-Bernard meant that there was no reverse slope at this point, behind which the battalion could take shelter. Like most veteran officers of the Peninsular War, Douglas did the only thing he could and ordered the men to lie down in the flattened rye, presenting a less visible target to the French gunners.[42]

Other regiments were also on the move. Through the smoke in rear of the battalion, Major Calvert of the 32nd Regiment of Foot could see the familiar figure of General Picton and shortly afterwards, a bugle call sounded for the soldiers to reform on the colours. Word was quickly passed from company to company and the men slowly ceased firing, disengaged and withdrew up the slope to the position from which they had commenced their advance. Some of the men passed French soldiers, wounded in the initial advance. Their knapsacks open, pointing to the withdrawing British that they might take anything they wanted, for fear that the 'Rosbifs' would otherwise slaughter them indiscriminately, fully aware that the actions of their own comrades to their wounded enemies might provoke such harsh treatment. No doubt with one or two exceptions, the men of Kempt's brigade were of a higher-minded nature and had more to occupy their thoughts than a little meat, a trinket or two, or a hard-won *Legion d'Honneur*.[43]

The tired British infantry sweated back up the slope, continuing to receive fire from the French, whose skirmishers once again passed through the hedges and fanned out in pursuit of the retiring redcoats. Now that their front was once more clear of their own troops, the French artillery had resumed its murderous fire and lashed Kempt's men as they sought the refuge of the reverse slope. Lieutenant Stephens was at the eastern end of the line, chivvying along his tired men:

> During this time I had received a grape shot, which tore the wing completely off my left shoulder and did me no more harm than bruising me. I received another slight contusion in my left thigh and was just congratulating myself on my narrow escapes, when a third ball (musket) passed directly through my left arm between the elbow and the wrist. I was obliged to leave the field.

The ragged and breathless line of men stumbled back over the chemin Bati-Saint-Bernard and sank exhausted into the field beyond it whilst the officers and sergeants endeavoured to restore order. In the distance, towards the Bois de l'Hutte, it appeared that the French were about to make a second attempt to seize the position.[44]

Within minutes, the battalion was led once more to the attack and the men streamed back down the slope, the bayonets glinting in the late afternoon sunshine. The ground was littered with the bodies of the killed and wounded and every now and then, men stumbled over them in the high wheat and rye. The fire of musketry and artillery, especially towards the centre companies and the colour party was constant in its intensity and savage in its outcome. As Ensign James McConchy struggled to keep the regimental colour aloft, a shell burst a short distance away and tore the silk away from the staff, causing carnage in the right section of No. 5 Company. The explosion blew Captain Whitty's head to atoms, spraying the men around him with blood, brain, hair and bone. The intended target, McConchy, was unaccountably only slightly wounded and the advance continued.[45]

The Battle of Quatre Bras

To McConchy's left, the Camerons were in a similarly exposed situation on the forward slope of the ridge. Swarms of French skirmishers had followed them back up the slope and were now peppering them with musketry. Face-down on the rich earth with the rest of his comrades was Private Vallence:

> We formed up at our station in the field of rye and were ordered to lie down for a short time to save ourselves from the deadly showers that the French were pouring upon us. While we lay flat on the ground amongst the rye, several of our men were killed and wounded; the man that lay next to me received a musket ball on the crown of his head, which killed him, and a musket ball struck my camp kettle and went through it and stuck in my knapsack. The French were advancing near us; we rose and commenced firing. Our bullets tumbled them down in heaps. They severely felt the force of British powder. Our captain always told us to take good aim and bring down the ruffians. While we continued to fire on each other, the French bullets were whizzing about our ears as thick as a shower of hail. My face, hands, clothes and belts were bespattered with the blood of my killed and wounded companions.[46]

General Kempt realised that if he allowed the fire fight to continue without some effort being made to drive the French back down the slope, the 79th Regiment of Foot, already dangerously low on ammunition as a result of its earlier advance, risked expending its supply entirely. It would then be being obliged to pull back and expose the flank of the remainder of the division. Colonel Douglas passed the word for the battalion to advance, an order which was welcomed by Captain Campbell, Vallence's fire-eating company commander. Leaving behind the motionless body of Private Peter Carrick and dozens of severely wounded comrades, Vallence and his fellow Highlanders were eager to get to grips again with 'Johnny':[47]

> We gave them three hurrays and again drove them through the hedges and returned to our former station in the field of rye. The French were again reinforced in great numbers and advanced near us. We thinned their ranks as we had done before with our well-directed deadly shower. My companions were killed and wounded in great numbers. Several bullets went through my clothes and cut my belts. We were ordered to charge the French. We gave them three cheers and charged them through the hedges with our bayonets and continued to fire on them for some time, and returned to our former station.[48]

Endnotes

1. Anonymous (Near Observer), p. 56. Aubrey-Fletcher, p. 371. de Bas &c., pp. 461–2. Clay. Fraser &c., p. 12. Lake. Master. Maurice, p. 12. Powell. Whitworth, p. 45.
2. de Bas &c., p. 461. Anonymous (Britain Triumphant). Anonymous (Near Observer), p. 56. Hamilton, p. 15. Lake. Maurice, p. 12. Powell.

'Sir Andrew pointed out which was the French'

3. Anonymous (Britain Triumphant). Anonymous (Near Observer), p. 56. Fraser &c., p. 12. Master. Powell. Whitworth, p. 45.
4. Clay.
5. Aubrey-Fletcher, p. 371. de Bas &c., pp. 461–2. Beamish, p. 532. Clay. Kuhlmann. Master. Powell.
6. Clay. Kuhlmann. Maurice, p. 12.
7. Fraser &c., p. 12. Master. Whitworth, p. 45.
8. Aubrey-Fletcher, p. 371. Clay. Fraser &c., p. 12. Master. Whitworth, p. 45.
9. Aubrey-Fletcher, p. 371. Clay. Lake. Maurice, p. 12. Powell. Whitworth, p. 45.
10. Bannatyne, pp. 320–1. Macready (I). Macready (IV), p. 389. Macready (V).
11. Powell. Standen (I). C. Wood, p. 806.
12. Banntyne, p. 321. Macready (I).
13. Brett-James, p. 62. Macready (IV), p. 389.
14. Hellemann.
15. Jackson (II), p. 17.
16. Bourdon de Vatry, p. 101. Jolyet, pp. 75–6. Leonhard. von Müffling (II). van Opstall. Reille. von Sachsen-Weimar (II), von Sachsen-Weimar (III). von Sachsen-Weimar (IV). F. Somerset, p. 9.
17. Bergmann. Bourdon de Vatry, p. 101. Houssaye, p. 115. Jolyet, pp. 75–6. Leonhard. von Muffling (I), pp. 4–5. von Müffling (II). van Opstall, von Sachsen-Weimar (II), von Sachsen-Weimar (III). von Sachsen-Weimar (IV). F. Somerset, p. 9.
18. de Jongh, p. 13.
19. Allebrandi. van Zuylen van Nyeveld (I), p. 57.
20. van Zuylen van Nyeveld (I), pp. 55–6.
21. F. Somerset, p. 9.
22. Anonymous (V. D. W.). de Bas &c., pp. 513–4. de Crassier. Grunenbosch. Hylckema. Koopman. van Opstall. van de Wall. Wassenaar van Sint-Pancras.
23. Caldwell and Cooper, p. 10. von Herzberg. Kincaid (I), pp. 316–7. Partridge and Oliver, p. 96.
24. Kincaid (I), pp. 316–7.
25. Girod de l'Ain, pp. 271–2. von Herzberg. Ney, p. 59. Langenstrasse. von Pivka (II), p. 21. Puvis, p. 116. Reille. W. Siborne (V), pp. 65, 76. Trefcon, p. 182. von Wachholtz, p. 27.
26. Bowden, p. 257. Hellemann. von Herzberg. Langenstrasse. Nafziger, pp. 252–4. von Pflugk-Harttung (II), p. 26. W. Siborne (V), p. 76. von Wachholtz, p. 27.
27. Delhaize and Aerts, p. 445. von Herzberg. Langenstrasse. van Noeyen, p. 23. von Pivka (III), p. 21. W. Siborne (V), pp. 76–7. von Wachholtz, pp. 28–9.
28. Anonymous (Letters), p. 255. Cathcart. Delhaize and Aerts, p. 453. Girod de l'Ain, p. 271. Gomm (III). Houssaye, pp. 114–5. von Müffling (I), pp. 4–5. Reille. W. Siborne (V), pp. 75–6. Swiney, pp. 112–3. Trefcon, p. 182.
29. Allan. Vallence.
30. Allan. Vallence.
31. Allan. Vallence. Archibald Forbes, p. 267. Swiney, pp. 112–3.
32. Calvert (III). Crowe. Stephens. Swiney, p. 116. Trefcon, pp. 182–3.

33. Dallas.
34. Calvert (III). Crowe. Ross-Lewin, pp. 256–7.
35. Crowe. Girod de l'Ain, pp. 271–2. Ney, p. 59. Reille. Ross-Lewin, p. 257. Stephens.
36. Anonymous (Near Observer), pp. 67–8. Douglas, p. 98. Leask and McCance, p. 334. Macdonald. Mudie (I). Mudie (II), p. 183.
37. Mudie (II), p. 183.
38. Anonymous (Near Observer), pp. 67–8. Douglas, p. 98. Leask and McCance, p. 334. Macdonald. Mudie (I).
39. Allan. Anonymous (Cameron), pp. 89–90. Calvert (III). Cornford and Walker, p. 105. Dewar. Alexander Forbes (II). Archibald Forbes, p. 267. Mackenzie &c., p. 56. Ross-Lewin, pp. 257–8. W. Siborne (V), p. 76. Swiney, pp. 112–3. Vallence.
40. Houssaye, p. 115. F. Somerset, p. 9.
41. Anonymous (Letters), pp. 224–5.
42. Allan. Anonymous (Cameron), p. 89. Dewar. Alexander Forbes (II). Mackenzie &c., p. 56. Vallence.
43. Allan. Calvert (III). Crowe. Ross-Lewin, p. 257. Swiney, p. 116. Stephens. Vallence.
44. Stephens.
45. Swiney, p. 116.
46. Allan. Vallence.
47. Allan. Vallence.
48. Allan. Vallence.

CHAPTER 13

In contrast to Private Vallence, exposed and under fire from artillery and musketry, Private Costello of the 95th Regiment of Foot was with the two companies detailed by Colonel Barnard to garrison the hamlet of Thyle. He was safely ensconced in one of the houses, grateful for the momentary respite from the small arms fire; it was not destined to last for long:

> We remained very quietly where we were until the French, bringing up some artillery, began riddling the house with round shot. Feeling rather thirsty, I asked a young woman in the place for a little water, which she was handing to me, when a ball passed through the buildings, knocking the dust about our ears. Strange to say, the girl appeared less alarmed than myself. Fearing that we might be surrounded, we were at length obliged to leave the building; in doing which we were fiercely attacked by a number of French voltigeurs, who forced us to extend along a lane, from whence we as smartly retaliated, and a galling fire was kept up for some time on both sides.[1]

As the riflemen pulled back to secure their flanks, Costello could not help but notice the contrasting fortunes of his inexperienced and veteran comrades:

> It is remarkable that recruits in action are generally more unfortunate than the old soldiers. We had many fine fellows, who joined us on the eve of our leaving England, who were killed here. The reason of this is that an old rifleman will seek shelter, if there be any near his post, while the inexperienced recruit appears as if petrified to the spot by the whizzing balls, and unnecessarily exposes himself to the enemy's fire.[2]

Pressured by the increasingly numerous French, Lieutenant Fitzmaurice and Captain Chawner pulled their men back, past the mill and down the lane towards the Bois des Censes. Pausing here and there to check the onrush of the tirailleurs, they eventually established a new line of defence along the chemin des Dames-Avelines, from which they managed to stem the French advance for some time. As the pressure continued to mount and the swarms of enemy skirmishers became ever more numerous, they were steadily pushed back through the wood and into the fields of rye to the south of the Ferme de l'Haute Cense. Somewhere in the tangled crops lay

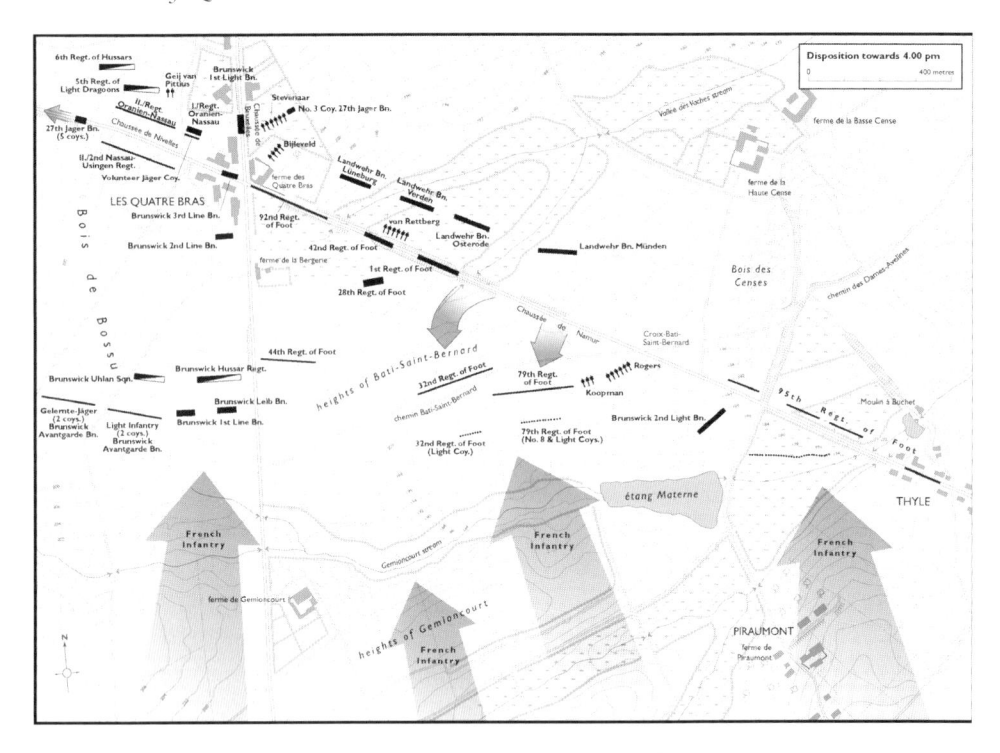

Lieutenant Fitzmaurice, a musket ball lodged deep in his thigh. Resigned to his fate, he realised that he would have to wait some time for his hard-pressed comrades to recover him.[3]

Seeing the defenders of Thyle pressed back, Barnard withdrew his skirmishers from the Namur road and with the Brunswickers maintaining their alignment on his right, he pulled back both battalions to a new position in rear of the Bois des Censes, at right angles to the chaussée. Thinking that the Brunswickers had somehow contrived to lose possession of the wood to the French and that it was their behaviour which had forced the riflemen to cede a hard-won and even harder-maintained position, the officers of Johnston's and Beckwith's companies were in an ungenerous mood towards their ostensible allies.[4]

Having reunited the battalion, Colonel Barnard realised that the French had to be driven back and the Namur road secured at all costs. With hostile infantry already across the chaussée, Wellington's rear was threatened and Picton's division was at risk of being cut off from the Brussels road. He could not allow his men any time to contemplate the danger of their position and ordering the swords to be fixed, he led the combined force forward through the fields in a sweeping counter-attack. The French tirailleurs, who had advanced through the Bois des Censes to its western edge, could not withstand the ferocity of the assault and fell back rapidly, the British and Germans clearing the wood with cold steel and pursuing their beaten opponents into the fields to the east. The main body of the French had already gained the Namur road, but Barnard pressed home his charge, crossing the road and ascending the slope opposite, towards the Ferme de Piraumont. As the British and Germans advanced, they ran into a heavy flanking fire from a French infantry battalion to their right, which was drawn up in line to the east of the étang Materne.[5]

Somewhere in the high grain was Private Costello:

> I was in the act of taking aim at some of our opposing skirmishers, when a ball struck my trigger finger, tearing it off and turning the trigger aside, while a second shot passed through the mess tin on my knapsack. Several of our men were killed by this volley, and Lieutenant Gairdner, a worthy little officer of the company, was wounded in the lower part of the leg. We wounded men made the best of our way to the rear and on my return to the house at the corner of the lane, I found the pretty Belgian still in possession, looking out of the window and seemingly unconcerned, although a dozen shots had perforated the house. All our entreaties for her to leave were in vain, as her father, she said, had desired her to take care of the place until he returned from Brussels.[6]

The combat ebbed and flowed across the fields, as each side sought to gain and hold ground, preventing the enemy from making further progress. Whilst the 95th Regiment of Foot was once more driving the hostile infantry back across the chaussée, French troops to the west of the étang Materne had pinned down the 79th Regiment of Foot and the Highlanders were suffering severely as the French artillery lashed the ridge. Men were tumbling everywhere; some killed; others with horrifying injuries. Private Vallence noticed that a slight breeze had sprung up, driving the smoke from the French guns across the valley into their faces, causing the infantrymen to choke on the acrid fumes. The metallic pounding of Captain Rogers' battery, just in advance and to the left was adding to the discomfort, the billowing clouds of smoke stinging the eyes and catching in the throat. Somewhere in the murk were the French infantry, the crackle of musketry and the flame from hundreds of priming pans confirming their nearby presence; when in doubt, the Camerons simply fired at where the smoke was thickest. Suddenly, a messenger appeared from General Kempt. The Colonel was to form in column on the road and thereafter act as circumstances might require. The battered battalion pulled back, forming up behind the embankment once more, the decimated companies now under the command of lieutenants and, in some cases, ensigns.[7]

The situation was becoming desperate. On the left flank of Kempt's brigade, the Camerons had had been pushed back to their starting line on the Namur road. The 32nd Regiment of Foot, with the Royals to their right, were barely holding their own in the central section of the heights of Bati-Saint-Bernard, with the 28th Regiment of Foot in reserve along the chaussée. The 44th Regiment of Foot, close to the Charleroi road, linked Picton's division with the Brunswick infantry to the west of the chaussée, whilst the Gordon Highlanders continued to occupy the vital crossroads. With their efforts to punch a hole through the eastern end of Picton's line frustrated by the tenacity of the Rifles, Rogers' guns and the 79th Regiment, the weight of the French attack shifted westwards. Before long, hostile infantry could be seen climbing the southern slopes of the heights of Bati-Saint-Bernard, slightly

The Battle of Quatre Bras

to the east of the Ferme de Gemioncourt. General Picton decided it was time to commit Pack's final reserve, the Royal Highlanders of the 42nd Regiment of Foot, which had had just fulfilled the earlier order to move down and occupy the Namur road, close to the Ferme des Quatre Bras.

Major Campbell had just halted No. 1 Company, when he noticed Sir John Elley, the Deputy Adjutant-General, ride up and order the men to lie down in the shallow ditch by the roadside. The men gratefully fell out and slumped down under cover of the modest bank on the southern side of the ditch, some tilting their heads back against the rolled blankets strapped to the top of their knapsacks, drifting off to sleep with the warm sun shining on their upturned faces. Suddenly, the familiar figure of Sir Denis Pack clattered up the cobbled road, reining in his horse close to where the commanding officer was halted. It was not to be Colonel Macara's day. Having castigated him in the early hours of the morning for the delay in assembling his battalion in the rue Royale, the volatile Pack proceeded to dress him down in full view of the men for not having the bayonets fixed; Macara, no doubt blushing a shade as crimson as his coat, immediately barked out the order and the line of men rippled as men wriggled awkwardly to extract bayonets from their scabbards beneath them. In Major Campbell's company, Sergeant Anton's blood was up:

> There is something animating to a soldier in the clash of the fixing bayonet, more particularly so, when it is thought that the scabbard is not to receive it until it drinks the blood of its foe. Call me not bloodthirsty for expressing myself in this unfeeling manner. It is harsh, but it is just.[8]

Brunswick Infantry in action to the west of the chausée de Charleroi. Richard Knötel.

'The clash of the fixing bayonet'

The symbolism of this order was not lost on anyone in the battalion, from the veterans of Alexandria, to the drafts from Aberdeen. Half the men had never been on campaign before. As their nervous bodies lay against the bank, the old campaigners taunted them with ghoulish stories of all they had seen and suffered, adding for good measure, some remarks likely to embellish their own reputations in the minds of the youngsters. Though their eyes were round as saucers with the fear of what the impending ordeal might hold for them, the pale-faced, sweating recruits were anxious to get on with it and have it done; stomachs churned. Each man's musket was loaded and they gripped Brown Bess tightly because their lives depended upon her. Corporals and sergeants checked flints and reminded the youngsters to remember to remove their ramrods from the muzzle after they had loaded the next time. Anxiety reached fever pitch. Elsewhere in the ranks, their backs raw and weeping from the flogging they had received, were a number of recalcitrants; men who had sold their blankets in exchange for gin. Unlike those whose feelings were animated by the highest ideals, these were men who had a bone to pick, a point to prove, and the 'Crapauds' were going to feel the consequences. Perhaps, they thought, the opportunity might arise in the confusion of battle to settle a few scores on their own side. Cheeks rested on the cool metal of the muskets. Some tested the point of their bayonets, or passed a canteen of gin around their mess-mates; Dutch courage. Eyes watched the officers and sergeants. Suddenly, Colonel Macara gave the order. The drums thumped and whistles blew.[9]

> We were all ready and in line. 'Forward!' was the word of command and forward we hastened, though we saw no enemy in front. The stalks of the rye, like the weeds that grow on the margin of some swamp, opposed our advance. The tops were up to our bonnets and we strode and groped our way through as fast as we could. By the time we reached a field of clover on the other side, we were very much straggled, however, we united in line as fast as time and our speedy advance would permit.[10]

Making their way through the fields, the men sweated profusely. The heat had become unbearable and as they floundered through the crops, they choked in a thick dust of cereal ears, husks and insects. The long incline told on the weary muscles and their bare legs were scratched, bruised and irritated by the crops. Irrespective of the discomfort, each man grasped his firelock tightly and through the rustling sound of his own advance, listened hard for any sign of an enemy stumbling equally blindly towards them.[11]

The long line gradually emerged from the trampled rye, having left a swathe almost two hundred metres broad in its wake and gained the open space of a field of clover. Companies halted to let others form up. Once the men had reassembled, the ranks were dressed and the battalion remained at ordered arms, waiting for Macara's next command. A sudden whooshing noise rent the air as the French artillery posted on the heights of Gemioncourt, barely seven hundred metres away, opened up, but it was French marksmen who drew first blood. Concealed in the folds of the ground and

The Battle of Quatre Bras

hidden in the nearby fields of standing grain, they immediately concentrated their efforts on the officers of the Highland regiment, many of whom made unnecessarily tempting targets by standing together, prominent in their red-striped grey trousers, the other ranks all wearing kilts. Suddenly a shot rang out and Lieutenant Robert Gordon crumpled to the ground, a gaping hole in his head where the musket ball had smashed into his skull. Lieutenant Duncan Stewart was mortally wounded, while others received less serious injuries, as the French skirmishers raked the ranks of the battalion with an accurate and galling fire. Behind the skirmishers, the field officers could see a number of columns steadily ascending the slope a short distance away.[12]

Suddenly, Sergeant Anton noticed some different skirmishers appear in front of the right wing of the battalion, whom he took for Belgians, on account of the unfamiliarity of their dress. The men were escaping prisoners, wounded and stragglers from Colonel Grunenbosch's 27th Jager Battalion, who had now been under fire for over two hours. The exhausted light infantrymen were being closely pursued by the enemy and hurriedly withdrew through the ranks of the 42nd Regiment of Foot:

> In an instant we were on their victorious pursuers. Our sudden appearance seemed to paralyse their advance. The singular appearance of our dress, combined no doubt with our sudden debut, tended to stagger their resolution. We were on them. Our pieces were loaded and our bayonets glittered, impatient to drink their blood. Those who had so proudly driven the Belgians before them, turned now to fly, whilst our loud cheers made the fields echo to our wild hurrahs. France fled or fell before us and we thought the field our own. We had not yet lost a man, for the victors seldom lose many, except in protracted, hard-contested struggles. With one's face to the enemy, he may shun the deadly thrust or stroke. It is the retreating soldier that destruction pursues. We drove on so fast that we almost appeared like a mob following the rout of some defeated faction.[13]

With adrenalin pumping through their veins, the men of the left wing of the Highland regiment pursued the enemy into the dense rye field whence they had emerged, oblivious to the danger within. The French gave way under the ferocious onset and blood-curdling yells and stumbled back down the slope as fast as they could, towards their formed battalions, which had been toiling up the slope in their turn. Here and there, the Highlanders discharged their muskets at the fugitives, the thick smoke obliterating the scene, as though a veil had been drawn over the tableau. Whilst the left of the battalion was entering the rye; the right, which had been halted in a field of rye adjoining the clover field to the west, moved forward, blind to the events transpiring as little as ten metres away. Shortly after the left wing entered the tall crops, the right wing emerged at last into the open; it could see the French withdrawing towards the enclosures of the Ferme de Gemioncourt, under the protection of several batteries that pounded the Allied ranks from the heights beyond.[14]

On the opposite side of the Charleroi road, this same artillery had long been a concern for the Duke von Braunschweig-Lüneburg, whose troops were holding the vital patch of ground between the highway and the Bois de Bossu, from which Stevenaar's wrecked brigade had been driven a short time earlier. His own troops were somewhat in advance of most of Picton's division and were consequently receiving a great deal of attention from several batteries. Calm though he remained on the exterior, the Duke was becoming increasingly exasperated at having to remain in such an exposed position without being able to close with the French or to respond to the continuous bombardment from the enemy guns a short distance away. Bijleveld's and Stevenaar's artillery was, to all intents and purposes, useless; the crews regrouping in the orchards behind the Ferme des Quatre Bras. The section of guns that had accompanied the Netherlands light cavalry brigade was similarly hors de combat, having been overrun in the cavalry engagement shortly before the Brunswick contingent had deployed. This left the Duke reliant upon the artillery brought by the British and Hanoverians from Brussels. With the cannonade showing no signs of abating on his part of the line, the toll was mounting and the covering sergeants were constantly bellowing at the young infantrymen and cavalrymen to close ranks. So far, the line had held firm, but for how long?

Eventually, frustrated that his own artillery had still not come up and desperate for some means of responding to the enemy provocation, he sent an officer to the Duke of Wellington, requesting the loan of some British guns. When the messenger arrived at Wellington's command post, Colonel Wood explained that there were only two brigades of artillery in the field. Major Rogers was supporting Picton's left flank, which had been so seriously menaced, whilst Captain von Rettberg's Hanoverian guns had been posted a short distance to the east of the Ferme des Quatre Bras, in support of Pack's brigade. With regret, he said, he had no guns to spare, but undertook to send some, as soon as reinforcements came up. In the meantime, von Rettberg would have to lend what aid he could to provide covering fire.[15]

The cannonade was relentless. Round shot moaned through the rye. Shells arched overhead, their spluttering fuses disappearing into the great iron balls, before detonating and hurling shards of ragged metal across the unfortunate ranks of troops below. In the four acre orchard behind the Ferme des Quatre Bras, hundreds of fruit trees had been smashed, lacerated or cut down by the round shot. Amongst the trees, the ammunition wagons and baggage vehicles were thrown into confusion.[16]

A short distance in advance of the crossroads, the young and inexperienced men of the Brunswick Leib-Battalion, the 1st Line Battalion and the Avantgarde-Battalion, already tormented by the fire of French artillery, were about to undergo an even greater trial. Runners from the skirmish line of the Avantgarde-Battalion came rushing through the rye fields, with word that the French infantry was on the move. Marching steadily through the tall crops on the edge of the Bois de Bossu was a battalion deployed in line, accompanied by what looked like a general officer and his staff. Immediately behind were two more battalions, supported closely by horse artillery. The nervous Brunswick soldiers could hear the wild cheering of the French infantry, though the height of the crops prevented them from seeing their enemy. Accompanied by the brassy din of regimental bands playing *'Veillons au salut de*

The Battle of Quatre Bras

l'Empire', the men in the enemy ranks could be heard belting out the refrain, with its exhortation to defend liberty, overthrow tyrants and protect *'la Patrie'*. They were the same noisy tunes and sanctimonious words that the Duke had fought against for the past nine years, but for the majority of his soldiers, this was their first experience of the battlefield and they awaited the noisy masses in silence, punctuated by the regular shouts of *'Auf geschlossen!'* as the sergeants thumped another unwilling soldier into the gap caused by a 6-pound ball. The cheering was heard by Colonel Frazer at Les Quatre Bras itself and there was speculation amongst Wellington's staff that only the presence of Napoleon himself could be responsible for 'the loud and continued cheering among the French troops'. In support of this infantry, a heavy column of cavalry could also be seen, burnished helmets glittering in the sunshine. Lancers? Cuirassiers? The great distance and the shimmering heat made it difficult to tell.[17]

At the crossroads itself, Lieutenant James Ross was certain they were cuirassiers and there was no doubt in his mind that the French were about to launch a combined-arms assault to seize the road leading to Brussels. Lieutenant Winchester shared his view, firm in the belief that the French were about to try and seize Les Quatre Bras by a *'coup de main'*. A few hundred metres farther forward, perhaps the Duke von Braunschweig-Lüneburg was thinking similar thoughts; if this did prove to be the case, he might find himself hamstrung if he remained in his present position.

The 1st Line Battalion and the Leib-Battalion were formed up between the Charleroi road and the Bois de Bossu, along with elements of the Avantgarde-Battalion. This meant that the Hussar Regiment was hemmed in by a combination of the wood to its rear and its own infantry to the left and front. He hurriedly sent orders for the three squadrons to cross the Charleroi road in order to deploy in the open ground to the east and there await developments. Major von Oeynhausen ordered 'Threes left,' and led the regiment through a gap in the hedge, across the chaussée and into a field to the south of the Ferme de la Bergerie, overlooked by the men of the 92nd Regiment of Foot formed up along the Namur road. By now, the leading French column had reached the right flank of the skirmish line formed by the two light infantry companies of the Avantgarde-Battalion. Weight of numbers began to tell. Slowly, the Brunswick skirmishers in the open ground withdrew through the ranks of the Uhlan Squadron, the companies of Gelernte Jäger in the Bois de Bossu also giving ground for fear of being outflanked.[18]

Once the hussars had moved off, the Duke turned to the Uhlan Squadron under Colonel Pott, whose front was now clear. Placing himself at their head, he led the horsemen forward, through the small gap between the right flank of the Leib-Battalion and the Bois de Bossu, towards the imposing mass of hostile bayonets, who were supported by what could now be clearly identified as a sizeable body of cuirassiers, followed by other mounted troops. With trumpets sounding the charge, the uhlans steadily gained momentum as they crossed the fields of rye, their charge directed at the left flank of the French advance, but as they rapidly closed the short distance, they were subjected to a shower of musketry from the ranks of the leading French battalion.[19]

'The clash of the fixing bayonet'

The presence of this handful of cavalry seemed to paralyse the advancing infantry and the French attack became bogged down as the battalions were forced to form square and drive the uhlans off with volley fire. With a grandstand view of this combat, the Brunswick infantry remained rooted to the spot, grateful for every minute of relief provide by their mounted comrades. Eventually, the patience of the French generals gave out and Pott suddenly found his front obstructed by an advancing line of green-coated *chasseurs à cheval*. Hurriedly disengaging, the Brunswickers sought to make an orderly withdrawal, but the enemy cavalry charged in close pursuit. Major Ferdinand von Metzner and his Adjutant, Captain von Aurich, hurriedly formed the 1st Line Battalion into square and opened a running fire on the French horsemen. A short distance away, Major von Pröstler and Captain von Mosqua carried out the same evolution with the Leib-Battalion and the French cavalry were forced to run a gauntlet of fire as they swept up the field to the gardens, enclosures and buildings to the west of the crossroads. Wellington was on foot at the crossroads at the time the French charged and was busy observing matters through his field glass.

A short distance away, Captain von Gagern was astonished by the brilliance of the enemy cavalry as it charged past, but was wounded shortly afterwards and forced to leave the field. Approaching the crossroads, the horsemen were met by a fusillade from the skirmishers of the 2nd and 3rd Line battalions. Many believed that the French had at last managed to seize Les Quatre Bras, but calmer minds prevailed and the cavalry were subjected to a murderous fire from the Brunswick infantry held in reserve. Hampered by the fences and hedges, forced into enclosures and narrow spaces, isolated French troopers were shot and bayoneted by the vengeful Brunswickers. Where a few moments ago, all had seemed lost, the French now wavered. All they had needed was for their infantry to dash forward and occupy the hamlet and Wellington's centre would be smashed, but the 'fantassins' were advancing at a snail's pace. Alarmed by the numbers of enemy troops in the vicinity, unsupported by their infantry and under a terrific fire from troops concealed in the houses and behind the fences, the French were forced to sound the withdrawal.[20]

With the Hussars already withdrawn to the east of the Charleroi road, the Brunswick battalions between the chaussée and the Bois de Bossu seemed to be all that stood in the way of a French assault on Les Quatre Bras itself. As soon as the uhlans had withdrawn, the French infantry had resumed its advance and was cautiously picking its way through the tall rye, as though expecting to find Allied infantry where there were none. The tirailleurs were soon firing on the 1st Line Battalion and within minutes, the leading French battalion emerged from the gloom and smoke, deployed in line. It immediately fired a thunderous volley into the head of the Brunswick column. Muffled shrieks and screams could be heard in the din as men fell in the dense ranks. Threatened by the presence of the *chasseurs à cheval* to their rear and therefore unable to deploy into line themselves, the Brunswickers could not match the hostile fire and were steadily forced back up the Charleroi road.

Major von Pröstler, aided by the Duke von Braunschweig-Lüneburg, was exerting himself strenuously to ensure that his inexperienced Leib-Battalion also completed

The Battle of Quatre Bras

its withdrawal in an orderly manner. The battalion had crossed the chaussée and was in the fields to the east of the Ferme de la Bergerie, making for the Namur road, but the volume of round shot ploughing through the column, the rapid pursuit by the French infantry and the advance of a body of cuirassiers up the highway, shattered their confidence and reduced the battalion to a disorderly mob. Some fled towards the crossroads, whilst others streamed across the pasture towards the Namur road.[21]

The Duke halted the battalion and was in the process of trying to rally the men when a musket ball struck him and knocked him from his horse. His aide-de-camp, Captain von Lübeck lifted him to the ground, aided by Corporal Külbel, Bugler Aüe and Jager Reckau of the Leib-Battalion. Major Friedrich von Wachholtz, the Deputy Quartermaster-General, hurried across and instructed them to carry the wounded man across the Namur road and behind the lines, lending his own strength to remove the Duke from the immediate danger of the field. Another officer sent a soldier to bring up the Duke's small carriage, thinking him perhaps only slightly wounded, whilst several other officers went off in search of a surgeon. As they carried him off, it became clear that their chief was in a great deal of pain, not only from his injuries and the manner in which he was being carried, but also from the fact that the men kept stumbling on his sash and sabre, which trailed along the ground. Setting him down for a moment, they removed both items and having procured a blanket, wrapped him in it and resumed their journey. A short distance to the north, the group was joined by Sergeant Kreibohm and some stragglers, who were added to the bearer party. The sombre group slowly made its way to the rear, passing the detachment of gunners commanded by Lieutnant Bredenschey and arriving at Maison Paquet, a small, single-storey cottage between Les Quatre Bras and La Baraque.[22]

> Despite the efforts made by several officers, it was not possible to find a surgeon immediately. The deathly pale of his face and his half-closed eyes indicated the worst. He then opened his eyes again, recognising those standing around him, enquired after Colonel Olfermann and asked for some water. However, there was none available at this moment. Rather than take the risk of leaving him to fall into the hands of the enemy in the event of a withdrawal, he was picked up again and carried along the paved road to the next houses, known as La Baracque. Staff Surgeon Dr. Pockels was here. He examined the wound and declared the Duke dead.[23]

It was determined that the Duke's mortal wound was caused by a ball which had passed through his right wrist and into the right side of his torso, just above the hip, before punching through his abdomen, through his liver and lung and exiting on the left hand side of his chest. Such was the end of a son whose father had also paid the ultimate price in challenging French imperial ambitions. When the officer who had ordered the Duke's carriage arrived to find his master dead, he reacted with 'inexpressible sorrow'. Unable to describe his feelings further, his sentiments were shared by every soldier in black and grey. They had lost their father, their leader and their lord. Leaving behind Majors von Grone and von Mahrenholtz to make arrangements for the evacuation of the Duke's remains, the other Brunswick officers returned to the fight.[24]

To the exultant French, it must have seemed that Les Quatre Bras was theirs for the taking; the Brunswick resistance had all but collapsed. Everywhere, panicked infantrymen were streaming away, jostling each other in their bid to reach the perceived safety of the Namur road. Others sought sanctuary with the 2nd and 3rd Line Battalions, still ensconced in the houses to the west of the crossroads. The most desperate made for the rear areas, where they had formed up earlier in the day. By now, French skirmishers were trading shots with the 'scharfschutzen' of the reserve Brunswick battalions over the garden hedges, fences and walls of the hamlet itself. The heat was infernal; the din even worse. From the opposite side of the crossroads, the redcoats of the 92nd Regiment of Foot peered through the dense smoke as the muskets crackled and popped, their balls buzzing through the sulphurous air. Their position had provided them with a grandstand view of proceedings, though as many had expected, the nearby presence of 'Nosey' had attracted much attention from the French artillery. Each battalion must fight or die where it stood. Amongst the throng of Brunswickers, Colonel Olfermann sought to regain control of the shattered Leib-Battalion. Wellington had just appointed him to command the division, but it was in danger of disintegrating before his eyes. As he sought to steady the infantrymen, his two aides, Captains Morgenstern and von Zweifel, helped the Quartermaster-General, Colonel von Heinemann, organise a defensive perimeter to the south-west of the hamlet itself. In an effort to buy time, an urgent order was sent to Major von Oeynhausen to throw the Hussar Regiment into the fray.[25]

To the east of the Charleroi road, in the lee of the heights of Bati-Saint-Bernard, the Brunswick cavalry had taken up a position in the pasture immediately in front of the 92nd Regiment of Foot, somewhat more sheltered than they had been on the opposite side of the road. Aware that the Leib-Battalion had disintegrated, Major von Oeynhausen was making strenuous efforts to keep his own young soldiers steady; the remorseless treatment they had received at the hands of the French artillery and the death of Major von Cramm had demoralised them greatly. Hoping that the men would maintain their nerve, von Oeynhausen turned to his trumpeter and ordered the regiment to march. The jostling column of men and horses started to move diagonally across the field, towards the Charleroi road. Gaining momentum, the three squadrons reached the highway to the south of the Ferme de la Bergerie, extending into the fields to the west of the road. As they passed by, the flank of the column was raked by fire from a French battalion that had advanced to within a short distance of the buildings. The formation staggered, as if encountering some unseen obstacle; men and horses tumbling to the ground in the long rye. Once over the causeway, the horsemen found themselves in the midst of several French battalions, who immediately opened a rolling fire on them. Skirmishers lining the Bois de Bossu joined in with a murderous fire of their own. Finding themselves alone in a sea of infantry, fired on at devastatingly short range by infantry and artillery, the morale of the Brunswickers was at breaking point. Their collective nerve now shattered and without waiting to come to blows, the panicked troopers wheeled their horses about and galloped helter-skelter back towards the crossroads, pursued yet so closely by French cavalry that some nearby Allied infantry took them to be a single body of friendly cavalry retiring.[26]

With the Hussars streaming back to the crossroads, pursued by the French cavalry, the Brunswick infantry in the buildings and gardens of the hamlet were once again thrown into the thick of the fighting. In the ranks of the 3rd Line Battalion was Ensign Anton Kubel:

> We formed only the third line and lost merely a few men and Ensign Diekmann, when suddenly the terrible news arrived that the Duke was badly wounded and had died shortly thereafter. Moreover, several of our battalions were almost annihilated, many of the officers of all ranks dead or wounded, for at that moment the French cuirassiers advanced on us through a village, and in our numbness and anger we would have been killed to the last man had our artillery not just arrived and thrown the enemy back.[27]

On the opposite side of the Charleroi road, the 44th Regiment of Foot had ascended the gentle slope of the heights of Bati-Saint-Bernard, some two hundred metres to the right rear of the 42nd Regiment of Foot. Moving through the pastures to the immediate south of the Namur road, the battalion steadily advanced in a two-deep line, to a point some two hundred metres past the Ferme de la Bergerie and with the Grenadier Company close to the chaussée. Lieutenant-Colonel George O'Malley, the second-in-command of the regiment, was riding alongside General Pack in the rear of his battalion when he suddenly noticed the cavalry on the opposite side of the road sweep past them, towards the crossroads. Though he could make out the black uniforms of the Brunswick Hussars, with their light blue facings and blue and yellow barrelled sashes, there seemed to be other cavalry amongst them. Friendly cavalry? The French? Lieutenant Riddock was convinced they were Belgian. The old soldiers on the right of the battalion, however, were certain that the cavalry was hostile and opened an oblique fire on the horsemen as the jostling mass swept past their flank. General Pack was furious, convinced as he was that the whole of the cavalry constituted Allied horsemen. Colonel Hamerton immediately gave the order to cease firing. The drums beat and the word was passed down the line, but it took some considerable time before the company officers were able to get their men back in order.[28]

Within moments of the cease fire, a part of this mass of cavalry, which O'Malley judged from their appearance to be lancers, wheeled around and rapidly approached the rear of the battalion. Both he and Pack were astonished. The men were confused and frightened. Suddenly, with no warning other than a thundering sensation, they were confronted by a wall of horseflesh, closing the distance at an alarming rate. Towards the west of the line, ferocious French troopers had already got in amongst the skirmishers and hacked, slashed and stabbed at the men as they swept towards

'The clash of the fixing bayonet'

the formed line. Screams rang out as steel clove into flesh and bone and men were bowled to the ground and trampled beneath the flying hooves.[29]

Hamerton could see that to form square would be impossible in the circumstances. The French would be amongst them whilst the companies were still running in, a situation which would leave the soldiers wholly unable to defend themselves or maintain any sort of order and discipline. In his mind, there was but one option and without a moment's hesitation, he bellowed the command: 'Rear rank, right about face!' The order rippled out from the centre of the battalion to the wings and within seconds, the men were back to back, the rear rank men facing the new threat. Lieutenant Riddock was pleased that his men executed the manoeuvre in what he deemed to be a characteristically cool manner. Despite the anxiety, no man lost his nerve. 'Make ready!' came the next order down the line and with a satisfying series of clicks, the muskets were ratcheted to full cock. The tension was unbearable; their commanding officer seemed to be waiting. With each second, the flying hooves came closer. Still no word of command was heard. Suddenly, Colonel Hamerton shouted 'Present,' and several hundred muskets were levelled, before 'Fire!' was repeated down the line and the firearms exploded in a roar as the battalion discharged half its weapons at a target now seemingly within touching distance. So well directed was the fire, felt Lieutenant Riddock, that it appeared few of the lancers had escaped its effects. The leading rank was virtually destroyed. Some of the horses crashed to the ground in a bloody tangle; others wheeled about, rider-less. Wounded troopers fell heavily to the ground, to be trampled by the succeeding ranks. The cavalry swept along the line towards the east, the more valiant individuals amongst them seeking targets of opportunity.[30]

In the centre of the line, James Christie, the senior ensign, was standing with the rest of the regiment's colour party, ready to defend the King's colour. Christie was an unusual phenomenon in the regiment and the army as a whole, having been promoted from Sergeant-Major in November 1812; a very experienced soldier, he would prove a redoubtable opponent. Suddenly, a grizzled lancer made an enterprising dash at the colour escort. As he came up to Christie, he lunged forward with his lance, almost three metres long, and drove the wicked point downwards into Christie's left eye with such force, that the tip skewered the officer's tongue and emerged below his jaw, the victim's blood saturating the lance's fluttering red and white pennant. As Christie slumped to the ground, the colour fell beneath him and the weight of his body pulled the lance from his assailant's grasp. Determined to secure his prize, the lancer stooped from his saddle and seized the bottom corner of the flag, trying to wrest it from Christie's hands, but succeeded only in tearing off a small triangle of the silk. Spurring his horse to get clear of the infantry, he was shot a few yards away and, tumbling from his horse, bayoneted for good measure, paying with his life for his intrepid attempt.[31]

The remaining horsemen, severely mauled by the brutal fusillade, careered along the length of the line, until they came to the Light Company. Captain Adam Brugh, its commander, had disregarded Hamerton's earlier order to fire, no doubt judging that the French were too distant at the time that it was given, but that they would pass along his company's front only a few seconds later. With muskets loaded and made ready, his men poured a devastating volley into the flank of the French horsemen as they dashed past; they were joined by the men on the left flank of the front rank, who emptied yet more saddles as the French sought to regain their own lines.[32]

A short distance to the south-east, Corporal McEween of the 42nd Regiment of Foot emerged into the open ground, just south of the chemin Bati-Saint-Bernard, overlooking the Ferme de Gemioncourt. The long line of the battalion stretched across the fields. It had taken them barely fifteen minutes to drive back the French infantry. A little to his right and in rear of the battalion, he too could make out some lancers appearing quietly and assumed they were a reconnaissance party, though he quickly changed his mind. Turning to his commanding officer, he shouted: 'Those are French lancers!' and received in reply the assurance that they belonged to the Prince van Oranje-Nassau. McEween was not about to be fobbed off, having been made prisoner by similarly-uniformed men in the Peninsula. Mistaking the faded red facing colours of the 6th Regiment of Chevau-Légers-Lanciers, he insisted that they were the 3rd Regiment, whose rose facings he recollected well from his time as their captive. Seeing that his warnings were having no effect, he obtained Lieutenant George Munro's agreement instead to fire a round at them in order to provoke a response and no sooner had McEween fired, than the lancers began to move in their direction.[33]

Sergeant Anton, had until now been far too busy herding the French infantry down the slope to notice the cavalry advancing, but gradually he and the remainder of the battalion became aware of its presence. On account of the Charleroi road being slightly elevated from the fields to either side, the horsemen appeared to have come from the Bois de Bossu. Though closer than Corporal McEween, he could not distinguish their identity and took them for Brunswickers, moving up to pursue the broken French infantry. Even the battalion's skirmishers, extended on the right of the formation did not appear unduly alarmed; indeed Major Campbell must have been of the same opinion, since he gave the order for the company to halt and give way to the horsemen. Gradually the shouts and cheers died down as the Highlanders advance petered out and an uneasy silence descended on the ranks:[34]

> They were approaching our right flank, from which our skirmishers were extended and we were far from being in a formation fit to repel an attack, if intended, or to afford regular support to our friends if requiring our aid. I think we stood with too much confidence, gazing towards them as if they had been our friends, anticipating the gallant charge they would make on the flying foe and were making no preparative movement to receive them as enemies, further than the reloading of the muskets, until a German orderly dragoon galloped up, exclaiming, 'Franchee! Franchee!' and, wheeling about, galloped off.[35]

The battalion had remained in line since advancing through the fields, but this was no formation in which to receive enemy cavalry. Nor was there time for the niceties of a conventional 'square'. The skirmishers ran in, shouting: 'Square! Square! French cavalry!' Realising the implications, Anton and the other experienced men instinctively began running in to form a rallying square, a dense thicket of men, bristling with bayonets. Those who had fired on the French infantry and had, as yet, found no opportunity to reload, were now frantically ramming home another ball with trembling hands, anxious lest any sweat drip into the priming pan and render their principal means of defence useless.[36]

The cavalry had gathered momentum and the horses' hooves were tearing up great divots of earth before entering the tall rye and mowing down the crops beneath an irresistible wall of horseflesh. Their ranks seemed to wheel to the left as they aligned themselves with their intended target. Here and there, Highlanders scurried, desperate to reach the sanctuary of the square. As the infantry jostled each other, or tumbled over the tangled stalks of wheat and rye, the horsemen reached the gallop, closing the distance rapidly as though sensing that a spectacular victory was within their grasp. The front face of the square had been successfully formed by No. 4 and No. 5 companies and the sides were largely complete, but there was a gaping hole in the rear of the formation, where the Grenadier and Light Companies should have been. Formed on the extremities of the line, these two companies had the furthest distance to cover to their post, yet with an irony so prevalent in warfare, they were responsible for that part of the human rampart closest to the enemy assault.[37]

Time had finally run out for Macara's men. Sweeping forward, the leading French squadron ran down the skirmishers and crashed into the confused mêlée of the flank companies, the leading rank spearing the helpless Highlanders at every turn, before the second rank drove into the mass of struggling men, hacking and stabbing at the unfortunate infantry. Their momentum carried some of the horsemen into the heart of the incomplete square, mingled with their hapless victims. The press of the scrum was tremendous. Recognising the absolute priority of closing the ranks, the officers and sergeants ignored the chaotic scenes in the centre and shouted orders for No. 1 and No. 8 companies to wheel back and form an improvised rear face. The men retired step by step, their packs pressing back the throng at the heart of the formation. Eventually, after a titanic effort of pushing and shoving, often aided by blows from the sergeants and corporals, the lancers and the remnants of the Grenadier and Light Companies were hemmed into the centre. Somewhere in the confusion, a French officer had been dismounted and as he struggled to regain his feet, he was attacked by a Highland sergeant, wielding a spontoon. Crying out 'Quarter! Quarter!' the only word of English he knew, the sergeant replied 'Och, och inteet, she's no' going to put you in quarters at aal, at aal, put shust in twa halves, inteet!' Cut off from their comrades, one by one the French horsemen were dismounted, bayoneted or shot at close quarters, until the only survivors, like the officer, were disarmed and taken prisoner.[38]

Outside the square, quarter was neither being requested nor given. Captain Archibald Menzies was fighting for his life in the midst of the wreckage of his Grenadier Company. He had decided to fight on foot and had left his charger in the

The Battle of Quatre Bras

care of one of the company's drummers. A powerful man, he stood just short of two metres tall, even without his impressive feather bonnet and was a natural target for the French lancers. Charged by several horsemen at once, he defended himself with his claymore and managed to kill or wound several of them, receiving seventeen wounds in return. A short distance away, Private Donald McIntosh was also in the thick of the action and fell to the ground, severely wounded. Seeing his plight, the drummer abandoned Menzies' horse and dashed forward to try and help him. As he did so, a French lancer galloped up and seeing the unattended animal, attempted to seize it as a prize. Private McIntosh shouted: 'Hoot man, ye manna tak that beast 't belongs to our captain here!' Ignoring the injured soldier, the French trooper continued his attempt to make off with the animal and McIntosh, using all his remaining energy, loaded his musket a final time and shot him dead. Weakened from loss of blood, Menzies himself had by now collapsed to the ground, but a French officer, still detecting signs of life, stooped from his saddle, in an attempt to run him through with his sword. Menzies, summoning the last of his strength, grappled with the Frenchman, seized his leg and managed to pull him from his horse. A nearby lancer, witnessing the struggle, came to assist his superior and jabbed his lance towards Menzies who, by a sudden jerk, contrived to manhandle the fallen officer in such a way that he and not Menzies, received the fatal blow. For ten minutes, Menzies lay pinned down under the weight of the Frenchman, gripping him tightly to prevent him using his sword, unaware that his adversary was already dying. Eventually, exhausted, he released his grip and his mortally wounded enemy raised himself from the ground, staggered a few yards and fell for a final time.[39]

Not far away, Colonel Macara was also wounded and disabled, having been caught in the open outside the square by a lancer. As the horsemen swept by, a party of four men were ordered to wrap him in a blanket and evacuate him to the rear; they had gone but a short distance, when they were ridden down by another party of lancers and killed out of hand. Seeing from Macara's bullion epaulettes and the embroidered star of a Knight Commander of the Order of the Bath, they finished off the defenceless officer at the same time, a lance being skewered through his chin and into his brain. When word was passed that Macara had been rendered hors de combat, Lieutenant-Colonel Robert Dick, awarded the gold medal at Busaco, Fuentes d'Oñoro and Salamanca, assumed the command, only to be wounded himself moments later. With Captain Menzies already severely wounded, Major George Davidson took control, before he too was wounded and command passed to Major Campbell. Menzies and Campbell seemed destined to share an unfortunate fate; they had both been wounded at the storming of Burgos in September 1812.[40]

Oblivious to the niceties of regimental and army seniority, Sergeant Anton was directing his men, whose rhythmic musketry was pouring an immense amount of fire into the French cavalry. The atmosphere was stiflingly hot, the smoke stinging his eyes and severely limiting his field of vision. Some of the lancers, aiming at the officers, hurled their weapons with considerable precision, reluctant to drive their horses onto the points of the glinting bayonets. Finally, the remaining lancers were driven off and one by one, the muskets fell silent as the drums and whistles signalled to cease firing. Men slumped, breathless and exhausted, their ears ringing with the sound of musketry and assaulted by the screams of the wounded and dying.[41]

Captain Menzies' plight had been noticed by one of his men in the ranks of the square and he rushed across and asked the wounded officer if there was anything he could do to assist him. 'Nothing, my good fellow,' replied Menzies, 'But load your piece and finish me.' The soldier was not so easily persuaded and said, 'But your eye still looks lively. If I could move you to the 92nd, fighting hard by, I think you would yet do well.' Calling across another soldier, the pair of them moved Menzies as gently as they could, struggling across the fields until they arrived at the Ferme des Quatre Bras. As they passed the Gordons, Colonel Cameron, to whom Menzies was well known, recognised his terribly injured friend. Summoning four of his own men, he ordered them to carry the casualty in a blanket to the field in rear of the farm and directed the two Black Watch men to rejoin their battalion. Turning to Menzies as he was about to be carried off, Cameron said, 'God bless you. I must be off. The devils are at us again. I must stand up to them.'[42]

Endnotes

1. Caldwell and Cooper, pp. 10–11. Costello, pp. 151–2.
2. Costello, p. 152.
3. Costello, p. 152. Fitzmaurice, p. 50. von Herzberg.
4. Anonymous (Near Observer), pp. 46–7. Cope, p. 198. von Herzberg. Leach, p. 375.
5. Cope, pp. 198–9. Costello, p. 152.
6. Anonymous (Waterloo Medal Roll), p. 318. Costello, p. 152. Dalton, pp. 197, 200.
7. Allan. Anonymous (Cameron), p. 90. Archibald Forbes (II). Mackenzie &c., p. 56. Vallence.
8. Anton, p. 190. Brett-James, p. 58. Campbell. Malcolm.
9. Anton, pp. 190–1. Malcolm.
10. Anton, p. 191. Brett-James, p. 58. Fitchett, p. 291. Malcolm.
11. Campbell.
12. Anton, p. 193. Campbell. Hope (II).
13. Anton, p. 191. Brett-James, p. 58. Campbell.
14. Anton, p. 191.
15. Anonymous (Das braunschweigische Korps). von Herzberg. Rudyerd. W. Siborne (II). W. Siborne (V), p. 77. Traupe, pp. 15–16. von Wachholtz, pp. 27–9. Wells. Winchester (III). Winchester (IV).
16. Anonymous (Account), p. 77. Anonymous (Near Observer), p. 77.
17. Anonymous (Near Observer), p. 77. Arcq, p. 70. de Bas &c., p. 401. Delhaize and Aerts, p. 445. von Herzberg. Houssaye, p. 115. Jolyet. Reille. Ross (II). W. Siborne (V), pp. 76–8. von Wachholtz, pp. 27–9.

The Battle of Quatre Bras

18. Anonymous (Das braunschweigische Korps). de Bas &c., p. 401. Archibald Forbes, p. 267. von Herzberg. J. Ross (II). W. Siborne (V), p. 77. von Wachholtz, pp. 27–9. Winchester (III).
19. Anonymous (Das braunschweigische Korps). Arcq, p. 70. Delhaize and Aerts, pp. 445–7. Archibald Forbes, p. 267. Gomm (IV). Henckens, p. 229. von Herzberg. Houssaye, p. 115. Langenstrasse. van Noeyen, pp. 23–4. von Pivka (II), p. 21. J. Ross (II). W. Siborne (V), p. 77. Traupe, pp. 15–16. von Wachholtz, pp. 27–30.
20. Henckens, p. 229.
21. Anonymous (Near Observer, pp. 62–3, 77). Delhaize and Aerts, pp. 445–7. Archibald Forbes, p. 267. Gunn. Henckens, p. 229. von Herzberg. van Noeyen, p. 24. W. Siborne (V), pp. 77–8. Traupe, pp. 15–18. von Wachholtz, pp. 27–9.
22. Anonymous (Das braunschweigische Korps). Anonymous (Journal), pp. 381–2. Anonymous (Near Observer), p. 77. Arcq, p. 70. Arthur, p. 597. de Bas &c., p. 515. Cathcart. Crummer (II). Delhaize and Aerts, pp. 445–7. Döring. Hellemann. von Herzberg. Houssaye, p. 115. Jackson (II), pp. 18–19. Kincaid (I), p. 319. Langenstrasse. Leach, p. 376. van Noeyen, p. 24. Olfermann. Ross-Lewin, p. 261. von Sachsen-Weimar (I). W. Siborne (V), p. 78. F. Somerset, p. 9. von Wachholtz, pp. 27–9.
23. Anonymous (Das braunschweigische Korps). Anonymous (Near Observer), p. 72. Batty, p. 52. Brett-James, p. 55. Delhazie and Aerts, pp. 445–7. Kincaid (I), p. 319. Langenstrasse. van Noeyen, p. 24. Olfermann. von Pflugk-Harttung (II), p. 26. W. Siborne (V), p. 78. von Wachholtz, pp. 27–9.
24. Anonymous (Das braunschweigische Korps). Anonymous (Letters), pp. 239–40. Anonymous (Near Observer), pp. 72, 77. Arcq, p. 70. de Bas &c., p. 515. Delhaize and Aerts, pp. 445–7. Frazer, p. 540. Gurwood, pp. 490–1. Hellemann. von Herzberg. Houssaye, p. 115. van Noeyen, p. 24. Olfermann. von Sachsen-Weimar (I). W. Siborne (V), p. 78. von Wachholtz, pp. 27–9. Wildman.
25. Anonymous (Das braunschweigische Korps). Anonymous (Letters), p. 226. Anonymous (Near Observer), pp. 62–3. von Herzberg. Olfermann.
26. Anonymous (Letters), p. 226. Anonymous (Near Observer), pp. 62–3. Batty, pp. 48–9. Cornford and Walker, p. 105. Creevey, p. 231. Delhaize and Aerts, p. 447. Archibald Forbes, p. 267. Frazer, p. 540. Gomm (IV). Henckens, p. 229. Langenstrasse. Leach, p. 376. de Mauduit (Volume II), p. 150. McEween. von Müffling (I), p. 5. O'Malley. Robertson, p. 146. J. Ross (II). W. Siborne (V), p. 78. F. Somerset, p. 9. von Wachholtz, pp. 27–9. Winchester (I).
27. Kubel.
28. Anonymous (42nd Regiment), p. 143. Carter, p. 94. Archibald Forbes, p. 269. McEween. O'Malley. Riddock. W. Siborne (V), p. 79.
29. Carter, p. 94. O'Malley. Riddock. W. Siborne (V), p. 79.
30. Carter, pp. 93–4. Archibald Forbes, p. 269. O'Malley. Riddock. W. Siborne (V), p. 79. Surtees, p. 73.
31. de Bas &c., pp. 514–5. Bukhari, p. 33. Carter, p. 94. Cornford and Walker, p. 106. Archibald Forbes, p. 269. Haythornthwaite (V). O'Malley. Riddock. W. Siborne (V), pp. 80–1. Surtees, p. 73.

32. Anonymous (Waterloo Medal Roll), pp. 243, 245. Carter, pp. 86, 94–5. Archibald Forbes, p. 269. Houssaye, p. 116. de Mauduit (Volume II), p. 152. W. Siborne (V), p. 80.
33. Anonymous (42nd Regiment), p. 142. Anonymous (Waterloo Medal Roll), p. 239. de Bas &c., pp. 514–5. Bukhari, p. 24. McEween. O'Malley.
34. Anton, p. 192. Brett-James, pp. 58–9. Ross-Lewin, p. 258. Wauchope, p. 48.
35. Anton, pp. 192–3.
36. Anonymous (42nd Regiment), p. 143. Anton, pp. 192–3. Batty, p. 49. Brett-James, p. 59. Cornford and Walker, pp. 105–6. Grant and Youens, p. 22. Malcolm. McEween.
37. Anonymous (42nd Regiment), p. 142. Anton, pp. 192–3. Brett-James, p. 59. Cornford and Walker, pp. 105–6. Archibald Forbes, p. 268. Grant and Youens, p. 22. Malcolm. Wauchope, p. 48.
38. Anonymous (42nd Regiment), p. 143. Anonymous (Cameron), p. 89. Cathcart. Cornford and Walker, pp. 105–6. Archibald Forbes, pp. 268–9. Gomm (IV). Grant and Youens, p. 22. P. Howard, pp. 52–3. Malcolm. McEween. Mudie (I). Ross-Lewin, p. 258.
39. Anonymous (McKenzie Papers). Anton, p. 193. Brett-James, p. 59. Haythornthwaite (I), p. 118. P. Howard, p. 53.
40. Anonymous (42nd Regiment), p. 143. Anonymous (Cameron), p. 89. Anonymous (Journal), pp. 382–3. Anton, p. 193. Batty, p. 53. Bowden, p. 251. Brett-James, p. 59. Cornford and Walker, p. 106. Dalton, p. 158. Dick. Archibald Forbes, p. 269. Grant and Youens, p. 22. Gunn. Ross-Lewin, p. 258.
41. Anton, p. 193. Brett-James, p. 59.
42. Anonymous (McKenzie Papers).

CHAPTER 14

Although the 44th and 42nd Regiments of Foot had borne the brunt of the charge by the French lancers, succeeding squadrons had swept through Picton's position and fallen upon the isolated battalions. The Royals had seen the Black Watch attempt to form square in the distance and as Lieutenant-Colonel Colin Campbell bellowed the command: 'Prepare to receive cavalry!' several squadrons could be seen bursting through the intervals between the 42nd and 44th Regiments of Foot, wheeling slightly to the north and pounding across the spine of the ridge towards his own position. His regiment, known as 'Pontius Pilate's Bodyguard', on account of a legend that Caledonian legionaries had guarded the tomb of Christ, was composed of many troops whose military service had commenced considerably later. Having fought at Salamanca, participated in the retreat from Burgos and shared in the glory of the battle of Vitoria, the climactic action of the Peninsular campaign, the thinned ranks had been supplemented with new recruits and drafts from the militia. In the scramble to prepare the battalion for active service, the depot had been emptied of every able-bodied soldier and shipped to Belgium. The reconstructed battalion was about to face its first trial and as the hostile horsemen swept across the ground towards them, the weeks of training, drill and target practice paid off. On the Colonel's command, a deafening roar erupted from the solid ranks, spewing a cloud of dirty smoke in the direction of the French, whose ranks were staggered by the shower of bullets. To the young soldiers in the front ranks, the kaleidoscope of colour and the cacophony of noise mingled with the stench of powder, sweat and horses. In the blink of an eye, the cavalry were gone, the ragged squadrons galloping onwards.

Major Ross-Lewin and the 32nd Regiment of Foot were formed up in column on the Namur road when officers posted on the embankment caught sight of the advance of the French cavalry and Colonel Hicks gave the precautionary order to form square. As the depleted squadrons swept towards them, their ranks dreadfully thinned and in considerable disorder, the infantry completed their square, a short distance to the south of the chaussée. In contrast, Colonel Best had led his brigade towards the Namur road. A little to the north of the highway, he had posted the Hanoverian Lüneburg and Osterode Landwehr Battalions in a skirmish line and these added the weight of their own fire to that of Picton's redcoats. Indeed, as the French horsemen approached, Lieutenant-Colonel von Ramdohr allowed them to close to within thirty paces of the

'Some had the audacity to draw their swords'

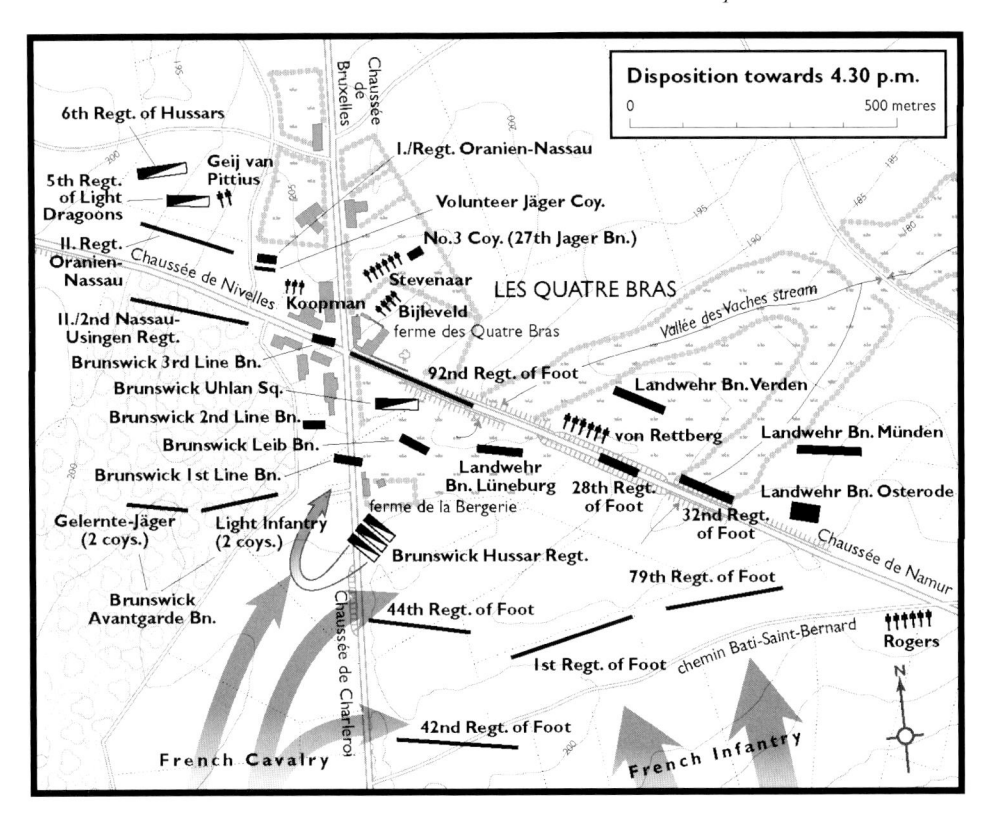

Lüneburg Landwehr Battalion, before driving them off with a murderous volley. The second battalion of the Regiment Oranien-Nassau also moved from its position to the north-east of the crossroads and took up ground on Best's right. The 79th Regiment of Foot slowly moved to the south of the Namur road and marched steadily once more into the open ground, churned up with cannon balls and littered with the dead and dying. Like a gigantic game of chess, each potential enemy move was countered by the Allies. To Lieutenant Forbes, it seemed as though each battalion had become an island in the sea of rye, independent of any other and adopting measures suited to its defence alone. There no longer seemed to be any cohesion in the deployment of the brigade. Gaps were beginning to open up, alignments disregarded and intervals ignored. It appeared as though the exhausted defenders could no longer mount an offensive action of their own, but were merely soaking up the punishment being meted out by the French and reacting breathlessly to everything that the enemy had thrown at them. The charge petered out, the horsemen once more turning to the south, to reform and renew their probing advances. At least, thought the tired infantry, the French battalions – still ranged in columns at the foot of the slope – were receiving a decided beating from Captain Rogers' 9-pounder guns. With a throaty roar the cannon spewed forth death into the densely packed Gallic ranks, the guns bucking on the carriages as the weary crews prepared for the next salvo. Unwilling to take on the shreds of the British infantry at the top of the slope and trapped without cover in the open fields, the French suffered terribly.[1]

The Battle of Quatre Bras

Towards 4.00 p.m., Colonel Belson galloped up the 28th Regiment of Foot and resumed the command. Shortly afterwards, a staff officer rode through the gloom and called out: 'What regiment?' Perhaps he was inexperienced, or his view was obscured by the thickness of the smoke, because the 28th was one of the most distinctive line infantry regiments in the entire British army, retaining the old 'stovepipe' shako, to the rear of which was affixed the 'back badge', awarded in commemoration of its services at Alexandria in 1801. 'The 28th,' he answered proudly. 'Who commands?' the staff officer enquired. 'Colonel Belson,' was the response. The formalities over, the messenger relayed his orders. 'Colonel Belson, form square and take up 42nd ground.' In an instant the battalion was in formation, the Colonel and colours in the centre. Maintaining its order, the square moved, crab-like, across the field to where the heaps of dead and dying bodies marked where the Black Watch had been virtually destroyed. Suddenly, a rushing sound was heard coming through the standing rye and shortly afterwards, a galloping wave of French lancers burst into view, lances couched low, sabres extended. The young men in the ranks of the North Gloucesters could feel the tonnage of horseflesh by the pounding of hooves on the ground and silently gripped their firelocks as the line of shouting cavaliers bore down on them. When it seemed the enemy were almost on them, Belson gave the command to fire and a single volley crashed out, shattering the impetus of the charge. Horses reared and men fell to the ground, whilst others wheeled about, eager to distance themselves from the murderous fusillade. No sooner had the leading squadron been driven off, than subsequent ones charged, their progress impeded by the writhing bodies of horses and troopers. To the men in the compact square, it seemed as though the charges were endless and that the ever-present whirl of cavalry just beyond their bayonets could not be withstood for ever.[2]

As one wave receded, General Kempt himself galloped up and waving his hat, shouted above the din, 'Bravo, 28th! The 28th are still the 28th and their conduct this day will never be forgotten.' Some flushed with pride. Others focused on the practical matters of reloading or keeping the hedge of bayonets intact. In the rear of the ranks, covering sergeants prowled, shouting words of encouragement. Suddenly, another charge was observed and the solid red line parted to allow General Kempt access to the interior, where the officers, drummers, colours and wounded sheltered within the human walls. Yet another volley crashed out and the French were driven back. Sensing the moment was right, Kempt ordered Belson to deploy the battalion into line and with three cheers, the two Knights Commander of the Order of the Bath led them in a bayonet charge against the retreating enemy.[3]

At the same time as General Picton had sent the messenger to Colonel Belson to take up ground to the right, he sent a second messenger across the Namur road to Colonel Best, ordering him to bring forward one of his battalions to replace the 28th Regiment of Foot in the front line. The Verden Landwehr Battalion advanced to the attack with its first company extended in a skirmishing line, which was joined a short time later by the second and third companies. Between them, the three companies managed to drive the French infantry back to a hedge, over which a fire fight ensued. Continuing to advance beyond this point, just over sixty men of the second company, led by Lieutenant von der Horst, Ensign Plate and Ensign Kotzebue, were surrounded and fell into enemy hands. Replacing them immediately in the firing line with further reinforcements, Major Christoph von der Decken managed to maintain his position, despite his men being inexperienced in this type of fighting. Stood, as they were, in an open field and exposed to a galling fire from the French tirailleurs, who were themselves under the cover of the hedge and some bushes, the Hanoverians found the experience very testing, but maintained their order. Other battalions of the brigade now entered the fray and were soon suffering a similar fate; a short distance away, Lieutenant Waegener and Lieutenant Jenisch of the Osterode Landwehr Battalion were shot. Frustrated at not being able to drive the French off by firepower alone, Lieutenant Hurtzig led an assault on the French position, which cost the Hannoverians severely. Lieutenant Hinüber fell, mortally wounded. Ensign Best, attached from the King's German Legion also fell and the gallant band were forced to pull back in order to avoid being outflanked by the French. The combat ebbed and flowed across the slopes.[4]

Meanwhile, Ensign Charles Mudie, was riding up to his own regiment, the Royal Scots, having earlier been tasked with depositing a large sum of money at Brussels. He had little opportunity to note the chaotic scenes, before his battalion was also committed:

> Sir Thomas Picton called out an old Peninsula battalion (3rd Battalion Royals) and, reminding them of their former deeds, led them in person away to the left, to attack a French column which threatened to turn it. This regiment deployed as usual (Picton's favourite theory and practice) and, giving a volley, rushed to the charge. The column was dispersed, and the gallant corps, being with difficulty brought back, was thanked by Sir Thomas in very handsome terms, and promised they should be publicly noted for their good conduct – his death prevented it. It was a bloody affair for those engaged and their troubles were not yet over; the French formed columns and other bodies of attack, under shelter of some very tall rye, with which the fields were covered at the time, and dashed out upon the poor Fifth Division, which, however, stood its ground manfully.[5]

Despite having beaten back the French columns, the Royals were once again subjected to the attentions of French tirailleurs, hidden in the rye and wheat, who took every opportunity to pepper the scarlet ranks with musketry. Through the gloom, the French guns continued to fire on them, the round shot moaning as they passed through the densely packed ranks. One projectile missed the head of one of the young ensigns bearing the colours by a matter of inches, its passage stunning him to such an extent that he lost consciousness, fell to the ground and was left for dead. The colour was wrested from his grasp by the covering colour sergeant and another young officer detailed to its defence. All along the line, men were falling in similar vein. How long could this continue?[6]

Close to the crossroads, Colonel Cameron was about to come under attack from the French cavalry that had bypassed Pack's brigade and had pressed the Brunswick Hussars back up the Charleroi road. All around him was the wreckage of the Brunswick division, the majority of which seemed to be on the verge of disintegration. The two infantry battalions that had fled back across the Namur and Nivelles roads were in such a shambles that they would need considerable time to regroup. The Brunswick battalions posted in the buildings about the crossroads were similarly shaky, having seen their leader dragged to the rear, mortally wounded. The 'Schwarzer Schar' had been decapitated.[7]

Cameron's own men, formed in a four-deep line, were the only steady Allied infantry available that had yet to be committed; the last line of defence in front of the crossroads, the evident target of the French assault. Wellington, dismounted in rear of the regiment with his staff, was of the same opinion and suggested that Cameron form an elongated 'square,' by wheeling his two flank companies back to form the east and west faces, using the garden wall as a makeshift northern face. There was little time left. The Brunswick Hussars, closely pursued by cuirassiers came galloping towards the crossroads. Cameron ordered Captain Campbell to wheel back the Grenadier Company, so that it formed at right-angles to the remainder of the battalion, which lined the ditch on the south side of the Namur road. Immediately afterwards, instructions were passed to these men in the ditches: on the Colonel's word of command, those that could were to open an oblique fire on the flank of the pursuing French horsemen. Until then, they were to remain under cover of the ditch, hidden from view. Muskets were loaded and cocked.

The long scarlet line held its collective breath as the broken Brunswick Hussars galloped pell-mell back towards the crossroads. The Duke of Wellington and his staff tried to bar the path of the fleeing horsemen as they eddied past, but their efforts were in vain. Heedless of rank, personage, command or threat, the panicked troopers nonetheless streamed back, masking the approach of the enterprising Frenchmen, who charged into the chaotic multitude. Appreciating they were now in real danger of being killed or made prisoner, Wellington and his officers immediately spurred their mounts towards the crossroads, pursued vigorously by the enemy. Their horses lathered with exertion, the French were determined not to let so rich a prize slip from their grasp and gouged the flanks of their horses with their spurs to coax the extra fraction of energy needed for glory. As the infantry surveyed the spectacle, 'Nosey' himself frantically gestured and shouted at them to lie down. Fortunately, Cameron understood his intent and gave the order for the battalion to crouch in the bottom of the ditch. Almost immediately afterwards, Wellington and his horse soared over their heads and clattered onto the roadway, followed by the horses of his staff. Almost as soon as they had passed, the Colonel shouted the order to 'Present.' The men stumbled to their feet and a long line of muskets were levelled at the approaching mêlée of horsemen, now almost on the point of their bayonets. The French troopers hacked at the Brunswickers, who desperately fought back with edge, pommel and guard, straining every nerve and sinew to preserve themselves from a fatal blow.[8]

'Some had the audacity to draw their swords'

Though the regiment had ceased to exist as a fighting unit, individual hussars displayed the spirit and loathing for the French that had animated their master. One officer of the 92nd Regiment of Foot, posted on the Namur road, witnessed such an example:

> One of his [the Duke von Braunschweig-Lüneburg's] soldiers was dismounted a little way in front of the 92nd Regiment, to which he fled for refuge. But before he attained his object, the Highland infantry had got orders to fire on the enemy's cavalry. Placed between the two fires, and not more than ten yards from us, he naturally enough thought that he was to be blown to pieces. He screamed dreadfully. His cries attracted the attention of our men, who called to him to come behind the bank. Having done so, his first salutation was, 'Oh! Comrades, my Prince be killed. My horse be killed by de French devils; but (drawing his pistols), 'Gott damn them, I have my pistols and my sword yet!'[9]

The mingled press of men and horses had swept up the road and was less than thirty paces from the grenadiers near the main gate of the Ferme des Quatre Bras when Wellington gave the command to present. With the front rank kneeling to form an impervious hedge of bayonets, the third rank took a half-step to the side and levelled their muskets in the interval between the files of the second rank. As soon as the bulk of the Brunswick fugitives had cleared the line, Cameron yelled the order, 'Fire!' and the air was rent by the crash of a volley into the flank of the pursuing cuirassiers, the heavy balls thudding into the yielding flesh of men and beasts. At such a short range, the iron cuirasses and helmets could not withstand the muzzle velocity of the musket balls and unless the bullets struck only a glancing blow, they punched through the metal, making a sound not dissimilar to that of hailstones on a pane of glass. In the hopeless confusion, some Brunswickers also fell victim to this fusillade and within seconds, the chaussée was littered with a writhing tangle of harness and horseflesh, the slaughter creating a gap into which the succeeding French squadron stumbled and was raked by musketry in its turn. Lieutenant Ross felt great sympathy for the Brunswick Hussars on account of the invidious position in which they had been placed; such was the misfortune and horror of war:[10]

> The cuirassiers having, in their charge, got amongst the Belgian cavalry, it was not of the power of the 92nd to refrain from firing one moment longer than it did, its own safety depending on its steadiness and the effects of its volley, as its formation at the time was a critical one to be charged by cavalry, viz., in line. Indeed the men were in the ditch that ran along the side of the road, having been ordered to take advantage of it before the cavalry came on and having been exposed to a severe cannonade, the enemy not being near enough for musket shots. Some of the Allied cavalry did fall at the time we gave the volley to the cuirassiers.[11]

Unaware of the carnage created behind them, or perhaps careless of it, some cuirassiers dashed through the hamlet, cutting down the stragglers, the walking wounded

The Battle of Quatre Bras

and the supernumeraries. The drivers of the carts and wagons parked to the north of the crossroads turned their teams around and fled for Brussels. Those horsemen that had remained at the crossroads met with less success. In the compressed space between the buildings, hampered by human and equine carcasses and with their horses skidding on the cobbles, the rearmost squadrons faltered. Musket balls from the nearby Gordon Highlanders and the Brunswick infantry in the houses and gardens, were punching through helmets and cuirasses. Having met with such a reception at a point where they had anticipated easy pickings and cheap glory, the fragile confidence of some of the horsemen gave way to panic; they clattered out of the farm buildings, only to be shot down by Cameron's grenadiers. Wheeling around, encouraging tired horses to find one last surge of energy, the troopers jabbed their spurs into weary flanks and cantered back down the road to the safety of the Ferme de la Bergerie, where they reformed the confused ranks and licked their wounds.[12]

Once the wave of armoured cavalry had receded, the Duke of Wellington and his staff, joined by Cameron's mounted officers, kept a keen watch on further developments. The cuirassiers were forming up once again into their respective troops and squadrons, evidently preparing for another attempt on the crossroads. The insistent sound of French trumpeters blowing the recall gradually emptied Les Quatre Bras of riders, save for those lifeless forms now carpeting the cobbles, or pinned beneath half a ton of quivering horseflesh. Under the observant eyes of their adversaries, the French gradually restored order and were reinforced by the arrival of a body of *chasseurs à cheval,* who formed up on their left.[13]

Maintaining the discipline that had made them the victors at Eylau, eight years before, the sparkling lines of horsemen once again launched themselves up the slope, this time across the trampled crops and through the pasture immediately to the south of the 92nd Regiment of Foot, where Ensign Gronow, General Picton's honorary aide-de-camp, only just managed to escape them on account of the superior speed of his Tattersall's mount; some cuirassiers coming to within thirty metres of him. Realising that the frontage of the French attack was narrower than that of the Highlanders, the Duke of Wellington ordered the left wing to fire obliquely to the right and the right wing to do likewise to the left; creating a convergent funnel of fire into which the unsuspecting French would gallop. With the battle at crisis-point and with little he could do until the arrival of desperately-sought reinforcements, Wellington had reverted to type as the commanding officer of an infantry battalion, a role he had first fulfilled over twenty years before. Amid the confusion, Wellington shouted: 'Ninety-Second, 'Don't fire until I tell you!' The word was quickly passed down the line to ensure that those deafened by the clamour understood the intention. Whilst the Scots checked their flints one last time, the ground shook as over a thousand horsemen, swords and sabres extended, charged up the slope, yelling *'Vive l'Empereur!'* It seemed to Sergeant Robertson, watching the spectacle from the covering file of the battalion, as though it was impossible to miss such huge men, mounted on such massive horses. When the leading rank was a matter of metres away, Wellington gave to order to fire and a volley crashed out, bringing down dozens of horses and riders. To Lieutenant Winchester, the volley seemed to claim an immense number of victims and he could not help admiring the courage of such an intrepid enemy. Colonel Frazer, immediately behind the infantry, thought that the cuirassiers were 'The finest fellows I ever saw', and was astonished at their boldness, riding into the very teeth of the infantry.[14]

The rattle of musketry filled the air. Leading from the front, as was their wont, the French officers suffered accordingly, animals and men being brought to ground. Beautiful chargers became nothing more than expensive carcasses as they fell, riddled with bullets. Dismounted horsemen seized the empty reins of rider-less horses, as they milled about in the confusion, whinnying with fear. *Chasseurs à cheval* swept around the right of the 92nd Regiment of Foot and once more imagined themselves masters of the crossroads. John Stewart, Assistant Surgeon of the Gordons was dressing a wounded soldier close to the farm, when he was felled by a blow from a sword which cut his bonnet in two. Other troopers managed to penetrate to the courtyard of the Ferme des Quatre Bras, where they sent surgeons, orderlies and wounded alike scurrying for cover inside the buildings. Isolated Brunswick hussars and French *chasseurs* and cuirassiers traded blows, but the sight of the two regiments of General van Merlen's brigade, a short distance to the north-west of the crossroads contained the impetuosity of the French. Other horsemen, disoriented and alarmed by the presence of the Scots infantry, attempted to make their escape by wheeling down the Namur road in rear of the Highlanders, perhaps mistaking it for the highway to Charleroi. Lieutenant Winchester, in rear of the centre of the battalion, saw one such Frenchman:

> At this time, a French officer of Light Dragoons, thinking his men were still following him, got too far to be able to retire by the way he had advanced, galloped down the road in rear of our regiment. The Duke of Wellington, observing him, called out, 'Damn it, 92nd! Will you allow that fellow to escape?[15]

A corporal of the 42nd Regiment of Foot, who had been separated from his own battalion while skirmishing and who had taken refuge in the ranks of the Gordon Highlanders dropped on one knee and levelling his musket, shot the horse dead, wounding the Frenchman in both feet. Shortly afterwards, a body of Brunswick light infantrymen, retreating across the field where the immobile young officer lay, could be heard speaking to him compassionately, telling him: 'Never fear, comrade.' Not everyone on the battlefield, however, was as honourable and the Scots noticed a villainous-looking camp-follower already looting the dead. He had picked up a sabre and was walking amongst the wounded, threatening to kill them unless they surrendered their valuables. Such behaviour was considered beyond the pale and several soldiers were sent forward to secure the casualties and prisoners. Not all the French were grateful for their protection; several perhaps having been veterans of the hulks and implacable enemies of the British. Sergeant Robertson, was surprised at the behaviour of some of these men:

Some of them had the audacity to draw their swords upon the men when in the act of taking them, but such temerity only served to accelerate their own destruction; for in the infuriated state of mind in which we were at the moment, those guilty of such conduct fared a worse fate than those who submitted without a murmur.[16]

These were clearly men who had never faced the British in the Peninsula and who had become hardened to the rule of 'No quarter!' when fighting the vengeful Prussians. Others, convinced that more could be expected from the 'Homards' than to have their skull pulverised by the musket butt of an enraged Brunswicker, surrendered more meekly. From these, Robertson and his comrades learned some useful snippets of information:

Napoleon himself was in the field, as were our old friends, Soult and Ney; and that Ney was directly in our front and had ordered the charge to be made upon us. We were very happy on hearing this intelligence, as the thought that the two great generals of the time were to meet each other on the field of battle, stimulated us to do our utmost to maintain unsullied the hard-earned reputation which the British army had gained in many a bloody battle field.

Despite this gritty determination, Robertson was somewhat under the spell of Napoleon's genius, though he could not recall the Emperor ever having crossed swords with the British. Could he repeat Lodi, Marengo and Austerlitz against veteran British infantry, commanded by experienced generals? For Robertson, being British meant being a part of that: 'One tiny isle of the sea that would brave his colossal strength and defy him to his teeth.'[17]

The intelligence gleaned from these prisoners was rapidly communicated to Wellington. Other captives revealed that the force he faced were the 1st Corps d'Armée of Count d'Erlon and the 2nd under Count Reille, along with a numerous body of cavalry; all told, 50,000 men. Prior intelligence estimates had suggested that Napoleon had only five infantry corps plus the Imperial Guard. Perhaps, thought Colonel von Müffling, Field Marshal von Blücher might even find himself with the advantage of numbers over Napoleon. Wellington would clearly be hard-pressed to maintain his position at Les Quatre Bras, never mind afford the Prussian army the assistance he had earlier promised. Maybe, in the scheme of things, it would no longer be necessary?[18]

The French cavalry, all impetus spent and having suffered severely in the contest, swept down the slopes to the east of the Charleroi road, forcing Picton's exhausted battalions to once again hurriedly form squares. From his position with the Cameron Highlanders, Lieutenant Forbes could pick out the glittering horsemen streaming past the Royals, the 28th and 42nd Regiments of Foot and he thought it remarkable that these battalions had somehow managed to preserve themselves. Major Rogers, still pounding away at the enemy infantry, also noticed the presence of a heavy body of cavalry, but although menacing, it did not seem inclined to charge in his direction. His attention and that of First Lieutenant George Maule, temporarily attached to his battery, was almost completely absorbed in firing round after round of spherical case shot into a French column which was attempting to turn Wellington's left flank, by manoeuvring past the étang Materne.[19]

Closer to the action, Lieutenant Hope was probably sensing a feeling of selfish relief as he watched the cuirassiers charge other targets in their withdrawal:

> Disappointed at Les Quatre Bras, the enemy turned his attention to the troops on the left, who were attacked with death-like fury by the French legions. The several regiments having formed themselves into solid squares, presented an impenetrable front to their assailants, who rode up to the very muzzles of our pieces, in order to provoke the soldiers to throw away their fire, that they might, with greater facility, penetrate our squares. All the attempts of the enemy to induce our soldiers to do so were fruitless. Irritated at their obstinacy, the enemy attacked our squares sword in hand, but were always beat back with great loss. By numerous trials of this kind, equally unsuccessful, the enemy lost a number of his bravest soldiers.[20]

On the forward slopes of the position, isolated groups of *chasseurs à cheval* regrouped and exchanged accounts of triumphs and losses. Leaderless warriors found new chieftains in the lesser ranks, who proudly formed up the depleted squadrons; the crossroads were choked with dead and wounded, the latter crying for water in the most piteous manner. Horseless troopers struggled towards their parent corps. Though some obtained remounts, most were forced to make their way to the rear; horsemen without horses. As soon as sufficient men had been collected to display a show of force, squadrons trotted forward several yards, as if intending to charge. The jittery Allied infantry flinched, but did not shift. To Lieutenant James Ross of the Gordons, the contest was over:

> This second repulse seemed to have made them abandon the idea of taking possession of the road to Brussels, although they made a short advance as if intending to try it again, but our fronts being clear on this occasion, we opened fire at a longer range and they did not attempt to charge.[21]

Whilst the 92nd Regiment of Foot retained its position on the high ground at Les Quatre Bras, the 44th Regiment of Foot had withdrawn some fifty metres into a bowl of ground that sheltered its shattered remnants somewhat. Virtually all the company commanders, who had been such prominent targets to the French skirmishers and gunners, had by now fallen. Colonel O'Malley was the only unwounded field officer amid the wreckage of the regiment, whose officer corps, 25 strong at the outset, now comprised Lieutenants Ralph Twinberrow, Nicholas Kingsley, Henry Martin, Alexander Riddock, Ensigns Gillespie Dunlevie and Thomas Sinclair. In four companies, the command had devolved upon sergeants.[22]

Captain Burney, dangerously wounded by a musket ball in the head and with a further severe wound to his leg, was being carried off the field by two of his sergeants. Passing the Duke of Wellington and his suite, he heard the voice of Lieutenant George Coles, who was serving as Staff Adjutant to Colonel Wood, commanding the Duke's artillery. Coles dismounted to take leave of his old, but dying friend. When Burney fainted, Coles immediately assumed the worst and directed the sergeants to take the body a short distance to the rear and to bury it in the next ditch. Fortunately, the sergeants disregarded his instructions and deposited him into the care of Assistant Surgeon John Collins. Calling over Surgeon Oliver Halpin and his fellow Assistant-Surgeon, William Newton, they examined Burney's head wound and declared the injuries survivable, but concurred that if the ball was not immediately removed, then the poor officer would die a maddening death. Collins instantly set to work with probes and forceps. As soon as he had located and extracted the flattened ball, he put it into Burney's coat pocket, along with a pencilled a note that said it had been removed from the head. If Burney survived, he would have a precious souvenir of the battle to show to his children and grand children.[23]

Still very much in the thick of the action, Lieutenant Riddock had been ordered by Colonel O'Malley to take command of an advanced party comprising his No. 9 Company and the Light Company of the battalion, which had been without officers since Captain Brugh and Lieutenant Robert Grier had both received severe wounds. Lieutenant Kingsley, his company commander had remained with the battalion to take command of the left wing. With this small force, Riddock was to advance within a short distance of the French and to suppress the fire of the enemy sharpshooters, giving O'Malley time to reorganise the remainder of the decimated regiment. Deploying the two companies in extended order, Riddock advanced to about thirty metres from the French skirmish line and opened fire. The bullets whipped through the rye as both sides traded shots at point-blank range. To Riddock, the French seemed to be picking off his men as fast as they could load and fire and it would clearly be impossible to hold this position indefinitely. As the long minutes passed, the ammunition in the men's cartridge pouches gradually dwindled and runners were sent back behind the ridge to request replenishment.[24]

With the cavalry threat receding and the French infantry still needing time to reorganise themselves for a further attempt to storm the heights of Bati-Saint-Bernard, a partial lull descended on the battlefield. Even the artillery fire slackened as French battery commanders gave orders to cease firing, the barrels of their pieces now red hot from several hours of use. To the north, the Allied artillery followed suit, the risk of misfire increasing with every round. Gunners were dispatched to the Vallée des Vaches stream to bring forward buckets of water to cool the gun tubes and sponge out the bores, already caked with powder residue. Though enjoying the respite from hauling the massively heavy carriages back to their firing positions, the men were now engaged in bringing forward more ammunition from the caissons, cutting the dead and wounded horses from the traces, replacing damaged wheels and effecting other running repairs. The battle remained to be won or lost.

Peering through the gloom from his position on the right of the line formed by the 92nd Regiment of Foot, Lieutenant James Ross could make out a body of French infantry moving forward along the Charleroi road, evidently with the objective of seizing the Ferme de la Bergerie, a few hundred metres to the south of the crossroads. Close to Ross, posted on the Namur road itself, the Duke of Wellington and his staff were watching the same infantry. Colonel Cameron, seeing the French advance, asked permission to charge them, to which Wellington replied: 'Have patience, and you will have plenty of work by and by.' As the infantry reached the Ferme de la Bergerie, Cameron again requested permission to launch a counter-attack, which Wellington once more refused. Shortly afterwards, a second column of infantry was seen, advancing in support of the first, along the hollow way that skirted the Bois de Bossu. Partially obscured from view by the dense smoke hanging in the still air, occasionally hidden by the folds of the ground and the building of the Ferme de la Bergerie itself, the advance of this body of infantry was unnoticed by all but the most observant. Concerned that the occupation of the sheep farm would again provide the French with a strongpoint from which they could launch an assault on the crossroads, Wellington sent General Barnes across to the right of the battalion to obtain a clearer view. If he considered the threat to be sufficiently great, Wellington added, he was to act on his own initiative and if necessary, commit the battalion to a counter-attack. The moment was desperate. Though General von Alten's infantry was now only a short distance away, it would need time to deploy and with the orphaned Brunswick infantry seemingly unable to remain formed, Wellington was forced to play his last card.[25]

Hurrying over to the right wing of the battalion, Barnes found it difficult to make out the intentions of the French and called out to Lieutenant James Ross: 'What have we got here?' Shouting up from the ditch as the Adjutant-General towered above him on his horse, Ross told him they were enemy infantry and warned him that they were moving to reinforce an earlier advance that had seized the building and enclosures of the Ferme de la Bergerie. Barnes, judging that any more delay would result in the concentration of an overwhelming force of infantry, decided that urgent action was required. He tore off his hat and waving it about his head, shouted: 'Ninety-second! Follow me!' Nudging his horse with his spurs, Barnes wheeled around on the chaussée shouting: 'Come on my old Ninety-Second,' before setting his horse at the ditch and leaping it in a single bound. Towards the centre of the line, the Duke had been watching Barnes and turned to Cameron: 'Now, Cameron, is your time – take care of that road,' he said, before riding behind the centre of the battalion and shouting: 'Ninety-second. You must charge these two columns of infantry.' After several hours of bombardment in the same position, the Highlanders needed no second invitation. Lieutenant Winchester was instantly urging his men to their feet. Within seconds, the entire battalion had scrambled from the ditch and formed up in a two-deep line on the lip of ground to the south.[26]

The battalion now advanced to the attack. On the right of the line, Barnes had been joined by Cameron and the two officers led the Grenadier and No. 1 Company onto the Charleroi road, forming them into a compact column. To the east, the remaining eight companies advanced in line. Those on the extreme left wheeled to remain aligned with the rest of the battalion as it steadily descended the slope, kilts swaying

The Battle of Quatre Bras

The Duke of Wellington leaps the ditch occupied by the 92nd Regiment of Foot. See page 274. Artist unkown.

and bayonets glittering. Several of the Duke of Wellington's staff, carried away by the moment, leaped the ditch and joined the regimental officers in the advance; among them Colonel Frazer, the commander of Wellington's absent horse artillery. For hours, the men had enjoyed the fragile protection of the roadside ditch. Now, they encountered the horribly accurate fire of the French skirmishers, as they raked the line with musketry in an attempt to draw its fire. Almost as soon as he had clambered from the ditch, Ensign John McPherson, bearing the Regimental colour, was shot through the heart and toppled back, motionless, the staff of the colour shattered into six pieces by three further balls. Ensign Robert Hewitt, bearing the King's colour, survived the fusillade unscathed, though the staff of his colour was also broken in two by a musket ball. Within minutes, the Highlanders had forced the most advanced skirmishers back to the Ferme de la Bergerie and its garden, the French marksmen taking shelter behind the hedges and walls of the enclosure. As the Gordons continued their rapid advance, they came under a heavy fire from the French, posted in the house and behind the hedge to the left of it. To Lieutenant Hope, it was one of the heaviest fires of musketry he ever witnessed.[27]

There was a tinkling sound as enemy musket butts put out the panes of glass in the windows of both storeys of the house and within seconds, the broken frames bristled with weapons. With a clear view of the advancing Scots, the 'fantassins' poured a heavy fire into the men of the 92nd Regiment of Foot, as they advanced towards the hedge. Suddenly, the hedge itself exploded in smoke and flames as the French defenders unleashed a short-range volley. In the thick of the action and immediately in front of Sergeant Robertson, was the Duke of Wellington, a prominent and tempting target, even in the dense smoke. Amid the groans and cries of the wounded, Wellington ordered Robertson to take a section and to drive the hostile infantry out of their improvised stronghold. The sergeant and his men broke into the kitchen garden and launched themselves at the French, killing several of the garrison with musket and bayonet, before eventually driving them back and securing the enclosure.[28]

Whilst Robertson and his men cleared the kitchen garden, others stove in the doors to the house, poured through the entrance and became embroiled in a vicious hand-to-hand struggle as the French resisted with the greatest courage. Eventually, having cleared both storeys of the house, room by bloodstained room, the Highlanders emerged on the main road:

'It was hot work then,' said an old Highland soldier. 'They were in the hoose like as many mice, an' we couldna get at them wi' oor shot when their fire was ca'in' doon mony a goot man among us ... oot o' that they had to come, or dee where they were; so we ower the hedge an' through the garden till the hoose was fair surrounded, an' they couldna get a shot oot where we couldna get ane in. In the end they were driven oot, an' keepit oot. Ay, but the French were brave men, an' tried again an' again to take it from us, but they only got beaten back for their pains, and left their dead to fatten the garden ground.'[29]

Robertson's blood was up. As he and his men emerged from the garden, they found themselves on the chaussée, with the rest of the regiment sweeping past on their left and right, a blur of scarlet and tartan. In contrast, about eighty metres away, the dark mass of the main body of the French column was drawn up. Though he was an experienced soldier, even Robertson must have baulked at the prospect of taking on these adversaries, for he estimated that the French force comprised between 1,200 and 1,500 men.[30]

The men of No. 6 Company had also gained the Charleroi road, on the far side of which they found a large, empty garden, which had not been occupied by the enemy when they had initially seized the house. The garden was enclosed by a thick thorn hedge and opened onto the chaussée through a small gate, with another gate at the western end opening into the fields beyond and a gravel path connecting the two. A short distance beyond the garden was another large body of hostile infantry, substantially more numerous than the Highlanders and drawn up in an imposing manner. Colonel Cameron was in a quandary. The position of this French infantry immediately behind the garden made an advance through it hazardous, but there was insufficient ground between the garden and the edge of the Bois de Bossu, for the whole of his battalion to pass around it. Such a manoeuvre would also necessitate withdrawing the companies of the left wing who had penetrated to the south of the house, as well as extricating the men of the centre companies, who had become wedged on the roadway between the house and the garden gate. In the midst of this latter group was Lieutenant Hope, eager to press forward and concerned that any indecision might result in the battalion being forced to yield what it had gained at such cost.[31]

> Although we had forced the enemy to relinquish their hold of the house and hedge on the left of it, the principal part of our duties remained to be performed. Although their advanced guard had been driven back, the main body showed no disposition to retire. On the contrary, they poured on us showers of musketry, sufficient to appal soldiers of more experience in those matters than one half of those who fought on the plains of Quatre Bras. In fact, it required no little exertion to keep some of the young soldiers in the ranks, for perceiving the French so much more numerous than themselves and that the garden hedge, though very thick, afforded them no protection, the danger appeared to some of them so very great, that but for their veteran companions and the attention of their officers to their duties, they might have been induced to retire. But from this disagreeable situation, we endeavoured to extricate ourselves in the following manner. The only obstacle between it and the enemy being the garden, it was proposed to take a portion of the battalion round and between it and the wood of Bossu, another division round the left, or lower side of the garden and a third to open a passage for itself through the garden, by entering at the front gate. Being of this party, we accomplished our task of forcing the gates with some little difficulty, for the fire of the enemy was truly dreadful and we could not take any steps to render it less effective, till the whole battalion could be brought to bear upon the enemy. At length, all the three columns arrived at their appointed stations. Seeing our friends on the right and left ready, we moved out at the rear gate and quickly formed in front of the hedge. On this formation being accomplished, the signal of readiness was given, when the whole joined in three hearty cheers and then, with the irresistible bayonet in their hands, advanced to the work of death.[32]

Whilst the enemy troops to the south of the garden poured a heavy fusillade into the part of the British battalion that had advanced through the garden and around its south-eastern corner, Colonel Cameron had passed the enclosure to the west with the Grenadier and No. 1 Companies. Here, he found himself close to the French column that had been advancing from the wood, but which now seemed disinclined to come to blows with the Highlanders and was retracing its steps. Cameron swept forward with his little band. Suddenly, the French halted, their rear ranks faced about and delivered a crushing volley at short range that caused terrible execution in the ranks of the two companies, dozens of officers and men falling to the ground within seconds. The hail of musket balls now claimed a more significant victim. Colonel Cameron, conspicuous on his horse and in the forefront of the advance, received a musket ball in the groin and his horse received four further balls, which caused it to stagger and wheel around. Seeing the courageous officer slump in the saddle, Colonel

Frazer, who was nearby at the time, supported him until help arrived in the form of two soldiers. These men led the horse back to the crossroads, where Cameron was lowered to the ground. His horse, mortally wounded, was dispatched with a pistol to the head. Cameron's groom, who had remained behind with his led horse, hurried to attend to his master, as did Colonel Frazer, who arrived at the crossroads shortly afterwards. Though the wound was clearly serious, Frazer hoped Cameron would do well and helped unbuckle his sword and scabbard, which was causing the Scotsman some distress. Handing these to a sergeant for safe-keeping, he also removed the officer's maps, before a party of men, including the Colonel's foster-brother, Ewen Macmillan, carried him a short distance to the rear and lifted him into a wagon that was evacuating the wounded to Genappe.[33]

Whilst the 92nd Regiment of Foot had advanced into action across the ground that had previously been occupied by the Brunswick infantry, Colonel Olfermann managed to restore order amongst his troops and led forward several battalions in support, taking up positions to the south of the Ferme de la Bergerie, in the fields between the Charleroi road and the Bois de Bossu. Colonel Best, also seeing the Gordon Highlanders move off, ordered Colonel von Ramdohr to occupy the vital crossroads with the Lüneburg Landwehr Battalion.[34]

The fire fight to the west of the garden was barely five minutes old. With each soldier mechanically firing between two and three rounds per minute, thousands of balls were flailing the opposing ranks, inflicting numerous losses. Every few seconds, men fell into the rye, some screaming, some already dead. To some officers, it seemed as if the battalion had but fifty men left standing, though in the pall of smoke they could distinguish little of what was going on more than a short distance away. Behind the Highland line, the sergeants were barking at the men to close the ranks. It seemed to some that they were now separated from the rest of the Allied army, alone and unsupported in this appalling carnage. As the minutes passed, those on the right of the line noticed a body of troops, who to some resembled a regiment of Foot Guards, moving up in their rear, though by this time a further thirty men had fallen. At last, the French column disengaged and slowly pulled back to the edge of the wood, all the while maintaining a tremendous fire. Lieutenant James Ross and the remaining officers and men pressed forward, not content to allow the French to remain in such an advanced position. Driving them back a substantial distance down the eastern edge of the Bois de Bossu, they were: 'Exposed to a galling fire of shot, shell, grape and musketry'. The French, attempting several times to establish a new line of defence behind successive hedges, were unable to resist the impetus of the Scots. Lieutenant Ewen Ross was wounded and carried from the field, yet another victim of the murderous exchange.[35]

It seemed to Lieutenant Hope that the enemy column closer to the chaussée had initially been unwilling to retire, but realising that the Scots battalion was determined to press home its attack and seeing their supporting column driven back, they promptly faced about and withdrew. Continuing to pour in volleys of musketry, the Gordons pursued them all the way to the edge of the Bois de Bossu, with Lieutenant Hope once again in the forefront of the chase:

> The loss of the enemy in this affair was terrible. At every step we found a dead or wounded Frenchman; some of them affected to treat the whole business very lightly; whilst others, even in the very agonies of death, never ceased to echo the cry of their brethren in the front, of 'Vive l'Empereur!' Our loss was also very great on this occasion, not caused by the fire of those to whom we were opposed, as by the fire of their artillery and light troops on our left flank.[36]

The depleted Highlanders continued the pursuit. The men, toiling through the much-trampled fields of tall wheat and rye were rapidly tiring. The baking heat, the exertion of maintaining the fire fight and the strain of the desperate counter-attack had drained them of energy. Shoulders throbbed from the recoil of muskets; mouths were dry and blackened with powder; heads ached from the relentless exposure to the burning sun. This physical suffering contrasted with the euphoria felt by others; advancing with the remnants of No. 1 Company, Lieutenant James Ross was extremely proud of the performance of his regiment:

> We had to occupy and defend ourselves on ground, that it surprises me we were not cut to pieces, as we were frequently as a battalion extended, acting as skirmishers, now and then throwing ourselves into square to repel cavalry, by which we were threatened and when we were sure to suffer severe loss from the enemy's guns, as they embraced every opportunity of bringing them to bear upon us, whenever they could, with a chance of annoying us.[37]

Officers were being picked off by French light troops at an alarming rate. Having assumed the command when Colonel Cameron received his mortal wound, it was only a matter of minutes before Lieutenant-Colonel James Mitchell also succumbed to the fire of the French tirailleurs and was himself wounded close to the edge of the Bois de Bossu. With Major Donald McDonald absent from the battalion, Captain George Holmes took charge. Almost as soon as he had assumed the command, he too fell wounded, to be followed closely by the next senior officer, Captain Campbell of the Grenadiers. The battalion had seen four commanding officers fall in as many minutes, before Captain Peter Wilkie took control. By now, the regiment was in a very dangerous position, having advanced some distance in the space between the Ferme de Gemioncourt and the edge of the Bois de Bossu. On the chaussée were a number of pieces of French horse artillery, though they remained limbered up, as if preparing to advance. Close by, between the road and the wood, were more French artillery which bombarded the flank of the advancing troops, forcing them back to the cover afforded by the edge of the wood. From here, the infantry made rapid progress and seemed to be turning the flank of the enemy troops to the south of the farm, though two French guns firing canister were causing mayhem in the ranks. The Highlanders impetuously rushed at the artillery, but the nimble gunners limbered up immediately and pulled back a short distance. Once again the Highlanders dashed forward, only for the artillerymen to withdraw tantalisingly out of their reach and resume the bombardment. Sergeant Robertson found this whole episode especially trying:

> We, however, still sustained considerable loss from the enemy's cannon, as we had none with which to oppose them and as so few of our troops had come up, we could not form a sufficiently strong column in one place to enable us to take any of their artillery from them.[38]

Having reduced the French infantry to a skeleton, the exposed position of the battalion had become a source of great anxiety for Captain Wilkie. Captain William Little, Lieutenant James Chisholm, and Ensigns Abel Becher and John McPherson were dead. Colonel Cameron and Captain William Grant were mortally and eighteen other officers less severely, wounded. Almost two thirds of the battalion's officers were hors de combat. Threatened once again by French cavalry at the south-eastern tip of the Bois de Bossu, pounded incessantly by the French guns posted nearby, he ordered the débris of the battalion to pull back into the wood itself. Here, unable to retire by the way they had advanced and virtually leaderless, the remnants of the battalion crossed the wood, having to contest several thickets with large bands of French infantry, before emerging into the Champ du Sarti, to the west of the Bois de Bossu. As more and more isolated groups of Highlanders appeared, the depleted battalion, exhausted and lacking ammunition, slowly made its way to the north and finally halted in the fields to the north-west of the crossroads. A summary headcount conducted by the remaining sergeants indicated that it had left behind at least 28 officers and 270 men killed, wounded and missing around the Ferme de la Bergerie, in the fields to the south-west and in the Bois de Bossu. Some of these missing men, however, many comprising large numbers of wounded, had somehow become detached from the main body and continued to line the ditch and the trees at the edge of the wood, among them the wounded Lieutenant Winchester and Sergeant Robertson.[39]

Endnotes

1. von Alten (I). von Alten (II). Anonymous (Near Observer), p. 68. de Bas &c., pp. 514–5. Best (I). Best (II). Eberhard. Alexander Forbes (II). von Herzberg. von der Horst. Leask and McCance, p. 334. Oppermann. Ross-Lewin, p. 258. van Zuylen van Nyeveld (I), pp. 56–7.
2. Daniell, p. 134. Glazebrook, p. 13. Seale, p. 8.
3. Daniell, p. 134. Glazebrook, pp. 14–15. Seale, p. 10.
4. Best (I). Best (II). von der Horst, de Mauduit (Volume II), p. 151. Oppermann. von Pflugk-Harttung (II), pp. 21–2.
5. Mudie (II), p. 174.
6. Mudie (II), p. 175.
7. von Pivka (III), p. 8.

The Battle of Quatre Bras

8. Anonymous (Letters), p. 227. Anonymous (Near Observer), pp. 62–3. Aubrey-Fletcher, p. 369. de Bas &c., p. 507. Batty, pp. 48–9. Cornford and Walker, p. 105. Creevey, p. 231. Delhaize and Aerts, p. 447. Archibald Forbes, pp. 267–8. Gomm (V). Hope (III), pp. 226–7. Robertson, p. 146. F. Somerset, p. 9.
9. Anonymous (Letters), pp. 278–9. Hope (III), p. 227.
10. Anonymous (Letters), p. 227. Anonymous (Near Observer), pp. 62–3. Cathcart. Cornford and Walker, p. 105. Delhaize and Aerts, p. 447. Alexander Forbes (II). Archibald Forbes, p. 267. Gomm (I). Gomm (IV). Hope (III), p. 227. Leach, p. 376. J. Ross (II). F. Somerset, p. 9. Winchester (II).
11. J. Ross (II).
12. Anonymous (Letters), p. 227. Batty, pp. 48–9. Delhaize and Aerts, p. 447. Archibald Forbes, p. 268. Henckens, p. 229. Hope (III), p. 227. Leach, p. 376. J. Ross (II). F. Somerset, p. 9.
13. Cathcart. Houssaye, p. 119. Robertson.
14. Anonymous (Letters), p. 228. Döring. Alexander Forbes (II). Frazer, p. 540. Gronow, p. 127. Hope (I). Hope (III), p. 227. Robertson. Winchester (II).
15. Anonymous (Letters), p. 227. Delhaize and Aerts, pp. 447–8. Archibald Forbes, p. 268. Henckens, pp. 229–30. Hope (III), p. 27. Jackson (II), pp. 26–7. Pattyn, pp. 18–19. F. Somerset, p. 9. Winchester (II).
16. Anonymous (Letters), p. 227. Delhaize and Aerts, pp. 447–8. Archibald Forbes, p. 268. Hope (III), p. 227. Martinien. Pattyn, pp. 18–19. Robertson, pp. 147–8. Winchester (II).
17. Robertson, pp. 147–8. Pigeard, p. 307.
18. Jecklyn. von Müffling (I), p. 5.
19. Alexander Forbes (II). Gomm (IV). Rogers (I).
20. Anonymous (Letters), pp. 227–8. Hope (III), pp. 227–8.
21. Henckens, p. 230. J. Ross (II).
22. Anonymous (Waterloo Medal Roll), pp. 240–5. Carter, p. 86. Dalton, pp. 161–3. Riddock.
23. Carter, p. 86.
24. Anonymous (Waterloo Medal Roll), p. 244. Riddock.
25. Anonymous (Letters), pp. 229–30. Anonymous (Near Observer), pp. 67–8, 77–80. Clerk, p. 79. Hope (I). Hope (III), pp. 229–30. J. Ross (II). Winchester (II). Winchester (III).
26. Anonymous (Letters), pp. 229–30. Anonymous (Near Observer), p. 77–80. Clerk, p. 79. Hope (I). Hope (III), p. 229. Robertson. J. Ross (II). Winchester (II). Winchester (III).
27. Anonymous (Letters), pp. 230–1. Anonymous (Near Observer), pp. 67–8, 77–80. Clerk, p. 79. Dalton, p. 194. Frazer, p. 541. Hope (I). Hope (III), p. 230. Robertson. J. Ross (II). Winchester (II).
28. Anonymous (Letters), p. 230. Clerk, p. 79. Hope (I). Robertson. J. Ross (II).
29. Anonymous (Letters), pp. 230–1. Gardyne, p. 355. Hope (I). Hope (III), pp. 231–2. J. Ross (II).
30. Hope (I). Robertson.
31. Anonymous (Letters), pp. 230–1. Hope (I). Hope (III), p. 231.
32. Anonymous (Letters), pp. 231–2. Hope (I). Hope (III), pp. 231–2.

33. Anonymous (Letters), pp. 230–1, 277–8. Anonymous (Near Observer), pp. 67–8, 77–80. Batty, p. 53. Clerk, p. 79. Frazer, p. 541. Hope (I). Hope (III), p. 231. Robertson. E. Ross. J. Ross (II). W. Siborne (V), p. 91. Sinclair-Stevenson, pp. 39–40. Winchester (I). Winchester (II).
34. Anonymous (Brunswick Officer). Best (I). Best (II). Olfermann.
35. Anonymous (Near Observer), pp. 67–8, 77–80. Alexander Forbes (II). J. Ross (II).
36. Anonymous (Letters), p. 232. Hope (III), p. 232. Winchester (I).
37. Hope (I). J. Ross (II). Sinclair-Stevenson, p. 39.
38. Anonymous (Letters), p. 232. Anonymous (Near Observer), p. 77–80. Anonymous (Waterloo Medal Roll), pp. 311–7. Dalton, pp. 193–6. Gardyne, p. 357. Hope (III), p. 232. Robertson. J. Ross (II). Winchester (II).
39. Anonymous (Near Observer), pp. 67–8. Anonymous (Waterloo Medal Roll), pp. 311–7. Best (I). Dalton, pp. 193–96. Gardyne, p. 357. Hope (I). Robertson. Winchester (II).

CHAPTER 15

As the Gordon Highlanders gathered to the north and west of the Bois de Bossu, the long-anticipated division of General von Alten was finally arriving on the field of battle. Towards 5.00 p.m., the 5th (British) Infantry Brigade halted at Croix-Gilbert, slightly to the north-west of the Bois de Bossu. The four footsore battalions were followed by General von Kielmansegge's 1st (Hanoverian) Infantry Brigade. General Halkett rode forward to assess the situation and seek orders.[1]

As his General rode away, Colonel Hamilton of the 30th Regiment of Foot, whose men had been marching steadily in the centre of the column, noticed a wounded staff officer emerge from the wood on horseback and gallop up to the battalion. Surgeon Elkington was immediately summoned. He instantly recognised the casualty as Major John Jessop of the 44th Regiment of Foot, serving in this campaign as an Assistant Quartermaster-General in von Alten's divisional staff. Jessop had been an aide-de-camp to Major-General Dunlop at the battle of Fuentes d'Oñoro in 1811, where the second battalions of both regiments had been brigaded together. The Major seemed agitated and believed the enemy to be so close by that he would not even dismount to have his wounded foot dressed. Not able to attend Jessop without dismounting himself, Elkington opened his case of instruments, and proceeded to clean the wound, whilst balls whizzed over their heads. As they talked, it emerged that Jessop had only been in the field for some fifteen minutes before he had been hit, which suggested to the surgeon that he would be kept very busy that afternoon. Having dressed Jessop's injuries as best he could, Elkington advised his patient to take himself off the field for further treatment. For the remainder of the campaign, his responsibilities would devolve upon his young deputy, Captain James Shaw-Kennedy. Realising that the battalion would soon be committed to action, Colonel Hamilton summoned Quartermaster John Williamson. If the fighting was as ferocious as Jessop described, there was no way he would risk his valuable charger in action; if killed, he would only receive £20 compensation from the Government. The Quartermaster agreed to exchange horses and to keep Hamilton's animal well to the rear.[2]

A few hundred metres to the west, another soldier was being examined by a surgeon. When General Halkett had halted his brigade, he had also sent orders to the commanding officers to have the muskets loaded. The ranks of the Grenadier

Company of the 33rd Regiment of Foot were carrying out the familiar drill, when Lieutenant Pattison received an unusual request:

> James Gibbons, one of my men, came up to me and, saluting me, said he was sick and wished to go to the rear. The request on such an occasion was altogether inadmissible, especially as this was not the first time he had shown the white feather and, had I complied, the consequences might have been dangerous as an example to others. I at once called for the Surgeon (Dr. Lever) to examine him and give his opinion of him. The doctor felt his pulse and told him there was nothing wrong with him and that he must return to the ranks at once.

Whether suffering from a premonition of his death, a nervous disorder, or sheer terror at the prospect of going into action, Gibbons complied and fell in alongside his comrades, who if they had not heard his request, could probably have guessed at its nature, being aware that he was: 'Not made of stern enough stuff to qualify him for a good soldier in the hour of danger.' A journeyman hairdresser before enlisting, he had proven useful to both officers and men in shaving, cutting hair and setting razors, but was more suited to the post of valet-de-chambre than that of an infantryman.[3]

The highway from Nivelles was crammed with soldiers from every battalion. The brigade's order of march had been somewhat disrupted by the need to bypass congestion along the route, with the battalions either marching along minor roads or sometimes entering the fields to either side of the chaussée. Somehow, Colonel Morice's 69th Regiment of Foot had ended up in the lead, followed by the 30th and 33rd Regiments of Foot, with Colonel Harris' 73rd Regiment of Foot bringing up the rear. To Lieutenant Pattison's astonishment, the fields that stretched into the distance to the north and south of the road were filled with Netherlands and Nassau soldiers. Unaware of the contribution these battered battalions had earlier made, ignorant of their losses and oblivious to their ammunition shortages, word rapidly spread that they: 'Being disaffected to the cause, had left the field like traitors'. Stretching along the Nivelles road into the distance behind Halkett's men was the 1st (Hanoverian) Infantry Brigade under General von Kielmansegge. At the head of the column was the Bremen Field Battalion, followed by its sister battalions from Verden, Osnabrück, Lüneburg and Grubenhagen; the Feld-Jager-Korps brought up the rear.[4]

On the battlefield itself, the battered remnant of Pack's brigade was exhausted and had been pressed behind the chemin Bati-Saint-Bernard, into the confined triangle of ground between the Ferme de la Bergerie and the Namur road. The shattered battalions had almost completely expended their supplies of ammunition. Here and there, soldiers picked up the muskets of the dead and wounded, looking for weapons to replace their own, now too fouled for use. The barrels were red hot to the touch. The ragged bands of men, faces blackened by powder smoke, their uniforms covered in dust and grime so as to be indistinguishable as friend

The Battle of Quatre Bras

or foe, mechanically continued to go through their evolutions. Little did they care about what was happening around them, knowing only that they had their backs to the wall – the Namur road – and that the coming minutes would determine who would triumph and who would fail. As the officers and sergeants tried to keep order, the skirmishers in advance continued their seemingly endless contest with the French tirailleurs, who had the all-important crossroads once more in sight and could perhaps, scent victory. Picton's division, it seemed, was a well-nigh spent force.[5]

General Halkett had just passed the northern tip of the Bois de Bossu and was approaching the crossroads when he received an urgent message from General Picton to General von Alten, whose whereabouts were still unknown. Picton's message had the tone of an order; had he been placed in command of Wellington's centre; or was his message simply a reflection of his no nonsense attitude? In either case, the request was for the left shoulders of the leading brigade to be brought forward, for it to move through the wood and if possible, to fall upon the left of the French army. Beyond these stipulations, it was suggested that von Alten was free to act as he thought most advantageous. General von Kielmansegge's brigade was to continue towards the left of the Allied position.[6]

As Halkett paused for a moment to marshal his thoughts, an aide-de-camp galloped up and saluted. He had come from General Pack, he said, whose brigade had expended nearly the whole of its ammunition. Breathlessly, the Captain stated that if General Halkett was not able to offer his support, then Pack would be compelled to abandon his post, which he stressed was of great advantage to the allied position. The leading element of Halkett's brigade was Major Lloyd's battery of 9-pounders, a short distance behind which was the 69th Regiment of Foot. Colonel Morice was sent for and Halkett informed him that his battalion was to be detached and seconded to General Pack. He was directed to move forward and to form up under cover of the Ferme de la Bergerie and from there, communicate with the General and act according to his orders. He was to also send Major Watson to Halkett, who had need of additional mounted aides, if he were to retain control of his brigade in such a confused situation.[7]

Halkett seemed to be a magnet for messengers. Soon after sending Morice back to his command, an aide-de-camp from the Duke of Wellington rode up to him and demanded to know why his brigade was stationary instead of attempting the flanking movement through the Bois de Bossu that Picton had earlier instructed him to undertake. Halkett was astonished; was 'Arthur' not aware that his centre was virtually destitute of troops? Remembering his place and curbing his tongue, Halkett replied that he felt he could not leave the situation he was in until further support moved up. A short time after this aide had departed, another galloped up and ordered Halkett to fall on the left of the French, if possible by passing through the wood. Clearly the Duke either felt that the attempt on the French left was worth the risk of the enemy punching through the centre, or he had already taken steps to reinforce the area between the Charleroi road and the Bois de Bossu with fresh troops. Halkett was just about to organise this attempt, when the first aide returned, with directions to remain on the ground he occupied and to use his initiative in its defence.[8]

As soon as Morice came galloping back to his battalion with Halkett's orders, the regimental officers dismounted and the servants removed the horses, some distance to the north-west of the crossroads. The colours were unfurled and the South Lincolnshires, accompanied by Rudyerd's section of two guns from Lloyd's brigade, moved off and passed through some houses in the south-west angle of the crossroads, before entering a field of tall green corn to the south. Ensign Ainslie, though aware from the volume of shot and shells passing beyond the advancing column that they were close to the front and no great distance from the French, could see very little on account of the crops and had no distinct notion of what was going on. Captain Barlow noticed that the ground seemed to comprise: 'Little dales and gently rising slopes, covered throughout with rye and wheat which here grew five or six feet high', but was more interested in how fine a summer's evening it had turned out to be. Such curious thoughts passed through the heads of each individual as he prepared in his own way to face the coming ordeal.

Shortly afterwards, the battalion crossed the Charleroi road slightly to the north of the Ferme de la Bergerie and entered a field of clover on the far side. Though more open ground, the depressed nature of the terrain afforded an even more limited view of what was going on, even a short distance away. When the battalion halted, Colonel Morice ordered the companies to close up and Rudyerd placed the two 9-pounders on his right. Overhead, black specks could be seen against the blueness of the sky, which ploughed into the fields in their rear and skidded across the chaussée. Within the space of a few minutes, Barlow's musings on the balmy nature of the evening were interrupted by great iron balls bounding through the densely-packed ranks and shells being lobbed high over his head, exploding in a shower of jagged chunks.[9]

In the meantime, a further messenger rode up to Halkett with an order from Wellington, stating that Major Lloyd was to immediately move up to the crossroads, with his remaining four guns. Once there, he was to take up a position on the Charleroi road, immediately in front of the farm at Les Quatre Bras. At last, within moments of his death, Brunswick's request for direct artillery support had been answered.[10]

Having issued the appropriate instructions, Halkett turned his attention to the situation at hand. In the midst of all this marching and movement, he noticed some infantry which appeared to be in a state of some confusion. It turned out to be the Brunswick Leib-Battalion and Avantgarde-Battalion, both of which had advanced a short time earlier in order to support the attack made by the 92nd Regiment of Foot. Though butchered by artillery and threatened repeatedly by French cavalry, they were retiring too hastily for Halkett's liking. Spurring his horse, he rode up to the officer in command, who introduced himself as Colonel Olfermann. The two men quickly conversed in German, during which Halkett expressed his

The Battle of Quatre Bras

concerns over the behaviour of the Brunswickers. After a brief horseback conference, Olfermann promised to restore order amongst his troops and undertook to bring them forward to the cover of a ditch that ran almost parallel to the enemy's line, on condition that Halkett guaranteed that his brigade would take up a position in their support. The Colonel would also bring forward the 2nd Brunswick Line Battalion to bolster the position. Until someone managed to establish communication with Halkett's divisional commander, or fresh orders to the contrary were forthcoming, the two officers judged that this course of action would be the most sensible in the circumstances.[11]

The Duke of Wellington was also concerned with the situation of the Brunswickers. Realising that Olfermann and his infantry were being pounded to destruction and that French artillery and infantry had advanced through the Bois de Bossu and were firing on the decimated battalions from a range of less than a few hundred metres, he sent Lieutenant-Colonel Dawson Kelly, an Assistant Quartermaster-General, with orders to Major Lloyd, for his artillery to advance in support of these troops. As soon as Kelly had transmitted Wellington's instructions, Lloyd notified Rudyerd to limber up and pull back to the main body of the brigade. Before the arrival of Rudyerd's section, Lloyd brought the four guns immediately at hand forward and established a battery on the right of the 1st Brunswick Line Battalion, in a field to the south-west of the crossroads, a short distance away from the houses on the Nivelles road. Even before the guns had unlimbered, their arrival provoked such a storm of shot and shell that within the space of a few minutes, some of the gunners were cut in two by French artillery projectiles, two of the guns were dismounted, three or four horses from each limber and wagon team were killed and wounded and several wheels were smashed, paralysing many of the vehicles.[12]

On the opposite side of the Charleroi road, Lieutenant Riddock had also been concerned by developments in the Bois de Bossu and by the fragile state of the Brunswick battalions between the wood itself and the Charleroi road. Though the 44th Regiment of Foot was bearing its share of the violence being meted out by the French, it was reassuring to see allied artillery inflicting the same punishment on the French infantry, even if he mistook Lloyd's brigade for Brunswick gunners:

> The forest on the right having been given in charge of a few Dutch and Belgians, the French retook it the same with little opposition or loss, but in retaking the forest again no doubt it cost us dear, but the French paid for their making themselves masters of it a second time. They supported their attack in the wood with an immense column skirting the wood, which was exposed to a well-directed and deadly fire from one brigade of Brunswick guns... The loss of the French was such, that the ground skirting the wood was literally covered with dead, so that the fall of the ground was totally invisible the next morning.[13]

Amid his sweating gunners and choking on the sulphurous fumes as his 9-pounders vomited their destruction, Major Lloyd himself was unsure whether the column had emerged from the wood. Irrespective of whether this was the case or not, he took great delight in seeing it hurriedly move into its shelter, though he also felt concern at what other forces might be waiting to emerge. The wood seemed to be swarming with French infantry. Blinded by the smoke, feeling isolated and considering that he had fulfilled his task in driving the French infantry off, Lloyd reluctantly decided to abandon the two damaged guns until such time as new carriages could be brought up, along with replacement horses to draw the limber; he then ordered the remaining guns to be limbered up and he calmly walked his brigade towards the Ferme des Quatre Bras and the main body of his division.[14]

Observing the withdrawal of the wrecked brigade was Sergeant-Major Ferdinand Nienburg of Captain von Rettberg's Hanoverian foot artillery, who noticed that the two dismounted pieces had been temporarily abandoned and were in danger of being lost to the French. Showing the same determination as at Talavera, where he had been severely wounded in the head, he hastily organised a team and limber and brought the two damaged pieces into cover at Les Quatre Bras, where the artificers could start the laborious process of repairs.[15]

The crossroads that he brought the guns back to was itself was a scene of utter mayhem, as were the surrounding fields. The buildings were wrecked by shot holes in their roofs and walls, their interiors choked with dead and dying soldiers:

> Not only was the corn entirely trodden down for a considerable distance on each side of the road, but it was cut up and trampled, just as may be seen on a London street on an occasion of sickness. The ground was strewed with battered helmets, damaged cuirasses, broken swords and muskets, shattered gun-carriages and other signs of fierce strife; and that it had been a bloody contest was shown by the manly form of many a bold cuirassier, lying stretched by the side of a dead opponent.[16]

With the 69th Regiment of Foot now committed to the west of the chaussée, Halkett and Olfermann once more led the remnants of the Brunswick Avantgarde-Battalion, Leib-Battalion and 1st Line Batallion a short distance forward, into the killing fields that they had occupied since their arrival about an hour and a half earlier. Here they were joined by the 2nd Brunswick Line Battalion. It was astonishing how many men could be killed and wounded in such a short space of time and as they advanced, the men were careful to avoid treading on the lifeless, mangled bodies of their erstwhile comrades. The butcher's bill was even higher in terms of the wounded and the piteous cries and moans that came from amongst the tangled crops plaintively fell on the ears of the exhausted young men. Once the four depleted battalions had re-established themselves in a flimsy defensive line, Halkett reassured Olfermann that he would soon deploy troops in their support and galloped back up the road towards Croix-Gilbert, turning his attention to the remaining three battalions of his command.

It was shortly after 5.30 p.m. when Halkett gave the order for the remainder of his brigade to advance. Marching up the chaussée towards Les Quatre Bras, the 30th, 33rd and 73rd Regiments of Foot passed isolated groups of officers and men from the Gordon Highlanders. Once this battalion had regained open ground to the rear of the Bois de Bossu, its officers and NCOs had begun the slow process of gathering in the fugitives and forming up in the fields to the north and west of the wood, though their depleted ranks told the story of their bloody counter-attack on the Ferme de la Bergerie. Lieutenant Hope was amongst their number and watched with relief as Halkett's brigade moved into action:[17]

> As the troops passed us on the road, we cheered them. Tears of joy bade them welcome to share our perils and our glory. Our feelings on this occasion, were very acute, but they were the feelings of men and of soldiers. We prayed for blessings to be showered down on our friends as they passed and our best wishes followed them, too many of them to their last and silent abode.[18]

The wave of relief that trembled through the hard-pressed soldiers of de Perponcher-Sedlnitzky's and Picton's divisions was palpable, but perhaps most especially for the 92nd Regiment of Foot, so long the bulwark that had kept the crossroads safe in Allied hands. Lieutenant Hope was leaning against a bank and watching the passage of these troops, when the 73rd Regiment of Foot approached, at the tail of the column:

> Unconscious at the time that I had the pleasure of being known to any member of that corps, I felt something like surprise when Lieutenant [John Acres], a genuine Irishman, jumped out of his place and grasping my hand as firmly as a vice, said, 'How are you, my old boy?'[19]

No doubt the battlefield was a strange place to make new acquaintances, but the minds of other officers perhaps fleetingly turned to social matters. General Barnes had been due to dine with Capels that afternoon at their 'Pick nick dinner and do', at the Château de Walcheuse, but was sure his absence would be understood by young Caroline. After all, Colonel Gordon and Captain Hill, aides to the Duke of Wellington; Major Dawson of the staff; and Captain Seymour, aide to the Earl of Uxbridge, would also be noticeable by their absence. He turned his attention to more pressing matters. Having had two horses killed beneath him, he was on foot and that would never do for a general.[20]

No sooner had Halkett ridden up to his leading battalion, the 30th Regiment of Foot, than he ordered it and the remaining two battalions to form open column; they would deploy in the strip of land between the Bois de Bossu and the Charleroi road. Colonel Hamilton ordered the regiment to march a short distance along the Nivelles road, then bring its left shoulders forward and pass around the tip of the Bois de Bossu and the enclosures to the west of the crossroads, advancing through the open field, in such a manner that it remained 'en echelon' to the 69th Regiment of Foot. The excitable Ensign Howard was delighted that musket balls were buzzing about his ears, whereas others, for which this infernal noise was less of a novelty, kept their heads down. Farther behind, the 33rd and 73rd Regiments of Foot were to move into the Bois de Bossu and pass through it to gain the open ground along its eastern edge.[21]

By this stage of the contest, the northern section of the Bois de Bossu had become a charnel house. Soldiers of the Regiment Oranien-Nassau rubbed shoulders with those of the Netherlands militia. Brunswick Jagers shared cartridges with their comrades from Nassau. The smoke-filled glades echoed with the rattle of musketry, the orange flash of the priming pans illuminating the sombre interior, where the undergrowth was littered with the corpses of the protagonists and the débris of the combat. The French skirmish line maintained its stranglehold on the bulk of the woodland, though it too was running short of ammunition and the fighting had somewhat declined in intensity.

The 33rd Regiment of Foot emerged from the tree-line of the Bois de Bossu and entered the open ground between the wood and the Charleroi road, moving forward steadily in column of companies at quarter distance. In the forefront was Lieutenant Pattison of the Grenadier Company, who noticed that the undulating ground was: 'In full crop of rye, which in that rich and luxuriant country grows excessively high and on this account hindered observation'. All he knew was that they were destined to support the right of Picton's division. Colonel Elphinstone, Major Edward Parkinson and Ensign Thain, the Adjutant, had an advantage over Pattison. Being mounted, they had some sort of view as they passed through the grain, leading the battalion towards the Charleroi road at the Ferme de la Bergerie, where on the opposite side of the road, the ragged remnants of Picton's redcoats appeared to be still clinging to their positions. Pausing momentarily, the battalion hurriedly dressed its disordered ranks, the intervals of the column having been disrupted; an unfortunate consequence of having moved through the tangled undergrowth. Whilst this necessary evolution was taking place, Ensign Thain urged his horse forward through the field and observed the 30th Regiment of Foot halted somewhat closer to the chaussée, with a number of infantry battalions in dark uniforms a short distance in front, between the road and the wood.

Lieutenant Pattison, also peering through the smoke, recognised these troops as Brunswickers, who it seemed were under a vigorous attack from the enemy's light troops, near the edge of the Bois de Bossu. Colonel Elphinstone ordered the men to lie down in the thickly planted field, concealing them more effectively from the musketry of the French skirmishers, who were also firing from the edge of the trees. Having passed on these instructions, Elphinstone took stock of his position and squinting in the shimmering sunlight, he too noticed the body of enemy troops advancing close to the skirts of the wood. The portents were threatening and he immediately had the battalion back on its feet, the rank and file cursing him no doubt for constantly changing his orders.[22]

The roar of the French artillery had diminished somewhat, both to permit the guns to cool down and to minimise the risk of the advancing French battalions being cannonaded in error by their own gunners. Despite this, the din of the battlefield was still deafening. The cries of officers shouting orders blended with the screams of wounded men, whilst the rhythmic beating of drums competed with the booming of the Allied guns as they tried to stem the advance of the French infantry. Advancing with the Grenadier Company, Lieutenant Pattison's ears were assaulted by the 'Shrill rattle of musketry' and the bitter scent of burnt powder filled his nose. Seemingly every sense was under assault.[23]

After the final battalions of Halkett's brigade moved off the Nivelles road, General von Kielmansegge's brigade doubled along the chaussée towards the crossroads, picking their way through the tangle of dead horses, smashed wagons and sullen Brunswick infantrymen. To the officers of the 92nd Regiment of Foot, it seemed as though the French mistook the arrival of these new red-coated infantry for the return of the Highlanders to their former post at the Ferme des Quatre Bras. As no sooner were the Hanoverians visible, than the French artillery opened up afresh, hurling an enormous quantity of ordnance across the seven hundred metres that separated their batteries from the column of reinforcements. Others mistook the renewed roar of the guns as a preliminary bombardment, evidence that the French were once again making an attempt to punch through Wellington's line.[24]

In contrast to the overwhelming superiority in artillery that the French had enjoyed for much of the day, the situation was slowly but surely turning to Wellington's advantage and at the head of General von Kielmansegge's column, the King's German Legion foot artillery brigade of 9-pounder guns under Captain Andreas Cleeves was one such example. The long column of guns, limbers and ammunition wagons creaked and groaned as it rumbled down the Namur road, the drivers flogging the exhausted animals. Shortly after its arrival at Les Quatre Bras, Colonel Wood had ordered it to take up a position to the north-east of the crossroads, in a field bounded by quick hedges. In this position, the brigade was targeted by French artillery and lost several horses and men and after suffering this fire for about half an hour, Cleeves was ordered to take up a new position to the south of the Namur road, whence he would be able to enfilade any French attack mounted towards the road junction. As the brigade moved onto the chaussée, it lost still more men from French fire; Gunner Friedrich Jahns was hit in the arm and was given permission to make for a nearby farm for treatment.

Eventually, the remaining gunners reached a point some seven hundred metres from the crossroads, where one of Picton's staff officers directed the column off the road and into a field to the south. Unhitching the pieces, the men lost no time in forming battery, breaking open the ammunition wagons and hurriedly stockpiling cartridges, whilst the drivers removed the limbers, wagons and horse teams behind the embankment of the Namur road in its rear. The enemy had established guns on the chemin Bati-Saint-Bernard, less than four hundred metres away; it would be a bloody affair. As they unstowed rammers, trail spikes and buckets, the more religious men in the brigade mumbled prayers under their breath: *'Vater unser im Himmel, Geheiligt werde dein Name.'*[25]

The prayer was doubtless being echoed in the column that had followed the artillery down the chaussée. The Bremen Field Battalion ran the gauntlet, followed by its sister battalions from Verden, Osnabrück, Lüneburg and Grubenhagen; the Feld-Jager-Korps brought up the rear. The jostling battalions doubled along the road, with muscles aching and blistered feet raising agonised objections. Muskets at the trail, the cartridge boxes bouncing on bruised hips, pack straps biting still further into sore shoulders, the infantry gradually moved towards the eastern end of the line, where Kempt's brigade, bloodied but as yet unbowed, was clinging to the Namur road with its little remaining strength. Just after the brigade passed Cleeves' guns, the Bremen Field Battalion was directed off the road and formed into a quarter-distance column, ordered to charge up the gentle northern slope of the heights of Bati-Saint-Bernard, followed by the Verden and Osnabrück battalions. As they advanced in the teeth of vicious musketry and artillery, they flushed out French tirailleurs and gradually, after a vigorous fire fight, managed to drive the French columns back across the high ground and regain the crest of the ridge.[26]

To Lieutenant Kincaid, on the extreme eastern flank of the Allied position, it had seemed until now that there had been a slight lull in the intensity of the artillery fire. Perhaps ammunition was running low, or gun barrels were overheating. Whatever the reason, it served to accentuate the continuous din of the artillery some distance to the west, indicating the Prussians were still hard at it. From early on in the engagement, he had been astonished by the tremendous volume of artillery and musketry fire from that direction, though the intervening high ground around Marbais, Villers-Perwin and Brye had prevented him from seeing any of the fighting. Suddenly, some of the men posted along the Namur road reported the arrival of a patrol of thirty or so Prussian dragoons, who had been sent to ascertain the situation at Les Quatre Bras. Having been completely absorbed in his own microcosm of fields, smoke, skirmishers and noise, Kincaid could not really be of assistance:

> Their day, however, was still to be decided and, indeed, for that matter, so was our own, for although the firing for the moment had nearly ceased, I had not yet clearly made up my mind which side had been the offensive, which the defensive, or which the winning. I had merely the satisfaction of knowing that we had not lost it, for we had met fairly in the middle of a field (or rather unfairly, considering that they had two to one) and, after the scramble was over, our division still held the ground they fought on.[27]

At least he and his men were fortunate in being in the position which they occupied, thought another officer of the same regiment, for the remainder of the division was being steadily annihilated, their files swept by artillery, their ranks subjected to desperate fire fights with opposing infantry and regularly charged by hostile cavalry, of which Wellington seemingly had little.[28]

The Battle of Quatre Bras

Whatever the case and wherever on the field soldiers found themselves, there were still several hours of daylight left and the outcome of both the fighting here and the conflict raging at Ligny, perhaps even of the war itself, still hung in the balance. A short while after this welcome interlude, the men skirmishing in the boggy fields to the east of the étang Materne noticed a sudden increase in the cannonade. Did this presage a general attack? Had French reinforcements arrived? Was the day lost? Captain Kincaid was sent to investigate:

> The enemy's artillery once more opened and, on running to the brow of the hill to ascertain the cause, we perceived our old Light Division general, Count Alten, at the head of a fresh British division, moving gallantly down the road towards us. It was, indeed, such a joyful sight, for as already mentioned, our division had suffered so severely that we could not help looking forward to a renewal of the action with such a disparity of force, with considerable anxiety.[29]

The troops at whose head von Alten was advancing were the Lüneburg and Grubenhagen Field Battalions, commanded by Lieutenant-Colonels August von Klencke and Friedrich von Wurmke respectively. Both were light battalions and wore a similar uniform to that of the 95th Regiment of Foot. The Lüneburg battalion sported the dark green jackets with three rows of pewter buttons, which they had inherited from the 1st and 2nd Light Battalions of the King's German Legion, whilst the Grubenhagen battalion wore a single-breasted variant. Both sported the 'stovepipe' shako, though those of the Grubenhagen battalion had no peaks. Both units were equipped with a mixture of muskets and rifles. In front were the two companies of the Feld-Jager-Korps, under the command of Captain von Reden. Perhaps General von Kielmansegge viewed these last with a critical eye; he had commanded a Feld-Jager-Korps of four companies during the campaigns in Germany and Holland in 1813 and 1814, though the two companies now under his command had been raised as recently as April 1815 from professional foresters and gamekeepers. Though excellent shots with their hunting rifles, this would be the first time they would see action.[30]

As he passed the Duke of Wellington, von Alten had been given orders to relieve any of Kempt's regiments that were no longer capable of remaining in line, to stabilise the situation on the left flank and if possible to seize Piraumont. Several of the battalions on this side of the battlefield were by now dangerously short of ammunition. As the Hanoverians approached the southern edge of the Bois des Censes, no longer sheltered by the cuttings of the Namur road, the French gunners to the south of the étang Materne threw everything they had at them.[31]

Captain Kincaid rode back and passed on the good news of von Alten's arrival to his commanding officer. A short while later, General von Kielmansegge rode up and introduced himself to Colonel Barnard. A reinforcement of ten light infantry companies, he said, was on the way. The situation in Barnard's sector, the Colonel explained, was fluid in the extreme. Faced by several French battalions

'The ground was literally covered with dead'

which were universally preceded by swarms of tirailleurs, his men and those of Major von Brandenstein had spent the best part of the past three hours skirmishing in the fields to either side of the Namur road. From time to time, the French dashed forward in battalion columns, upon which the 95th Regiment of Foot and 2nd Brunswick Light Battalion formed up more regularly and drove them off. On occasions where the French skirmishers became too bold, a swift counter-attack with the wicked looking sword bayonets had proved sufficient to discourage any further attempts. Though on occasion Barnard's men had pursued the enemy as far at Thyle, he had been content for some time simply to hold the line of the chemin des Dames-Avelines. Behind this line of riflemen, he kept his reserve companies sheltered in the Bois des Censes, whilst the Brunswickers held the open ground between the Namur road and the étang Materne. Conscious of a dwindling amount of ammunition, concerns had been growing in Barnard's mind, over how long he would be able to maintain himself in this position. With reinforcements, there was perhaps now an opportunity to apply some pressure to the French right, possibly even one to make an assault on Piraumont. The two men set to work planning their attack.[32]

Whilst General von Kielmansegge and Barnard were holding their horseback conference, fresh troops were arriving to shore up the centre of Wellington's position. By now, the 33rd Regiment of Foot was very much advanced in the open ground between the Bois de Bossu and the Charleroi road and the grenadiers of Captain Colclough's No. 3 Company were in the forefront of the battalion as it moved for-

Lieutenant-General Sir Carl von Alten. Thomas Heaphy. *Historisches Museum, Hanover*

ward in the tall rye. It descended the slope from the edge of the Bois de Bossu under fire from the French gun crews on the spur of high ground to the west of the Ferme de Gemioncourt. To Private Hemingway, the cannon balls seemed to be flying about his head 'As thick as hail stones' and the men, weighed down by almost forty kilogrammes of equipment, involuntarily hunched forward to avoid their effect. Within minutes, the advance was hampered by falling bodies; the nervous infantrymen pressed on. Eventually, after what seemed an eternity, the battalion reached its assigned position, behind the unfamiliar formations of Brunswick infantry. Here, Colonel Elphinstone deployed the battalion into line and ordered the companies to lie down in order to make themselves less conspicuous.[33]

Following them into action, Private Morris of the 73rd Regiment of Foot was startled by the extraordinary height of the crop, which covered the ground as far as the eye could see. Morris was by no means the smallest man in his regiment, but the rye was at least half a metre above his head, so that only the tips of the bayonets could be seen by the French, who were no doubt observing their progress. He himself could see nothing except the men to his front and beside him. Moving forward with a measured tread, the battalion came to a swathe of twisted, broken and trampled rye which denoted the passage of a body of troops. Here, the ground was littered with mangled corpses and pitifully wounded men; they had reached the bloody path of the earlier counter-attack of the 92nd Regiment of Foot. As the battalion passed over the ground, Private Morris met a Highlander who was slowly making his way back towards the crossroads. His arm had been removed by a cannon ball and judging by the exposed sinews, shattered bone and shredded muscle, he must have been in the most excruciating torment:

> On passing us, he exclaimed, 'Go on 73rd, give them pepper! I've got my Chelsea commission!' Poor fellow! I should think, from the nature of his wound, he would bleed to death in half an hour, unless he obtained the most prompt and efficient surgical attendance, which he was not likely to, as there were so many wounded waiting their turn to be attended to. I never was struck by a ball, but I have often noticed that those who are, do not always feel it at the time.[34]

Suddenly, a body of enemy infantry was spotted through the drifting smoke, making for the gap between the 33rd Regiment of Foot and the Bois de Bossu. Without hesitation, Colonel Elphinstone had the men once more on their feet. Advancing to meet the threat, Ensign Thain recalled that the battalion 'poured in the most beautiful volley and charged, but they ran faster than our troops, already fatigued, could do and we consequently did not touch them with the bayonet'. Although the immediate threat had been met and dealt with, the battalion was now some way in advance of the remainder of the brigade and in a very exposed situation. Whilst the men were being reformed from line into an open column, Thain noticed that the French had assembled a battery of five guns, which seemed to be specifically aimed at his regiment. Firing at virtually point-blank range, these pieces were soon wreaking havoc with the ranks and files, the balls bounding through the dense mass and bowling men over like ninepins. Here and there, howitzers showered the battalion with deadly iron balls and razor-sharp fragments of shell casing; the murderous fire continued, unabated. The infantry, helpless to do anything other than follow the commands of their officers, endured.[35]

Oblivious to these events, General Halkett was busy. Leaving Colonel Olfermann to restore the confidence of his young battalions, he decided to undertake a reconnaissance of his own and summoning his aides, they galloped off towards the French, intending to ascertain what was happening in the area to the south of the Ferme de Gemioncourt. They passed the Gemioncourt stream and breasted the rise to the west of the farm, behind which they encountered a large body of cavalry, forming by detachments.

To Halkett, it seemed they were trying to create the impression of moving forward to water the horses in the stream that he and his companion had just crossed, but he was too experienced a soldier to fall for such a ruse. The General and his staff immediately turned about and galloped back up the Charleroi road to rejoin the brigade, just as a tremendous cannonade erupted from the French artillery, the shot and shells straddling the chaussée itself and the adjacent fields.

Realising that the 69th Regiment of Foot was but a short distance away, Halkett sent Major Watson with an urgent message to Colonel Morice, to inform both him and General Pack that he expected the cavalry to advance, that he believed the sudden cannonade was further evidence of this intent and that the battalion was to prepare to receive cavalry immediately.

His obligations to Morice and Pack fulfilled, he then dispatched Captain Baron Heinrich von Marschalk and Captain Alexander Home to the remaining battalions of his brigades, to pass the order to prepare to receive cavalry. A short while later, as he continued to await the onset of the French, Major Watson returned with confirmation from Colonel Morice that his order had been received and that he had carried out Halkett's instructions.[36]

Judging it appropriate to send word to the Prince van Oranje-Nassau, posted with his staff a short distance away, Halkett entrusted Watson with this task, but as Watson galloped across the fields at full speed, his horse received a bullet through its head, wheeled quickly around and crashed lifeless to the ground. Winded, concussed and bruised, Watson found himself trapped beneath the horse and had great difficulty in extricating himself.[37]

As Watson wrestled to free himself, General Pack received Halkett's intelligence and gave the order for the remaining battalions of his brigade to form square, before sending word to the same effect, to the 69th Regiment of Foot. The air quivered as the French artillery on the heights of Gemioncourt continued the bombardment, but positioned as it was in the hollow ground immediately behind the heights of Bati-Saint-Bernard, Colonel Morice's men were relatively shielded from its worst effects, though the shallow depression they occupied, combined with the height of the surrounding crop, further inhibited the view of both officers and men. In such a situation, the slightest credible rumour spread like wildfire. Several of the soldiers were aware that Major Watson, returning from the front, had brought news that the French cavalry were on the move along both sides of the main road, a short distance to the battalion's right. Colonel Morice immediately ordered the battalion to form square, but as the companies were manoeuvring to take up their respective positions, another horseman approached through the smoke from the direction of Les Quatre Bras and shouted across to Morice to ask him the object of his movement. 'I am forming square,' replied the Colonel, 'To resist cavalry.' The anonymous horseman responded by angrily shouting: 'There are none coming!' and ordered Morice to 'Deploy at once into line.' As the smoke cleared somewhat and the horseman came closer, it became apparent that it was none other than the Prince van Oranje-Nassau. Colonel Morice was in a quandary. In forming square, he was carrying out the explicit order of his brigadier; indeed, he had already sent word back to General Halkett that he had followed his order, yet here was his corps commander, countermanding it. Compelled to respect rank over common sense and nobility over prudence, Morice grudgingly acceded to the Prince's demands.[38]

Even those battalions with a far better view of the battlefield were surprised by the rapid turn of events. So sudden and unexpected was the appearance of the French, that Ensign Thain of the 33rd Regiment of Foot supposed that the cavalry had been lying in ambush behind the solid red-brick farm buildings of the Ferme de Gemioncourt. From the ranks of the same battalion, Lieutenant Pattison suddenly heard a voice, calling out: 'Cavalry, cavalry, form square, form square!' Halting his company, he waited nervously as those in the ranks behind ran to right and left to form on the Grenadier Company and take up their respective positions in the hollow, rectangular, formation. As he waited, he took advantage of the position that the battalion had occupied on a spur of high ground, jutting from the Bois de Bossu, to observe the rapid approach of the French horsemen. At first, it had appeared to him that his own corps was the intended target of the cavalry, but now it seemed as though the direction of their charge had shifted somewhat farther to the east. Perhaps the French were put off by the fact that the battalion appeared steadily formed, with its square now complete; perhaps they were seeking more vulnerable targets elsewhere. The cavalry swept past, the sunshine of the late afternoon reflecting on burnished helmets, glittering breastplates and sparkling swords. Cuirassiers! The fabled cavalry that had terrorised much of Europe for the past twenty years![39]

On the far side of the Charleroi road, a short distance from Colonel Morice's command, stood the mutilated remains of the 42nd Regiment of Foot. Whilst the earlier rallying square had done its job temporarily, Major Campbell now realised that his battalion, lacking in officers and in some cases with sergeants commanding the companies, was desperately in need of reorganisation. Reaching the conclusion that this could not be brought about in such an exposed position, he had pulled the battalion back to the north of the heights of Bati-Saint-Bernard.

An attempt was now made to form us in line, for we stood mixed in one irregular mass, grenadier, light and battalion companies. A noisy group. Such is the inevitable consequence of a rapid succession of commanders. Our covering sergeants were called out on that purpose, that each company might form on the right of its sergeant, an excellent plan, had it been adopted, but a cry arose that another charge of cavalry was approaching and this plan was abandoned. We now formed a line on the left of the grenadiers.[40]

In front of the battalion, Corporal Alexander McEween and the survivors of No. 8 Company were alongside their comrades of the Light Company, busily exchanging fire with the French skirmishers, when they also spotted the powerful column of cavalry that had alarmed General Halkett. Disengaging from the enemy, the Highlanders hurriedly ran in to the main body of the battalion, which was again taking heavy casualties from the nearby French batteries. With its skirmishers shouting, 'Cavalry! Cavalry!' the battalion's collective instinct for self-preservation kicked in and the unequalised companies once again formed a ragged square. Across the smoke-filled fields, McEween could make out several other battalions to the north and east; all were hurriedly emulating the Highlanders; suddenly, the roar of the cannon fell silent, to be replaced by a rushing sound. As the horsemen swept past on the chaussée, they seemed so close that one could almost reach out and touch them. Ignoring the Highlanders, the French seemed intent upon pressing home their charge on the crossroads, though being presented with such an inviting target, the British infantry were not inclined to allow them to pass without opening fire. Noticing that the volley had not yielded the anticipated casualties among the blue-cloaked troopers, and that some of the horsemen had merely reeled in the saddle, someone shouted: 'They are in armour. Fire at the horses!' The cuirassiers, however, were already gaining momentum and heedless of the musketry, pressed on towards the crossroads. As soon as the cavalry had passed, the French skirmishers resumed their fire, peppering the ranks of the depleted square.[41]

The French heavy cavalry gained momentum, extending into the fields to the west of the road towards Major Watson, who was still trapped by the half-tonne carcass of his horse. With the thundering hooves pounding in his ears and the blood-curdling cries of the enemy cavalry rapidly approaching, he eventually managed to extricate himself and abandoning his cloak, valise and pistols, he fled back to the 30th Regiment of Foot, a short distance away. The bruised Major had left 'Pagan', his other charger, as well as his bât horse at Horrues and being unable to procure another, realised that he would have to fight on foot for the remainder of the battle, or somehow procure a replacement. As soon as the opportunity arrived, he resolved to return to his own regiment and resume the command of the Grenadier Company.[42]

The battalion in which he was temporarily sheltered had been alerted to the advance of the horsemen and the order: 'Prepare to receive cavalry' had been given. A short while after the square had been completed, Colonel Vigoreux hurried up with the three companies that formed the composite 'Light Battalion' of the

The Battle of Quatre Bras

brigade, minus the missing Light Company of the 30th Regiment of Foot, which had not yet rejoined. As they took up position on the southern and eastern faces of the square, they gave it a lop-sided and uneven appearance, the walls of men being six deep instead of the regulation four. Having so far remained with his battalion, Surgeon Elkington judged this to be an opportune moment to move to the rear, whilst the cavalry were still some distance away. The front line was no place for supernumeraries; he and his two Assistant Surgeons, John Evans and Patrick Clarke would have a busy enough afternoon and evening ahead of them, without running the risk of being unnecessarily killed or wounded themselves. Together with his Hospital Sergeant and the bât horse that carried their instruments and medicines, they would head for the Namur road and establish an aid post there, a short distance to the east of the crossroads.

As soon as they arrived on the chaussée, the three men contented themselves with avoiding the worst of the French cannonade and watching the movements of their parent battalion, which they could clearly identify from the grey horse ridden by Lieutenant Matthias Andrews, the Adjutant. The French gunners were doubtless also grateful to Andrews for giving them such an excellent target at which to aim, and the battalion was soon engulfed in smoke and iron. Within minutes, individual soldiers could be seen staggering from the ranks and small parties, evacuating wounded comrades in blood-soaked blankets, toiled across the fields towards the Namur road. The three surgeons would shortly have their first patients and hurried to prepare themselves.[43]

Endnotes

1. Barlow. Batty, pp. 49–50. Brereton and Savory, p. 144. Cleeves. Elkington (I), p. 12. Gomm (I). Gomm (IV). Gomm (V). Hope (I). Hope (III), p. 228. J. Howard. Kincaid (I), pp. 320–1. Macready (V). Morris, p. 67. Pattison (I). Pratt. Riddock. C. von Scriba (I). C. von Scriba (II). Thain (I). Thain (II).
2. Dalton, pp. 37, 143–44. Elkington (I), p. 12. Elkington (II). Powell. Shaw-Kennedy (I). Shaw-Kennedy (II), p. 17.
3. Pattison (II), pp. 3–4.
4. Halkett (I). Hofschröer (III), p. 38. Pattison (II), p. 4. von Pflugk-Harttung (II), p. 22. Rudyerd. C. von Scriba (I). C. von Scriba (II).
5. Butler, p. 78. Halkett (I). Halkett (II). Pattison (I). Pratt.
6. de Bas &c., p. 516. Halkett (I). von Pflugk-Harttung (II), p. 22. Tincombe.
7. Butler, pp. 78–9. Archibald Forbes, p. 270. Grant and Youens, p. 23. Lomax, p. 125. Halkett (I). Maugham, p. 7. Rudyerd.
8. Halkett (I).
9. Ainslie, pp. 14–15. Bannatyne, p. 314. Barlow. Butler, p. 79. Halkett (I). Lomax, p. 125. Macready (V). Pattison (I). Rudyerd.
10. de Bas &c., p. 516. C. Hamilton, p. 4. Rudyerd.

11. Anonymous (Das braunschweigische Korps). Halkett (I). Gurwood, pp. 490–1. Olfermann. Von Wachholtz, pp. 27–9.
12. Anonymous (Das braunschweigische Korps). Anonymous (Near Observer), pp. 67–8. Beamish, p. 489. Frazer, p. 541. von Herzberg. von Pivka (III), p.21. Rogers (I). Rudyerd. W. Siborne (I). W. Siborne (II). W. Siborne (V), p. 77. Wells.
13. Riddock.
14. Frazer, p. 545. Halkett (III). Rudyerd. Wells.
15. Beamish, p. 489. Frazer, p. 545. von Herzberg. von Wachholtz, p. 28.
16. Jackson (II), pp. 26–7.
17. Hope (III), p. 228. Pattison (II), p. 8.
18. Anonymous (Letters), pp. 228–9. Hope (I). Hope (III), pp. 228–9. Winchester (III).
19. Hope (I). Lagden and Sly, p. 3.
20. G. Paget (I), pp. 106, 113.
21. Arthur, p. 598. Bannatyne, p. 314. Elkington (II). Halkett (I). von Herzberg. Howard, p. 245. Lee, p. 227. Lomax, p. 125. Macready (IV). Macready (V). Thain (II). Tincombe.
22. Dalton, pp. 149–50. Halkett (I). Hemingway. Lee, p. 227. Pattison (I) Pattison (II), p. 5. Thain (I). Thain (II).
23. Kincaid (I), pp. 320–1. Leach, pp. 376–7. Pattison (II), p. 3.
24. Anonymous (Letters), p. 229. Arthur, p. 598. Gomm (V). Halkett (I), von Herzberg. Hope (I). Hope (III), p. 229. Lee, pp. 226–7. von Pflugk-Harttung (II), pp. 15–17, 22. Thain (II). Tincombe.
25. Anonymous (Cameron), pp. 90–1. Cleeves. Heise (II). Jahns. von Pflugk-Harttung (II), pp. 5–13, 22. von Rettberg (I). von Rettberg (II). Rudyerd.
26. Anonymous (Letters), p. 229. Hope (I). von Pflugk-Harttung, pp. 33–5.
27. Kincaid (I), pp. 319–20.
28. Anonymous (Near Observer), p. 46.
29. Kincaid (I), pp. 320–1. Leach, pp. 376–7.
30. Caldwell and Cooper, p. 11. McGuigan. von Pflugk-Harttung (II), p. 22.
31. Anonymous (Journal), p. 383. de Bas &c., p. 516. Gomm (IV). Kincaid (I), pp. 320–1.
32. Anonymous (Journal), p. 383. de Bas &c., p. 516. Gomm (IV). Kincaid (I), pp. 320–1. Leach pp. 376–7.
33. Hemingway. Thain (II).
34. Morris, pp. 68–9.
35. Hemingway. Pattison (I). Thain (II).
36. Barlow. Archibald Forbes, p. 270. Halkett (I). Halkett (II). Lomax, p. 125. Maughan, pp. 7–9. van Zuylen van Nyeveld (I), p. 57.
37. Myddleton, pp. 93–4.
38. Arthur, p. 598. Barlow. Black. Brereton and Savory, p. 145. Brett-James, p. 55. Butler, p. 79. Delhaize and Aerts, p. 460. Archibald Forbes, p. 271. Halkett (I). Halkett (II). Lomax, p. 125. Macready (I). Maughan, p. 7. Pattison (I).
39. Brereton and Savory, p. 145. Hemingway. Lee, p. 227. Pattison (I). Pattison (II), p. 5. Thain (II).
40. Anton, pp. 193–4.

41. Arthur, p. 598. Gomm (IV). McEween. Mudie (I). W. Siborne (V), p. 83.
42. Myddleton, pp. 93–4.
43. Dalton, p. 140. Elkington (I), p. 12. Elkington (II). Harty. Macready (IV), p. 393. Myddleton, p. 93. Tincombe.

CHAPTER 16

By 5.30 p.m. the Light Company of the 30th Regiment of Foot was but a short distance away to the west:

> At length we had a confused view of the field, with our troops and the enemy firing away under their sulphurous canopy. Clouds of birds were flying and squealing above the smoke. We loosened our ammunition, and pushed on for it. Hedges, streams, and ditches were passed like thought. After scrambling thro' a thick, thorny plantation, we found ourselves close to a body of men with whose uniform we were unacquainted. Not above twenty of our company were present. We advanced to these people and found them to belong to the Nassau-Usingen contingent. They had just been driven from the wood of Bossu, which was in front of us, and between ourselves and the army. We made for it, and came up with Sir George Berkeley, Adjutant-General to the Prince's corps, who had just escaped from the lancers. He told us our regiment had entered the field about a quarter of an hour before, and that they were on the other side of the wood, which we must pass on the left, near Quatre Bras, as the enemy occupied the whole of it.[1]

After leaving the Nassauers to the west of the Bois de Bossu, the men of the Light Company of the 30th Regiment of Foot had skirted the wood, convinced from the volume of fire emanating from it that the French must be in complete possession and had even brought up artillery, so numerous were the round shot that bounded out of it. One particular shot splashed the entire company with a large quantity of dirt and mud, leading to nervously humorous comments about the men having received their baptism. Indistinct shapes in blue, white and grey were skirmishing at the very edge of the wood, the rattle of musketry now very real. As he toiled breathlessly towards the Nivelles road, Ensign Macready noticed that it was lined by men of the 92nd Regiment of Foot, returning fire as best they could. The small party hurried on, passing the right flank of the Gordons, behind which several Highlanders were lying dead and wounded. As they approached the crossroads at Les Quatre Bras, Terry O'Neil, an old campaigner roared: 'Close your ranks and hold up your heads, my lads.' At such a moment, Ensign Macready could not help but feel a thrill as he found himself 'bodily in the battle':

The roaring of great guns and musketry, the bursting of shells and shouts of combatants raised an infernal din, while the squares and lines, galloping horses mounted and riderless, the mingled crowds of wounded and fugitives (foreigners), the volumes of smoke, and flashing of fire, struck out a scene which accorded admirably with the music.[2]

Not wishing to obstruct the front of Major Lloyd's battery, now established in the south-west angle of the crossroads, Lieutenant Rumley pressed on for the crossroads itself, where having ascertained the direction in which their parent battalion had deployed, they turned south and doubled down the Charleroi road. The ground between the crossroads and the Ferme de la Bergerie was littered with lifeless corpses and mutilated men of numerous nationalities, but most noticeably with the unfortunates of the 92nd Regiment of Foot, whose bodies had, in some places, fallen across each other in gruesome piles. Passing to the south of the Ferme de la Bergerie, they came across evidence of the 44th Regiment of Foot's ordeal at the hands of the French lancers, little over an hour or so beforehand. Clumps of wounded men lay in the fields to the east of the chaussée, some unable to move, others managing to drag themselves towards the road, in the hope of reaching the Ferme de la Bergerie, Les Quatre Bras, or even a water-filled ditch. Despite their desperate plight they still had sufficient breath and spirit to cheer on Macready and his men:

> As we passed a spot where the 44th, old chums of ours in Spain, had suffered considerably, the poor wounded fellows raised themselves up and welcomed us with faint shouts, 'Push on old three tens – pay 'em off for the 44th – you're much wanted, boys – success to you, my darlings.'[3]

A moment later, a more familiar figure appeared on the road, riding towards them. It was Colonel Hamilton, shot through the leg. As he came up to the band of warriors, he tried to present a cheerful aspect. He pointed to his shattered limb and joked: 'They've tickled me again, my boys – now one leg can't laugh at the other.'

Ensign Macready was exhausted; everything seemed surreal; a disjointed sequence of images. He didn't know what his sensations would have been, had he entered the field coolly, but he was 'so fagged and choked with running, and was pressed so suddenly into the very thick of the business', that most of the events around him were a blur, except that it seemed as if with every step he took, his foot stumbled over the dead and wounded Highlanders who were 'most provokingly distributed'. Lieutenant Rumley asked the Colonel where the main body of the regiment was and Hamilton pointed to a square of white-trousered infantry on a knoll some distance farther to the south.

Scattered across the fields to the west were other clusters of British troops in different formations. Could the front line really be this close to Les Quatre Bras? Quickly saluting his commanding officer, Rumley once more cajoled his men's tired legs into a run towards their parent battalion:

We reached it just as a body of lancers and cuirassiers had enveloped two faces of its square. We formed up to the left and fired away. The tremendous volley our square (which, in the hurry of formation, was six deep on the two sides attacked) gave them, sent off these fellows with the loss of a number of men and their commanding officer. He was a gallant soul; he fell while crying, 'Avancez, mes enfants! Courage! Encore une fois, Français!'[4]

Despite the exhortations of their chief, many of the lancers could not encourage their mounts to press the charge home against the dense hedge of bayonets. The French cavalry attacking the southern and eastern faces of the square, suffered volley after volley as they flashed by in a blur. Macready thought that they were 'Savage looking fellows'. Savage or not, the firepower of the British infantry was murderous, reinforced as it was by the presence of Colonel Vigoreux's 'Light Bobs' and the steel cuirasses and helmets proved no protection against the short-range musketry. As the French cavalry surged past, Captain Joseph Harty, commanding the Light Company of the 33rd Regiment of Foot in Vigoreux' battalion, saw General Picton ride up. Having been present nearby during the cavalry charges, he had been impressed with the battalion's steadiness and firepower. Summoning Major Thomas Chambers, he told him that: 'They were a noble set of fellows' and that he would report their gallant conduct to the Duke. These warm remarks quickly passed by word of mouth down the ranks and the men laughed, shook hands and cheered wildly, exhilarated by their experience, convinced of their invincibility and delighted with the prospect of such recognition. His pleasure turning immediately to anger, however, the mercurial Sir Thomas bellowed: 'Damn you all for making such a noise! Have you no officers amongst you?'[5]

Having run the gauntlet of the 30th Regiment of Foot, two squadrons of cuirassiers, supported by a body of lancers, continued their charge towards the glittering bayonets of the 73rd Regiment of Foot, just visible above the thick corn in the distance. The battalion had almost completed its deployment from quarter-distance column into line, when Colonel Harris, Major Archibald Maclean and Ensign Patrick Hay, the Adjutant, noticed the French approaching rapidly. Aware from the shouts of their officers and sergeants that French cavalry were coming on, but unable to see for themselves on account of the height of the crop, Private Morris and several other soldiers of the Grenadier Company panicked and ran back to the edge of the wood, convinced that there was no time to form square. The majority of the battalion stood its ground, however, though the left wing pulled back some distance in a confused manner. Fortunately, the cavalry did not press home its attack and after some minutes, Captain Alexander Robertson, aided by Lieutenant John Acres, his 'officier en second', managed the establish some order in their company. Acres using his gigantic stature and enormous strength to physically push the men into their ranks. Once back in line, the regiment changed front to the south, pivoting on Robertson's men in a regulation and orderly manner; the crisis had passed.[6]

To the east of the Charleroi road, and oblivious to the events unfolding on the opposite side of the chaussée or to the south, the 69th Regiment of Foot was busy

The Battle of Quatre Bras

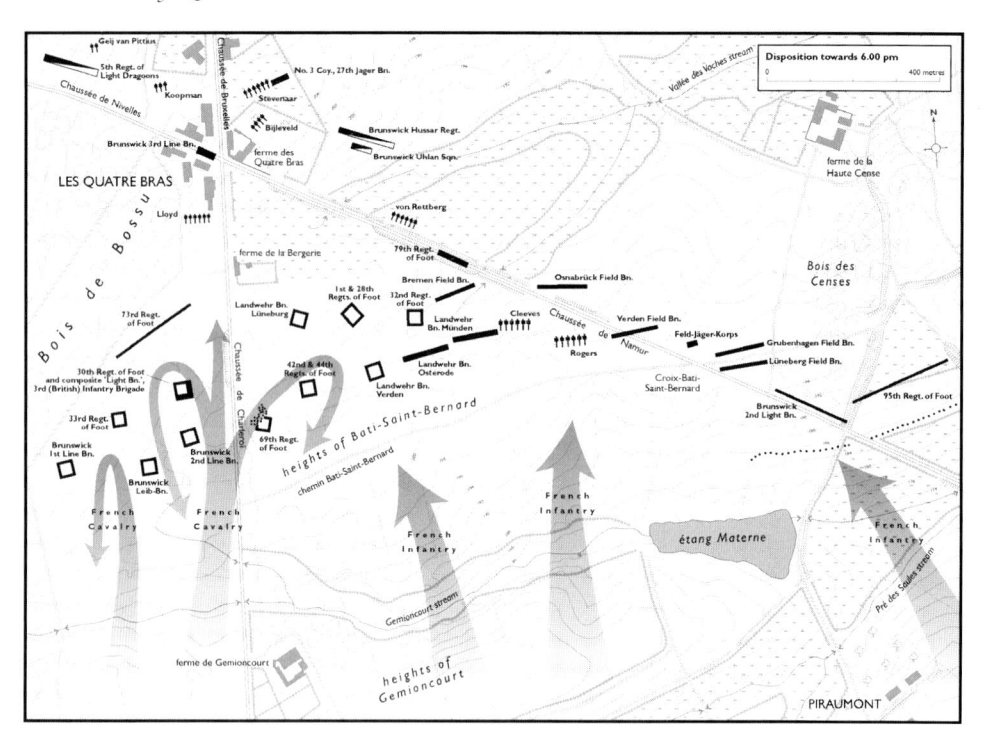

carrying out the Prince van Oranje-Nassau's order. To cover the evolution, Morice had sent forward No. 8 Company to form a skirmish line. Behind this screen were No. 4 and No. 5 Companies, the square having been formed on the centre of the battalion. The commanding officer paused for a moment, wondering how best to carry out the Prince's order? Change from square into open column and then deploy into line; or wheel back the sections and deploy? Events were about to overtake him. Colonel Morice ordered the three right-flank companies to wheel and form line to the right of No. 5 Company. The men were running into place when the bombardment ominously died away; it was the calm before the storm. Now, a new kind of vibration replaced that of projectiles in the quivering air. This time it was the thunder of hooves, transmitted through the ground. The sensation was accompanied by a moaning sound, as the massive chests of heavy horses drove through the thickly planted rye, trampling it beneath their pounding legs. 'Cavalry are coming!' went up a shout from somewhere in the confused crowd and Colonel Morice hurriedly bellowed the order to again form square; it was too late. Suddenly, less than fifty metres from the Grenadier Company and slightly in rear of its flank, a squadron of French cuirassiers appeared over the rising ground, thundering towards them, their horses kicking up great clods of earth and tangled rye as their armoured riders leaned forward in the saddle, long straight swords seemingly pointed at the heart of every British soldier. Unsure of what formation they were in and ignorant as to how to obey their commanding officer, the troops were paralysed; easy pickings for the cuirassiers, whose reputation had been forged on the fields of Essling, Wagram, Borodino and Leipzig.[7]

In the noise and confusion, however, Major Henry Lindsay and Lieutenant Brooke

Pigot had managed to form the Grenadier, No. 1 and No. 2 Companies into an open column. They were moving back as quickly as possible to close the north-west corner of the square, which had been formed on No. 5 Company and was largely complete. With the cavalry gaining ground, Lindsay now made an error that was to haunt him for the rest of his life. Instead of urging his men to run as fast as they could and close the square, he halted the small column, faced it right about and ordered the men to open fire on the cuirassiers, who by this time were virtually on top of them. With most of their front obscured, only the Grenadiers had a clear shot at the French and they fired a hurried volley, at thirty paces, supported by a few files on the flank of the column. They were joined in their volley by fire from No. 3 and No. 4 Companies, forming the south-west corner of the incomplete square. Though the fusillade staggered the French squadron, horses and men tumbling to the ground, their momentum was by now unstoppable; they smashed into Lindsay's hapless column, driving their swords into the unresisting bodies, bowling over the defenceless infantrymen and trampling them underfoot. Witness to the massacre being carried out a few metres to their front and aware of the gaping hole in the wall of bayonets where the victims of the butchery should have been, the morale of the battalion disintegrated, the square imploded and the men fled to the rear or towards the closest Allied squares, seeking sanctuary. There was no time even to form a rallying square.

Their confidence shattered, the 'Saucy Greens' ran blindly in all directions, seeking to avoid the onrushing cavalry, trampling each other in their desperation to escape. Whether too exhausted, or demonstrating great presence of mind, others threw themselves to the ground to avoid being spitted by the steel-clad giants, the hooves of the horses flashing by terrified faces. Screams mingled with shouts of triumph; images of steel, sweating horseflesh and implacable, moustached faces flashed before men's eyes. The majority of the officers and men from the southern and eastern faces of the square fled to the nearby 42nd and 44th Regiments of Foot, where they took cover under the bayonets of the kneeling front rank. Amongst them was Captain Barlow:

> When he [Barlow] saw the game was up and all resistance useless and some of the armour-bearing cavaliers close at his back, he had the presence of mind to throw himself on the ground. The enemy passed by and over him. He had often heard of their 'ruse' and being incapable of running he had no other resource left. He waited awhile and then getting on his legs made the best of his way to the square of the 42nd Regiment, which saved him.[8]

Lieutenant Wightwick of No. 1 Company, Lieutenant Pigot's second-in-command, was trampled into the rye, mortally wounded and within minutes, some 150 men of the regiment joined him. The impetuosity of the charge and the viciousness of the struggle made the French disinclined to take prisoners; those that threw down their weapons and held their arms aloft in supplication were simply killed or ignored altogether. Major George Muttlebury was one of only four mounted officers with the battalion and spurring his horse, he galloped off towards the Namur road, closely pursued by two French lancers. Ahead of him, he noticed two 9-pounder guns of Captain Cleeves' brigade of King's German Legion foot artillery, whose crews had just loaded their pieces. Uncertain whether to cross their front as they were about to discharge, he instinctively pulled hard on his reins, bringing his charger to a stand and causing the pursuing lancers to overshoot and sweep across the front of the artillery, where they were shredded by canister. Slightly to the east, Colonel Morice and Lieutenant Henry Oldershaw – his Adjutant – escaped a chasing pack of twenty cuirassiers by riding through a Hanoverian battalion, which they passed through so quickly, that they did not recognise its identity.[9]

In the centre of the abandoned battalion, a small body of men formed a scrum around the battalion's two colours. Ensign Ainslie, as the junior officer, was bearing the Regimental colour, a large flag with a green field and a small union flag in the upper canton. Close by was Ensign Keith with the King's colour. The flags were virtually new, the regiment having had the misfortune to have lost both its colours at Bergen-op-Zoom the previous year. Protected only by sergeants wielding spontoons that would not have looked out of place on a medieval battlefield, the two officers and their charges were immediately obvious to the cavalry and a knot of horseman made straight for them. The colour party stood rooted to the ground, seemingly left to its fate by the remainder of the battalion. Major Lindsay, perhaps in an effort to redeem himself, made a gallant attempt to protect the colours and fell, severely wounded. At his side, Lieutenant Pigot also went down. Ensign Ainslie could no longer think and was acting on a combination of adrenalin and instinct:

> When I saw the cuirassiers riding down our rank, and that our own men fled in every direction, my first impulse was to throw myself flat on the ground with my colour; but whilst in the act of doing so, it was taken from me by one of the colour sergeants, whose duty it is to take charge of the colours in moments of emergency. I am not certain of the fact, so great was the confusion of the moment, but I think this man, either by accident or design, fell to the ground with me.[10]

With the regimental colour now hidden from view beneath the prone bodies of Ainslie and his colour sergeant, the French were instead distracted by the small band of men surrounding the King's colour and a fierce struggle commenced for its possession. In the midst of the pack was Christopher Clarke, a cadet from the Military College, who had joined the battalion as a 'gentleman volunteer', seeking glory and perhaps a battle-field commission in the shoes of a dead officer. Ensign Keith fell to the ground, bowled over by a cuirassier. The colour was torn from his grasp, whether by a colour sergeant, Volunteer Clarke or a cuirassier, he could not make out. Clarke struggled to maintain his own grip on the colour and succeeded in killing three cuirassiers, earning 23 wounds in return, several of which were to deprive him of the use of an arm for the remainder of his life. Around him, the armoured horsemen continued to hack and stab at his tormented body, but heedless of the pain, Clarke clung on to the symbol of the battalion's

'Push on old three tens – pay 'em off for the 44th'

Royal allegiance. Weak from loss of blood, concussed and dazed, he eventually slumped unconscious into the rye, his coat in tatters and his body covered in blood from the deep wounds he had endured in its defence. The fluttering silk was instantly in the hands of the cavalry and for the second time in less than a year, the regiment would endure the shame of losing its colour. Victorious, the group of cuirassiers rode off towards their own positions, doubtless arguing who had delivered the killer thrust, or whose hands had been on the staff. *Quel exploit glorieux!* Cantering back down the Charleroi road with their prize, they paraded it before the cheering ranks of the French infantry, who were forming up for yet another attack. Surely the English were finished?[11]

In the square of the 42nd Regiment of Foot, Major Campbell had been joined by General Pack. Also occupying the centre of the square were the handful of remaining officers, the drummers, the tattered colours and several wounded French infantry, who at first were convinced they were about to be put to death by the fearsome-looking Highlanders; these, in contrast, were careful not to trample on the casualties and prisoners as they took up their respective places in the formation. The varying losses suffered by each of the companies made the square somewhat lopsided, no time having been available to redistribute the survivors between the companies. Despite this, the formation remained steady and the last file had just managed to run in, when the cuirassiers, their helmets and breastplates glinting in the afternoon sunshine, rode towards two faces of the square. Fortunately for the Highlanders, the French cavalry had lost momentum and came to a halt instead of pressing home the charge onto the hedge of bayonets. To the exhausted men in the ragged square, it had seemed inevitable that the enormous warhorses and their steel-clad riders would simply smash through their flimsy ranks, but the French commanding officer had seen enough of war to realise that a steady square was virtually impregnable. 'Why don't you surrender?' he called across. 'Surrender. You know you are beaten!'[12]

> A moment's pause ensued. It was the pause of death. General Pack was on the right angle of the front face of the square and lifted his hat towards the French officer, as he was wont to do when returning a salute. I suppose our assailants construed our forbearance as an indication of surrendering, a false idea. Not a blow had been struck nor a musket levelled, but when the General raised his hat, it served as the signal, though not a pre-concerted one, but entirely accidental, for we were doubtful whether our officer commanding was protracting the order, waiting for the General's command, as he was present. Be that as it may, a most destructive fire was opened. Riders, cased in heavy armour fell, tumbling from their horses. The horses reared, plunged and fell on the dismounted riders. Steel helmets and cuirasses rung against unsheathed sabres, as they fell to the ground; shrieks and groans of men, the neighing of horses, and the discharge of musketry, rent the air, as men and horses mixed together in one heap of indiscriminate slaughter.[13]

Those cuirassiers who survived the fusillade fled back across the road towards the Bois de Bossu, which seemed to Sergeant Anton to be bristling with troops. The repeated volleys necessary to drive off the cavalry, combined with the earlier infantry fire fights, had taken its toll on the ammunition pouches and as men reached behind them to pull out a fresh cartridge, more and more realised that their supply was exhausted and reported the fact to their corporals and sergeants. As soon as the danger had passed, Major Campbell ordered the battalion to once more deploy into line and directed the men to empty the pouches of the dead and dying and to share the cartridges out. As soon as this was complete, he once again led his battalion forward.[14]

As the Scots advanced up the gentle slope, the cannon balls came bounding over the ridge, spreading death and destruction. Ever solicitous for their welfare, Campbell ordered the men to lie down in a clover field, just to the north of the chemin Bati-Saint-Bernard and though this gave the men some shelter from the projectiles ploughing across the rutted track, they found that they had advanced some way from the other battalions of the brigade. A short distance away, some adventurous French infantry advanced through the rye field on the opposite side of the lane and fired with great effect at the huddled line of redcoats, who tried to conceal themselves in a position almost devoid of cover of any description. Musket balls whizzed by, embedding themselves in knapsacks, chinking off bayonets and passing through the men's bonnets. Any opportunity, however dangerous, to rest their weary limbs for some minutes was welcome, though few men were in the mood to doze, despite the warmth of the sun on their backs.[15]

The Allies were exhausted. The relentless bombardment, the murderous short-range sharpshooting and the continuous see-saw of attack and counter-attack had almost bled the army to death. Perhaps General Picton thought it was all over. Perhaps his premonition was to come true after all. His division was in desperate straits; having sustained crippling casualties, his battalions could now only muster a few hundred men, but perhaps more alarmingly, even the survivors would soon be unable to fight for want of ammunition. In the ranks of the 42nd Regiment of Foot, Sergeant Anton fished about in his cartridge box for his few remaining rounds:

> We had wasted a deal of ammunition this day and surely to very little effect, otherwise every one of our adversaries must have bled before this time. Our commanding officer cautioned against this useless expenditure and we became a little more economical.[16]

Anton was not alone. In the nearby 44th Regiment of Foot, Colonel O'Malley and Lieutenant Riddock were amongst many officers equally concerned at the want of ammunition; a predicament worsened by the astonishingly high losses in officers and men. Improvisation was required on a grand scale and General Pack decided to combine the depleted 42nd and 44th Regiments of Foot into a single formation, with which he would remain. With the Royal Scots seconded to Pack's brigade and the Gordon Highlanders effectively hors de combat, Pack's brigade now consisted of a depleted battalion, with a general as the commanding officer and Major Campbell of the 42nd and Colonel Hamerton of the 44th Regiments of Foot acting as majors.

Despite this drastic measure, the combined battalion was barely able to hold its own on the chemin Bati-Saint-Bernard, against the French skirmishers in the tall crops between there and the enclosures of the Ferme de Gemioncourt and the short-range fire of the enemy artillery. Picton realised the absolute necessity of moving up reinforcements. Accompanied by Colonel Gomm, he galloped across the field towards the Namur road, where he found the 28th Regiment of Foot drawn up in what he thought was a square. On approaching closer, he realised that the 'square' comprised only three faces in reality, the north face being formed by the deep cutting through which the Namur road passed at this point, making the regiment impervious to assault by cavalry on this side. He also noticed that the ranks contained many soldiers of the Royal Scots, perhaps as many as an entire wing. Major Robert Macdonald, commanding the left wing of the Royals, was better informed. After a prolonged fire fight with the French infantry close to the Gemioncourt stream, the battalion had formed into a quarter-distance column and withdrawn. Pressed by clouds of skirmishers and with many of the officers already killed and wounded, the formation had collapsed into a shambolic press of men, which was driven back as far as the Namur road and saved from destruction only by the 28th Regiment of Foot, which emerged from the gloom and drove the French back over the chemin Bati-Saint-Bernard. Bereft of orders and threatened by cavalry and infantry alike, the two battalions had combined and had spent a considerable time in line, holding back Bachelu's more adventurous skirmishers and forming square when threatened by cavalry. Many soldiers were totally unaware that their battalion had been merged with another, such was the confusion, noise and smoke.[17]

In these hastily amalgamated ranks was Lieutenant James Crummer, in a despondent mood and convinced that: 'All was nearly up with us'. The sight of the cuirassiers overrunning the 69th Regiment of Foot and swirling around the fields close to the Ferme de la Bergerie, had not brightened his mood, but things were about to change. Picton and Kempt held a brief horseback conference. Explaining Pack's predicament, Picton ordered Kempt to reform the two regiments in a single column and move towards the south-west, where it could come into action on the flank of the French horsemen, as they swept up the Charleroi road. Within minutes, the formation was complete and the composite column covered some four hundred metres towards the position occupied by the 42nd and 44th Regiments of Foot. The phalanx advanced unhindered, despite the presence of a large body of enemy cavalry in its front, until it reached the spot determined by Picton, where it formed an impenetrable square, with four ranks on each face and the two general officers in its centre.[18]

Farther to the east, Colonel Hicks spotted the movement of the battalion on his right. His own command was on the verge of collapse; half of his company commanders were casualties and he estimated that he had lost two thirds of his strength killed, wounded or missing. The territory that his battalion had contested was covered with the corpses of the fallen. From the crushed wheat and rye came moaning and sobbing, occasionally punctuated by a howl or shriek. The more fortunate wounded could stagger back across the chaussée towards the Ferme de l'Haute Cense, in search of a surgeon or simply some water. Others dragged themselves a few yards on shattered stumps, until their blood-soaked trail ended in a sanguine pool, already infested with flies. The least fortunate were pinned under the cadavers of their comrades, in tangled heaps where the dead and dying remained locked in a macabre embrace, the victims of a sudden volley or lethal discharge of canister. As they gazed up at the blue sky, what would their final thoughts have been? The survivors were inured to such scenes and although the carcasses of scarred, battered and bloody flesh were their mates, their most immediate concern was self-preservation.

Others were suffering the same fate. The threat posed by French artillery to Captain Cleeves' guns of the King's German Legion had proven itself to be very real. As the French horse artillery engaged them from a range of less than four hundred metres, First Lieutenant Heinrich Hartmann was wounded, as was Second Lieutenant Carl Ludwig. Still the round shot came bounding through the gun line. Finally, when First Lieutenant Wilhelm von Goeben was also hit, the Captain was obliged to send a message to Rogers' brigade – still heavily engaged in the open fields to the east – asking for assistance in the form of a spare officer. To the German's relief, a short while later, First Lieutenant Robert Manners hurried up to his position and, saluting his new commanding officer, immediately set about restoring some order to the exhausted brigade.[19]

As he galloped tirelessly from one decimated battalion to the next, General Picton's horse received a mortal wound and collapsed on top of its rider. His aide-de-camp, Captain Gore, immediately dismounted, dragged Picton clear and was offering his own horse to his winded and bruised chief, when a round shot passed between them with an enormous rush of air, terrifying Gore's charger, which broke away and galloped into the smoke, leaving them both dismounted and vulnerable. Whether by virtue of his fall, the passage of the cannonball, or the impact of a spent musket or canister ball, two of the General's ribs were broken and his coat torn on one side; unaware that his master was injured, Gore helped him to the safety of a nearby square.[20]

Into this charnel house, General von Kielmansegge deployed the three remaining battalions of his brigade. Lieutenant-Colonel Wilhelm von Langehr brought up the Bremen Field Battalion on the left of the 32nd Regiment of Foot, whilst Major Julius von Schkopp deployed the Verden battalion farther to the east. In support were Major Baron Carl von Bülow and the Osnabrück battalion, formerly known as the Duke of York Field Battalion, in honour of King George's son. Once again, a thin red line of defence was established in the exposed area between the Namur road and the étang Materne. Fresh meat was ready for the grinder and it was not long before the French gunners found the range and the three battalions started taking casualties.

With the Hanoverian troops taking up ground to his left, Hicks' own battalion edged farther and farther to the west, following to some extent in the wake of the combined column of the 1st and 28th Regiments of Foot, an involuntary and crab-like advance that at least brought him into the protective lee of the heights of Bati-Saint-Bernard. After a short period of time had elapsed, the remnants of Kempt's brigade took up ground a short distance to the south-east of the Ferme de la Bergerie, the 32nd Regiment of Foot forming up a short distance to the left rear of the newly-combined 1st and 28th Regiments of Foot.[21]

From his position on the slope to the east of the Ferme des Quatre Bras, Captain von Rettberg and his battery had been engaged for what seemed a lifetime, but in reality had been less than a few hours. Around him was the litter of war: dead horses, damaged vehicles and killed and wounded artillerymen. Earlier, he had seen Captain Cleeves pass along the road with his company of King's German Legion foot artillery and take up a position in front of the Namur road, some seven hundred metres from the crossroads, where the chaussée became embanked. Now, von Rettberg received an order to take up a position on Cleeves' left; apparently, General von Alten's division was short of artillery. Perhaps Major Lloyd's brigade was deemed sufficient to cover the centre of the position; perhaps other artillery were about to deploy. Then again, perhaps each general was only concerned with shoring up his own individual portion of the line. Whatever might prove the case, von Rettberg immediately saw that his new position was considerably closer to the French artillery; so much so that he could make out the barrels of the guns, which also appeared to him to be far superior in numbers. With judicious presentment, he placed his pieces as far apart as possible and gave orders for the ammunition wagons to be sheltered behind the embankment to the north of the road. It would make no sense for these to be needlessly exposed. In taking up his position, he gained an unexpected reinforcement:

> A second Captain from Captain Lloyd's battery, whose name I forget, came with a howitzer and placed himself voluntarily under my command, while the other guns of Captain Lloyd's battery were under fire by the enemy.

The new arrival was Captain Rudyerd, who had mistaken von Rettberg's battery for those of his parent brigade as he withdrew his guns on the orders of his battery commander. Realising his error, but with the intervening ground now full of French cavalry rampaging and Major Lloyd's guns under sustained fire, he would need to choose the timing of his dash carefully. Rudyerd was astonished by what he had seen. It seemed as though he had hardly left the 69th Regiment of Foot before it was engulfed by the cuirassiers, which appeared to have come from the direction of the Bois de l'Hutte. As the infantry disintegrated before his eyes, he had noticed Colonel Morice and Lieutenant Oldershaw making their escape to the east. Through relentless blasting away at the cuirassiers, Rudyerd was of the opinion that he and his men saved what remained of Morice's unfortunate battalion. To the west of the road, he caught sight of a British battalion in white trousers and mistook it for one of Cooke's Guards regiments, unaware that these were still some distance away to the west. The soldiers in fact belonged to the 30th Regiment of Foot, which had remained in square, almost parallel to the position that had been occupied by the unfortunate South Lincolnshires.[22]

The Battle of Quatre Bras

Shortly after it had taken up its new position, another charge was made by French lancers and cuirassiers on the square of the 1st and 28th Regiments of Foot, the front rank kneeling and presenting an impenetrable hedge of bayonets, whilst the rear three ranks blasted away at the steel-jacketed cavalry from a distance of less than fifty metres. The British probably welcomed the presence of the armoured horsemen; at least in this situation, the infantry could cause some damage whilst not taking casualties from infantry or artillery fire. A Hanoverian battalion to the north, and the combined square of the 42nd and 44th Regiments of Foot to the south poured volley after volley into the vulnerable flanks of the French charge. Trapped in this blind alley, realising the danger of their own situation and subjected to a storm of musketry, the French at last wheeled about and once more passed over the wreckage of the 69th Regiment of Foot, having suffered substantial losses in killed and wounded. His spirits lifted somewhat, Lieutenant Crummer became convinced that by this bold manoeuvre, Picton had 'restored the balance of victory' in the favour of the Allies.[23]

As the cavalry swept off to the south, an eerie silence replaced the clash of steel, the jingling of harness and the cries of the struggling combatants. Ensign Ainslie cautiously raised his head from the rye and looked about himself:

The capture of the King's colour of the 69th Regiment of Foot. Print after Robert Desvarraux. See page 314. (Author's collection)

The colour prior to restoration. (Author's collection)

> When I saw that the body of cavalry which had charged our regiment had retired, I got up and walked towards the road in front of the farm of Quatre Bras, which was but a few hundred yards distant. In doing this, I found myself on an open space, where the balls of friends and foes were whizzing past me every instant and many struck the earth close to me. I found, on reaching the road, that I had approached it in the very face of one of our regiments, which was concealed by a bank running parallel to it and from whence it maintained a heavy fire whenever any of the enemy approached the village. Here, I overtook one of our own men, bearing the regimental colour, from whom I learned that it had been passed through several hands. I rejoined the remnant of my regiment. We were particularly cast down by the severe loss we had sustained, particularly as this was the first general action in which the second battalion of the 69th Regiment had ever been engaged.[24]

Aside from the heap of killed and wounded in the rye fields, the remainder of his battalion had disintegrated, blown like chaff before the wind. Some remained with the square of the 42nd and 44th Regiments of Foot; others had found sanctuary farther to the east with the 1st and 28th Regiments of Foot; still more lay beneath the protection of the bayonets of Hanoverian infantry battalions. Across the battlefield, the demoralised men, many of whom no longer had muskets or accoutrements, trembled as they recalled the experience. Major Watson had at least been spared the horror that had engulfed the rest of his regiment and had taken shelter with the 30th Regiment of Foot. Once the cavalry charge receded, he made the best of his way on foot to the shattered remnant of his battalion, which the surviving officers were attempting to rally close to the crossroads. As the subaltern and non-commissioned

The Battle of Quatre Bras

officers tried to sort out the confusion and form up the ruined companies, the Major was rejoined by General Halkett. Evidently taking the view that defeat was probable, Halkett advised him to instruct his family to proceed to Brussels: 'For if the army was obliged to retire, it would be on that city and Antwerp'. Contriving to find some paper, he scribbled a hasty note to his wife, adding that although his horse had been shot, he was unharmed. Entrusting the note to his servant, Paget, he set about the duties of company commander.[25]

Several hundred metres to the south, Lieutenant Riddock had just survived his own ordeal. He had been posted some distance in advance of his battalion when enemy cavalry had suddenly come into view, though not so close that Riddock felt obliged to close up and form a rallying square. Riddock had now been detached for about half an hour and his ammunition supply had reached a crisis point. It would be impossible for the resupply parties to pass over the open ground between the battalion and the advanced party, but it would be equally impossible to repulse a cavalry charge with bayonets alone, nor to prolong the fire fight with the French tirailleurs without any ammunition. To stay exposed in his present situation would result in the almost certain destruction of his command. Fortunately, at this point, his brigade commander was a short distance away and Riddock deemed it proper to call General Pack's attention to his predicament:

> His orders were to close my men to the centre and join my regiment. I did so insofar, but ere this time a number of squadrons of French cuirassiers and lancers were sweeping the field in the rear, round and round every square, showing no mercy, dashing at and striking the helpless wounded officers and men that unfortunately lay without the protection of the square. I could compare them to nothing but a swarm of bees. At this time, I and my men were cut off from the regiment. I instantly formed four deep and charged bayonets, the rear rank with ported arms and fought my way through the French cavalry, until I reached the south side square of my regiment, but so hot and hard pressed was the regiment on all sides, that I could gain no admittance and my ammunition being totally gone, as before mentioned, we had no alternative than lie down flat close to the square and crave their friendly protection. The loss of the French cavalry at this time was very great, in proportion to the British infantry.[26]

Colonel O'Malley, Riddock found, was still unwounded and in command, but the battalion was so depleted in both officers and men, that he had been forced to form his command into four small companies and combine these with the 42nd Regiment of Foot. As these men popped away at the retiring horsemen, General Pack rode up to the bayonets, waved his hat in his hand and shouted for the troops to cease fire. With ammunition running low, little prospect of replenishment and the men exhausted, it seemed only a matter of time before yet another massive charge of enemy cavalry washed away the last vestiges of resistance, but the stoic islands of red in the sea of rye still remained, diminished, but not quite defeated. Sensing the need to lift the spirits, Colonel O'Malley, who had only recently assumed the command and was largely unknown to the men, shouted: 'You are as brave as lions! Attend to my orders and we shall yet repulse them!'[27]

The depleted skirmishers of the 42nd Regiment of Foot were still contesting the heights of Bati-Saint-Bernard, though their ammunition was virtually spent. Their antagonists were so close that the men could make out the numbers of the French regiments on the painted shako covers of the infantrymen. This type of fighting was up close and personal, requiring the soldier to keep his wits about him, make the best of any cover available, always ensure one soldier's piece in each pairing was ready to fire and, above all, to remain aware of the position of the enemy and one's own battalion. As the skirmish line ebbed and flowed, men took the opportunity to rifle the pockets or empty the knapsacks of the fallen and letters, shirts, spare shoes and all manner of objects littered the fields. Others satisfied themselves with emptying the gourds of wine or canteens of gin and water, for it was thirsty work as the sun beat down. The Highlanders, however, enjoyed one slight advantage over their French rivals: because the bore of the 'Brown Bess' musket was slightly larger than the French *Charleville*, any spare ammunition that the Scots found in the pouches of the French dead and wounded could be used as an alternative, though the excessive 'windage' would render the shot significantly less accurate. At close range, down to your last cartridge, however, it might make all the difference. For Corporal McEween, it had all become academic. The adage that 'Every bullet has its billet', had been proven after all and he had finally been hit by a French tirailleur. Keeping his wits about him, he made his way back across the wreckage of the battlefield towards the rear.[28]

Hundreds of wounded men and fugitives were streaming from the field, but still the French could not deliver the knockout blow. When the cuirassiers swept back down the road in confusion, they were replaced once more by the dreaded lancers. Despite the damage inflicted on the crops by the movements of British infantry battalions and the swathes of rye trampled down by the horses of preceding charges, these horsemen, advancing in support of the heavies, found it difficult to precisely locate the British squares, hidden by the drifting grey smoke. Suddenly, Major Llewellyn, on horseback in the combined square of the 1st and 28th Regiments of Foot, noticed a daring lancer emerge from the gloom and gallop up to the regiment. When he arrived within a few metres of the startled infantrymen, he raised his right arm and drove the iron ferrule of his lance into the ground almost at the foot of the front rank, before galloping off to safety.

Though the men in the ranks may have been confused by the man's actions, Llewellyn understood his purpose perfectly. At nearly three metres long, the fluttering red and white pennon at the other end of the lance was perfectly visible above the highest of the stalks of grain and served as a marker on which the French cavalry could charge in perfect order, building momentum over distance and timing the acceleration for maximum impact. Having previously come across infantry unexpectedly in the earlier stages of the battle without the time or space to properly charge, the French lancers had learned a valuable lesson, or perhaps the veterans in the ranks had used the technique elsewhere.

A few moments later, the ground shook again, as a squadron of lancers closed in on the square. Remaining steady, the infantry fired a volley at point-blank range, but as the smoke cleared, several lancers who had survived the discharge rode up close enough to the ranks to stab at the hapless infantrymen whilst they reloaded. Even though the lance pennon had served its purpose, the momentum of the charge had completely disappeared and the lancers were reduced to making individual sorties on different faces of the square in an attempt to stab or slash an opening in the wall of redcoats, or to ride up and discharge pistols or musketoons into the faces of the British.[29]

A short distance outside the southern face of the square, Captain William Irving had been posted with the skirmish line and was astride a rocky bank, which he had mounted in order to direct the fire of his marksmen. Along with Lieutenant William Irwin of the Light Company, reputed to be the strongest man in the regiment, he witnessed the French lancers furiously charging the square on its western side, only for their ranks to be broken up. Small parties of lancers were forced to disperse into the tall rye, which was so immensely tall that he likened it to: 'A wall surrounding the square'. Though the two officers could no longer see the cavalry once they had passed into the rye, they knew they were present because they were close enough to hear the snorting of the horses and the cry of orders as the French regrouped their squadrons. Just as a body of cuirassiers 'Burst out of the rye', Irwin was severely wounded in the leg. As he fell to the ground, another face of the square was enveloped by lancers and *chasseurs à cheval,* but the determined infantrymen continued to blast away with volley fire. Inside the square, Colonel Belson, his horse wounded in two places and with blood streaming down its side, rode calmly back and forth, exhorting the men to remain steady. The cavalry threat eventually receded, replaced by yet another violent cannonade and Irwin took the opportunity to drag himself across the beaten down rye, until some men of the battalion noticed his predicament, broke ranks and dragged him back into the centre of the square, where they were also joined by General Kempt and his staff. Within minutes, the cavalry resumed its onslaught.[30]

Throughout the confusion, General Picton could be heard bellowing: 'Twenty-Eighth! Remember Egypt!' and those old soldiers who had fought back to back at Alexandria once more rammed home the ball cartridge and muttered words of encouragement to the recruits from the militia. After several minutes of stalemate, 'Johnny' was once again driven off by the usual combination of cold steel and firepower. As the threat receded, Picton was heard by some to return thanks to the regiment, pledging that he would: 'Recommend them to the government to wear feathers'. Elsewhere, Captain Cadell was told that the General had said: 'Twenty-Eighth, if I live to see the Prince Regent, I shall lay before him your bravery this day.' Cadell was immensely impressed by the way in which the cool and intrepid behaviour of the infantry had overcome the several gallant charges of the enemy cavalry, but had lost count of the number of times they had been charged; was it four times? Isolated in a field and surrounded by lancers one minute and cuirassiers the next, the images fused in his mind and further disoriented him. As the horsemen ebbed away, the command: 'Cease firing!' could be heard along the ranks. So deafened were some of the men, however, that many continued to mechanically load and fire their muskets:

> Private Tom Patten, a loyal old soldier of the 28th, full of misplaced initiative, was standing in the second file of the Grenadier Company. Seeing a junior French officer who was encouraging his troopers to break into the square, he quickly lifted his musket and shot him. An officer struck Patten across the face with his drawn sword, and when the latter asked why he had been struck, the officer replied, 'For firing without orders,' and something of an argument began, but General Kempt overheard the argument and called out, 'Silence gentlemen; let the men alone. They know their duty better than you. The men please me, so not a word, gentlemen.'

With the muskets falling silent, men of the 1st Regiment of Foot took advantage of the lull in the cavalry charges to recover the firelocks of the killed and wounded. Where they were successful in securing a weapon with a superior lock, they tossed aside their own fouled, red-hot pieces with glee.[31]

Captain Cadell, a private soldier in the ranks of the 42nd Regiment of Foot was also counting the number of charges; was that the third charge they had repulsed or the fourth? He could not understand how the French could sustain such losses and yet return for more; their gallantry was astonishing. Other soldiers were too busy to concern themselves with such thoughts: flints needed changing; fouling around the priming pan needed scraping off and the vent pricking; dwindling supplies of ammunition were redistributed. As if in punishment for allowing his mind to stray from the task in hand, an opportunistic French tirailleur took careful aim and fired into the face of the square, the ball smashing through the right arm of the unfortunate private, passing through his chest and lodging in his back. Slowly, the blood welled up and he slumped into the trampled rye, another nameless victim. The corn was only partially trodden down and though there were many dead and wounded, it was difficult to see more than a few at a time. As the battalion changed formation or shifted its ground, the men picked their way through the stalks not wishing to add to the suffering of friend or foe alike by a misplaced boot. Bodies littered the ground, recumbent in every attitude, but generally on their backs, their eyes staring unseeing into the blue sky, expressions betraying nothing of the suffering of their last moments. The wounded lay or sat mutely resigned, bearing the torment of hunger, pain and thirst with resignation. They were no longer part of the ranks of the living and could not expect any aid until the fight was fought.[32]

Through the smoke, a lone horseman galloped up to Wellington, who had taken shelter in one of the squares. It was Captain Wildman of the 7th Hussars, aide-de-camp to the Earl of Uxbridge, commander of Wellington's cavalry reserve. He had searched for the Duke at Braine-le-Comte and Nivelles, before hearing the considerable sound of firing and riding onwards to Les Quatre Bras.

On the way, Captain Wildman had passed the divisions of Generals von Alten and Cooke, summoned to reinforce de Perponcher-Sedlnitzky's and Picton's divisions. Wellington instructed him to ride back to Braine-le-Comte as fast as he could and to bring up all the cavalry and another infantry division that he would find there. Taking a brief moment to absorb the spectacle of the wheeling, repeated charges by lancers on the infantry squares, Wildman tugged on the reins and spurred his tired horse back toward the west.[33]

Endnotes

1. Bannatyne, p. 321. Brett-James, p. 62. Henckens, p. 229. Kellermann. Macready (I). Ney, p. 9.
2. Anonymous (Waterloo Medal Roll), p. 203. Bannatyne, pp. 321–2. Macready (I). Macready (III), p. 389. Macready (IV). Macready (V).
3. Macready (I). Macready IV).
4. Bannatyne, pp. 321–2. Elkington (II), p. 12. Macready (I). Macready (IV), pp. 389–94. Macready (V).
5. Bannatyne, pp. 315, 317, 322. Elkington (II), pp. 12–13. Harty. Macready (I). Macready (III), p. 390. Macready (IV), pp. 390–1. Tincombe.
6. Dalton, p. 175. Halkett (III). W. Harris. Ladgen and Sly, pp. 3–4, 193. Lloyd. Macready (IV), p. 393. Morris, p. 68.
7. Ainslie, p. 15. Anonymous (Y.Z.). Barlow. Brereton and Savory, p. 145. Bukhari, p. 41. Butler, pp. 79–80. Archibald Forbes, p. 271. Lomax, p. 125. Maughan, p. 7. Mudie (I). Pattison (I). Riddock.
8. Ainslie, p. 15. Anonymous (Y.Z.). Anonymous (Waterloo Medal Roll), p. 277. Bannatyne, p. 318. Barlow. de Bas &c., p. 524. Brereton and Savory, p. 145. Butler, pp. 79–80. Archibald Forbes, p. 271. Halkett (I). Lomax, p. 125. Mudie (I). Myddleton, pp. 93–4. Pigot. Riddock. Surtees, p. 73.
9. Ainslie, p. 15. Anonymous (Near Observer), p. 285. Anonymous (Waterloo Medal Roll), pp. 276–80. Anonymous (Y.Z.). Barlow. Butler, pp. 79–80. Dalton, pp. 175–7. Archibald Forbes, p. 271. Maughan, pp. 4–5, 8. Pigot. Riddock. Ross-Lewin, p. 259. Rudyerd. W. Siborne (V), p. 93.
10. Ainslie, pp. 16–18. Anonymous (Y.Z.). Dalton, pp. 175–6. Archibald Forbes, p. 271. Haythornthwaite (V). Lomax, pp. 125–6. Pattison (II), p. 5. Pigot. Rudyerd. Surtees, p. 73.
11. Ainslie, pp. 15–16. Anonymous (Y.Z.). Barlow. de Bas &c., p. 524. Butler, pp. 79–80. Cotton, p. 109. Archibald Forbes, p. 271. Halkett (I). Halkett (II). Haythornthwaite (V). Kellermann. J. Leslie (II). Lomax, pp. 125–6. Maughan, p. 7. Morris, pp. 68, 90. Pattison (I). Pattison (II), p. 5. Riddock. Surtees, p. 73.
12. Anton, p. 194. Fitchett, p. 293. Gomm (IV). P. Howard, p. 53. McEween. Mudie (I).
13. Anton, p. 195.
14. Anton, p. 195.
15. Anton, pp. 195–6.
16. Anton, p. 196.

17. Anton, p. 196. Butler, p. 78. Carter, p. 98. Crummer (I). Crummer (II). Dalton, p. 116. Douglas, p. 98. Archibald Forbes, p. 270. Fosten, p. 27. Glazebrook, pp. 14–15. Gomm (IV). Grant and Youens, pp. 22–3. P. Howard, p. 54. Leask and McCance, p. 333. Macdonald. Martin (I). Mudie (I). O'Malley. Seale, p. 9. Wauchope, p. 49.
18. Anonymous (Near Observer), pp. 67–8. Carter, p. 98. Daniell, p. 135. Fosten, p. 27. Gomm (IV). Gomm (V). Grant, p. 23. Leask and McCance, p. 333. Macdonald. Martin (I). Mudie (I).
19. Anonymous (Royal Artillery). Cleeves. Dalton, p. 226. de Goeben. von Pflugk-Harttung (II), p. 40.
20. Gore. Mansell. H. Robinson, p. 562.
21. Carter, p. 98. Gomm (IV).
22. Anonymous (Cameron), pp. 90–1. Cleeves. Fletcher (I), p. 63. Lomax, p. 125. Macdonald. Macready (V). von Rettberg (I). von Rettberg (II). Rudyerd.
23. Anonymous (Near Observer), pp. 67–8. Barlow. Carter, p. 98. Crummer (I). Gomm (IV). Grant and Youens, pp. 22–3. Halkett (I). Leask and McCance, pp. 333–4. Martin (I). Mudie (I). W. Siborne (V), p. 86.
24. Ainslie, pp. 16–17.
25. Myddleton, pp. 81–2.
26. Riddock.
27. O'Malley. Riddock.
28. McEween.
29. Fosten, p. 30. Glazebrook, pp. 14–15. Llewellyn. Seale, pp. 9–10.
30. Fosten, pp. 27–30.
31. Black. Cadell (I). Cadell (II), p. 233. Crummer (I). Douglas, p. 98. Fosten, p. 30. Glazebrook, pp. 14–15. Gomm (IV). Leask and McCance, pp. 333–4. Llewellyn. Macdonald. Mudie (II), p. 183. Ross-Lewin, p. 258. Seale, pp. 9–10. W. Siborne (V), p. 84.
32. Anonymous (Near Observer), pp. 61–2. Jackson (II), pp. 27–8.
33. G. Paget (II), p. 127.

CHAPTER 17

As the cavalry poured back across the fields towards their own lines, they were replaced yet again by advancing infantry, preceded by the usual swarms of skirmishers. Exposed in an open field to the south of the chemin Bati-Saint-Bernard, the battered hulk of the 1st Regiment of Foot had once more deployed in line on the right of the 28th Regiment of Foot, the shadows of the men lengthening across the trampled crops. A stone's throw away, French skirmishers were again subjecting the battalion to a galling fire. As ever, they were targeting the officers. Ensign James Kennedy was killed and his colour fluttered to the ground, though Colonel Campbell remained miraculously unwounded, despite being prominent on horseback. Perhaps he wondered how the 'Forty Thieves', the name he had given to the draft from the fourth battalion, were getting on. Conscious from the diminution of fire from his own skirmishers that ammunition was once again running low, he rode up behind No. 8 Company, where he spotted Private Henry O'Connor. The face appeared familiar and he realised that this was the man he had recently reduced from sergeant to the rank and pay of a private soldier in consequence of having allowed Drummer Duffey, a soldier who was: 'No favourite of the Adjutant', to escape from arrest whilst in his charge. Perhaps wishing to offer him a chance of redemption, Campbell ordered him to go to the rear and bring up more ammunition. Corporal Douglas, a short distance away, watched O'Connor leave the ranks, but an unfortunate fate was to befall him before he had gone but a short distance:

> He received a ball in the buttock on which he sang out 'What the devil would I care, but to be hit in so disgraceful a place!' The colonel, overhearing the remark, cried out, 'Make that fellow sergeant again!' Thus, if he was disgracefully wounded, which could not be denied, he was honourably restored to his former rank.[1]

Not everyone was as fortunate. A short time earlier, the 32nd Regiment of Foot had been reinforced by a battalion of Hanoverian Landwehr from General Best's brigade. In order to counter the continued pressure being exerted by the French tirailleurs, the young men of the German battalion were deployed into open order and moved forward to engage the enemy with great determination. The nearby officers of the British regiment were very impressed by its steady conduct, but it soon became clear that the untried militia had never been trained in this type of warfare. The much more experienced French skirmishers, taking advantage of every fold in the ground and firing alternately in pairs, caused the Hanoverians considerable damage and within minutes, scores of militiamen had been rendered hors de combat in this unequal contest. Neither was the 32nd Regiment of Foot, similarly engaged with the same skirmishers, immune from such punishment. In the Grenadier Company alone, Captain Jacques Boyse was mortally wounded and Lieutenant James Robinson also hit. Suddenly a musket ball punched through the sleeve of Lieutenant Stephens' coat, passing directly through his arm. As he staggered away to have his wound dressed, Lieutenant Henry Butterworth was obliged to assume command of the company. Having endured the worst of the musketry and artillery fire and conscious from the slightly diminished sound of gunfire that the battle was possibly reaching its conclusion, some men had premonitions of death whilst others became ever more convinced of their invulnerability. Captain Whitty was showing Major Ross-Lewin a number of holes torn in his coat by musket balls, canister and shell fragments and remarking what a number of escapes he had clearly had; when his banter was interrupted by a musket ball, which smashed into his mouth and penetrated his brain, killing him instantly.[2]

If the situation on the heights of Bati-Saint-Bernard was precarious, so too was that faced by Halkett's recently deployed battalions in the space between the Charleroi road and the Bois de Bossu. Safe behind the bristling bayonets of the 33rd Regiment of Foot's square, an incredulous Lieutenant Pattison had witnessed the charge of the French cavalry, the muscular sheen of their magnificent horses rippling as they snorted through the fields, churning up great divots of earth, their riders cheering *'Vive l'Empereur!'* Rank after rank had whirled past: cuirassiers on massive Norman horses; green-coated *chasseurs à cheval*; and menacing chevau-légers-lanciers with their barbaric spears. The kaleidoscope of colour blinded the men with its brilliance, whilst the pungent aroma of sweat, horses and trampled crops filled their nostrils. These were the most vaunted cavalry in Europe, but in Pattison's mind, if infantry in square remained cool, it was invulnerable to cavalry and the horsemen 'Might as well try and ride over Saint Paul's, as to break them.[3]

Though the men in the southern and eastern faces of the square had laughed at the cuirassiers with scorn as they declined to engage the battalion and made off in search of easier pickings, the French had stealthily brought forward two batteries of artillery. The industrious gunners now halted their teams and unlimbered the fearsome cannon at point-blank range; an ominous silence fell amongst the ranks. Far from being in an impregnable position, as they had felt when threatened by cavalry, the square now took on a very vulnerable aspect. The smug sense of superiority faded, it was as if they were 'A beacon in the presence of the enemy'. One thing was certain; the destruction, when it came, would be awful.[4]

With an ominous flash from the muzzles and a simultaneous throaty boom, the artillery opposite the square fired its first salvo and was instantly shrouded in smoke. Seconds later, the earth was filled with the whooshing, moaning noise of the projectiles as they smashed into the densely-packed ranks and tore through the formation, bounding across the ground. To Lieutenant Pattison, it was as though his men were hay, before the scythe of the mower. Towering above him was Lieutenant Arthur Gore, his subaltern, an exceedingly handsome man. Both officers tried to set an example by standing unflinchingly as the hail of round shot, canister and shell consumed the battalion. Suddenly, a 6-pounder shot bounced up and smashed Gore's head into fragments, drenching the shakos, faces and coats of Pattison and the officers and men standing near him in a mush of brain, bone and blood. 'Like a stately oak from the last blow of the hewer', his body toppled into the trampled rye, pumping out the remaining lifeblood into the rich soil. Someone immediately exclaimed: 'That's poor Pat!' to which Pattison shouted back: 'It is not I. It is Arthur.' The twitching body was now unrecognisable, the fine scarlet coat, with its richly embroidered wings and grenade symbols contrasting strangely with the gruesome appearance of the headless torso. Ensign Andrew Watson, Gore's 'Young and most intimate friend . . . sat down and cried like a child'. Those even a few ranks away were oblivious to this horror and were concerned more with their own survival. Involuntarily, the men in the front face of the square recoiled from the bombardment, the centre of the line bowing in, as they flinched and fell. The artillery was well beyond the range of the muskets and the battalion was therefore unable to retaliate. From his post behind No. 5 Company, Captain John Haigh was anxious that the ranks might break at any moment and with it the morale of the battalion. The sergeants, halberds across the packs of the rear rank men, tried to maintain the dressing with main force, but were being pressed back by weight of numbers. Haigh immediately left his place and greatly excited, flourished his sword, yelling: 'Keep up! Keep up! I say keep up!'[5]

> The words were vibrating on his lips, when a cannon ball hit him on the abdomen, and cut him nearly in twain. He fell on his back; the separation between soul and body was most appalling. His eyes strained as if they would leap from their sockets, and the quiver of the lip with the strong convulsion of his whole frame, showed unquestionably how unwilling his spirit was to be driven in this ruthless way from her clay tenement. His poor brother who was standing by was thrown into a terrible state of grief and anguish. Expressing his feelings by the wringing of his hands, and shedding a flood of tears over the lifeless body, he cried aloud with a bitter lamentation, 'Oh! My brother; Oh! My poor brother; my dear brother! Alas! Alas! My poor old father!'[6]

Pattison was aghast; he would later write: 'Were I to live a thousand years this scene could never be effaced from my mind.' Leaving Lieutenant Thomas Haigh weeping over his brother's lifeless remains, the officers and men in the covering file strained to maintain the formation. In the jostling ranks was Private Hemingway. To him, it seemed as though

> The cannon shot from the enemy broke down our square faster than we could form it, killing nine and ten men every shot, the balls falling down amongst us just at the present and shells bursting into a hundred pieces. We could not be accountable for the number of men that we lost there.

The battalion was in danger of annihilation.[7]

Colonel Elphinstone, realising that he could not stand idly by as his command was butchered, ordered the battalion to form line and the order was drummed out by the musicians. Relieved to be active once more, the sections and companies scrambled into their respective positions, until a long line was formed, fronting the Bois de Bossu. As soon as this was complete, the order was given to march on a point some two hundred metres in advance, in the teeth of the most violent barrage from the French. Within the space of a few minutes, the regiment had closed the distance and engaged the French gunners with a vigorous fire of musketry for a considerable time, eventually forcing them to limber up and withdraw.[8]

As the enemy made off, however, they revealed the advance of several battalions of French infantry and the redcoats and Les Bleus, spontaneously blazed away, each side lashing the other with musket balls. Lieutenant John Boyce was killed instantly by the fusillade; his earlier premonition of death had proven correct. A short distance away, the tall figure of young Ensign James Furlong staggered past. His body was bent double, his breath rasping from the sucking wound caused by the ball that had struck the right side of his chest. He staggered a few steps, leaning on his sword to remain upright and a non-commissioned officer hurried across and supported him until men could be organised to carry him to the rear. Gently lowered onto the crushed rye, choking on his own blood, he blurted for someone to fetch Ensign Howard, not realising that his friend was skirmishing with Vigoreux's Light Battalion. Convinced that he was dying, he entrusted his watch to one of the men and asked him to ensure that Howard received it. All along the line, men fell to the ground, many to rise no more. To the right, some Brunswick hussars had advanced along the fringes of the Bois de Bossu and some battalions of Brunswick infantry could be made out through the thick smoke, fiercely engaged with French infantry, close to the edge of the wood. Gradually, the pressure started to tell and the Brunswick Hussars, dashing forward, eventually forced the veteran French battalions to give ground.[9]

Pressing on, the 33rd Regiment of Foot manoeuvred towards the Brunswickers, with the intention of forming up on their left in order to create a stable defensive line, but within minutes, a loud cry was heard. Cavalry were approaching the rear of the battalion at the charge. Being as they were in the dead ground to the west of the chemin Bati-Saint-Bernard, little could be seen in the direction of Les Quatre Bras, but whether real or imaginary, the very prospect was sufficient to shatter the fragile confidence of the battalion. Any attempt to form square in the face of the French infantry would result in the battalion's firepower being reduced by three quarters, even if the manoeuvre could be completed in time. Alternatively, any attempt to face the rear rank right about would probably end in catastrophe; in the event, neither option was taken.

As Elphinstone dithered, the entire battalion disintegrated and fled towards the Bois de Bossu, some 200 metres to the west. One of the closest to the wood, Private Hemingway ran as swiftly as he could, encumbered as he was by musket, pack, haversack, canteen and cartridge box. He was convinced that if he did not make its sanctuary, he and his comrades would be 'Cut in pieces by the cavalry and trampled upon by their

The Battle of Quatre Bras

horses'. Perhaps, he wondered, whether his friend Private William Illingworth would make it, posted as he was with the unfortunate Captain Haigh's No. 5 Company, close to the regiment's colours in the centre of the line. Perhaps he was already dead and would no longer dally with Hemingway's sister, Martha. In all directions, men fled the marauding cavalry, a split-second decision governing who would live and who would die. Whilst some men were hacked down remorselessly by French horsemen, others met a more charitable enemy. Sergeant-Major James Colbeck was pursued, wounded and seized, to spend the next three weeks of his life in French captivity. Spurring his horse towards the edge of the Bois de Bossu, Major Parkinson was shot and severely wounded, but managed to reach the security of the wood, where he fell in with Captain Charles Knight, Lieutenant Pattison of the Grenadiers and Ensign Thain, the battalion's Adjutant. Gathering together the men closest to them, Knight formed an improvised company of some 60 men from the right wing of the battalion and deploying them into a line, the small band moved south through the thick woodland, in the direction in which they expected to find the enemy.[10]

Corporal William Holdsworth had been cut off from the main body of the battalion along with Lieutenant Arthur Trevor and concealing themselves in the standing corn, the two managed to avoid being taken prisoner:

> When I looked up, I saw a cuirassier with one of our colours, which he was bringing off, shouting. I said to Mr. [Arthur Trevor], 'We are disgraced for ever, for there is our colour; but if you will allow me, I'll fire at that man.' He replied, 'It is as much as our lives are worth if you do, but I won't say you shall not.' On which I fired, when the Frenchman was very near us; he fell; and I stripped the colour (or cut it) from the staff, gave it to Mr. [Trevor] and told him to get away with it into the wood, which he reached safely. I reloaded and fired again, but without effect, and was soon surrounded by the French, when I threw down my musket and cried 'Prisoner.' They seized my fob, in which I had two francs, and one of them cut it off, which I resisted, for which I got some blows with the flat of a sword and was marched off. Among other prisoners they had got the sergeant-major of our regiment, and we were standing together whenced the Brunswickers charged. We took to our heels, ran in among the horses, and escaped. When I rejoined without arms and belts, I was questioned, and Mr. [Trevor] having told the commanding officer that a corporal, whose name he did not know, had given him the colour, etc., but that he must be killed or taken; the Colonel told me that if we both survived he would try and do something for me.[11]

A short distance away, but hidden from Captain Knight by the foliage and undergrowth of the wood, another large portion of the regiment had taken shelter. The battalion was now experiencing the paralysis that accompanies heavy casualties amongst the officer cadre. Captain Haigh was dead, as were Lieutenants Boyce and Gore. Major Parkinson, Captain McIntyre, Lieutenants James Markland and James Ogle, and Ensigns Furlong and John Alderson were all wounded. The men milled about in confusion. As the horsemen swept past the perimeter of the wood, those

'The separation between soul and body'

with the discipline and presence of mind to line the ditch opened fire and killed and wounded several of them, dissuading the Frenchmen from approaching too closely. Colonel Elphinstone and Captains Ralph Gore and John Longden, along with the surviving subalterns, desperately tried to fashion some order from the chaos, but in the confines of the wood, it proved impossible. To re-form the men, balance the numbers in each company and redistribute the officers to create a workable command structure would require time and space. Elphinstone therefore decided to pull the battalion out of the fight. The word was passed for every man to retire through the wood, to its northern edge and to assemble in the open ground beyond.[12]

Whilst Elphinstone was instructing the men in the wood to pull back, others had fled back through the fields over which they had advanced, individuals chancing that the presence of so many would reduce the probability of them falling victim to the swords, carbines and pistols of the enemy. Within minutes, they arrived close to where General Halkett had posted himself, a short distance from the square of the 73rd Regiment of Foot. As soon as the cavalry had passed, the enraged General spurred his horse forward and rode up to the noisy group. Unable to get them under control, he did the only thing he could that would shame the men into forming up. Riding up to the ensign holding one of the colours, he seized it and walked his horse some distance away from the mob, towards the enemy. Almost immediately, the panic subsided, the shouting died away and the men fell into what appeared to him to be a steady formation.[13]

In the meantime, Captain Knight's party had become hopelessly disoriented amongst the trees and rather than risk their safety by some injudicious movement, he too withdrew along one of the tracks that intersected the wood and emerged into the Champ du Sarti, close to Croix-Gilbert. As they reached the open ground, they found Colonel Elphinstone and the main body of the battalion, formed up as best they could in the circumstances. To Lieutenant Pattison: 'The morale of the men was as good, nay, even better than when they first entered the field.' Those that stood in the depleted ranks had suffered the combined effects of the French infantry, cavalry and artillery and were still alive. As soon as Captain Knight's contingent had fallen into the ranks, the muster was taken and revealed the loss of over a hundred men killed, wounded or missing.[14]

Even as Elphinstone's scattered battalion streamed from the western edge of the Bois de Bossu, Cooke's exhausted division was approaching Croix-Gilbert, just under a kilometre short of the crossroads at Les Quatre Bras and over forty from its starting point at Enghien, having halted briefly as it passed through Houtain-le-Val in order once again to close up and collect its stragglers. It was close to 6.00 p.m. The men were worn out, their sweat-soaked red coats thick with dust, their parched mouths desperate for a cooling drink of water and a rest in some shaded place. It was a far cry from St. James' Palace or the barracks of the third battalion of the 1st Regiment of Foot Guards on Birdcage Walk. Whilst the four battalions halted at the crossroads, the twelve pieces of the two batteries commanded by Captain Charles Sandham and Major Kuhlmann trundled past towards Les Quatre Bras itself, staff officers directing them to take up a position to the east of the crossroads.[15]

Artillery was now pouring into Wellington's line. As the artillery of the 1st (British) Infantry Division moved up, a battery of Brunswick horse artillery, clattered up the road to the north of the crossroads, having been urged into a trot in an effort to bring some much needed ordnance to the support of the Allied army. A short distance behind came Major von Moll's foot artillery battery, the gunners jogging alongside the limbers, breathlessly trying to maintain the pace. As each battery arrived, Major Mahn directed it across the fields to the north-east of the Ferme des Quatre Bras and ordered the commanding officers to unlimber their pieces on the high ground overlooking the Namur road, to the east of Major Lloyd's guns, which were maintaining a very effective fire. Here, they were joined shortly afterwards by Lieutenant Koopman and the three guns of Bijleveld's troop, which had come forward from its position to the north-west of the crossroads. Before long, however, as the Netherlands troop commander himself rode up and ordered Koopman to rejoin the rest of the troop in rear of the crossroads. To the right of the Brunswick artillery, the 1st and 3rd Light Battalions, urged on by Major Werner von Holstein and Major Ludwig Ebeling came doubling up the road and were directed into positions in support of battalions still occupying the buildings and gardens of Les Quatre Bras itself.[16]

Another arrival approached Wellington through the gloom, in the uniform of a Prussian General Staff Officer. It was Lieutenant von Wussow, sent from the Prussian headquarters to brief Wellington on the fighting at Ligny and to assess the state of play at Les Quatre Bras. After a brief word with Colonel von Müffling, he saluted Wellington and proceeded to give his report in French:

> At the time of my riding away from the battlefield, we occupied all of the villages that constituted our position behind the Ligny brook, from Sombreffe to Ligny, Saint-Amand-La-Haye and Wagnelée, and have maintained them despite the unrelenting French attacks and their loss and recapture. However, in doing so, our losses are increasing substantially. Since the possibility of reinforcement by Bülow's Corps has disappeared altogether, it will be possible at best to maintain the battlefield until nightfall. A greater success was not to be expected.

The officer also expressed the request of the Prussian staff that perhaps a strong offensive by the English could prevent the Emperor Napoleon from using his forces with devastating effect against the Prussian army. Wellington probably asked von Wussow to inform Gneisenau that it had become very difficult to oppose the violent attacks by the superior French forces; that he would try with the reinforcements – which he thought we approximately 20,000 men at his disposal – to attempt a strong offensive and by doing so assist the Prussian army.[17]

General Cooke, Colonel Rooke and Captain Disbrowe had ridden forward to the crossroads and were met by a scene of appalling carnage. The buildings, enclosures and gardens close to the junction were choked with the wreckage of cannon, caissons and wagons, through which individuals and small groups of men, wounded and unwounded, were streaming away to the rear. To the south, like islands in the fields of trampled grain, were small clumps of troops in red, black, grey and blue uniforms, exposed to a storm of shot and shell.[18]

Ensign Lake and other officers of the brigade could now distinctly make out the rattle of musketry and the smell of gunpowder was heavy in the late afternoon air. All around them was the evidence of a fierce struggle, with damaged wagons and smashed limbers strewn across the road. Parties of men dragged away their mutilated comrades in blankets to the aid stations in the rear, where the surgeons and their assistants performed roadside amputations and probed for bullets, their screaming patients being restrained by medical orderlies or their own friends. The alcohol had long since run out. Whilst the most severely wounded casualties were left by harassed medical staff to slowly bleed to death, parties of bandsmen and other supernumeraries loaded those with a greater prospect of survival on wagons that already groaned with the wounded of several nationalities. Some officers noticed other injured men in unfamiliar uniforms, which they took to be Belgian, making the best of their way off the field. Elsewhere, pitiful remnants of human beings and horses were heaped on the sides of the road, filling the ditches and littering the fields, their unmoving and mangled remains provoking pity in some and anger in others. The majority, it seemed to Lieutenant-Colonel Hon. James Stanhope, were British. Though many of the officers of the second battalion of the 1st Regiment of Foot Guards had experienced the consequences of battle in the Peninsula, France and the Netherlands, this particular scene demanded 'Every better feeling of the mind to cope with its horrors'. The majority of the soldiers in the Coldstream Guards, thought Ensign Short, were probably too fagged to even notice. Nearby, the Acting Adjutant of the battalion, Captain William Walton perhaps ruefully reflected that his mother, the Dowager Lady Strachan, would be raising a glass in honour of his birthday. Amongst the crowds of wounded, Captain Powell noticed Major Jessop, an old acquaintance of his from the 44th Regiment of Foot, but serving in this campaign on the staff as an Assistant Quartermaster-General. He had earlier been shot through the foot and treated by Surgeon Elkington of the 30th Regiment of Foot, but despite his pain, encouraged Powell and the other officers of the battalion to: 'Get on, as the action was going on badly'.[19]

Amid the clouds of smoke billowing across the road and fields from the northern end of the Bois de Bossu, men could be seen emerging, sometimes alone and sometimes in isolated groups. Some parties halted as they came into the open, the flames of their priming pans flaring vividly as they turned to fire at their pursuers. Others seemed more concerned about getting to the north of the Nivelles road, but whether they were pursuers or the pursued, it was difficult to tell. The silhouettes of shakos and colours of coats were too indistinct to identify for certain in the gloom.[20]

Maitland passed instructions to the commanding officers to get their men into battle order. Some of the officers had, quite naturally, congregated with their friends on the march and orders were passed down the column for them to return to their companies. All the officers, with the exception of staff officers, regimental field officers and adjutants, dismounted and gave their horses into the charge of their servants and grooms, some emptying their pockets of valuables, others kissing miniature portraits, whilst those

The Battle of Quatre Bras

of a more sanguine frame of mind entrusted their retainers with letters: 'To be sent in the event of their death'. Captain Thomas Brown of the second and Captain Grose of the third battalion of the 1st Regiment of Foot Guards were stood together by the side of the road when the column of the third battalion halted a short distance away. They noticed a colour-sergeant hand Ensign Master the King's colour – the 1807 Major's colour – who unfurled it and shook out its crimson folds and tassels, the golden dragon and battle honours of Lincelles, Corunna and Barrosa catching the sun's powerful light. Anyone bearing such a prize would be a prime target for the French. Exchanging a chuckle, they walked across and told him that they: 'Would not give sixpence,' for his chances, before they hurried back to the head of the column to take up their posts.[21]

In both battalions of Maitland's brigade, sergeants and corporals were passing along the ranks of exhausted men, ensuring that each had untied a bundle of ten rounds of ammunition from the sixty that had been issued at Enghien and checking that the cartridges were correctly stowed in the drilled boxes inside the cartridge pouch. Woe betide any man who had disposed of this government property, or whose flint was not in working order. As soon as this inspection was complete, the men were brought to attention, muskets loaded and the order, 'Fix bayonets!' given. The ranks rippled as, in succession, some two thousand socket bayonets were drawn from their leather scabbards and with a metallic clang, were twisted onto the muzzles of the muskets.[22]

At the head of the column, Colonel Lord Saltoun was preparing the combined light companies of the 1st Regiment of Foot Guards for their coming ordeal. It appeared that his arrival had been a timely one; all around, groups of exhausted British, Nassau and Netherlands troops, many of whom were wounded or completely destitute of ammunition, were streaming across the road into the fields to the north. Standing close by, Lieutenant Hope of the 92nd Regiment of Foot reflected that seldom had an army received a more seasonable reinforcement. The Prince van Oranje-Nassau galloped up on his tired horse, in a state of some considerable agitation. Catching sight of Saltoun and taking him for the commanding officer of the battalion, he breathlessly ordered him to advance with his men into the wood on the right of the road and to drive the enemy from it. The Prince had been brief with his instructions and had galloped off before providing the Colonel with either intelligence as to the position and strength of the enemy or what action he was to take once the task was accomplished. Someone said the French had two battalions in the wood. Not one to waste time, however, or to question the commands of his superiors, Saltoun immediately formed his two companies into a skirmish line and advanced into the wood, where it abutted the chaussée de Nivelles. The light infantrymen moved steadily into the trees and were immediately engaged by the French. Within seconds, their view of the enemy was obliterated as several hundred muskets erupted with fire and smoke. Moving steadily forward, the Colonel was anxious to keep his men in order and not to lose control of them in the confusion.[23]

On the instructions of the Prince van Oranje-Nassau, General Maitland ordered Colonel Askew to immediately support the light companies with the second battalion of the 1st Regiment of Foot Guards. The General directed that the battalion be committed in 'grand divisions'. Having been drilled repeatedly in these tactics, companies quickly formed into column and took up positions in pairs, the senior company 'en échelon' to the fore. As soon as the Grenadier and No. 1 Company had formed up, they advanced across the fields. With Maitland waving his hat in encouragement, the men gave three cheers and dashed forward into the wood, somewhat to the west of where Colonel Lord Saltoun's men had entered. Isolated French soldiers who had advanced beyond the trees fell back as soon as the battalion commenced its assault, although one unfortunate Frenchman mistimed his escape and was killed by the grenadiers as he sought to regain the cover of the trees. No. 2 and No. 3 Companies moved forward in a second wave, followed closely by No. 4 and No. 5 Companies. Bringing up the rear was a somewhat larger final group, comprising No. 6, No. 7 and No. 8 Companies, the natural partner of No. 6 Company, the Light Company, being detached.[24]

The cheering men dashed into the woods, at once being enveloped in the gloom of the dense smoke, periodically illuminated by orange and yellow muzzle flashes as the retiring French opened fire on the leading elements. The advance was too much for some of the young men, who collapsed at the vital moment, complaining of exhaustion. Their comrades passed by, some perhaps assuming they had been shot; whilst others, more familiar with this pusillanimous behaviour, perhaps ridiculed them. The sergeants following in rear of the line treated them to kicks, threats and liberal pokes from their spontoons, as well as the prospect of 500 lashes at the triangle for cowardice in the face of the enemy; the soldiers somehow summoned sufficient energy to find their feet and resume their advance.[25]

The remainder of the battalion poured into the wood, the stench of powder filling their nostrils as they blindly stumbled through the thick undergrowth, feet trampling the huddled, shuddering bodies of wounded men. In some parts: 'The trees were so thick that it was beyond anything difficult to effect a passage.' In others, the undergrowth was so dense that the ranks became ragged as the soldiers used their muskets to force a way through the tangled vegetation. Voices in familiar and unfamiliar tongues echoed in every direction. The confused situation was rendered more chaotic by the difficulties of maintaining a clear sense of direction in a place that lacked visual reference points. After entering the trees, Colonel Lord Saltoun's men had veered to the left, sweeping aside the small numbers of French they encountered, but as succeeding companies entered the fray, they found it difficult to trace the path that their predecessors had taken or even to maintain formation with the company in their pairing. The wood soon swallowed up the second battalion.[26]

Though in some parts of the wood, the companies pressed forward quickly, with the French retiring in haste, in other parts the enemy contested every bush and the Guards ran into a withering frontal fire from sizeable bodies of French troops hidden amongst the trees, which the light companies had unwittingly bypassed. As they struggled to return fire, their ranks were decimated by an accurate fusillade from French voltigeurs who had concealed themselves in the ditches that lined the edges of the wood.[27]

Shadowy figures loomed through the haze. Were they friends or foes? Grey-coated Brunswickers from the Avantgarde-Battalion joined in with the advance. Where the redcoats were unable to establish the identity of the troops milling about amongst the trees, they blazed away regardless. Some companies came under fire from the rear and returned it with gusto, only to find that they were firing at their own infantry, the instinct for self-preservation in some cases overcoming the ability of the officers to control the fire of their men, who were inclined to shoot first and worry about the consequences later. The air became thick with bullets being exchanged indiscriminately between British, Brunswick, Nassau, Netherlands and French troops.[28]

Muskets belched smoke and fire into the forest and dozens of men dropped to the ground, limbs torn away, leaving stumps of shredded sinews and splintered bone. Balls smashed into torsos, creating sucking wounds of torn flesh, contaminated with leather and cloth. The brains of some men spattered across the faces of others, jaws were ripped away and horrified screams rang out as young men realised that the great gouts of blood pumping from severed arteries were their own, their short lives gradually ebbing away into the mulch that would be their final resting place. All around, the wounded whimpered, at first numbed by the shock of their injuries, then tortured by the excruciating pain. Men called for their mothers, for water, for their friends to shoot them. The leading wave of the battalion, the Grenadier and No. 1 Companies, was decimated. As the combat heightened in its intensity, Sergeant Wood watched in disgust as the French bayoneted the British wounded, ran them through with their swords, or stove in their heads with musket butts. These were not the men he had become accustomed to fight against in the Peninsula. There, each side had behaved with honour. Here, no quarter was being given. Whilst the dying gazed at the clear blue sky through the leafy canopy of the woods, the living instinctively cowered behind trees and bushes, frantically loading and priming their muskets. This was not about glory, patriotism or preservation of the established order; it was about survival, sticking with your mates and the honour of the regiment.[29]

Once the second battalion had moved forward into the wood, the third battalion entered the fields to the south of the Nivelles road, parallel to the chaussée, close to where its sister battalion had entered the trees. Nobody seemed to know whether this signified that they were about to be fed into the struggle in turn, or were to be held in reserve should Maitland's attack proved unsuccessful. Some had heard rumours that the French were using the wood to try and outflank Wellington's position and to prevent him being reinforced by way of the Nivelles road; perhaps the battalion would be used to counter that movement? Drawn up on the chaussée nearby was Byng's brigade, the second battalion of the Coldstream Regiment of Foot Guards in front and that of the 3rd Regiment of Foot Guards to their rear. Colonel Macdonell, with the two light companies, was halted in a field to the north of the road into which he had led them when Maitland's brigade had advanced. The men fidgeted and speculated, mostly oblivious to their surroundings, their world becoming an introspective place as they prepared themselves for the fighting to come. Those of a more observant nature spent the time studying their surroundings or observing the suffering of others.[30]

Fugitives continued to pour from the wood and across the fields to the west; Brunswickers, Nassauers, Netherlanders and large numbers of British. Mixed up in the throng were the distinctive red facings of the 33rd Regiment of Foot, the remnants of which were falling back with their commanding officer, Colonel Elphinstone, a man

'The separation between soul and body'

well-known to many in the Guards. Ensign Lake watched with interest as the Colonel and his officers attempted to reform their scattered men on the highway, a short distance away. The battalion was a wreck and its sergeants had their hands full organising the ragged line of panicky young soldiers that had so far collected, many of whom had lost their weapons and accoutrements. The massive and reassuring presence of Byng's brigade went a long way, however, to instil some confidence in the young soldiers and Lieutenant Pattison was no doubt amongst several officers filled with great 'Joy and satisfaction' by their proximity and set to work with enthusiasm to re-form his men and renew the struggle with the enemy.[31]

At last, the order was received for the third battalion of the 1st Regiment of Foot Guards to follow the second battalion into the wood and Colonel Stuart deployed the companies into grand divisions in the same manner. Holding the King's colour aloft in the centre of Lieutenant-Colonel George Fead's Company, Ensign Master became the focus of attention for a number of French voltigeurs and as he advanced to the attack, he could distinctly hear: 'The whishing of the balls' as they whipped past his head. Pressing on into the wood, the orderly ranks of the battalion were immediately disrupted by the thickets and the men instinctively spread out into skirmish order. The battalion entered a veritable charnel house, the undergrowth choked with the dead and wounded of all nationalities. Moving rapidly through the trees, the rattle of musketry to the south indicated where the fire fight was continuing. Here and there, they came upon powerful groups of French infantry, which Askew's battalion had swept past without noticing and the two sides became engaged in fierce musketry from behind the trunks of trees, in shallow ditches and banks, or from the scant cover of bushes and shrubs. Slowly, the superior numbers of the British began to tell and the French were pushed back, sending scattered shots among their pursuers as they effected their escape.[32]

In the open ground between the Bois de Bossu and the Charleroi road to the east, Colonel Vigoreux had ordered his Light Battalion of General Halkett's Brigade to deploy in open order and advance in the wake of the withdrawing French cavalry. The four companies immediately detached themselves from the square of the 30th Regiment of Foot and formed up in an extended line. When all was ready, Vigoreux gave the order to advance at the double, the light infantrymen jogging through the wrecked crops and towards the cavalry, who were forming up some distance to the south. In the surrounding fields, British and Brunswick infantry battalions were deploying into line and restoring the order they had lost in their hurried efforts to receive the cavalry in square. As he advanced, Ensign Macready could hear the heavy firing in the wood to his rear, with the smoky interior occasionally lit up by a flaring light as muskets were discharged on one side or another. Shortly afterwards, musketry of another kind brought his attention back to the job in hand as the British skirmishers were brought up by a line of tirailleurs. Forming up once again, the combatants traded a brisk fire across the open fields, the space between them filled with billowing grey smoke and burnt cartridge paper. The air was suffocatingly hot.[33]

Macready was with his company, directing the fire of the handful of men remaining, when he was joined by Lieutenant Purefoy Lockwood of the Grenadier Company and the two officers fell into conversation as the bullets whistled past their heads. Suddenly, Lockwood slumped to the ground, a gaping hole in his forehead. As ever, the tirailleurs had chosen their mark carefully and conscious that the young man's campaign and possibly his life were over, Macready ordered two of his men to drag the semi-conscious officer back to the surgeons.[34]

The order to advance had also been passed to the Brunswick Leib-Battalion and the 2nd Line Battalion, which had earlier been brought forward from the reserve at Les Quatre Bras to replace the 1st Line Battalion, exhausted by the vicious fighting of the late afternoon. Farther to the north, the 73rd Regiment of Foot was also on the offensive. With the enemy cavalry now some distance away, across the fields to the south, Colonel Harris was in the process of dressing the line formation he had ordered, when word arrived that the battalion was to advance in support of the 30th Regiment of Foot and drive back the French infantry, who were barely visible in the distance. As the battalion moved off with its drums rolling, the tempo and volume of artillery fire from the crossroads behind them increased. The sound of the combat in the Bois de Bossu was also moving south; the entire Allied line, it appeared, was on the counter-offensive.[35]

As the battalions moved away from the indescribable din of the Allied artillery at Les Quatre Bras, the fire from the French guns seemed to diminish in comparison. Was 'Johnny' running short of ammunition? Had the enemy guns been silenced by counter-battery fire? In the packed ranks, it was difficult to tell. Hurrying through the rye, Harris's men came up with the other advancing battalions. Suddenly, the men came across the Gemioncourt stream, choked with bodies on both banks, some of whom had tumbled into the water, which was tinged with their blood. Desperately thirsty, those with stronger stomachs filled their canteens or cupped mouthfuls of the tainted liquid before they swept on.

Having advanced about a thousand metres, Colonel Askew and the leading companies of the second battalion of the 1st Regiment of Foot Guards also found themselves at the Gemioncourt stream, which flowed between steep banks as it passed through the wood. Though not a significant obstacle in itself, the ditch of the stream was choked with brambles, nettles and thorns; the French having been forced by weight of numbers to cede ground, had chosen this feature as a defensive position. Askew's men cautiously advanced, guided only by the fire of the enemy and ran headlong into a murderous volley from the French formed up on the other side. The ravine was too wide to be jumped and the men stumbled into the ditch and through the stagnant water, before scrambling up the other side, boots squelching and trousers covered in slime. Thorns and brambles clawed at their faces and hands, but the British were determined to drive the French back. Faced by these dust-coated, bloodied and cheering adversaries in seemingly unstoppable numbers, the French line of resistance at last melted away.[36]

French artillery fire had once again resumed, as word was passed that the British were counter-attacking in the wood. Their guns, sited a short distance away in the open ground along the ridge between the Ferme du Grand-Pierrepont and Delsot, fired salvo after salvo into the forest, shattering trees, bringing down huge branches and a rain of twigs and leaves on the heads of the British infantry, killing and wounding a number of men. At ground level, iron projectiles and shards of wood cut through the already ragged ranks of the redcoats. Deep in the centre of the wood, a cannon ball tore a branch from a tree, causing Colonel Stanhope to fall from his horse, with more injury to his pride than his person.[37]

Askew's men reached the southern face of the wood within minutes, in time to see the defeated French infantry streaming away across the fields to the south, seeking the shelter and protection of friendly forces behind which to regroup and resume the contest. To the east, Colonel Lord Saltoun and the light companies of the brigade encountered parties of men from the 92nd Regiment of Foot, including Lieutenant Winchester, dug in at the edge of the wood. As the Guards moved forward, a relieved Winchester gave orders for his men to cease firing. It was time to find out what had happened to the remainder of the battalion and orders were given for the men to make their way back to the crossroads.

Colonel Lord Saltoun exited the eastern edge of the wood opposite the Ferme de Gemioncourt and found himself with the sunken chemin de Gemioncourt on his immediate right. About 150 metres away to his left rear, he could also just about make out another British battalion, perhaps elements of the 33rd Regiment of Foot, posted behind a 'Low scrubby hedge'. Separated from the remainder of the brigade by a tongue of woodland, Saltoun was unaware that the second battalion had been committed. Seemingly alone as they issued from the modest cover of the wood, the ranks were raked by round shot and canister from the French guns on high ground less than three hundred metres away. These same guns also targeted the companies of the second battalion of the 1st Regiment of Foot Guards, as they emerged into the open fields somewhat to the west. Not seeing the sunken lane to his front that could have afforded the men a temporary shelter whilst they reorganised, Askew hurriedly gave the order to retire back into the wood and to await reinforcements. The attack had got out of hand. General Maitland was nowhere to be seen; neither was the Duke, though it was said that one of his aides-de-camp had been sent to try and stop them. Remaining in the open, Saltoun's men were also taking punishment. Down went Private William Hoyles, his left thigh smashed by a ball; somewhere in the tangled rye was Private James Graham, his right arm hanging from his shoulder by threads of shredded muscle and sinew; whilst Private Thomas Minchell was making his painful way to the rear, his shattered left hand wrapped in a blood-soaked cloth. With men being killed and wounded at an alarming rate, the Colonel withdrew his men to the sanctuary of the woods.[38]

Here they joined the remaining companies of the battalion, who had not yet reached the open ground. Now they too began to feel the effects of the enemy cannonade. Since their own infantry had evacuated the wood, the French gunners could fire with impunity into the trees, the flashes of red and white confirming the presence of British infantry along its edge. Round shot and canister ploughed into the vegetation, bowling over men and smashing into the trunks of the trees, bringing large boughs down on the heads of the infantry as they struggled through the thick undergrowth. Finding it virtually impossible to maintain order even in the interior of the wood, Colonel Cooke gave the order for his company to withdraw several hundred metres towards

The Battle of Quatre Bras

the Gemioncourt stream in an effort to cushion his men from the ferocious bombardment. Benefiting from this manoeuvre, Lieutenant Powell and Ensign Bathurst sought to restore some order in the ranks, aided by Ensign Fletcher Norton.[39]

To the east of the Bois de Bossu, the 73rd Regiment of Foot was suffering similarly heavy casualties. The battalion had advanced towards the Gemioncourt stream and come up against skirmishers, supported by formed French infantry. Shouting encouragement, Colonel Harris gave the order to charge and the cheering soldiers ran headlong into a violent shower of balls. Captain William Wharton collapsed, both thighs smashed by musket balls; Lieutenant John Lloyd fell, severely wounded; 18-year-old Ensign Robert Hesilrige was also slightly wounded. At least thirty other ranks became casualties.[40]

> Ensign Deacon, of our regiment, was on my right, close to me, when we were charging the enemy and a private on my left, being killed by a musket ball through the temple, the officer said, 'Who is that, Morris?' I replied, 'Sam Shortly' and, pointing to the officer's arm, where a musket ball had passed through, taking with it a portion of the shirt sleeve, I said, 'You are wounded, Sir.' 'God bless me! So I am!' said he and, dropping his sword, made the best of his way to the rear.[41]

The Brunswickers were faring little better. Major von Strombeck, the commanding officer of the 2nd Line Battalion had fallen, as had Captain von Bülow. Captain von Schwarzkoppen assumed the command and continued to encourage the men forward. Despite these casualties, however, the combined impetus of the British and Brunswick troops drove back the wavering French, now under pressure seemingly on every part of the line.[42]

Endnotes

1. Dalton, p. 119. J. Douglas, pp. 96–8.
2. Ross-Lewin, pp. 259–61. Stephens. Swiney, pp. 115–6.
3. Pattison (I). Pattison (II), p. 5.
4. Nafziger, p. 252. Pattison (I). Pattison (II), p. 5, Thain (II).
5. Brereton and Savory, p. 145. Myddleton, p. 99. Pattison (I). Pattison (II), pp. 5–6. Thain (II).
6. Pattison (I). Pattison (II), p. 7.
7. Hemingway. Pattison (I). Thain (II).
8. Pattison (I). Pattison (II), p. 7.
9. J. Howard, p. 246. Lee, p. 227. Pattison (I). Pattison (II), pp. 7–8.
10. Anonymous (O). Arthur, p. 599. de Bas &c., p. 525. Batty, p. 50. Colbeck. Dalton, p. 151. Hemingway. Lee, p. 227. Pattison (I). Pattison (II), p. 7. Thain (I). Thain (II).
11. Anonymous (33rd Regiment). Haythornthwaite (V), p. 55. Trevor.
12. Brereton and Savory, p. 145. Dalton, pp. 149–50. Hemingway. Lee, pp. 227–31. Pattison (I). Pattison (II), pp. 5–8. Thain (II).
13. Halkett (III). Pattison (I). Surtees, p. 73.
14. Halkett (III). Hemingway. Lee, p. 227. Pattison (I). Pattison (II), p. 8.

15. Anonymous (Cameron), p. 90. de Bas &c., pp. 516–7. Batty, p. 50. Clay. Duncan, p. 421. Archibald Forbes, pp. 265, 270. Fraser &c., p. 12. Frazer, p. 540. Gomm (I), pp. 7–8. Kuhlmann. MacKinnon. Master. May. J. Paget (I), p. 85. Powell. Rooke (II). Saint-John. Short. F. Somerset, p. 9.
16. Anonymous (Das braunschweigische Korps). Brett-James, p. 55. Charras, p. 208. Drude. Hellemann. von Herzberg. Houssaye, p. 122. Koopman. Kubel. von Pivka (III), p. 22. Schütte. W. Siborne (V), p. 98. Starklof, p. 141. Traupe, p. 16. von Wachholtz, p. 32.
17. von Damitz, p. 214. Hervey. Houssaye, p. 383. von Ollech, pp. 139–40.
18. Clay. Rooke (II).
19. Dalton, p. 37. Elkington (I), p. 12. Elkington (II). Lake. Powell. Walton. Whitworth, p. 45.
20. Anonymous (Near Observer), pp. 49–52, 56–7. Aubrey-Fletcher, pp. 370, 372. Batty, p. 50. Haythornthwaite (I), p. 114. Lake. Maitland, pp. 20–1. Master. Pattison (II). Ross-Lewin, p. 259. Standen (I). Whitworth, p. 46. C. Wood, p. 806.
21. Braddon, pp. 111–12. Fraser &c., p. 12. Master. Powell. Whitworth, p. 45.
22. Anonymous (Britain Triumphant). Anonymous (Near Observer), pp. 49–52. Aubrey-Fletcher, p. 372. de Bas &c., pp. 517–8. Powell. Whitworth, p. 45.
23. Anonymous (Letters), p. 228. Anonymous (Near Observer), p. 49–52. Clay. Fraser &c., p. 12. F. Hamilton, p. 17. Hope (I). Hope (III), p. 228. Maitland, pp. 20–1. Maurice, p. 12. Powell. Rooke (II). Standen (I). Standen (II).
24. Anonymous (Near Observer), pp. 49–52, 56–7. Aubrey-Fletcher, p. 372. Batty, pp 50–1. Lake. Maitland, p. 21. Pattison (II), p. 8. Powell. Saint-John. Standen (I). Stanhope.
25. Anonymous (Near Observer), pp. 49–52.
26. Anonymous (Near Observer), pp. 49–52. Powell. Standen.
27. Anonymous (Near Observer), pp. 49–52, 56–7. Blake.
28. Blake. Fletcher and Poulter, p. 198. Standen (I).
29. C. Wood, p. 806.
30. Anonymous (Britain Triumphant). Anonymous (Near Observer), pp. 49–52. Mackinnon, p. 211. Powell. Short.
31. Clay. Hemingway. Lake. Pattison (II), p. 8.
32. Anonymous (Britain Triumphant). Aubrey-Fletcher, p. 372. de Bas &c., pp. 517–8. Batty, p. 50. Green. Master. Powell.
33. Macready (I). Macready (III).
34. Bannatyne, p. 322. Macready (I). Macready (III).
35. von Herzberg. Morris, p. 68.
36. Anonymous (Near Observer), pp. 49–52,. 56–7. Green. Lake. Master.
37. Powell. Stanhope.
38. Anonymous (Near Observer), pp. 56–7. Aubrey-Fletcher, pp. 372–3. de Bas &c., pp. 517–8. Chambers, pp. 343, 417, 534. Clay. A. Fraser (II). Maurice, p. 12. Standen (I). Whitworth, p. 46. Winchester (II).
39. Aubrey-Fletcher, pp. 372–3. Powell.
40. Dalton, pp. 185–8. von Herzberg. Lagden and Sly, pp. 98, 126, 243. Morris, pp. 68–70.
41. Morris, p. 69.
42. Hellemann. von Herzberg. Morris, p. 68. von Pflugk-Harttung (II), p. 26.

CHAPTER 18

Farther to the west, Colonel Stuart's third battalion of the 1st Regiment of Foot Guards finally entered open ground, having passed through the centre of the wood. Like its sister battalion, the fire of the French artillery and the difficult terrain of the Bois de Bossu had disrupted the formation and as companies exited, they gradually formed a line, the right of which rested on the edge of the wood, where the chemin d'Houtain-le-Val entered the trees. When No. 3 Company in its turn emerged into the open, William Blake, the battalion's Drum-Major advanced through the thick grain behind it, trying to stay as close as he could to Colonel Miller, his company commander. Despite being a veteran of Holland, Portugal, Spain and France, Blake had seldom endured such a cannonade. All around, hidden in the densely planted rye, concealed in the shallow folds of the ground, in ditches or behind the banks that bounded the fields, were French tirailleurs, who were deliberately targeting the officers, sergeants and drummers. Musket balls slapped through the air, lodging themselves in flesh, striking the metal of the muskets and bayonets and even becoming lodged in knapsacks. Suddenly, as the company approached the fragile cover of a hedge, their Captain tumbled from view amongst the high crops. A number of men rushed to his assistance, but it rapidly became clear that Miller was seriously injured and could not continue in command. A man was sent to the rear of the company, in search of Captain Hon. Robert Clements. Having handed over his command, Miller, who seemed to know almost from the moment of being wounded that his injuries were not survivable, was carried off to the rear. Miller was not the only unfortunate. Elsewhere, a French round shot pitched up and smashed into Captain Adair's thigh; it would take him a week to die.[1]

Ensign Master was observing the scene to his front. This, so it was said, was where Marshal Ney wanted to push through Wellington's front. To the east of his position, the second battalion was still in the greatest disarray, owing to the confused manner in which it had entered and moved through the wood. Disordered companies emerged from the trees and hastily formed a ragged line on the left of the third batallion in the area between the south-eastern tip of the Bois de Bossu and the Ferme de Gemioncourt. As the soldiers came forward, sergeants and corporals posted them in two ranks, irrespective of company, until gradually some semblance of order was restored. This was no time for the niceties of Saint James' Palace. It was vital that the battalion be restored to some degree of regularity before the next French assault.

'Now men, let us see what you are made of'

Dotted here and there in the ranks were men of the 33rd Regiment of Foot, fugitives from the broken 69th Regiment of Foot and even some Gordon Highlanders, survivors of Colonel Cameron's earlier counter-attack on the Ferme de la Bergerie. They had been swept up by the advancing infantry and pressed back into service. In some places, the continuity of the red line was interrupted here and there by the uniforms of men from the Netherlands, Nassau and Brunswick, as they also took up positions. Within minutes, the appearance of a considerable, steady and organised body of troops was created in front of the sergeant's spontoons.[2]

Drawn up to their front were several French infantry battalions, which quickly advanced until they were a short distance from the British companies, apparently in an effort to separate Maitland's brigade from the Charleroi road. As soon as the range had closed sufficiently, Askew's men opened fire, the disciplined enemy infantry proceeding to calmly deploy under intense musketry. Once they had established a three-deep line, the 'fantassins' returned the compliment and a fierce fire fight ensued, which ended in the ragged and depleted British being once again pushed back a short way. In the meantime, three French battalions, supported by two guns, fought it out with the third battalion. Recognising that a great effort was required and, shouting encouragement to the officers and men, General Maitland ordered both battalions to fire a final volley before charging across the ground that separated them from their enemies with their wicked looking bayonets levelled. Demoralised by the appearance of this line and having already sustained numerous casualties from the disciplined British musketry, the French were reluctant to become involved in hand-to-hand fighting with the more numerous redcoats. Their shaky confidence eventually gave way and they hurriedly retired in turn towards their own gun line, the exhausted but triumphant British soldiers trailing in their wake.[3]

The cheering Allies swept across the bowl of ground, pausing here and there to pass through hedges and to negotiate the sometimes deeply sunken lanes. From every possible place of concealment and benefiting from their years of experience of open order fighting, French tirailleurs peppered them with highly accurate shots, their fire being concentrated on the officers, sergeants and drummers. Without leaders, nor the means to convey commands, the battalions would simply become uncontrollable mobs, with the tendency that mobs have towards self-preservation. Conspicuous in the throng were those few officers that regulations permitted to be mounted. One of these was General Maitland, accompanied by Captain Gunthorpe, the Adjutant of the third battalion, who was serving as his Major of Brigade. Completing his staff was Ensign Lord Hay, his aide-de-camp. The General himself, resplendent in his scarlet coat and bullion epaulettes was a prime target for the French sharpshooters and attracted a particularly lively fire as he moved up and down the line, urging his men forward. Suddenly, unheard amongst the crackle and popping of the muskets, a ball sang through the air and struck Lord Hay, killing him instantly, his body falling across Maitland's horse before falling heavily to the ground. He would not, after all, be able to fulfil the promise he had made to Maria Capel at the Duchess of Richmond's ball.[4]

In the woods, buildings or on the roadside, the surgeons were hard-pressed to keep up with the flow of wounded men making their way back through the fields to the makeshift dressing stations. Faint from loss of blood, Colonel Hamilton at last found the aid post of the 30th Regiment of Foot on the Namur road. With Hamilton refusing to dismount, Surgeon Elkington did what he could to staunch the bleeding from the Colonel's leg, but it was useless; the prognosis was not good. After an animated discussion, Elkington eventually convinced his chief that he required surgery and directed him towards the temporary field hospital that had been established in the Ferme des Quatre Bras. Here, he was prepared for surgery, the tourniquet tightened, but the surgeon was called away; Hamilton would have to wait. A while later, the tourniquet was once more applied, only for the surgeon to be called away to deal with a higher priority case. When this happened for the third time, Hamilton complained bitterly and after an examination of the leg, the surgeon and his patient decided to let it take its chance.[5]

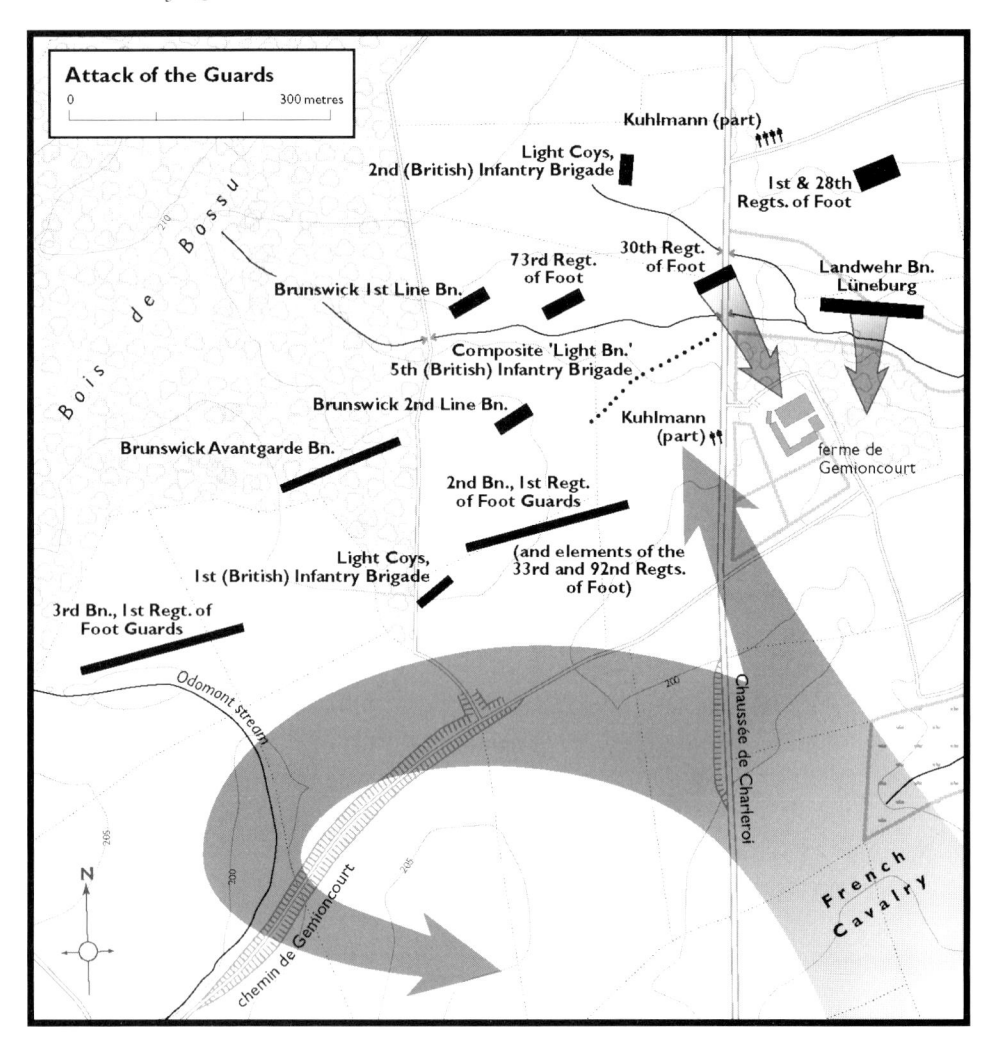

Whilst the fate of Hamilton's leg was decided, Elkington had continued to treat casualties in the open and under fire. The medical teams were also kept updated on the progress of the battle, as each soldier brought back news of the fighting from the firing line. In this manner, he heard of the congratulatory remarks that Picton had made to his regiment, but as was so often the case with messages passed in the heat of battle, in this version it was Picton's aide and not the General himself, who had congratulated the men and not content with being brought to the attention of the Duke of Wellington, a personage no less than the Prince Regent would be informed of their gallantry![6]

Shortly afterwards, the party of soldiers carrying the grievously wounded Lieutenant Lockwood reached the improvised operating theatre and set the young officer's unconscious body down on the cobbles. Examining the wound carefully with a probe and deftly removing pieces of shako felt, cords, bone, hair and metal with his sequestrectomy forceps, Surgeon Elkington surmised that a musket ball must have entered Lockwood's skull, in the region of the frontal sinus. It was not the sort of injury best treated by the side of the road and he instructed the soldiers to remove the casualty to the Ferme des Quatre Bras. Once he was finished here with men who had a reasonable chance of survival, Elkington would do what he could for those such as Lockwood, whose wounds were almost certainly mortal; triage on the field of battle paid no respect to commission dates and seniority.[7]

The stream of wounded was endless. Men came in with gunshot wounds to the skull, arms and thighs; neat little entry wounds disguised large and gruesome exit wounds, if the victim had been lucky enough for the low-velocity balls to completely pass through the flesh, bone, cartilage and muscle. The trauma was as varied as it was voluminous; arterial damage, swelling, severe bruises from spent bullets, raw burns, sabre cuts, stab wounds and fractured or severed limbs.

Elkington was working his way through the growing queues of men, the orderlies doing their best to reassure the impassive lines of less seriously wounded, when a messenger arrived from Major Chambers; he was to remove himself to the front line and attend to a group of wounded men of the regiment in advance. Leaving Assistant-Surgeon Evans in charge, Elkington duly mounted his horse and along with his Hospital Sergeant and bât horse, picked his way across the pasture, through the heaps of corpses and prostrate wounded men, as far as the Charleroi road. As he gained the chaussée, however, he found it choked with dead and dying cuirassiers and their horses; the carnage was horrific. Mangled bodies, wrecked equipment and twitching horse-flesh combined to carpet the road to the extent that, despite his best encouragement, Elkington could not persuade his horse to pass over it. Instead, he rode back into the fields to the east of the road and shortly afterwards arrived at the Ferme de la Bergerie, where he found a number of wounded men and set to work dressing their injuries as best he could. All around were the pitiful corpses of the Gordons, liberally matched by those of the French.[8]

Shortly afterwards, having patched up as many men as possible, he mounted his horse and – once again avoiding the horrors of the highway – made his way back to the charnel house that was the Ferme des Quatre Bras. Every part of the courtyard was filled with wounded men in varying states of distress. Some sat, dumbly, like animals awaiting the slaughter; others bore their misfortune with a resigned countenance; yet more writhed on the ground in the most hideous torment. The living lay side by side with the dead. Here and there, orderlies carried mangled men into the barns, where the surgeons, operating on kitchen tables, barn doors laid across makeshift trestles and other improvised operating tables sawed and sliced through mutilated limbs and sometimes the tables themselves, the agonised patients pinned down by burly assistants. In the corner, a heap of severed hands, arms, feet and legs steadily grew into a hideous mound of amputated tissue.

Finding Lockwood, Elkington once again examined him and removed more débris from the wound. Clearing away the worst of the mess, he finally located the path of the ball and – again using his forceps – managed to extract what he thought was its entirety, before binding Lockwood's head with a bandage. Little was he to know that what he had managed to remove was not the whole ball, but simply a portion of it. The poor officer still had the other half lodged in his sinus, but this was to remain undiscovered for some weeks to come. Having done his best for the young man, Elkington returned to the thankless task of attending the others.[9]

Abandoning the hellish scenes of the battlefield, those still able to stagger made their way to the rear along the Brussels road, where they reassured Lieutenant Jackson and Colonel Nicolay that Wellington 'Was still maintaining himself' at the crossroads. Curiously, thought Jackson, the cannonade seemed to be coming from the east and not the south. Had the battle ended? Had the fighting shifted? A little farther on the road, two sombre Brunswickers informed him that their Duke was dead and Jackson was saddened, having frequently seen the Duke on ceremonial occasions and having admired his: 'Soldier-like appearance and gallant bearing'. Nearing Les Quatre Bras, they passed a groom, leading off a splendid-looking horse that Jackson thought looked somehow familiar and as he searched his mind for the reason, they came across an extraordinary scene:

> We fell in with a remarkable group of human beings, clustered upon some sort of wheel carriage, that turned out to be a Dutch 12-pounder gun, upon which sat or clung a dozen or more wounded men, bloody and dirty, with head or limb bound up, and among them two or three females. It was with great surprise that I heard my name issue from the cluster, and, on close inspection, perceived that it came from Brough, of the 44th, whom I had last seen at Bergen-op-Zoom. He said that Picton's division had suffered very severely, but kept its ground; that he was himself wounded, and but too happy to avail himself of his present seat on the gun carriage, feeling, however, as if the jolting would kill him outright, and exclaiming, 'Oh! That I had my horse.' How his countenance gleamed when I told him that we had just passed his handsome Andalusian, an animal he had brought from Spain, and of which he was exceedingly proud.[10]

Even as the mutilated survivors were fleeing the carnage, fresh victims were being rushed into the slaughter. With evening falling, General Byng ordered Colonel Macdonell, commanding both light companies of the brigade, to skirt the wood by way of the crossroads. He was then to advance along its eastern edge, thereby providing support to the 1st Regiment of Foot Guards in the open ground to the south. In the ranks of Colonel Dashwood's Light Company of the 3rd Regiment of Foot Guards, Private Clay recollected how they were led through the enclosures at Les Quatre Bras:

> We loaded our muskets and very hastily advanced up the rising ground in the open field. The shots from the enemy were now whizzing amongst us and we quickly attained the summit and, bringing our left shoulders forward, the enemy retired before us. We had arrived near to a building against the walls of which the shots from the guns of enemy intended for us were freely rebounding. We were just within range of our guns and our skilful commander led us through an enclosed yard where several bodies of the enemy's cavalry lay, slain before our arrival, through an adjoining garden a short distance to our right, which concealed our advance from the enemy's view and we passed singly through a gap in the hedge at the end of the garden nearest the enemy. We immediately formed in the field into which we had entered and were at the same time joined by our light artillery guns, which had been brought round the outside of the enclosure through which we had passed. They immediately opened their fire upon the enemy, who hastened their retreat and we at the same time advanced through the rye, which was trampled down and passed over the numerous bodies of the dead, more particularly near to a fence enclosing a house and garden, which clearly showed that there had been a severe contest for the possession of it . . . Most of the dead were English, Brunswickers and Highlanders. The majority were the latter.[11]

The house that Clay could see was the Ferme de la Bergerie and, though his mind was preoccupied with preserving his safety, doing his duty and surviving the day, he could not fail to notice the trampled rye fields that told the terrible story of sacrifice. The Guards passed through the pitiful wake left by the counter-attack of the Gordon Highlanders, past the place where Colonel Cameron had received his mortal wound and through the débris of Halkett's 5th (British) Infantry Brigade and the long-suffering Brunswickers.[12]

A short distance in front of Clay was the 73rd Regiment of Foot. His exhausted men breathless in consequence of their rapid advance and under fire at close range once more from French artillery, Colonel Harris ordered the battalion to lie down in the trampled crops. Before long, however, the close advance of a body of French tirailleurs compelled him to detach two companies to combat this new menace. As ever, Private Morris was in the thick of it:

> The colonel ordered two companies out skirmishing. The Light Company and the company to which I belonged were detached to this duty, but not together. Our company was unfortunately commanded by a captain, sixty years of age; who had been upwards of thirty years in the service, but was never before in action. He knew nothing of field movements, and when going through the ordinary evolutions of a parade, the sergeant was obliged to tell him what to say and do. He now led us forward, and we fired a few shots at a portion of the enemy who were within reach.[13]

Across the chaussée from Morris, in the fields to the north of the Ferme de Gemioncourt, Ensign Macready was similarly engaged with the remnants of the Light Company of the 30th Regiment of Foot:

> On the left of our company were some Hanoverian Jägers, one of whom covered a soldier of ours named [Private Thomas] Tracy. A tirailleur dashed out from their line and shot the German thro' the head; upon which Tracy ran over to him, and before he could get off blew his skull to pieces. This enraptured their officers; who, to say the truth, were marvellously distempered with drink or choler, and they were lauding us with praises, such as, 'Englees and Hanover fiell good for the Franceosens – Franceosens à la monde capote, etc.'[14]

Time had now lost its meaning and the light was beginning to fade when, farther to the east, Colonel von Klencke and Major von Dachenhausen led the Lüneburg Field Battalion from its position in rear of the Namur road, across the highway and through the gap between the chaussée and the étang Materne. In the face of this powerful column, accompanied on its left flank by the 95th Regiment of Foot and the 2nd Brunswick Light Battalion, the French infantry hurriedly pulled back to the shelter of Piraumont, taking up positions in the farm and cottages. So rapid was the Allied advance, the French were only just able to bring off some artillery which had been engaged at short range. With support arriving in the shape of the Grubenhagen Field Battalion, the Hanoverians pressed home the attack. Farther east, the Rifles advanced between the chemin de Piraumont and the edge of the Bois de l'Hutte, but soon came under fire from French infantry on their right and a number of officers and men were killed and wounded, including Lieutenant Gairdner, who fell with a severe wound to the lower part of his leg. Driving the French from the buildings of the hamlet, the two Hanoverian battalions were also brought up by the fire of a swarm of French skirmishers to the west; the impetus of the assault was checked and the Hanoverians forced to abandon their gains. To the west of the étang Materne, on the ground so bitterly contested by Kempt's battalions, French infantry advanced to within fifty metres of the Bremen Field Battalion, but came under fire from Rogers' and Cleeves' batteries and the remainder of von Kielmansegge's brigade. As the French in turn wavered, two companies of the Feld-Jäger-Corps drove them off, supported by the 1st and 8th companies of the Bremen battalion under Ensigns Brüel and Meyer. With the Osnabrück Field Battalion also advancing, the French suffered heavy casualties and were forced once again to abandon the heights for the final time.[15]

Even whilst the Hanoverians were trading shots with the French at the eastern end of the battlefield, Colonel Macdonell was preparing his own light companies to move into the front line in the centre of Wellington's position. These were drawn up in the open ground between the Ferme de la Bergerie and the Bois de Bossu, amongst the corpses of the Highlanders and Brunswickers who had fought so hard to hold the ground. On the opposite side of the chaussée, Major Kuhlmann had brought his troop a little farther in advance in order to provide close-range artillery support to the remnants of Halkett's brigade and the Brunswick troops, with Lieutenant Speckmann's section of two guns on the chaussée de Charleroi and the remaining four behind the Namur road to the east. Nearby, Private Clay was preparing to go into action:

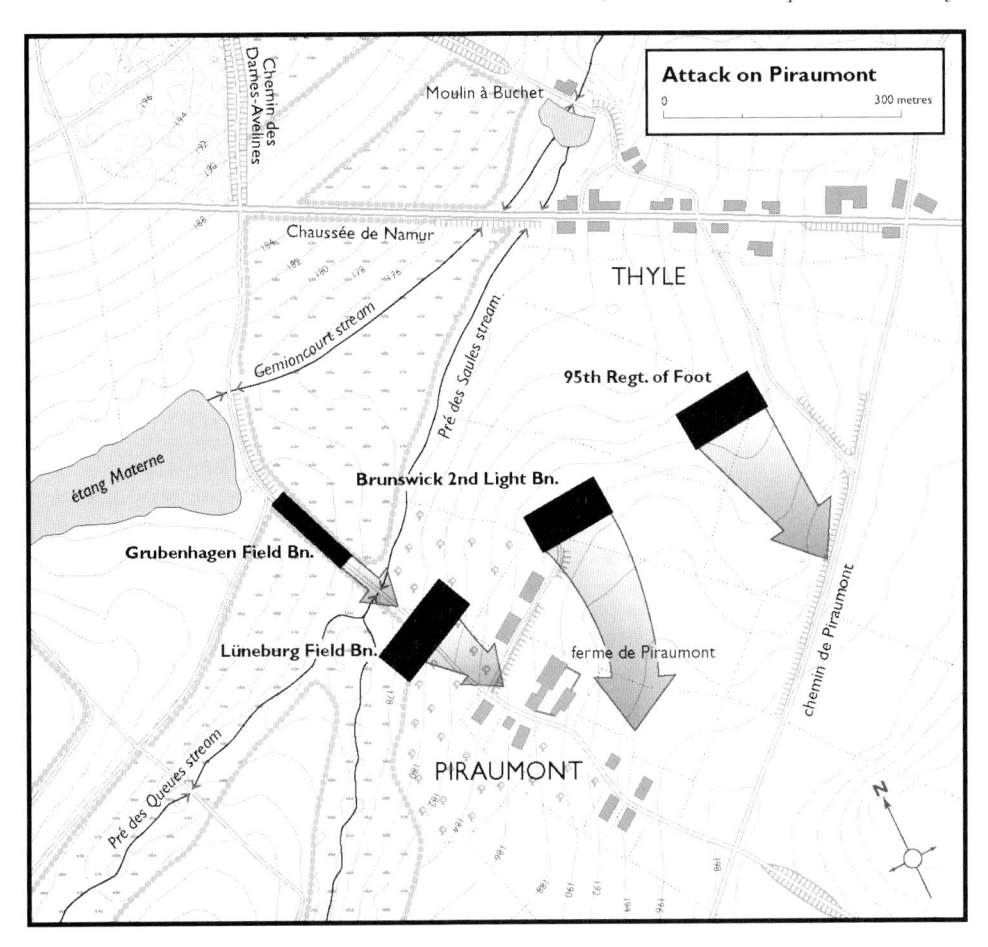

> We halted for a short time whilst our brigade of guns, which was a little farther to the left, exchanged shots with the enemy. Lieutenant-Colonel Dashwood, being in command of the Light Company, 3rd Regiment, took the opportunity of placing himself in front of the company and with cheerful countenance and manner addressed us, saying, 'Now men, let us see what you are made of.'[16]

Ahead of Macdonell's two companies, the Brunswickers of the 2nd Line Battalion, accompanied by Colonel Olfermann, had advanced along the eastern edge of the wood and were approaching a position opposite the Ferme de Gemioncourt, from where they could link up with elements of the second battalion of the 1st Regiment of Foot Guards in the open ground a short distance in front of the Bois de Bossu. Sensing, however, the failing energy of the British advance and once more animated with the confidence so typical of their veterans, the French infantry suddenly coun-

The Battle of Quatre Bras

ter-attacked and pressed the British back towards the woods. As the fighting ebbed and flowed, the pursuing 'Fantassins' gave way to a hitherto unseen but substantial body of French cavalry, including lancers of the Imperial Guard, which emerged from the slight dip in rear of the ridge, moved up in support and appeared ready to charge. The companies being jumbled together, the ground being deemed unsuitable and the enemy being only a very short distance away, the probability of successfully forming square was considered so poor that General Maitland hastily ordered the men to retire to the edge of the wood.[17]

The moment that the Guards dashed for the trees, the advancing 2nd Brunswick Line Battalion, maintaining its discipline and cohesion, immediately halted between the Ferme de Gemioncourt and the Bois de Bossu, closed its column and opened a heavy fire on the approaching French, causing the horsemen to veer off towards the west. The cavalry charged the Allied infantry, who scurried for the ditches that separated the wood from the fields of grain, but not everyone made this feeble sanctuary and the French horsemen did great execution as they got in amongst the stragglers. Once the bulk of the British battalion had formed up at the edge of the trees, they opened up a destructive fire against the cavalry, killing and wounding significant numbers. In places, some of the cavalry got across the ditches and in amongst the infantry, but their advantage was negligible once confined by the closely planted trees. Others shouted: 'Pardon!' and casting away their arms, were made prisoner and led to the rear, their horses being collected to provide remounts for the British officers, most of whom were fighting on foot with their men. The more fortunate horsemen managed to regain the open ground outside and cantered off, peppered from all sides by musket balls.[18]

Farther to the west, the third battalion had, like the Brunswickers, managed to form square, in the midst of which Ensign James Butler stood with the Regimental colour. As the French approached, they were met with volley after volley and suffered severely. Their formation in tatters and their prospects of breaking the square negligible, the French wheeled about and galloped off. As they swept away to the south, the companies of the second battalion once again ventured out into the open, supported to the east by the Brunswick battalion.

Whilst this cavalry was attacking the southern face of the Bois de Bossu, further squadrons had bypassed the Brunswickers and had charged once again towards the crossroads, impeding the advance of the light companies of Byng's brigade. In the forefront was Private Clay:

> Our commander found it necessary to form us into a square to oppose the enemy's cavalry, who were constantly menacing us on our advance. Our square was compactly formed and prepared to receive cavalry. Whenever they bore off, the enemy's artillery would alternately annoy us with their shells, which were skilfully directed but which were equally skilfully avoided through the tactics of our commander. All our movements now for a time were performed while in square for the reasons given above, with the officers in the centre and I had frequent opportunities for observing the keen watchfulness of our commander, who was mounted on his charger and who could undoubtedly,

from his elevated position, distinctly see the preparation of the enemy for the renewed attack upon us, by the united force of infantry, cavalry and artillery. Being foiled by the timely movements of our square and ever obedient to the commander, we escaped the destructive effects of the well-directed shells of the enemy, who, no doubt having observed our repeated escapes from the goring fire of their artillery, menaced us more daringly with their cavalry and prevented our taking fresh ground until their artillery had thrown their shells amongst us. By this means, we had a more narrow escape than before, being compelled to remain longer in our position to resist the cavalry. I, being one of the outward rank of the square, can testify as to the correct aim of the enemy, whose shells having fallen to the ground and exploded within a few paces of the rank in which I was kneeling, a portion of their destructive fragments in their ascent passed between my head and that of my comrade next in the rank. Its force and tremendous sound caused an unconscious movement of the head not to be forgotten in haste.[19]

The skirmishers of the 73rd Regiment of Foot had also seen the approach of the horsemen and, for Private Morris, his concerns over Captain Robertson's capabilities were about to prove correct:

He was then at his wits' end, and there is no doubt we should all have been sacrificed, had we not been seen by the adjutant of our regiment, a fine-spirited fellow, who had been our regimental surgeon, but through the interest of the colonel, exchanged to Ensign and Adjutant. On seeing us in this perilous position, he immediately rode up, and exclaimed, 'Captain Robinson [sic], what are you about? Are you going to murder your men?' He directly ordered us to make the best of our way to the regiment, where we arrived just in time to form square; and on the cuirassiers coming up, and finding us so well prepared, they wheeled off to the left, receiving from us a volley as they retired. They then attacked the 42nd, by whom they were again repulsed, and compelled to retire.[20]

Before the milling horsemen disengaged, however, one cuirassier exacted some compensation for the Grenadier Company's lucky escape. Riding close to the bristling face of the square, the Frenchman braved the musketry and with his pistol extended, shot Lieutenant Acres in the back of the neck, before riding off. The bullet smashed through bone, muscle and sinews, coming to rest in Acres' mouth, from which he was able to remove it. Though his throat and mouth were choked with blood, he managed to turn to Colonel Harris and joke: 'See, Colonel, I've got my allowance,' before collapsing; the wound would prove mortal. Those horsemen who had spurred themselves on towards the crossroads now came under fire at close range from several brigades of Allied artillery, notably Lieutenant Speckmann's two guns on the highway in front of Les Quatre Bras. They also suffered from the lively musketry of the four companies of the right wing of the Coldstream Regiment of Foot Guards, which had been led forward by Colonel Daniel MacKinnon to their support, as well as the Lüneburg Landwehr Battalion. For the final time, the valiant cavalry foundered within pistol shot of the crossroads.[21]

Despite their courageous efforts to stem the increasing pressure being exerted by the Allies, Ensign Macready felt that the French charge had been a 'Faint one, very tame and lukewarm', when compared to the dash, vigour and enthusiasm of their previous efforts. In the literal sense, it appeared they were simply going through the motions. Perhaps, he thought, they only intended to put a decent face on their retreat. As soon as the horsemen had trotted exhaustedly towards the next battalion or the wave had receded to the south of the Ferme de Gemioncourt, Macready and his men were instantly back at their skirmish line, where shortly afterwards, they were joined by the remainder of the battalion. Forming quarter-distance columns, they moved down the slope obliquely to the south-west, towards a heavy body of French infantry. Supported on their left by the remnants of the Royal Scots, the Grenadier Company fired a volley into the ranks of the French battalion a short distance to their front, which the French reciprocated in a violent manner. After a short fire fight, however, the enemy was at last driven back into the Gemioncourt enclosures, the British infantry cheering as they rushed forward, eager to keep the French on the move.[22]

In the meantime, Major Kuhlmann had ordered Lieutenant Speckmann to advance with his, in support of the Brunswickers. Galloping forward, Speckmann unlimbered his section on the highway, close the junction of the chemin de Gemioncourt and the chaussée. As these guns formed up, Maitland concentrated his efforts on restoring the line of his brigade. Almost as soon as this had been effected, more French cavalry appeared, sending the infantry once again running for the protection of the trees. Even the third battalion, which had been about to advance towards the Charleroi road, had no time to form square and withdrew instead to the shelter of the Bois de Bossu.

The Brunswickers, some six hundred metres to Ensign Batty's left, formed what looked like: 'A flèche, or two sides of a square, with the salient angle towards the enemy, and were of great use in covering the retreat of the Guards into the wood'. To Ensign Master, Captain Powell and others, closer to the action, they seemed to be in a perfectly formed square. One body of lancers dashed impotently past the bristling tree-line, suffering further casualties without result until they too, were forced to withdraw. Another column, charging forward along the chaussée itself, seemed to be intent on seizing the two guns, perhaps with a view to turning them against the flank of the second battalion, close to the chemin de Gemioncourt. As the French clattered up the road, they received a point-blank discharge from Speckmann's guns, as well as a vicious volley into its flank from two companies of British infantry which had established themselves behind a dung hill close to the farm buildings. The head of the column disintegrated in a tangle of flailing limbs, gun smoke and gore as the iron and lead projectiles tore through the tightly-packed formation. The remnants of the cavalry, assailed on all sides and unable to complete their charge over the writhing bodies fled back down the road in confusion.[23]

The 30th Regiment of Foot had advanced a considerable distance to the south and Ensign Macready had a grandstand view of the fighting:

> The enemy was retiring from the wood, and the Guards pressing them very closely. A retrograde movement was perceptible along their whole line and it was performed in beautiful style; their columns and skirmishers kept their alignment and distances as if on a parade. The dimness of the evening made the firing doubly vivid, and, above this roar, one occasionally heard German bugles sounding the, 'Advance and fire'. We had no cavalry to spoil this spectacle, but the light troops pushed rapidly from hedge to hedge.[24]

The whole line was advancing and the bugle calls that Macready could hear in the gloom came from the eastern side of the Charleroi road, where von Kielmansegge's battalions, supported by Best's Landwehr, pushed the remnants of the French infantry back to the hedge that bordered the Gemioncourt stream. The fading light and the drifting smoke made it increasingly difficult to pick out friend and foe.

The infantrymen pressed forward, firing at anything; there would be time enough to ponder mistaken identity and express regrets later. Sergeant Robertson, Lieutenant Ross and several other officers and men of the 92nd Regiment of Foot had remained in the Bois de Bossu since their regiment's earlier counter-attack and had been warmly engaged there for the best part of two hours. They could see Brunswickers and other infantry advancing in the open ground as far as the chaussée and as they saw men from the Guards coming up in the wood behind them and to each side, they again determined to advance and attempt to capture some enemy artillery that had been engaged a short distance away. As the tired men dashed forward, Robertson cheered them on, until something smashed into his head and he dropped to the ground, stunned. The shock, the heat, his thirst and anxiety overcame him and he retched into the rye. Lieutenant Ross called Surgeon George Hicks over and asked him to escort the stupefied Sergeant to the rear, where his wound could be examined and dressed.[25]

By this time, the much-battered 30th Regiment of Foot had reached the Ferme de Gemioncourt, into which a substantial body of enemy infantry had withdrawn. As the Netherlands infantry had found out that morning, the French would find it difficult to defend the buildings and enclosures:

> Major Chambers of ours was pushing on with two companies towards a house in our front, and I joined him with as many of the light infantry as I could collect. We rushed into the court-yard, but were repulsed; he re-formed us in the orchards, directed the men how to attack, and it was carried in an instant, by battering open the doors and ramming the muskets into the windows. We found 140 wounded and some excellent beer in the house.[26]

In the open ground to the south of the Bois de Bossu, the second battalion of the 1st Regiment of Foot Guards was steadily pressing the French infantry back, the ebb and flow of the fighting leading to individual trials by combat. Ensign Joseph Saint-John was in the thick of the fighting and noticed one such incident:

The Battle of Quatre Bras

A sergeant of the French came up with his bayonet fixed to one of our officers who is a very little fellow, and told him that he must surrender himself prisoner. 'No,' says our officer, 'You forget that you are a Frenchman and I am an Englishman, so you are my prisoner.' 'Eh bien,' says the Frenchman, 'Chacun son lot, et je me rends votre prisoner.'[27]

With the French cavalry once again driven back, the implacable line of Guards moved towards the high ground between the Charleroi road and the chemin du Pierrepont, a short distance to the south of the Ferme de Gemioncourt, supported by the Brunswickers and the remnants of Halkett's brigade. A little later, they were joined by the cheering ranks of Colonel Macdonell's light companies and Maitland, seeing that the French displayed no inclination to continue the action, decided to a halt on the summit of the ridge from which the French had observed the dispositions of the Prince van Oranje-Nassau earlier that morning. After the harrowing experience of the Bois de Bossu, neither side seemed prepared to engage in further bloody hand-to-hand combat.[28]

By now, the ranks of the 1st Regiment of Foot Guards were dreadfully thinned, severely depleted of officers and non-commissioned officers alike, the victims of French artillery and the deliberate and accurate attentions of enemy marksmen. Of the second battalion, Ensign Hon. Samuel Barrington was dead, his body lying somewhere in the wood or fields. Colonel Askew had been severely wounded in the hip, with Captain Simpson and Ensigns Thomas Croft and George Fludyer similarly suffering severe wounds. Command of the battalion now devolved upon Colonel Richard Cooke, who consequently delegated his company to the care of Captain Powell. Despite its apparent order, losses were just as severe in the third battalion. Colonel Stuart's arm was shattered in the final attack, with Colonel Miller and Captain Adair both receiving wounds that would prove mortal.

Losses in No. 7 Company were especially heavy, both Lieutenant-Colonel Horatio Townshend, the company commander and Captain Thomas Streatfield, his second-in-command, having been severely wounded. Responsibility now devolved upon 18-year-old Ensign Charles Vyner, an officer of less than two years' service, but fortunately, he could rely on the experience of Thomas Cooper, a sergeant with over ten years of soldiering under his belt. The light companies of the 1st Regiment of Foot Guards had suffered more than most. Captain Grose was dead, as was Captain Brown, who had both mocked Ensign Master's chances of survival but a short while earlier. Amongst the piles of severely wounded men lay Ensign William Barton, though Captain Ellis' severe bruising was not sufficient to prevent him from fulfilling his duties. The majority of the killed and wounded choked the fields to the south of the Bois de Bossu, with clumps of dead and injured men at the south-east corner marking the place where Colonel Saltoun's two companies had undergone their ordeal by fire.[29]

Maitland halted the second battalion a short distance to the south of the chemin de Gemioncourt, establishing a line of pickets on the high ground to observe the French. The third battalion took up ground to the right, its skirmishers extending towards the Ferme du Grande-Pierrepont. Gradually, the firing died away.[30]

'Now men, let us see what you are made of'

A short time later, his depleted brigade was joined by the full-strength 2nd (British) Infantry Brigade of General Byng. Towards 8.30 p.m., a messenger had galloped up from General Cooke, with orders for Colonel Woodford to form the remaining five companies of his second battalion of the Coldstream Regiment of Foot Guards into line, to advance through the Bois de Bossu and on arriving at its southern end, to charge the French. As the third battalion of the 3rd Regiment of Foot Guards entered the wood in their wake, Ensign Standen took care to avoid the scattered corpses and the fearfully mangled wounded; to him, they all seemed to be British. He had heard that they were to go on picquet duty, which he thought must surely be a mistake? As he marched through the Bois de Bossu, he noticed small groups of Netherlands infantry and cavalry and unaware of the sacrifices made by these troops earlier in the day, he and his brother officers quickly jumped the conclusion that they were shirkers.[31]

From 9.00 p.m. onwards, only desultory firing could be heard. Exhausted, in disarray and lacking ammunition, the Allied battalions were content to let the enemy slip away into the twilight.[32]

At the eastern extent of the battlefield, the Brunswickers of the 2nd Light Battalion took up positions between the villages of Thyle and Piraumont. The latter had been secured by the Lüneburg and Grubenhagen Field Battalions, but between 9.00 p.m. and 10.00 p.m., these were relieved by the Verden Field Battalion and two companies of the Osnabrück Field Battalion, the remaining six companies of which took up positions at the eastern end of the heights of Lairalle. A short distance to the northwest of this battalion, on the heights of Gemioncourt, the Bremen Field Battalion occupied Colonel Grunenbosch's former position, with Captain von Ehlern's No. 3 Company deployed in a picquet line some one hundred metres to the south, observing the enemy watch fires. Extending along the heights towards Gemioncourt itself were the companies of the Feld-Jager-Korps under the command of Captain von Reden. For a brief period, they were joined by Lieutenant Müller and two guns, but in the gathering gloom, no one was really quite sure whence they had come and where they subsequently went.[33]

Almost at the exact place where Bijleveld's troop had fired off the first Allied artillery rounds of the day, Major Kuhlmann had reunited his own troop and here they went into bivouac. A little to the south-west, a field on the high ground between the Charleroi road and the chemin de Gemioncourt, became the bivouac of the third battalion of the 1st Regiment of Foot Guards and Ensign Master was pleased to find his friend Ensign Pardoe safe and well. Both officers had a raging thirst:

> No water near, we so thirsty, when to Pardoe and my surprise, one of our corporals comes up saluting and offering us his shako, full of water he had fetched for me, he said a long way off. What an attention and what a pleasure this kind spontaneous act gave, I shall never forget.[34]

In their rear, between the Ferme de Gemioncourt and the Bois de Bossu, elements of the Brunswick division took up positions for the night, with the 1st Light Battalion

The Battle of Quatre Bras

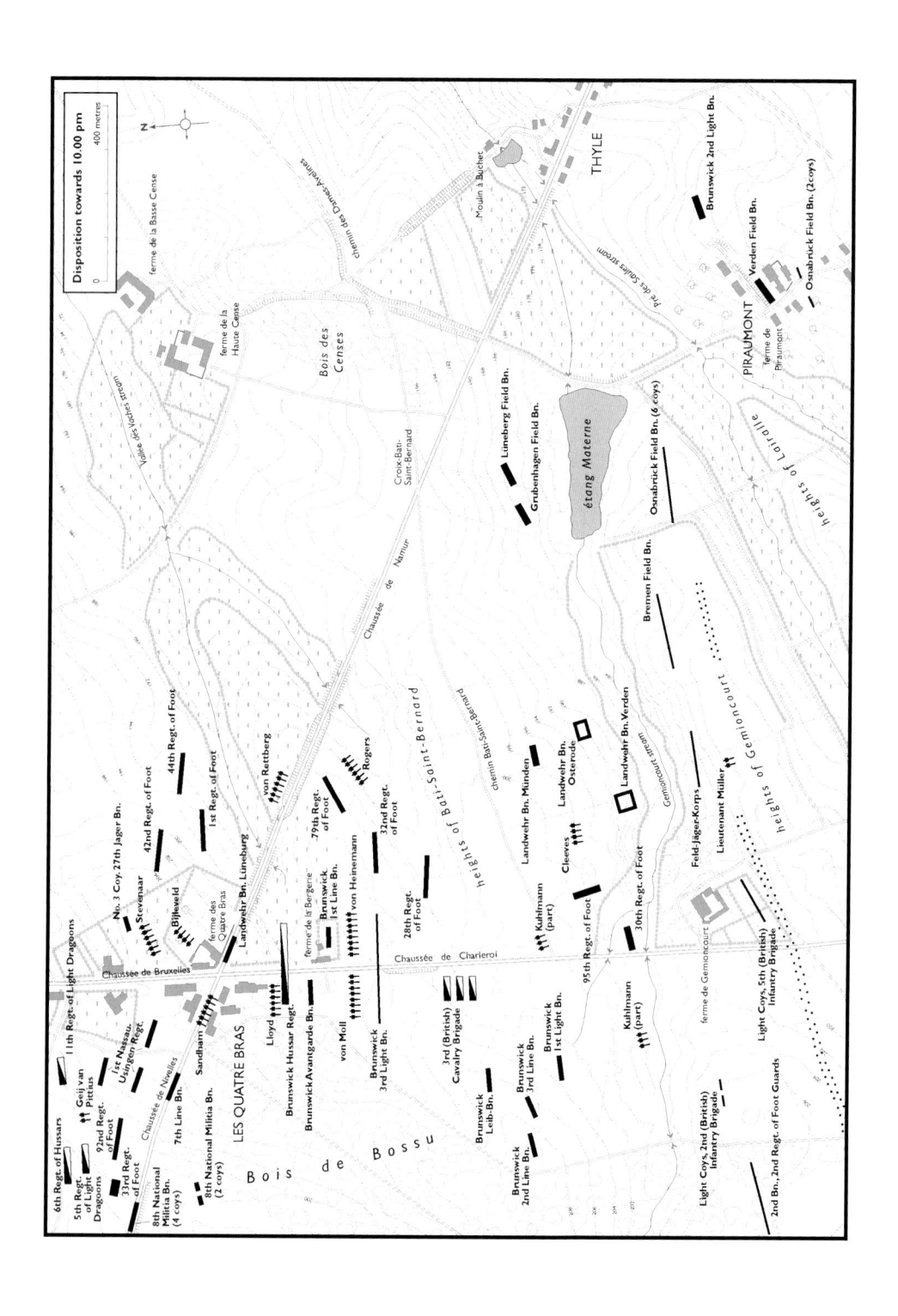

'Now men, let us see what you are made of'

in advance and the Leib-Battalion and 2nd and 3rd Line battalions a little to the north-west, close to the wood itself. Not far from Les Quatre Bras, amid the heaps of dead and dying on both sides of the chaussée de Bruxelles, the exhausted Avantgarde-Battalion was camped with the 1st Line Battalion, 3rd Light Battalion, artillery and Hussar Regiment. The Uhlan Squadron had been told off to provide picquets to the west of the Bois de Bossu. Despite having only had dry biscuit to eat, the men were exhausted from seventeen hours of marching and fighting and dropped to ground at the first opportunity. Almost as soon as it had taken up its bivouac for the night, orders arrived for the 3rd Light Battalion to join its sister battalion between Thyle and Piraumont and the grumbling infantrymen once more stowed their kettles, rolled their blankets and unpiled the arms before moving off across the eerie landscape, accompanied by two guns and a patrol of hussars. In the ranks was Corporal Bollmann, who before the night was finished would capture a French tirailleur who had already shot several Brunswickers, by rushing the man and seizing his musket before he could reload.[35]

After the fighting had come to an end, General Barnes rode up to General Halkett and ordered him to bivouac a short distance to the north of the Gemioncourt stream, between the Charleroi road and the Bois de Bossu. The 30th Regiment, having secured the Ferme de Gemioncourt, took up ground slightly to its north, no doubt enjoying the beer they had earlier liberated:

> Our regiment piled arms about ten o'clock at night, and laid down to sleep, covered by the ravine in our front. The dead and the dying were around us, but no-one slept the worse. Military men know this, but it appears incredible to the uninitiated that a few hours of glory should give the heart such a stoical insensibility. [Lieutenant William] Warren and I pig'd [sic] together under a cuirassier's cloak, and Jack Rumley made a pillow of my buttock.[36]

They were joined, shortly after 11.00 p.m., by the 95th Regiment of Foot, which had been relieved from its position in and around the Bois de Censes by troops from General Kielmansegge's brigade. They had been marched down to the area north of the Ferme de Gemioncourt and ordered to bivouac in ranks, the officers on the inner flanks of each company, in the event that the alarm be raised and the battalion thrown into action:

> Our slumbers were not destined to be of long duration; as we were suddenly broad awake and standing to our arms in consequence of the pickets of both armies blazing away at each other, from some unknown cause, which kept us on the alert.[37]

The fields to the north and south of the heights of Bati-Saint-Bernard were choked with bodies of the living, wounded, dying and dead. The Verden Landwehr Battalion bivouacked in a square, whether to defend itself from the French or from the ghouls that remained invisible in the surrounding fields, no one could tell. Not far away, the

Osterode and Münden Landwehr Battalions sat around their flickering fires, reflecting on the trials of the day. No one had seen the Lüneburg Landwehr Battalion since it had replaced the 92nd Regiment of Foot at Les Quatre Bras.[38]

Also occupying ground between the chaussée de Charleroi and the chaussée de Namur were the remnants of Kempt's three remaining battalions. As the 1st (Hanoverian) Infantry Bigade had deployed in the centre, the 32nd Regiment of Foot had taken up ground closer to the Brussels road and went into bivouac here, along with the 28th and 79th Regiments of Foot. To the north of the Namur road, Pack's brigade slept on their arms in the fields to the north-east of Les Quatre Bras, with General Picton for company.[39]

In the orchard of the Ferme des Quatre Bras, Bijleveld's and Stevenaar's gunners and artificers shared the task of repairing the matériel, sleeping and eating. Lieutenant Winsinger's section had never rejoined and was reported to be in bivouac to the west of the Bois de Bossu. Colonel von Sachsen-Weimar had managed to assemble three of his battalions in the Champ du Sarti, occupying the fields between the Bois de Bossu and the Nivelles road. To the south of the road were the first battalion of the Regiment Oranien-Nassau and the second and third battalions of the 2nd Nassau-Usingen Regiment. On the other side of the road were the second battalion of the former and the first battalion of the latter regiments. Also to the north of the Nivelles road was the 7th National Militia Battalion and the 5th National Militia Battalions, accompanied by No. 3 Company of the 27th Jager Battalion, the remaining companies of which General de Perponcher had ordered to Nivelles in order to re-arm and replenish its ammunition supply. Somewhat closer to the crossroads, the 8th National Militia battalion posted two companies near the edge of the Bois de Bossu and kept the remaining four on the Nivelles road, to the north of which General van Merlen's two cavalry regiments were posted. The 7th Line Battalion was close to the crossroads itself.[40]

As the exhausted troops slept amid the corpses, wrecked vehicles and trampled crops, their generals were somewhat more fortunate. At about 9.00 p.m., Wellington and his staff left the battlefield for Genappe, where headquarters was established at the Hôtel du Roi d'Espagne. He dictated a brief message for Picton, ordering him to continue to occupy the same ground and to place picquets to his front. He then dictated a letter to Colonel De Lancey for the Prince van Oranje-Nassau:

Genappe, June 16 1815

The troops to continue on the same ground as they occupied at the close of the action this day, placing picquets in their front and communicating to their right and left. The 1st Brigade and 2nd Brigade of Guards to bivouac in rear of 4 Bras [sic] having their light companies in their front. The Brunswick battalions and Nassau troops to occupy the wood on the right of the position and placing picquets round the wood and communicating with the cavalry on their right.

Wm. De Lancey QMG General.

HRH the Prince of Orange is requested to communicate this order to the Brunswick and the Nassau troops.

W. de Lancey.

He went on to issue further orders to summon General Hill and the 2nd and 4th (British) Infantry Divisions to move at daybreak to Les Quatre Bras and Nivelles respectively, for the reserve artillery to move on Les Quatre Bras and to General Sir John Lambert to march with his 10th (British) Infantry Brigade from Asse to Genappe. Towards midnight, he went to sleep.[41]

The Prince van Oranje-Nassau had also left the battlefield with General de Constant-Rebecque and arrived at the headquarters of the 2nd (Netherlands) Infantry Division towards 10.00 p.m., where they dined together and reflected on the events of the day. It appeared that de Constant-Rebecque's orders for the removal of the Prince's headquarters from Braine-le-Comte to Nivelles had not been attended to and before retiring to his own quarters at the residence of Madame Robin, the General made his own arrangements for its departure. The Prince, meanwhile, slept fitfully, before waking at 2.00 a.m. and writing a detailed letter to his father, King Willem, which he completed by stating:

> It is with the greatest satisfaction that I can assure Your Majesty that the troops have fought with much bravery, particularly the infantry and the artillery. Circumstances do not permit me to receive the states from the different corps which certify the losses that we have experienced, but I shall have the honour to place these before your eyes as soon as it will be possible.[42]

During the course of the evening and throughout the night, reinforcements steadily arrived on the field. The first and second battalions of the 1st Nassau-Usingen Regiment had arrived at about 8.00 p.m., being joined by their third battalion towards 9.30 p.m. These troops took up position to the right of the chaussée de Bruxelles, to the north of Les Quatre Bras. The first British cavalry on the field was Lieutenant-Colonel James Sleigh's 11th Regiment of Light Dragoons, which arrived too late to see action, but bivouacked to the north-west of Les Quatre Bras, with a squadron pushed forward on picquet duty. It was followed during the night by five more cavalry brigades and a number of troops of horse artillery.[43]

Significantly, the only additional infantry that reached the battlefield before dawn was Colonel Ompteda's 2nd (King's German Legion) Brigade, which had been relieved at Arquennes by Colonel Detmers' troops and arrived shortly before 1.00 a.m. In its ranks was 22-year-old Lieutenant Edmund Wheatley:

> We marched nearly three hours unknowing every step was bringing us nearer and nearer to the scene of slaughter. The crowd of mutilated, lacerated objects soon increased, which I only discovered by their cries and groans as they passed. At length, we arrived

on a wide plain. The road more elevated. Broken muskets, soldier's caps and shoes were strewed on the road; and on each side were numerous blankets stretched out, under which lay the pining, forsaken, wounded soldiers. A strong melancholy seized me as I marched by these moaning heaps of bruised valour. At times I could perceive by the starlight a feeble motion in the white coverings; and a painful scream would accompany the attempt to ease the shattered limb. A few hours ago, they were enjoying low jokes and converse. One small moment has produced more contrition in the heart than ten thousand pathetic admonitions could effect. And the feverish tongue now pronounced 'My God!' which days before prophaned the sacred word in utterance.[44]

Endnotes

1. Batty, p. 5. Blake. Chambers, p. 143. Dalton, p. 101. F. Hamilton, pp. 22–3. Master. Powell. Whitworth, p. 47.
2. Anonymous (Near Observer), pp. 56–7. Aubrey-Fletcher, pp. 372–3. Batty, p. 51. A. Fraser (II). von Herzberg. Powell. Standen (I).
3. Anonymous (Near Observer), pp. 56–7. Aubrey-Fletcher, pp. 372–3. Batty, p. 51. Maitland, p. 21. Powell. Whitworth, p. 46.
4. Anonymous (Near Observer), pp. 49–52. Anonymous (Waterloo Medal Roll), p. 139. Dalton, p. 25. Maitland, p. 21. Powell. Whitworth, p. 46.
5. Dalton, p. 141. Elkington (I), p. 12. Elkington (II). Macready (I).
6. Elkington (I), p. 12.
7. Elkington (I), p. 12. Elkington (II). Tincombe.
8. Bannatyne, p. 347. Dalton, p. 104. Elkington (I), p. 12.
9. Elkington (I), p. 12. Elkington (II).
10. Jackson (II), pp. 18–20.
11. Clay. Powell. Short. Standen (I).
12. Pattison (II), p. 5.
13. Morris, p. 69.
14. Anonymous (Waterloo Medal Roll), p. 207. Macready (I). Macready (III), p. 390.
15. von Alten (I). von Alten (II). Anonymous (Das braunschweigische Korps). von Bülow. Caldwell and Cooper, pp. 10–11. Delhaize and Aerts, p. 464. Gairdner. Müller. von Pflugk-Harttung (I), pp. 30–4. von Pflugk-Harttung (II), pp. 10–11. C. von Scriba (I). C. von Scriba (II). Reille. Simmons (I).
16. Clay. Kuhlmann. May.
17. Anonymous (Near Observer), pp. 49–52, 56–7. Aubrey-Fletcher, pp. 372–3. de Bas &c., pp. 517–8. Batty, pp. 51–2. Fraser &c., pp. 12–13. von Herzberg. Master. Powell. Ross-Lewin, p. 259. Saint-John. Standen (I). Starklof, p. 209. von Wachholtz, p. 32. Whitworth, p. 46.
18. Anonymous (Near Observer), pp. 49–52, 56–7. Batty, pp. 51–2. von Herzberg. Powell. Standen (I). von Wachholtz, p. 32. Whitworth, pp. 46–7.
19. Clay.
20. Lagden and Sly, pp. 192–3. Morris, pp. 68–69. Wauchope, p. 49.

21. Best (I). Best (II). Kuhlmann. Lagden and Sly, p. 4. MacKinnon, p. 211. Mercer, p. 144. Morris, p. 68.
22. Macdonald. Macready (I). Macready (III), p. 390. Macready (IV), p. 391. Mudie (I), p. 168.
23. Anonymous (Near Observer), pp. 49–52, 56–7. de Bas &c., pp. 517–8. Batty, p. 52. Clay. Elkington (II). Kuhlmann. Master. May. Powell. Ross-Lewin, p. 259. Standen (I).
24. Macready (I). Macready (III), p. 390.
25. Anonymous (Waterloo Medal Roll). Robertson. J. Ross (II). Winchester (II).
26. Bannatyne, pp. 322–3. Macready (I). Macready (V).
27. Saint-John.
28. Anonymous (Britain Triumphant). Anonymous (Near Observer), pp. 56–7. Aubrey-Fletcher, pp. 372–3. de Bas &c., pp. 517–8. Batty, p. 52. MacKinnon, p. 211. Rooke (II). F. Somerset, p. 10.
29. Aubrey-Fletcher, pp. 372–3. Batty, p. 53. Chambers, pp. 79–715. Dalton, pp. 95–104. F. Hamilton, pp. 19, 29. d'Oyly. Whitworth, pp. 46–50.
30. Anonymous (Britain Triumphant). Anonymous (Near Observer), pp. 68–9. Beets. A. Fraser (II). Frazer, pp. 539–40. MacKinnon, p. 211. Master. Powell. Rooke (II), Whitworth, p. 47.
31. Short. Standen (I).
32. Best (II). Caldwell and Cooper, pp. 11–12. Finlayson. Alexander Forbes (II). Gairdner. Houssaye, p. 122–3. Kincaid (I), p. 321. Leach, p. 377. D. Mackenzie. Oranje-Nassau (II). von Pflugk-Harttung, pp. 1–3. Puvis, p. 116. Reille. Riddock. C. von Scriba (I). Standen (I). Trefcon, p. 184.
33. von Bülow. von Herzberg. Müller. C. von Scriba (I). von Scriba (II). von Pflugk-Harttung, pp. 9, 11. von Wachholtz, p. 32.
34. Heise (II). Master.
35. Anonymous (Das braunschweigisches Korps). von Herzberg. von Wachholtz, p. 32.
36. Macready (I). Pratt.
37. Caldwell and Cooper, p. 12. Kincaid (I), pp. 321–2. Leach, p. 377.
38. Best (I).
39. Calvert (II). Macdonald. Ross-Lewin, p. 260.
40. de Bas &c., pp. 527–8. de Constant-Rebecque (I). Grunenbosch. de Jongh. Leonhard. van Opstall. Scheltens, p. 199. Wirths. van Zuylen van Nyeveld, p. 57.
41. Gurwood, p. 475.
42. Gurwood, p. 475.
43. H. von Gagern. von Kruse, p. 122. von Pivka (II), p. 27. Schreiber. Wheatley, p. 60.
44. Wheatley, p. 60.

EPILOGUE

Aside from some desultory skirmishing between the outposts, the combatants busied themselves with the practicalities of existence. For many, having marched and fought for most of the day under a broiling sun, the most urgent priority was water; but it was in short supply on the battlefield. Those who had fought on the heights of Bati-Saint-Bernard were aware of the Gemioncourt stream and the étang Materne. The remnants of Pack's brigade had fortuitously found themselves bivouacked close to the Vallée des Vaches stream, across which they had earlier made their way into action. For those to the west of the Charleroi road, and for those camped about the cross-roads itself, water was very hard to come by. Amongst those who went searching was Militiaman Allebrandi of the 7th National Militia Battalion:

> It was between 11.00 p.m. and midnight – about half an hour after the firing ceased – when I went to a nearby house with my canteen; it was a gin distillery. I found the house choked with Allied troops, who had all come for the same reason. It took a lot of effort to enter, which at first was badly rewarded. Although the store was full of strong drink, such that one waded through gin as through a stream of water, I did not find what I so eagerly yearned for. At last, a delightful sight presented itself to my eyes: a pump, to which I hastened and which – Oh joy! – I found full of water as clear as crystal. Here I filled my canteen and got on my way, fully content with the result of my expedition.[1]

Elsewhere on the battlefield, Private Clay was motivated by the desire to help those unable to make such expeditions:

> Being now settled in our position for the night and as there were numbers of wounded men lying close around my post who begged for water and assistance, my comrade and I, being on duty, were also suffering severely from thirst. Being the older soldier of the two, he proposed to keep watch whilst I attended to the wounded and I went in the dark in search of water . . . I took a camp kettle from off the knapsack of a dead man, wended my way a short distance to the rear of the posts, where I had observed the appearance of water when advancing after the enemy on the previous afternoon and found a narrow channel of water in a ditch which I traced into the wood. It was from here that our brave comrades of the 1st Guards had driven the enemy in the evening. There was a

pond from which I filled my kettle and drank freely from its contents, enjoying it much, whilst in the dark I found my way back to my post, where my comrade and the poor sufferers from wounds gladly partook of the contents of the same.[2]

The battlefield took on an eerie aspect in the gloom of the summer night. Captain Kincaid was bivouacked close to Gemioncourt with the 95th Regiment of Foot and later recollected that: 'The fields were strewed with the bodies of men, horses, torn clothing and shattered cuirasses.' A little to the north of Clay and Kincaid, Private Morris of the 73rd Regiment of Foot was: 'Awakened about midnight and was sitting, meditating on the occurrences of the past day and thinking of the poor fellows we had lost and wondering whose turn it would be on the morrow'. His battalion had been fortunate in comparison to most. When going into action, it had a strength of 27 officers and 530 men. By nightfall, it had suffered casualties of four men killed and four officers and 27 men wounded. Amongst the injured was Lieutenant Acres, who would reach the hospital at Antwerp over the coming days, only to succumb to his wound there. Even those who had survived were probably contemplating their chances on the morrow. Captain Robertson, the company commander about whom Private Morris had expressed such reservations earlier in the day, would be killed at Waterloo in less than 48 hours' time.[3]

As Morris pondered these questions, Colonel Harris and some other officers had formed a circle around Lieutenant Joseph Strachan, who had just arrived from England. Learning upon his arrival at Ostend that an engagement was probable, he had travelled post-haste to reach the battlefield. Expressing his disappointment in not having arrived until the fighting was over and not sharing in the glories of the fight, Harris retorted: 'If you are fond of such glory, you will have plenty of it tomorrow.' 'I hope so,' replied the young officer. Little did either know that the new arrival would be in his grave before the day was out, the victim of an accidental discharge from the musket of Private Jeremiah Bates. A stalk of corn would become entangled around the trigger, sending a ball through Strachan's heart.[4]

Some distance to the north, Ensign Deacon of the regiment was making his way to Brussels on foot, having had his wound dressed by a hard-pressed hospital sergeant at one of the makeshift aid stations. He then went in search of his wife and children amongst the baggage guard, but without success. Exhausted, in shock and at the end of his strength, he was evacuated to Brussels. His wife in the meantime, having heard that her husband was wounded, searched in vain amongst the casualties as they passed. Learning that he had been transported to Brussels, she made her way through the most appalling conditions, to find him there on the morning of 18 June: 'Faint, exhausted and wet to the skin, having no other clothes than a black silk dress and a light shawl', she was found accommodation with her husband and gave birth to a daughter the following day, which they duly christened 'Waterloo Deacon.'[5]

Deacon was one of the lucky ones. He had been evacuated and would later recover. For many, however, the battlefield would be their final resting place. In the area between the road from Nivelles to Namur in the north, from the western edge of the Bois de Bossu to the village of Thyle and as far as the heights of Gemioncourt

The Battle of Quatre Bras

stream in the south, were the bodies of some 771 Allied soldiers who had been killed in action, amongst them some forty officers. A further 3,608 officers and men were wounded to varying degrees, many still on the field, many making their way to the aid posts, dressing stations or temporary hospitals. Every building was choked with casualties. Private Costello had made his way to a farm house some distance from the Namur road, most probably the Ferme de la Haute Cense, in which numbers of other walking wounded had taken shelter:

> The house became soon thronged with the wounded of our division, who were momentarily brought in, until the out-houses, courtlages, &c., were literally crammed. All the straw and hay that could be obtained was procured, of which, fortunately, there was plenty, and strewed everywhere to lay the men on. To sleep was impossible with the anguish of my shattered hand and the groans of my fellow sufferers.[6]

The vast majority of the casualties filling the farm were from General Kempt's brigade, which had gone into action with 2,742 officers and men. Three officers and 68 other ranks had been killed, with a further 567 officers and men wounded. Almost a quarter of the brigade was hors de combat. Especially hard hit was the 79th Regiment of Foot, which had suffered losses of thirty killed and 275 wounded, including almost half the officers. Captain Robert Mackay and Lieutenant Kynock, the Adjutant, were dead. Captain Neil Campbell would die of the injuries he had sustained in the days to come, his mother Catherine, receiving a pension of £50 per annum to compensate for her loss. Command now devolved upon Captain Peter Innes, with Colonel Douglas wounded in the knee and Lieutenant-Colonels Andrew Brown and Duncan Cameron both wounded. During the course of the afternoon, all the field officers had seen their horses killed beneath them. Private Vallence had come through unscathed, but was in a melancholoy mood as he surveyed the scene:

> Many of the slain were shockingly mangled, some of their innards torn out and scattered all over the ground, others with their heads severed from their bodies, the heads lying, a shapeless mass, covered with blood and brains.[7]

Amongst the heaps of corpses was Corporal James Marshall from Angus; he would never make sergeant. Nor would Privates Gilbert McArthur and Gilbert McIntosh ever see their native Glasgow again. The former weavers, tailors, labourers of Scotland, Shropshire, County Antrim and Lancashire who now lay unseeing on the slopes of the heights of Bati-Saint-Bernard, would be joined in the coming months by a further 26 comrades who would subsequently die of their wounds.

The 32nd Regiment of Foot, which had spent much of the afternoon and evening to the right of the Cameron Highlanders had also suffered severely. Captain Whitty was dead and his two best friends, Captains Jacques Boyse and Edward Cassan, would eventually die the following day. Lieutenant Stephens had been shot through the arm, but ball had not broken the bone. He had been fortunate, unlike Lieutenants George

Epilogue

Barr and Henry Quill, whose injuries he believed were life threatening; both, however, would go on to make a full recovery. Of his brother officers in the Grenadier Company, only Lieutenant Butterworth was uninjured. The battalion had left 28 of its private soldiers in the fields to the south; they would be tumbled into burial pits in the coming weeks. A further 168 officers, sergeants, drummers and private soldiers who had been wounded in the action, either remained where they had fallen, or made their uncertain way back to the surgeons.[8]

In contrast to the losses suffered by the 32nd and 79th Regiments of foot, the remaining battalions of Kempt's brigade got away comparatively lightly. The 95th Regiment of Foot had benefited from the cover afforded by the houses at Thyle and the trees of the Bois de Censes. They suffered a loss of eight men killed. A further nine officers were wounded, of which one, First Lieutenant William Lister, would die of his serious stomach wound in a house at Les Quatre Bras the following day. Captain Johnstone was possibly counting his blessings. He had acquired a slight wound to complement the shattered arm he had received as part of the storming party at the siege of Badajoz on 6 April 1812, but was to receive yet another during the fighting at Waterloo. Both Gentleman Volunteer Robert Kellett and Charles Smith were wounded, but only Smith would recover sufficiently to be promoted ensign on 19 July. At least one of the 51 sergeants and private soldiers wounded in the battle owed his survival to the efforts of Lieutenant Simmons:

> A man of ours was left near the French. When it fell dark, I went with three men to fetch him away. Both the poor fellow's legs were broken. I deposited him in a house and rejoined my regiment.

Simmons himself would benefit from the care of others two days later; at Waterloo he would be shot through the liver and break two of his ribs.[9]

The 28th Regiment of Foot had been similarly fortunate in that only eleven men had been killed and a further 64 wounded, including four officers and four sergeants. Captain Irving's adventures with the skirmishers had ended up with him being shot in the thigh and through his right arm, but he had crawled to safety and sheltered under the bayonets of the Grenadier Company. Lieutenant William Irwin, whom Captain Cadell considered 'The strongest man in the regiment', was wounded. Major Meacham, the senior company commander had survived unscathed, but would be killed instantly at Waterloo by a musket ball through his heart. Major Llewellyn was similarly unharmed, news which would have delighted the Waldies but his luck too would run out at Waterloo, where he would be severely wounded in the leg. Despite this, he would survive for a further 52 years.[10]

To the north of the Namur road, the depleted battalions of General Pack's brigade were hunched around flickering watch fires. At about 10.00 p.m., one of the surviving pipers of the 92nd Regiment of Foot tuned his bagpipes and played for some considerable time in an effort to rally the wounded and missing men to the colours. Four officers and 35 men could no longer answer the call. Their mangled bodies

The Battle of Quatre Bras

marked the point of the battalion's staunch resistance at Les Quatre Bras and traced the path of its bloody counter-attack on La Bergerie. Lieutenant Winchester, though wounded, had remained with the regiment and recollected a visit from General Picton, the divisional commander:

> Not knowing that we had been engaged till he saw the remains of the regiment, when he enquired what this was, he was told it was the 92nd, on which he asked, 'Where is the rest of the regiment?'

The battalion had arrived at Les Quatre Bras with 38 officers and 661 other ranks and now barely 60 per cent of that strength remained. Captain Little had been killed, along with Lieutenant Chisholm and Ensigns Becher and McPherson. After the arrival at the crossroads of the mortally wounded Colonel Cameron, he had been attended to by his foster brother, Ewen Macmillan.

> Carrying him, with the aid of another private, beyond reach of the firing, he procured a cart, whereon he laid him, carefully and tenderly propping his head on a breast than which none was more faithful. The life-blood, however, was ebbing fast, and on reaching the village of Waterloo, where so many other brave hearts were soon after to bleed, Macmillan carried Fassiefern into a deserted house by the road side, and stretched him on the floor. He anxiously enquired how the day had gone, and how his beloved Highlanders had acquitted themselves. Hearing that, as usual, they had been victorious, he said, 'I die happy, and I trust my dear country will believe that I have served her faithfully.'

He was interred by the side of the Allée Verte, to the north-east of Brussels, during the violent storm of the following day, but would later be disinterred and buried at Kilmallie Church in Lochaber, his aged parents unable to make the journey to his graveside. The baronetcy that Ewen Cameron would receive could never assuage his grief. Captain Grant had also received a wound which would prove mortal, his widow receiving a £60 pension in return for her loss. Somewhere in the gloom, a tired surgeon was amputating the right leg of Ensign John Bramwell; he would survive and be promoted as a one-legged lieutenant on 18 July. Amongst the 245 wounded officers and men was Assistant-Surgeon John Stewart, who had earlier been sabred by French cavalry and Lieutenant James Ross, who would die a retired major-general in April 1872. The wreckage of the battalion was now commanded by Captain Wilkie, though he would also fall victim at Waterloo, as would Lieutenant Hope, who had emerged from the fighting miraculously unscathed. Lieutenant Claude Alexander, who only the night before had supervised the display of highland dancing, was now the third senior officer and would go on to command a wing of the battalion for the rest of the campaign.[11]

Alongside the Gordon Highlanders in Pack's brigade, the 42nd Regiment of Foot had shared in the trials of its sister battalion. With three officers and 42 other ranks killed, the regiment had suffered the highest number of fatalities of any British infantry regiment. From a starting strength of 613 officers and men, a mere 322 remained. As well as its commanding officer, Colonel Macara, Lieutenant Gordon and Ensign George Gerard had been killed at a relatively early point in the action and Major Davidson would die of his wounds shortly afterwards in Brussels. Captain Menzies was more fortunate, he would survive the sixteen wounds he had sustained, perhaps owing his survival to being evacuated to the protection of the square of the 92nd Regiment of Foot. As for Colonel Dick, his wound would not curtail his already glittering career and he would be killed in action against the Sikhs as a major-general at the battle of Sobraon in 1846. The majority of the fifteen officers, fourteen sergeants, single drummer and 216 private soldiers wounded during the fighting had been victims of the French artillery and the incessant musketry of French tirailleurs. When morning came, Sergeant Anton in particular would be reluctant to leave any of the wounded on the field, especially a young man who had been wounded in the forehead, from which the brain protruded. Though his eyes were open, they had a death film over them and he was destined to remain in this state until death released him, by which time his comrades would be some distance to the north. In common with most of Picton's battalions, the Royal Highlanders had suffered heavier losses at Les Quatre Bras than they would subsequently sustain at Waterloo. In their case, seeing only a further 50 casualties of all ranks during the remainder of the campaign.[12]

The third battalion of the 1st Regiment of Foot had also suffered during the course of the afternoon, losing a total of 26 killed and 194 wounded, a third of its strength. Of the six officers killed, the most tragic had been the death of Captain William Buckley. He would not see the birth of his fourth child a mere three weeks later and his widow, Mary, would be forced to raise his family on the Government's pension of £60 per annum. The most courageous, yet futile death had been that of 16-year-old Ensign James Kennedy:

> He was carrying a colour in advance of the battalion and was shot in the arm, but continued to advance. He was again shot, but this time killed or mortally wounded. A sergeant then attempted to take the colour from him, but could not disengage his grip, so he then threw the body over his shoulder and rejoined the ranks of the battalion ... the officer commanding the French battalion opposed to the Royals ... ordered his men not to fire on the sergeant.

On a happier note, the family of Ensign Charles Graham would be distraught to see him returned as killed when the official casualty return was published in the London Gazette on 3 July 1815. Perhaps he would find time to communicate to them that he had only been wounded and would fully recover. By the close of the action, four of the battalion's six captains were casualties, eight of its companies were in the charge of lieutenants and command had devolved upon Major Robert Macdonald.[13]

In contrast, to the sufferings of the Scots, the men of the 44th Regiment of Foot had got away lightly, despite its desperate encounters with French cavalry. Of an opening strength of 530 of all ranks, the battalion had lost twelve killed and 109 wounded. Amongst these was Corporal John Conway, who had gone to his maker with an empty stomach. Although overall casualties were modest in comparison to other battalions, seventeen of the battalion's complement of 25 officers were hors de combat. Though 26-year-old Ensign Peter Cooke had been killed whilst carrying the King's colour, Ensign Christie, who had earlier suffered such an agonising wound in the defence of the same, would survive and be promoted to lieutenant on 26 October. Perhaps the whole experience somewhat put him off the military life, for he exchanged to half-pay the following year.[14]

In contrast to the British brigades, Colonel Best's Hanoverian militia had benefited from the protection of the ground and the embankments of the Namur road. The brigade had suffered Lieutenant Wägener and 43 men killed. Captain von Witzendorf, Lieutenant von Hinüber, Ensign Best of the King's German Legion and an unidentified officer were wounded, along with a non-commissioned officer, a drummer and seventy-seven men. In addition, a further two subaltern officers, six non-commissioned officers and ninety men were missing, many never to be recovered from the tangled crops on the heights of Bati-Saint-Bernard.[15]

Similar losses had been suffered by General von Kielmansegge's 1st (Hanoverian) Infantry Brigade, which had relieved several of Pack and Kempt's battalions in the closing stages of the action. The most heavily engaged had been the Lüneburg Field Battalion, which lost two killed and 56 wounded, including Lieutenants Volge and von Weyhe, who were severely wounded and Lieutenant von Plato and Ensign Sachs, who received minor injuries. In addition, eight men missing were missing in the high crops, one of whom was Captain Korfus. These casualties had mostly been sustained in the course of its attack on Piraumont. The Bremen Field Battalion had been more fortunate, losing only Captain Count Bazoldo and sixteen other ranks wounded and a further two men missing. In total, the brigade had lost fourteen killed, 154 wounded and seventeen missing, from a starting strength of 3,315.[16]

To the west of the Charleroi road, the fields were full of the dead and dying from Halkett's brigade, the Brunswick Division and the 92nd Regiment of Foot. For Ensign Ainslie of the 69th Regiment of Foot, the thing he noticed the most was the deathly smell:

> The smell proceeding from a field of battle, even after the short interval which had, in this instance, taken place, is sickening to a degree which can scarcely be imagined. It is a combined effluvium arising from the bodies and from the crushed grass.

Given its experiences at the hands of the French cavalry, his battalion was fortunate not to be making a more substantial contribution to the corpse-strewn landscape. The 'Saucy Greens' had lost 37 killed and 137 wounded of all ranks. Lieutenant Wightwick, who had but a short time earlier returned the borrowed newspapers to Mrs Watson, had suffered a severe wound, from which he would die near Brussels the following day. Lieutenant Henry Anderson may have been congratulating himself

Epilogue

that the effect of the ricocheting bullet that had hit and slightly wounded him was not too severe. He would continue to serve and would be shot through the left lung at Waterloo, breaking his scapula in the process. Gentleman Volunteer Clarke, who had suffered some 22 wounds in the defence of the King's colour would receive his reward. He was promoted ensign in the 42nd Regiment of Foot. The rest of his military career would not be as glittering as this, his finest hour. He died as a lieutenant in the 33rd Regiment of Foot some seventeen years later.[17]

The very same regiment not suffered as severely, losing nineteen killed, including Private Gibbons, and 101 wounded of all ranks. Having witnessed the carnage around him, Lieutenant Pattison was reflecting on his own good fortune:

> The multitudinous thoughts which arose and passed through my mind in quick succession after the termination of this bloody conflict, were so complex and anomalous that to attempt an analysis of them were altogether vain. The most prominent of these thoughts, however, was a deep sense of gratitude and thankfulness to the God of Battles, who gives the victory to whom He pleases, for shielding me from those winged messengers of death that had cut down so many of my comrades on my right hand and my left.

Lieutenant John Boyce, who had earlier shared with Pattison the concern that he felt certain to be killed had tempted fate and lost his life. In the ranks of the living was Captain Haigh, lamenting the loss of Captain Gore. Unlike Pattison, he would not enjoy divine protection and would be shot through the neck and mortally wounded at Waterloo.[18]

The 30th Regiment of Foot barely suffered at all, losing a total of five killed and 34 wounded from a strength of 682 all ranks. Ensigns John James and James Bullen would, however, succumb to their injuries and die of their wounds. They had both had their legs removed by round shot. Lieutenant Lockwood would continue to suffer surgeons fishing around inside his head until, with the wound clear of all the wreckage, he was fashioned an oval plate manufactured from silver and inscribed with the words 'Bomb Proof'. Wearing a black silk bandana, he would survive for another 31 years, living proof of the enormous capacity for suffering that the generation which fought at Les Quatre Bras possessed. Colonel Hamilton's wound had obliged him to hand over his command to Major Chambers, Major Bailey being absent from the battalion. During the evening, Sir William Ponsonby came to hear that Hamilton was wounded and therefore would probably not require the horse that he had left in the charge of Quartermaster Williamson. He sent an aide-de-camp across with an offer to purchase the animal but Hamilton declined. This would prove fateful for Ponsonby, he would be bogged down in a field at Waterloo and killed by French lancers, for want of a suitable mount.[19]

The senior Allied casualty of the battle of Les Quatre Bras was the Duke von Braunschweig-Lüneburg, who – like his father before him – had been mortally wounded while fighting the French. After the pronouncement of Doctor Pockels;

A proud survivor of both Quatre Bras and Waterloo. Private Thomas Weaver of the 30th Regiment of Foot. *Courtesy Terry Weaver*

Majors von Grone and von Mahrenholtz made preparations for the disposal of his remains. They would escort their chief to his final resting place. His body was removed that evening and arrived at Laeken the following day. From there, it was transported to Antwerp, where it remained overnight at the Hôtel du Grand Laboureur in the Place de Meir. It finally arrived at Brunswick on 22 June and was buried in the crypt of Saint Blasius Cathedral on 3 July.[20]

The death of the Duke had a dispiriting effect on the soldiers of the Brunswick Division, a circumstance heightened by the heavy losses amongst the troops that had been engaged. Despite being wounded in the leg, Lieutenant Hylckema of the 27th Jager Battalion had earlier made his way back to a barn at the crossroads and was an eyewitness to the collective grief of the officers and men:

> When I entered the barn, one surgeon had just amputated the leg of a Brunswick-Oels lancer above the knee and another was busy with a severely wounded man. Standing with the lancer, I asked him how he felt. 'Oh, entirely well,' was his answer, 'Had not our brave Duke been killed.' Never will I forget the tearful tone with which these words were spoken, nor the deathly-pale face with the jet-black, drooping moustache ... One should feel almost ashamed to be in that barn without having lost an arm or leg.[21]

Epilogue

Sergeant Langenstrasse recollected that: 'It was a bad night. The heavy losses, the long corn and nothing to eat meant that the men and horses suffered.' He would be amongst the burial party for Major von Cramm the following day. Amongst the slain was Captain von Pavel of the Hussars, who had been killed not far from Langenstrasse himself. The infantry had fared little better. Major von Strombeck, commanding the 2nd Line battalion was dead, as was Captain von Bülow and Ensign Herge of the 1st and 2nd Line Battalions. Major von Rauschenplatt of the Avantgarde Battalion had been seriously wounded in his upper left arm. Captains von Brömbsen and von der Heyde of the Leib-Battalion were severely wounded; Lieutenant Eduarts less so, with a minor injury to his left hand. Though Ensigns Parren and Hollern of the same battalion had suffered minor wounds to the foot and arm, Ensign Bosse had sustained a more serious wound to his upper thigh. Amongst the 21 officers and 505 other ranks wounded in the action were Captain von Pussinsky, Lieutenant Ahrberg and Ensign Gerlach of the Avantgarde Battalion, Captain Ludovici and Lieutenant Scheffler of the 2nd Light Battalion and Lieutenant von Specht of the 3rd Light Battalion. Lieutenant Hanstein of the 1st Line Battalion had been slightly wounded in the thigh, but his fellow officers in the 2nd Line battalion, Captain Schleiter and Lieutenant Müller, had been more seriously wounded in the knee and chest respectively.[22]

Many of the Brunswick casualties had made their way back to the crossroads, where Militiaman Allebrandi of the 7th National Militia Battalion came upon a scene that would be etched in his mind forever:

> Arriving at the corner of Les Quatre Bras, I became aware of a horrible scenery. Thousands of bodies lay piled on top of each other ... Yet many amongst this terrifying mass of heaped-up bodies were not entirely lifeless; confused and dismal cries for help, lamentations in different languages confirmed this. Here a French *chasseur à cheval* called for the compassion of those passing by; yonder a Scotsman or Hanoverian groaned ... Full, completely full, were the ambulances, while wagons with wounded covered the road to Brussels, and everywhere means of transportation were requisitioned from those farmers who had not fled the fighting ... A certain farm or inn had been requisitioned as an ambulance. In front of it was a wagon full of wounded, ready to depart for Brussels, and which only awaited one Brunswicker, whose second leg had been shattered by a bullet and was amputated by a surgeon; the other leg had been shot away below the knee. As soon as the operation had been carried out, the mutilated man was laid down in the wagon and sang the popular song 'Unser alter Stadtverwalter.' Truly a feat of warrior stoicism! Having gone a long way in the direction of our bivouac, I suddenly fell down and touched something soft and slippery with my hands. At first, I imagined it was the discarded entrails of a few pigs, which were slaughtered here during the morning ... but I noticed that my fall had been caused by a human body, that of a Brunswicker, who had been killed by a bullet in the stomach, which had left his bowels hanging out. Motionless and with my hands together, I gazed on this horrid scene for quite some time.[23]

Perhaps the body that Allebrandi had stumbled over was that of Sergeant Wagenknecht of the Uhlan Squadron? More likely it was one of the 103 other sergeants, corporals, drummers or private soldiers who had been killed during the day and who would find their final resting place in one of the anonymous burial pits that would scar the landscape for months to come. The Leib-Battalion, engaged for much of the day, had suffered losses of 126 officers and men. The 2nd Line Battalion had sustained even greater casualties, with 191 of all ranks killed and wounded. In all, some 846 Brunswickers were killed, wounded or missing by nightfall on 16 June. Amongst the casualties was Sergeant-Major Kinkel, badly wounded in the face. Sergeant Fuhr had been more fortunate; he had been slightly wounded whilst carrying his battalion's colour, but his luck would run out at Waterloo, where he would be severely wounded, shouting: 'Somebody take the colour before I am lost!' Sergeant Fischer had come through the ordeal unscathed, despite the gallantry he had displayed in the skirmish line. All three would receive the Ducat of Honour for their bravery. A further 210 men were missing, possibly lying wounded in the trees and crops, disorientated and lost, or simply too terrified by the ordeal to return to the ranks. At least ten men had been confirmed taken prisoner by the French.[24]

Though it is not known how many men were captured on either side, a mere 100 Frenchmen are recorded as being taken by British forces at Les Quatre Bras, including five men of the Imperial Guard. Sergeant-Major Colbeck of the 33rd Regiment of Foot, who had been taken prisoner late in the afternoon, was destined to spend the next three weeks in the hands of the French. On 4 July, he noted in his journal that: 'On the enemy learning the rapid advance of the Prussians, we were marched out of prison with an intention of being put out of reach and had we marched another quarter of a mile, we would have been retaken by the Prussians.' He would eventually be liberated on 7 July and would rejoin his battalion at its camp in the Bois de Boulogne, near Paris. Private Smith Fyfe of the 42nd Regiment of Foot was released from captivity somewhat earlier. He was one of six private soldiers of the battalion who had fallen into enemy hands, but was by far the shortest, being only about five feet high. A passing French general was said to have hauled him off his feet by his collar or breeches, roaring to the nearby French infantry: 'Behold the sample of the men of whom you seem afraid!' Fyfe returned a few days later, dressed in the clothing of a French grenadier. In a typical example of regimental humour, he was saluted by his comrades as Napoleon until the day he was discharged.[25]

The buildings around the crossroads were filled with wounded men. A British commissariat officer, overseeing an issue of rations, entered one such house:

> A house had been filled with wounded men, chiefly of the Guards, amongst whom a few French had also crept in for shelter. The English rations of provisions were brought, when our men asked if there was any for what they called the poor French, and being answered no, they immediately shared their own small allowance with them.[26]

One of the largest improvised casualty clearing stations was the inn at Les Quatre Bras itself. One German officer, writing on 16 July, recollected the scene:

Epilogue

> At the inn by the crossroads, the contest was hottest. Here are the most graves. The wounded reeled into the inn yard, leaned against the walls, and then sank down. There are still traces of blood on the walls, as it spouted forth from the wounds with departing life.[27]

Lieutenant Hope of the 92nd Regiment of Foot was bivouacked behind the Ferme des Quatre Bras, which had been in use throughout the day by the medical services:

> The yard, I have been assured by a surgeon, who dressed a number of the wounded, at one time contained upwards of a thousand soldiers of the 3rd and 5th Divisions. The ground, inside of the yard, was literally dyed with blood, and the walls very much stained. In short, the interior of that place presented to the eye a scene of unparalleled horror.[28]

During the night, Chief Medical Officer Mergell reached the field. Arriving at Nivelles, earlier in the evening, he had found that the hospital and ambulance of the 2nd (Netherlands) Infantry Division had been sent towards Brussels. Having dispatched one order to recall it and another to Surgeon-Major Scharten to bring his own equipment to Nivelles, Mergell had left for Les Quatre Bras:

> I arrived around 11 o'clock in the evening at the battlefield and met General van der Wijk returning to Nivelles (where His Royal Highness would spend the night), who told me that everything had ended well and there was to be no retreat. He indicated to me the position of the 2nd Division and I wandered around in the dark and got between the French outposts and ours, without being able to locate the staff of the 2nd Division. I remained there until 2 o'clock in the night, collected about a hundred of our wounded, as well as those of our Allies and had them transported to Nivelles.[29]

Whilst the surgeons and their teams worked tirelessly to relieve the suffering, those of a less humanitarian nature were busy prowling the gloomy fields and woods in search of plunder. Private Vallence noticed that some of his fellow sentries passed the time by examining the knapsacks of the slain, but their searches yielded little of value. A more fortunate looter had come across the lifeless body of Ensign Lord Hay and was sufficiently attracted by the young officer's riding boots that he made off with them. The following morning, Ensign Lake and Ensign David Baird of the 3rd Regiment of Foot Guards would find the body and he would be buried in his blue-striped boot stockings. Elsewhere, marauding infantry of all nationalities would not only steal from the dead, but would also rob the living, an unknown number being murdered if they showed any sign of resistance.[30]

Ensign Short of the 2nd Regiment of Foot Guards spent the best part of the night with the outlying picquet, the first time he had been detailed for such a task. Keeping a sharp lookout and placing the sentries carefully, he was much distracted by the groaning of the wounded. The majority of those suffering in the dark fields

The Battle of Quatre Bras

around him were of the two battalions of the 1st Regiment of Foot Guards. In passing through the Bois de Bossu and during the course of the succeeding fighting in the open fields to its south, they had sustained fearful losses. The second battalion had lost two officers and 23 men killed and further four officers and 256 men wounded; a quarter of the battalion's strength. Captain Brown and Ensign Barrington were dead and Colonel Askew, Captain Simpson and Ensigns Fludyer and 16-year-old Croft wounded. Simpson would live for a further fifty-three years, during which he would succeed Wellington's Military Secretary, Colonel Somerset, in command of the British Army in the Crimea. If the second battalion had been hard hit, the third battalion had fared no better. A total of 262 officers and men were killed or wounded.[31]

Private Clay was still doing his bit to ease the plight of the wounded:

> I groped my way about the amongst the sufferers and placed them in as easy a position as I could. Many had fallen in uneasy postures and the fact that they were altogether helpless increased their sufferings. Some had fallen with their legs doubled underneath them, others lay with the weight of the dead upon them.[32]

Amongst its casualties was Captain Adair, struck by a cannonball which had shattered his thigh near the hip. The shot had torn away the flesh and bone fragments were sticking out in splinters near the hip. Assistant-Surgeon Frederick Gilder no doubt looked in despair at the mess. His knife was already blunt from the number of amputations he had already conducted. Though Adair must have suffered the most excrutiating torment, he had the wit to remark: 'Take your time, Mr Carver.' He would linger in torment for another nine days before eventually dying of his wounds at Brussels on 25 June.[33]

Colonel Miller's suffering would be somewhat shorter, he would only survive until 18 June. Before his evacuation to Brussels, he sent for his friend, Colonel Thomas and murmured some parting words:

> 'I feel I am mortally wounded, but I am pleased to think it is my fate rather than yours, whose life is involved in that of your young wife.' After a pause, he said, 'I should like to see the colours of the regiment before I quit them for ever.' They were brought and his countenance brightened, he smiled, declared himself well satisfied, and was carried from the field.[34]

Amongst the survivors was Ensign Pardoe, whose bad luck had been the subject of much chafing by Ensign Master in the early hours of the morning. Master would live for a further 58 years, but young Pardoe's luck would run out on the field of Waterloo, where he would be killed in action. Perhaps the d'Oyly brothers searched for each other in the bivouacs, keen to reassure themselves of their sibling's survival. Little did Henry know that he would be writing to their parents to inform them of Sir Francis' death by a musket ball at the close of the fighting at Waterloo.[35]

Epilogue

Elsewhere, to the north-west of the Bois de Bossu, other men were checking on friends and relations. Sergeant Döring was not amongst the 34 men killed and wounded of the first battalion of the Regiment Oranien-Nassau:

Before all of the corps had assembled for our bivouac, chance led me to my uncle, [Major Gottfried] Hegmann. While we were talking about the day's events, my uncle said, 'I think we are going to have a hot day tomorrow' and offered me a golden pocket watch which chimed the hours. I believed by this offer that we would not meet again, although if the same fate befell us, he, as a staff officer, would receive more care than I as an NCO.

Perhaps the conversation was a prophetic one; Hegmann would lose his left leg at Waterloo.[36]

The first battalion of the Regiment Oranien-Nassau had suffered few casualties, though Lieutenant Schlarbaum had been killed and Lieutenant Engel would die at Genappe of the wounds he received at Les Quatre Bras. The second battalion, on the other hand, which had taken no active part in the fighting, recorded no casualties at all. The three battalions of the 2nd Nassau-Usingen Regiment had also got off lightly, with Captain Weilburg of the second battalion and Captain von Gödecke of the third battalion the only officer casualties. The first battalion had sustained losses of forty officers and men killed, wounded or missing, von Normann's second battalion thirty and the third battalion 35. In contrast, van Bijlandt's brigade had suffered 201 killed and 360 wounded, but the lion's share of these losses was borne by the two battalions that had been most heavily engaged in the early afternoon. The 27th Jager Battalion lost eleven killed and 133 wounded, in addition to which a further 118 officers and men were posted as missing, some to rejoin, others who had simply melted away and yet more who would be buried as unidentified corpses in the rich soil where they fell. Captain de Nave was dead; Colonel Grunenbosch, Captains Eichholtz and van Heekeren van Waliën, along with Lieutenants de Croes and Hylckema were wounded. The Prince van Oranje-Nassau considered the state of the battalion so serious, that he ordered five of its six companies to march on Nivelles, where they would be re-armed, re-equipped and issued with ammunition. As had been the case all afternoon, No. 3 Company would remain behind with the artillery.

A similar story was true of the 5th National Militia Battalion. It had left behind seventy killed, including Lieutenants Boltjens, de Haan and Wijnoldie, and 122 wounded, amongst whom were Captains Forsten, van Gorkum, Mollinger and van Tol. Lieutenant Klein, struck down as the battalion advanced into action, would die of his wounds. Five of the battalion's six company commanders were out of action. A further 102 men were missing in the darkness. The 7th Line Battalion had suffered most of its 182 killed, wounded and missing when routed by French cavalry, including Lieutenants Gérards and Scheltens. Of the two remaining battalions of the brigade, there is no record of the casualties suffered by the 7th National Militia

Battalion, but it is likely they suffered only slight losses. Colonel de Jongh of the 8th National Militia Battalion had been wounded, as had his surgeon, Wilson. They were amongst a total of 27 killed, 48 wounded and 13 missing, presumed prisoners of the French. On completing the returns, the Colonel was informed that 9,650 rounds had been expended. In addition, 28 muskets, sixteen ammunition pouches and seven sabre-briquets had been lost. Doubtless the men responsible would incur the necessary stoppages to their pay.[37]

In percentage terms, the most severe losses amongst the Netherlands troops had been suffered by Captain Stevenaar's foot artillery, with the battery commander and 28 men killed. In addition, Lieutenants Ruysch van Coeverden, van de Wall and van Gahlen were wounded, together with 59 other ranks. A further 31 men were missing. In contrast, Bijleveld's battery was virtually unscathed, with a single fatality; Gunner van Raij's head had been blown off by a cannonball. The poor man had been unlucky, only seven gunners and drivers were wounded during the entire afternoon. Losses to matériel were also a cause for concern in Stevenaar's bivouac. One gun had been irreparably damaged and three further pieces needed remounting. Work continued throughout the night to effect the repairs. Whilst the wheelwrights, artificers and other specialists went about their business, the ammunition caissons were replenished. The same was true for the British, King's German Legion and Hanoverian artillery, whose supplies were running low. Major Rogers' company had fired eleven shells and ninety round shot. Captain von Rettberg's guns had fired the greatest quantity of ordnance; 24 shells and 270 round shot. Major Lloyd's company had expended thirty shells and 94 round shot, with its sister battery, Captain Cleeves' company accounting for a further seventeen shells and 205 round shot. Arriving on the scene much later, Major Kuhlmann's troop of KGL horse artillery were in need of 31 shells and 130 round shot to make up the deficiencies, whilst Sandham's company, kept in reserve until the close of the action, only managed to fire eight rounds in total. Expenditure of canister rounds was unknown.[38]

As for the generals and their staffs, they had led from the front and had suffered the consequences. Though the Duke of Wellington and his staff were miraculously unharmed, General Picton was suffering severely, though his injuries were not revealed to anyone but the servant who helped bind his wounds. Captain Algernon Langton, one of his aides-de-camp was wounded. Another aide, Captain Newton Chambers, would be killed at Waterloo with his chief. Only Captain Tyler would survive the campaign. Major Charles Smyth, Pack's 29-year-old Major of Brigade was mortally wounded. Even as his life ebbed away, his parents John and Georgiana continued to pray for his safe return to Wakefield. Captain Jessop, treated by Surgeon Elkington would live to the ripe old age of ninety and his young protégé, Captain Shaw, would receive a brevet-majority for his services. Colonel Gomm would survive for another sixty years, ending his military career as field marshal and commander-in-chief in India; his fidgety horse, George, would live for 26 of these, dying of old age at Stoke House, near Windsor. Others would be less fortunate. Colonel Somerset would lose his right arm at Waterloo; Colonel Bradford of the staff of Cooke's divi-

Epilogue

sion would eventually die of the consequences of a Waterloo wound on 7 December 1816. Incredibly, the Prince van Oranje-Nassau was unharmed, though Major van Limburg-Stirum of his staff was wounded. General de Perponcher-Sedlnitzky was the senior Netherlands casualty, though he had been only slightly wounded, as had Captain von Gagern of his staff, who had been so active the previous night. At brigade level, Colonel von Sachsen-Weimar's self-inflicted sabre cut would not keep him out of action and he would command his troops at Waterloo, where General van Bijlandt would also become a casualty.[39]

Irrespective of rank, those in the darkened fields, overcrowded buildings and dim forests who had participated in the struggle for Les Quatre Bras were united by an intense personal experience in which some would take great pride and others do their best to forget. That they had held the battlefield at the close of the action confirmed in the thoughts of most that they were not yet defeated; that the contest was not yet over. As to what would happen next, none was the wiser. That was a business for the generals. The exhausted infantrymen, troopers and gunners were united by an anxiety that the carnage would resume with the dawn, or that Wellington would be forced to retreat. What they did not yet comprehend was that the blood spilt by those 5,000 victims of the fighting, as well as that shed by some 20,000 of their Prussian allies on the field of Ligny, had bought the Allies time to fashion the victory that would be won at Waterloo in two days' time. The outcome of the campaign had, to a great extent, already been decided. Thirty-eight hours after the first news of invasion had reached the outpost at Saint-Symphorien, the Allies had inflicted a reverse on the supposedly invincible French that would doom their ultimate prospects of victory, but it had been a very, very close run thing.

Endnotes

1. Allebrandi.
2. Clay.
3. Dalton, p. 185.
4. Lagden and Sly, pp. 15–16, 224. Morris, pp. 71–2.
5. Brett-James, pp 61–2. Lagden and Sly, pp. 52–5. Morris, pp. 69–70.
6. Barnett, p. 201. Chandler (II), pp, 11,18.
7. Anonymous (Cameron), p. 91. Dalton, pp. 187, 191. Alexander Forbes (II). Gomm (I), p. 27. Hamilton, p. 23. Mackenzie et al., p. 56. Siborne (V), p. 555. Vallence.
8. Dalton, pp. 145–8. Gomm (I), p. 27. Hamilton, p. 23. Ross-Lewin, p. 285. Siborne (V), p. 555. Stephens. Swiney, p. 115.
9. Dalton, pp. 197–200. Gomm (I), p. 27. Hamilton, p., 23. Simmons, pp. 363–4, 368, 374.
10. Dalton, pp. 135–9. Cadell, p. 234. Crummer (I). Daniell, pp. 136, 140. Gomm (I), p. 27. Hamilton, p. 23. Siborne (V), p. 555.
11. Clerk, pp. 79–81. Dalton, pp. 193–6. Gomm (I), p. 27. Hamilton, p. 23. Hope (I). Robertson, pp. 149–50. Siborne (V), p. 555. Sinclair-Stevenson, p. 42.

12. Anonymous (Near Observer), pp. 61–2. Anton, p. 201. Cornford and Walker, p. 108. Dalton, pp. 157–160. Archibald Forbes, p. 273. Gomm (I), p. 27. Grant and Youens, p. 23. Groves, p. 14. Hamilton, p. 23. P. Howards, p. 53. Siborne (V), p. 555. Wauchope, p. 50.
13. Dalton, pp. 116–9. Gomm, p. 27. Hamilton, p. 23. Leask and McCance, p. 335. Siborne (V), pp. 555.
14. Carter, p. 104. Dalton, pp. 161–3. Gomm (I), p. 27. Hamilton, p. 23. Martin (I). Siborne (V), p. 555.
15. Best (I). Best [II]. von Pflugk-Harttung, pp. 9–10.
16. von Pflugk-Harttung, pp. 16, 31, 35.
17. Ainslie, p. 15. Anonymous (Near Observer), p. 285. Dalton, p. 175–8. Hamilton, p. 23. Lomax, p. 126. Myddleton, p. 78. Siborne (V), p. 555.
18. Dalton, pp. 149–52. Elphinstone. Hamilton, p. 23. Lee, p. 231. Pattison (II), pp. 3, 10, 28. Siborne (V), p. 555. Thain (II).
19. Dalton, p. 140–4. Hamilton, p. 23. Macready (I). Macready (IV), p. 400. Siborne (V), p. 555.
20. von Herzberg. Olfermann. Traupe, p. 15. von Wachholtz, pp. 30–1
21. Hylckema.
22. Anonymous (Das braunschweigisches Korps). von Herzberg. Langenstrasse. Olfermann.
23. Allebrandi.
24. Anonymous (Das braunschweigisches Korps). von Herzberg.
25. Anton. Chamberlain, p. 26. Colbeck.
26. Anonymous (Journal), p. 427.
27. Anonymous (Near Observer), p. 72.
28. Anonymous (Letters), pp. 235–6.
29. Mergell.
30. Anonymous (Near Observer), pp. 51–2, 69. Aubrey-Fletcher, p. 343. Dalton, pp. 97–106. Hamilton, pp. 22, 25, 45. Master. Powell. Short. Siborne (V), p. 555. Whitworth, p. 47.
31. Dalton, pp. 97, 101. Hamilton, p. 22. Short.
32. Clay.
33. Fletcher and Poulter, p. 201. Gronow, pp. 145–6. Hamilton, p. 22.
33. Dalton, pp. 97, 101.
34. Dalton, pp. 97–8, 104. Master.
35. Döring.
36. Dellevoet, p. 36. Grunenbosch. de Jongh. Knoop (II), p. 193. von Pflugk-Harttung, pp. 213–5. Starklof, p. 142. Wüppermann, pp. 106, 109. 111.
37. Bijleveld. Delhaize and Aerts, p. 455. Koopman. van Zuylen van Nyeveld (I), pp. 57–8.
38. Anonymous (Near Observer), pp. 51–2, 69. Dalton, pp. 9, 11–2, 15–16, 18, 20–1, 25, 27, 30–1, 36–7, 99. Hamilton, pp. 2, 25, 47. Master, Powell. Siborne (V), p. 555.

THE ARMY OF THE LOW COUNTRIES

Staff

Commander-in-Chief	Field Marshal Arthur Wellesley, Duke of Wellington
Military Secretary	Lieutenant-Colonel Lord Fitzroy Somerset
Aides-de-Camp	Colonel the Hereditary Prince of Nassau-Usingen
	Lieutenant-Colonel John Fremantle
	Lieutenant-Colonel Charles Canning
	Lieutenant-Colonel Hon. Sir Alexander Gordon
	Lieutenant Lord George Lennox
Extra Aides-de-Camp	Major Hon. Henry Percy
	Captain Lord Arthur Hill
	Lieutenant Hon. George Cathcart
Military Commissioners	Colonel Baron Friedrich von Müffling (Prussia)
	Lieutenant-Field Marshal Baron de Vincent (Austria)
	Lieutenant-General Count Carlo Pozzo di Borgo (Russia)
	Lieutenant-General Don Miguel de Alava y Esquivel (Spain)
	Major-General Count van Reede (Netherlands)
Quartermaster-General	Lieutenant-General Sir George Murray (absent)
Deputy Quartermaster-General	Colonel Sir William Howe de Lancey
Adjutant-General	Major-General Sir Edward Barnes
Aide-de-Camp	Major Andrew Hamilton
Deputy Adjutant-General	Colonel Sir John Elley
Headquarters Commandant	Colonel Sir Colin Campbell
Head of Communications	Lieutenant-Colonel Sir George Scovell
Commander Royal Artillery	Colonel Sir George Wood
Staff Adjutants	Lieutenant John Bloomfield
	Lieutenant George Coles
Chief-of-Staff	Colonel Sir John May
Royal Horse Artillery	Lieutenant-Colonel Sir Augustus Frazer
Staff Adjutant	Lieutenant William Bell
KGL Artillery	Lieutenant-Colonel Sir Julius Hartmann
Major of Brigade	Captain H. Baynes

The Battle of Quatre Bras

Commander Royal Engineers	Lieutenant-Colonel James Carmichael Smyth
Engineer Staff	Captain Sir George Hoste
	Captain John Oldfield
	Captain Frank Stanway
	Captain Alexander Thomson
	Lieutenant John Pringle,
	Lieutenant Marcus Waters
	Lieutenant Francis Head
	Lieutenant Francis Gilbert
	Lieutenant John Sperling
	Lieutenant Andrew White
Chief Medical Officer	Inspector Sir James Grant

I Corps

Staff

General Officer Commanding	General Prince Willem van Oranje-Nassau
Adjutants	Colonel L. du Caylar
	Colonel Baron J. de Knijff
	Lieutenant-Colonel Guillaume Wauthier
	Lieutenant-Colonel Count Henri de Cruquembourg de Vichte
	Major Count Otto van Limburg-Stirum
	Major Paulus van Hooff
	Major N. Ampt
	Major Count D. Duchatel
Aides-de-Camp	Lieutenant-Colonel Baron Ernst Tripp
	Captain Lord John Somerset
	Captain Hon. Francis Russell
Extra Aides-de-Camp	Captain Charles Lennox (Earl of March)
	Captain Augustus Keppel (Viscount Bury)
	Lieutenant Henry Webster
Quartermaster-General	Major-General Baron Jean-Victor de Constant-Rebecque
Aide-de-Camp	Captain Baron Charles Nepveu
Assistant Quartermaster-General	Colonel Hon. Alexander Abercromby
Adjutant-General	Major-General Lord Herman van der Wijk
Aide-de-Camp	Second-Lieutenant Lord Carel van der Wijk
General Staff Officers	Lieutenant-Colonel D. Arnould
	Lieutenant-Colonel J. Herdeboudt
	Major E. van Gorkum
	Major J. Hulst
	Captain Willem Schröder

The Army of the Low Countries

	Captain A. Engelen
	Captain G. von Rothmaler
	Captain J. van der Hoeven
	Captain Baron R. van der Capellen
	Captain A. van Panhuijs
	Lieutenant G. Muller
Commandant of Headquarters	Lieutenant-Colonel Count L. de Hardy de Beaulieu
Commanding Mounted Guides	Captain Baron K. van Heinecken (66 all ranks)
Commanding Marechaussee	Lieutenant G. Leutner (60 all ranks)
Commanding Artillery	Major-General Carel van Gunkel
Adjutant	Lieutenant F. Teyler van Wall
Chief-of-Staff	Major James de la Sarraz
Artillery Staff Officers	Captain Jean van Osten
	Lieutenant Count P. van Limburg-Stirum
Inspector of Artillery Train	Captain J. Reitz
Headquarters' Engineers	Captain Johannes Ninaber
	Captain F. Cochius
	Lieutenant Cornelius van Kaps
	Lieutenant P. Eckhardt
	Lieutenant F. Baud
Commanding Corps Engineers	Captain J. Esau (66 all ranks)
Administrative Inspector	Colonel J. Reuther
Assistant Inspectors	B. Prevost
	J. Piepers
Chief Medical Officer	K. Mergell
Hospital Administration Agent	M. Uhlens
Apothecary	B. Krabbendam

1st (British) Infantry Division

Staff

General Officer Commanding	Major-General George Cooke
Aide-de-Camp	Captain George Disbrowe
Extra Aide-de-Camp	Ensign Augustus Cuyler
Asst. Quartermaster-General	Lieutenant-Colonel Sir Henry Bradford
Asst. Adjutant-General	Lieutenant-Colonel Henry Rooke
Commanding Artillery	Lieutenant-Colonel Stephen Adye

1st (British) Infantry Brigade

General Officer Commanding	Major-General Peregrine Maitland
Aide-de-Camp	Ensign James, Lord Hay
Major of Brigade	Captain James Gunthorpe

The Battle of Quatre Bras

2nd battalion, 1st Regiment of Foot Guards (Colonel Henry Askew)
                    35 officers and 1,054 men
3rd battalion, 1st Regiment of Foot Guards (Colonel Hon. William Stuart)
                    36 officers and 1,096 men

2nd (British) Infantry Brigade

General Officer Commanding	Major-General Sir John Byng
Aides-de-Camp	Captain Henry Dumaresq
	Lieutenant William Brereton
Extra Aide-de-Camp	Ensign Hon. Edward Stopford
Major of Brigade	Captain William Stothert

2nd battalion, 2nd (Coldstream) Regiment of Foot Guards (Colonel Alexander Woodford)
                    36 officers and 1,085 men
2nd battalion, 3rd Regiment of Foot Guards (Colonel Francis Hepburn)
                    35 officers and 1,139 men

Artillery

No. 9 Company, 3rd Battalion, Royal Regiment of Artillery (Captain Charles Sandham)
                    5 officers and 219 men
                    five 9-pounder guns and one 5½″ howitzer
2nd Horse Troop, King's German Legion Artillery (Major Heinrich Kuhlmann)
                    5 officers and 220 men
                    five 9-pounder guns and one 5½″ howitzer

2nd (Netherlands') Infantry Division

Staff

General Officer Commanding	Lieutenant-General Baron Henri Baron de Perponcher-Sedlnitzky
Aides-de-Camp	Major Jan van de Poll
	Captain Baron T. de Smeth van Duerne
Chief-of-Staff	Colonel Baron Pieter van Zuylen van Nyevelt
Major of Headquarters	Major Baron G. Taets van Amerongen
General Staff Officers	Captain Baron Frederick von Gagern
	Lieutenant Chalmers
	Lieutenant C. Hoynck van Papendrecht
Commanding Artillery	Major Cornelius van Opstall
Commanding Engineers	Captain Albert Gobelet
Inspector of Administration	J. de Sturler
Chief Medical Officer	Dr F. Kühn

The Army of the Low Countries

1st Brigade

General Officer Commanding	Major-General Count Willem van Bijlandt
Aide-de-Camp	Captain Lord P. Rendorp
Major of Brigade	Captain Baron Philip van Zuylen van Nyeveld
General Staff Officers	Captain Count G. van Hogendorp
	Lieutenant Baron C. van Haren

27th (North Netherlands') Jager Battalion (Lieutenant-Colonel Jan Grunenbosch)
23 officers and 739 men

7th (South Netherlands') Line Battalion (Lieutenant-Colonel François van den Sanden)
23 officers and 666 men

5th (North Netherlands') National Militia Battalion (Lieutenant-Colonel Jan Westenbergh)
21 officers and 454 men

7th (North Netherlands') National Militia Battalion (Lieutenant-Colonel Henry Singendonck)
22 officers and 622 men

8th (North Netherlands') National Militia Battalion (Lieutenant-Colonel Wijbrandus de Jongh)
22 officers and 502 men

2nd Brigade

Officer Commanding	Colonel Friedrich von Gödecke
Adjutant	Lieutenant Friedrich von Steprodt
Major of Brigade	Captain Alexander van Coustoll

Regiment Oranien-Nassau (Colonel Prince Bernhard von Sachsen-Weimar)
   1st Battalion (Lieutenant-Colonel Willem von Dressel)
28 officers and 849 men

   2nd Battalion (Major Christian Schleyer)
22 officers and 666 men

Volunteer Jäger Company (Captain Emilius Bergmann)
5 officers and 172 men

2nd Nassau-Usingen Regiment (Major Johann Sattler, vice Lieutenant-Colonel Baron Ernst von Umbusch, absent)
   1st Battalion (Captain Moritz Büsgen, vice Major Johann Sattler)
28 officers and 880 men

   2nd Battalion (Major Phillip von Normann)
28 officers and 850 men

   3rd Battalion (Major Gottfried Hegmann)
28 officers and 855 men

Artillery

Foot Artillery Battery (South Netherlands') (Captain Emmanuel Stevenaar)
3 officers and 107 men
six 6-pounder guns and two 5½" howitzers

Artillery Train (First-Lieutenant F. von Gahlen)
         2 officers and 126 men
Horse Artillery Battery (North Netherlands') (Captain Adriaan Bijleveld)
         5 officers and 100 men
         six 6-pounder guns and two 5½″ howitzers
Artillery Train (First-Lieutenant Jacobus van der Hoeven)
         2 officers and 109 men

3rd (British) Infantry Division

Staff
General Officer Commanding	Lieutenant-General Baron Carl von Alten
Aides-de-Camp	Major Augustus Heise
	Lieutenant William Havelock
Chief-of-Staff	Colonel August von Berger
Asst. Quartermaster-Generals	Major Friedrich Kuntze
	Major John Jessop
Commanding Artillery	Lieutenant-Colonel John Williamson

1st (Hanoverian) Infantry Brigade
General Officer Commanding Major-General Count Friedrich von Kielmansegge
Lüneburg Field Battalion (Lieutenant-Colonel August von Klencke)
        22 officers and 595 men
Osnabrück (Duke of York) Field Battalion (Major Carl Baron von Bülow)
        25 officers and 607 men
Grubenhagen Field Battalion (Lieutenant-Colonel Friedrich von Wurmke)
        22 officers and 621 men
Verden Field Battalion (Major Julius von Schkopp)
        26 officers and 533 men
Bremen Field Battalion (Lieutenant-Colonel Wilhelm von Langehr)
        21 officers and 512 men
Feld-Jäger-Korps (Captain von Reden, vice Lieutenant-Colonel August von Spörken, absent)
        10 officers and 321 men

1st (King's German Legion) Infantry Brigade
Detached at Arquennes. Did not rejoin until the evening of 16 of June 1815.

5th (British) Infantry Brigade
General Officer Commanding	Major-General Sir Colin Halkett
Aides de Camp	Captain Baron Henry von Marschalk
	Captain Alexander Home
Major of Brigade	Captain William Crofton

The Army of the Low Countries

2nd battalion, 30th (Cambridgeshire) Regiment of Foot (Lieutenant-Colonel Alexander Hamilton)
38 officers and 644 men

33rd (1st Yorkshire West Riding) Regiment of Foot (Lieutenant-Colonel William Elphinstone)
36 officers and 548 men

2nd battalion, 69th (South Lincolnshire) Regiment of Foot (Colonel Charles Morice)
28 officers and 580 men

2nd battalion, 73rd (Highland) Regiment of Foot (Lieutenant-Colonel William Harris)
27 officers and 530 men

Artillery

No. 2 Company, 10th Battalion, Royal Regiment of Artillery (Major William Lloyd)
5 officers and 219 men
five 9-pounder guns and one 5½" howitzer

No. 4 Company, King's German Legion Artillery (Captain Andreas Cleeves)
5 officers and 209 men
five 9-pounder guns and one 5½" howitzer

Netherlands' Cavalry Division

2nd (Netherlands') Light Cavalry Brigade

General Officer Commanding	Major-General Baron Jean-Baptiste van Merlen
Aide-de-Camp	Captain J. de Bellefroid
Major of Brigade	Major J. de Paravicini di Capelli

5th (South Netherlands') Regiment of Light Dragoons (Lieutenant-Colonel Edouard de Mercx de Corbais)
18 officers and 379 men

6th (North Netherlands') Regiment of Hussars (Lieutenant-Colonel Lord Willem Boreel)
28 officers and 549 men

Horse Artillery Half-Battery (Captain Adrianus Geij van Pittius)
2 officers and 63 men
three 6-pounder guns and one 5½" howitzer

Artillery Train (Second Lieutenant Camise)
2 officers and 53 men

The Battle of Quatre Bras

4th (British) Infantry Division

Artillery
2nd (Hanoverian) Foot Artillery Brigade (Captain Carl von Rettberg)
        5 officers and 233 men
        five 5-pounder guns and one 5½" howitzer

5th (British) Infantry Division

General Officer Commanding	Lieutenant-General Sir Thomas Picton
Aides-de-Camp	Captain Algernon Langton
	Captain J. Tyler
	Captain Newton Chambers
Extra Aide-de-Camp	Captain Barrington Price
Asst. Quartermaster-General	Lieutenant-Colonel Sir William Gomm
Commanding Artillery	Major Augustus Heise

8th (British) Infantry Brigade

General Officer Commanding	Major-General Sir James Kempt
Aide-de-Camp	Captain Hon. Charles Gore
Major of Brigade	Captain Charles Eeles

1st battalion, 28th (North Gloucestershire) Regiment of Foot (Lieutenant-Colonel Sir Charles Belson)
        34 officers and 592 men
1st battalion, 32nd (Cornwall) Regiment of Foot (Lieutenant-Colonel John Hicks)
        38 officers and 651 men
1st battalion, 79th (Cameron Highlanders) Regiment of Foot (Lieutenant-Colonel Neil Douglas)
        41 officers and 735 men
1st battalion, 95th (Rifles) Regiment of Foot (Lieutenant-Colonel Sir Andrew Barnard)
        29 officers and 622 men

9th (British) Infantry Brigade

General Officer Commanding	Major-General Sir Denis Pack
Aide-de-Camp	Major Edmund L'Estrange
Major of Brigade	Major Charles Smyth

3rd battalion, 1st (Royal Scots) Regiment of Foot (Lieutenant-Colonel Colin Campbell)
        37 officers and 624 men
1st battalion, 42nd (Royal Highland) Regiment of Foot (Lieutenant-Colonel Sir Robert Macara)
        31 officers and 582 men

2nd battalion, 44th (East Essex) Regiment of Foot (Lieutenant-Colonel John Hamerton)
25 officers and 505 men
1st battalion, 92nd (Gordon Highlanders) Regiment of Foot (Colonel Sir John Cameron)
38 officers and 661 men

Artillery
No. 2 Company, 3rd Battalion, Royal Regiment of Artillery (Major Thomas Rogers)
3 officers and 216 men
five 9-pounder guns and one 5½″ howitzer

6th (British) Infantry Division

4th (Hanoverian) Infantry Brigade
General Officer Commanding   Colonel Carl Best
Landwehr Battalion Verden (Major Christoph von der Decken)
21 officers and 621 men
Landwehr Battalion Lüneburg (Lieutenant-Colonel Ludwig von Ramdohr)
23 officers and 624 men
Landwehr Battalion Osterode (Major Baron Claus von Reden)
23 officers and 677 men
Landwehr Battalion Münden (Major Ferdinand von Schmidt)
20 officers and 660 men

Brunswick Division

Staff
General Officer Commanding	Duke Friedrich-Wilhelm von Braunschweig-Lüneburg
Aides-de-Camp	Captain Lübeck
	Captain Bause
Corps Commandant	Colonel Elias Olfermann
Aides-de-Camp	Captain Morgenstern
	Captain von Zweifel
Quartermaster-General	Lieutenant-Colonel von Heinemann
Deputy Quartermaster-General	Major Friedrich von Wachholtz
General Staff Officers	Colonel von Herzberg
	Major von Grone
	Major von Mahrenholtz
Commanding Cavalry	Major Friedrich von Cramm
Commanding Artillery	Major von Lubecq
Police Hussars	1 officer and 13 men
Supply Train	Captain Warnecke and 50 all ranks

The Battle of Quatre Bras

Avantgarde
Avantgarde Battalion (Major Adolf von Rauschenplatt)
   2 companies of Gelernte-Jäger (Professional Riflemen)
   2 companies of Leicht-Infanterie (Light Infantry)
                     34 officers and 679 men

Light Infantry Brigade
Officer Commanding   Lieutenant-Colonel Wilhelm Treusch von Buttlar
Leib-Battalion (Major August von Pröstler)
                     34 officers and 672 men
1st Light Battalion (Major Werner von Holstein)
                     34 officers and 672 men
2nd Light Battalion (Major Heinrich von Brandenstein)
                     33 officers and 672 men
3rd Light Battalion (Major Ludwig Ebeling)
                     33 officers and 672 men

Line Infantry Brigade
Officer Commanding   Lieutenant-Colonel Friedrich von Specht
1st Line Battalion (Major Ferdinand von Metzner)
                     34 officers and 672 men
2nd Line Battalion (Major von Johann Strombeck)
                     33 officers and 672 men
3rd Line Battalion (Major Gustavus Normann)
                     34 officers and 672 men

Cavalry
Hussar Regiment (Major von Braun)
                     36 officers and 727 men
Uhlan Regiment (Lieutenant-Colonel Carl Pott)
                     12 officers and 246 men

Artillery
Horse Artillery Battery (Captain von Heinemann)
                     5 officers and 162 men
                     eight 6-pounder guns
Foot Battery (Major Carl von Moll)
                     7 officers and 223 men
                     eight 6-pounder guns

BIBLIOGRAPHY

Adkin, Mark. *The Waterloo Companion,* Aurum, London, 2001.
Adye, Lieutenant-Colonel Stephen. *MS letter to Lieutenant William Siborne, dated Woolwich Common, 6 December 1834,* British Library, London, BL Add MS 34,704, ff. 7-8.
Ainslie, Ensign George. *Memoir.* See Maughan, pp. 12-27.
Allan, James M. *Extract from a Narrative of the Battle of Quatre Bras by a Soldier of the 79th Highlanders,* published in The Waterloo Journal, Volume XXI, No. 2, August 1999, pp. 14-16.
Allebrandi, Militiaman Sebastian. *Herinneringen uit mijn tienjarige militaire loopbaan door S.A.,* Amsterdam, 1835.
Allen, Mark D. *The Highlanders at Quatre Bras,* published in The Waterloo Journal, Volume XXI, No. 3, December 1999, pp. 29-33.
von Alten (I), Lieutenant-General Baron Carl. *MS transcript of extract from despatch,* British Library, London, BL Add MS 34,708, ff. 368-9.
von Alten (II), Lieutenant-General Baron Carl. *Report of Lieutenant General von Alten to the Duke of Cambridge on the conduct of the Hanoverian troops in the engagement at Quatre Bras, dated Brussels, 20 June 1815.* See von Pflugk-Harttung (II), pp. 13-14.
Anonymous (33rd Regiment), *The 33rd Regiment at Quatre Bras,* published in The United Services Journal, June 1845, pp. 292-293.
Anonymous (42nd Regiment). *Historical Record of the Forty-Second or The Royal Highland Regiment of Foot,* Parker, Furnivall and Parker, London, 1845.
Anonymous (Account). *An Account of the Battle of Waterloo,* W. Falconer, Glasgow, 1816.
Anonymous (Belgian Bibliography). *Bibliographie d'histoire militaire belge des origins au 1er août 1914,* Centre d'Histoire Militaire, Musée Royal de l'Armée, Brussels, 1979.
Anonymous (Belgian Notions). *Belgian notions of the battle of Waterloo,* published in The United Services Journal, July 1842, pp. 391-5.
Anonymous (Britain Triumphant). *Britain Triumphant on the Plains of Waterloo: being a correct and circumstantial narrative of that memorable battle with biographical and characteristic anecdotes of the principal commanders,* John Tregortha, London, 1817.
Anonymous (Cameron). *Historical record of the Queens Own Cameron Highlanders (Volume I)* William Blackwood, Edinburgh, 1909.
Anonymous (Das braunschweigische Korps). *Das braunschweigische Korps im Feldzug in Brabant und die Teilnahme an der Schlacht bei Quatre-Bras am 16. Juni 1815,* published electronically on www.braunschweiger-feldkorps.de.
Anonymous (Incoming Register). *Register of Incoming Correspondence of the Quartermaster-General's Department of the Field Army.* Archive of the Field Campaigns of Quartermaster-General de Constant-Rebecque, Nationaal Archief, The Hague, NA 2.13.14.01;7.
Anonymous (Jérôme). *MS memorandum of conversations with Jérôme Bonaparte and Count Bertrand, dated Rome, 10 May 1823, Paris, 2 August 1824 and Paris, 3 August 1824,* British Library, London, BL Add MS 34,703, ff. 65-75.

Anonymous (Journal). *Journal of an officer in the Commissariat Department of the Army,* printed for the author, London, 1820.
Anonymous (Letters). *Letters from Portugal, Spain, and France during the memorable campaigns of 1811, 1812, & 1813 and from Belgium and France in the year 1815,* Michael Anderson, London and Edinburgh, 1819.
Anonymous (McKenzie Papers). *Undated MS account of an incident involving a Major of the 42nd Regiment,* National Army Museum, London, Archive 6807/125.
Anonymous (Namenslisten). *Namenslisten der bei Waterloo Gefallenen, Verwundeten und Vermissten der Nassauischen Brigade,* Hessisches Hauptstaatsarchiv Wiesbaden (HHStaW), Abt. 202, No. 450, f. 79.
Anonymous (Near Observer). *The Battle of Waterloo: containing the series of accounts published by authority British and Foreign with circumstantial details, previous, during and after the battle from a variety of original sources with relative official documents, forming an historical record of the operations in the campaign of the Netherlands, 1815, and also of the co-operative movements of the Russians, Austrians, Bavarians, &c. (6th edition),* J. Booth, London, 1815.
Anonymous (Order Book). *MS Small Holland Order Book of the second battalion, 3rd Regiment of Foot Guards,* private collection.
Anonymous (Outgoing Register). *Register of Outgoing Correspondence of the Quartermaster-General's Department of the Field Army.* Archive of the Field Campaigns of Quartermaster-General de Constant-Rebecque, Nationaal Archief, The Hague, NA 2.13.14.01;6.
Anonymous (Popular Errors). *Popular errors respecting the battle of Waterloo,* published in The United Services Journal, June 1839, pp. 198-201.
Anonymous (Record). *Record of the Services of the 33rd (the Duke of Wellington's) Regiment of Foot,* published in The United Services Journal, December 1869, pp. 510-22.
Anonymous (Regimental Order Book). *MS Regimental Order Book of the first Battalion, 92nd Regiment of Foot.* Gordon Highlanders Museum, Aberdeen.
Anonymous (Royal Artillery). *Undated MS memorandum referring to Royal Artillery officer casualties,* British Library, London, BL Add MS 34,707, f. 8.
Anonymous (Small Order Book). *Small Order Book of the second battalion of the 2nd Regiment of Foot Guards,* private collection.
Anonymous (V. d. W.). *Account of Bijleveld's Horse Artillery,* published in The Bredascher Courant, No. 80, 5 July 1840, pp. 2-3.
Anonymous (Waterloo Medal Roll). *Waterloo Medal Roll, compiled from the muster rolls,* Naval and Military Press, Dallington, 1992.
Anonymous (Y.Z.). *Regimental Colour captured at Quatre Bras,* published in The Journal of the Society for Army Historical Research, Volume IV, pp. 53-4.
Anton, Sergeant James. *Retrospect of a military Life during the most eventful periods of the last war,* W. H. Lizars, Edinburgh, 1841.
Arcq, Alan. *La Bataille des Quatre-Bras,* Historic'One Editions, Annecy-le-Vieux, 2005.
Arthur, Captain Sir George. *The Story of the Household Cavalry (Volume II),* Archibald Constable, London, 1909.
Asquith, General W. H. *List of Officers of the Royal Artillery from the Year 1716 to the Year 1899 (4th edition),* William Clowes, London, 1900.
Atteridge, A. H. *Marshal Ney: The Bravest of the Brave,* Naval and Military Press, Uckfield, 2001.
Aubrey-Fletcher, Major H. L. *A History of the Foot Guards to 1856,* Constable, London, 1927.
Aumüller, Lydia. *Die 'Nassauer' kämpften mit Blücher und Wellington gegen Napoleon,* published in Jahrbuch für den Kreis Limburg-Weilburg, Bd. 2001, pp. 169-72.
van Balveren, Major Baron Walraven Elias Johan. *MS letter to E. van Löben-Sels, dated Nijmegen, 25 May 1841,* van Löben-Sels Family Archive, Stads-en-Streekarchief, Zutphen, Folder II, No. 5, Letter 2.
Bannatyne, Lieutenant-Colonel Neil. *History of the Thirtieth Regiment, now the First Battalion East*

Lancashire Regiment, 1689-1881, Littlebury, Liverpool, 1923.

Barlow, Captain George. *Letter to his father, Sir George Barlow Bart., dated Paris, 7 July 1815*, National Army Museum, London, 6507-1. See also Owen, pp. 38-44.

Barnett, Corelli. *Napoleon Bonaparte,* Hill and Wang, New York, 1978.

Barre, First Lieutenant J. L. *MS letter to E. van Löben-Sels, Harderwijk, dated Nijmegen, 22 September 1841,* van Löben-Sels Family Archive, Stads-en-Streekarchief, Zutphen, Folder II, No. 3, Letter 10.

de Bas, F. *Prins Frederik der Nederlanden en zijn tijd (Volume III),* H. E. M. Roelants, Schiedam, 1904.

de Bas, F. and de T'Serclaes de Wommersom, Count J. *La campagne de 1815 aux Pays-Bas, d'après les rapports officials Néerlandais (Volume I),* Albert Dewit, Brussels, 1908.

Basslé, Lieutenant J. F. L. *Report to General Tindal, dated 16 June 1815.* See Couvreur (II), pp 76-7.

Batty, Ensign Robert. *An Historical Sketch of the Campaign of 1815, illustrated by plans of the Operations and of the Battles of Quatre Bras, Ligny, and Waterloo (2nd edition),* Rodwell, Martin Clarke and Egerton, London, 1820.

Beamish, N. Ludlow. *History of the King's German Legion (Volume II),* Naval and Military Press, Dallington, 1997.

Becke, A. F. *Napoleon and Waterloo. The Emperor's Campaign with the Armée du Nord 1815,* Greenhill Books, London, 1995.

Beets, Militiaman Dirk. *Undated MS Journal,* Instituut voor Militaire Geschiedenis, The Hague, 101/8.

van Bentinck tot 't Nyenhuis, Lieutenant W. *MS letter to E. van Löben-Sels, dated Dordrecht, 30 November 1841,* van Löben-Sels Family Archive, Stads-en-Streekarchief, Zutphen, folder II, No. 4, Letter 11.

Bergmann, Captain Emilus. *Undated letter to the Duke of Nassau.* See Domarius, pp. 18-20.

Berlemon, J. H. M. *Quatre Bras en Waterloo, Juni 1815, paarden die deee haver verdienen,* published in Ons Leger, 67e Jaargang, No. 6, June 1983, pp. 32-8.

Bernard, Gilles and Lachaux, Gérard. *Waterloo Relics,* Histoire et Collections, Paris, 2005.

Best (I), Colonel Carl. *Letter to Lieutenant-General Count von Alten, dated Bavay, 22 June 1815.* See von Pflugk-Harttung (II), pp. 18-19.

Best (II), Colonel Carl. *IV. Infanterie-Brigade. Bericht der Sclacht bey Quatre-bras, den 16. Juni 1815, und des darauf am 17. Juni erfolgten Rückzuges, eigesanndt vom General-Major Best.* See von Pflugk-Harttung (II), pp. 19-25.

van Bijlandt, Major-General Count Willem. *MS Letter written on his behalf by his son, E. van Bijlandt, to E. van Löben-Sels, dated The Hague, 31 May 1841,* van Löben-Sels Family Archive, Stads-en-Streekarchief, Zutphen, Folder II, No. 3, Letter 6.

Bijleveld, Captain Adriaan. *MS Letters to E. van Löben-Sels, dated Breda, 3 June and 4 August 1841,* van Löben-Sels Family Archive, Stads-en-Streekarchief, Zutphen, Folder II, No. 4, Letters 7-8.

Bikar, Colonel A. *Bulletin de la Société Belge d'Études Napoléonien,* No. 23, 1994, pp. 14, 32-4.

Black, Private J. C. *MS letter to his father, dated 10 July 1815,* National Library of Scotland, MS10488.

Blake, Private William. *MS letter to his sister, dated Paris, 19 January 1816,* private collection.

Bluth, B. J. *Marching with Sharpe,* Harper Collins, London, 2001.

Boersma, Hans. *A bibliography of the Army of the Kingdom of the Netherlands in the Waterloo Campaign, 1815,* published electronically, December 2001.

Bonaparte, Napoleon. *La Correspondance de Napoléon Ier (32 Volumes),* Imprimerie Impériale, Paris, 1858-1870.

Bosscha, J. *Het Leven van Willem den Tweede, Konig der Nederlanden en Groothertog van Luxemburg,* C. M. van Gogh, Amsterdam, 1854.

Boulger, Demetrius. *The Belgians at Waterloo (with translations of the Reports of the Dutch and Belgian Commanders),* published by the author, London, 1901.

Bourdon de Vatry. See Grouchy, pp. 98-116.

Bowden, Scott. *Armies at Waterloo. A detailed analysis of the armies that fought History's greatest battle,*

Empire Games Press, Arlington, Texas, 1983.

Braddon, Russell. *All the Queen's Men. The Household Cavalry and the Brigade of Guards,* Hamish Hamilton, London, 1977.

Brander, A. Michael. *The Royal Scots (The Royal Regiment),* Leo Cooper, London, 1976.

Brandis, Captain. See Dehnel, pp. 247-260.

Braun, Captain Wilhelm. *State of losses,* Niedersächsiches Hauptstaatsarchiv (NHA), Hanover, Hann. 38D, No. 200.

Brereton, J. M. and Savory, A. C. S. *The History of the Duke of Wellington's Regiment (West Riding) 1702-1992,* published by The Duke of Wellington's Regiment (West Riding), Halifax, 1993.

Brett-James, Antony. *The Hundred Days. Napoleon's last campaign from eye-witness accounts,* Ken Trotman, Cambridge, 1989.

Bronkhorst, Captain Abraham G. *Letter to unknown addressee ('Anette'), dated Péronne, 9 July 1815.* See Berlemon, pp. 32-8.

Bukhari, Emir. *Napoleon's Cavalry,* Osprey, London, 1979.

von Bülow, Lieutenant. *MS letter dated 26 August 1815.* See Kannicht, p. 205.

Bunsen (I), Baron Christian. *MS letter to Captain William Siborne, dated London, 14 January 1848,* British Library, London, BL Add MS 34,708 ff. 265-9.

Bunsen (II), Baron Christian. *MS letter to Captain William Siborne, dated London, 3 February 1848,* British Library, London, BL Add MS 34,708 f.280.

Burney, Captain William. See Carter, pp. 82-3.

Burrows, John William. *The Essex Regiment (2nd edition),* John H. Burrows, Southend-on-Sea, 1931.

Butler, W. F., *A narrative of the historical events connected with the Sixty-Ninth Regiment,* W. Mitchell, London, 1870.

Cadell (I), Captain Charles. *Narrative of the campaigns of the Twenty-Eighth Regiment since their return from Egypt in 1802,* Whittaker, London, 1835.

Cadell (II), Captain Charles. *MS letter to Captain William Siborne, dated 28 March 1837,* British Library, London, BL Add MS 34,706, ff. 282-3.

Caldwell, George and Cooper, Robert. *Rifles at Waterloo,* Bugle Horn Publications, 1995.

Calvert (I), Major Felix. *MS letter to Lieutenant William Siborne, dated Ware, 19 April 1835,* British Library, London, BL Add MS 34,705 ff. 169-70.

Calvert (II), Major Felix. *MS letter to Lieutenant William Siborne, dated London, 11 March 1837,* British Library, London, BL Add MS 34,706 ff. 256-8.

Cameron (I), Lieutenant-Colonel John. *MS letter to his father, Ewen Cameron, dated Brussels, 29 May 1815,* private collection.

Cameron (II), Lieutenant-Colonel John. *MS letter to his father, Ewen Cameron, dated Brussels, 12 June 1815,* private collection.

del Campo, W. J. *Het leven en de krijgsbedriven van David Hendricus Baron Chassé, in leven generaal der infanterie enz,* Gebroeders Muller, Den Bosch, 1849.

Campbell, Major John. *MS letter to an unknown addressee, dated Liverpool, 15 March 1838,* British Library, London, BL Add MS 34,706 ff. 451-4.

Cannon, Richard. *Historical Record of the Seventy-Third Regiment,* Parker, Furnival and Parker, London, 1851.

Carman, W. Y. *The Royal Artillery,* Osprey, Botley, 1973.

Carter, Thomas. *Historical Records of the Forty-Fourth or the East Essex Regiment of Foot (2nd edition),* Gale and Polden, Chatham, 1887.

Cathcart, Lieutenant Hon. George (Second Earl Cathcart). *The Military Journal and Correspondence of George Cathcart, A.D.C. to the Duke of Wellington, describing the campaigns of Dresden, Leipzig and Waterloo, 1813-1815,* transcription of original MS by Michael McGarvie, private collection.

Chamberlain, Paul. *From Waterloo to Dartmoor: Prisoners of war during the Waterloo campaign,* published in The Waterloo Journal, Volume 23, No. 1, April 2001, pp. 25-31.

Bibliography

Chambers, Barbara. *The men of the 1st Foot Guards at Waterloo and beyond (2 volumes)*, published by the author, Letchworth Garden City, 2003.

Chandler (I), David G. *The campaigns of Napoleon (12th edition)*, Weidenfeld and Nicholson, London, 1993.

Chandler (II), David G. *Waterloo. The Hundred Days*, Osprey, London, 1993.

Charras, Lieutenant-Colonel Jean-Baptiste-Adolphe. *Histoire de la Campagne de 1815. Waterloo (Volume I)*, Paris, 1869.

Chassé, Lieutenant-General Baron David. *Letter to the Prince van Oranje-Nassau, dated Montmorency, 3 August 1815.* See Köffler, p. 24.

Chesney, Colonel Charles. *Waterloo Lectures*, Greenhill Books, London, 1997.

Christemeijer, J. B. *Herinneringen van een oud-strijder van 1813-1815 aangaande Quatre-Bras en Waterloo*, Keminck, Utrecht, 1865.

von Clausewitz, General Carl. *Der Feldzug von 1815 in Frankreich*, Dümmler, Berlin, 1835.

Clay, Private Matthew. *A narrative of adventures at the battle of Quatre Bras*, published in The Household Brigade Magazine, Autumn 1958, pp. 139-42.

Clayton, Herbert B. *Born on the field of Waterloo*, published in Notes and Queries, 9th Series, X, 26 July 1902 (July-December 1902).

Cleeves, Captain Andreas. *Bericht der 4. Batterie der Deutschen Legion über ihren Anteil am Gefechte bei Quatrebras, dated Wunstorf, 25 November 1824.* See von Pflugk-Harttung (II), pp. 39-41.

Clerk, Reverend Archibald. *Memoir of Colonel John Cameron, Fassiefern, K.T.S., Lieutenant-Colonel of the Gordon Highlanders, or 92nd Regiment of Foot*, privately published, Glasgow, n.d.

Colbeck, Sergeant-Major James. *MS Journal of Stages on the March in the 33rd Regiment*, Duke of Wellington's Regimental Archive, Halifax.

de Constant-Rebecque (I), Major-General Baron Jean-Victor. *MS Journal*, Nationaal Archief, The Hague. C22259, Collection 66.

de Constant-Rebecque (II), Major-General Baron Jean-Victor. *Letters received by de Constant-Rebecque, April 1814 to January 1816, Archive of the Field Campaigns of Quartermaster-General de Constant-Rebecque*, Nationaal Archief, The Hague, NA 2.13.14.01;8.

Cope, Sir William H. *The History of the Rifle Brigade (The Prince Consort's Own), formerly the 95th*, Chatto and Windus, London, 1877.

Cornford, L. Cope and Walker, F.W. *The great deeds of the Black Watch*, J. M. Dent, London, 1915.

Costello, Edward. *Military Memoirs. Edward Costello. The Peninsular and Waterloo campaigns (edited by Antony Brett-James)*, Longmans, Green, London, 1967.

Cotton. Sergeant-Major Edward. *A voice from Waterloo*, Naval and Military Press, Uckfield, 2001.

Couvreur, H. J. *Le drame Belge de Waterloo*, Brussels, 1959.

Couvreur, Pierre. *Historique du 108è de Ligne qui s'illustra à Genappe-Quatre Bras le 16 juin 1815*, Association Franco-Européenne de Waterloo, Syndicate d'Initiative de Genappe, n.d.

Cox, First Lieutenant John. *MS Letter to Lieutenant William Siborne, dated London, 14 March 1837*, British Library, London, BL Add MS 34,706 ff. 262-3.

Crowe, Captain John. *MS letter to Lieutenant William Siborne, dated Buleford, 10 May 1837*, British Library, London, BL Add MS 34,706 ff. 320-1.

de Crassier, Captain L. W. J. *MS letter dated Sertry, 26 June 1815*, Archive of the Department of War, Nationaal Archief, The Hague, No. 2.13.01. inv177.

Creevey, Thomas. *A Selection from the Correspondance and Diaries of the Late Thomas Creevey, M. P. Born 1768; Died 1838 (edited by Sir Herbert Maxwell) (Volume I)*, John Murray, London, 1904.

Croker, J.W. *The Croker Papers 1809-1830 (Volume II)*, Jennings, London, 1885.

Crummer (I), Lieutenant James. *MS letter to his father, Samuel Crummer, dated Amouville, 4 July 1815*, State Library of New South Wales, Sydney, Australia.

Crummer (II), Lieutenant James. *MS journal*, State Library of New South Wales, Sydney, Australia.

Crumplin, M. K. H. and Starling, P. *A Surgical Artist at War. The Paintings and Sketches of Sir Charles Bell 1809-1815*, Royal College of Surgeons of Edinburgh, Edinburgh, 2005.

Dallas, Ensign Charles R. K. *MS letter to his cousins, dated 25 June 1815,* private collection.

Dalton, Charles. *Waterloo Roll Call, with biographical notes and anecdotes (2nd edition),* Eyre and Spottiswoode, London, 1904.

von Damitz, Carl. *Geschichte des Feldzüges von 1815 in den Niederlanden und Frankreich als Beitrag zur Kriegsgeschichte des neurn Kriege (Volume I),* Berlin, Posen and Bromberg, 1837-1838.

Daniell, David Scott. *Cap of Honour. The Story of the Gloucestershire Regiment (the 28th / 61st Foot) 1694-1950,* Harrap, London, 1951.

Deebetz, First Lieutenant J. J. *Undated MS note of conversation with E. van Löben-Sels,* van Löben-Sels Family Archive, Stads-en-Streekarchief, Zutphen, Folder II, No. 5, Letter 5.

Dehnel, Heinrich. *Erinnerungen deutscher Offiziere in britischen Diensten aus den Kriegsjahren 1805 bis 1816; nach Aufzeichnungen und mündlichen Erzählungen zusammengetragen, und mit einzelnen geschichtlichen Erlauterungen begleitet.* C. Rümpler, Hannover, 1864.

van Delen, Major Leonhard Albrecht Carl Baron. *Statement as to the conduct of the Third Division of the Royal Netherlands Army on the days of 15th, 16th, 17th, and 18th, up to the morning of the 19th June, 1815, dated 11 November 1815.* See Boulger, pp. 43-5.

Delhaize, Jules and Aerts, Winand. *Études relatives à la campagne de 1815 en Belgique (Volume I),* Brussels, 1915.

Dellevoet, André. *Cowards at Waterloo? A re-examination of Bijlandt's Dutch-Belgian Brigade in the campaign of 1815,* published in Napoleon, No. 16, Summer 2000, pp. 18-36.

Dewar, Sergeant William. *MS letter to his brother, dated 5 August 1815,* National War Museum of Scotland, Edinburgh, M1960.2.

Dick, Lieutenant-Colonel Robert Dick. *MS letter to Lieutenant William Siborne, dated 29 November 1834,* British Library, London, BL Add MS 34,703 ff. 274-5.

Domarius, M. *Die Oranien-Nassauischen Freiwillige Jägerkompagnie,* published in Nassauische Heimatblätter, 1915, pp. 15-24.

van Doren, J. B. J. *Strategisch verhaal van de veldslagen tusschen het Fransche Leger en dat der Geallierden op 15, 16, 17 en 18 Juni 1815, op Mont-Saint-Jean,* Amsterdam, 1865.

Döring, Sergeant Heinrich. *Die Belagerung von Mainz und die Schlacht bei Waterloo aus der Sicht eines Sergeanten des 1. Bataillons Oranien-Nassau (1813-1815),* published in Heimatblätter für das Dillgebiet, den östlichen Westerwald und das hessische Hinterland, Historische beilage zur Dill-Zeitung, 56. Jahrgang, Nos. 11-12, November-December 1988.

von Dörnberg, Major-General Sir Wilhelm. *MS Account of the start of the Waterloo campaign.* See Hussey (I).

Douglas, Corporal John. *Douglas' Tales of the Peninsular and Waterloo,* Leo Cooper, London, 1998.

Douglas, Lieutenant-Colonel Neil. *MS letter to Lieutenant William Siborne, dated Broughty, 22 November 1834,* British Library, London, BL Add MS 34,703 ff. 309-11.

Drude, Surgeon. *MS diary,* Geheime Staatsarchiv Preussischer Kulturbesitz, Berlin, Gneisenau Papers, Rep 92, A, Abt., Pkt 3.

Duncan, Major Francis. *History of the Royal Regiment of Artillery, compiled from the original records (2nd edition),* John Murray, London, 1874.

Dyneley, Second Captain Thomas. *Letters written by Lieutenant-General Thomas Dyneley C.B. R.A., while on active service between the years 1806 and 1815 (edited by Colonel F. A. Whinyates),* Trotman, London, 1984.

Eaton, Charlotte A. *The days of battle, or Quatre Bras and Waterloo, by an Englishwoman resident at Brussels in June 1815,* Henry G. Bohn, London, 1853.

Eberhard, Captain C. F. *Nassauische Erinnerungen an Waterloo,* published in Der Uhrturm, Heft 27, July 1940, p. 552.

Eenens, Lieutenant-General Alexis M. *Dissertation sur la participation des troupes des Pays-Bas à la campagne de 1815 en Belgique,* Ghent, 1879.

Elkington (I), Surgeon James. *Extracts from the Diary of Surgeon James Goodall Elkington,* published in XXX Magazine, June 1911, pp. 11-13.

Bibliography

Elkington (II), Surgeon James. *MS letter to Major Edward Macready, dated Dublin, 14 March 1845,* British Library, London, BL Add MS 34,708 ff. 183-5.

Elphinstone, Lieutenant-Colonel William. *MS Letter to Major-General Count Count Friedrich von Kielmansegge, dated 25 June 1815,* British Library, London, BL Add MS 34,703 ff. 50-1.

Fairfield, Captain Charles. *MS Letter to Lieutenant William Siborne, dated Mount Eagle, 6 August 1836,* British Library, London, BL Add MS 34,706 ff. 129-31.

Finlayson, Assistant-Surgeon D. *MS letter to Mr. Somerville, dated 25 June 1815,* National Library of Scotland, Edinburgh, MS 9236.

Fitchett, W. H. *Wellington's Men. Some Soldier Autobiographies,* Smith Elder, London, 1976.

Fitzmaurice, Lieutenant G. *Biographical sketch of Major-General John Fitzmaurice,* privately published, Anghiari, 1908.

Fletcher (I), Ian. *Wellington's Foot Guards,* Osprey, London, 1997.

Fletcher (II), Ian. *A Desperate Business. Wellington, the British Army and the Waterloo Campaign,* Spellmount, Staplehurst, 2001.

Fletcher, Ian and Poulter, Ron. *Gentlemen's Sons. The Guards in the Peninsula and at Waterloo, 1808-1815,* Spellmount, Speldhurst, 1992.

Forbes, Lieutenant Alexander (I). *MS letter to Lieutenant William Siborne, dated Dublin, 25 March 1835,* British Library, London, BL Add MS 34,705 ff. 105-9.

Forbes, Lieutenant Alexander (II). *MS letter to Lieutenant William Siborne, dated 3 May 1837,* British Library, London, BL Add MS 34,703 ff. 1-2.

Forbes, Archibald. *The Black Watch. The Record of an Historic Regiment,* Cassell, London, 1896.

Fosten, Bryan. *Brass before and brass behind: the 28th Regiment of Foot (the North Gloucestershire) during the battle of Waterloo,* published in Campaigns Magazine, n.d., pp. 26-30.

Fraser (I), Lieutenant-Colonel Alexander (Lord Saltoun). *MS letter to Lieutenant William Siborne, dated Brampton, 29 January 1838,* British Library, London, BL Add MS 34,706 ff. 431-4.

Fraser (II), Lieutenant-Colonel Alexander (Lord Saltoun). MS letter to Lieutenant William Siborne, dated Brampton, 29 January 1838, British Library, London, BL Add MS, 34,706, ff. 431-4.

Fraser, General Sir David; Marrion, R. J. and Fosten, D. S. V. *The Grenadier Guards,* Osprey, London, 1978.

Fraser, Sir William. *Words on Wellington: the Duke; Waterloo; the Ball,* Routledge, New York, 1905.

Frazer, Colonel Sir Augustus. *Letters of Colonel Sir Augustus Frazer, K.C.B., commanding the Royal Horse Artillery in the army under the Duke of Wellington, written during the Peninsular and Waterloo campaigns (edited by Major-General Edward Sabine),* Longman, Brown, London, 1859.

von Gagern, Captain Baron Friedrich. *MS letter to E. van Löben-Sels, dated 16 Deventer, December 1841,* van Löben-Sels Family Archive, Stads-en-Streekarchief, Zutphen, Folder II, No. 3, Letter 3.

von Gagern, Ensign Heinrich. *MS letter to his mother, dated 26 July 1815* (edited by Wolfgang Klötzer), published as *Ein unbekannter Waterloo-Brief Heinrich von Gagerns,* in Nassauische Heimblätter, 46 Jahrgang, 1956, pp. 17-18.

Gairdner, First Lieutenant James. *MS Diary,* National Army Museum, London, No. 6902-5.

Gardiner, Lieutenant John. *Transcript of undated MS letter to an unknown addressee,* private collection.

Gardyne, Lieutenant-Colonel C. Greenhill. *The Life of a Regiment. The History of the Gordon Highlanders, from its formation in 1794 to 1816 (Volume I),* The Medici Society, London, 1929.

Geij van Pittius, Captain Adrianus. *MS Letter to his brother, Karel Geij van Pittius, dated Saint-Symphorien, 15 June 1815,* Boreel Family Collection, Nationaal Archief, The Hague, No. 462A, 2.21.071 Coll. 123, No. 188.

Girod de l'Ain, Maurice. *Vie militaire du Général Foy,* Plon, Nourrit, Paris, 1900.

Glazebrook, Brigadier T. N. *The 28th Regiment in the Waterloo Campaign,* unpublished MS, Soldiers of Gloucester Museum, Gloucester.

Glover, Gareth. *Letters from the battle of Waterloo. The Unpublished Correspondence by Allied Officers from the Siborne Papers,* Greenhill Books, London, 2004.

Glover, Michael. *Wellington as Military Commander,* Batsford, London, 1968.
de Goeben, Lieutenant Wilhelm. *MS letter to Lieutenant William Siborne, dated Celle, 7 February 1835,* British Library, London, BL Add MS 34,704 ff. 226-7.
Gomm (I), Lieutenant-Colonel Sir William. *Letters and Journals of Sir William Maynard Gomm in the Waterloo campaign,* FSP Books, Darlington, n.d.
Gomm (II), Lieutenant-Colonel Sir William. *MS letter to Lieutenant William Siborne, dated Teignmouth, 12 November 1834,* British Library, London, BL Add MS 34,703 ff. 213-4.
Gomm (III), Lieutenant-Colonel Sir William. *MS letter to Lieutenant William Siborne, dated London, 9 April 1836,* British Library, London, BL Add MS 34,705 ff. 144-5.
Gomm (IV), Lieutenant-Colonel Sir William. *MS letter to Lieutenant William Siborne, dated London, 7 December 1836, enclosing an MS copy of the journal of operations of the army under the Duke of Wellington from the 15th of June,* British Library, London, BL Add MS 34,706 ff. 179-84.
Gomm (V), Lieutenant-Colonel Sir William. *MS letter to Lieutenant William Siborne, dated London, 5 January 1837,* British Library, London, BL Add MS 34,706 ff. 200-6.
Goodinge, Antony. *The Scots Guards (the 3rd Guards),* Leo Cooper, London, 1969.
Gore, Captain Hon. Charles. *MS Account,* Schalk Collection, United States of America.
van Gorkum, Major E. J. See Koolemans-Beijnen.
Gourgaud, Colonel Baron Gaspard. *The Campaign of 1815; or a narrative of the military operations which took place in France and Belgium during the Hundred Days,* London, 1818.
Grant, Charles and Youens, Michael. *The Black Watch,* Osprey, London, 1971.
Green, Private Samuel. *MS letter to his brother and friends, dated Paris, 12 July 1815.* See Chambers, pp. 351-2.
Gregory, Rev. E. Tighe. *MS letter to Captain William Siborne, dated Kilcock, 8 November 1842,* British Library, London, BL Add MS 34,707 ff. 460-1.
Grehan, John. *Quatre Bras confusion,* published in The Waterloo Journal, Volume XIX, No. 3, December 1997.
Gronow, Captain Rees Howell. *Captain Gronow. His Reminiscences of Regency and Victorian Life 1810-60 (edited by Christopher Hibbert),* Kyle Cathie, London, 1991.
Groos, Helmut. *Briefe einheimischer Soldaten aus den Befreiugsriegen,* published in Heimatnachrichten von Aar und Siegbach, Bd. 2004/2005, 2005, pp. 60-5.
de Grouchy, Emmanuel Marquis. *Mémoires du Maréchal de Grouchy, par le Marquis de Grouchy (4 volumes),* E. Dentu, Paris, 1874.
Groves, Lieutenant-Colonel Percy. *History of the 42nd Royal Highlanders, The Black Watch, now the first battalion The Black Watch (Royal Highlanders), 1729-1893,* W. and A. K. Johnston, Edinburgh and London, 1893.
Grunenbosch, Lieutenant-Colonel Willem J. *MS letter to E. van Löben-Sels, dated Utrecht, 26 May 1841,* van Löben-Sels Family Archive, Stads-en-Streekarchief, Zutphen, Folder II, No. 3, Letter 7.
Gunn, Private James. *The Memoirs of Private James Gunn (edited by Dr. R. H. Roy).* Journal of the Society for Army Historical Research, Volume XLIX, 1971, pp. 90-120.
Gurwood, John (editor). *The Dispatches of Field Marshal the Duke of Wellington during his various campaigns in India, Denmark, Portugal, Spain, the Low Countries and France from 1799 to 1815 (Volume XII),* John Murray, London, 1838.
Guy, Alan J. (editor) *The Road to Waterloo. The British Army and the struggle against Revolutionary and Napoleonic France, 1793-1815,* National Army Museum, London, 1990.
Hafner, Dietrich. *Hans Carl Ernst Graf von Zieten,* published in Militärisches Wochenblatt, No. 1, Leipzig, January 1896.
Halkett (I), Major-General Sir Colin. *MS letter to Lieutenant William Siborne, dated London, 21 March 1837,* British Library, London, BL Add MS 34,706 ff. 276-9.
Halkett (II), Major-General Sir Colin. *MS letter to Lieutenant William Siborne, dated 20 May 1839,* British Library, London, BL Add MS 34,707 ff. 37-8.

Bibliography

Jahns, Gunner Friedrich. *Account.* See Usinger, pp. 221-44.

Jecklyn, Captain Friedrich. *MS letter to his mother and mother-in-law, dated 14 July 1815,* Hessisches Haputstaatsarchiv, Wiesbaden, HHStAW Abt 1042, No. 1.

Jolyet, Chef de Bataillon Jean-Baptiste. See Teissedre (II), pp. 63-88.

Jones, Alun (Lord Chalfont, editor). *Waterloo. Battle of Three Armies,* Sidgewick and Jackson, London, 1979.

de Jongh, Lieutenant-Colonel Wijbrandus A. *Aanteekeningen over 1815; uit de nagelaten papieren van den Kolonel de Jongh,* published in De Nieuwe Spectator, 20ste Jaargang, Thieme, Arnhem, 1866, pp. 1-49.

Jonxis, J. P. *Quatre-Bras,* van Hinloopen-Labberton, Doesborgh, 1875.

Jung, Monika. *Das Herzoglich-Nassauische Militär bei der Schlacht von Waterloo,* published in Jahrbuch für den Kreis Limburg-Weilburg, Bd. 2005, S. pp. 265-75.

Kannicht, Joachim. *Un dalles wegen Napoleon. Aus den Kriegstagebuch des Georg von Coulon, Major der Königlich Deutschen Legion, und den Briefen seiner Frau Henriette 1806-1815,* Koblenz, 1986.

Kellermann, Général de Division François-Etienne comte. *Report, to Maréchal de l'Empire Michel Ney, dated 16 June 1815,* Service Historique de l'Armée de Terre, Château de Vincennes, Carton C15, No. 5.

Kelly, Christopher. *The Memorable Battle of Waterloo,* Thomas Kelly, London, 1817.

Kincaid (I), First Lieutenant John. *Adventures in the Rifle Brigade in the Peninsula, France, and the Netherlands from 1809 to 1815,* T. and W. Boone, London, 1830.

Kincaid (II), First Lieutenant John. *MS letter to Lieutenant William Siborne, dated Blackfriars, 27 May 1839,* British Library, London, BL Add MS 34,707 ff. 39-41.

Knoop (I), W. J. *Beschouwingen over Siborne's Geschiedenis van den Oorlog van 1815 in Frankrijk en de Nederlanden,* van Gulick en Hermans, Breda, 1846.

Knoop (II), W. J. *Quatre Bras en Waterloo. Krijgskundige beschouwingen,* Gebroeders Muller, Den Bosch, 1855.

Köffler, G. C. E. *De Militaire Willemsorde 1815-1940,* The Hague, 1940.

Koolemans-Beijnen, General G. J. W. *De order van den Prins van Oranje aan Chassé uit St.-Symphorien in den vroegen morgen van den 14en Juni 1815,* published in De Militaire Spectator, 1910, pp. 567-77, 1911, pp. 384-404, 1912, pp. 203-4.

Koopman, Second Lieutenant Wijnand. *MS letter to E. van Löben-Sels, dated Amersfoort, September 1841,* van Löben-Sels Family Archive, Stads-en-Streekarchief, Zutphen, Folder II, No. 4, Letter 9.

von Kortzfleisch, Gustav. *Geschichte des Herzoglich Braunschweigischen Infanterie-Regiments (2 volumes),* Braunschweig, 1898.

von Kruse, Major-General Baron August. *MS Report, dated 7 January 1836,* Hessisches Hauptstaatsarchiv, Wiesbaden, HHStAW Abt 202/1372.

Kubel, Ensign Anton. *MS Letter to his parents, dated 22 June 1815,* Niedersächsisches Staatsarchiv Wolfenbüttel, 249 AN 190.

Kuhlmann, Major Heinrich. *MS report,* Niedersächsisches Hauptstaatsarchiv (NHA), Hanoverm Hann. 41, XXI, No. 151, pp. 134-7.

Lachouque, Henry. *Waterloo,* Purnell, London, 1975.

Lachouque, Henry, Tranie, J. and Carmigniani, J.C. *Napoleon's War in Spain,* Arms and Armour Press, London, 1993.

Lagden, Alan and Sly, John. *The 2/73rd at Waterloo including a roll of all ranks present with biographical notes,* privately published, 1998.

Lake, Ensign Charles. *Waterloo reminiscences of Ensign Charles Lake, Third Guards,* published in The Scots Guards Magazine, 1961.

Langenstrasse, Sergeant Wilhelm. *MS letter to his brother, dated St Denis, 2 August 1815,* Niedersächsisches Staatsarchiv Wolfenbüttel, 249 AN 192.

Laws, Lieutenant-Colonel M. E. S. *Battery Records of the Royal Artillery, 1716-1859,* Royal Artillery Institute, Woolwich, 1952.

Leach, Major Jonathan. *Rough sketches in the life of an old soldier,* Longman, Rees, Orme, Brown and Green, London, 1831.

Leask, J. C. and McCance, H. M. *The Regimental Records of the Royal Scots (the First or Royal Regiment of Foot),* Thom, Dublin, 1915.

Lee, Albert. *The History of the Thirty-Third Foot, Duke of Wellington's (West Riding) Regiment,* Jarrold, Norwich, 1922.

Léfèbvre-Desnoëttes, Général de Division Count Charles. *Report to Maréchal de l'Empire Michel Ney, dated 15 June 1815.* Service Historique de l'Armée de Terre, Château de Vincennes, Carton C14, No. 5.

Lemonnier-Delafosse, Lieutenant-Colonel Jean-Baptiste. *Souvenirs militaires du Capitaine Jean-Baptiste Lemonnier-Delafosse,* Le Livre Chez Vous, Paris, 2002.

Leonard, Neil. *Wellington's Army recreated in Colour Photographs,* Windrow and Green, London, 1995.

Leonhard (I), Private Johann Peter. See Peter Wacker, pp. 93-111.

Leonhard (II), Private Johann Peter. See Aumüller, pp. 169-72.

Leslie, Major J. H. (I) *Tradition in the Royal Regiment of Artillery. How it can best be preserved. A lecture delivered at the Royal Artillery Institution, Woolwich, on 17 October 1912,* published in The Journal of the Royal Artillery (Volume XXXIX), Leng, Sheffield, 1916.

Leslie, Lieutenant-Colonel J. H. (II). *The Home-coming of the King's Colour of the 2nd Battalion 69th (or the South Lincolnshire) Regiment of Foot, captured by the French at Quatre Bras on 16 June 1815,* published in The Journal of the Society for Army Historical Research, Volume IX, pp. 129-133.

Leslie, Lieutenant Kewan. *MS letter to unknown addressee (probably Lieutenant William Siborne), dated 16 April 1835,* British Library, London, BL Add MS 34,705 ff. 159-61.

von Lettow-Vorbeck, Major-General Oskar. *Geschichte der Befreiungskriege 1813-1815. Napoleons Untergang 1815,* Berlin, 1904.

van Limburg-Stirum, Major Count Otto. *MS letter to E. van Löben-Sels, dated 5 August 1841,* van Löben-Sels Family Archive, Stads-en-Streekarchief, Zutphen, Folder II, No. 3, Letter 4.

Linck, Tony. *Napoleon's Generals.* Emperor's, Chicago, 1994.

Llewellyn, Major Richard. *MS letter to Lieutenant William Siborne, dated Leatherhead, 16 March 1837,* British Library, London, BL Add MS 34,706, ff. 264-5.

Lloyd, Lieutenant John. *MS letter to unknown addressee (probably Captain William Siborne), dated 6 February 1845,* British Library, London, BL Add MS 34,708 ff. 172-4.

van Löben-Sels, Ernst. *Bijdragen tot de Krijgsgeschedenis van Napoleon Bonaparte (Volume IV),* de Erven Doorman, The Hague, 1842.

Logie, Jacques. *Waterloo. L'évitable défaite,* Bibliothèque d'Histoire Duculot, Paris, 1989.

Logie, Jacques. *Waterloo 1815: L'Europe face à Napoleon,* Credit Communal, Brussels, 1990.

Logie, Jacques. *Waterloo. La Campagne de 1815,* Éditions Racine, Brussels, 2003.

Lomax, Major-General C. E. M. *The History of the Welch Regiment,* Western Mail and Echo, Cardiff, 1932.

Longford, Elizabeth. *Wellington. The Years of the Sword,* Weidenfeld and Nicholson, London, 1969.

Macdonald, Major Robert. *MS letter to Lieutenant William Siborne, dated Southsea, 14 February 1839,* British Library, London, BL Add MS 34,707 ff. 3-6.

Mackenzie, Lieutenant Donald. *MS letter,* Black Watch Regimental Archive, Dalhousie Castle, Perth, No. 414.

Mackenzie, Norman. *The Escape from Elba,* Oxford University Press, Oxford, 1982.

Mackenzie, Captain T. A., Ewart, Lieutenant J. S. and Findlay, Lieutenant C. *Historical Records of the 79th Queen's Own Cameron Highlanders,* Hamilton, Adams, London, 1887.

MacKinnon, Colonel Daniel. *Origin and Services of the Coldstream Guards (Volume II),* Richard Bentley, London, 1833.

Mackworth, Captain Sir Digby. *The Waterloo Diary of Sir Digby Mackworth,* published in The Army Quarterly, Volume XXXV, January 1938, William Clowes, London, 1938.

Bibliography

Macready (I), Ensign Edward. *The Journal and Opinions of Edward Nevil Macready* (unpublished transcription by Lieutenant-Colonel John Downham), n.d.

Macready (II), Ensign Edward. *Letter to his father, Mr. W. Macready, dated Bois de Boulogne, 7 July 1815,* published in The East Lancashire Regimental Journal, Volume III, March 1933, pp. 41-3.

Macready (III), Ensign Edward. *MS letter to Lieutenant-Colonel Gawler, dated Kandy, 30 November 1836,* British Library, London, BL Add MS 34,708 ff. 253-7.

Macready (IV), Ensign Edward. *On a part of Captain Siborne's History of the Waterloo Campaign,* published in The United Service Magazine, March 1845, pp. 388-404.

Macready (V), Ensign Edward. *MS letter to Captain William Siborne, dated London, 25 December 1845,* British Library, London, BL Add MS 34,708 ff. 227-9.

Maitland, Major-General Peregrine. *Letter to the Duke of York, dated Nivelles, 19 June 1815.* See F. Hamilton, pp. 20-1.

Malcolm, Lieutenant John. *MS account,* Black Watch Regimental Archive, Dalhousie Castle, Perth, No. 220.

Manchot, Roland. *Notice biographique sur le général-major Edouard de Mercx de Corbais,* Namur, 1855.

Mansell, First Lieutenant John. *MS letter to Captain William Siborne, dated Limerick, 9 December 1842,* British Library, BL Add MS 34,707, ff. 515-6.

Martin (I), Lieutenant Henry. *MS letter to his father, Reverend Joseph Martin, Dated Roye, 29 June 1815,* The Essex Regiment Museum, Chelmsford.

Martin (II), Lieutenant Henry. *MS letter to his mother, Mrs Joseph Martin, dated Clichy, 20 August 1815,* The Essex Regiment Museum, Chelmsford.

Martinien, A. *Tableaux par corps et par batailles des officiers tués et blesses pendant les guerres de l'Empire (1805-1815) aux Archives Historiques de la Guerre,* Éditions Militaires Européennes, Paris, n.d.

Master, Ensign Richard Thomas. *A Remembrance of Younger Days in the Army. Richard Master, Grenadier Guards,* private collection.

Mathieu, Claude. *Braine-le-Comte. Présence des troupes Alliés en 1815,* Braine-Le-Comte, 1970.

de Mauduit, Hippolyte. *Les derniers jours de la grande armée. Documents et correspondence inédite de Napoléon en 1814 et 1815 (2 volumes),* H. de Mauduit, Paris, 1854.

Maughan, Stephen. *With the 69th in the Waterloo campaign,* FSP Books, Darlington, n.d.

Maurice, Major-General Sir F. *The History of the Scots Guards, from the creation of the Regiment to the eve of the Great War (Volume II),* Chatto and Windus, London, 1934.

Maxwell, Sir Herbert. *The Life of Wellington. The restoration of the martial power of Great Britain (Volume II),* Samson, Low, Marston, London, 1899.

May, Lieutenant-Colonel Sir John. MS letter to Captain Edward Whinyates, dated 5 April 1816, Royal Artillery Institute, Woolwich, No. MD 1438.

McEween, Sergeant-Major Alexander. *Undated MS account,* British Library, London, BL Add MS 34,706, ff. 455-6.

McGuigan, Ron. *Hanoverian Light Battalions 1813-1815,* published electronically on www.napoleon-series.org.

Meijer, Sergeant Carel. *MS letter to his brother, Frederik, dated Nivelles, 22 June 1815,* private collection.

Mercer, Second Captain Alexander Cavalié. *Journal of the Waterloo campaign, kept throughout the campaign of 1815,* Da Capo, New York, 1995.

de Mercx de Corbais, Lieutenant-Colonel Edouard A. J. C. *Letter to General Rénard, dated Namur, 17 January 1855.* See Manchot, p. 75-7.

Mergell, Chief Medical Officer K. G. E. *MS letter dated Soultain, 3 July 1815,* Nederlands Instituut voor Militaire Historie, The Hague, No. 58/3.

Miller, David (I). *Lady De Lancey at Waterloo,* Spellmount, Staplehurst, 2000.

Miller, David (II). *The Duchess of Richmond's Ball,* Spellmount, Staplehurst, 2005.

Mittelacher (I), Martin. *Die Nassauer bei Waterloo. Aus der Sicht neuerer englisch-sprachiger Literatur,* published in Nassauische Annalen, Volume CIX, Bd 109, 2001, pp. 265-75.

Mittelacher (II), Martin. *Wellingtons Nassauer. Die Verteidiger der Domäne Hougoumont in der Schlacht bei Waterloo,* published in Nassauische Annalen, Volume CXII, Bd 112, 2001, pp. 329-48.

Mollinger, Captain F. R. *MS letter to E. van Löben-Sels, dated Bergen-op-Zoom, 19 August 1841,* van Löben-Sels Family Archive, Stads-en-Streekarchief, Zutphen, Folder II, No. 3, Letter 8.

von Morenhoffen, Lieutenant-Colonel. *Übersicht des Anteils der Herzoglich Nassauischen Truppen an der Campagne 1815 gegen Frankreich,* House-Archives of the Grand Duke of Luxembourg, Duke of Nassau and Weilburg, Wiesbaden.

Morice, Colonel Charles. *Letter to his father, dated Hoornes, 11 June 1815.* See Maughan, p. 31.

Morris, Thomas. *Military Memoirs. Thomas Morris. The Napoleonic Wars,* (edited by John Selby), Longmans Green, London, 1967.

Morrison, B. L. *Phases of the Moon, 1800-1939,* published in Circular, No. 112, US Naval Observatory, 1966.

Mudie (I), Ensign Charles. *MS journal,* Regimental Museum of the Royal Scots, Edinburgh Castle. Also published in The Thistle, Regimental Journal of the Royal Scots, April, July and October 1931.

Mudie (II), Charles. *Operations of the Fifth or Picton's Division in the Campaign of Waterloo,* published anonymously in The United Services Journal, June 1841, pp. 170-203.

von Müffling (I), Colonel Baron Friedrich Carl Ferdinand. *History of the campaign of the British, Dutch, Hanoverian and Brunswick armies, under the command of the Duke of Wellington and of the Prussians under that of Prince Blücher of Wahlstadt, in the year 1815,* T. Egerton, London, 1816.

von Müffling (II), Colonel Baron Friedrich Carl Ferdinand. *Passages from my life, together with memoirs of the campaign of 1813 and 1814 (2nd edition),* London, 1853.

Muilwijk, Erwin. *The participation of the Netherlands Mobile Army in the Waterloo Campaign,* unpublished manuscript, Bleyswyk, 2006-2008.

Müller, Major. *Bericht des hannoverschen Feldbataillons Bremen über seinem Anteil am Gefechte bei Quatrebras, dated 9 December 1824.* See von Pflugk-Harttung (II), pp. 29-32, 127-32.

Myddleton, Frances Penelope. *Reminiscences of a Military Life by a Soldier's Daughter,* privately published, Sleaford, 1879.

Nafziger, George. *Imperial Bayonets. Tactics of the Napoleonic battery, battalion and brigade, as found in contemporary regulations,* Greenhill, London, 1996.

Neumann, J. *Great Historical Events That Were Significantly Affected by the Weather. Part II. Meteorological Aspects of the Battle of Waterloo,* published in The Bulletin of the American Meteorological Society, Volume LXXIV, No. 3, March 1993.

Ney, Général Michel (Duke d'Elchingen). *Documents inédits sur la campagne de 1815,* Paris, 1840.

van Noeyen, José. *Le duc de Brunswick aux Quatre-Bras,* published in Bulletin de la Societé Belge d'Études Napoléonien, No. 10, 1953, pp 121-6.

Nofi, Albert A. *The Waterloo Campaign, June 1815,* Greenhill Books, London, 1993.

Norden, J. *Het leven en de lotgevallen van den gebroeders J. en A. Norden,* Lagerweij, Dordrecht, 1856.

North, René. *Regiments at Waterloo,* Almark Publications, New Malden. 1971.

von Olfermann, Colonel Elias. *Bericht des Obersten Olfermann an das Fürstliche Geheime Rats-Kollegium zu Braunschweig über das Gefecht bei Quatrebras.* See von Pflugk-Harttung (II), pp. 25-7.

von Ollech, General Karl. *Geschichte des Feldzüges von 1815 nach archivalischen Quellen,* Berlin, 1876.

O'Malley, Lieutenant-Colonel George. *MS letter to Lieutenant William Siborne, dated 10 May 1837,* British Library, London, BL Add MS 34,706 ff. 322-5.

van Omphal, Major A. *MS biographical notes (4 volumes),* Nederlands Instituut voor Militaire Historie, The Hague, No. 104/7.

von Ompteda, L. *Ein hannoversch-englischer Offizier vor hundert Jahren – Christian Friedrich Wilhelm Freiherr von Ompteda, Oberst und Brigadier in der Königlich Deutschen Legion – 26. November 1765 bis 18 Juni 1815,* Hirzel, Leipzig, 1892.

O'Neil, Charles. *The Military Adventures of Charles O'Neil,* Spellmount, Staplehurst, 1997.

Oppermann, Fahnrich. *Letter to his parents, dated 23 June 1815.* See Kannicht, p. 203.

Bibliography

van Opstall, Major Cornelius. *MS letter to E. van Löben-Sels, dated Geertruidenberg, 22 July 1841 and MS report of the Artillery of the 2nd Division in the actions of 1815,* van Löben-Sels Family Archive, Stads-en-Streekarchief, Zutphen, Folder II, No. 4, Letters 1 and 3.

van Oranje-Nassau (I), General Prince Willem. *MS Letter to Field Marshal the Duke of Wellington, dated 16 June 1815,* Koninklijke Huisarchief, Paleis Nordeinde, The Hague, No. A 40 VIC W 10.

van Oranje-Nassau (II), General Prince Willem. *Report to his father, King Willem I, dated 17 June 1815.* See Boulger, pp. 20-21.

van Osten, Captain J. B. *MS letter to E. van Löben-Sels,* dated Zutphen, 20 July 1841, van Löben-Sels Family Archive, Stads-en-Streekarchief, Zutphen, Folder II, No. 4, Letter 4.

Owen, Colonel Edward (editor). *The Waterloo papers: 1815 and beyond,* Army Quarterly and Defence Journal Publications, Tavistock, 1997.

d'Oyly, Lieutenant-Colonel Hon. Henry. *MS letter to his mother, dated Paris, 4 July 1815,* East Sussex Record Office, Lewes, AMS6185.

Paget, Lieutenant-General Henry (Marquess of Anglesey, Earl of Uxbridge). *Undated MS letter to an unknown addressee,* British Library, London, BL Add MS 34,703 ff. 5-10.

Paget, Sir George (I), Marquess of Angelesey (editor). *The Capel letters, being the correspondence of Lady Caroline Capel and her daughters with the Dowager Countess of Uxbridge from Brussels and Switzerland (1814-1817),* Jonathan Cape, London, 1955.

Paget, Sir George (II), Marquess of Anglesey. *One leg. The life and letters of Henry William Paget, First Marquess of Anglesey, 1768-1854,* Leo Cooper, 1996.

Paget, Julian (I). *The Story of the Guards,* Osprey, London, 1976.

Paget, Julian (II). *Hougoumont,* Leo Cooper, London, 1992.

Partridge, Richard and Oliver, Michael. *Napoleonic Army Handbook. The British Army and her Allies,* Constable, London, 1999.

Pattison (I), Lieutenant Frederick. *MS letter to his brother John Pattison, dated Dalmain, 6 December 1842,* British Library, London, BL Add MS 34,707 ff. 509-12.

Pattison (II), Lieutenant Frederick. *Personal Recollections of the Waterloo Campaign in a series of letters to his grand-children (2nd edition),* privately published, Glasgow, 1873.

Pattyn, Jean-Jacques. *Blessé aux deux pieds et aux Quatre Bras!* Published in Bulletin de la Societé Belge d'Études Napoléonien, No. 36, 2000, pp 18-23.

Pawly (I), Ronald. *The Red Lancers. Anatomy of a Napoleonic Regiment,* The Crowood Press, Marlborough, 1998.

Pawly (II), Ronald. *Wellington's Belgian Allies, 1815,* Osprey, Oxford, 2001.

Pawly (III), Ronald. *Wellington's Dutch Allies, 1815,* Osprey, Oxford, 2002.

de Perponcher-Sedlnitzky, Lieutenant-General Baron Henri-Georges. *Report of the 2nd Division on the Battles of Quatre Bras and Waterloo, dated 11 July 1815.* See Boulger, pp. 47-49.

von Pflugk-Harttung (I), Dr. Julius. *Vorgeschichte der Schlacht bei Belle-Alliance. Wellington,* Berlin, 1903.

von Pflugk-Harttung (II), Dr. Julius. *Belle-Alliance (Verbündetes Heer). Berichte und Angaben über die Beteiligung deutscher Truppen der Armee Wellingtons an dem Gefechte bei Quatrebras und der Schlacht bei Belle-Alliance,* R. Eisenschmidt, Berlin, 1915.

Pigeard, Alain. *L'Armée de Napoleon: organisation et vie quotidienne,* Bibliothèque Napoléonienne, Bibliothèque Napoléonienne Tallandier, Paris, 2002.

Pigot, Lieutenant Brooke. *MS letter to Captain William Siborne, dated Mansfield, 7 July 1844,* British Library, London, BL Add MS 34,708 ff. 146-7.

Pinstock (I), Private Johann Pfillip. *Letter dated 22 June 1815.* See Groos.

Pinstock (II), Private Johann Pfillip. *Letter dated 2 September 1815.* See Groos.

von Pivka (I), Otto. *Dutch-Belgian troops of the Napoleonic Wars,* Osprey, Oxford, 2000.

von Pivka (II), Otto. *Napoleon's German Allies (2): Nassau and Oldenburg,* Osprey, Oxford, 2001.

von Pivka (III), Otto. *Brunswick Troops 1809-15,* Osprey, Oxford, 2001.

von Plotho, Carl. *Der Krieg des verbündeten Europa gegen Frankreich im Jahre 1815,* Berlin, 1818.

Powell, Captain Henry. *Undated MS letter to Lieutenant William Siborne,* British Library, London, BL Add MS 34,704 ff. 143-6.

Pratt, Lieutenant John. *MS letter to unknown addressee (probably Lieutenant William Siborne), dated London, 23 March 1835,* British Library, London, BL Add MS 34,705 ff. 88-94.

Puvis, Chef de Bataillon Théobald. *Souvenirs,* published in Revue historiques des armées, 1979, No. 3, pp. 101-29.

Reid, Stuart. *British Redcoat (2) 1793-1815,* Osprey, Oxford, 1997.

Reille. Général de Division Count Honoré. *Report to Maréchal de l'Empire Michel Ney, dated 16 June 1815.* Service Historique de l'Armée de Terre, Château de Vincennes. Paris, Carton C15, No. 22.

Rem, Militiaman Jan. *Aanteekeningen van een Veteraan,* published in the Purmerend Waterloo Courant, Schuitemaker, Purmerend, 18 June 1865.

Renard, Général B.J. *Réponse aux allegations anglaises sur la conduite des troupes belges en 1815, par un officier general. Lettres adressées à l'Indépendance belge,* Brussels, 1855.

Rens, Arie. *Het Regiment Huzaren Prins Alexander. De geschiedenis van het 'Hofregiment' 1672-1994,* Managements Press, Amsterdam, 1994.

Rentenaar, R. *MS Account,* private collection.

Répécaud, Colonel. *Napoléon à Ligny et le Maréchal Ney à Quatre Bras,* Arras, 1849.

von Rettberg (I), Captain Carl. *Bericht der hannoverschen 2. neunpfünder-Batterie von Rettberg über ihnen Antheil am Gefechte bei Quatrebras.* See von Pflugk-Harttung (II), pp. 42-4.

von Rettberg (II), Captain Carl. *MS letter to Lieutenant William Siborne, dated Stade, 10 February 1835,* British Library, London, BL Add MS 34,704, ff. 229-34.

von Rettberg (III), Captain Carl. *MS letter to Lieutenant Ludwig Benne, dated Stade, 25 July 1836,* British Library, London, BL Add MS 34,706, f. 377.

von Reuter, E. *Erinnerungen eines Preussischen Artillerieoffiziers aus den Jahren 1798 bis 1815,* published in Militär-Wochenblatt, Berlin, 1890.

Riach (I), Lieutenant W.A. *Letter to Miss Eliza Riach, dated 18 June 1815,* published in The 79th News, July 1938, pp. 367-8.

Riach (II), Lieutenant W.A. *MS letter to Lieutenant William Siborne, dated Manchester, 20 September 1839,* British Library, London, BL Add MS 34,707 f. 129.

Richardson, Ethel M. *Long forgotten days (leading to Waterloo),* Heath Cranton, London, 1928.

Riddock, Lieutenant Alexander. *MS letter to Lieutenant William Siborne, dated Kirktown of Deskford, 11 April 1837,* British Library, London, BL Add MS 34,706 ff. 293-8.

Robertson, Sergeant David. *The Journal of Sergeant D. Robertson, late 92nd Foot: comprising the different campaigns, between the years 1797 and 1818 in Egypt, Walcheren, Denmark, Sweden, Portugal, Spain, France and Belgium.* J. Fisher, Perth, 1842.

Robinson, Major-General Sir C.W. *Wellington's Campaigns. Peninsula-Waterloo, 1808-15 (for military students),* Hugh Rees, London, 1927.

Robinson, H. B. *Memoirs of Lieutenant-General Sir Thomas Picton, including his correspondence, from originals in possession of his family (Volume II),* Richard Bentley, London, 1836.

Rogers (I), Major Thomas. *MS letter to Lieutenant William Siborne, dated Woolwich, 9 February 1837,* British Library, London, BL Add MS 34,706 ff. 227-30, 233.

Rogers (II), Major Thomas. *MS letter to Lieutenant William Siborne, dated Woolwich, 25 February 1837,* British Library, London, BL Add MS 34,706 ff. 240-1.

Roijen, Captain H. *Undated MD letter written on his behalf by Captain Wiltbrennick to E. van Löben-Sels,* van Löben-Sels Family Archive, Stads-en-Streekarchief, Zutphen, Folder II, No. 5, Letter 6.

Rooke (I), Lieutenant-Colonel Henry. *MS Notebook,* private collection.

Rooke (II), Lieutenant-Colonel Henry. *Letter to his father, Colonel Charles Rooke, dated 19 June 1815* (edited by Gareth Glover), published as, *Communications. A Guardsman at Waterloo,* in Journal of the Society for Army Historical Research, Volume LXXXIII, 2005, pp. 345-50.

Bibliography

de Roo van Alderwerelt, J. K. H. *Geschiedenis van het Zevende Regiment Infanterie*, Arnhem, 1857.

Ropes, John Codman. *The Campaign of Waterloo. A Military History*, Worley Publications, Felling, 1995.

Ross, Lieutenant Ewen. *The Death of Colonel Cameron of the Gordon Highlanders*, published anonymously in The United Services Journal, June 1850, pp. 293-4.

Ross, Lieutenant James (I). *MS letter to Captain William Siborne, dated Edinburgh, 25 November 1834*, British Library, London, BL Add MS 34,703 ff. 341-5.

Ross, Lieutenant James (II). *MS letter to Captain William Siborne, dated Dunse, 10 March 1837*, British Library, London, BL Add MS 34,706 ff. 252-5.

Ross-Lewin, Harry. *With the 'Thirty-Second' in the Peninsula and other campaigns* (edited by John Wardell), Hodges Figgis, Dublin, 1904.

Rudyerd, Second Captain Samuel. *MS letter to Lieutenant William Siborne, dated London, 6 May 1838*, British Library, London, BL Add MS 34,706 ff. 473-7.

von Sachsen-Weimar (I), Colonel Prince Carl Bernhard. *Report to General de Perponcher-Sedlnitzky, dated 15 June 1815*. See Starklof, p. 135.

von Sachsen-Weimar (II), Colonel Prince Carl Bernhard. *Letter to his father, Carl August, Grand Duke von Sachsen-Weimar-Eisenach, dated Waterloo, 19 June 1815*. See Anonymous (Near Observer), pp. 75-6.

von Sachsen-Weimar (III), Colonel Prince Carl Bernhard. *MS letter to E. van Löben-Sels, dated Oisterwijk, 29 August 1841*, van Löben-Sels Family Archive, Stads-en-Streekarchief, Zutphen, Folder II, No. 3, Letter 5.

von Sachsen-Weimar (IV), Colonel Prince Carl Bernhard. *MS Diary*, Grossherzogliches Hausarchiv, A.XXIV.30, Thüringischen Hauptstaatsarchiv, Wiesbaden.

Saint-John, Ensign Joseph. *MS letter to his mother, dated Bavay, 22 June 1815*, private collection.

Saltoun, Lord. See Fraser, Lieutenant-Colonel Alexander.

Sattler, Major Friedrich. *Bericht des nassauischen 2. Regiments über seinem Anteil an den Gefechten bei Frasnes und Quatrebras*, published in von Pflugk-Harttung (II), pp. 47-50.

Saunders, Edith. *The Hundred Days*, Longmans, London, 1964.

Scheltema, Jacobus. *De Laatste Veldtogt van Napoleon Bonaparte*, Hendrik Gartman, Amsterdam, 1816.

Scheltens, Colonel Chrétien H. *Souvenirs d'un grognard belge. Mémoires du Colonel Scheltens*, Charles Dessart, Bruxelles, n.d.

Schom, Alan. *One Hundred Days: Napoleon's Road to Waterloo*, Michael Joseph, London, 1993.

Schreiber, Captain James. *MS letter to Lieutenant William Siborne dated 21 October 1839*, British Library, BL Add MS 34707, ff. 145-6.

Schütte, Company Surgeon Wilhelm. *Brief des Kompagnie-Chirurgen Wilhelm Schütte an seine Eltern über die Tätigkeit der braunschweigischen Truppen bei Quatrebras und Belle-Alliance*. See von Pflugk-Harttung (II), pp. 239-40.

von Scriba (I), Captain C. *Bericht des hannoversches Feldbataillons Bremen über seinem Anteil am Gefechte bei Quatrebras und am 17 Juni, dated Stade, 4 December 1824*. See von Pflugk-Harttung (II), pp. 32-37.

von Scriba (II), C. *Das leichte Bataillon der Bremen-Verdenschen Legion in den Jahren 1813 bis 1820*, Nienburg, Hameln 1849.

von Scriba. *Einige allgemeine Bemerkungen über den Feldzug im Jahre 1815 und besonders über die Schlachten von les Quatre Bras und Waterloo*, published in Internationale Revue über die gesamten Armeen und Marine, Berlin, 1892, pp. 200-214 and 293-301.

Seale, T. P. *The 28th (or the North Gloucestershire) Regiment of Foot in the Waterloo Campaign*, unpublished MS, Soldiers of Gloucester Museum, Gloucester.

Shaw-Kennedy (I), Captain James. *Undated MS letter to Lieutenant William Siborne*, British Library, London, BL Add MS 34,708 ff. 307-8.

Shaw-Kennedy (II), Captain James. MS letter to Lieutenant William Siborne, dated Manchester,

The Battle of Quatre Bras

25 April 1836, British Library, London, BL Add MS 34,706 ff. 82-8.

Shaw-Kennedy (III). General Sir James. *Notes on the battle of Waterloo,* Spellmount, Staplehurst, 2003.

Short, Ensign Charles. *MS letter to his mother, dated Nivelles, 19 June 1815,* National Army Museum, London.

Siborne, Major-General H.T. (editor). *Waterloo Letters,* Greenhill Books, London, 1993.

Siborne, Lieutenant William Siborne (I). *MS letter to an unknown addressee, dated Dublin, 3 April 1836,* British Library, London, BL Add MS 34,706 ff. 68-70.

Siborne, Lieutenant William (II). *MS letter to Major Samuel Rudyerd, dated Dublin, 23 May 1836,* British Library, London, BL Add MS 34,706 ff. 473-7.

Siborne, Lieutenant William (III). *MS letter to Second Captain Samuel Rudyerd, Dated Dublin, 30 April 1837,* British Library, London, BL Add MS 34,706 ff. 473-7.

Siborne, Lieutenant William (IV). *MS letter to an unknown addressee, dated 24 February 1838,* British Library, London, BL Add MS 34,706 ff. 445-50.

Siborne, Captain William (V). *History of the Waterloo Campaign,* Greenhill Books, London, 1990.

von Sichart, Major-Generals U. and R. *Geschichte der Königlich-Hannoverschen Armee (Volume V),* Hahn'sche Buchhandlung, Hannover and Leipzig, 1898.

van Sijpestein, Lord J.W. *Geschiedenis van het Regiment Nederlandsche Rijdende Artillerie,* Zalt-Bommel, 1852.

Simmons (I), First Lieutenant George. *MS account,* National Army Museum, London, 6804-2.

Simmons (II), Major George. *A British Rifle Man. Journals and Correspondence during the Peninsular War and the Campaign of Wellington,* Greenhill, London, 1986.

Sinclair-Stevenson, Christopher. *The Gordon Highlanders,* Hamish Hamilton, London, n.d.

Somerset, Lieutenant-Colonel Lord Fitzroy. *Lord Fitzroy Somerset's Account of the events from 15-18 June 1815.* See Owen, pp. 6-15.

Somerset, Captain Lord John. *MS letter to Captain William Siborne, dated London, 26 November 1842,* British Library, London, BL Add MS 34,707 ff. 484-5.

Standen (I), Ensign George. *Undated MS letter to Captain William Siborne,* BL Add MS 34,708 ff. 324-7.

Standen (II), Ensign George. *Undated MS letter to Captain William Siborne,* BL Add MS 34,708 ff. 334-5.

Stanhope, Lieutenant-Colonel Hon. James. *MS letter to the Duke of York, dated Nivelles, 19 June 1815,* British Library, London, BL Add MS 34,703 ff. 22-4.

Stanhope, Philip Henry Mahon, (Fifth Earl Stanhope). *Notes of conversations with the Duke of Wellington 1831-1851,* Prion, London, 1998.

Starklof, Richard. *The life of Duke Bernhard of Saxe-Weimar-Eisenach, General of the Infantry of the Royal Dutch Army (translated and edited by William Jeronimus),* University Press of America, Lanham, Maryland, 1996.

Stephens, Lieutenant Edward. *MS letter to his mother, dated Antwerp, 19 June 1815,* published in The One and All, The Journal of the Duke of Cornwall's Light Infantry, Volume XVIII, May 1953, p. 8.

Stewart, Captain John. *The Royal Highland Regiment. The Black Watch Medal Roll,* Constable, Edinburgh, 1913.

Storm de Grave, Captain Lord Carel Willem. *Undated MS letter to E. van Löben-Sels,* van Löben-Sels Family Archive, Stads-en-Streekarchief, Zutphen, Folder II, No. 5, Letter 7.

Surtees, Major-General G. *British colours in the Waterloo campaign,* published in Journal of the Society for Army Historical Research, Volume XLIII, 1965, p. 75.

Sutherland, John. *Men of Waterloo,* Frederick Muller, London, 1966.

Swiney, Colonel G. C. *Historical Records of the 32nd (Cornwall) Light Infantry, now the 1st Battalion Duke of Cornwall's Light Infantry,* Simpkin, London, 1893.

Swinton, the Hon. J. R. *A sketch of the life of Georgiana, Lady de Ros, with some reminiscences of her family and friends, including the Duke of Wellington,* Murray, London, 1893.

Teissèdre (I), Fabrice. *Waterloo. Récits de combatants,* F. Teissèdre, Paris, 1999.
Teissèdre (II), Fabrice. *Souvenirs et correspondance sur la bataille de Waterloo,* F. Teissèdre, Paris, 2000.
Thain (I), Ensign William. *Undated MS letter to an unknown addressee,* Duke of Wellington's Regiment Archive, Halifax.
Thain (II), Ensign William. *MS diary,* Duke of Wellington's Regiment Archive, Halifax.
Thain (III), Ensign William. *Letter to his father, dated 19 June 1815, published in The Iron Duke,* No. 2, November 1925.
Tincombe, Lieutenant Francis. *Letter to his brother, dated Paris, 5-15 July 1815,* published in XXX Magazine, September 1911, pp. 2-3.
van Toll, Captain Dirk. *Account of the 5th National Militia Battalion,* published anonymously in De Nieuwe Spectator, 5e Jaargang, 1851, pp. 380-9.
Traupe, Karl. *Le Corps de Brunswick aux Quatre-Bras et à Waterloo en juin 1815,* published in Bulletin de la Societé Belge d'Études Napoléonien, No. 10, 1989, pp. 11-17.
Trefcon, Colonel Jean. *Carnet de campagne du colonel Trefcon 1793-1815,* André Lévi, Paris, 1914.
Trevor, Lieutenant Arthur Hill. *MS letter to Captain William Siborne, dated London, 22 December 1842,* British Library, London, BL Add MS 34,707 ff. 537-9.
Urban, Mark. *Rifles. Six years with Wellington's legendary sharpshooters,* Faber and Faber, 2004.
Usinger, R. *Soldate-Briefs aus dem Feldzuge des Jahres 1815,* published in Zeitschrift des historischen Vereins für Niedersachsen, 1864.
Usinger, R. Soldaten-Briefe aus dem Feldzuge des Jahres 1815. p.225-230 van Uythoven, Geert. *Nassauers in Netherlands Service,* published in Age of Napoleon, Nos. 34 and 35, 2000.
Vallence, Private Dixon. *Extract from a narrative of the Battle of Quatre Bras by a soldier of the 79th Highlanders,* published in The 79th News, No. 5, Malta, 1 July 1892.
Vels Heijn, Dr. N. *Waterloo. Glorie zonder helden,* De Bataafsche Leeuw, Amsterdam, 1990.
Verhülsdonk, Torsten and Schulze, Carl. *German Napoleonic armies recreated in colour photographs,* Crowood, Ramsbury, 1998.
Verhulst, Jean. *Genappe en 1815. Histoire et Tourisme,* Syndicat d'Initiative et de Tourisme de Genappe, Genappe, n.d.
Vivian, Major General Sir Hussey. *MS letter to Captain William Siborne, dated London, 3 June 1839,* British Library, London, BL Add MS 34,707, ff. 50-55.
Vrijthoff, L. B. A. *Eene onuitgegeven bijdrage tot de geschiedenis van den slag van Waterloo,* Maastricht, 1861.
von Wachholtz, Major Baron Friedrich. *Geschichte des Herzoglich Braunschweigschen Armee-Korps,* Brunswick, 1816.
Wagner. *Plane der Schlachte und Treffen,* 4. Heft, Berlin, 1825. Wakker, P. *Aanteekeningen van een Veteraan, dato 16 Aug. 1815,* J. Schuitemaker, Purmerende, 1863.
Wacker, Peter. *Das herzoglich-nassauische Militär 1813-1866,* Taunusstein, 1998.
van der Wall, First Lieutenant Charles E. *MS letter to E. van Löben-Sels,* van Löben-Sels Family Archive, Stads-en-Streekarchief, Zutphen, Folder II, No. 4, Letter 2.
Walton, Captain W. L. *MS letter to his mother, Lady Strachan, dated 22 June 1815,* National Army Museum, London, Archive 7608-14.
Wassenaar van Sint-Pancras, Second Lieutenant Willem. *MS letter to E. van Löben-Sels, dated Breda, 30 April 1841,* van Löben-Sels Family Archive, Stads-en-Streekarchief, Zutphen, Folder II, No. 4, Letter 5a.
Wauchope, Captain A. G. *A Short History of The Black Watch (Royal Highlanders),* William Blackwood, Edinburgh and London, 1908.
Webb-Carter, B. W. A line regiment at Waterloo, published in Journal for the Society of Army Historical Research, Volume XLIII, 1965, pp. 60-6.
Weller, Jac. *Wellington at Waterloo,* Greenhill, London, 1992.
Wellesley, Arthur (Second Duke of Wellington) (Editor). *Supplementary Despatches, Correspondence, and Memoranda of Field Marshal Arthur, Duke of Wellington (Volume X)* London, 1863.

Wells, First Lieutenant Fortescue. *MS letter to Lieutenant William Siborne, dated Kingsbridge, 13 March 1837,* British Library, London, BL Add MS 34,706 ff. 259-61.

Welter, Cadet Sergeant. *MS letter dated Péronne, 1 July 1815,* Volkersz Family Archive (private collection), Stony Brook, United States of America.

Westenbergh, Lieutenant-Colonel Jan. *MS letter to J. Scheltema, dated 7 February 1816,* Handwriting Collection, de la Fontaine Verwey Room, University of Amsterdam Library, No. Ay112.

Wheatley, Lieutenant Edmund. *The Wheatley Diary. A Journal and Sketchbook kept during the Peninsular War and the Waterloo Campaign* (edited by Christopher Hibbert), Windrush Press, Gloucestershire, 1964.

Wheeler, Private William. *The letters of Private Wheeler, 1809-1828,* Michael Joseph, London, 1951.

White, Captain Charles. *MS letter to Captain William Siborne, dated Château de Chokier, 31 July 1845,* BL Add MS 34,708 ff. 202-3).

White, Arthur S. *A Bibliography of Regimental Histories of the British Army,* Society for Army Historical Research, London, 1965.

Whitworth, Major-General R. H. *The Grenadier Guards (The First or Grenadier Regiment of Foot Guards),* Leo Cooper, London, 1974.

de Wilde, Dr F. G. *De uniform van de Prins van Oranje,* published in Armamentaria, Volume I, 1966, pp. 19-21.

Wildman, Captain Thomas. *MS letter to his mother, Sarah, dated Brussels, 19 June 1815,* private collection.

Winchester (I), Lieutenant Robert. *MS letter to Lieutenant William Siborne, dated Londonderry, 7 February 1837,* British Library, London, BL Add MS 34,706 ff. 216-23.

Winchester (II), Lieutenant Robert. *MS letter to Lieutenant William Siborne, dated Edinburgh, 2 March 1839,* British Library, London, BL Add MS 34,706 ff. 242-7.

Winchester (III), Lieutenant Robert. *MS letter to Lieutenant William Siborne, dated Birr, 6 March 1839,* British Library, London, BL Add MS 34,706 ff. 248-9.

Winchester (IV), Lieutenant Robert. *MS letter to Lieutenant William Siborne, dated 15 July 1839,* British Library, London, BL Add MS 34,707 ff. 9-10.

Winstock, Lewis. *Songs and music of the Redcoats. A history of the War Music of the British Army 1642-1902,* Leo Cooper, London, 1970.

Wirths, Captain Ludwig. *Aus der Schlacht bei Waterloo,* published in Nassovia, 1935, pp. 142-144.

Wise, Terence. *Flags of the Napoleonic Wars (1),* Osprey, Oxford, 2001.

Wise, Terence. *Flags of the Napoleonic Wars (3),* Osprey, Oxford, 2001.

de Wit, Pierre. *The campaign of 1815. A study,* published online at www.waterloo-campaign.nl.

Wood, Sergeant Charles. *Letter to an anonymous addressee, dated Paris, 29 July 1815.* See Chambers, pp. 806-7.

Wood, General Sir Evelyn. *Cavalry in the Waterloo Campaign,* Worley Publications, Felling, 1991.

Wootten, Geoffrey. *Waterloo 1815. The birth of Modern Europe,* Osprey, London, 1992.

Wüppermann, W. E. A. *De Vorming van het Nederlandsche Leger na de opwenteling van 1813 en het aandeel van dat leger aan den Veldtocht van 1815,* De Koninklijke Militaire Academie, Breda, 1900.

Young, Julian Charles. *A memoir of Charles Mayne Young, tragedian, with extracts from his son's journal (Volume II),* Macmillan, London. 1871.

van Zuylen van Nyeveld (I), Colonel Pieter Hendrik. *Koninklijke Nederlandsche Armée. Veltocht van 1815. Historick van de 2e Divisie Infanterie. Includes, Historisch verhaal der 2de Divisie voor de Batailles van Les Quatre Bras en Waterloo,* Instituut voor Militaire Geschiedenis, The Hague. See also Boulger, pp. 49-65.

van Zuylen van Nyeveld (II), Colonel Pieter Hendrik. *MS letter to E. van Löben-Sels, dated Utrecht, 24 February 1845,* van Löben-Sels Family Archive, Stads-en-Streekarchief, Zutphen, Folder II, No. 3, Letter 11.

INDEX

Abercromby, Col. Alexander 80, 149, 157-8, 171
Acres, Lt John 296, 311, 353, 365
Adye, Lt-Col. Stephen 100, 233-4
Ainslie, Ensign George 48-9, 80, 115, 188, 293, 314, 320, 370
Alexander, Lt Claude 108, 368
Allebrandi, Militiaman Sebastian 149, 210, 213, 238, 364, 373-4
Alten, Lt-Gen. Baron Carl von 24, 37, 40, 49, 74, 98, 114, 120, 129, 138, 148, 152, 157 *passim* 170, 172, 187, 233, 281, 290, 292, 300, 319, 216
Amerongen, Major Baron Taets van 166
Anton, Sergeant James 110, 147, 217, 254, 256, 264-6, 315-6, 369
Antwerp 25, 77, 81-2, 100, 116, 146, 172, 322, 365, 372
Apsley, Lord Henry 70, 92
Army units, British
    1st (British) Infantry Division 24, 37, 82, 115, 117, 132, 155, 334
    2nd (British) Infantry Division 100, 117, 155, 361
    3rd (British) Infantry Division 24, 37, 49, 114, 117, 129, 151, 155, 233
    4th (British) Infantry Division 93, 100, 128, 155, 198, 361
    5th (British) Infantry Division 24, 77, 108-9, 124, 128, 144, 214, 228
    6th (British) Infantry Division 24, 40, 108, 128
    7th (British) Infantry Division 24
    3rd (British) Cavalry Brigade 30
    6th (British) Cavalry Brigade 74
    2nd (British) Infantry Brigade 119, 357
    5th (British) Infantry Brigade 49, 187, 290, 349
    8th (British) Infantry Brigade 125
    9th (British) Infantry Brigade 125
    10th (British) Infantry Brigade 361
    1st Regiment of Foot Guards 10, 33, 47, 109, 116, 119, 128, 150-1, 232, 234-6, 333, 335-6, 339-41, 344, 349, 357, 375
    2nd Regiment of Foot Guards 115, 375
    3rd Regiment of Foot Guards 46-7, 82, 232-4, 236, 338, 349, 357, 375
    1st Regiment of Foot 105, 197, 214-5, 325, 328, 369
    7th Regiment of Foot 76
    28th Regiment of Foot 23, 53, 117, 126-7, 145, 156, 197, 211, 216, 253, 272, 317, 328, 367
    30th Regiment of Foot 8, 10, 15, 49, 52, 70, 74, 115, 168, 187, 134-5, 290, 296-7, 305-6, 309, 311, 319, 321, 335, 339-40, 346, 350, 354-5, 371
    32nd Regiment of Foot 79, 105, 126, 145, 156, 197, 214, 216, 220, 242-3, 245, 247, 253, 318-9, 328-9, 360, 366
    33rd Regiment of Foot 18, 23, 49, 73, 114, 130, 157-8, 188-9, 270, 291, 297, 301-2, 304, 311, 329, 331, 338, 341, 345, 371, 374
    42nd Regiment of Foot 103, 110, 126-7, 144, 147, 156, 186, 216, 254, 256, 277, 304, 315-16, 322-3, 325, 368, 371, 374
    44th Regiment of Foot 51, 103, 127, 146, 186, 217, 253, 262, 264, 279, 290, 294, 310, 316, 335, 369
    54th Regiment of Foot 94
    60th Regiment of Foot 74
    69th Regiment of Foot 48-9, 52, 80, 158, 169, 188, 291-2, 295, 297, 303, 311, 317, 319-20, 345, 370
    73rd Regiment of Foot 73, 80, 115, 130, 152, 159, 168, 296, 302, 311, 333, 340, 342, 349, 353, 365
    79th Regiment of Foot 92, 96, 110, 126, 146, 156, 164, 171, 186, 197, 214, 216, 219, 241, 244, 248, 253, 271, 366
    92nd Regiment of Foot 71, 93, 104, 108-9, 124, 126-7, 132, 146, 218, 229, 246, 258, 261, 275-7, 279-80, 282, 285, 293, 296, 298, 302, 309-10, 336, 341, 355, 360, 367, 369-70, 375
    95th Regiment of Foot 72, 77, 96, 125, 127, 144, 146, 163, 193, 197, 199, 214, 219-20, 251, 53, 300-301, 350, 359, 365, 367
Army units, Brunswick
    Brunswick Division 24, 95, 133, 164, 172, 197, 229, 274, 357, 370
    Uhlan Squadron *see also* Uhlans 133, 164, 258, 359, 374
    Avantgarde Battalion 21, 133, 143, 164, 225-6, 241, 257-8, 293, 295, 337, 359, 373
    Leib-Battalion 123, 147, 257, 293, 340
    1st Light Battalion 95, 357
    2nd Light Battalion 239, 301, 350
    3rd Light Battalion 95, 133, 334, 359, 373
    1st Line Battalion 225-6, 257-9, 340, 359, 373
    2nd Line Battalion 29, 133, 164, 226, 340, 342, 351

3rd Line Battalion 133, 164, 226, 259, 261-2, 359
Army units, Hanoverian
  Hanoverian Reserve Division
  1st (Hanoverian) Infantry Brigade 20, 290-91, 370
  4th (Hanoverian) Infantry Brigade 20, 148, 227
  5th (Hanoverian) Infantry Brigade 198
  2nd (Hanoverian) Brigade of Foot Artillery 127, 229
  Feld-Jäger-Korps 20, 70, 291, 299-300, 350, 357
  Bremen Field Battalion 73, 291, 299, 318, 350, 357, 370
  Duke of York's Field Battalion *see* Osnabruck Field Battalion 318
  Grubenhagen Field Battalion 291, 299-300, 350, 357
  Lüneburg Field Battalion 227, 300
  Osnabruck Field Battalion 291, 299, 318, 350, 357
  Verden Field Battalion 73, 227, 291, 299, 318, 357
  Lüneburg Landwehr Battalion 271, 285, 353, 360
  Münden Landwehr Battalion 227, 359
  Osterode Landwehr Battalion 227, 359
  Verden Landwehr Battalion 272, 359
Army units, King's German Legion (KGL)
  King's German Legion (KGL) 19-20, 24, 76, 128, 173, 233, 273, 298, 300, 314, 318-19, 361, 370, 378
  3rd Hussar Regiment (KGL) 76
Army units, Netherlands
  1st (Netherlands) Infantry Division 24
  2nd (Netherlands) Infantry Division 24, 41, 77, 151, 153, 155, 157, 169, 233, 361, 375
  3rd (Netherlands) Infantry Division 24, 29, 91, 233
  Netherlands Cavalry Division 91, 117, 143, 156
  1st (Netherlands) Light Cavalry Brigade 57
  Netherlands Indian Brigade 24, 76
  5th (South Netherlands) Regiment of Light Dragoons 22
  6th (North Netherlands) Regiment of Hussars 22, 28, 199, 204, 239
  27th Jager Battalion 55, 74, 79, 113, 119, 129, 134, 139, 149, 169, 176, 182-4, 202-3, 206, 209, 211, 239, 256, 360, 372, 377
  35th Jager Battalion 29
  36th Jager Battalion 30
  2nd Line Battalion 29, 133, 164, 226, 340, 342, 351, 373-4
  3rd Line Battalion 133, 164, 226, 259, 261-2, 359
  7th Line Battalion 55, 79, 87, 113, 130-2, 153, 157, 171, 181-2, 184-5, 192, 202-3, 206-8, 360, 377
  12th Line Battalion 143
  3rd National Militia Battalion 30
  4th National Militia Battalion 29-30
  5th National Militia Battalion 58, 70, 113, 130-2, 149, 166, 181-4, 201-4, 206-7, 209, 239, 360, 377
  6th National Militia Battalion 29, 128
  7th National Militia Battalion 58, 74, 79, 113-14, 130-2, 149, 166, 181-2, 184, 190, 199, 210, 222, 226, 238, 360, 364, 373
  8th National Militia Battalion 53, 58, 74, 113, 129, 149, 166, 180, 186, 190-1, 202, 206, 210-11, 238, 360, 378
  10th National Militia Battalion 29-30
  17th National Militia Battalion 29-30, 128
  19th National Militia Battalion 29
Army units, Nassau
  1st Nassau-Usingen Regiment 24, 62, 361
  2nd Nassau-Usingen Regiment 21, 38, 43, 51-2, 57, 59, 63, 66, 68-9, 85, 97, 96, 118, 129, 133, 135-6, 149, 153, 162, 166-7, 180, 190, 195, 201, 209-10, 225, 237-8, 360, 377
  Regiment Oranien-Nassau 37-8, 52, 57, 66, 68-9, 85, 149, 166-7, 180, 185-6, 190, 195, 198, 209-11, 222, 225-7, 238, 271, 297, 360, 377
  Volunteer Jäger Company 37, 52, 57, 68-9, 85-6, 118, 166, 180, 237, 239
Army units, Prussian
  1st (Prussian) Infantry Brigade 28, 163
  2nd (Prussian) Infantry Brigade 33-4
  4th (1st Silesian) Hussar Regiment 33, 59, 114
French
  1st (French) Corps de l'Armée 78, 278
  2nd (French) Corps de l'Armée 27
  4th (French) Infantry Division 77
  6th Chasseurs à Cheval 27-8, 223
  Garde Nationale 17
  Imperial Guard 56, 61, 78, 148-9, 180, 186, 278, 352, 374
Arquennnes 55, 87, 91, 117, 120, 130, 138-9, 143, 149, 158, 171, 173, 199, 361
Bailén, Battle of 14
Bailey, Lt-Col. Morris 50
Barnard, Lt-Col. Sir Andrew 92, 97, 126, 146, 193-4, 200, 240, 251-2, 300-301
Barnes, Major-Gen. Sir Edward 81, 281, 296, 339
Barrington, Ensign Hon. Samuel 356, 376
Bathurst, Earl 18, 22, 70
Bathurst, Ensign Hon. Seymour 92, 342
Baume 30, 128, 130-1
Bean, Major George 94, 100
Beaulieu, Major Baron Du Val de 224
Sattler, Major Johann 43, 53, 57, 61, 68, 85, 166
Sattler, Major Johann 43, 53, 57, 61, 68, 85, 166
Beckwith, Major Charles 201, 252
Belson, Col. Sir Charles 23, 53, 272, 324
Bergerie, Ferme de la 68, 203, 205-7, 211-12, 216, 218, 222-3, 225, 258, 260-2, 276, 281-2, 285, 287, 291-3, 296-7, 310, 317, 319, 345, 347, 349-50, 368
Bergmann, Capt. Emilius 37, 68, 85, 118, 166, 180, 237, 239
Berkeley, Lt-Col. Sir George 36-7, 55, 98, 117, 309
Best, Col. Carl 20, 148, 169, 172, 192, 214, 227, 270-2, 286, 370
Bijlandt, Major-Gen. Count Willem 10, 22, 53, 55, 58-9, 74, 78-9, 88-9, 96, 100, 112-13, 130-2, 139, 171, 207, 212, 216, 229, 236, 239, 377, 379
Bijleveld, Capt. Adriaanus 175-85 *passim*, 201-2, 206, 211, 219, 239, 257, 334, 357, 366, 378
Binche 24, 27-36, 51, 55-6, 71, 74, 78, 88, 96, 113, 143, 155-6, 178
Black Band, the, *see also* Brunswick Division 20-21
Black Watch, the, *see also* 42nd Regiment of Foot 13, 267, 270, 272

Index

Blücher, Field-Marshal Prince Gebhard Lebrecht von 17, 77, 79, 94, 97, 100-101, 105, 112, 124, 137, 143, 154, 163, 168, 192-3, 278
   and supply problems 25
   early plans 33
   confidence in 71
   at Ligny 145
   at Brye 189
   Wellington unhappy with deployment 189
Bois de Bossu 62-3, 66, 68-9, 86, 118-19, 134-5, 150, 156, 165-7, 171, 174, 176, 180-1, 183, 185, 190, 195, 199, 204, 207, 209-11, 215, 222, 225-6, 237-9, 257-9, 261, 264, 281, 283, 285-7, 290, 292, 294, 296-7, 301-302, 304, 309, 315, 329, 331-3, 335, 339-40, 342, 344, 350-2, 354-60, 365, 376-7
Bois des Censes 194, 214, 219, 228, 239, 251-2, 300
Bonaparte, Prince Jérôme 128, 169
Bonaparte, Napoleon, Napoleon I 16-18, 21-3, 25, 34, 39, 49, 56, 61, 71-2, 92, 90, 94-5, 97, 101, 112, 124, 142-3, 145-6, 167-8, 173, 214, 225, 234, 258, 278, 334
   abdication and exile to Elba 14-15
   escape from Elba 15-16
   appeals for peace 16
   arrival at Paris 16
   Acte Additionel aux Constitutions de l'Empire 17
   leaves Paris 26-7
   headquarters at Avesnes 27
   rumoured to be at the head of the army 94
Boreel, Lt-Col. Lord Willem 28, 199, 204-6, 208
Bowles, Capt. George 108, 111, 119
Boyce, Lt John 188, 331-2, 371
Bradford, Lt-Col. Sir Henry Hollis 46, 378
Braine-le-Comte 24, 27, 30-1, 33-5, 38, 41, 46, 48, 54-6, 75, 79-80, 82, 87-9, 91, 98-100, 110, 114-15, 117, 120, 129-31, 138-9, 144, 146, 150-2, 155-7, 163, 167-8, 170, 192, 232-3, 325-6, 361
Brandenstein, Major Heinrich von 219, 239, 301
Braun, Capt. Wilhelm 20
Braun, Major von 240
Braunschweig-Lüneburg, Duke Wilhelm von 20, 108, 133, 145-6, 168-70, 218, 225, 227, 241, 256, 258-9
Bredenschey, Lt Friedrich 123, 236, 260
Bronkhorst, Capt. Abraham van 199
Bronkhorst, Capt. Jan van 199, 204, 223
Brown Bess, musket 38, 216, 255, 323
Brückmann, Lt-Col. Heinrich 19
Brunneck Major von 137-8, 154, 162-3, 189
Burgos 23, 266, 270
Burney, Capt. 51, 89, 103, 217, 279-80
Busaco 23, 266
Büsgen, Capt. Moritz 43, 180, 190, 237
Byng, Major-Gen. Sir John 46, 119, 235-6, 338-9, 348, 352, 357
Cabrera 15
Cameron, Col. 109-10, 126, 146, 193, 227, 267, 274, 281, 283-7, 345, 349, 368
Cameron Highlanders 127, 145, 187, 214, 220, 278, 366

Campbell, Lt-Col. Colin 270
Campbell, Major John 217
Campbell, Col. Sir Neil 15, 94
Capel, Lady Caroline 81, 123, 133
Capel, Lady Harriet 32
Capel, Hon. John 32, 106
Capel, Lady Maria 109, 345
Casualties 366-79
Champ du Sarti 68, 166, 171, 238, 287, 333, 360, 384
Charleroi road 39, 58, 61, 68, 85, 129, 134-5, 150, 153, 162, 165-6, 170 174-7, 180-2, 185, 202-3, 205, 209, 211, 218, 222, 225, 227-8, 241, 241, 253, 258-64, 274, 281, 283, 292-7, 301-4, 310-11, 315, 339, 354-9, 364, 370
Chassé, General Baron David 22, 24, 29-230, 32, 34-6, 41, 48, 78, 88, 96, 98-100, 120, 128, 131, 143, 148, 154-7, 171, 173, 233
Chasseurs à Cheval 27-8, 78, 134, 148, 204-8, 223-4, 259, 276-7, 279, 324, 329
Christie, Ensign James 263, 370
Clarke, Count d'Hunebourg and Duke de Feltre 89
Clarke, Gentleman-Volunteer Christopher 314, 371
Clarke, Patrick, assistant surgeon 306
Cleeves, Capt. Andreas 20, 159, 298-9, 314, 318-9, 35, 378
Coeverden, Lt Ruysch van 206, 378
Colbert-Chabanais, *Général de Division* Count Edouard 61
Coldstream Guards see also 2nd Regiment of Foot Guards 108, 116, 119, 236, 335, 339, 353, 357
Cole, Lt-Gen. Sir Lowry 40
Coles, Lt George 280
Collins, John, assistant surgeon 280
Cooke, Major-Gen. George 24, 37, 40, 46, 98, 100, 138, 151, 154-7, 163, 170, 232-3, 236, 319, 326, 333-4, 341, 357
Corruna 23, 116, 127, 336
Costello, Private 96, 127, 144, 251, 253, 366
Cramm, Major Friedrich von 226, 240, 261, 373
Crowe, Capt. John 221
Croy, Capt. van der Bruggen van 210
Cuyler, Ensign Augustus 46, 115, 150
Dashwood, Lt-Col. Charles 233, 349, 351
d'Aubremé, Major-Gen. Count Alexandre 29-30, 128, 143
Dawson, Major Hon. George 81, 294, 296
Deacon, Ensign Thomas 115, 342, 365
de Collaert, Lt-Gen. Baron Jean-Marie 27, 32, 41, 56-7, 78, 80, 88-91, 98-100, 114, 117, 120, 130, 143-4, 148-9, 154, 156, 171, 173
de Constant Rebecque, Major-Gen. Baron Jean-Victoir 22, 27, 30-37, 41, 53-4, 56, 80, 87-9, 98-100, 117, 120, 128, 130-4, 136, 151, 157, 171, 173, 361
   receives orders to stand-down 78
   perplexed by Wellington's orders 97
   ordered back to Nivelles 148
de Corbais, Lt-Col. Edouard de Mercx 27, 158, 199, 212, 222-4, 226

413

de Crassier, Capt. 79, 129, 167, 175, 177, 182, 204, 209, 213, 249
de Jacobi, Major Frederik 205
De Lancey, Col. Sir William Howe 69, 71, 75, 95, 101, 154, 360
De Lancey, Magdalene 70, 80
de la Sarraz, Major James 150, 169, 202, 239
de Jongh, Lt-Col. Wijbrandus 53, 58, 113, 128, 166, 186, 90, 192, 373
de Looz-Corswarem, Major Count Jean-Joseph-Benjamin 223-4
de L'Etang, General Count Pierre Dupont 14
de Perponcher-Sedlnitzky, Lt-Gen. Henri-Georges 24, 32, 38, 41-5, 52-7, 61, 68-70, 72-3, 77-80, 86-8, 99-101, 113-14, 117-18, 120-22, 128-9, 149, 153, 162, 165-7, 169-71 182-4, 189-90, 198, 206, 210, 227, 238-9, 326
   and loss of Charleroi 95
   decides to reinforce Les Quatre Bras 112
   briefs the Prince van Oranje-Nassau 134
   at the crossroads 195
   wounded 379
de Piré, *Général de Division* Count Hyppolyte 78
de Poll, Major Jan van 113
der Decken, Major Christoph 273
d'Erlon, *Général de Division* Count Jean-Baptiste Drouet 78, 278
der Wijck, Major-Gen. van 181
de Smeth van Derne, Capt. Baron Frederik 113
de Tolly, Field-Marshal Barclay 17
de Witterzee, Lt Chevalier Adolphe de Cléty 158
Dibbettz, Lt Frederik 43, 135, 202, 223
di Capelli, Major de Paravicini 33-5
Dick, Lt-Col. Robert 266, 369
Disbrowe, Capt. George 46, 150, 334
Dörnberg, Major-Gen. Sir Wilhelm von 30-1, 34-5, 48, 55, 75, 91, 101, 146, 153, 163-4, 189
Douglas, Lt-Col. Neil 110, 220, 242, 245, 248, 328, 366
Douro 23
Dressel, Lt-Col. Wilhelm von 37-8, 52, 68, 165-6, 190
Drummond, Ensign Barclay 48
Duhesme, Count Philibert 168
Durutte, *Général de Division* Count Pierre 78
Egypt 23, 93, 324
Elba 14-16, 61
Elkington, James, surgeon 15-16, 49, 188, 290, 306, 335, 346-8, 378
Elphinstone, Lt-Col. William 114, 158, 188, 297, 302-3 331, 333, 338
Evans, John, assistant surgeon 306, 347
Fitzgerald, Capt. Edward 46, 77, 82, 115
Fitzmaurice, Lt John 97, 193-4, 199, 251-2
Fleurus 33, 35-6, 51, 56, 73, 77, 90, 112, 115, 154, 163, 189
Fraser, Lt-Col. Alexander, Lord Saltoun 119
Frazer, Lt-Col. Sir Augustus 93-4, 97, 99-100, 136, 142, 216, 258, 277, 282, 285
Gagern, Capt. Baron Friedrich von 53, 57, 61, 66, 69, 78-9, 87-8, 100, 259, 379

Gemioncourt, Ferme de 62-3, 68-9, 85, 129, 134, 166-7, 176-7, 180-6, 189, 193, 195, 201 218, 222, 237, 240-1, 254, 256, 264, 286, 302-4, 341, 344, 350-2, 354-7, 359
George III 20, 318
Ghent 16, 18, 25, 39, 77, 81, 90, 100, 104, 158, 172
Gneisenau, General Baron August Niedhardt von 18, 25, 90, 165, 334
Gomm, Lt-Col. Sir William 77, 197-9, 211-12, 214, 378
Gordon Highlanders *see also* 92nd Regiment of Foot 23, 108, 126, 187, 228, 253, 276-7, 285, 290, 296, 316, 345, 349, 368
Gorkum, Major van 31, 35, 170, 232, 377
Gosselies 33, 35-6, 39, 42, 51, 53, 55-6, 58-9, 70-3, 78, 114, 138, 148, 163
Grier, Lt Robert 280
Grunenbosch, Col. Jan 112, 129, 134, 167, 174, 176-7, 182-4, 203, 209, 256, 357, 377
Graham, Lt-Gen. Sir Thomas 15
Grenadiers 43, 68, 85, 130, 145, 188-9, 209, 235, 262, 265, 274, 281, 284, 286, 290, 297-8, 304-5 311-13, 325, 329, 332, 337-9, 353-4, 367
Grose, Capt. Edward 151, 336, 356
Gunkel, Major-Gen. Carel van 151
Haigh, Capt. John 330, 332, 371
Halkett, Major-Gen. Sir Colin 49-50, 73, 114-15, 152, 168, 173, 187-8 290-6, 298, 303, 305, 322, 329, 333, 349, 351, 356, 359, 370
Halpin, Oliver, surgeon 280
Hamerton, Lt-Col. John 103, 217-18, 262-3, 316
Hamilton, Lt-Col. Alexander 74, 290, 296, 310, 346, 371
Hardinge, Lt-Col. Sir Henry 19, 189
Harris, Lt-Col. William 115, 130, 152, 291, 311, 340, 342, 349, 353, 365
Hawker, Lt-Col. James 93
Heinemann, Col. Von 95, 261
Hepburn, Col. Francis 47-8, 82
Hicks, Lt-Col. John 221, 242-3, 270, 317-18
Hill, Lt-Gen. Lord Rowland 24, 107, 155, 198, 361
Hobhouse, Capt. Benjamin 48, 80
Horse artillery 21, 29, 34, 42, 57, 93, 130, 148, 157, 165, 204, 223, 239, 257, 282, 334, 361, 378
   French 31, 149, 211, 257, 286, 318
Hôtel de Miroir 31, 48, 80, 88-9
Howitzers 20, 31, 43, 57, 85, 132, 135, 150, 180, 199, 202, 219, 223, 228-9, 303, 319
Ireland 19, 23, 152
Irwin, Lt William 324, 367
Jessop, Major John 290, 335
Kellermann, *Général de Division* Count François 78
Kempt, Major-Gen. Sir James 77, 79, 93, 125-6, 168-72, 197, 211-12, 216-21, 239, 241, 245-8, 253, 299, 317, 319, 324-5, 350
   lines the Namur road 214
   urges on the 28th 272
   losses to brigade 366-7, 370
Kennedy, Ensign James 328, 369

Index

Kielmansegge, Major-Gen. Count Friedrich von 20, 73, 114, 148, 173, 187-8, 290-292, 298, 300-1, 318, 350, 355, 359, 370
Kincaid, Lt John 72, 144-6, 186, 193-4, 200, 239, 299-300, 365
Kingsley, Lt Nicholas 279-80
Klencke, Lt-Col. August von 300, 350
Krahmer de Bichin, Capt. Carel 30, 157
Kruse, Major-Gen. Baron August von 24
Kuhlmann, Major Heinrich 19, 150, 233, 333, 350, 354, 357, 378
Lake, Ensign Charles 47
Lallemand, *Général de Division* Baron François 78
Léfèbvre-Desnoëttes, *Général de Division* Count Charles 78
Lennox, Charles, Duke of Richmond 112
Lennox, Capt. Charles, Earl of March 32-3, 37, 55, 80
Liège 25
Ligny 145, 228, 300, 334, 379
Lille 16
Limburg-Stirum, Major Count Otto van 88-9, 100, 112, 120, 191-2, 208, 379
Lindsay, Major Henry 312-4
Llewellyn, Major Richard 7, 117, 323, 367
Lloyd, Major William 159, 189, 292-5, 310, 319, 334, 342, 378
Louis XVIII 14-16, 18, 81, 90
Lubecq, Major von 236
Lyons 16
Macara, Lt-Col. Sir Robert 110, 147, 156, 217, 254-5, 265-6, 369
Macdonell, Lt-Col. James 119, 338, 348, 350-1, 356
Maclean, Major Archibald 311
Mahrenholz, Major von 260, 372
Maitland, Major-Gen. Peregrine 46, 128, 235-6, 335-8, 342, 341, 345, 352, 355, 356,
Malcolm, Rear Admiral Sir Pulteney 74, 92
Marshall, Capt. William 108, 220
McConchy, Ensign James 247-8
McEween, Corporal 264, 323, 305
Menzies, Capt. Archibald 265-7, 369
McPherson, Ensign John 282, 287, 368
Merlen, Major-Gen. Baron Jean-Baptiste van 22, 27-9, 32-7, 48, 56, 130, 144, 149, 199, 204-5, 208, 222-3, 277, 360
Metzner, Major Ferdinand 259
Meuse 17
Miller, Lt-Col. William 151, 235, 344, 356, 376
Mitchell, Lt-Col. James 286
Moll, Major Carl von 123, 334
Mollinger, Capt. 183-4, 377
Morice, Lt-Col. Charles 48, 50, 115, 158, 188, 291-3, 303-5, 312, 314, 319
Müffling, Col Baron Friedrich von 56, 90, 153-4, 278, 334
  Dispatch to Blücher 100-1
  Reports intelligence to Wellington at Quatre Bras 163-4
Mühlmann, Capt. von 43, 53-4

Napoleon I *see* Bonaparte, Napoleon
Nepveu, Capt. Baron Charles 99, 128, 131, 133
Ney, Maréchal de l''Empire Michel, Duke d'Elchingen, Prince de la Moscowa 78, 158, 278, 344
Niel, Capt. Baron 27-8
Nivelle, Battle of 23
Nixon, Lt-Col. Robert 53, 127, 211-12
Normann, Major Philipp von 39, 42-3, 51, 53, 55, 59-63, 66, 68, 72, 78-9, 135, 148, 162, 180, 225-6
Nyeveld, Col. Baron Pieter van Zuylen van 77, 95-6, 113-14, 185
Olfermann, Col. Elias 95, 146, 260-1, 268, 285, 293-5, 303, 351
O'Malley, Lt-Col. George 262, 279-80, 316, 323
Ompteda, Col. Baron Christian von 114, 149, 171, 173, 361
Opstall, Major Cornelius van 131, 169, 203, 206, 227
Oranje-Nassau, Prince Willem Frederik van 16, 24, 27, 29-34, 36-7, 41, 77, 80, 87, 88, 91, 99-100, 107, 117, 120, 131, 143, 148-51, 153-5, 157, 164-5, 168-70, 176, 178, 180-208 *passim*, 218, 225, 227, 232, 238, 264, 303, 312, 336, 356, 360, 379
  declared Prince-Sovereign 21
  'Slender Billy' nickname 49
  and Duchess of Richmond's Ball 110-11
  to Nivelles 129
  at Quatre Bras 133-8
  commits 5th Rgt of Light Dragoons 222
  commits last reserves 239
  leaves battlefield 361
  re-equips at Nivelles 377
Oudenaarde 75-6, 91, 128
Pack, Major-Gen. Sir Denis 77, 100, 125, 146, 156, 170, 172, 197, 211, 214, 216-18, 227, 229, 254, 257, 262, 274, 291-2
Paget, Lt-Gen. Henry, Earl of Uxbridge 24, 50, 322
Paris 12, 14, 16-17, 26-7, 234, 374
Paris, Treaty of 21
Pattison, Lt Frederick 49, 114, 130, 152, 188, 291, 297-8, 304, 329-30, 332-3, 339, 371
Petter, Capt. Abraham 57, 130
Picton, Lt-Gen. Sir Thomas 32-3, 40, 53, 125, 128, 132, 197, 199-201, 214, 216, 218, 220, 227-8, 241-3, 247, 252-4, 257, 270, 272-3, 276, 296-8, 311, 316-18, 320, 324, 326, 347, 360, 368-9, 378
  'Fighting Third' 53
  ordered to attack the Ferme de la Bergerie 211
  Division links with Brunswick infantry 253
  Division exhausted 278, 292, 316-7, 348
  Division relieved 296-7
  'restores the balance of victory' 320
Piraumont 85, 119, 129, 134, 165, 167, 169, 174-5, 177, 192-3, 201, 214, 219, 252, 300-301, 350, 357, 359, 370
Piraumont, Ferme de 69, 201, 252
Pirch, Major-Gen. Otto von 78
Pittius, Capt. Adrianus Geij van 29, 31, 34, 130, 199, 204, 208, 223, 239
Pott, Col. Carl 164, 226, 258-9

Powell, Capt. Henry Weyland 23, 335
Pratt, Lt John 144, 151
Pröstler, Major August von 147, 236, 259
Ramdohr, Lt-Col. Von 270, 285
Rauschenplatt, Major Adolf von 225-6, 241, 273
Reille, *Général de Division* Count Honoré 78, 148, 278
Rettberg, Capt. Carl von 20, 127-8, 229, 257, 295, 319, 378
Ridesdale, George, surgeon 187
Rhine 17, 95
Robertson, Capt. Alexander 312, 354, 365
Robertson, Sgt David 93, 104, 127, 132, 169-70, 188, 218, 227-8, 276-8, 285, 287, 356
Rogers, Major Thomas 124, 219-20, 239, 278, 318, 352, 378
Rooke, Lt-Col. Henry 46, 115-6, 335
Ross, Lt James 93, 97, 275, 279-81, 285-6
Ross, Lt-Col. Sir Hew 93-4
Ross-Lewin, Major 79-80, 145, 168, 214-15, 222, 243, 270, 329
Royal Highlanders *see also* 42nd Regiment of Foot 216, 254, 369
Royal Scots *see also* 1st Regiment of Foot 105, 187, 316-17, 354
Russell, Capt. Hon. Francis 32, 77, 89
Sanden, Lt-Col. François Van den 55, 79, 87, 132, 157-8, 171, 184-5, 202
Sandham, Capt. Charles 333, 378
Sachsen-Weimar, Col. Prince Bernhard von 37-8, 43, 51-2, 55, 57, 61, 68-70, 78-9, 85-7, 89, 96, 98, 112-13, 118, 122, 129, 134-5, 139, 165, 173, 185-6, 198, 209-10, 236, 379
  snubbed by Wellington 154
  falls back on Houtain-le-Val 238
  at Champ du Sarti 360
Sattler, Major Johann 43, 53, 57, 61, 68, 85, 166
Scheltens, Lt Chrétien 22, 158, 182, 207, 377
Schleyer, Major Christian 37, 52
Schwarzenberg, Field-Marshal Prince Karl von 17
Scott, Capt. Thomas 219
Shaw-Kennedy, Capt. James 290
Somerset, Lt-Col. Lord Fitzroy 32-3, 37, 55, 75, 90, 143, 153, 164, 192-4, 238, 246, 376, 378
Steinmetz, Major-Gen. Carl von 28, 31, 33-6, 78, 163
Stevenaar, Capt. Emmanuel 74, 113, 130-2, 139, 165, 176, 180-1, 183, 185, 201, 203, 206-7, 222-3, 257, 360, 378
  arrives at Les Quatre Bras 149-50
  guns unprotected 205
Seymour, Capt. Horace 74, 81, 92, 96
Seymour, Lady Isabella 81
Simmons, Lt George 53, 97, 127, 144, 194, 201, 367
Soignies 24, 29, 49-53, 58, 73-4, 80, 113-4, 117, 119, 149, 152, 236
Stewart, Lt-Gen. Lord Charles 22
Stewart, Lt Duncan 256
Stewart, John, assistant surgeon 277, 368
Strombeck, Major Johann von 164, 226, 342, 378

Talavera 18, 23, 129, 295
Thyle 192, 201, 237, 251-2, 301, 357, 359, 365, 367
Tirlemont 25
Toulouse 23, 127
Tournai 25, 82, 156
Townshend, Lt-Col. Hon. Horatio 116, 356
Trip, Major-Gen. Lord Albert 56, 130, 173, 199
Trip, Lt-Col. Baron Ernst 32
Uhlans 21, 42, 59, 133, 164, 214, 226, 258, 359, 374
Vallence, Private Dixon 92-3, 96, 145, 156, 164, 171, 174, 187, 197, 220, 241-2, 245-6, 248, 251, 253, 366, 375
Vienna, Congress of 15-16, 18, 26
Vigoreux, Lt-Col. Charles 52, 305, 311, 331, 339
Vitoria 23, 270
Vivian, Major-Gen. Sir Hussey 73, 107
Wachholtz, Major Friedrich von 260
Waldie, Charlotte 39-40, 57, 76, 94-5, 105, 109, 117, 123, 125, 367
Waterloo 7, 10, 79, 128, 133, 136, 144, 146, 152, 154, 156, 163, 169, 173, 236, 365, 367-9, 371-2, 374, 376-9
Watson, Fanny 15, 49-50
Watson, Major Lewis 15, 50, 115, 292, 303-5, 321, 330
Wellington, Arthur Wellesley, the Duke of
  at Brussels 40-1, 55-6, 71
  and Duchess of Richmond's Ball 46, 106-112
  first memorandum re: dispositions 75
  worries over Nivelles 120
  unimpressed by von Blücher's deployment 189
  concerns over left flank 193, 201, 211
  sees importance of Quatre Bras 198
  and French snipers 220
  and Ferme des Quatre Bras 228, 275-6
  and Bois de Bossu 238
  in personal danger 274-5
  and Ferme de la Bergerie 282-3
  and artillery advantage 298, 334
  leaves battlefield 360
  and *passim*
Winchester, Lt Robert 145, 156, 218, 227-8, 258, 277, 281, 287, 341
Winzingerode, Field-Marshal Ferdinand 17
Wirths, Capt. Ludwig 38, 59, 63
Wood, Col. Sir George 94, 100, 116, 119, 136, 235, 257, 280, 298, 338
Ypres 15, 25
Zieten, Lt-General Count Hans von 55-6, 90

Hofschröer (IV), Peter. *Black Brunswickers at Quatre Bras,* published in Military Illustrated, No. 169, June 2002, pp. 40-5.

Hofschröer (V), Peter. *Busting the myths about Blücher,* published in Military Illustrated, No. 179, April 2003, pp. 32-9.

Hofschröer (VI), Peter. *Wellington's last-minute victory,* published in Military Illustrated, No. 181, June 2003, pp. 32-9.

Holighausen, Private Johann Jost. *Die Geschichte des Johann Jost Holighaus. Dieser hat 1815 als einfacher Soldat an der Schlacht von Waterloo teilgenommen,* published online at www.widerhallderzeit.de/index.html.

Holle, Lieutenant Hendrik. *MS letter dated Passey, 10 July 1815,* Blussé Family Collection, Stadsarchief Dordrecht, Inventory 68-21, No. 21.

Hooper, George. *Waterloo. The Downfall of the First Napoleon. A History of the Campaign of 1815,* Smith Elder, London, 1862.

Hope (I), Lieutenant James. Undated MS extracts from *'The military memoirs of an infantry officer 1809-1816,'* British Library, London, BL Add MS 34,703 ff. 18-21.

Hope (II), Lieutenant James. *MS letter to Captain William Siborne, dated Liverpool, 4 January 1842,* British Library, London, BL Add MS 34,707 ff. 336-7.

Hope (III), Lieutenant James. *The Iberian and Waterloo Campaigns. The Letters of Lieutenant James Hope* (edited by S. Monick), Naval and Military, Dallington, 2000.

Horricks, Raymond. *Marshal Ney. The Romance and the Real,* Archway, London 1998.

von der Horst, Lieutenant. Account, published in Hannoversches Magazine, 95e Stück, 1816, pp. 1507-11.

Hourtoulle, F. G. and Jirbal, J. *L'Épopée Napoléonienne,* Histoire et Collections, Paris, 1997.

Houssaye, Henry. *Napoleon and the Campaign of 1815.* Waterloo, Worley, Felling, 1991.

Howard, Ensign James. *Letter to an unknown addressee, dated Paris, 8 July 1815.* See Lee, pp. 245-8.

Howard, Philip. *The Black Watch (Royal Highland Regiment, the 42nd Regiment of Foot),* Hamish Hamilton, London, 1968.

Hoynck van Papendrecht, Lieutenant-Colonel Arend. *Undated MS report to Major-General Baron Jean-Victor de Constant-Rebecque,* van Löben-Sels Family Archive, Stads-en-Streekarchief, Zutphen, Folder II, No. 8, Letter 6. See also Boulger, pp. 67-8.

Hughes, Major-General B.P. *Honour titles of the Royal Artillery,* Henry Ling, Dorchester, n.d.

Hussey (I), John. *Conversations with the Duke of Wellington. Dörnberg's account of the start of the Waterloo campaign,* First Empire, No. 73, 2003, pp. 9-15.

Hussey (II), John. *Müffling, Gleig, Zieten and the 'missing' Wellingtonian records: the 'compromising' documents traced,* published in The Journal of the Society for Army Historical Research, Volume LXXVII, 1999, pp. 250-68.

Hussey (III), John. *At what time on 15 June 1815 did Wellington learn of Napoleon's attack on the Prussians?* published in War in History, No. 6, 1999, pp. 88-116.

Hussey (IV) John. *Towards a better chronology for the Waterloo campaign,* published in War in History, No. 7, 2000, pp. 463-80.

van Hylckema, Second Lieutenant C. Frisius F. *MS letter to W. Eekhoff, dated Sondel, 8 July and 6 August 1865,* Correspondance of W. Eekhoff, Collection Fries Genootschap, Tresoar Archief, Provincial Library of Friesland, Leeuwarden, Nos. 1229 and 1229a.

Jackson (I), Captain Basil. *Major Basil Jackson respecting the Prussians at Waterloo,* published in The United Services Journal, August 1841, pp. 541-3.

Jackson (II), Captain Basil. *Recollections of Waterloo, by a Staff Officer,* published in The United Services Journal, August 1847, pp. 1-11.

Jackson (III), Captain Basil. *Notes and reminiscences of a Staff Officer, chiefly relating to the Waterloo campaign and to St. Helena matters during the captivity of Napoleon* (edited by R. C. Seaton), Murray, London, 1903.

Bibliography

Halkett (III), Major-General Sir Colin. *MS letter to Lieutenant William Siborne, dated Calais, 5 June 1839,* British Library, London, BL Add MS 34,707 ff. 58-9.

Halkett (IV), Major-General Sir Colin. *MS notes of an conversation with Captain William Siborne, dated April 1846,* British Library, London, BL Add MS 34,708 ff. 249-50.

Hamilton, Clive. *Quatre Bras Memorial. Project Update,* published in The Waterloo Journal, Volume 22, No. 2, September 2000.

Hamilton, Lieutenant-General Sir F.W. *The origin and history of the First or Grenadier Guards, from documents in the State Paper Office, War Office, Horse Guards, contemporary history, regimental records, etc. (3 volumes),* John Murray, London, 1874.

Hamilton-Williams, David. *Waterloo. New perspectives. The great battle reappraised,* BCA, London, 1994.

Harris, James (First Earl of Malmesbury). *A series of letters of the First Earl of Malmesbury, his family and friends, from 1745 to 1820 (Volume II),* Bentley, London, 1870.

Harris, Colonel William. *MS letter to unknown addressee, dated Belmont, 23 January 1845,* British Library, London, BL Add MS 34,708 f. 171.

Hartmann, Major Augustus. *MS letter to Lieutenant William Siborne, dated Hildesheim, 9 February 1835,* British Library, London, BL Add MS 34,704 ff. 227-8.

Hay, Captain William. *Reminiscences 1808-1815 under Wellington (edited by Mrs. S.C.I. Wood),* Simpkin, Marshall, Hamilton and Kent, London, 1901.

Haythornthwaite (I), Philip. *Uniforms of Waterloo,* Blandford Press, London, 1974.

Haythornthwaite (II), Philip. *Napoleon's Line Infantry,* Osprey, London, 1983.

Haythornthwaite (III), Philip. *The Napoleonic Source Book,* Arms and Armour Press, London, 1997.

Haythornthwaite (IV). *Waterloo Men. The Experience of Battle 16-18 June 1815,* The Crowood Press, Ramsbury, 1999.

Haythornthwaite (V), Philip. *Save the Colours! Napoleonic heroism,* published in Military Illustrated, No. 153, February 2001, pp. 52-5.

Head, Michael. *French Napoleonic Artillery,* Almark, London, 1973.

Heise (I), Lieutenant Ludwig. *MS letter to an unknown addressee, dated Hanover, 23 April 1835,* British Library, London, BL Add MS 34,705, f. 190-1.

Heise (II), Lieutenant Ludwig. MS letter to Captain Ludwig Benne, dated Hanover, 20 February 1837, British Library, London, BL Add MS 34,706, ff. 375-6.

Hellemann, Oberfeuerwerker August. *MS letter to his parents and sisters, dated 20 June 1815,* Niedersächsisches Staatsarchiv Wolfenbüttel, 249 AN 190.

Hemingway, Private George. *MS letter to his mother, Elizabeth Hemingway, dated 16 August 1815,* published in The British Library Journal, Volume VI, No. 1, Spring 1980.

Henckens, E. F. C. A. (editor). *Mémoires se rapportant à son service militaire au 6ème Régiment de Chasseurs à Cheval Français de Février 1803 à Août 1816,* Martinus Nijhoff, The Hague, 1910.

Henderson, Ernest F. *Blücher and the uprising of Prussia against Napoleon 1806-1815,* G. P. Puttnam, New York and London, 1911.

von Herzberg, Lieutenant-General August. MS Report of the Corps of the Duke of Brunswick from the 15th to the 18th June 1815, British Library, London, BL Add MS 34,706, ff. 23-46.

Hervey, Colonel Felton. *A contemprorary letter, etc.,* published in Nineteenth Century Magazine, March 1893, p. 432.

Heymès, Colonel. *Relation de la campagne de 1815, dites de Waterloo, pour servir à l'histoire du Maréchal Ney,* Paris, 1829.

Hibbert, Christopher. *Wellington. A Personal History,* Harper Collins, London, 1997.

Hofschröer (I), Peter. *1815. The Waterloo Campaign. Wellington, his German Allies and the Battles of Ligny and Quatre Bras,* Greenhill Books, London, 1998.

Hofschröer (II), Peter. *1815. The Waterloo Campaign. The German Victory,* Greenhill Books, London, 1999.

Hofschröer (III), Peter. *The Hanoverian Army of the Napoleonic Wars,* Osprey, Oxford, 2000.